THIS IS YOUR *Georgia*

THIS IS YOUR

Georgia

Bernice McCullar

VIEWPOINT PUBLICATIONS

P. O. BOX 2205

MONTGOMERY, ALA. 36106

AMERICAN SOUTHERN PUBLISHING COMPANY•NORTHPORT, ALABAMA

This book is dedicated to the thousands of Georgia students of Georgia history and their teachers who shared my television programs "This Is Your Georgia" and whose inquiring minds, adventurous searching and generous responses made my work more interesting and taught me much about Georgia history.

FOREWORD

History is studied for many reasons. The one most commonly advanced is that history is our social memory. Our memories tell us who we are, where we belong, what has worked and not worked, and where we seem to be going.

Some historians insist that history is basically a question-answering activity. Others see it as a means to get us out of the present.

In the first part of the Nineteenth Century coordinated efforts by Georgians, historical societies and scholars led to the collection of materials for a more thorough and comprehensive history of our state.

Georgians have never before been as interested in the founding and development of their state as they are today. The many studies in recent years have helped them to realize that they have a past and are no longer young. That past is essentially our own, and different from that of other states in many respects.

Growing out of the feeling of the need to know about Georgia, its history has been almost completely rewritten. New facts have been discovered; new interests have developed.

A generation ago those versed in history had limited records of the state's past. They were still chiefly concerned with political and military events.

Today our whole culture is their province, and the public which reads Georgia's history has widened with the broader visions of the historians.

The history of our state is no longer the concern of a few. The use of the results of researches are sought by many.

It is the hope of the writer to challenge every student to make contributions in aiding in further research of his native state.

Dr. James S. Peters, Chairman of the Georgia State Board of Education

This Georgia history is written to give to students a clearer idea of Georgia's great resources and possibilities; that it will enable them to glimpse the progress and potential of today; that it will give them an appreciation of the things their forefathers died for.

This writer would fail in her duty if she did not give to the rising generations and those to follow, a clear account of Georgia's historic past and the deeds and heroic lives of those who made this state a great commonwealth.

Our state history is a moving tale that stirs the blood and moves men and women to high endeavor.

James S. Peters
Chairman, Georgia
State Board of Education

CONTENTS

UNIT EIGHT:
GEORGIA IN THE NEW SOUTH

UNIT NINE:
BEFORE THE FIRST WORLD WAR

UNIT TEN:
GEORGIA IN THE WILSON ERA

UNIT ELEVEN:
THE ROOSEVELT IMPACT

UNIT TWELVE:
GEORGIA NOW

POSTSCRIPT:

PHOTO CREDITS

INTRODUCTION

HISTORY SHOULD TELL A STORY

"History should tell a story," says historian Henry Steele Commager.

Georgia's history unfolds a drama more absorbing than any novel, more interesting than a television spectacular. No spot on earth has a more remarkable story than Georgia.

Some chapters are thrilling stories of splendid achievement, like Atlanta's rebuilding itself from the ashes after Sherman burned it, or Margaret Mitchell's writing *Gone with the Wind,* a bestseller read around the world, or Georgia's helping FDR conquer polio. Some parts of the story are of spine-chilling horror, like the incredible battle of Chickamauga. There in a golden wood on a September morning, 36,000 Americans lay dead, dying, or wounded, and the creeks ran red with blood. "I could have walked a mile on dead bodies, not once putting my foot to the ground," said an old Georgia woman who had been a little child there. Such a tale reminds one of Dickens' Fat Boy saying, "I wants to make yer flesh creep." Or Shakespeare's lines in "Hamlet":

> "I could a tale unfold whose slightest word
> Would harrow up thy soul, freeze thy young blood,
> Make thy two eyes, like stars, start from their
>   spheres,
> Thy knotted and combined locks to part
> And each particular hair to stand on end,
> Like quills upon the fretful porcupine."

Georgia's history is a fascinating story, like the one described by Sir Philip Sidney: "A tale to draw children

1

from their play and old men from their chimney corners."

Tremendous changes have come to Georgia through the years. Today is different from the way it was yesterday, and tomorrow will not be like any of the time that came before. Sometimes the change was slow as shadows: sometimes like morning light spreading over the land. There were changes like people moving from farm to city and changing Georgia from a rural to an urban state, or Negroes changing status from slaves to citizens. At other times, the changes were sad and sudden, swift and shattering, like the British capturing Savannah by surprise and a secret path. Or the quick tragedy of the flu in 1918, like a plague from the Dark Ages, killing people faster than they could be buried.

There are grave and profound questions that make one think. Was there a better way to have solved the Indian problem than moving the Indians West? What if the South had won the Civil War? How did some honest men happen to get involved in the scandalous Yazoo Fraud? How did Georgia move so far ahead of other states in granting the vote to eighteen-year-olds? Why did Georgia create so many counties? Did we hang an innocent man in Leo Frank? How can we achieve harmony in race relations, and how shall we educate all our people? Provocative and disturbing questions grow out of our history.

No dry-as-dust dates, no dull and static facts make up the Georgia story. Dates are important only because on that date something important happened to people. What? Why? How did it affect them? What did they do about it? That's history. G. K. Chesterton said there is not the shadow of a reason why the picturing of history should not be picturesque.

Besides the actual story itself, there's the legend and lore that add drama. You have to be able to tell fact from fancy. There are the ghosts of the headless children that dance around the pool, the ghosts of Barnsley Castle where two brothers dueled with drinks of deadly poisoned wine, and the Coast ghost with the long arms. Fancies, all! But such fascinating fancies.

All good history leads to more history. Once you glimpse the wonders of history, you will see your own community with fresh eyes. What is really written on that

2

monument you pass every day? That soldier there —
statued in stone forever, like the figures on Keats' urn —
represents a warm and living boy who had to leave his girl
and go away to war. Did he ever come home again? Perhaps
there's a yellowed old letter in somebody's attic, or a memo
in a family Bible. Look for original documents. Go to the
source for facts.

Walk up and down among the shelves of your library.
Find biographies of Georgians who interest you, or a history
that tells you more about an era that arouses your curiosity.

What's the history of your community? Who was there
before you came? What kind of history are you helping make
today for students to read about the day after many tomor-
rows?

SETTING

FOR THE

STORY

UNIT 1

THE GEORGIA MAP – WHERE EXCITING HISTORY HAPPENED!

CHAPTER 1. The Land That Helped Shape Our History

CHAPTER 2. History Happened Along the Rivers

CHAPTER 3. Georgia's Golden Islands

CHAPTER 4. Georgia's Seven Wonders

CHAPTER 5. Names and Symbols Make a State More Interesting

CHAPTER 1

THE LAND THAT HELPED
SHAPE OUR HISTORY

HOW THE SHAPE OF THE STATE HAS CHANGED

Once Georgia was a narrow strip between the Savannah and the Altamaha rivers, and stretched from the Atlantic to the Pacific oceans, including the present site of Los Angeles, California. It looked like this, when King George II granted its charter on June 9, 1732:

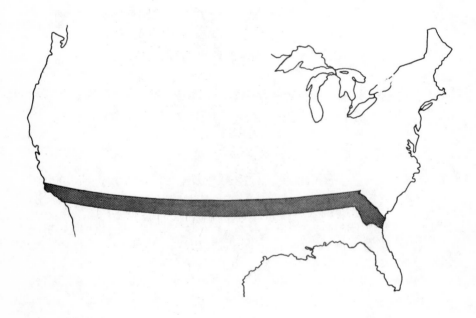

Today, it is about 250 miles long and 320 miles wide, covers 59,878 square miles, and looks like this:

This is the way Georgia looks in the southeast:

IF A GIANT COULD FEEL GEORGIA WITH HIS FINGERS

What would a great giant feel if he could reach down and run his finger tips over Georgia? Across the top, mountains, then a plateau, then a great coastal plain, then 126 miles of coast with the blue waters of the Atlantic splashing over the bronzed marshes and the golden islands.

The sea used to cover most of Georgia. You can still find sea shells far up in the state.

What does the "fall line" mean? That's where the rivers fall because the soil changes. The fall creates water power, and here factories were first set up, and power plants and manufacturing developed. Where is the fall line? It is an imaginary line that you could draw from Columbus through Macon to Augusta.

THE BOUNDARY IS STILL IN DISPUTE

Georgia's boundary is not settled yet, even after two and a half centuries. Georgia and Tennessee still disagree about who owns a strip of land on Georgia's northern border.

The state is bounded by Tennessee and North Carolina on the north, by the Chattahoochee River and Alabama on the west, by the crooked St. Marys River and Florida on the south, and by South Carolina, the Savannah River, and the Atlantic Ocean on the east. The boundary lines are usually started at Nickajack, site of an old Indian town on top of Nickajack Mountain. There's a stone there that serves as a marker.

The center of the state, geographically, is southeast of Macon, where Town and Savage creeks join, but near Hartwell is a site that the Indians called "Center of the

8

World." It was the center of their world. Their paths to trading stations and battles crossed here. The Indian name for it was Ay-ye-li-a-lo-hee. Passenger pigeons darkened the sky above it.

Georgia's Mountains Are Older Than The Rockies Or The Alps!

Georgia's mountains, a part of the Appalachian range, are older than the Rockies or the Alps! Geologists say they are over 300 million years old. The Appalachian system runs 1,600 miles from Canada's Gaspe Peninsula, through Georgia, to Alabama. Some peaks in Georgia are nearly 5,000 feet above sea level. In Georgia, the Blue Ridge foothills start climbing toward the Great Smokies, which became a U.S. National Park on February 6, 1930. "Of all the world's mountains, I love the Appalachians best," said U. S. Supreme Court Justice William O. Douglas. Georgia's own mountain region has scenery as picturesque as any in Europe. The Cherokee Indians once called this "the Enchanted Land." The mountain area of Georgia covers about 1,850 square miles, stretching 48 miles down from the northern boundary.

GEORGIA'S MOUNTAIN NAMES ARE PICTURESQUE: Lost Mountain, Blood Mountain, and Slaughter Mountain (on both of these the Indians once waged savage war), Doubleknob, Buzzard Peak, Mt. Yonah or Bear Mountain, Pickens' Nose, Snake Mountain, Slipdown Mountain, Tickanetly Peak, Blue Mountain, Lavender Mountain. There are gaps where the pioneers crossed: Woody Gap, Unicoi, Tesnatee, Gooch's Gap, and Frogtown Gap, among the many.

GEORGIA'S HIGHEST MOUNTAIN PEAK

The highest mountain peak in Georgia is Mt. Enotah, often called Brasstown Bald, which means "the place of the green valley." This peak is 4,768 feet above sea level. It is located on the divide between the Hiawassee and Nottely rivers, seven miles southeast of Young Harris College.

The Cherokee Indians, who lived among these mountains, thought that odd folk lived here: tiny Yun-wee-chuns-dee, who dwelt in caves and looked especially after children and lost men among the mountains, and the Nunnehi, who made magic and music that echoed among the peaks. They believed that a great frog, which they called Walasiyi, and thought to be as big as a house, hopped across the valleys, especially Sapphire Valley. An inn named Walasiyi is at Vogel Park today.

From Georgia's Rabun Bald Mountain, which is only 72 feet lower than Brasstown Bald, one can see three states: North Carolina, South Carolina, and Georgia. This peak is two miles from the North Carolina border. Fourteen mountain peaks in this area are more than 4,000 feet high. The Chattahoochee National Forest is here.

The spectacular waterfalls, like Amicalola, near

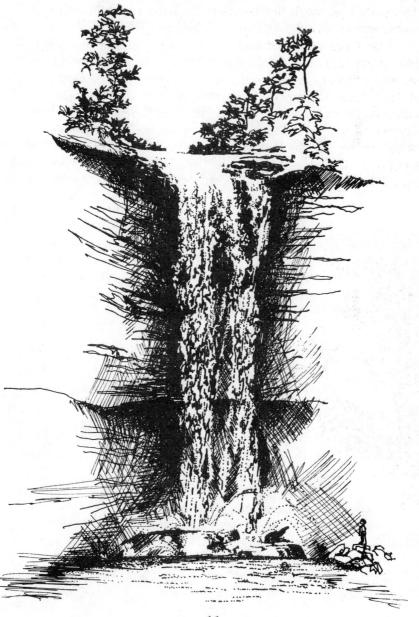

Ellijay, Annie Ruby near Helen and Tallulah, and Toccoa
Falls in Stephens County, add to the beauty of Georgia's
mountains. There are 136 kinds of trees growing in the
mountain country, like the hemlock (whose fatal poison
Socrates was made to drink by his fellow Greeks), poplar,
maple, pine, basswood, white and red oak, ash, and the
cucumber tree! Here are the exquisite mountain blossoms
like rhododendron, mountain laurel, and azalea. And here
grow many of the 800 plants and herbs that the Indians
knew. The cool crystal lakes often reflect the blossoms
and the tall trees, the misty mountain peaks, and the quiet
clouds floating.

There are many state parks, like Vogel. Vogel was
given to Georgia by Fred and August Vogel, who had bought
65,000 acres in north Georgia as a source of tanbark for
their leather factory in Milwaukee. Then they discovered
that tannic acid from the quebracho tree that grows in South
America was cheaper. In 1928, they gave Georgia 248 acres
for a state park.

Among the beautiful lakes in the mountains are Lake
Winfield Scott, named for the U. S. Army commander-in-
chief who was sent to Georgia to supervise the removal of
the Cherokees west in 1838, and Lake Trahlyta, named for
the Indian maiden said to have bathed in the fountain of
youth, and now buried in a cairn in the middle of the highway
nine miles north of Dahlonega.

BLOOD MOUNTAIN IN UNION COUNTY

Blood Mountain, and nearby Slaughter Mountain, were
the scenes of vicious battles between the Cherokees and
other Indians. Blood ran down the mountain sides and
colored the waters. Other fierce battles were fought on
Slipdown Mountain and Rocky Knob. (Near here is buried
an Indian Queen named Anawaqua.)

THE APPALACHIAN TRAIL BEGINS IN GEORGIA

For 2,065 miles across the mountains from Georgia
through Maine runs the longest continuous hiking trail in
the world, the Appalachian Trail. It starts at Springer
Mountain in North Georgia and goes past Mt. Katahdin in
Maine. Once it started at the 3,290-foot-high Mt. Oglethorpe,

but vandals destroyed the markers there and its entrance was moved. About 76 miles of the Appalachian Trail are in Georgia. The Trail crosses thirteen states.

At the Georgia entrance are these words:

"To enjoy nature in its primitive beauty, unspoiled by man's greed, to leave civilization behind, with its cares, worries, and annoyances; to rest tired minds and souls and nerves that are jangled and out of tune; to gain fresh strength for the battles of life by contact with the wind and trees, earth and sky, the firmament that showeth God's handiwork."

Blood Mountain was named for Indian battles fought there.

MT. LECONTE WAS NAMED FOR A GEORGIAN

Mt. LeConte in North Carolina, not far from the Georgia line, on the Appalachian Trail, was named for Joseph LeConte, Georgia teacher and scientist who taught at the University of Georgia. He was a native of Liberty County, where he and his brother John were once taught by

13

Alexander Stephens.

Mt. LeConte was one of the last peaks to be explored. Its best entrance is from Gatlinburg. It is eight miles to the top. Among the sites are Hoot Owl Holler, Trillium Gap, Huggins Hell, and Rainbow Falls. Alum Cave is on the side.

After the Civil War, the LeConte brothers, John and Joseph, went to California, and established the University of California. John LeConte was a professor too.

There is also a peak on the Trail named for Sequoyah, who invented the Indian alphabet.

The Chattahoochee National Forest Stretches Across the Appalachian Mountain Area

In 1936, President Franklin D. Roosevelt proclaimed as a national forest much of the old mountain area of the Cherokee Indians. In the Chattahoochee National Forest some of the mountain peaks are nearly a mile high. The Forest spreads over some twenty counties with nearly two million acres. Many acres within its boundaries are still privately owned. It was created out of the Cherokee and Nantahala forests.

More than fifty kinds of trees grow within the forest. Deer, turkey, bear, ruffled grouse, squirrel, raccoon, and

many fish, including mountain trout and bass, draw sportsmen. There are over 800 miles of trout streams. Over 300 kinds of birds are here.

Great rivers begin in this forest: the Chattahoochee, the Coosa, the Tennessee, and the Savannah. From the Blue Ridge Divide, some waters flow to the Atlantic Ocean, some to the Gulf of Mexico.

Dogwood, laurel, rhododendron, azaleas, and the famous sourwood, from which the bees make delicious honey, grow here. Here in spring dogwood foams up like soapsuds, and in the autumn the mountainsides are a glory of burnished gold and scarlet.

Picturesque names of the recreation areas here are Unicoi Gap, Warwoman Dell, DeSoto Falls, Deep Hole, Nancytown Lake, Panther Creek, Chenocetha, and Enota Glade.

CHAPTER 2

HISTORY HAPPENED
ALONG THE RIVERS

Georgia has more than 75 rivers. Not all of them flow down to the sea. Three, the Chattahoochee, the Flint, and the Suwanee, flow to the Gulf of Mexico.

The Savannah River,
Where the Story Started

The Savannah is the river up which Oglethorpe and his first little band of colonists sailed on February 12, 1733, found a high bluff and started Georgia! An old story recounts that as early as 1603 boats of the Spaniards were coming up the river to buy sassafras from the Indians. The Indians used sassafras root as a medicine.

The 31-mile river forms the boundary between Georgia and South Carolina and drains 10,000 square miles of Georgia. The Indians called the river the "I-sun-de-ga," or "the river of the blue waters," but its waters were never blue. The Spanish called the river "Rio Dulco." There is a bend in the river known as "the Devil's Elbow."

Long before Oglethorpe came, DeSoto crossed the river, after spending two months in Georgia in the spring of 1540. George Washington was rowed down the river from Purrysburg, when he visited Georgia in 1791.

On this river, William Longstreet sailed his steamboat before Robert Fulton invented one. On this river, too, the *Savannah*, first steamship to cross the Atlantic, plied up and down taking people on excursions. One celebrated rider was President James Monroe.

Confederate President Jefferson Davis and Vice-President Alexander Stephens were taken down this river

The illustration contains the following labels:

1791 — Longstreet's steamboat
1733 — George Washington was here
1603 — First colonists arrive
1540 — Spanish buy sassafras
De Soto crosses
Jefferson Davis goes to prison
The "Waving Girl"
Today there are lakes, locks, and dams

to Savannah, there to be put on the ship *Clyde* that took them to prison after the Confederacy fell.

On Elba Island, near Savannah, Florence Martus, Georgia's famous "Waving Girl," began waving to passing ships, a handkerchief by day, a lantern by night. Her brother was lighthouse keeper there. Sailors from all over the world learned to watch for her friendly wave.

The Savannah's waters are transformed into power by many dams and hydroelectric plants. The Clarke Hill Dam, with its lake, is 22 miles above Augusta. The lake has a 1,200-mile shore line. This dam was named for General Elijah Clarke, the valiant old Revolutionary hero. Not far away is the Elijah Clarke State Park. Hartwell Dam and Lake, seven miles east of Hartwell, Georgia, has a 960-mile shoreline. An atomic energy plant is across the Savannah.

The Chattahoochee River
Was Made Famous By A Poem

Sidney Lanier, Georgia's first great poet, wrote, "The Song of the Chattahoochee," and made this 436-mile river famous.

This mighty river begins with a little trickle of water near Poplar Stump by Horse Trough Mountain up in Union County. After it gets to West Point, it forms the boundary line between Georgia and Alabama. Down at the very corner of the state it joins the Flint to form the Apalachicola, then flows to the Gulf of Mexico.

17

The Indian name "Chattahoochee" means "painted rock." Somewhere along its banks the Indians found their materials for war paint. One U. S. Commissioner reported, "I tried many times to get them to show me where, but they invariably refused."

Spanish and French explorers had been here along the river before the English came. Spanish friars sought to set up missions here. In 1679 Father Juan Ocon came to Coweta, and in 1681 Franciscans came to Coweta Town below Columbus, but the Indians drove them all out. Some white men had trading stations at Cusseta.

The Chattahoochee, like other Georgia rivers, now creates great centers of power and of recreation. Lake Lanier, near Gainesville, with its 550-mile shoreline, is named for the poet who wrote about the river. The beautiful Dunaway Gardens near Newnan are on a creek that flows into this river. At Columbus, Ft. Gaines, and Bainbridge are other power dams and reservoirs.

Stephen Foster Never Saw
The Suwannee River

The Suwannee River is thought to rise somewhere in the soft, weird depths of Georgia's Okefenokee Swamp. It flows through Florida, and on to the Gulf of Mexico. Its name "Suwannee" means "the river of the deer."

Stephen Foster, the man who set the world singing about the river, never laid eyes upon its black waters. A memorial, a three-ton granite shaft, to him is at Fargo, Georgia. About 35 miles below the Georgia border, at White Springs, Florida, is the Stephen Foster Memorial, with shrine and chimes and museum.

Foster was writing songs for Christy's Minstrels in New York. He had written a song about a river, and he needed a name for the river. He considered the Pee Dee, which South Carolina calls "the mighty Pee Dee." He discarded that. Then he thought of Yazoo, the name of a river in the Mississippi country. This name, once associated with a very strange chapter in Georgia's own story, means "river of death," and is not very musical. Finally, putting his finger on the map, he came upon the Suwannee River.

Stephen Foster never saw the Suwannee River.

19

When he published the song, nobody he found had ever heard of the Suwannee River so he called the song "Old Folks at Home."

George Gershwin, composer of "Porgy and Bess," titled his first hit tune "Suwannee." Al Jolson often sang Foster's song on the stage. January 13 is Stephen Foster Day, by Act of Congress. Foster, who was born on July 4, 1826, had a sad life, and died in New York's Bellevue Hospital, a haven for the mentally and emotionally troubled, on January 13, 1864.

The Suwannee River has a ghost, so legend says. Her name is Hannah and she is a part of the Suwannee folklore. She is said to have been a pretty girl deserted by her lover, a British soldier. Legend says she stands on the banks of Hannah's Island, here in this river, and calls to boatmen, "Throw me your rope and I'll tie it." And then she screams!

The Coosa,
A River With A Mystery Name

The 285-mile Coosa is the river that Georgia shares with Alabama. It is formed at Rome of the 99-mile muddy Etowah and the swift 45-mile Oostanaula. The name "Etowah" means "place of the dead wood." The name "Oostanaula" means "the rock that bars your way."

Indians paddled up and down the Coosa in their hollowed-out logs and canoes. The Cherokees had a post office there, called "Head of Coosa." A small village called Chihaha grew up; it became Rome.

The Coosa leaves Georgia 30 miles west of Rome, crosses into Alabama, joins with the Tallapoosa and forms the Alabama River.

The Altamaha,
River of Mary Musgrove And Fannie Kemble

The Altamaha is made up of two rivers, the Oconee and the Ocmulgee. The mighty Altamaha River was, until 1763, the southern boundary of Georgia. The original grant for the little colony covered a strip of land between the

Savannah and the Altamaha. At the end of the French and Indian War in 1763, England acquired the land below the Altamaha, and Georgia's territory was doubled.

Oglethorpe brought Scotch Highlanders over as the war with the Spaniards from Florida approached, and they settled at Darien, the mouth of this mighty river. He also sent Mary Musgrove and her husband to set up a trading post on the river and keep the Indians friendly. Her story is elsewhere in this book.

From her husband's rice plantation, still to be seen just below Darien, the British actress Fannie Kemble journeyed by boat down to the other Butler plantation on St. Simons. She also went by canoe up and down the river, as did William Bartram, the naturalist, when he visited it years before, studying and writing about the plants and wild life. He borrowed a boat and rowed 50 miles upstream.

The Ogeechee, From Oglethorpe's Time To Henry Ford

The 250-mile Ogeechee tidal river flows parallel to the Savannah River. It rises in Greene County in the Piedmont Plateau, flows by Louisville, the old state capital, and enters the Atlantic by way of Ossabaw Sound.

Oglethorpe sent eighteen families to live on the banks of the Ogeechee soon after he had established Savannah. The first royal governor, John Reynolds, tried to move the capital from Savannah to a site on this river, which he wanted to name Hardwicke. A marker on the Savannah-Darien Highway points to this site.

During the Civil War, Sherman's men captured Fort McAllister, the Confederate stronghold on the Ogeechee.

The Flint River, That Desoto Crossed

The 330-mile Flint, which starts near Atlanta, was one of the rivers crossed by DeSoto in 1540. The Indians called it "Thronateeska."

Once boats carried cargo and passengers up and down

21

this river. Some of the boats had odd names: "The Joke," "Hard Times," "The Flint Bride," and "Flint Fanny."

At the southwest tip of Georgia, the Flint joins the Chattahoochee to form the Apalachicola, and flows to the Gulf of Mexico.

On the Flint once stood the Old Creek Agency, where Benjamin Hawkins, the remarkable agent to the Indians, lived with his library, his gardens, and often his illustrious guests. At Bainbridge there once was an Indian trading village, run by an Englishman who had married an Indian girl. Now at Bainbridge, Georgia's chief inland port, stands a million-dollar dock and the great Jim Woodruff Dam, forming Lake Seminole.

The Crooked St. Marys River, For Which Three Nations Fought

The St. Marys River, part of Georgia's southern boundary, is one of the crookedest rivers in the world. Of its 180 miles, 175 meander between two points which are only 65 miles apart by straight line. (Georgia has another smaller stream named Crooked River.)

Once ports and trading posts were all along the river. It was also a favorite site for pirates and smugglers. Once smugglers lifted a horse, stolen from Reverend Horace Pratt, into the vestibule of the church at St. Marys to attract the attention of people while they unloaded smuggled cargoes of gin and rum and sped out to sea.

Four hundred years ago, three powerful nations were struggling for control of this quiet river: France, Spain and England.

DeSoto may have seen the river. But there are those who doubt it, and believe that Jean Ribaut, the French explorer, was, in 1562, the first to find it. He sailed up the coast from St. Augustine and came upon this river on May 1. He thereupon named it "the river of Mary." He wrote of its beauty: "... we entered the river and veued the country thereabouts, which is the fairest, frutefullest, and pleasantest in all the world."

Two years later, Reni Laudonniere, another Frenchman, came and established a settlement, called "La

Pirates unload smuggled cargoes.

Caroline" near the present town of St. Marys. In less than a year, the Spanish governor Menendez had destroyed it. The Timucuan Indians lived along the banks, but they were finally driven out.

By 1800, many trading stations were along the river, sending out from their docks schooners and later steamboats with lumber, turpentine, furs, rice, beef, hides, and later cotton, and bringing in the things the settlers needed. St. Marys was the fifth largest town in Georgia about 1810. This little town had been started before the Revolution by wealthy Englishmen, on Buttermilk Bluff. It was the site of an old Indian town, part of a 1,672-acre tract bought for $38. A British fort and soldiers protected it. An American surveyor, Absolom Jackson, often entertained the officers at his home. One Christmas Day, after he had guests there for dinner, he sat on his porch, waiting for them to return

23

from a walk with his wife. Boisterous drunken soldiers passed, taunted him with not inviting them, and pushed him off his porch. He died of a concussion.

Lumber from along this river went to build ships in New England. The famous Indian Treaty of Coleraine was signed near the banks of this river.

The St. Marys River may start at Billy's Lake in the Okefenokee Swamp. The St. Marys enters the Atlantic at Cumberland Sound between Cumberland Island and Fernandina Beach. Near the Atlantic it becomes about a thousand feet wide, classed as a tidal river and one of the deepest rivers for its width in the United States.

The Indian name for this river was Thathlothlaguphka. It means "rotten fish."

CHAPTER 3
GEORGIA'S
GOLDEN
ISLANDS

WHY THE "GOLDEN" ISLANDS?

Some authorities say the islands along Georgia's 126-mile Atlantic coast were called golden because here the pirates hid their gold. Others say they are called golden islands because they are splashed with golden sunshine that draws people from the wintry climates elsewhere to the warmth and brightness of the Georgia coast.

The islands are haunted with legend. They are also rich in history. It was here that the Spanish tried to establish a stronghold with forts and missions. Frenchmen sailed along the coast and up the rivers. Dashing Englishmen like Sir Francis Drake plundered and burned coastal settlements. Indians warred here. Pirates buried their gold here, legend says.

The chief islands are Ossabaw, St. Catherines, Sapelo, Blackbeard's, Sea Island, St. Simons, Jekyll, and Cumberland. Spanish moss and gnarled old trees shaped and twisted by many storms add to the picturesque beauty of the islands.

Ossabaw,
Where Deer Hunters Came In 1687

This island, with St. Catherines and Sapelo, was reserved by the Indians when they granted the other land to Oglethorpe and the colonists in 1733. The three islands later figured in the settlement made with Mary Musgrove, who had been interpreter for Oglethorpe. Ossabaw is 20 miles below Savannah, and is the northernmost of the golden chain of islands on Georgia's coast.

Bear River runs along the south of the island. Other streams are Queen Bess Creek, Big Tom Creek, Little

Tom Creek. There is a spot called Polly's Point.

War has touched the island three times: The Revolution, the War of 1812, and Civil War. Hurricanes have driven residents off. Patriots fled to the island from Savannah, too, when the British took that city in 1778. People who lived here once grew indigo, rice, cotton, and timber.

Once Ossabaw was overrun with wild hogs; in 1924 cowboys were brought from the West to round them up. This island has long been a favorite of hunters. South Carolina hunters were stalking deer here as early as 1687. Now hunters seek wild ducks, turkeys, pheasants, marsh hens, and deer.

Trees grow to strange shapes on these islands, twisted by winds and storms. One with grotesque form was called the "Gnome Tree." Another, where hunters left early snacks, was the "Breakfast Tree." On this and all the islands, turtles crawl up to lay their eggs in the sand. Sometimes, 100 turtles come in one night. Each lays from 85 to 150 eggs, weeping all the while; nobody knows why they weep. Some turtles are thought to be 500 years old.

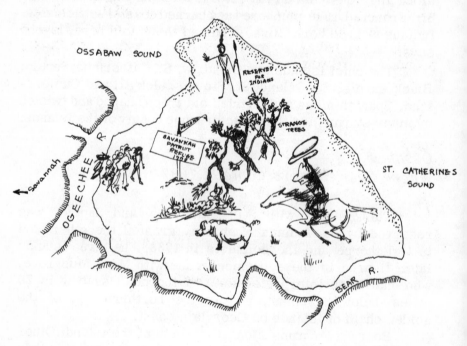

26

St. Catherines,
Where America's First Book Was Written

This 25,000-acre island is known as the former home of Button Gwinnett, most famous of Georgia's three signers of the Declaration of Independence. He bought land from Reverend Thomas Bosomworth, third husband of Mary Musgrove. Gwinnett was in and out of the neighboring port of Sunbury and the Midway settlement of the Puritans and of his friend Dr. Lyman Hall. An old legend says two ghosts of Gwinnett haunt the island: one on his horse returning from Philadelphia, the other at the helm of his boat, "Beggar's Benison."

It was to this island that the Spanish governor Menendez came up from St. Augustine in 1566 to talk with Indian Chief Gaule, who gave him permission to put forts and missions along the coast. It may have been on this island that Brother Domingo wrote a grammar, about 1568, to use in teaching the Yemassee Indians. It is sometimes referred to as the first book written on the American continent. It was lost. Five priests were savagely murdered here when Indians rebelled at their strict religious rules.

St. Catherines was the headquarters of Chief Guale of the Guale Indians, and the whole area was called Guale, pronounced "Wally."

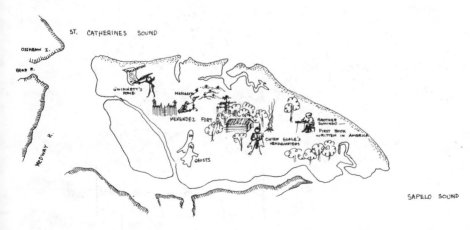

Blackbeard's Island,
Where A Pirate Hid Gold?

This 5,600-acre island, tucked into the side of Sapelo, was once the haunt of Blackbeard the Pirate, an eighteenth century rascal, who may have hidden much of his stolen loot here. He was Edward Teach or Thache or Tache. He was hanged in 1718, captured by Robert Maynard at Ocracoke Inlet, North Carolina. Sailors thought he was the devil himself.

He was plundering coastal ships from Nova Scotia to the West Indies in his ship *Queen Anne's Revenge* about 1702, after the Spanish missions had gone and before the first colonists came. He came last in 1717. A picture of him, imaginatively drawn by a visitor and now in the main house on the island, showed a fierce-looking man, with bulging, bloodshot eyes, and heavy black beard, filthy and matted, which he tied with tiny bows. Each bow was said to represent a wife that he had along the seaboard. He used to braid his hair, stick slow-burning ropes into the braids, and with knives shining and guns blazing, terrify the passengers of the ships he plundered. If they were slow to give up rings, he chopped off their fingers. Many other pirates hid treasures along the shore, and went in and out the old Pirate's House in Savannah. Robert Louis Stevenson drew the character of Long John Silver in *Treasure Island* from one of these fierce fellows.

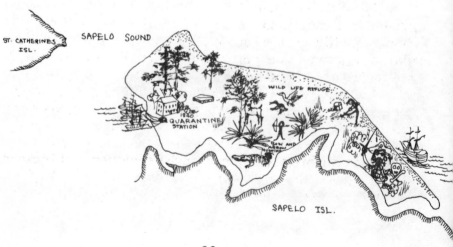

In 1914, Woodrow Wilson had the 87.5-square-mile island made into a wildlife range especially for water fowl. About 20,000 ducks spend the winter here. Deer roam through the sun and the silver fog. Men had to be hired to kill the alligators that overran the place. There are also curlews, sandpipers, coons, hoot owls, bald eagles, ospreys, red-tailed hawks, turtle doves, rabbits, snakes, and many other specimens of wild life, but reputedly no possums, polecats, or squirrels. Hunters have long been allowed to shoot game here only with bows and arrows. Alligators infest the island; 150 must be killed each year.

Once there was a quarantine house here, and a crematorium where the bodies of the sailors and others who died in the plague of yellow fever were burned. A grim coffin-shaped crematorium among the lush pines, palmettos and oaks reminds one of this macabre chapter in coastal history.

The island has been under five flags. One was the "skull and crossbones" of the pirates.

Sapelo Island,
The French Noblemen, And Three Millionaires

Three wealthy men have owned Sapelo Island: Thomas Spalding, Howard Coffin, and Richard J. Reynolds. Its story is also entangled with the French Revolution and its Reign of Terror.

Spalding, known as "the laird of Sapelo" was a great plantation owner, and the first of Sapelo's wealthy owners. Howard Coffin was an automobile magnate from the North who developed much of the Georgia coast. Richard J. Reynolds was the heir to a tobacco fortune.

But before the millionaires there were French noblemen, who settled here February 1, 1789. They were fleeing the Reign of Terror of the French Revolution, in which many wealthy Frenchmen lost their heads on the guillotine. Carlyle, in his history of the French Revolution, and Dickens in *Tale Of Two Cities* have written vividly of the guillotine. Another is the recent *Paris In the Terror* by Stanley Loomis. They fled first to the West Indies, but a revolt in Haiti led by Toussaint L'Ouverture (called the "Black Napoleon"), sped them to the Georgia coast. Five of them, including the colorful Christopher Poulain duBignon, who later owned Jekyll, planned to raise and sell slaves here. The other four Frenchmen were Francis Marie Says Bumossay Delavaux, Pierre Caesar Picot de Boisfeuillet, Nicolas Francis Mazon de la Villa Huchet, and "Le Grande" Colosmezle. They quarreled and the scheme came to naught. (Four later bought Jekyll.) Another Frenchman, the gentle Marquis de Montelet, who built the "chocolate house" and led a pig on a leash looking for truffles, lived here. Perhaps the most interesting of the Sapelo Island personalities was a giant Mohammedan overseer of Spalding's.

Sapelo, called "Zapala" by the Spanish, was one of the three islands which the Indians reserved for themselves when they made their treaty with Oglethorpe. It later became a part of the settlement that the British government made with Mary Musgrove.

Sea Island,
From Audubon to O'Neill

This island, now famous for the Cloisters, a well-known resort, was once Retreat Plantation, home of Thomas Butler King and his wife, who had been Ann Page. King, who had come here from Connecticut with a sick brother, was a famous statesman and was sent about the world on government missions. His wife had grown up as an only child here, and had been rowed across to the mainland every Monday by four slaves to share a governess with the Floyd children. She tended the plantation in his absence, and raised sea island cotton that brought the highest prices on the coast. In their yard they built Grasshopper Hall, to which their sons brought guests from college. The Kings were once hosts to John James Audubon, who had been in Savannah taking orders for his book, *Birds of America,* at $1,000 a copy. King ordered a set. Audubon wrote his wife Lucy, a school teacher, of this chance visit to the Kings: "Our boat was passing the island when a sudden storm drove it on to land. I made for the shore, and met a gentleman named King on the beach. I presented him my card and was immediately invited to dinner. I visited his garden and got into such agreeable conversation and quarters that I was fain to think that I had landed on one of those fairy islands said to have existed in the golden age."

The series, not even published then, had 435 life-size bird prints. Audubon traveled all over America to find and paint them. Mice destroyed 200 plates, which it took three years to do. He sold 89 advance subscriptions, and the series finally brought $200,000.

ST. SIMONS ISL.

Neptune, a family slave, went to war with Captain Henry Lord King, a son of the family, and when the boy was killed, brought him back from a Virginia battlefield to lie in Christ Churchyard. Then he went back to be with another son in battle. Together, the boy and the old man would dream of home. Neptune would say, "Water's high on the bar tonight."

Ann Page King died in 1859, just before her world fell apart in a sad, strange war.

The corn barn of the King plantation is now a part of the golf club of the Cloisters, and an old slave cabin stands nearby.

The Cloisters, now a famed resort, was opened October 12, 1928, on the site of Retreat Plantation, by Howard Coffin, a Northern industrialist who had become interested in developments on the Georgia coast. He and his partner developed the islands as two other friends, John Couper and James Hamilton, had done a century before. Mr. Coffin, taking a page out of the old days of Chaucer and the innkeepers long ago, greeted his guests wearing his night clothes and cap and bearing aloft a candle. Coffin and his wife are buried in Christ Churchyard, the only graves placed north and south. They always changed beds in hotel rooms in that direction. The hotel attracts world celebrities, and many honeymooners. It was to the islands once that a newly married couple came on their honeymoon, and — in those days of long visits — remained as guests until after their second child was born! Many celebrities came to Sea Island; among them were Queen Juliana of Holland and President Calvin Coolidge. Each of them planted a tree here.

Here on Sea Island, Eugene O'Neill and his wife Carlotta built the first real home that the restless playwright ever had. He used $100,000 of the money he had made from his play *Mourning Becomes Electra*. The house, which was green and white, was named "Casa Genotta," a combination of their names Gene and Carlotta. His own study was designed like the cabin of a ship's captain. Here he worked on his plays *Days Without End* and *Ah, Wilderness.*

The island had been suggested to them by Ilka Chase, actress and author. O'Neill sent her a copy of *Mourning*

Becomes Electra, inscribed, "To Ilka, who found our blessed isles for us." The O'Neills lived here from July 1932 to 1936. Then they moved to the West Coast.

St. Simons, Wesley, and a Pink Chapel

It was on St. Simons Island that Oglethorpe defeated the Spanish at Bloody Marsh. Here, too, was Oglethorpe's only home in Georgia, Orange Hall. The village and fort of Frederica, were excavated and established as a national park. It is one of the few in the nation that go back to colonial days.

Here the Wesleys and Whitefield once preached under "Wesley's Oak" near where Christ Church was later built. The congregation was established under the Church of England in 1736. Here John Wesley once walked with Sophey Hopkey, the Georgia girl he thought of marrying. She was visiting here from Savannah, where their romance flowered. The church, center of much community life for the plantation owners and their guests, assembled so many that the postman delivered the mail here. In the quiet church-yard lie many remarkable people of an earlier day. A plantation owner who killed a neighbor found chill hostility, and built the "Pink Chapel" for the private devotions of his family thereafter. Its ruins still stand.

A Methodist center on this island is named Epworth-by-the-Sea, for John Wesley's home in England.

Here came such famous visitors as Fannie Kemble, brilliant British actress who wrote a bitter book against slavery, and Aaron Burr, vice-president of the United States, fleeing the ghost of Alexander Hamilton whom he had killed in a duel.

Spanish priests, first the Jesuits and later the Franciscans, had missions here. It was here that the beloved big priest Velascola, known as the Cumbrian giant, was fatally tomahawked by Indians in 1597.

St. Simons, like the other islands, has its ghosts. At Ebo Landing, a group of Africans in chains dashed into the water and drowned rather than become slaves. The superstitious say their tribal death chant, which they sang as

33

they died, can still be heard on dark nights. A light in the graveyard is supposed to shine from a candle lighted by a husband for his wife who was afraid of the dark. On the Cater's Kelvin Grove Plantation, next to Oglethorpe's Bloody Marsh, are other ghosts. There the owner was killed by his overseer, and his ghost is said to return and walk about seeking his murderer. Two headless children are supposed to dance about the pool on moonlit nights. Another specter is "the ghost with the long arms" that walks and wails and beckons when the night is dark and stormy. The gray, ghostly moss and the eternally lonely sound of the sea make the coast a good place for telling shivery tales.

The historic ship "Old Ironsides," officially the U.S.S. *Constitution*, had in it timbers cut on St. Simons. After the colorful career of the old vessel, it was restored with pennies and nickels and dimes of the nation's school children. It was sailed down the coast, and docked at Brunswick for a while. Georgia school children, many of whom had given their piggy-bank contents to help restore the old ship, went on board to see it. It was later sent to the Boston shipyard. Stephen Decatur, who helped defeat the Barbary Pirates for the United States, and for whom Georgia named a town and county, once commanded this ship.

Dr. Oliver Wendell Holmes, father of the late Justice Holmes and the son of Reverend Abiel Holmes who was once

34

"Old Ironsides"

pastor at Midway, was angry when he heard that the old ship was to be discarded. He wrote a poem that stirred the imagination of the nation, and saved "Old Ironsides."

A way of life grew up on St. Simons that has now vanished from existence. The plantation owners sent to Europe for their clothes, books, and furniture. Tutors from Harvard and Yale and governesses from England were obtained for their children. Guests from all over the world were entertained lavishly. Some plantation owners made or lost a hundred thousand dollars in one year on crops, depending on the weather and plagues.

St. Simons life centered about Christ Church. This church, destroyed in many wars, was rebuilt with the money of a bride named Ellen Dodge, who died on her bridal trip around the world. She was brought back and buried under the altar, but later her body was moved to the churchyard outside. Nearby are buried her husband, Reverend Anson Dodge, who built the church and became its pastor, and his second wife and their little son, who died in a fall from a pony. A stained glass window in the church depicts the father and the child in whose memory a school was established on the island.

Jekyll Island, *Where The Millionaires Relaxed*

This island, since 1947 a resort belonging to the people of Georgia, was once one of the most famous resorts in the world. From 1886 to 1947, it belonged to 100 millionaires who were said to control one sixth of all the money in the world. On their yachts they came here each winter, escaping from the busy world. One of them was blind Joseph Pulitzer, once penniless and later a millionaire newspaper editor. He was on his way in his yacht "Liberty" for the annual retreat on Jekyll in 1911 when he died on the Carolina coast. It was Pulitzer who set up the famed Pulitzer Prizes, which have now been won by a number of Georgians for distinction in writing. Bricks from the Pulitzer cottage are in the golf club now.

One millionaire, George Gould, was so grieved when his son was killed by a wild boar in a hunting accident on Jekyll that he had his home there torn down, all except two stone lions at the entrance. These are still there. They were modeled on the famous "Lion of Lucerne" in Switzerland.

Another millionaire, a thirty-seven-year-old New York banker named McEvers Bayard Brown, built a honeymoon cottage for his prospective bride, who changed her mind about marrying him. Only the chimney remains today. He boarded his yacht, *Valfreya,* sailed for England, kept a crew waiting to sail back for 36 years but never did.

"Indian Mound," the William Rockefeller cottage, with 25 rooms and 15 baths, is now the Georgia history museum. The millionaires finally gave up their retreat. Some say they were bored. The fact is they were disturbed by German submarines which torpedoed a tanker along the coast during World War II. The U. S. government encouraged them to leave, lest such a concentration of wealth should tempt another German attack. They did not return. The end of an era had come. After they left, Jekyll was occupied for a while by the U. S. Coast Guard.

In 1947, Georgia bought the island for $650,000. Now a playground and convention resort, it is valued at over $20,000,000. The millionaires had bought it from the heirs of Christopher duBignon for $125,000. DuBignon, who is buried by a tree there on the island, was a colorful figure who had fought with Clive in India. "He was always found where life was the most exciting," wrote a friend. He was one of the Frenchmen who had come to the Georgia coast when the terror of the French Revolution was cutting off the heads of noblemen in France. DuBignon bought Jekyll in 1791. He lived on the island until his death at eighty-seven in 1825.

This island, with its 11,000 acres, and ten miles of beach, and beautiful buildings, is now a showplace. Some say Oglethorpe named it for his friend, Lord Jekyll, whose portrait hangs over the mantel in the Museum, once the red-carpeted Rockefeller cottage. Lord and Lady Jekyll had given Oglethorpe 600 pounds to help him with his Georgia colony. Legend says that Lord Jekyll was a distant kinsman of the Doctor Jekyll made famous by Robert Louis Stevenson in his story *Doctor Jekyll and Mister Hyde* but it is doubtful that the author would have used real names. Some say that the island was called "Jake's Isle" for a pirate by that name whose favorite haunt it was, and that it became

known by his name as "Jake-isle." The Indians called it Ospo. Among its interesting sites are the carved ebony Chinese wishing chair in the Museum, said to have taken a man 27 years to complete, and the mess kettle from the last slave ship, *The Wanderer,* which landed on the islands with smuggled slaves on a stormy November night in 1858. The kettle has been there over a hundred years. It stands in front of the Jekyll Island Museum.

Cumberland Island, Where Lee's Father Died

The Indians called this island "Missoe." Oglethorpe changed that to Cumberland at the request of Tooanahowi, the adopted son of Tomochichi. The Indian boy, who went to England with Oglethorpe in 1734, had been given a gold watch by the young Duke of Cumberland. He wanted the island named for the English boy.

On this island General Nathaniel Greene had built a home and lumber business just before his death at Mulberry Grove. In 1818, when the Greenes' daughter lived there, the father of Robert E. Lee died at Dungeness, and was buried for 90 years on Cumberland. Mrs. Nathaniel Greene, the charming Kitty who was Washington's favorite dancing partner and who encouraged Eli Whitney to invent the cotton gin, is buried here. She died at fifty-nine. Her epitaph reads, "Catherine Miller, widow of General Greene, commander in chief of the American Revolutionary Army, who died September 1, 1814, age 59. She possessed great talents and exalted virtues."

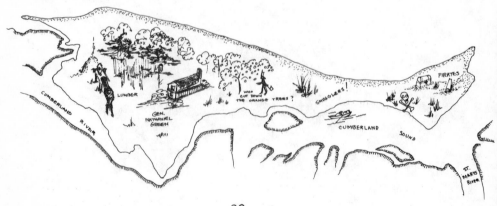

Her second husband Phineas Miller, who had been tutor to the Greene children, and farm boss, died here of blood poisoning in 1806. A thorn had stuck in his hand when he was transplanting an orange tree. All the orange trees there were cut down by the British in the War of 1812.

General Lachlan McIntosh, who killed Button Gwinnett in the famous duel, owned property here. William Bartram, the famous naturalist, visited here. In 1932, an old canoe used by the Timucuan Indians was found here and sent to the Smithsonian Institution in Washington, D.C.

In modern times the island was bought by the Carnegies, relatives of Andrew Carnegie, the steel millionaire who gave money to build the Carnegie libraries all over America.

There were pirates on Cumberland. They are thought to have buried treasure on this island. Smugglers hid their cargoes here. There is an island nearby called Hush Your Mouth Island. In 1965, the Secretary of the Interior visited Cumberland to consider it as a national park.

CHAPTER 4

GEORGIA'S SEVEN WONDERS

The ancients had their "seven wonders of the world." Now when something seems marvelous, people sometimes refer to it as "the eighth wonder of the world." The seven wonders of the early times were these: The Pyramids of Egypt, The Hanging Gardens of Babylon, Phidias's Statue of Zeus, The Temple of Diana at Ephesus, The Tomb of Mausolus (Mausoleum), The Colossus of Rhodes, The Pharos Lighthouse at Alexandria. They are all man-made.

Here are seven of Georgia's natural "wonders": Okefenokee Swamp near Waycross, Warm Springs, Amicalola Falls near Ellijay, Providence Canyons near Lumpkin, Radium Springs near Albany, Tallulah Gorge in Habersham County, and Stone Mountain near Atlanta.

The Weird Okefenokee Swamp

This weirdly beautiful, mysterious swamp is the second largest freshwater swamp in the United States. The Indian name for it was O-wa-qua-phenoga. It means "The Land of the Trembling Earth." Dark comes quickly in this Poe-like place. It resembles the Everglades in Florida and the Dismal Swamp in Virginia. William Bartram wrote about its gloomy beauty in 1774. In 1889, the Swanee Canal Company bought the swamp from Georgia for $62,000 and spent over a million dollars trying to drain it for rich farming land. The venture failed. In 1937, President Franklin D. Roosevelt designated it as a wildlife refuge. The Laura Walker State Park is on the Swamp's Waycross side.

The Swamp was once part of the ocean. It was cut off

by Trail Ridge when the rest of Georgia rose out of the sea, which once covered most of the state. This 130-mile ridge, which still cuts the Swamp off from the Atlantic, is about 250 feet high at Stark, Florida, and descends to 160 feet about two miles south of St. Marys River. The Swamp, which is 166 miles square, is at the head of this river; and the famous Suwannee, of Stephen Foster's song, is said to rise in the Okefenokee. The Swamp's wildlife, including alligators and colorful birds, together with its beautiful trees and plants make it a wonderland of nature. Vereen Bell, Georgia novelist who died in World War II, based his novel *Swamp Water* on life in the Swamp. It was filmed by Hollywood. The eerie Okefenokee is said to have been the refuge of the last Indian in this section.

Among the starkly beautiful growing things in the old Swamp are cypress, black gum and bay trees, draped with old Spanish moss. People have been lost in the Swamp.

Among the plants there is the dropwort or hemlock.

The earth actually does quiver beneath men's feet because of the peculiar sponge-like quality of the soil and the water under it. There are 40 kinds of frogs here. One is the "carpenter frog," which makes a sound like a man hammering nails.

THE GOLDEN MICE IN THE OKEFENOKEE

In 1903, a visitor to the Swamp caught two tiny mice of a strangely golden color, with bright brown eyes. It was 1921 when these little Swamp creatures were noticed again. A Cornell professor, Dr. Francis Harper, heard natives talking about the little mice, and searched until he found a nest. Dr. Harper described the golden mice in his book *The Mammals of the Okefenokee Swamp Region of Georgia.* People who once lived deep in the Swamp but have now been moved outside once had rat hunts to kill the ravenous little creatures that devoured their grain and food. (The entire population of the United States could live for a year on all the food destroyed annually by rats, insects, and fungi!) It is likely that in the general rat-killing forays, they might have killed a number of these little golden mice, too. But after they found out that scientists were searching for them, they helpfully searched, too.

Billy's Island in the Swamp was named for the Indian

chief Billy Bowlegs, who once lived here. General Charles Floyd was in charge of ousting the last of the Indians from deep in the Swamp.

THE CREATURES OF THE SWAMP

The crawling, dangerous alligators, fish hawks that swoop, the beautiful blue herons and white egrets, lizards, possums, coons, bears (which used to steal hogs from the Swamp people), and once panthers, tigers, catamounts, and dozens of various beautiful birds and fish make the Swamp a favorite haunt of sportsmen. It is a U.S. Wildlife Refuge of 400,000 acres covering 660 square miles, bought from private owners in 1937 by the United States government.

FDR's Warm Springs

Warm Springs, where the Indians brought their wounded from the wars to be healed in the gentle waters, is located about forty miles north of Columbus, in Meriwether County. It became world-famous when Franklin D. Roosevelt went there in search of treatment for polio. The Warm Springs Foundation was established by him and his friends. The Little White House nearby became a historic site after Roosevelt became President. The March of Dimes, and the coming of the famous and the helpless to these Springs, drew the attention of the world to the old healing waters of the Georgia Indians.

Roosevelt sent geologists to Warm Springs to find out why the water was warm. The geologists put gauges on the top of Pine Mountain and on other high places. They measured the amount of the water flow from the Springs, and sought to learn the source of the water which formed them. They decided that the rain that falls on the high places penetrates the rock strata which carry the water at least 2,800 feet into the earth's depth and that this causes the warmth of the spring. The temperature of the water is about 87 degrees. This provides warm water in which patients crippled with polio can exercise their limbs. The temperature of the water in the springs goes up one degree for every 90 feet that the rain penetrates the earth. A break in deep rock strata under Warm Springs lets this warmed water get to the surface. Oddly enough, about a mile away from the warm springs there is a very cold spring where the water remains at a temperature of 63 degrees.

Warm Springs is a part of the story in many books about FDR. The Little White House and the Warm Springs Foundation here attract million of visitors. Here he died in April, 1945, as his portrait was being painted.

Amicalola Falls, A Crystal Glory

The name means "tumbling waters," from the two Indian words "ami," water, and "calalah," tumbling. The Falls are in Dawson County, between Dawsonville and Ellijay, near the Georgia end of the Appalachian Trail. They have a fall of 729 feet. Seven waterfalls cascade over Amicalola

Ridge, pouring their waters into the Amicalola River, a crystal-clear, sparkling mountain stream in which trout fishermen like to fish. It is a tributary of the Etowah River in northwest Georgia.

The falls, a spectacular sight, can be seen from the main highway. For a closer view, there are roads leading to the top and bottom. The falls are now part of Amicalola Falls State Park.

Providence Canyons,
The Gobbling Monster

The canyons, sometimes called the Little Grand Canyons, are eight miles west of Lumpkin in Stewart County, near the Chattahoochee River.

The canyons are a phenomenon of land erosion. Some people believe the canyons started with rain falling off a barn roof. Like a great hungry monster out of mythology, the canyons have devoured half the county's farming fields, part of the forest, and even houses. The rain wore into the earth and simply crumbled it. Below the topsoil was a 100-foot layer of loose clay sand overlying blue marl, a hard clay limestone. Scientists say the water has for centuries eaten away marine sands deposited when this was the floor of the ocean.

Twisting chasms, trees growing on the deep floor, rainbow-hued earth colors, are all in the view as one stands on the edge and looks down 250 feet where the earth has vanished. It has 43 different soils. Azaleas and partridge berries are all over the banks. Strange desert vegetation also grows here. The cliffs shade from dazzling white through bright red, candy pinks, fudge brown, sky blue, sunset yellow, and purple like far-off mountain peaks. The range from red clay to white kaolin is a spectacle.

Adventurous explorers among the visitors have left initials carved all over the chasm, even on the sheerest cliffs.

The canyons get their name from the Providence Methodist Church in the vicinity. Old Indian trails once crossed here.

The terrible erosion started only about 150 years ago. Some of the chasms are now 200 to 300 feet deep and cover a thousand acres. One family saw the canyon take its fields,

44

then its barn and yard, the family residence, and last of all a fig tree by the door.

Radium Springs,
A Mystery

Glitteringly beautiful springs four miles below Albany are now the center of a hotel resort. Their cool waters, 68 degrees, were also considered by the Creek Indians to be healing, as the warm waters of Warm Springs, some hundred miles north. The springs were known as Blue Springs. The Indians thought their blue color dropped from the blue skies. The main spring is the largest spring in Georgia, with 70,000 gallons a minute flowing out. The deepest spring is 30 feet deep.

The source of Radium Springs is secret. The mystery of just where the cold waters come from has never been solved.

The last of the Creeks left this area in 1836, although most of their tribe had left middle Georgia in the 1820's.

The modern spring was developed by Byron Collier in 1925.

Spectacular Tallulah Gorge

Tallulah Gorge in Habersham County is a dramatic sight. It looks like a canyon with thick swamps growing in it, even on its steep, rugged sides. The Tallulah River once flowed here. Its course was diverted to create more power for a hydroelectric power dam. A tunnel was built for more than a mile right through the side of a mountain! The water now has a 602-foot drop. The Terrora Powerhouse is located at the Tallulah Reservoir.

Tallulah Falls here was for many years one of the South's popular resorts, one of the first to draw summer visitors. Special trains were run to and from here in summer. There were seven hotels here. Georgians, and visitors from far away, spend weeks here in the summer. The Falls were one of the state's first tourist attractions.

Now people come to see the spectacular gorge, and to visit Tallulah Falls School nearby. This school is known as the "Light in the Mountains."

Legends cluster about Tallulah. Indians are said to have avoided it in fear of evil spirits. The Indian word "Tallulah" means "terrible."

A curious story of an occurrence at Tallulah Falls is told by the historian, George White. A Presbyterian

minister named Hawthorn arrived to preach at Clarkesville and disappeared at the falls on July 5, 1837. He went with some friends, saw the falls, and decided to swim in the pool beneath. The other men accompanied the ladies to the carriage. When they came back to the Falls, his clothes were on a rock. He had disappeared. They never found his body.

Before the river was dammed and diverted for electric power in 1913, there were six beautiful waterfalls. Highest was the 89-foot Tempesta. One called Hurricane was 76 feet high. Smallest was Sweet Sixteen, which fell only 16 feet. The others were Bridal Veil, Oceana, and Lodore. This last one was thought to have been originally named L'eau D'Or, meaning "water of gold" because the sun glinted on it, making it shiningly beautiful.

No Indian artifacts were found in the Gorge, even though Indians lived in the vicinity. They had a superstitious fear of the site because they thought that a cave on the side of the Gorge was the entrance to the Happy Hunting Ground. An old story said that only one Indian who went near the site was ever seen again, and that he died soon after he told of it.

Georgians once considered making a state park out of the Falls, and they also asked the Department of the Interior about making it a national beauty site. But it was bought by industrialists who saw its value as a source of hydro-electric power.

One of the spectacular events that occurred here during the days when trains brought visitors from New Orleans, Jacksonville, and all parts of Georgia, was J. A. St. Johns' walking across the chasm on a cable on July 4, 1884.

Stone Mountain

Georgia's oldest and newest scenic attraction is Stone Mountain. This great granite monolith, the largest exposed granite rock in the world, looks like a gigantic monster left over from the world's morning. Geologists say it is over 200 million years old!

The Indians called it Crystal Mountain, held councils on its summit, built campfires there, and sent smoke signals from its top. DeSoto may have seen it when he came through Georgia, though most historians doubt that he got that near. They say the writers who came with him and wrote so much about the Georgia of 1540 would hardly fail to note such a sight as Stone Mountain, and there is not a

word about it in their chronicles.

It is more likely that the first white man to see the mountain was Captain Juan Pardo, famous as the discoverer of "Pardo's Diamond." He is thought to have seen it in 1567. Pardo had been sent to Georgia to build some forts that were to have been part of a string of forts that stretched to Mexico. He noted that rubies and diamonds could be found lying around "Crystal Mountain."

Earlier in the twentieth century, the United Daughters of the Confederacy set up plans for the carving of a gigantic memorial on the mountain, with figures of Lee, Davis, and Jackson. The sculptor Gutzon Borglum had started the carving on the mountain. On the shoulder of Lee, he entertained 40 guests at breakfast! The completed figure of Lee was to be 130 feet high, including his horse Traveller. The money ran out and disagreements set in, and the memorial was not finished.

In recent years, the State of Georgia bought the mountain and a tourist center has been developed there. It includes Magnolia Plantation, a typical ante-bellum home (not white or with Greek columns), a ski lift to the mountain top, a scenic railroad, and other attractions.

The mountain is 16 miles from Atlanta. It covers 563 acres, is 650 feet high, two miles long, and seven miles around. It is 1,683 feet above sea level. Water falling off one side of it runs to the Atlantic Ocean; from the other side, it goes to the Gulf of Mexico.

CHAPTER 5

NAMES AND SYMBOLS MAKE A STATE MORE INTERESTING

*Such Interesting Place Names
Are On Georgia's Map!*

Who named Atlanta! Or Attapulgus? Whence came such Georgia place names as Too Nigh, Fashion, Between, Split Silk, Yahoo, Buttermilk Bottom, Snuffbox Swamp, Aska, Nickajack, Sawdust, Gratis, Six Mile, Doctortown, Hard Cash, Roosterville, Headlight, and Fairyland? There's a place called Nameless and a Nowhere Road, and a place called Santa Claus. Woven into the history and folklore of Georgia are the names of the cities, the little towns, the villages, the rivers and creeks and lakes and waterfalls, the roads, and country lanes. A search to find out who named these spots and why they chose these names, and why sometimes the names were changed reaches back into dim and shadowy yesterdays. The names range from Atlanta and Attapulgus to Zuta and Zellabee.

Among Georgia's unusual place names, some found on the big map, and others only on county maps or on no map at all, but known to the people who live around little ghost towns or by the streams, are these: Trickum, Wayback, Nebula, Serepta, Six Mile, Luxomi, Whistleville, Licklog, Pumpkin Center, Po Biddy and Nowhere roads, Lost Mountain, Saw Dust, Dot, Hobby, Social Circle, Tell, and Snapfinger. There are places called Rockalo, Oasis, Subligna, Leaf, Linger. An art show is held each autumn at a North Georgia place called "Plum Nelly" because "it's plum outa Tennessee and nelly outa Georgia."

In White County are Pink Mountain and Blue Creek! There are names that sound like a bright, shiny morning in the country: Crabapple, Happy Valley, May Day, Sycamore, Rosebud, Persimmon, Mayapple Knob, Flowery Branch, Elmodel, Dewey Rose, Shady Dale, Apple Valley, Sapphire Valley, and Sunnyside.

There are shivery names that sound as if they had come from an Edgar Allan Poe story that would do to tell on Halloween: Hush Your Mouth Hollow, Bloody Bucket, Pirate Island, Tiger (named for old Indian Chief Tiger Tail), Old Screamer, so named because a frightened Indian squaw once screamed all night at its top, Booger Hollow, Dismal Mountain, Modoc, Boneville, Lordy Mercy Cove, Hoot Owl Hollow, Fighting Town, Mystic, Thunderbolt, and Black Cat.

On the other hand, there are place names that are soap-bubble light and as gay as if they had come out of a Gilbert and Sullivan operetta: Ty Ty (named for the ti ti bush), Chalybeate, Yahoo, Kinderloo, Calico Corners, Checkero, Tuckaho, Tickanetly, Tip Top, Lickskillet, Barefoot, Nankipoo, Scataway and Scuffletown, Bugscuffle Branch, and Ypsilanti, which was named for a Greek general who freed his people from the Turks.

There are dozens of girls' names, like Rebecca, Edith, Lula, Hortense, Aline, Vanna, Emma, Roberta, and Camilla, Roxanne, Thelma, Hepzibah, Adelaide, Agnes, Adabelle. Atlanta, which was first called Terminus, was later named Marthasville for the daughter of Governor Wilson Lumpkin. An old tale tells that it was changed to Atlanta only because a rival railroad, a competitor for one in which Lumpkin had an interest, was ready to open its

line from this city to the Atlantic, and did not want to advertise the Lumpkins and their railroad, and so changed the place name that the road would run from the Atlantic to Atlanta! Alma was not named for a girl. It is a name made up of the first letters of four Georgia capitals: Augusta, Louisville, Milledgeville, and Atlanta. The government stayed for ten years in Augusta until Louisville could be made ready to succeed Savannah as the seat of government.

Boys' names are on the map, too. Among them are Cecil, Carl, Douglas, Chester, Dudley, Hiram, Jasper, Nelson, Grady, Homer, Barney, Aaron, Byron, and Hubert.

There's a Summerville and a Winterville. There are Scienceville, Starve All, Pinch Gut, and Persimmon. Bible names are on the map, names that St. Paul would recognize: Corinth, Bethlehem, Antioch, Mt. Zion, Shiloh, Sardis, Eden, Calvary, and Damascus. There are names out of history: Athens and Sparta and Rome. Some place names are identical with those of places in the Old World: Florence as in Italy, Manchester as named for the manufacturing town in England, Warsaw as in Poland, Bremen and Berlin as in Germany, Canton, where silk was once made, as in China, Darien as in Panama, Lisbon as in Portugal, Amsterdam as in Holland, Cairo as in Egypt, and Aberdeen and Bannockburn as in Scotland. Some are named for the countries themselves, like Egypt, Scotland, Holland. Buda and Pest, in Haralson County, were named by 400 Hungarian winemakers who came to Georgia with their priest to plant vineyards and make wines. But early prohibition laws defeated them and they had to find other employment.

Many place names are associated with figures important to history. Lafayette, a town in North Georgia, and the county of Fayette are named for the French nobleman who helped America in the Revolution and was later imprisoned in France during the French Revolution. He came to Georgia in 1825. LaGrange in Georgia was named for his plantation in France. Washington, Georgia, is thought to have been the first of scores of places in the country named for George Washington, who visited Georgia in 1791. Mt. Vernon was named for Washington's home on the Potomac. Arlington was named for the mansion of General and Mrs. Robert E. Lee, confiscated by the Union after the Civil War broke out. The original Arlington, now a shrine, is also

51

the site of the national cemetery where the late President John F. Kennedy is buried. Columbus and Americus were named to honor America's discoverer and the reporter who wrote about it.

Buena Vista and Resaca are associated with the Mexican War. A place in northwest Georgia was once named Kin Mori, by a man who had married a Japanese wife who was homesick for her native land. He even built a few Japanese buildings there, with curved roofs, for her to look at. Some names have been changed. Winder was once Jug Tavern, Dahlonega was known as Lick Log, Tennille was Station 13, Kennesaw was Big Shanty, Buena Vista was Pea Ridge, and Gainesville was Mule Camp Springs.

One Georgia town was named Enigma, and its origin is really an enigma; nobody knows where the name came from, or why.

A small town once in south Georgia long ago was called Ruskin, for John Ruskin, the English essayist and art critic. It was a communal venture, like Hawthorne's Brook Farm. Its school had the first twelfth grade in Georgia.

Indian names are all over the map, on towns, counties, rivers, streams, mountains, and trails. They are usually musical sounds. An odd thing happened about one of them. People in Webster County first named their county Kinchafoonee. But, one historian reports, "a ripple of laughter went over the state," and they changed it to the more prosaic name of Webster, for Daniel Webster. The lovely name of Kinchafoonee is now on a library in that section.

Indian names have interesting meanings: Choestoe, "where the rabbit danced"; Chestatee, "the place of the lights," where hunters for deer carried torches.

Ichawaynochaway means "the place where the deer sleep." Yonah means "big bear." Omaha means "against the wind." Unocoi means "white." Ellijay means "the place of green, growing things." Toccoa means "beautiful" and Tallulah means "terrible." Dahlonega means "yellow gold," Nottley means "daring horseman"; Hiawassee, "pretty fawn"; and Nacoochee, "Evening Star." Chickamauga, which the Indians spelled Tsikamegi, means "the place of death," and it turned out to be a name that fit when 36,000 Civil War soldiers lay dead, dying, or wounded there in September, 1863.

Other Indian names still on Georgia's map are Talla-poosa, Montezuma, Cusseta, Ochlochee, Ludowici, Attapulgus, Nootootly, Chippewa, Pocataligo, Ohoopee, Sutalee, Upatoi, Willacoochee, and many others.

Talking Rock (named because of an echo nearby) was known by the Indians as Nuny-gunswani-ski. Ball Ground got its name because it was the site of fierce games between Cherokees and Creeks. Much land changed ownership on the outcome.

Counties that were given Indian names are Cherokee, Seminole, Muscogee, Chattooga, Catoosa, Coweta, Chatta-

GEORGIA'S SIGNS, SOUNDS, AND SYMBOLS

Georgia's Seal,
With Plato's Words

The Georgia seal is seen in many places: on doors, on papers, in the stone floors of the State Capitol. The words "Wisdom, Justice, and Moderation" are from Plato's *Republic.* This seal, and important state papers, were hidden by Secretary of State Nathan Barnett and his wife under this house as Sherman's soldiers advanced on Milledgeville, then the state capital, in 1864. The Federals ordered an artist to make an identical seal. But he put the sword in the other hand of the soldier. This made it possible later to detect the spurious state papers.

The Great Seal of State was authorized by the legislature in 1799. It was designed by Daniel Sturges, state surveyor. Governor James Jackson put an advertisement in the "Louisville Gazette," February 26, 1799 and had invited artists to submit designs for a seal. He offered a prize of thirty dollars for the winning design.

The gates at the University of Georgia are in the shape of the arch of this seal.

The Georgia Flag

Georgia's present flag was adopted in 1956. It is red, white and blue, like the Star Spangled Banner. It has at left a vertical blue broad stripe, with the Georgia seal in blue and white. The right side has the Stars and Bars of the Confederacy on a red background, and the thirteen white stars.

Many flags have flown over Georgia, flags of many nations and of many explorers. Once in 1715 a pirate's flag was stuck in the soil on Blackbeard's Island. Spanish explorers set the scarlet flag of Spain along the coast in the sixteenth century. The Flag of France flew briefly along the seashore as the French explorers sought new lands. The British "Union Jack" flew over Georgia until the Revolution ended England's reign in America.

The Liberty Boys had a blue flag, with the word "Liberty" in white letters. Later there was a red and white Georgia flag with the words "American Liberty." The State of Georgia long had a flag with three stripes. The present flag combines symbols of the state's beginning, of its experience as a part of the Confederacy, and of its history as one of the fifty states in the nation. It was the youngest of the thirteen original colonies.

The Georgia Flower

The Georgia flower is the Cherokee Rose. It is a native of China, and came to this country by way of England about 1757. Its botanical name is *"rosa laevigata Michaux."* Andre Michaux, a Charleston botanist born in France, was the first to describe this flower.

It grows in parts of Georgia, often wild. It blooms in early spring, and sometimes blooms again in the autumn. It has bright green leaves, many thorns, and blossoms of creamy velvety texture with centers of bright gold. It was officially adopted by the legislature in 1916.

The legend of the Cherokee Rose is one of the favorite Indian stories still told in Georgia. The Cherokee Indians in north Georgia once captured a young chief of the Seminole Indians in a battle. He was badly wounded. They decided to let him get well before putting him to death. He was nursed by the pretty daughter of a Cherokee chief, and the two young people fell in love. Knowing that their tribes, which were bitter enemies, would never agree to their marriage, they fled into the night. The Indian girl crept back, after they had gone a little way, to dig up a rooted rose to carry with her. She wanted something to plant in her new home with the Seminoles that would remind her of the mountains of her old home, where her people the Cherokees lived.

Georgia has counties named for both of their tribes, the Cherokees and the Seminoles.

The Georgia Tree

Georgia's state tree is the live oak. It is one of 250 native trees that grow in the state. Oglethorpe found these great live oaks growing here in 1733. He gave orders that they be left standing wherever possible.

They live to great age. An old saying is that they are "300 years growing, 300 years grown, and 300 years dying." The live oaks sometimes grow 40 to 50 feet high, and have a spread of 100 feet. A 300-year-old live oak in Thomasville has grown to 55 feet in height, is 25 feet around its trunk, and 170 feet across. It is enrolled as the twenty-fourth member of the National Live Oak Association. Indians valued live oaks for their shade. They used the acorns for roasting, boiling, or seasoning venison stew.

Once a Georgia tree owned itself. Colonel William H. Jackson, its owner, willed the tree to itself at his death. The official deed in Clarke County read like this: "I, W. H. Jackson, of the County of Clarke, State of Georgia, in consideration of great affection for said tree and a desire to see it protected, convey unto said tree entire possession of itself and of land 8 feet around it on all sides." It became famous throughout the land as "The Tree That Owned Itself."

At St. Marys, Georgia, stands the Washington Oak, one of four planted the day George Washington died, December 14, 1799. It is the only one of the four still living.

Georgia's Official Bird

The brown thrasher is Georgia's official state bird. Sometimes it is confused with the brown thrush. But the brown thrasher is rusty-brown color, with white stripes, and yellow eyes; the brown thrush has white spots and dark eyes.

The brown thrasher was made Georgia's official bird by proclamation of the governor on April 6, 1935.

It is one of America's finest songbirds, and one of about 250 kinds of birds found within Georgia.

Athos Menaboni, Georgia artist, has painted the picture of it that most Georgians know best. Audubon probably saw this bird when he was in Georgia.

The Georgia Song

"GEORGIA" was made the official song of the State of Georgia by act of the General Assembly 1922.

This arrangement was adopted by act of General Assembly 1958.

GEORGIA

Words by Robert Loveman

Music by Lollie Belle Wylie
Arr. by Esther Wilburn Barnes
1958

1 From the mountains to the sea, Where her riv-ers
2 Georgia, land of our delight, Haven of the

Roll, there I ever long to be. O, my heart my soul. By her meadows let me lie, In her vales re-main
blest, Here by happy day and night, Peace enthrones the breast. Georgia, Georgia, dearest earth Underneath the blue

1st ending

Underneath her rooftree sky Watch the seasons wane.
Clime that ev-er giveth (birth to the brave and true)

Optional 2nd ending

birth to the brave and true.

THE STORY

UNIT 2

STRANGE LITTLE COLONY AND HOW IT CHANGED

STRANGE LITTLE COLONY AND HOW IT CHANGED

The colony of Georgia started on a bleak, wintry February day in 1733 when George Washington was a baby not quite one year old.

Thirty-five families from England sailed in little boats down the coast from Carolina and eighteen miles up the Savannah River. They put up four white tents — and a new colony was started in the new world. It was the youngest of thirteen colonies here. It was to have a rough time. Once it almost disappeared.

The little colony of Georgia may have got its start just when it did and just the way it did because a rich Englishman wanted to make some repairs on his town house in London. That rich man came to Georgia, a site he had already chosen, with the first 114 colonists that February day. He had wealth and luxury in England. He did not have to concern himself with the problems of poor people coming to the hardships of a new home on the frontier of a new land, but he did. He would stay with them ten years, except for a few business trips back to England. His name was James Edward Oglethorpe. He was a very remarkable fellow. His name is all over the Georgia map, and his statue and picture are in many places. Yet when he finally sailed for England, on a ship named the *"Success,"* he felt he had been a failure.

History does not have a more absorbing story than that of the little colony, of how it changed, of the people who transformed it eventually into the present state of Georgia. That is the story in this book.

But many things had already happened here in this place before there was a colony. What were these things, and who were the people here when they happened?

CHAPTER 6

WHO WAS HERE
BEFORE THE
COLONISTS CAME?

Whose feet first touched the earth that is now Georgia after the Atlantic Ocean no longer washed up beyond Macon and Augusta?

The answer is lost in the mists of time. But more than ten thousand years ago, perhaps 25,000, there were men of mystery here whom we call the Mound Builders. Mounds they built still exist at Kolomoki near Blakely, at Ocmulgee near Macon, and at Etowah near Cartersville. There are others that are smaller. There are effigy mounds, made in the shape of creatures, like the Rock Eagle Mound in Putnam County, now the focus of the 4-H Camp. There are mysterious markings left by the men of long ago, like the curious scribblings on Track Rock Gap near Blairsville in the North Georgia mountains.

WHO WERE THE MOUND BUILDERS?

Nobody really knows who the Mound Builders were, where they came from, how they disappeared, nor why they built the mounds. Historians now are inclined to think they were early Indians. But the Indians who were here when the first white men came knew no more about the Mound Builders than the white men did. The Creeks especially held the mounds in superstitious awe, and would not disturb them. Many people, including Thomas Jefferson, have tried to solve the mystery of the mounds.

The Mound Builders had no wheels and no domesticated animals. They built the mounds by carrying millions of basketfuls of earth. They did not have even a wheelbarrow. It was labor as long and hard as that of the Egyptians who built the pyramids, or the Chinese who built the Great Wall. These mystery men in future Georgia evidently used the mounds for holding councils, for religious worship, for watch towers, for signal stations, for the chief's residence, and for burying their dead. Why did they stop building the mounds? Nobody knows.

Science has provided a way of finding out how old things are. The process is known as carbon 14 dating. It was discovered after World War II by W. F. Libby, a Chicago chemist, and was a by-product of atomic research. By measuring the amount of radioactive carbon 14 in plant and animal matter left over from long ago, and comparing it with that found in living things today, it is possible almost to pinpoint time. By this method we know that the Mound Builders were here at least ten thousand years ago. There was a time when the arrow was their "new weapon." It made possible the support of more people in a smaller area. This gave rise to their villages.

Mounds and Mysteries

Within Georgia are three of the four most important Indian mounds in the southeast. The fourth is near St. Louis, Missouri. The largest mounds in Georgia are the Kolomoki Mounds, the Ocmulgee Mounds, and the Etowah Mounds.

THE KOLOMOKI MOUNDS: These mounds are near Blakely, Georgia, in the southwest corner of the state. They are on Kolomoki Creek, about fifteen miles east of the Chattahoochee River. There is a museum here, with exhibits to help visitors understand the site.

Historians and archeologists believe that these people were wandering through this region in search of food more than ten thousand years ago. They were living in family groups. By five hundred years before Christ, they were using a new weapon, the bow and arrow. It was more effective than the spear in getting food. There were certainly settlements here during the years 800 to 1200 B.C., though the nomadic tribes had wandered through here long before that.

The Temple Mound, which is the largest of the Kolomoki group, is ascended by many steps.

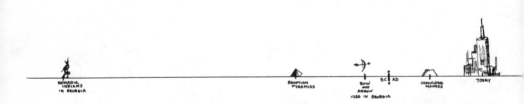

THE OCMULGEE MOUNDS: These mounds are near the banks of the Ocmulgee River just outside of Macon in middle Georgia. At least six different groups lived here over a period of ten thousand years. The mounds themselves date back to at least 900 A. D. Creek tradition held that Ocmulgee was the first Creek settlement in this area. It was from here that Emperor Brim was, in 1715, to set up headquarters for his savage but ill-fated attempt to drive the white men from the Carolinas. He had moved his camp there from

64

Coweta Town near Columbus to organize his war. White men
followed him back and burned the Ocmulgee settlement. He
went back to Coweta Town on the Chattahoochee River, on
the Alabama side. But that came much later than the time of
the Mound Builders. General Walter Harris, writing Brim's
biography, titled it *Emperor Brim, The Most Remarkable
Indian.*

The Ocmulgee Old Fields had existed long before
Brim's time. There is some evidence that this ancient
council town could have been set up by the Mayas, who later
went on to Yucatan in Central America.

A circular row of fifty seats show where the old
rulers sat. The oldest relics include the Folsom spear
points of the wandering hunters who were here thousands of
years ago. The Ocmulgee Old Fields were described by

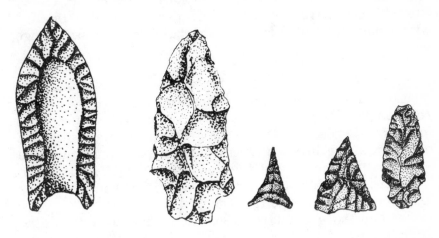

William Bartram in his book about his travels through Georgia. He had been here with his father in 1765, and returned alone in 1773. His book of travels has been re-issued in recent years, edited by Mark Van Doren.

The Ocmulgee Mounds extended 20 miles down the river. The original residents had abandoned the site before DeSoto was here in 1540, but other groups settled here later.

THE ETOWAH MOUNDS, near Cartersville in upper Georgia were, about 1000 to 1500 A. D., the center of vigorous Indian life. Early inhabitants came here from hundreds of miles away for festivals and for trading. Here was the largest of more than a hundred settlements throughout the Etowah River Valley. This was their political, economic, and religious headquarters. They were skilled in shaping objects from clay, bone, shell, wood, and copper. They made cloth and wove baskets.

Here the chief lived. He decided what crops they would grow (usually beans, corn, and pumpkins), and how they would share their food.

In the museum here are two grotesque marble figures, male and female. There is a skeleton in an open grave. There are objects here that are not native to the region, evidence that early people came here from far away for the assemblies.

There was a moat around the settlement. It may have been built for several reasons: protection from enemies, irrigating crops, and trapping fish. In an arts and crafts shop on these grounds is an artist's drawing of the way Etowah may have looked in the days when it was alive with sound and color and the vigorous life of these strange people.

THE ROCK EAGLE EFFIGY MOUND is a different kind of mound. This is not simply heaped-up earth; it is a great rock eagle, designed and built by some shadowy people of long ago. Legend has it that the great mound was built by a chieftain whose little child was carried away by an immense eagle, but the fact is that eagles do not carry off children.

The great bird has a wingspread of 120 feet, and is 102 feet from top of head to tip of toe.

Near the great bird, which is the center of one of the world's largest youth camps, is a marker with these words:

66

Tread softly here, white man,
For long ere you came strange races
Lived, fought and loved.

(Copied from Monument)

The Rock Eagle Mound is said to be the most perfect effigy mound in North America.

SMALLER MOUNDS: At various places throughout Georgia, there are smaller mounds and other traces of these men of long ago who dwelt here before there was a Georgia.

The waters of the newly created lakes along the rivers have covered some of these traces. Archeologists and their students and others interested in antiquities rushed to dig in the sections before the waters covered the earth.

67

Twelve miles south of Cumming, in northwest Georgia, there are several small mounds. These may be old Indian graves. Two miles northwest of Cumming, there is a big mass of granite, carved with mysterious figures, most of them enclosed in circles. The meaning is a mystery, like the markings at Track Rock Gap. These Cumming mounds and mysteries are just examples of others that are here and there about the state. On Enchanted Mountain, ten miles north of Blue Ridge, there is the track of a six-toed foot.

THE CURIOUS MARKINGS AT TRACK ROCK GAP: On a great rock on the side of a mountain road near Blairsville are strange markings on soapstones. The site is on the old Choestoe ("where the rabbit danced") Indian Trail. It is near Blood Mountain.

The markings seem to be both animal and human footprints. There are markings like bird tracks, too. There are also geometric squares, circles, crosses and straight lines in no special order.

Were they messages of meaning, or were they just the doodlings of hunters or warriors resting there? The Cherokee Indians later said these marks were there when they first came into Georgia.

An old legend says that it rains when white men approach this spot because the Great Spirit is angry. Another tale tells of a flood that once drowned people in this spot, and says that on moonsilvered nights, their spirits return and cluster here.

The Indians That Were Here When The White Men Came

The Indians are thought to have been Asiatics, judging from their black, straight hair, high cheek bones, and copper skin. They came over to the American continent either in boats or probably from Inner Mongolia by land when Bering Strait was a land bridge from the present Alaska to Asia. They filtered down through both of the American continents. Some stopped in one place; others traveled on. The Incas went to Peru in South America; the Aztecs settled in Mexico. Both were to be cruelly conquered later by the Spaniards. Their story is well told in books by William Prescott, a

courageous historian who wrote very readable histories
despite one blind eye and another which he could sometimes

use for only a half hour. His blindness had started when a
fellow student at Harvard threw a piece of bread that damaged
his eye. Fortunately Prescott had money, and could spend
his life as he liked. He had to hire people to read his books
of research. He had research done in Spain and Mexico and
Peru. His books are invaluable sources of history.

Georgia's story includes a part of the history of
three Indian groups: the Cherokees, who belonged to the
Iroquois tribe, made familiar by Longfellow in his legend
about Hiawatha (another Hiawatha formed them into a confederacy about 1250 A.D.); the Creeks, who were Muscogeans
and came to be known as "Creeks" because the British
found them living by the creeks in the southeast; and the
Seminoles, who dwelt along the lower border of Georgia and
in upper Florida. The descendants of the Seminoles live
in the Florida Everglades and make the palms Americans
use on Palm Sunday. All Seminoles never surrendered
their lands or went west as many other Indians did. The
Lower Creeks were in middle Georgia. They were friendly
to whites; the Upper Creeks or Red Sticks, who lived in
Alabama, were not. The Cherokees lived above the Creeks,
in the mountains. The line that divided them ran somewhere
about Elberton to Atlanta to Cedartown. In Banks County,
a marker stands on the line, and there is a "Line" Church.

There had once been 850,000 Indians in the United States; there were probably 200,000 between the Atlantic and the Mississippi, and 25,000 in Georgia.

THE FIRST EUROPEAN SETTLERS IN GEORGIA

Three powerful nations struggled to possess the New World, including the land that was to become Georgia. They were Spain, France, and England.

Shadowy legend also tells of Norsemen from the frozen countries coming along the shore. Icelanders with Leif Ericson, sailing in 1000 A. D. for Greenland, were said to have been blown off course and landed on this continent, probably near Nova Scotia. They later may have sailed down the Atlantic coast, some writers have suggested.

Spain Came First

Spain was first to claim the New World because the Italian, Christopher Columbus, had been sailing for Spain, financed by King Ferdinand, Queen Isabella, and the Pinson brothers, when he found this land in 1492. Though he had made four voyages in all, he had never touched the main continent. Columbus, who had read Marco Polo's tales of the fabulous East, had married the daughter of a mapmaker, Bartholomew Perestrello, navigator for Prince Henry of Portugal, and inherited her father's maps. He came to believe, as some other men also believed then, that the world was round and that he could reach the East by sailing west. The reason men wanted to reach the East was that they had discovered that there were fabulous treasures to be had there. Not only silks and jewels, but also spices that possessed some of the riches of the Orient. Another source was the Italian named Marco Polo, who had gone from Venice with his father and uncle, and lived in the rich kingdom of China for several years. He had come back and written a book about it that set men wild with eagerness to find a way to get there and possess some of the riches of the East. They did not want to go by land because the roads in those days were full of bandits who were quick to kill.

COLUMBUS BELIEVED HE COULD FIND A WAY BY WATER. People thought he was crazy. Every schoolboy knows the story of how people warned him that he would fall off the edge of

70

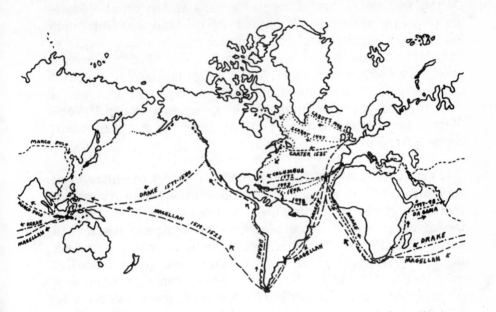

an earth they believed to be flat, or encounter monsters
that would devour his ships and sailors. Thousands of
pictures have made the world familiar with his three little
ships, the Nina, the Pinta, and the Santa Maria. Joaquin
Miller's poem tells the tale of the sailors about to mutiny,
wanting desperately to turn back, and of Columbus saying,
"Sail on! Sail on!" When they finally saw land and landed on
the island of Santo Domingo, Columbus claimed the land for
Spain. He did not know that he had found a new world; he
thought he had found India. He called the copper-colored
people he found here "Indians." It was a mistake, but they
have been known as Indians ever since. Sometimes they are
called "the American Indians" to distinguish them from the
people who live in India, the land that Columbus was really
seeking. He later took some of the dark-skinned people back
to Europe with him. People there had never seen Indians
before.

Columbus was deprived of having the world he had
found named for him because a Florentine explorer who was
on one of the voyages wrote letters about it to Lorenzo de
Medici, and the letters became well known in Europe. A
mapmaker, "Hylacomylus," or Martin Waldseemuller, director of the French academy, who may never have heard of

Columbus, had heard about the letters of Americus Vespucius, and put the name "America" on the land that Columbus had found. But many cities — including one in Georgia — and other sites have been named for Columbus, whose voyages were made in 1492, 1493, 1498 and 1502. The poetic name for America, used in many songs and stories, is "Columbia," as in "Columbia, the Gem of the Ocean." Vespucius is believed to have sailed along the coast himself, about 1501.

PONCE DE LEON DISCOVERED FLORIDA: Columbus died May 20, 1506 without having set foot on the North American continent. It was a Spaniard who had been with Columbus on one of his voyages who discovered the continent itself. His name was Ponce de Leon. When he was young, he was a page at the court of King Ferdinand and Queen Isabella, and later he fought the Moors in Spain. Ponce de Leon was governor of Haiti, and later of Puerto Rico, where he became rich from gold mines. He was thirty-two years old, and he did not want to grow old.

He had heard of a fabled "fountain of youth," and thought it was on the island of Bimini. He was searching for that island when he landed near the present site of St. Augustine, Florida, on Easter, March 13, 1513, just twenty-one years after Columbus had found the New World. Easter in Spanish means "festival of flowers," so Ponce de Leon named the land he had discovered "Florida," which means "the place of flowers." Easter was for them a festival of flowers. He sailed down the coast as far as Cape Canaveral, now Cape Kennedy, then up the west coast. Catusa Indians almost massacred his men at a place now called "Monstanza," meaning "massacre." He also fought the Carib Indians, for whom the Caribbean Ocean was named.

Dr. John R. Swanton, writing in a bulletin published by the Smithsonian Institution, says that in 1526 — just five years after Ponce de Leon's settlement at St. Augustine — about six hundred Spaniards stayed for a little while near the mouth of the Savannah River, led by Lucas De Allyon, in a temporary settlement known as San Miguel de Guadalupe.

VASQUEZ DE ALLYON   had first started to the New World in 1520, seeking Indians for slaves. He had grown rich

72

working Indian slaves in his mines in Santo Domingo. Many died or were killed by cruelty and he needed others to replace them. Once he took 150 from along the southeastern coast, but many died on the voyage to Santo Domingo. When the ship landed, the island's governor, Diego Columbus (son of Christopher Columbus), freed them. De Allyon went to Spain to get permission to settle a colony somewhere near the American coast. It may have been on the Savannah River. He had five hundred men and six ships. Once he sent two hundred inland exploring, but angry Indians drove them back.

De Allyon decided to abandon the settlement. He became ill and died on the ship and a storm washed his body overboard. De Allyon's settlement could have been the first entry into Georgia by white men, or Ponce de Leon himself could have crossed over into present Georgia territory in his search for the Fountain of Youth. However, the best-known story is that a brave and cruel Spaniard named DeSoto was, in 1539, the first white man to set foot in what is known today as Georgia.

WHICH WAY DID DESOTO GO?　　People argue to this day about which route DeSoto took through Georgia. Did he enter just above Tallahassee and leave just below Augusta and never come back into Georgia? Or did he later turn back from the Carolina country — before he went west, where he met his tragic doom — into the Coosa country? Was he once in Rome, as a plaque in that Georgia city maintains?

Before we consider which way he went, we must consider who he was, why he was here at all, and what he did.

Fernando deSoto (called Ferdinand deSoto by Americans) had been a six-year-old boy in Spain when Columbus discovered America. By the time he became a teen-ager, his uncle had been appointed governor of Darien, now Panama, where the famed Panama Canal is located. This uncle brought DeSoto to Darien.

When DeSoto was a young man, he went with Pizarro on the 1531 conquest of the Incas in Peru. They looted the Incan treasures, just as Spain's Cortez had conquered and looted the Mayas of Mexico in 1513. DeSoto's share of the gold was said to have been $100,000. He determined to use it to find more gold in the northern section of America.

73

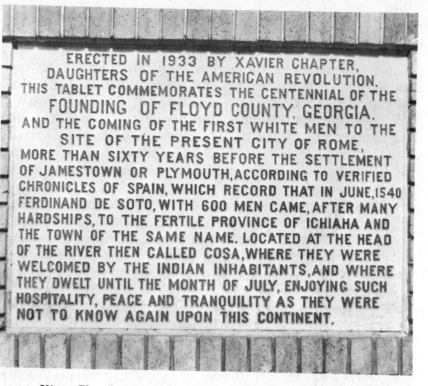

ERECTED IN 1933 BY XAVIER CHAPTER, DAUGHTERS OF THE AMERICAN REVOLUTION. THIS TABLET COMMEMORATES THE CENTENNIAL OF THE FOUNDING OF FLOYD COUNTY, GEORGIA. AND THE COMING OF THE FIRST WHITE MEN TO THE SITE OF THE PRESENT CITY OF ROME, MORE THAN SIXTY YEARS BEFORE THE SETTLEMENT OF JAMESTOWN OR PLYMOUTH, ACCORDING TO VERIFIED CHRONICLES OF SPAIN, WHICH RECORD THAT IN JUNE, 1540 FERDINAND DE SOTO, WITH 600 MEN CAME, AFTER MANY HARDSHIPS, TO THE FERTILE PROVINCE OF ICHIAHA AND THE TOWN OF THE SAME NAME. LOCATED AT THE HEAD OF THE RIVER THEN CALLED COSA, WHERE THEY WERE WELCOMED BY THE INDIAN INHABITANTS, AND WHERE THEY DWELT UNTIL THE MONTH OF JULY, ENJOYING SUCH HOSPITALITY, PEACE AND TRANQUILITY AS THEY WERE NOT TO KNOW AGAIN UPON THIS CONTINENT.

King Charles V of Spain had appointed DeSoto governor "for life" of Cuba and Florida. ("Florida" at that time meant the entire southeast and beyond!) But DeSoto's life was not to be very long.

After he decided to explore the North American continent in search of gold, he went to Spain to get permission — and to promise the king a share of the riches he expected to find in future Georgia and the rest of the continent.

In 1538, he assembled men and ships and provisions in Spain for his venture into the north of the New World. He went back to Cuba. He left his wife, Dona Isabel, the daughter of the Dovila of Nicaragua, who was never to see him again. She was left to govern the island in his absence.

DeSoto and his men left Cuba in nine ships on May 18, 1539. There were about six hundred soldiers and many other attendants of various kinds, including priests and writers. There were also Portuguese noblemen with him. They all landed at Tampa Bay on May 30, 1539. (The DeSoto Oak, near the landing site, stands at the University of

DeSoto in Georgia

Tampa.) He brought two hundred horses and many dogs, a huge chair to sit on — like a throne when he dealt with the natives — and crucibles for refining the gold he expected to find. He also brought chains and irons and handcuffs for the prisoners he expected to take.

Not all the Indians he first encountered were friendly. Those around the Tampa area had seen white men before, and had not liked them. The historian L.O. Wilmer suggests that their hostility to DeSoto was due to the cruel treatment they had received from another European, probably Panfilo de Narvaez, who made a tragic trip along the Gulf in 1528. This first one had cut off the nose of an Indian chief, Cacique Ucita, and allowed wild dogs to attack the chief's mother when she protested their treatment of an Indian girl. DeSoto found in this area a man named Ortiz, who had been with Narvaez and had been held prisoner and tortured by the Indians for twelve years. Porcallo, a rich man from Havana who was with one of the exploring groups, captured Indians to work his mine.

DeSoto's men saw many sights that were strange to them. One field of corn was six miles long! At Taolli, in what is now Irwin County, they found houses roofed with cane stalks. They saw Indian women wearing shawls of linen-like cloth made from a mulberry bark. They also saw Indians who wore nothing at all.

DeSoto and his men came into Georgia in the spring of 1540, near the site of Bainbridge and the Ochlocknee River, starting March 3. They had spent the winter near Tallahassee, which was then an Indian village called Anhayca. They also went along the Suwannee, or "River of the Deer."

Their route up through the state carried them through what is now Bainbridge, Leesburg, Hawkinsville, Cordele,

Dublin, and on toward Silver Bluff below Augusta. Along the way, many things happened. They crossed the Flint River on March 13, 1540. Just below Cordele, they put up a cross and observed the first Easter ever celebrated in Georgia.

Sometimes DeSoto gave the Indians gifts; at other times, he treated them cruelly. One of his own writers, known as "the gentleman of Elvas," noted this in his report, *Travels Of A Portuguese Gentleman:* "The Governor is very fond of the sport of shooting Indians." He allowed his men to rob them, and sometimes even to plunder the graves of their dead, searching for the gold they had come to find.

At a town called Yupaha, ruled by a woman, they saw Indians wearing gold trinkets. DeSoto asked them the source. They kept pointing northward. This may have been a trick to get rid of this Spanish intruder. DeSoto kept going north. One Indian lad even described how the gold was dug and mined.

At first the soldiers tried to march in their heavy armor. The weather was getting hot, the mosquitoes and sandflies pestered them, and they never knew when an Indian arrow would whiz into their midst. Many were sick and homesick. It was hard to get through the thick and tangled swamps, and across the big rivers, which had no bridges.

Sometimes their food ran low. Once they were reduced to eating the wild dogs and horses they had brought. The Indians had never seen horses. At first they thought that horse and rider were one animal.

Sometimes the Indians were friendly and shared their food. One of the writers with the expedition reported, "As the Governor (DeSoto) came to the town called Conaysago, twenty Indians met him, each laden with baskets of mulberries, butter, and honey." Sometimes they also brought corn (which they called maize), and beans and pumpkins. Now and then they gave the white men fish and turkey and quail. The Indians knew how to roast meat slowly over glowing coals. The Spaniards called this "barbecue." Once the Indians at Guaxale gave the Spaniards three hundred dogs, which Indians themselves never ate, but the Spaniards did if they got hungry enough.

An Indian princess met him at Iotatachachequi near Silver Bluff floating on a barge, like Cleopatra. She had rowed over from an Indian settlement, said to have been ruled by her mother, who was hostile to the strangers. The princess was friendly. She brought DeSoto many pearls and skins. He gave her a ruby ring from his own fingers.

There were thousands of pearls in this vicinity. Some were no good because the Indians had burned them in the fire or bored holes in them. But many were valuable. There were so many that one of DeSoto's men, Juan Perron, got tired of carrying his sackful. He twirled the sack around his head and spilled the pearls. (These "shell pearls" were from fresh water mussels in the mountain streams, because oysters that make regular pearls live only in salt water.)

Fernando de Soto

Despite her kindness, DeSoto captured the Indian princess and forced her to go with him. She carried with her a *petaca* or cane trunk, filled with her treasures. Even some of DeSoto's own men thought he repaid her friendship cruelly. The reporter noted, "It was not so good usage as she deserved for the goodwill she showed and the entertainment she made him." Soon the princess escaped into the green swamps and DeSoto never found her again.

DeSoto must have sent many of his men on side trips while he himself stayed on the main route. There are many legends, and some evidence of Spanish men being in places where historians say DeSoto himself never was. Some of his men found a dagger and armor said to have been left by De Allyon.

In Nacoochee Valley, in White County, there is a legend about the DeSoto journey.

An Indian queen named Oohooee, so that story goes, was persuaded to reveal to Lorenzo, one of DeSoto's men, the secret of where her tribe's treasure was hidden, at the foot of Mt. Yonah. ("Yonah" means "big bear.") Wahoo, the tribal chief, killed Lorenzo for trying to steal the treasure. The Indians drowned Oohooee and Eola, one of her daughters. They also threw her other daughter Nacoochee into the water, but she was saved by her lover, an Indian lad named Sautee, who was just sixteen and a member of another tribe. Not allowed to marry, says the legend, these two leaped off Mt. Yonah to their deaths. They were buried under the Nacoochee Mounds. Nacoochee ("Evening Star") Valley and the village of Sautee are named for them.

In the Mt. Yonah area, where some of DeSoto's men were at the village of Xulla, in May, 1540, the gold they were searching for was found nearly three hundred years later! In 1829 thousands came swarming to Duke's Creek, in this area, in the nation's first gold rush twenty years before the "Forty-niners" rushed to California to dig gold at Sutter's Creek in 1849. DeSoto's men never found Georgia gold, however.

After two months in Georgia, they crossed over the Savannah River into the Carolina country. Soon they turned back toward the west, but this is the part still argued about: Did DeSoto re-enter Georgia after he had crossed the Savannah River in May, 1540? A plaque in the City Hall at Rome, Georgia, bears these words:

More than sixty years before the settlement of Jamestown or Plymouth, according to verified chronicles of Spain, in June, 1540, Ferdinand DeSoto, with six hundred men, came, after many hardships, to the fertile province of Iahaha and the town of the same name, located at the head of the river then called Coosa, where they were welcomed by the Indian inhabitants, and where they dwelt until July, enjoying such hospitality, peace, and tranquillity as they were not to know again upon this continent.

But the United States Commission, set up to plan for the observance in 1940 of the four hundredth anniversary of DeSoto's journey, reported their belief that once he had left Georgia, he did not enter it again. They thought that the best evidence showed that DeSoto went from the Carolina country westward through the future site of Chattanooga, then down the Tennessee River into Alabama. Nobody really knows. There is a legend that some of DeSoto's men built the peculiar fortifications on Fort Mountain, which rises 2,855 feet in elevation, near Chatsworth. But most authorities say they did not stay in one place long enough to have built these. Indians said they were built by a race of "moon-eyed people who could see to work only at night." Some believe Indians built it as a refuge from DeSoto.

At Mabila, in Alabama, there was a fearful battle between DeSoto's men and Indians under the giant Chief Tuscaloosa, known as the "Black Warrior." The Indians resisted when DeSoto tried to take their food, molest their women, and press Indians into service as burden bearers.

The battle was fought October 18, 1540, and lasted all day. Even Indian women and children fought. The Spaniards, who had iron armor and crossbows, killed 2,500 Indians, and lost only 20 of their own men.

During the battle, DeSoto heard that a Spaniard named Captain Francisco Maldonado was at the Indian village of Achusi on the Gulf of Mexico, with ships and supplies for him. But DeSoto turned northward instead of going toward the ships, though he desperately needed the supplies. He believed that once his men saw the ships, they would rebel against him and return to Cuba, and he was still determined to find gold.

He pushed on west, camping near Tupelo, Mississippi. during the 1540-41 winter. He discovered the Mississippi

80

River, and went on beyond it into future Arizona and Texas territory. Then he turned back toward the great river. Many of his men had died of fevers. Some had been killed.

Some had grown weak from hunger and perished. About a hundred were left. DeSoto himself became ill with fever, and on May 21, 1542, two years after he had left Georgia, he died in Louisiana. His men, fearful that the Indians would attack their weak little band if they knew the leader was dead, buried him at night in the river, weighting his hollowed-out oak tree coffin with wet sand. For four hundred years his bones have been at rest at the bottom of the river that Mark Twain was later to make famous as the haunt of his "rascals," Huck Finn and Tom Sawyer.

DeSoto had named Luis de Moscoso as his successor, and Moscoso and the remaining handful of men struggled on to Texas, trying vainly to reach Mexico by land. Failing that, they turned back to the Mississippi River, built seven brigantines, and boarded them, with the 22 horses that they had left of the original 243. They got so hungry that they ate the horses, one by one, until less than a half dozen were left, and these they turned loose. Not more than forty of DeSoto's men got back to Cuba, from whence they had started. They had trudged more than four thousand miles through Georgia and the rest of the southeast looking for gold. It was sometimes under their feet, especially in North Georgia, where it would be found about 300 years later, but they never found it.

DeSoto's wife, who was rich, had sent many searching parties to find her husband before she received the news that he was dead. She died soon after.

Isabella, Wife Of DeSoto.

The historian Bourne says that DeSoto's journey through the southeast, comparable in courage and resourcefulness to Byrd's expedition to the South Pole, is one of the most remarkable ventures in history. DeSoto's name is on many towns, streams, waterfalls, trees, and other things in Georgia and elsewhere today.

The report, which was written by the Portuguese who accompanied DeSoto, has this notation on the English translation: "DeSoto's Travels 'written by a Portugal gentleman of Elvas emploied in all the action,' and translated out of the Portuguese by Richard Hakluyt, 1609."

THE SPANISH KING SENT OTHERS:　　　King Phillip of Spain was enraged by attacks on Spanish ships that were bringing gold and other treasures out of Mexico. He began to send men to see about setting up settlements along the Gulf of Mexico, and later the coast of Georgia, as bases for the protection of Spanish interests.

In 1558, he ordered his Mexican viceroy, Luis de Vasco, to send men from Mexico to Mobile Bay to select a site for a colony. But it was another Spaniard, Tristan de Luna, who in 1560 came into the southeast hoping to set up a permanent settlement, to build a string of forts, and to mine gold. He followed part of DeSoto's route. There is some evidence that De Luna proceeded "to the Appalachy Mountains" and the Indian town of Xualla, where DeSoto had once been about twenty years earlier. He had with him about a half dozen of the men who had been with DeSoto. In 1840, Meriweather and Lumsden found in Duke's Creek in White County, Georgia mining equipment that gave evidence of the presence of Europeans long before. Johannes Lederer, German traveler, says Spaniards mined in Georgia until 1670. Indians did not mine for gold, and even if they did, they would not have had metal equipment. The Georgia Indians were still in the Stone Age when Europeans had entered the Iron Age. At places like the Etowah Mounds, where festivals drew Indians from a thousand miles, there have been found some bits of copper, brought by visiting Indians from the North, but it was not in use by Georgia Indians then.

Many of De Luna's people starved. Some were so hungry that they ate leaves from the trees. Some died from eating poisonous plants. Some soldiers boiled the leather

De Luna Had Ships Like These.

of their garments and ate it. De Luna's men followed part of DeSoto's route in reverse, and were probably in what is now Georgia at some time. He came up the Coosa and explored the valley land there. He was not only searching for gold, but had plans for establishing forts and settlements. But he failed as DeSoto had failed, and he left the area in April, 1561.

In 1565, King Phillip of Spain had sent Spaniards to St. Augustine — where the Spanish Ponce de Leon had tried to establish a colony in 1521 — to drive out what he considered the "intruders" from other nations. Because Columbus had discovered America when he was sailing from Spain, and because Ponce de Leon and DeSoto had been exploring for Spain, the king believed that all the new country was his.

MENENDEZ AND THE GOLDEN AGE OF SPANISH MISSIONS:
Pedro Menendez, the first to set up a permanent Spanish colony in Florida, was commander of the Spanish fleet in Cuba. He was also a religious fanatic. The reason he happened to come to the mainland was that King Phillip II

of Spain was enraged at the news that France had dared to set up a little settlement on the St. Johns River. He ordered Menendez to destroy it and to drive the French off the American shores. "Root out the Huguenots," ordered the Catholic king of Spain. Menendez said, "I come to hang and behead all the Lutherans I can find. . . ."

On September 8, 1565, seventy-three years after Columbus discovered America, Menendez, who had been appointed Governor of Florida, arrived near St. Augustine with nineteen ships and fifteen hundred soldiers, plus others, or 2,436 in all. He soon attacked the French Protestant colony that Jean Ribaut and Reni de Laudonnierre had set up, burning the village and shooting or hanging those that could not escape in time. For this, he was actually honored in Europe. His portrait was painted by Titian.

In 1566, the year after he had done this, he sailed up the Georgia coast to talk with the Indians. He wanted to put forts on their islands to protect Spanish interests. He also wanted to set up Catholic missions there to convert the Indians. He had heard that they made human sacrifices. The Spanish usually had two chief purposes in a new country: finding gold and converting the natives to Catholicism. Menendez had a third purpose: to keep other explorers and settlers out of the southeast.

He landed on St. Catherines Island. He sat on the beach and ate biscuit and honey with old Guale, who, with his brother, ruled over the territory known as Guale. This was the name by which Georgia first came to be known by the Spaniards, who regarded it as a part of Florida.

Menendez left his nephew and another soldier on the island while he went with his men and some Indians to look at South Carolina. When he returned, the Indians welcomed him because they thought a cross he set up had brought rain, breaking a long drought.

The chief gave Menendez permission to put a fort with thirty soldiers on the island. The Spanish governor also put missions along the coast and some far inland, near Stone Mountain and on the Chattahoochee River. He sent his two aides, Boyano and Pardo, to explore the interior of Georgia and the Carolina country. They were to open up a road that led from St. Augustine to Mexico, which the Spaniards called "New Spain." They explored the country,

The Indians Thought A Cross Brought Rain.

built some forts, and continued the search for gold. Boyano was reported to have found a fabulous gem that came to be known to historians as "Boyano's Diamond."

By 1575, Spaniards were shipping wild turkeys, sassafras, and furs from Georgia back to Spain.

What happened to Menendez? He was later appointed governor of Cuba. In 1572, he finally departed from America. He had made fifty voyages, and was made captain in a powerful fleet, ships which the Spanish king called "the invincible Spanish Armada." He became ill; perhaps he was poisoned. He died on September 17, 1574, leaving his family in dire poverty.

In 1588, England defeated "the invincible Spanish Armada" and Spain's power in the world began to wane.

FIRE AND MURDER DESTROYED THE SPANISH MISSION: The Jesuits were the first of the Spanish religious leaders to settle on the Georgia coast. They made the Guale region their headquarters. At first the Indians were friendly. Then they rebelled at the strict disciplines of the church. They attacked some of the missions, and murdered the men who had come to do them good.

After the Jesuits left, the Franciscans came. They set up the San Pedro Mission on Cumberland Island. Later came other missions like the San Buena Ventura on St. Simons, San Jose on Sapelo, Santa Catalina on St. Catherines, and Santo Domingo on the mainland near the Altamaha River. There were others inland. Some historians say the missions were established as far inland as the Flint and the Chattahoochee rivers, and near Stone Mountain. Others dispute this. But the "golden age of Spanish missions" lasted about a hundred years; then the bells were silenced, and the gardens quiet again. Georgia's Spanish missions are twenty years older than those in California. The largest and best preserved of them are the Santa Maria Missions near St. Marys.

The priests planted figs, oranges, lemons, melons, pomegranates, grapes, peaches, and olives in their gardens. They grew vegetables, and they raised medicinal herbs. They rowed in their little boats among the islands — where the inland waterway boats skitter through the bright waters today — teaching the Indians, tending the sick, baptizing the natives, comforting the troubled. The Spanish conquistadores came for gold and glory; but the gentle priests came for the glory of God.

The Indians grew restive under the discipline of the church. Some chiefs wanted to have more than one wife. They wanted to drink the "fire water" that made them savage. They grew tired of observing the holidays of the church. Both Indians and pirates attacked the missions at one time or another. When their missions were destroyed, the Spanish sometimes built them again.

In 1597, Juanillo, Indian heir to the mico of Guale, led a frightful attack in which Catholic priests were brutally

87

murdered. He had resented the gentle remonstrance of Father
Pedro de Corpa over his wild ways and his many wives. He
fled to the woods, rounded up other young Indians and led a
savage massacre of the priests. They killed Father Corpa
with a hatchet, as he knelt in prayer. By this time, French
corsairs and English adventurers were also raiding the
Georgia coasts. Raiding parties based in the Carolinas
destroyed thirteen Spanish missions. But at first, the Spanish kept rebuilding them.

    In 1606, Don Diego, the Bishop of Cuba, visited the
Georgia coastal missions and received more than a thousand
Indian converts into the Church. Cuban Bishop Altamirans
spent three months on the coast in 1606 and reported the
conversion of 2,074 Indians and 370 whites. By 1655, five
missions had been rebuilt in Guale. By 1680, the Spanish

had pushed far into the interior, set up the Savacola Mission on the Chattahoochee, and the Santa Cruz de Savacola Mission where the Flint and the Chattahoochee join.

By 1696, Pensacola had been established as a fort, and the Spanish had another foothold in the area.

One of the priests slain at the Georgia coastal missions of the Spaniards was the gentle Cumbrian giant, Father Valascola. Another was Jesuit Father Augustin Baez Domingo, who had written a grammar book with which to teach the Indians. It is thought to have been the first book written on this continent, but it was lost. A Franciscan friar, Father Pareja, wrote books for the Timucuan Indians.

Some of the priests died of malaria and yellow fever. By 1686, there were no Spanish settlements above the St. Marys River. By 1700, the Spanish in this area had been pushed back to the St. Johns River.

But the Spanish shadow loomed long over Georgia. Spain had not objected greatly to the founding of the Carolina colony at Charleston in 1670, but had insisted that no colony be established south of it.

The French Changed The Names Of The Rivers

King Francis I of France did not like the way things were going in the New World. When he heard that the Pope at Rome had issued a "bull" dividing South America between Spain and Portugal, in 1493, he said, "I would like to see that paragraph in Father Adam's will that divided the world between Spain and Portugal." (The effect of the Papal Bull was modified in 1494 by the Treaty of Tordesillas between the two countries.)

France began to send its own explorers up and down the coasts and the inland rivers of North America. Some went in through northern rivers, explored the Great Lakes region, sailed down the Mississippi and settled in along the Gulf of Mexico and New Orleans, pushing toward Florida. Others sailed along the Atlantic coast.

Verazzano, an Italian hired by France, may have sailed up the Savannah River about 1525. He described a river very much like it. Panfilo de Narvaez, beginning his terrible and tragic journey through the southeast in 1528, may have set foot in Georgia, but there is no proof. Other Frenchmen explored the Satilla River as a possible site for a colony, and then decided to settle at Port Royal in South Carolina.

Ribaut was the Frenchman who changed the name of Georgia's rivers. Captain Jean Ribaut of Dieppe, France, sailing under the orders of Admiral Coligny (the Protestant leader who was killed August 24, 1572 in the St. Bartholomew's Massacre), left LeHavre, France, February 18, 1562, with two ships, headed for America. They were loaded with French Protestants of the sect known as Huguenots. There was terrible rivalry between Catholics and Protestants in the Old World; sometimes one was in power; sometimes, another. Ribaut's first lieutenant was Reni de Laudonnierre, who was later to head another French expedition.

Ribaut's shipload of Protestants were looking for a place to settle. They landed near St. Augustine. Three years later, they would meet their doom.

They did not settle in St. Augustine. They sailed on up the Georgia coast. Ribaut gave the Timucuan Indian chiefs blue robes with a gold *fleur de lis,* and he gave the Georgia rivers new names, French names. He changed the St. Marys to the Seine; the Altamaha to the Loire; the Ogeechee to the Garonne; and the Savannah to the Grande. Nobody at all paid any attention to the change in names. The rivers went on being the St. Marys, the Altamaha, the Ogeechee, and the Savannah.

Ribaut liked Georgia. He kept written records of his voyage, and he wrote down his impressions of the Georgia and Florida coast. It was all called Florida then. Though he settled his Huguenots at Port Royal instead of on a Georgia river, he wrote about the Georgia land in his report titled, "The True and Last Discoveries of Florida Made by Captain Jean Ribaut in the year 1562." He wrote, "This is the fairest and pleasantest, the fruitfullest land we have seen." He found the Indians growing maize, peas, cucumbers, gourds and other things. He had explored the Satilla River because he though he might settle his colonists there on its banks. He visited the old Indian town of St. Marys which is now located on the St. Marys River. But he finally settled at Port Royal, known as Santa Elena, and later as Beaufort, South Carolina. The French colony there was soon destroyed by Catholic Spain. Another colony, called Charlesfort, was also destroyed.

Then, in 1564, Ribaut came back down to the coast to help another Frenchman, Reni de Laudonnierre, establish a settlement for the Huguenots. It was called Fort Caroline, and it was located on the St. Johns River in Florida.

This was the French settlement that Menendez was sent by the Spanish king to destroy in 1565, just a year before he came up the coast to talk to the Guale Indians about putting forts and missions on the Georgia coast.

Menendez, who had settled St. Augustine in 1565, to keep the French out, destroyed Fort Caroline on September 20, 1565. He had been sent to do it by King Phillip of Spain. Ribaut was among the 133 murdered when they refused to give up their Huguenot faith. Menendez explained, blandly, "We did not destroy them because they were Frenchmen, but because they were Huguenots."

Menendez wrote, of the death of Ribaut by the Spanish, "He was put to the knife for the glory of God and of your Majesty. . . .He was the most experienced seaman I know and very skillful in the navigation of this coast."

The French Huguenots, like the Swiss Calvinists, the German Lutherans, and the Scotch Presbyterians, were all a part of the early "protestants" against certain practices of the Catholic Church as it was then set up. More than forty thousand left their homes for other countries, including America.

About two million people lost their lives in the wars between the Protestants and Catholics, which lasted from 1562 to 1629. About fifty thousand of them died in the St. Bartholomew's Day Massacre.

On April 13, 1598, the Edict of Nantes, signed by Henry IV of France would guarantee freedom of worship to Protestants as well as Catholics, but in 1685 it would be revoked by King Louis XIV.

OTHER FRENCHMEN CAME WITH SWISS CAPTAIN JEAN PURRY:
It was 1732 when 120 French and Swiss colonists came with the Swiss leader, Jean Purry, and settled Purrysburg on the South Carolina side of the Savannah River. They too had explored the Georgia coast. They had considered settling

on this side. Purry called this section "Georgia." He had probably seen it on the 1715 map.

He was the first to predict that the rich forests of the southeast would produce valuable things: lumber, turpentine, pitch, and other naval stores. He was proved right in a few years.

The English Came Last,
On Cabot's Claims

John Cabot, on whose explorations in 1497 England claimed the New World, sailed to America because he had read the reports of the voyages of Columbus. Cabot had gone from his native Italy to live in Bristol, England. He had been sailing for a company that shared its profits

with the Tudor King, Henry VII. The king noted in his journal that he had paid "To him that found the new isle, 10 pds." Cabot explored the coast as far as Labrador and Newfoundland. His son Sebastian also sailed along the Atlantic coast, going down as far as Florida and reporting that he turned back to England because his "victuals" gave out and he had also despaired of finding India by this route.

DARING DRAKE

During the sixteenth century, the daring English explored the coast of the southeast. They were seeking riches and glory for their queen, Elizabeth I. In 1588, Sir Francis Drake, who is famed for his part in the defeat of the Spanish Armada, sailed along the southeast coast of the New World in his ship the *Golden Hind*. His ship was fitted with the finest furniture, rich carpets, the best silver, and carried private musicians. He tried to drive Spain's ships from the sea. As terrifying as any pirate, the young nobleman, who had once sailed with the famous Sir John Hawkins, plundered St. Augustine and damaged the missions on the Georgia islands.

Heady with power after defeating the "invincible Spanish Armada," in 1588, the Elizabethans sailed the seas of the world in search of more power and glory and gold. Drake, who had attacked and pillaged St. Augustine in 1586, reported to Queen Elizabeth this startling account about the Georgia coast: "We attacked the island (thought to be Jekyll, then called Ospo), hung and burned the Spanish captain and 17 other Spaniards, but having in mind the merciful disposition of your Gracious Majesty, we did not kill the women and children, but having destroyed upon the island all their provisions and property and taken away all their weapons, we left them to starve."

SIR WALTER RALEIGH

One of the most colorful of the noblemen in Queen Elizabeth's court was the tragic, doomed, and romantic Sir Walter Raleigh.

Raleigh, known to many school students first through the myth that he attracted the queen's attention by putting his velvet coat over a mud puddle so she would not get her feet wet, was interested in America. He spent more than a million dollars exploring the coast of the southeast. This was the first real threat to Spanish control.

Queen Elizabeth I was reluctant to let Raleigh leave her court. He often had to send his expeditions, though he longed to go himself.

Raleigh supported the growing of tobacco in the new country. An old tale says that once his servant, seeing him smoking, thought he was on fire and dashed a bucket of water over him.

Raleigh's colony landed at Roanoke Island, North Carolina, 1585. Virginia Dare was born there, the first white child to be born on this continent, August 18, 1587 to a member of Raleigh's second colony. She and her parents and the other colonists disappeared mysteriously while her grandfather, the leader of the colony, went back to England for supplies. Only the word "Croatan" carved on a tree gave any clue to the mystery. Unsolved to this day, it is presented each summer in the pageant, "The Lost Colony," by Paul Green, on Roanoke Island on the North Carolina coast.

Raleigh, once the royal favorite, fell from grace even in Queen Elizabeth's time. He was imprisoned in the Tower of London. Later, James I, who succeeded Elizabeth, let him out to find riches in America again. He failed, and was finally beheaded. He had acquired malaria somewhere in the jungles of the New World, and had chills and fever. One chill was upon him as he was led out to have his head cut off. The executioner offered to wait a little. "No," said Raleigh, "another will come again. I am sure my enemies will say I am shaking from fear."

Some believed that Raleigh had been in Georgia, and among these was Oglethorpe, who founded the Georgia colony in 1733. He brought with him to Savannah a copy of Raleigh's diary. But historians say that Raleigh was never in this section at all. The "bearded young explorer" which the natives talked about was probably Captain Jean Ribaut, whose Carolina colony had been the first Protestant settlement in North America.

A DOOMED KING GAVE GEORGIA TO HIS FRIENDS: King
Charles I, the only king ever beheaded by the British, included the area that is now Georgia in a grant which he
made a friend. The friend was Sir Robert Heath, his
attorney. The land was granted to Heath in 1629, twenty
years before Oliver Cromwell's civil war, which resulted
in the king's execution. The grant stretched from Virginia

ENGLISH
SETTLEMENTS
IN AMERICA

to Cumberland Island on the Georgia coast, but was never settled by Heath. It reverted to the Crown. It had also been owned briefly by the Royal Physician, Daniel Coxe, who did not settle it either.

In 1663, the doomed king's son, Charles II, who had been restored to the throne in 1660, after Cromwell's death, granted the same land again. He sold it to eight friends, known as the Lords Proprietors. They named it in his honor: "Carolina." Two years later, in 1665, he extended the grant so that it included the Spanish colony of St. Augustine, which had existed exactly a century by that year. Spain naturally objected. In 1670 a treaty between England and Spain returned the Georgia coast to Spain and recognized England's claim as far south as Charleston, South Carolina, which had just been founded that year on the Ashley River.

But the treaty really settled nothing permanently, and the two countries continued their quarreling about the ownership of Georgia for another century. Spain resented the coming of Oglethorpe and his colonists, and continually caused trouble for Georgia. By this time, the French had begun to push in and the struggle became three-cornered. The European wars in the Old World constantly waged among England, France, and Spain in their mighty struggle for power touched off explosions in America, and were fought here on a smaller scale. Among these were Queen Anne's War, or the War of the Spanish Succession, and the War of Jenkins' Ear. In 1670 Charleston was established with 150 colonists. The Proprietors soon realized that their colony was in some danger from the Spanish in Florida and from Indians who did not want any white men to settle on this continent. The Proprietors needed a "buffer" colony to protect them. Spain had not objected to Charleston, but insisted that no more English colonies be established south of it. The British had other plans, and they paid no attention to Spain's objections.

In 1685, Dr. Henry Woodward, an Englishman who had settled there, began to lead groups of traders across Georgia and over the Chattahoochee River to the Indian country. He also traded with Indians at Cusseta in Georgia, and Coweta Town just across the river below Columbus. Woodward learned the Indian language and made friends with the red men. On his last journey he fell ill and had to be carried the long way home on a litter.

MONTGOMERY AND HIS MARGRAVATE: In 1717, glowing ads began to appear in the London papers describing a proposed new colony. Sir Robert Montgomery, a Scotch nobleman, described the land as a "paradise on earth." The area was between the two rivers, Savannah and Altamaha, in what is now Georgia. It included the islands of St. Simons, Ossabaw, Sapelo, and St. Catherines, and was to be part of South Carolina. Montgomery planned to rent it from the Lords Proprietors for a penny and one fourth an acre, and a half of any gold, silver, or precious stones he might find. They agreed, but specified that the land must be settled within three years. They wanted a colony to protect them from Spaniards and Indians. He said his Margravate would do this. By this time, most of the English colonies had begged London to send them more protection.

Montgomery expected to be "margrave," or governor for life. He planned to call his new colony "The Margravate of Azilia." In 1720, he wrote a pamphlet titled "A Description of the Golden Island," which he hoped would attract settlers to the area. He described it as a veritable "Paradise" where the climate was delightful and almost anything would grow. This was more than a decade before Ogle - thorpe's settlement. Montgomery did all he could to advertise his new venture, but nobody came. One writer suggests that it could not survive the weight of its name!

FORT KING GEORGE AND THE LONELY GRAVES: About a mile east of Darien in a marsh is a reminder of the first actual English settlement in Georgia, Fort King George. The reminder is a small area of shallow thirty-inch-deep graves, with weathered gray tombstones.

The fort was established in 1721 by Colonel John Barnwell, a planter from South Carolina, known as Tuscarora Jack, with the aid of the governor of that colony. Barnwell was an Irishman who had come to America in 1701, when he was thirty, and had grown rich. He saw the increasing threat to British business from the encroaching Spaniards, who were pushing in from Florida, and the French, who were already on the northern rivers and looking toward the Gulf of Mexico, from where they could threaten the British area. Frenchmen had settled Biloxi in 1699, and Mobile in 1702. In 1718 the French built a fort on the Apalachicola and were actually claiming the Altamaha. They built Fort Toulouse near the Coosa and Tallapoosa rivers. Bienville had just founded New Orleans in 1718. The Spanish, who had claimed the region since DeSoto's landing at Tampa in 1539, established Pensacola on the Gulf of Mexico in 1698.

Barnwell had fought the Indians and had much experience in frontier warfare. He went to Britain about 1720 and talked with the king and his ministers about the coming danger in America. They gave him permission

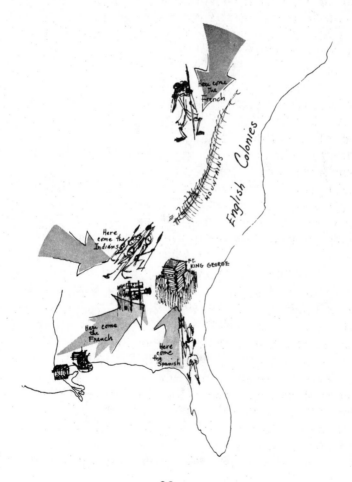

to set up a chain of protective forts. The first he established was Fort King George at the mouth of the Altamaha, near Darien where the Scotch Highlanders would come in 1736. This was 150 miles below the South Carolina settlements. Fort King George lasted six years, from 1721 to 1727, with the Spanish protesting its existence all the time. Soldiers of His Majesty's Independent Company were there, but never more than one hundred at a time. They lived in a small cypress blockhouse, about twenty-six feet square and twenty-three feet high, with four small rooms. They were attacked by Indians, and suffered from malaria and other diseases. They frequently mutinied. During one year, two-thirds of the soldiers died. Many years later rows of skeletons were found at the location of the Fort. They were buried in shallow graves that may nave been dug hastily during an attack. But the graves were row on row, in military precision. In 1727 the Fort burned, and was not rebuilt. It had lasted just six years.

The site of Fort King George was bought by the State of Georgia in 1938. It is now a part of the State Parks System. Many stop to visit the lonely graves, location of the first English settlement on Georgia soil. This was also once the site of an Indian village and of the Spanish mission Santo Domingo de Telaxe. Oglethorpe later built a small fort here, but higher than the marsh.

In 1965, the governor made available $50,000 to start reclaiming the old fort.

CUMMING FIRST TOOK INDIANS TO ENGLAND: In 1730, Britain sent Sir Alexander Cumming, a Scot from Aberdeenshire, who had been at Charleston, South Carolina, on a secret mission to the Indians in the southeast. The French and the Spanish were making friends among the Indians and getting more and more of their trade away from the British. Governor Moore, of South Carolina, had led a war against Indians, who had been molesting South Carolina colonies. British merchants and traders were beginning to worry about these Indian raids.

Cumming boldly walked into a council meeting with his hand on his sword, and demanded that the Indians declare allegiance to the British Crown. They were awed by such boldness.

The Indians liked Cumming. He talked with the Upper

100

Creeks, and with about three hundred of the Cherokees at a meeting at Keowee. One special friend that Cumming made among the Indians was Attakullakulla, a very small chief whose name meant "Little Carpenter."

Sir Alexander Cumming

As Columbus had done earlier, and as Oglethorpe was to do later, Cumming took Indians back to Europe on a seven-month visit. One of them was Attakullakulla. They met the King and Queen at Windsor Castle. "Little Carpenter" was impressed with the might and power of Britain and by the friendly attention his people received. He remained the warm and loyal friend of Britain to the end of his life.

There was more and more talk of the need of a colony between the British in the Carolinas and the Indians, French, and Spanish, who encircled them. The land which had been called first a part of Florida and later a part of Carolina was about to become a new colony named Georgia. The time was right and the stage was set for Oglethorpe and his first colonists. There was one good reason why the British were destined to be more permanent colonists than the

Spanish or the French. They brought their families, put
down roots, and built homes. They came to stay.

CHAPTER 7
HOW GEORGIA BECAME A COLONY

There had long been talk in the coffee shops and elsewhere in England of the need for another colony in the New World. For one thing, the English colonies already here, in the Carolinas and Virginia, wanted protection from the Indians, who wanted to drive them out. Some Indians were friendly, but some were not. The Emperor Brim, operating from his Georgia headquarters at Ocmulgee Old Fields near Macon and with a supply base at his permanent capital, Coweta Town, had almost destroyed the English South Carolina settlement in the War of 1715. It is probable that the only reason his savage attack failed was that the Cherokees would not join him. Though the white men had followed Brim back to Georgia and burned the Ocmulgee Old Fields base, they never knew when the unfriendly Indians might attack them again. They also wanted protection from menacing Spaniards in Florida, who had already destroyed colonies set up by other nations along the coast.

Then something happened that brought all this vague and scattered interest to focus. It concerned General James Edward Oglethorpe, who was to become known as the Father of Georgia, the youngest of the thirteen English colonies in America.

How Oglethorpe Got The Idea For Georgia

For some time there had been talk around London about starting another colony in the New World. The Bray Associates were interested in missionary work here. England's businessmen were interested in developing new sources of raw materials such as silk, for which they were having to pay very high prices on the continent, and in expanding the market for British goods. Proprietors of colonies already established in America, not to mention the colonists who were living in the Carolinas and Virginia, urged the need for a buffer state that would protect them from the Indians and from the Spanish who had settled Florida and claimed the whole southeast.

General James Edward Oglethorpe

So the time was ripe for what happened.

Sir James Edward Oglethorpe, born December 22, 1696, member of a powerful and wealthy English family, was in Parliament. He had been to Oxford University and had studied the arts of war under the famous Prince Eugene of Savoy. He was the son of Sir Theophilus Oglethorpe, British army officer, and Lady Eleanor Oglethorpe, lady-in-waiting to Queen Anne. His father and older brother had died and he had come into his inheritance as master of a great estate. He had also taken his place in Parliament, representing a district in Surrey.

When he needed an architect to do some work on his house in London, he found that his friend, Robert Castell, a brilliant architect, who had written *Villas Of The Ancients,* had been jailed for debt and had died of small-pox in a filthy British prison.

About four thousand Englishmen were jailed yearly for debt. They even had to pay seven shillings a day for their own imprisonment. This had been going on since 1283, when British merchants had got the Statute of Merchants passed to insure the practice. Conditions in the prisons had become horrible. Later the novelist Charles Dickens was to describe the prisons in his novels, especially in *David Copperfield.*

Oglethorpe was so shocked by the death of his friend that he demanded that Parliament investigate the prisons. He was made chairman of the committee. They brought in a blistering report that shocked England from end to end. Many jailers were fired, and about ten thousand debtors were freed.

The publicity given to the plight of poor people who had become entangled with the economics of making a living brought to a focus the old talk about a colony in the New World. (Few of the debtors ever came to the new colony, but others who needed a land of beginning again, or were attracted by the promise of the New World, did come.)

Oglethorpe and his friends set about raising money and stirring up interest in their proposed venture. Parliament agreed to provide some money for such a colony. Oglethorpe put his own money into it, and private individuals gave money. William Penn's son sent a hundred pounds from Pennsylvania. Oglethorpe knew of a haberdasher's will that had left 15,000 pounds for charity, and he applied for it. Heirs tried to break the will, but Oglethorpe got this money. By the time the Trustees gave up the charter in 1752, Parliament would have invested a great amount of money in this, the thirteenth and youngest colony in America.

Oglethorpe, rich and living in comfort in England, agreed that if such a colony could be started, he would come with the colonists to the new and dangerous land and help them get established here.

Now the problem of the Trustees who were interested in the new colony was to persuade King George II to sign a charter. He was not greatly in favor of granting such charters to private companies. He favored the idea of royal provinces in the New World. The question now was whether Oglethorpe and his associates could persuade him to sign a charter.

King George II

The king they asked to grant the charter for Georgia was the second of the Hanoverian kings that had been invited to come over from Germany to rule England. The British novelist Thackeray was later to lecture in Georgia on "The Four Georges." The fifth and sixth were quite unlike the first four. King George V and King George VI were grandfather and father, respectively, of Queen Elizabeth II. (The British rulers during World War I changed their family name to Windsor.)

King George I, descendant of the ill-fated Scotch queen Mary Stuart, who was beheaded by her cousin, Queen Elizabeth I, had come from Germany to ascend the British throne when Queen Anne died in 1714. All her children had died before her and she had no heirs. Powerful men in England, preferring a Protestant on the throne to the Catholic claimant in exile in France, offered the throne to George of Hanover. He was a great-grandson of Sophie, daughter of Mary Stuart's son, King James I. George did not want to come, and he spent most of his time back in Germany. He never even learned to speak the English language. It was because of this that England's prime ministers began to acquire such power. George I died in 1727, and was succeeded by George II, who stayed in Germany a great deal also. While George II was away in Germany, his picture was propped up on the English throne. He had married Queen Caroline, and it was this queen to whom Oglethorpe would take the first silk to be made in the little colony of Georgia after it got started.

Oglethorpe and his friends went to King George II to ask for the granting of the charter for the little colony in the New World which they planned to name "Georgia" in his honor.

This would not be, however, the first time that the name "Georgia" had been given to this land. Jean Purry had once put the same name on this territory. As early as 1715, an old map drawn by Herman Moll, probably for Sir Robert Montgomery's proposed "Margravate of Azilia," had shown the place with the name "Georgia."

King George II

It was 1729 when Oglethorpe and his associates asked for a charter to start a colony in America. It was three years later — June 9, 1732 — that the king finally signed the charter for "21 Trustees for 21 years."

The Crown had some years earlier bought back (for 22,500 pounds) the land sold earlier to the Lords Proprietors. (This was the same land that Montgomery included in the Margravate.) That is, King George II had bought back seven-eighths of it. Lord Carteret did not want to sell his eighth, though he did later relinquish this to the Trustees. But his refusal at first is the reason why the Georgia charter specified only a "seven-eighths interest in all those lands, countries, and territories situated, lying, and being in that part of South Carolina in America which lies from the northern-most part of a stream or river there, commonly called the Savannah, all along the sea coast to the southward into the Altamaha, and westerly, from the heads of the said rivers respectively, in direct line to the South Seas." Georgia was carved out of South Carolina, and this was to cause trouble later when that state claimed that the land below the Altamaha, not described in the charter, was still a part of its area. The charter stretched Georgia from sea to sea, Atlantic to Pacific. The Pacific Ocean was at that time called "the South Seas."

King George II was reluctant to sign this charter. He had to be talked into it. He wanted American colonies to be royal colonies, directly under the control of the Crown and its ministers, and not granted to private people, even a philanthropic group that was not seeking profit from it.

This charter that had been drawn up, and which now awaited the signature of King George II, cut right through lands claimed by Spain and France.

The charter clearly states the three purposes for establishing the colony: (1) The relief of poor subjects who, through misfortune and want of employment, were reduced to great necessity, (2) The increase of trade, navigation, and wealth in the realm, and (3) The establishment of a barrier for the defense of South Carolina and the provinces farther north, but the wording was not that short.

The quaint words of the charter — a document that fills several pages — begin like this:

108

"George the Second, by the grace of God, of Great Britain, France, and Ireland, King and Defender of the Faith, To All Whom These Presents Shall Come, Greeting: Whereas, we are credibly informed that many of our poor subjects are, through misfortune and want of employment, reduced to great necessity inasmuch as by their labor they are not able to provide a maintenance for themselves and their families. . .wish to go to America. . .where they might gain a comfortable subsistence. . .and also strengthen our colonies and increase trade, navigation and wealth of these our realms. And whereas our provinces in North America have been frequently ravaged by Indian enemies. . . laid waste by fire and sword and great numbers of English inhabitants miserably massacred. . .We think it highly becoming our crown and royal dignity to protect all our loving subjects, be they ever so distant from us ...."

On June 9, 1732, the king signed the charter for the Trustees to establish Georgia.

Egmont Became President of The Trustees

The man who probably did most to help Oglethorpe persuade the king to sign the Georgia charter and get the little colony planned never set foot in Georgia. His name was Egmont. There was another Egmont, his grandson, who was on the Board of Trustees when they gave up the charter twenty years later. This later Egmont owned land on Amelia Island, off the Georgia coast.

The first Earl of Egmont was Lord Percival. He and Oglethorpe, both wealthy and powerful British noblemen, had worked together in the British Parliament. Egmont had also been, since 1723, one of the associates of Dr. Thomas Bray, who worked to found charitable enterprises beyond the bounds of England. Egmont was one of those British leaders who had offered the British crown to fat, gruff George I of Hanover, and had been at the ship when the German ruler arrived to mount the English throne in 1714, after Queen Anne's death.

He and Oglethorpe and their friends talked to many people about the plans for the little colony in the New World. The very first mention of the colony of Georgia is in Egmont's diary, dated February 13, 1730. He later kept a

"Journal of the Transaction of the Trustees." Georgia bought this manuscript in 1946 for $16,000, and it is now in this state; it is called "Georgia's birth certificate." Egmont liked to keep a diary, and usually got up at four o'clock in the morning to write in it.

Egmont knew many important men of his time who could help. He knew Addison and Steele who wrote and published a newspaper called *The Spectator*. He knew Oliver Goldsmith, who wrote plays, and little, deformed Alexander Pope, who was very bitter and wrote poetry. He also knew King George II, son and successor of the king he had met at the boat and who had died in 1727.

Egmont noted in his diary that up to 1741, the Trustees paid the way of 1,810 colonists to Georgia and that 1,021 had come at their own expense. He also recounts that of the original 114 colonists, 29 died the first year, 47 within ten years, and that 20 others had left for South Carolina or to return to England. He gives the population of Georgia in 1743 as 2,092.

Egmont does not mention any of the English debtors, who had been freed from the prisons, as coming to Georgia. There are historians who say that about a dozen came. Because of the fact that the imprisonment of debtors had been the factor that brought the plans to a focus, some writers have reported that Georgia was a colony composed of debtors. Many people of excellent character were sometimes imprisoned for debt in England, and later even in America.

Egmont had to resign from the Georgia Trustees' Corporation after some years because of his wife's ill health. When he was twenty-seven he married sixteen-year-old Catherine Baker. He had once refused to marry a girl his cousin had picked out for him because she had red hair!

Egmont died on May 1, 1748, four years before the Trustees gave up their charter (a year before it expired) and turned the little colony of Georgia back to the king to become a real province.

The Trustees And What They Did

They decided to take only those people of good character if possible, to let each man have fifty acres

110

(those who paid their own way could get five hundred) and to supply them with provisions for a year. No debtor was accepted without the consent of the creditor, and few debtors came. Every two weeks the list of approved applications was published in the London papers.

The Trustees had a seal made. On it was their motto, *Non Sibi Sed Aliis,* which means, "Not for Ourselves but for Others." No Trustee could hold office, own a foot

of land in Georgia, or make a profit from the new colony. Benjamin Martyn, their secretary, noted in the minutes, "England will get rich by sending its poor abroad."

Their official title was "The Trustees for Establishing the Colony of Georgia in America." They decided to allow men of all faiths except Catholic to come to Georgia. (Oglethorpe paid no attention to the rule against Catholics, and permitted Catholics, who were often among the colony's finest citizens.) There were probably two reasons why the Trustees wanted to exclude them: there had just been a Jacobite rebellion in England, and it was also possible that Catholics in Georgia might ally themselves with the menacing Catholic Spaniards in Florida who wanted to drive the English out of America.

They made some rules that the colonists, as it turned out, did not like: no rum was to be allowed (only wine and beer); the colonists could not own slaves; and a man could not own his land outright. These regulations were finally changed, but it took a long time. They were not called "laws" because laws were usually subject to the king's veto.

The Trustees believed that since Georgia was in about the same general latitude as the Madeira Islands where fine grapes grew to make excellent wines, that wine would be made in the new colony. They especially wanted colonists to produce silk, which was costing English

111

merchants too much to buy from other sources. They also thought that flax, potash, hemp, and indigo would be profitable products here. All of these turned out to be impractical, and the colonists would later turn to more profitable things like lumber, leather, tobacco, corn, livestock, and later, cotton.

As it turned out, Georgia produced only about a thousand pounds of raw silk in its first twenty years(the span of the Trustees' rule), and most of that was produced by the Salzburgers at Ebenezer, and not by the original colonists.

A Ship Carrying Mulberry Plants To Virginia

These Trustees were not the first people to believe that silk could be produced in America. King James I (the same one who authorized the King James Version of the Bible, and who was the son of the tragic Mary, Queen of Scots) had the same idea back in Shakespeare's time. James had insisted that the British colony of Virginia, founded in 1607, grow silk "instead of that noxious weed tobacco." The actual shipwreck in *The Tempest* was the wreck of a ship that was carrying in its cargo some mulberry plants to Virginia to feed silkworms. Virginians had actually produced a little silk, and some of it was sent back to England for the coronation robes of King Charles I, the tragic King who was later to be beheaded. Virginia was still growing a little silk in George Washington's time, and planters gave some to Mrs. Washington for a ball gown.

The Trustees were mindful of cultural things, too. They ordered, according to their minutes, "Plato's Works, Bibles, Catechisms, Greek and Latin, and his Republique bought for the use of the Mission in Georgia."

Many years later, Georgia's permanent motto, "Wisdom, Justice, and Moderation," was to come from Plato's *Republic*.

Eleven of the twenty-one Trustees had served on the committee that investigated the prisons. Five of the twenty-one were ministers. One of them, Reverend Stephen Hale, collected more than a thousand books for the new colony. Some Trustees were noblemen. During the twenty years that they ruled Georgia, there were seventy-two who served. When they gave up the charter, a year before it was to expire, six of the original trustees were still serving.

Sir Robert Walpole was the Prime Minister with whom the Trustees had to deal. They did not like him, this huge, red-faced man who liked to munch little apples. The ballad singer referred to him as "Fat Robin." John Gay based a character in his play *The Beggar's Opera* on Walpole, who was in office from 1722 to 1742.

Churchill, who called Georgia a "polyglot community" — meaning that people of many kinds and faiths were allowed to come — wrote of Walpole in his *History Of The English -Speaking People.* Walpole, a Whig who had once been put into prison by the Tories, was a brother-in-law of "Champagne Charlie" Townsend, whose tax policy was to hasten the Revolution many years later. It was only when a crash and panic came that England turned to him to head the government. The king, George I, was nearly always in Germany and Walpole practically was the government. George II fired him but had to ask him to write a speech. The queen, Caroline, supported Walpole, so he was put back into office, and was still powerful when the Trustees began to plan for Georgia. Churchill calls him "the first great House of Commons man in British history."

How The First
Colonists Were Picked

Hundreds of people wanted to come to the new colony. The Trustees interviewed more than six hundred during the summer of 1732.

They could take only 114. Each man was to get free passage over, fifty acres of land and a year's support for his family until he could start making his own way in the new land, and getting a living out of his own land. A man who paid his own way over could get five hundred acres, tax-free for ten years. He had to plant a portion of this land in mulberry trees, and so did the man with fifty acres. The ones who paid their own way could bring as many as ten servants.

The Trustees tried to select younger men, insofar as possible, who would be able to work hard in a new land. They also tried to get a variety of talents and abilities among the first comers. Curiously enough there were no lawyers allowed. They were regarded as "the pest and scourge of mankind." Many later came, and were elected governors, senators, and, in time of danger, military commanders. Five months after the charter had been signed, by November 17, 1732, the Trustees had picked thirty-five families, and had chartered a ship. They were delighted that Oglethorpe, a rich man, offered to come with the colonists. Reverend Henry Herbert, a Church of England clergyman, was also named to come with the colonists.

114

CHAPTER 8

TOWARD
THE NEW
VENTURE

The Good Ship Anne *Sailed For Georgia*

About the middle of November, 1732, a ship named for England's late Queen Anne was lying in the harbor at Gravesend, on the River Thames, awaiting the gathering of the passengers who were coming to Georgia. Lord Percival, the Earl of Egmont, who kept the records of the Georgia venture, recorded that 114 had been "mustered on board." The London newspapers carried stories about the ship, whose captain was John Thomas, and its passengers. The English sang a ballad about the ship:

> A capital ship for an ocean trip
> Was Oglethorpe's Good Ship Anne;
> No wind that blew dismayed her crew
> Or upset the captain's plan.
> Through raging seas and howling gales
> That o'er the seas did blow
> They bravely rode with tattered sails
> Oglethorpe's Good Ship Anne.

> Three cheers for Good Ship Anne
> A ship with a pioneer band
> Who gladly sailed from England's shore
> So let the music play.
> They crossed the raging main
> Their fortune to regain.
> Three cheers! Three cheers
> For the Good Ship Anne
> That sailed to Georgia land.

The colonists spent some of their last day on English soil at prayer. They thanked God for the chance at a new life, and they prayed for a safe voyage. The Trustees came to say goodbye and wish the group Godspeed. Oglethorpe was never actually named governor because such a title would have tacitly implied that his authority came directly from the king instead of from the Trustees. He was officially "Resident Trustee." The colonists called him "Father Oglethorpe."

Most of the group were young, though one, George Symes, was fifty-five. Thomas Pratt was only twenty-one. All had been chosen for their useful abilities, as well as their attitude and need. Oglethorpe's friend and neighbor, Noble Jones, who was skilled in both carpentry and medicine, was on board. With him were his wife Sarah, their son Noble Wymberly Jones, ten, their daughter Mary, three, and two young servants, Thomas Ellis, seventeen, and Mary Comstock, twelve. The Jones family was to become one of Georgia's most prominent. The son was to diverge from his father's views and become known as "the Morning Star of Liberty," while his father, rooted deep in old England, remained a king's man. The Joneses were to become owners of Wormsloe, the beautiful Isle of Hope estate still in their family today. Jones leased it in 1736 from Oglethorpe, and got the grant of it in 1756.

On the ship were the things the colonists would need in the new land: tools, seeds, guns, clothes, and more than a thousand books.

The ship sailed at high noon on November 17, 1732. Twice daily they held prayer services on board. They stopped by the Madeira Islands to pick up other wines and grape seedlings. They spent Christmas on the cold and lonely ocean. The voyage took two months and one week. Two babies, one eight months old, died on the way over, and were buried at sea. Four babies were born on the voyage across the Atlantic.

South Carolina Welcomed Their New Neighbors

On January 13, 1733, the ship *Anne*, with Georgia's first colonists, came into the harbor at Charleston, South Carolina, then it went down the coast to Beaufort, South

116

Carolina. There the colonists got off the ship, to set up housekeeping temporarily in a new barracks. This was loaned them by South Carolina authorities. It had been built for soldiers who had not yet moved in. The Georgia colonists were to stay there for a little while, waiting for Oglethorpe to go down the coast and pick out a site within the boundaries of the charter.

There is some mystery about what became of the ship *Anne* after it put the colonists off on the Carolina shore. When they were ready to come to Georgia, they came in four little boats, not in the ship. It had discharged passengers and cargo and sailed away. Where?

The people and the government of South Carolina were warm, gracious, and generous to the weary new colonists. In future years there would be bitter quarrels between the two states about several things, disputed title to the land below the Altamaha, Georgia's refusal to be absorbed into South Carolina, and Georgia's delay in joining in plans for the American Revolution, but at first there was no sign of these future disagreements. The Carolinians were glad to have another colony between them and the Spanish, the French, and the Indians, who had come so near destroying them and driving them out in 1715 in the Yemassee War.

South Carolina gave Georgia more than two thousand pounds in money, twenty barrels of rice, a hundred cows, thirty hogs, and many horses, sheep, and oxen. The residents of Edisto sent them sixteen sheep, from that one little settlement. One man named Hume sent a silver spoon to be given to the first baby born in Georgia.

Governor Robert Johnson gave Oglethorpe seven horses and offered him a boat on which to travel down the coast and some men to go with him. Said the governor, "I would go with you myself, but our legislative assembly is in session and I cannot leave." Several men did come, however. One of them was William Bull, an engineer, for whom Bull Street in Savannah was named. Oglethorpe named Johnson Square for the South Carolina governor.

CHAPTER 9

THE LITTLE COLONY
FINALLY GOT STARTED

THE FIRST COLONISTS
STARTED WITH FOUR WHITE TENTS

Oglethorpe and the South Carolinians who came with him were rowed down the coast in a little boat by sailors until they came to Savannah River. Then they went up the river about eighteen miles. There Oglethorpe saw a high bluff, which would make it easy to defend this little colony from any attack. The river was navigable at that place, and ships could easily go in and out. There were trees which they could cut down to build houses and furniture. The soil was fertile and he thought it would grow good crops.

He called the place Savannah, probably from the river, which may itself have been named for the Shawnee Indians. "Shawnee" may have meant "southerners." There was also, on the South Carolina side of the river, a trading post called Savannah Town. Some authorities think the name Savannah may have come originally, however, from the word "sabana" meaning "flat country."

The little group sailing in four ships landed at Savannah and put up four tents to shelter them until they could build their houses. Oglethorpe had a tent under a pine tree. A white stone bench marks the spot in Savannah. Later, he rented a room from the Widow Everend at #1 Jekyll Tithing, and still later had, on St. Simon, the only home he ever owned in Georgia.

The colonists gathered in front of "Father Oglethorpe's" tent that first morning for prayers by Reverend Henry Herbert. Oglethorpe gave them a fatherly talk; then everybody went to work. Oglethorpe wrote, "The very first house was started this afternoon." The General expected everybody to work, even the boys and girls. The people were not used to this kind of work and the houses went up slowly. Sand flies and mosquitoes annoyed them, too. They had to haul their supplies up the steep bluff, and cut timber for their houses. The chimneys were built after the houses were finished. The first, in 1733, was for Reverend Samuel Quincy. Oglethorpe ordered that widows' houses usually get chimneys first.

Three weeks later, Oglethorpe wrote the Trustees, "Our people still live in tents, there being only three clapboard houses and three sawed houses framed. Our crane, our battery of cannon and magazines are finished. This is all we have been able to do, by reason of the smallness of our number, of which many have been sick, and others unused to labor, though I thank God the sick are pretty well now and we have not lost one since our arrival."

Soon there was a store, a grist mill, a public bakery, a good water supply, and a sun dial. In a few weeks, Oglethorpe moved ten families to the banks of the Ogeechee River eighteen miles away, and started Fort Argyle. This was at the spot where the Indians crossed into South Carolina. Oglethorpe laid out Savannah by a design from the book *Villas of the Ancients.*   It had been written by his friend, Robert Castell, whose misfortune and death had started the investigation that hastened Georgia's founding. On a square tract of 15,360 acres, Oglethorpe planned homes for 240 families.

Tomochichi And Mary Musgrove Helped Oglethorpe With The New Colony

Even though the king had granted a charter for the colony, Oglethorpe tactfully wanted to get the consent of the Indians. There had already been an agreement with them that no more colonies would be located below the Carolina colony.

Three miles from the high bluff, called Yamacraw Bluff, which he climbed up from the river, Oglethorpe found the only Indian tribe living within fifty miles of the place. About a hundred Yamacraw Indians lived there. The name Yamacraw is a mystery, because they were Indians of the

Muscogean tribe, and there is no sound of "r" in the Muscogean language. Tomochichi, a six-foot-tall Indian, who was already ninety years old, was their chief or mico. He was a man of mystery; he had been banished from the Yamacraw tribe, and many other Indians had come with him. Nobody ever knew why he was exiled. He did not talk about it; he felt no bitterness toward them, and they spoke well of him. Tomochichi had settled with his little group there near the river. He greeted Oglethorpe with quiet kindness, even though these Indians were not happy to see more white men come.

They needed an interpreter. They sent for Mary Musgrove, the half-breed wife of John Musgrove, a white trader who was the son of a South Carolina official. His father had been sent to Georgia in 1716 by South Carolina to make a trade treaty with the Creeks. The Indians called Mary "Coonaponeeska." She had been sent to South Carolina when she was ten to go to school. She was the daughter of a white trader and an Indian woman. Her mother was a sister of Emperor Brim who had tried, in the terrible war in 1715, to drive the white man out of the southeast.

Mary Musgrove was a tiny woman, about five feet tall. She was about thirty-three years old at this time. She wore her hair in two long braids, with a band of beads across her forehead, and a feather stuck into the band. One record says that when Oglethorpe and his party first saw her, she was "an Indian woman in mean and lowe circumstances, being only clothed in a red stroud petticoat and an osnaburg shift." Mary later denied this, saying that she and her husband had a prosperous trading station there, got twelve hundred deerskins each year from the Indians and were "on the verge of great riches."

Oglethorpe hired her as his interpreter and agreed to pay her a hundred pounds, English money. For many years, she was a good friend to Georgia, but after Oglethorpe left, she was to cause much trouble to the colony.

Tomochichi, however, was a staunch friend all the days of his life. He told Oglethorpe that his own tribe would befriend the whites, and would come to welcome them as soon as they were settled, but he advised the general to summon the chiefs of the other tribes and talk with them and get their permission also to make a new settlement here. This, thought Oglethorpe, was good advice. Tomochichi promised to send runners to summon the other Creek chiefs to meet with Oglethorpe in the weeks to come, "You can have big talk. I will help you to make them your friends." The old Indian was very much interested in Oglethorpe's gun, which he called a "fire stick."

After he had picked the site and talked with Tomochichi, Oglethorpe went back to bring his colonists from South Carolina to their new home. To show his appreciation of the kindness which the people of South Carolina had shown, he gave a barbecue. On the menu were a hundred chickens and ducks, two English beef cows, and rum, punch, and wine; but the old records state that no man drank too much.

The colonists got into four small boats and sailed down the coast and up the Savannah River to their new home. It was what is now February 12, 1733. On August 13 1909, the Georgia legislature officially designated February 12 as Georgia Day. Actually, by the old Julian calendar, the colonists had arrived on February 1, but by the new Gregorian calendar, adopted by England in 1752, the date was February 12. In the year that the calendar was changed September had — for that year — only nineteen days!

Georgia was the only one of the thirteen colonies to be established in the eighteenth century: February 12, 1733. Twelve had already been established before 1700: Massachusetts, New Hampshire, Rhode Island, Connecticut, New York, New Jersey, Pennsylvania, Delaware, Maryland, Virginia, and North and South Carolina.

The Yamacraws' Greeting

One morning about eleven o'clock, the colonists heard the most frightening noises — strange shouts and the sound of drums. Looking down toward the swamps, they saw the Indians approaching. They were frightened. They gathered around Oglethorpe's tent. The men had their guns.

Oglethorpe said, "Do not be alarmed. The Indians are coming to welcome us." Tomochichi had said, "As soon as your people are settled, we will come to welcome them."

In front of the Indians was their priest or medicine man, gaudily dressed with bright feathers and beads and clanging bells. He leaped and strutted grotesquely while the Indians chanted, "Ugh!" "Ugh!" There was a sudden

silence, and the medicine man came up to Oglethorpe, stroked him with a feather fan and said, "May there be always peace between our people and your people."

Then Tomochichi gave Oglethorpe a buffalo robe. The old chief said, "We have come to welcome you, as I promised. I have brought you a present. This is the skin of a buffalo, which is the strongest of all beasts. Inside, you see painted the head and feathers of an eagle, which is the swiftest of all birds and flies farthest. So the English are the strongest of all people and nothing can withstand them. They have a swift and far flight like the eagle. They have flown hither from the uttermost part of the earth over the vast seas. The eagle's feathers are warm and soft and signify love. The buffalo robe is warm and signifies protection. Therefore, love and protect our little families."

Oglethorpe made a speech, too. He also gave presents to the Indians. To each man he gave a hatchet and a blanket. To each of the three women who came he gave a string of beads and a mirror. They were intrigued with mirrors. For Tomochichi he had a special gift: a bright scarlet robe, with heavy fringe.

The colonists rallied around to make the Indians feel welcome. The women prepared food and the men offered warm hospitality to their new neighbors. The Indian women were interested in seeing how the colonial women kept house. The men wanted to see the guns and the buildings.

The Indians liked Oglethorpe. He was fair and friendly. He hunted bison and other game with them. He learned from them and shared with them. Tomochichi was eager for Oglethorpe to talk with other Indians, stronger than the small Yamacraw tribe, "They are stronger than we are and we cannot defend you from them. You had better talk with them," he said.

Oglethorpe Met With The Other Creek Chiefs

Tomochichi had done just what he said at the very first he would do. He sent runners to all the other eight towns of the Creeks, and asked the chiefs and their leaders to come to Savannah and talk with Oglethorpe. The other Indian groups among the Creeks in this area were the Chehaws, the Eufaulas, the Cowetas, the Echotas, the Oconees, the Oswegas, the Cussetas, and the Pallachuolas.

Some Indians came in canoes down the river, but most of them came on foot. Many walked over a hundred miles to get there. On May 21, 1733, there were fifty-six of them there, including eight chiefs, in their feathered costumes, with their long black hair, and their painted faces. The meeting was held in the largest house in Savannah. The Indians sat cross-legged on the floor, the chiefs in front and the warriors in back of them. Oglethorpe passed out gifts; he gave the visitors coats, hats, shirts, mantles, cheap jewelry, and trinkets, especially mirrors, which they liked best of all.

Tomochichi talked with them. Tomochichi's brother, Queekachumpa, a wrinkled old man known as Long King, chief of the Oconas, made a speech. He said, "We are glad you have come. The Great Spirit who dwells in heaven and all around and who has given breath to all men, has sent you here to help us. We need help. You must protect us from our powerful enemies. You may settle in our land anywhere you please, for we have more land than we can use. But you must not disturb our hunting grounds nor our homes. You must protect us from our powerful enemies. Do not let your traders cheat us. Do not trade with any Indians but us. Teach us wise things. Instruct our children. You must let us forever keep our islands." They granted Oglethorpe the other land between the Savannah and the Altamaha. The islands that they wanted to keep were St. Catherines, Ossabaw, Sapelo, and a strip between Savannah and Pipemaker's Bluff.

A long time afterward, old Tomochichi said, "We were a small, weak tribe, and we were afraid the white man would drive us away and take over our lands. But they promised not to harm us. They gave us gifts, and promised to protect us and be our friends. So we brought them gifts too."

They all smoked together the peace pipe, which was called the calumet. They wanted Oglethorpe to decide how much the trading things would be worth. What price would be fixed for a deerskin, for instance, when the white man bought it from the Indian? These prices were settled upon to discourage unfair trading. The Trustees later required all white traders to get official licenses. Other colonies objected. "We were trading with the Indians for years before Georgia was started. Now we have to go miles

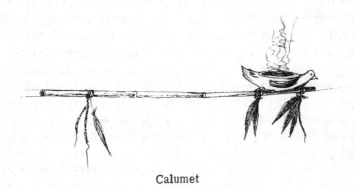

Calumet

out of the way to get permission."

The chiefs and Oglethorpe signed the treaty of friendship on May 21, 1733, and it was ratified by the Trustees in London on October 18, 1733.

The Indians granted the white men the lands in the tidewater region between the Savannah and the Altamaha rivers. They reserved only the three islands, and a council and camping spot near Savannah. Of course, the king had already granted this land to Oglethorpe and the colony, and Oglethorpe could have simply moved in. But he had tact and honor and he recognized the rights of the Indians. This was one of the reasons why these Indians became the friends of England, and remained loyal to that nation throughout the wars ahead.

The Ship That Won The Gold Cup

The Trustees had offered a golden cup to the first ship to arrive at Savannah after the new colony started. The prize was won by *The James*, commanded by Captain Goakley. It arrived May 14, 1733, bringing food, clothes, tools, and other supplies the colonists needed. It also brought the Piedmontese who were to teach the colonists how to grow silk. It was the first ship to unload at Savannah.

Problems The Colonists Had

It was not easy to start a new home in the wilderness of a new land. The first colonists had many problems. Sometimes they were discouraged. Like most human beings, they were homesick now and then, they got tired, they quarreled, and some moved away. But most of them worked hard.

SICKNESS PLAGUED THE LITTLE COLONY

One of their major problems was simply to stay alive. Malaria weakened them; other diseases attacked them. About thirty of the colonists died that first summer; that was a fourth of those who had come over on the ship "Anne." In Georgia, Mary Musgrove lost four sons and her husband, John. Their pastor, Reverend Henry Herbert, died as he started back to England. The three Milledge children lost both of their parents; and the oldest, John, tried to look after the younger two, Sarah and Richard. Peter Tondee, who was later to own the tavern where the Liberty Boys met, lost his father. Noble Jones, a doctor and a carpenter, was helpful to the colonists during these days. He had been a neighbor of the Oglethorpes in England, born near their estate "Godalming," and he had done some surveying for them.

126

BUILDING WAS SLOW

Because many of the colonists were not accustomed to hard labor with their hands, building was slow. But by March, 1734, ninety-one houses had been built. These were log houses that faced the Savannah River. The colony did not yet have a church, but the pastor held services in the open or in one of the tents. By November 13, 1736, they had built the famous lighthouse "of the best pine, with brickwork around the bottom." This was in the upper end of Tybee Island, built to guide the ships in from the sea. They had also built The House of Strangers, for hospitality to those who came.

INSECTS BOTHERED THEM

Thomas Causton, the storekeeper, wrote his wife, "We are much pestered with a little Fly they call a Sand Fly.... But every insect here is stronger than in England. The ants are half an inch long and they say will bite desperately...."

Many were unused to the hard work that it took to grow crops in the sandy soil, and by 1739, Oglethorpe was offering bonuses to those who would grow corn and potatoes.

UNFAIR LAWS CAUSED DISSATISFACTION

Three of the laws with which the colonists were most dissatisfied were those laws about land, slaves, and liquor. It was hard for the Trustees to pass wise laws in London that would work well three thousand miles away in Georgia.

The Trustees had a law that prohibited land from being sold, deeded away, mortgaged, or willed to daughters. If there were no sons to whom a man could leave his land, it went back to the Trustees. They had felt that if the colonists were allowed to borrow money on their land, or sell it, they could soon be as poor as many of them had been in England.

Oglethorpe and the other trustees were emphatic about not allowing slaves. They thought that the raising of silk was light work, and that there was no need for slaves. They feared also that the Spanish, who encouraged slaves to run away from South Carolina and come to Florida, might stir up insurrections. The colonists wanted slaves to help them do the hard work in the hot fields and they pointed out that South Carolina had slaves. They tried to evade the law against slaves by hiring "for life" Negroes from South

Carolina and paying as hire the entire value of the slaves.

They wanted rum and other liquors. But the trustees had seen the trouble that drink had caused poor people in England and they forbade liquor in Georgia. They allowed light drinks such as wine and ale.

Later, all three of these laws were relaxed or changed, and some people who had left Georgia came back.

A South Carolinian visiting Georgia reported in the *South Carolina Gazette* on March 22, 1733, "Mr. Oglethorpe is indefatigable. He is extremely well-beloved by all his people; they called him 'Father.' If any of them is sick, he immediately visits them and takes a great deal of care of them."

The Trustees' Garden And The Curious Silkworm

The Trustees ordered ten acres set aside for a "public" garden. Oglethorpe laid it out as soon as he could. It provided vegetables and fruits for the colonists to eat. Moreover, the colonists could get their mulberry trees and other plants here. Here also, a gardener could carry on experiments to see just what would grow best in Georgia and what would be hurt by frost or drought. This was the first agricultural experiment station in Georgia. It was modeled after the Chelsea Botanical Garden in London. Here they grew potatoes, cabbages, wheat, peas, corn, beets, celery, fruit and many other things. A fence enclosed the garden. Cross walks were lined with orange trees. Each family in the colony was assigned fifty acres, divided into three sections: a 30' x 90' house lot in Savannah, five acres on the edge of town, and the rest in the countryside nearby. They were also given beef or pork, Indian corn, peas, flour, molasses, cheese, butter, spices, vinegar, sugar, salt, lamp oil, spun cotton, and soap. The men could have beer or ale, but nothing stronger.

They got their little farms started, and went to the Trustees' Garden to get cuttings and plants and mulberry trees. Here, on the river bank east of town, was the nursery where they could learn how to grow white mulberry trees (to feed the silkworms that were to produce the silk), orange trees, peach trees, grape vines, fig trees, medicinal herbs, and many other things.

An old record says, "Vine dressers from Portugal were employed, and choice cuttings of Malaga vines were planted, resulted in a few gallons." The vineyards were soon abandoned.

"The olive trees from Venice, the barilla seeds from Spain, the kale from Egypt, and other exotics, obtained at much expense, after a short season withered and died in the public garden. The hemp and flax...never warranted the charter of a single vessel...and indigo did not commend itself to general favor." The colonists had to battle for food and clothing and to raise what the soil would yield. They had no time for costly experiments in agriculture. Even silk raising had to be abandoned in view of the necessity of other things.

Dr. William Houston, a botanist who taught at the University of Edinburgh in Scotland, was hired for three years to travel over the world, especially to South America, and find plants that were suited to the climate of Georgia. His collection was shipped to Savannah, but he died of tropical fever in Jamaica in 1733. The collection included two tubs of grapevines, one from Jamaica and one from Madeira. Later, Robert Miller was employed to look for medicinal herbs and plants for the garden, especially the quinine barks that the Jesuits had used to cure malaria. Frost and drought hurt the garden now and then. Wealthy men like Sir Hans Sloane, the Duke of Richmond, the Earl of Derby, and others sent money or plants for the garden.

The Trustees hired silk experts from the Piedmont section in Italy to come to Georgia to instruct the colonists in silk culture. Chief of these was Nicholas Amatis, whose brother Paul Amatis had come over on the *Anne*. Nicholas was to be paid twenty-five pounds a year for four years, a

Silkworm and Cocoon

129

hundred acres of land, a year's provisions and passage back to Italy in the fifth year. Later, he was fired. His brother became angry, and both moved to South Carolina.

Oglethorpe believed that since mulberry trees, on which silkworms feed, would grow along the Savannah River, a fine quality of silk could be made in Georgia. This could save England hundreds of dollars she was then paying to foreign countries for silk.

The colonists tried hard to grow silk. Cocoons cost them three shillings a pound. They got their mulberry trees, upon whose leaves the silkworms were to eat, from the Trustees' Garden, and planted them on their land. Each man had to plant ten of his fifty acres in mulberry trees; if he did not, his land could be forfeited. James Habersham named his plantation "Silk Hope." But the weather affected the cocoons and the trees. Corn, beans, pumpkins, potatoes, peaches, figs, grapes, rice, indigo, watermelons, and other plants grew well, however. Some settlers raised livestock, others fished in the rivers and ponds. Many hunted in the forests for deer, birds, rabbits, wild turkeys, and raccoons, which the Spanish had called "the little dogs that didn't bark." They learned the value of timber and other products of the forest. Eventually, Georgians also developed a brisk trade in exporting furs, deerskins, cowhides for shoes, and lumber to make the fine furniture the English bought in London. Rice became a more and more important crop until Europeans began to prefer homegrown Irish potatoes and the bottom dropped out of the rice market.

In 1755, the ten acres that had been the old Trustees' Garden was given to Captain John Reynolds, the first Royal Governor. In 1762, a fort was built on the site. During the Revolution it was renamed Fort Wayne, in honor of General "Mad Anthony" Wayne who had pushed the British back into Savannah and surrender.

In recent years, much of the area around the old Garden has been restored and changed into charming, picturesque homes. A restaurant, "The Pirates' House," with red checked tablecloths and seafood is said to be housed in the favorite haunt of real pirates. Legend says that the original pirate from which Robert Louis Stevenson drew Captain Flint died upstairs in this house, attended by Long John Silver, of *Treasure Island* fame, Billy Bones, and

Thomas Morgan. A trapdoor through which sailors were said to have been "shanghaied" from the rum cellar into service on foreign ships to far-off ports, gives cold shivers to the imaginative. The ghost of Captain Flint is said to haunt this place!

Charming gates open onto green growing things that preserve a little of the old Trustees' Garden. The old Savannah lighthouse is now the Trustees' Garden Center, and Oglethorpe's tool shed is now the Herb House.

Georgians were growing cotton as early as 1738. For five hundred years wool had been a chief item of trade in England; then cotton cloth from India became profitable. India had been making cotton cloth (called calico, from Calcutta, India), for hundreds of years. They had even devised a crude gin to separate the seed from the lint. Great rivalry grew up between the East India Company, which brought cotton from India, and England's wool merchants. The merchants had even got a law passed in 1666 that the dead could be buried only in woolen shrouds. By 1720, raw cotton could be carried into England, but not spun there. Later all this was to change because of new machines, the Industrial Revolution and the Georgia cotton gin.

Europeans were surprised that cotton was grown in Georgia. When the first eight bags were shipped by the firm of Habersham and Harris, they were held up by the customs officer. He thought they had come from some other source, and that somebody was violating the British trade laws.

Oglethorpe Took Indians And Silk To England

When Oglethorpe left on a business trip to England, April 7, 1734, he took with him a group of Indians. They sailed on the ship *Aldborough*. After a voyage of seventy days, they landed on the Isle of Wight. The Georgia leader wanted the Indians to see the power and wealth of England. He thought also that the British would be more interested in his colony if they could see the Indians. He also took the first Georgia silk to Queen Caroline on this trip. She expressed her "great satisfaction for the beauty and fineness of the silk and the richness of the pattern, and of seeing, so early, a product from the colony." She had the silk made into a beautiful dress. Tomochichi, his wife Senauki, and their nephew and adopted son, Tooanahowi, were among those who went to England. Others were Senauki's brother, Umpichi, chief of the Palischicolas. They landed June 16 at the Isle of Wight. Oglethorpe took them to his home "Godalming," and on June 20, 1734, they went to London.

They were a sensation in England, though other Indians had visited Britain. Many people remembered the Indians that Cumming had brought four years before, yet crowds swarmed after the Georgia Indians to get a sight of these strange red people. King George II and Queen Caroline entertained them at Kensington Palace. Egmont gave Tomochichi a silver snuff box which the old Indian said he would wear on a string around his neck, close to his heart, all his life. Senauki, who was a remarkable woman, made a speech at court just as her husband had done. Tooanahowi repeated the Lord's Prayer for the King and queen. When the Indians visited Eton, Tomochichi asked that the students be given a holiday.

Many people gave parties for the Indians. The red people wanted to go to the parties just as they dressed in Georgia, with very little covering on their bodies, but Oglethorpe tactfully suggested that they wear colorful red and blue robes he provided. They rode in a carriage drawn by six horses.

The king allowed them twenty pounds a week. People gave them many gifts. The Trustees had a famous artist named Verelet paint Tomochichi and Tooanahowi. The painting hung for many years in the Trustees' Room in London. Reproductions of the painting have often been in Georgia. Tooanahowi is holding an eagle in his hands. A picture of Oglethorpe presenting the Indians at court hangs in the Smithsonian Institution in Washington, D. C.

Tomochichi, who was more than ninety years old, asked the British a question: "Why do men, who are on earth so short a time, build houses that last so long?" He made a speech to the King. This is what he said:

"This day I see the majesty of your face, the greatness of your house, and the number of your people....I am come for the good of the children of all the nations of the Upper and Lower Creeks, that they may be instructed in the knowledge of the English.

132

Oglethorpe Took Tomochichi To England

133

"These are the feathers of the eagle which is the swiftest of birds, and who flieth all 'round our nations. These feathers are a sign of peace in our land...and we have brought them over to leave them with you, O Great King, as a sign of everlasting peace."

Senauki's brother, Umpichi, who was in the party that went to England, died of smallpox. He was buried in St. John's Cemetery in Westminster Abbey, with his weapons, beads, feathers, and silver money. His death made the Indians long for home, and they began to think of getting back to their native Georgia. The British gave Tomochichi presents to take back to his people in Georgia.

Tomochichi hated to part from Oglethorpe, who had not yet finished his business in England and was not sailing back to Georgia with the returning Indians. Tomochichi said to Oglethorpe, "I am glad to be going home. But to part from you is like the day of death to me."

He said to Oglethorpe at another time, "You have never made a difference between our people and your people. You have never broken a promise to us. When I die, I want to be buried in the white man's town, and not in the forest."

The Indians came back on a ship named the *Prince of Wales*, sailing on October 30, 1734. It arrived in Savannah in December, 1734. Tomochichi and the other chiefs who went, war chief Hillispilli, chiefs Apahowtski, Stimalchi, Sentauchi, and Hinguitti, had many tales to tell to their people in Georgia about what they had seen in England. So did Senauki and Tooanahowi.

When Oglethorpe came back to Georgia in 1736, so many people came with him that the voyage was known as the Great Embarkation. Much of the new interest of these newcomers to the colony had been stirred up by the visit of the Indians to England.

Chapter 10

OTHER GROUPS JOINED THE FIRST COLONISTS

Several groups followed the first colonists to Georgia. Some, like the Moravians, stayed only a little while and then moved on. Others remained and have descendants in Georgia now. The Jews came first, than the Salzburgers, the Moravians, and the Scotch Highlanders. The Trustees had granted 57,000 acres for further settlements. Swiss, Dutch, Italians, Greeks, and French came to early Georgia; so did Quakers.

Forty Jews Brought the Book of the Law

The first people of the Hebrew faith who came to Georgia were forty who arrived in Savannah in a chartered ship on July 11, 1733. They came during the very first year of the colony, about eleven months after Oglethorpe and the first colonists came. They brought with them the *Sefar Torah*, or *Book of the Law*, and the *Echal* or Ark. The Trustees did not want them to remain, but Oglethorpe appreciated their value as citizens and allowed them to stay. (Some soon moved to South Carolina.) He wrote the Trustees, "We have not better citizens than they are." One was skilled in grape culture. Another, Samuel Nunez, ministered to the colonists during the hard winters. Once he almost single-handedly saved them in an epidemic. The little town of Nunez in Emanuel County was named for him He also ran a drugstore, getting medicine from Europe. By 1741, ninety-two Jews had come. Others came later. They were a great help to Oglethorpe. The Trustees wrote, "Reward them suitably...but not with lands in Georgia."

The Nunez family had fled from Spain, where they had elegant homes and other property that had been confiscated by the officers of the Spanish Inquisition. One story says that the Nunez family escaped from Spain in the following manner. Among the guests they had at dinner one day was an English captain, whose ship was in the harbor. While the spies of the Inquisition watched and listened, the ship captain invited all the family and their guests to go down to the seashore and "visit" his ship. The government spies did not know that plans were already made for escape. The women had sewn their jewels in their dresses, and the men had concealed what money they could take in their belts. They left their homes and other property, all of which was confiscated by the government. They even left their dinner uneaten on the table. They went first to England. There they encountered Oglethorpe, heard of his Georgia colony, and came

to Georgia. Among them were the Minus, DeLyon and Sheftall families.

Many of them served Georgia well. One of these was Sheftall Sheftall. His son Mordecai Sheftall, who was born in Georgia on December 16, 1735, when the colony itself was not yet two years old, became commissary-general for Georgia during the Revolution. The British described him in the *Royal Gazette* as "a great rebel." He spent much of his own money for supplies, most of which he never recovered. The vouchers had been destroyed by the British. He applied to the legislature to get back the money he had spent, but they refused. He said sadly, "Ingratitude is not confined to individuals." His deputy was his son, Sheftall Sheftall, who was named for his grandfather. Both of them were captured by the British in 1789, and carried on a prison ship to Antigua in the West Indies; they were later paroled. The father, Mordecai Sheftall, was later elected to the legislature. The son was a lawyer in Savannah and was an honored guest when President Monroe visited Georgia.

When the first charitable organization in Georgia was begun, the three organizers were Peter Tondee, Catholic; Richard Milledge, Presbyterian; and Benjamin Sheftall, Jew.

Some of the first Jews who came left Georgia and went to Charleston and elsewhere, but many remained and helped build the colony into a great state. A later governor, David Emanuel, of the Jewish faith, fought in the Revolution. Captured, he was nearly hanged, but escaped and fled through the darkness after his clothes had been given to a slave. A county is named for him. He named all of his children from the Old Testament.

The Moravians and Their School Named "Irene"

Moravians, a German-speaking group, as the Salzburgers were, came over from Bohemia in Europe on the same ship with Oglethorpe and John and Charles Wesley in 1736, though a few had come in 1735. John Wesley was greatly impressed by their brave faith.

Wesley said later that he sometimes thought he had not been really converted until he saw the staunch faith of the Moravians in action. Later, in Georgia, he often went to consult them about his problems, including whether he should marry the pretty Georgia girl named Sophie Hopkey.

The Moravians settled between New Ebenezer and Savannah. Wesley helped the Moravians with their school, which they established in 1735 for Indian children, the first such school in Georgia. It was located on an island five miles above Savannah, on Pipemaker's Creek. The school, which they called Irene, was operated for five years, from 1735 to 1740. The Irene Mounds have been studied by archeologists in recent years. Tomochichi was interested in this school, and visited it. Benjamin Ingham was the teacher. He wrote a Creek grammar. Excavations in 1937 unearthed the cellar of this old school. Near this site was the New Yamacraw Indian village.

The Moravians did not stay in Georgia long. There were never more than fifty. Of the forty-seven that came, ten died the first year. Some stayed in Savannah; some lived by the Ogeechee River. They were pacifists, now called "conscientious objectors," and did not believe in fighting. They refused to perform military duty and they would not carry guns. This made them unpopular with the other colonists. About 1740, the Moravians left the little settlement that was between the Salzburgers at Ebenezer and the first colonists in Savannah, and went to Pennsylvania. They repaid the Trustees the money advanced for their passage to Georgia.

Their leader, Count Zinzendorf, a Bohemian Protestant, had first had ideas of establishing in Georgia a colony in which his group could live like the early Christian apostles. He had asked Oglethorpe for five hundred acres for this purpose and got permission to come, but never did.

The Moravians later sent their missionaries back into North Georgia to establish missions and help educate the Indian children. They were a compassionate people, as evidenced by the fact that they had previously left their property near Savannah to Whitfield to use for a hospital for the sick and the poor.

Sometimes the Moravian pastors went to jail for their beliefs. Descendants of the Moravians settled in North Carolina, especially in the vicinity of Winston-Salem. They still have beautiful Easter services which annually draw hundreds there at sunrise on Easter morning.

The Moravians had begun to leave their homes in Europe after the burning at the stake for his beliefs of a minister named John Huss in one of civilization's tragic moments of religious intolerance.

The Salzburgers and the Swan on the Church Steeple

In Effingham County there still stands Jerusalem Church, built by the Salzburgers, with the glistening golden swan from the coat-of-arms of Martin Luther, on top of the steeple. The Salzburgers were one of the Protestant

sects that had grown vigorous in Europe following the leadership of Martin Luther. Luther, a monk, had rebelled at practices which he did not approve of in the Catholic Church. He had written a list of the things to which he objected and nailed them on the door of the Catholic Church in Worms, Germany. This was the beginning of the Reformation. Thirty thousand Salzburgers left their beautiful home in the mountain valley. The church in Georgia was named for the Church of the Apostles at Jerusalem. Nearby is the churchyard in which are buried some of these Salzburgers who came to Georgia and two of their pastors. It was from the Salzburger community that Georgia's first governor would come, many years later. He was staunch old John Adam Treutlen, who disappeared from history as if he had been a ghost.

The Salzburgers had lived in Europe by the river Salza in Austria, in the region where the famous Salzburg music festivals were later held. The ruler Leopold had ordered them to abandon their religion. He burned their homes and Bibles. Finally the Emperor ordered Leopold to let them go. This was near the spot where Hitler later had his mountain retreat, Berchtesgaden. They made wooden clocks. The Salzburgers, a Protestant sect, were persecuted for their religion, and left Austria. Allowed to bring out only their clothes, from 1730 to 1732 hundreds left. Their Bibles and hymn books were burned in bonfires. Oglethorpe invited some of them to Georgia. Seventy-eight sailed in October, 1733, at the expense of the Trustees, in the first group. They arrived at Charleston and came on to Savannah March 11, 1734. Others came later, until there were about fifteen hundred in all. (In the first group were forty-two men, fifty-seven more in 1735, and eighty in 1736.)

Their pastor, John Martin Bolzius, wrote of the new land:

"We lay at anchor off our dear Georgia in a very lovely calm, and heard the birds singing sweetly. We were received with joy, friendship and civility. Even the Indians reached out their hands to us. A good dinner was prepared for us."

Oglethorpe told them they could have any place not reserved by the Indians. They wanted to live among the hills to remind them of home.

Oglethorpe went with their leader, Baron von Reck, and some Indian guides to pick out a place about twenty-five miles above Savannah for their new home. It was on a creek, six miles from the Savannah River.

The colonists in Savannah gave them ten cows and calves. Leather from these cows was shipped to England and made into boots and shoes. The Indians were so fascinated with the tinkle of the cowbells around the necks of the cattle that they sometimes stole the bells, but rarely took the cows. The Indians taught the Salzburgers about herbs, and how to grow and market sassafras root. The Salzburgers also made their own candles, of green wax from myrtle trees. The new settlers found honey in hollow trees, caught channel catfish and perch in the streams, and hunted in the woods for wild turkeys and partridges.

Each person had a two-acre lot in the village and fifty acres outside. They named their new home Ebenezer, which means "Stone of Help." Whitefield considered the Salzburgers Georgia's best colonists. He patterned his orphanage at Bethesda on the small one Bolzius had started at Ebenezer.

They worked hard, but the soil was not fertile there. The location was unhealthy and many had malaria. The creek was so shallow that boats could not get up to them. They asked Oglethorpe for permission to move to Red Bluff. He reluctantly granted it. They spent two years moving their cabins and possessions to this new site directly on the Savannah River. This they named New Ebenezer. It is within what is now Effingham County, near Springfield.

The Salzburgers now began to raise silk. They grew more silkworms and produced more silk than any other group in Georgia. About 1738, they experimented with cotton. They also raised peaches. They were good farmers, and they began to diversify their crops. Pastor Bolzius studied agriculture and, on Sundays after the sermon, instructed the men.

They started their little church in 1767, with bricks bought from across the sea. During the Revolution, the British used it first for a hospital and later as a stable for their horses. Jerusalem Church, where the ministers preached in German until 1824, still draws Salzburgers back to the spot to worship under a swan-topped steeple.

The Salzburgers who stayed in Savannah organized a Lutheran congregation there in 1744, and in 1756 built a church on the site of the present Lutheran Church of the Ascension which was built in 1843. Some of the Salzburgers went to Frederica, were their settlement was known as the "German Village," but most of them stayed at New Ebenezer.

PASTOR BOLZIUS' JOURNAL: The pastor of the Salzburgers, Reverend John Martin Bolzius, kept a diary. He wrote, "A man just brought me, as I wrote this, a bowl of blue grapes from the woods." The day by day living of these people is described in his pages. When he died later, he was succeeded by the assistant pastor named Israel Gronau. They are both buried in the churchyard there. Here are a few other entries that he made in his diary in 1734:

March 15: This day, Mr. Oglethorpe arrived here and received our Salzburgers and us in a friendly manner and we dined with him. He being very solicitous that these poor Indians should be brought to the knowledge of God, has desired us to learn their language, and we, with the blessing of God, will joyfully undertake the task.

Tuesday, March 26: It is a great pleasure to us that Mr. O. approved of our calling the river and the place where our houses are to be built, Ebenezer.

April 13: No coffins for the dead — Lackner, having been very long sick, died last night. (This man was to have had a coffin made for him, the pastor related, but the Salzburgers thought it unnecessary. They were not accustomed to burying anybody in a coffin except women who had died when their babies were born. So they dressed the body of Lackner, after it was washed, and laid him upon a board, and after he was brought to his grave, with a procession, they wrapped him in a cloth and let him down into the ground. Lackner left a little money, and they put this into the beginning of a collection for the poor.) Ebenezer, Tuesday, May 7: Today I had the happiness of seeing Ebenezer. The good people are already much advanced in tilling the ground.

The first teacher in Georgia was Christopher Ortman, who came in this group of Moravians. He was old, did not know English very well, and did not please the pastor. He was dismissed and became an object of charity.

Bolzius, their pastor, died on November 19, 1765.

142

The Salzburgers suffered greatly during the Revolution, both physically and mentally. They felt a deep loyalty to England because the Trustees had befriended them and paid their passage over, but they wanted to be loyal to their patriot neighbors, too.

Goethe, the great German poet, has written the sad story of their persecutions in Europe in his poem "Herman and Dorothea." Their Georgia story was written by Reverend P.A. Strobel. It is titled *The Salzburgers and Their Descendants*. Thousands of the descendants of these people are in Georgia today. Of them, about 450 still go back to the little Jerusalem church periodically. A Salzburger festival is held in the community from time to time.

The Scotch Highlanders Brought Golf to Georgia

When Oglethorpe needed more brave men and good soldiers to defend the struggling little colony of Georgia from the threat of the Spaniards in Florida, he sent Lieutenant Hugh Mackay as a messenger to the Highlands of Scotland. Parliament had appropriated 26,000 pounds Sterling to bring soldiers. Some of the finest of the Scots had sided with the exiled Stuart king and had had their property confiscated in the rebellion of 1715. A few had come to Georgia in 1734. Others Mackay brought were interested in Oglethorpe's offer of a new home in a new land. On October 18, 1735, they boarded the ship "Prince of Wales" bound for Georgia.

They came swirling their colorful kilts and skirling their tuneful bagpipes, and settled at Darien on the Altamaha, near Cat River. Other groups of them came later. McIntosh County was named for one of these Highlander families. They first named their settlement New Brunswick, but it became known as Darien. An old Indian settlement called Huspaw Town was there in 1716. The Indians in it were driven out by Carolina colonists after the 1715 Yemassee uprising of Emperor Brim's War.

The first road built in Georgia connected Darien with Savannah and was known as Oglethorpe's Road.

The Indians liked the colorful Highlanders, and hunted and played games with them. The Scots played a form of golf in Georgia, the first in this state.

143

Once when Oglethorpe went to Darien, he, too, wore kilts to honor them. The clan chief offered the general his bed, but Oglethorpe slept by the campfire, and the Scot chiefs lay down beside him there. Their clan chief was John Mohr McIntosh, a hero for whom tragedy lay ahead. The religious leader of the Scots was Reverend John McLeod.

McIntosh was about to go to Scotland to receive his inheritance when he decided to delay the trip to accompany Oglethorpe on his siege of St. Augustine. McIntosh was taken prisoner by the Spaniards and sent to a prison in Spain, where he was kept several years and suffered much. When he came back to Georgia, his health was broken.

Many of the Scotch leaders, with their jaunty courage, played valiant roles in the Battle of Bloody Marsh.

In the middle of the quiet little town of Darien, which they named for a settlement in South America that the Spaniards had destroyed forty years earlier, there is a pink marble monument to them. In stone, the Highlanders march forever across the top of it, like the figures on John Keats' Grecian urn. The inscription reads, "To the Highlanders of Scotland who founded New Inverness in 1736. Their valor defended the struggling colony from the Spanish invader. Their ideals, traditions, and culture enriched the land of their adoption."

On the monument is the Cherokee rose, Georgia's state flower, and the Scotch thistle, symbol of Scotland. It was said to have been chosen as the Scottish emblem when an enemy soldier, about to attack a Scotch camp, stepped on a thistle and alarmed the camp with his pained cry. These Scotch, who "came from the hills of heather, where the black night comes over the land" added colorful chapters to Georgia's history and have many descendants in the state today.

Now and then a jaunty Scotch Highlander officer comes to study or serve at Fort Benning, wearing his kilts and making people who see him think of his brave ancestors in Scotland.

Many people in Georgia proudly trace their ancestry back to the Scotch, and know the different clans and plaids and coats-of-arms. In Atlanta, there is a Burns Club which built a replica of the home of the famed Scotch poet, Robert Burns.

Chapter 11

COLORFUL PEOPLE
AND NEW PLACES

COLORFUL PEOPLE
CAME TO PREACH AND TEACH

Georgians needed somebody to educate their children, and religious leaders to look after their spiritual welfare. Sometimes the teachers were also preachers: the Wesleys, George Whitefield, and his assistant James Habersham who became a prosperous businessman too. Sometimes the teachers and preachers taught and preached among the Indians as well as the colonists. Charles Delamotte, who had come in 1735, taught the first regular school in Savannah. The Trustees paid only his expenses.

John and Charles Wesley in Georgia

The two great Methodist leaders, John Wesley and his brother Charles, came with Oglethorpe (who had been a friend of theirs at Christ Church College) when he returned to Georgia from England in 1736. They arrived in Savannah on February 6, 1736. But they were not Methodists then; they were ministers of the Church of England. Later they became founders of the Methodist denomination. Wesley said his experience as a Church of England minister in Savannah was one of the reasons for his founding Methodism when he returned to England. They were two of the nineteen children of Reverend Samuel Wesley (a college classmate of Daniel Defoe, author of *Robinson Crusoe*) and his wife Susannah, who was herself one of twenty-five children. When the Wesley brothers came to Georgia, John was thirty-three and Charles was twenty-nine.

John Wesley

Charles Wesley, who wrote over six thousand hymns and came to be known as "the sweet singer of Methodism," went to Frederica in a month to become secretary to General Oglethorpe. He also preached. He was very strict, and the colonists were compelled to attend daily services, summoned by drums of the army. The somewhat rough and careless soldiers there were impatient with his stern edicts. He and Oglethorpe had a few misunderstandings, and Charles Wesley grew very unhappy here. Meddlesome women, especially Beata, wife of Dr. Thomas Hawkins, tried to tell him how to run his parish, and misrepresented him to others. On the other hand, Susannah, wife of Samuel Davison, whose husband was the village carriage- and gun-maker and also kept a tavern, nursed Charles Wesley through a serious illness and welcomed him to her home and family life when he first came. When Frederica was excavated during its restoration in recent years, the foundations of the houses of the Hawkins and Davison families were still there. Among the things found were bits of fine porcelain, snuff and ink bottles, and some medicine jars in which Dr. Hawkins, who kept an apothecary shop, had sold ointments. The Hawkins and Davison families had come with the very first settlers.

Charles Wesley wrote to friends in England, "It has became unpopular even to speak to me. Those who washed my clothes now send them back unwashed. Thank God it is not yet a capital offense to give me a morsel of bread." Sick, neglected, and longing for home, he once had a hard time finding a bed in which to sleep during the last weeks he was there. A soldier gave up his own bed for the unhappy young minister, but the bed fell down during the night. Oglethorpe was too busy about his many duties to comfort young Wesley, and besides, gossipy tongues had made trouble between the two. Wesley wrote, "I would not spend another six days like the last six for all of Georgia." Little could he dream that one day he would be honored by Georgia and all the rest of the world.

Finally Oglethorpe sent Charles back to England to carry some important papers. On July 26, 1736, he sailed for England. He and Oglethorpe remained friends, however, and many years later, the General attended a violin recital given by Charles Wesley's young son.

JOHN WESLEY AND HIS UNHAPPY GEORGIA ROMANCE

John Wesley, who was older than his brother, had remained mostly in Savannah, although he went several times to preach at Frederica and to be with his brother there. Wesley had been eager to preach to the Indians. He went to talk with Tomochichi and two chiefs of the Mingos. But his doctrines were too strict for the Indians. He became discouraged, especially when Tomochichi did not like him. Wesley's greatest achievements thereafter were among the colonists. He preached to the English and Germans. He also studied Spanish so he could preach to the Jews from Spain. Wesley was a small man, only five feet and five inches tall. He had long hair, which he wore hanging over his shoulder, and bright blue eyes. He wore a long black coat, knee breeches, and a three-cornered hat such as most Englishmen of that time wore. "A great little man,"

wrote one historian.

Wesley walked tirelessly from one village to another, preaching to the people and trying to teach the Indians. But they never understood him, nor he them. Tomochichi, who was very fond of Oglethorpe, never had much to say to John Wesley. Tomochichi had asked that a preacher be sent to his Indians, and Wesley spoke English, French, German, and Italian. But Wesley made many staunch friends in Georgia. He and Delamotte, who had come with him, founded the world's first Sunday School, fifty years before one was started at Gloucester, in England by Robert Raikes, a newspaper publisher. Once when boys laughed at a child who came barefooted to Sunday School, Wesley himself came barefooted the next Sunday. He took the first (unofficial) census ever taken in the colony, and reported that there were 518 people living in Savannah. (The first official U. S. Census was taken in 1790.) He was once a guest of Mary Musgrove and her first husband, John, at a barbecue. John Musgrove, a trader, sometimes acted as Wesley's interpreter, as his wife Mary Musgrove did for Oglethorpe.

John Wesley had an unhappy romance in Georgia. Oglethorpe had tried to encourage a match between the young minister and a pretty girl named Sophie Hopkey, niece of the colony's storekeeper, Thomas Causton. The two young people seemed very much interested in each other. Once they were together on a boat that was bringing some people from St. Simons back to Savannah. A storm came up and the boat had to land on St. Catherines Island. The damp passengers built a campfire. Sophie later reported that during the entire evening there by the glow of the campfire, Wesley quoted scripture to her. But sometime during the week he said to her, "Miss Sophie, I would count myself happy if I could spend the rest of my life with you." Later she claimed that this was a proposal.

Wesley seriously thought of marrying the pretty Georgia girl. But first he thought of asking the advice of the Moravians, whose opinion he deeply respected. They liked Sophie, but they advised against their marriage because they felt that she was too young and frivolous to be able to settle down to the serious role of a minister's wife.

Sophie married William Williamson, and stopped attending church. When she finally went back, Wesley refused to allow her to take Holy Communion because of her absence. It was a rule of the church. But for a young matron in that time, this was considered an insult. She and her family, indignant, brought suit against Wesley. Others who had considered Wesley too strict joined in the hue and cry against him. He was arrested and taken into court. The summons read:

"Georgia. Savannah. s.s.

"To all Constables, Tythingmen, and others whom these may concern:

"You and each of you are hereby required to take the body of John Wesley, Clerk: and bring him before one of the Bailiffs of the said Town to answer the complaint of William Williamson and Sophie his wife, for defaming the said Sophie, and refusing to administer to her the Sacrament of the Lord's Supper in a public Congregation without cause, by which the said William Williamson is damaged One Thousand Pounds Sterling. And for so doing this is your Warrant, certifying what you are to do in the premises.

"Given under my hand and seal of the 8th day of August: Anno. Dom: 1737.

Th CHRISTIE."

When Constable Jones arrested Wesley and took him to court, Sophie's husband, William Williamson, was waiting there. He demanded that the minister give bail (pay money to guarantee his appearance for trial). But the judge, who knew this good man who was later to become one of history's most famous figures, said, "Mr. Wesley's word alone is sufficient."

Wesley maintained that the court did not have jurisdiction. His refusal to give Sophie Communion, the chief reason for which he was being sued by her family, was a purely ecclesiastical matter, he pointed out. He was indicted in the court on ten counts, some as absurd as having had only two witnesses when three were customary for some rite, and damages of 1000 pounds were assessed against him.

Wesley had already been planning to leave Georgia and had advertised for the return of his books that were out on loan. Now he saw his further presence would only cause turmoil. He quietly left Georgia on December 21, 1737. In his remarkably candid and interesting diary, he wrote, "I saw clearly that the hour was come for leaving this place; and as soon as the evening prayers were over, about 8 o'clock in the evening, the tide then serving, I shook the dust of Georgia off my feet and left, having preached the gospel there not as I ought but as I was able for one year and nine months." This same journal relates his unhappy marriage later to a widow named Molly whom he met when he slipped on the ice and broke his ankle near her home. It is likely that his personal unhappiness spurred him to greater efforts for his church, and he became one of history's greatest preachers. Later, when they met in England, Oglethorpe bent to kiss John Wesley's hand.

Wesley's life, as reflected in his astonishing journals, reveals not only his own thoughts but much of the background of life in England during the century which his life almost spanned. (He was born in 1703 and lived until 1791.) He wrote of great things and small, of sad things and happy ones. He told of his journeys up and down England, preaching often many times in one day. He tells candidly of his wife's leaving their home when they grew too unhappy, and of his not knowing where or when she died. There is in the diary also such little amusing things as a recipe to cure baldness! One commentator says, "... this was an honest man who wrote clearly, concealed nothing, set down naught in malice, much in candor, and never used two words when one would do." His journals were not interpreted until 119 years after his death. Like those of Samuel Pepys, they were written in cryptic symbols. A man finally decoded them, so Ripley's *Believe It Or Not* records say, because of a dream.

Wesleyan College in Macon is named for this great man. At Emory University in Atlanta, there is an excellent collection of things relating to his life, from a small wooden pulpit to a baby cap. There is also a small ledger and a motal box that he had while in Georgia.

On Cockspur Island near Savannah, the site is marked where Wesley first landed on February 6, 1736, and knelt to thank God for a safe journey. On St. Simons Island is the Wesley Center, Epworth-by-the-Sea, named by the Methodists for the Wesley home in England. Here thousands of Methodists gather for various meetings. A sign at the entry tells of Wesley, and of how he was "snatched as a brand from the burning" once when his family home caught fire, and was thus convinced that God had spared him for some purpose. His purpose became to convert men to God and this he did with mighty results. The site of his first sermon in Georgia is marked in Savannah.

Augusta Was Named For A Princess

Augusta had been set up in 1736 as a fort. A trading station had been put there in 1735. Only twenty soldiers were stationed there at first. Traders came to Augusta, some Frenchmen from as far away as Louisiana, to trade with the Indians: salt, gunpowder, hats, mirrors, cloth, trinkets, deer hides, and beaver skins. A hat was worth eight buckskins, and a calico petticoat, twelve skins.

A Celtic cross marks the site of the old fort. The cross stands back of St. Paul's Church, the fourth church to be built on this site. The first was built in 1750, fifteen years after the fort was established there. It had a hundred members; the first pastor was Reverend Johnathan Copp, of the Church of England. He wrote some very sad letters back to his friends in London about the hardships of life on the Georgia frontier and the danger of savage attacks from the Indians. During wars, the churches on this site were used as barracks and hospitals In the churchyard many

A Celtic Cross Marks The Site Of Fort Augusta.

years later would be buried Governor George Mathews, Commodore Oliver Bowen, and steamboat inventor William Longstreet. Under the altar, in the basement, Civil War Bishop-General Leonidas K. Polk, killed on Pine Mountain, would lie buried for years. His body was later removed to his native Louisiana. Augusta was destined to play an important role in Georgia's years.

Fort Augusta was named for the Princess of Wales, whom the twenty-nine-year-old Frederick had married April 27, 1736. She was the daughter of the Duke of Saxe-Gotha. When the British captured Fort Augusta during the Revolution, they changed the name temporarily to Fort Cornwallis. By 1740, the road had been built connecting Augusta with Savannah, and from there, with Oglethorpe at Frederica. There was also mail service.

Frederica Was Named For A Crown Prince Who Never Became King

The Trustees did not want Oglethorpe to settle

152

Frederica on St. Simons Island. They believed it was dangerously near the Spaniards. It was outside the boundary of the charter. They thought Oglethorpe should keep the colony focused around Savannah. They said at first that if he settled it, he would have to look to the government and not to them for money to run it. But later they helped him.

Oglethorpe needed Frederica as a base to use in the coming showdown with the Spanish, so he built it anyhow. He laid out a fort and a village on the site where the Indians had once had a forty-acre cornfield. Here, on September 26, 1736, he brought 227 soldiers, and started building.

In laying out Frederica, Oglethorpe followed the plans of Monsieur Vaubon, France's great military genius who had revolutionized the art of warfare. It was star-shaped with thick walls and a moat. He left the great live oaks standing.

Oglethorpe wrote the Trustees about the building of the village and fort:

"....as soon as we got there, we immediately got
up a house, thatched it with palmetto and dug a
cellar, and traced out enough of the ramparts for
a sample for the men to work on."

They built temporary shelters to use until the houses were ready.

The first shelters were made of palmetto leaves. A Jewish soldier who had been in Brazil showed Oglethorpe how to use these leaves for building. Later, buildings were made of "tabby." This is a word of African origin meaning "wall of earth or masonry." "Tabby," first used here by the Spanish, was a mixture of lime, seashells, sand, and water. It dries rock hard, and was used for most buildings

along the coast in that era. Tabby ruins may be seen along Georgia's coast to this day. (Later, after about 1890, coquina took the place of tabby for building. Coquina is a shell rock.)

The soldiers built a narrow military road from one fort to another fort on the south end of St. Simons Island. It was just wide enough for two to walk abreast.

Oglethorpe also started a mail service, the first in Georgia. He paid the postman, William Forrester, twelve pence a day to carry mail from one fort to the other and back. There was also established a mail service between St. Simons Isand and Savannah and Augusta.

At its peak, Frederica had a thousand residents. Oglethorpe encouraged the soldiers to bring their families, and some did. They built houses in the little village next to the fort.

Among them were Dr. Thomas Hawkins and his wife Beata, known as a mean woman, and Samuel Davison, who made chairs and gunstocks and kept a tavern in his house, and his wife, Susannah. They and their families had come with the very first settlers to Frederica, and were granted building lots one and two.

Frederica was named for Frederick, the Prince of Wales. He was the oldest son of King George II, who had signed Georgia's charter. Frederick was heir to the throne, but his father did not love him. This was often true with the Hanoverians. (A recent biography of King Edward VII points out that he was unloved by his mother, Queen Victoria, who did not think he was smart enough to be king, and also believed his conduct had hastened his father's death.)

Frederick had an allowance of fifty thousand pounds a year and wasted it, mostly on horse racing. In 1751, he was hit in the eye by a ball, developed an abcess and died. His father was glad to be rid of him, and gave him a shabby funeral.

Oglethorpe really built two forts, Frederica on the west side of the island, and Fort St. Simons on the south end. But the people lived in the tiny village next to Frederica. It was a wonderful site for a fort. There Oglethorpe could see both north and south, up and down the river, there behind the islands that bordered the Atlantic. He put five cannons on Yamacraw Bluff near Savannah, built Fort Argyle on the Ogeechee, Fort St. Andrew and Fort Williams on Cumberland Island, and set up Fort St. George on small San Juan Island at the mouth of the St. Johns River.

The General's Own Home

The only real home Oglethorpe ever had in Georgia was in Frederica. He called it "The Farm"; later, the Spaldings who bought it called it "Orange Hall." It was built on a three-hundred-acre tract just where the road turned into the woods, and was a one-and-a-half-story cottage. In the garden were oranges, figs, grapes, and other fruits. He could look out across the road and see the great oaks, sweet gums, and pine, the draped moss and the jasmine as yellow as sunshine. The bronze marshes stretched away into the distance. Here were rice birds, mockingbirds, deer, rabbits, raccoons, turkeys, doves, heron, marsh hens, and wild geese.

Once Oglethorpe was sick here for many weeks, and William Stephens, in his diary kept for the Trustees, recorded in 1740 that, "The General stays upstairs on his bed and hardly comes down. He has been sick with a lurking fever, for a long time past, that has worn away his strength." The house was occupied after he left by William Horton, who succeeded him as military commander. Horton also had a home on Jekyll made of tabby. Its ruins still stand on the Island of Jekyll today.

The Oglethorpe House and fifty acres were bought in 1771 by James Spalding. It was in this house, called "Orange Hall," that Thomas Spalding, later "the Laird of Sapelo," was born. In 1786 Spalding sold this house and moved to Sapelo. During Jefferson's presidency, many years later, the son of Oglethorpe's sister Eleanor tried to get title to Oglethorpe's American property, but there was none.

A Strange Prisoner Was At Frederica

One of the strangest figures among the Cherokees in early Georgia was the brilliant Gottlieb Christian Priber, a German Jesuit, who came to live among them in 1736. He knew their language, wore their costumes, and made himself secretary to the tribal chief. He was thought to be an agent of the French. His purpose was to keep them on the side of

155

the French, and against Oglethorpe and the British. Priber was a dramatic fellow, and he arranged colorful ceremonies to proclaim the Indian chiefs. He gave them very impressive titles, and deferred to them flatteringly, though he subtly influenced their actions. Priber called himself the "royal secretary," and carried on correspondence for the chief with the white men. He once wrote a letter ordering the South Carolinians to get out of the country. The Governor of South Carolina sent officers to arrest him but the Cherokees would not give him up.

Finally, he was arrested at Tallapoosa Town and, as a captured prisoner, was sent to Frederica to be tried. Oglethorpe was surprised to find him a polished European who spoke many languages and several Indian dialects. Priber told Oglethorpe that he wanted to help the Indians "throw off the white man's yoke," and that he planned to get up at Cusseta a town where any persecuted man could find a haven from oppression. He was put into prison at Frederica and died there, but before his death he said, "Believe me, before this century ends, the Europeans will have a very small footing on this continent."

Oglethorpe recognized Priber as a very dangerous force against the British. It was vital to keep British power strong among the Indians; Britain would need them as allies in the war with Spain, which was now coming closer and closer.

Whitefield Started America's First Orphanage Here

Reverend George Whitefield, one of the most eloquent preachers in England, came to Georgia May 7, 1738. John Wesley had invited him, but Wesley fled Georgia in 1737 before Whitefield arrived. James Habersham came with Whitefield. Habersham was later to serve as assistant to the royal governor, and partner in the first importing business with Francis Harris.

Whitefield had been sick on the voyage over, and when he landed he was pale as a ghost, and his cheeks were as puffy as those of a squirrel with nuts in its jaws. Wesley believed that the young minister, who had been drawing crowds by his preaching since he was twenty-three, was needed in this new land.

So the blue-eyed, twenty-five-year-old Whitefield
came. He had, as he wrote, "... found in Georgia many poor
orphans ... some likely to have no education at all." Whitefield and Habersham actually started their orphanage in
Savannah earlier than they had planned because they found so
many orphans here. Later Habersham picked a site on the
Isle of Hope, ten miles from Savannah, for their permanent
buildings, and moved the school and orphanage there. Then
John Dobell, who had been an assistant, was hired by the
Trustees as the teacher in Savannah. He taught the first
free school there. It became free to all children because
many people had resented the "poor" law that made school

The Rev.ᵈ George Whitefield A. M.
late Chaplain to the R.ᵗ Hon.ᵇᵉ the
Countess of Huntingdon.
Born Dec. 16. 1714 O.S. Died Sep: 30: 1770.

Reverend George Whitefield

157

free only to charity pupils, as in England. They refused to send their children until this stigma was removed and it was made free to all. On April 18, 1743, it became free to any child, irrespective of ability to pay. Not all Georgia orphans wanted to go to the home. Young Richard Milledge, whose parents had died earlier, took his young brother and sister out and made a home for them himself.

Oglethorpe and John Wesley had suggested that Georgia needed an orphanage. Many parents had died in the first hard years of the colony, and children were left. The Salzburgers had an orphanage at Ebenezer for twelve years. Whitefield visited there, and was inspired to establish one for the colony. He went back to England and got a grant of five hundred acres. He named the place Bethesda, meaning "house of mercy," because he hoped it would be a "house of mercy for many souls." The orphanage and school were set up about twelve miles from Savannah. It is still in operation as a school for boys.

Whitefield went up and down the land and back to England, preaching to raise money for these poor boys. Though he had not been an orphan, he had known what it was to be poor. He had been born December 16, 1714, to parents who kept a tavern. There he had to sweep floors, wash mops, and serve ale to the customers. He somehow got to college, where he came under the influence of the Wesleys. (He later broke with Wesley and became a Calvinist.) Whitefield was a fiery preacher who "lit the land with flame." He preached 18,000 sermons, in churches when they let him, in the field when they would not.

Whitefield disagreed with the Georgia Trustees about slavery, and bought a farm in South Carolina, where he had slaves to raise vegetables and meat for his Georgia orphanage. Indians brought deer and other food from the forests and the field to the door of Bethesda.

How successful Whitefield was in raising money for Bethesda is illustrated in a story told by Benjamin Franklin (who was later to become Georgia's Colonial Agent). In Pennsylvania, Franklin had started schools that included the sciences and vocational education, in contrast with the traditional academics. In Franklin's famous autobiography, he wrote about Whitefield:

> "I happened to attend one of his sermons.
> I perceived early that he meant to take up a col-
> lection. I silently resolved that he should get
> nothing from me. I had in my pocket a handful
> of copper money, three or four silver dollars, and
> five pistoles of gold. As the sermon progressed,
> I began to soften and concluded to give the copper.
> Another stroke of oratory made me ashamed and
> determined me to give the silver; and he finished
> so admirably that I emptied my pockets into
> the collection dish, gold and all."

Franklin had opposed building the orphanage in Georgia where workmen and materials were scarce, and often had to be brought in. He thought it would be simpler to carry the orphans to Philadelphia and build there.

At the orphanage-school, Whitefield himself laid the first brick for Bethesda on March 25, 1740. There the boys were taught regular school subjects and also trained to work. By 1741, there were sixty-eight boys at Bethesda. Habersham taught them while Whitefield raised the money to support the place.

Whitefield, who had helped found the University of Pennsylvania, had hoped to make a college at Bethesda, too, since there was not a college south of the College of William and Mary in Virginia. The church authorities told him that it would have to be headed by an Anglican clergyman and that the liturgy of the established church would have to be used. Since money for the place came from people of many denominations, Whitefield refused. The orphans themselves were of more than one denomination. Peter Tondee, a Catho-lic, was a student there. He later became known as the proprietor of Tondee's Tavern, where the Liberty Boys plotted Georgia's part in the American Revolution.

Whitefield had married a woman ten years older than he on one of his trips back to England. He crossed the Atlantic thirteen times in behalf of his orphanage and school. The founder of Bethesda died in this country, at the home of Reverend Jonathan Parsons, pastor of the First Presby-terian Church in Newburyport, Massachusetts, where he was spending the night. Suffering from asthma, Whitefield was going up to bed with a candle when the townspeople, having heard he was there, swarmed to the door. He turned and preached to them from the stair landing. He died about six o'clock the next morning, September 30, 1770, and was buried under the crypt of the church there.

In Savannah, people bought up every yard of black cloth they could find to use in mourning for him. He left Bethesda to Lady Selina, the Countess of Huntingdon, who had helped him finance it. Her portrait is in the Art Museum in Atlanta. One painted by Sir Joshua Reynolds is owned by the Georgia Historical Society. Fire, lightning, water, and a tornado brought havoc to Bethesda, but it was reestablished. At Christmas time the boys have an English Festival there,

complete with Yule log and boar's head. A tiny chapel, a replica of the one at which Whitefield preached in England, is on the grounds. A stained glass window is a memorial to

James Habersham, who later became famous as assisant to Royal Governor Wright, and a businessman in Savannah.

Lord Chesterfield said that Whitefield was the greatest orator he ever heard in all his life. Another contemporary said that Wesley gripped the common people, and Whitefield fascinated the upper classes. Georgia named a county for Whitefield.

The Union Society, organized by a Catholic, a Jew, and a Protestant ten years after the orphanage was founded, has long sponsored Bethesda, and bought it in 1854.

Chapter 12

HOW OGLETHORPE STRENGTHENED HIS COLONY AND RETURNED TO ENGLAND

Oglethorpe knew Georgia had to develop strength to resist the Spanish from Florida when the showdown came. He worked hard toward this end.

WILLIAM STEPHENS, "THE MAN WITH THE DIARY": Oglethorpe was so busy setting up defenses for the new colony and helping the people with their problems that he did not have time to write to the Trustees in London as often as they thought he should. They said they could not ask Parliament for any more money until they had a report on what was being done in Georgia. The Earl of Egmont had heard of William Stephens, a former member of Parliament and colleague of Oglethorpe, who had gone from England to Ireland and then to America, where he was hired to oversee some lands in South Carolina. Young Stephens had graduated from college, married a very beautiful woman, and been elected to Parliament from Newport. After he lost that seat, and his money, he got a job in Carolina as a clerk and surveyor. He was a man who kept voluminous survey diaries and wrote many letters. He seemed just the man to send to Georgia, so he was appointed secretary in April, 1737.

The Trustees wanted a report on

"the true state of the colony, settting out the number of inhabitants, their settlements and progress in cultivation, their ability or inability to support themselves by labor, the nature of the climate and soil as near as may be computed,

162

the produce that may be raised for trade by the inhabitants, the nature of the goodness of the coast and harbors, and the defensible state of the colony, together with the benefit Great Britain enjoys by settling and fortifying it and may reasonably be expected to enjoy by the produce silk, wine, oil, cotton, and cochineal."

Oglethorpe had been too busy to report on all these things, so Stephens was sent to help him, and was ordered to report on these things immediately. The colony's new secretary was amazed to contemplate the work involved in gathering so much information. Stephens arrived in Georgia November 1, 1737. He wrote the Trustees about the crops, the weather, the people, how they worked and whether they went to church, and the problems. Some considered him a nosy busybody, but he had been hired to make detailed reports, and this he did. When sending the reports back to England, he weighted them so they would go down if the ship sank. His diaries were later published, much to his embarrassment, by the Trustees in London; seventy copies were printed and then the Trustees ordered the "presses to be broke." The diaries, which began October 20, 1737, have been reprinted in recent years by the University of Georgia Press.

Stephens was sixty-six years old when he came to Georgia. He did everything he could to help Oglethorpe, and was deeply apologetic to the General when his son Thomas Stephens joined the opposition and actually went to London on April 30, 1742, to complain about Oglethorpe's strict discipline. In his diary, Stephens refers to his son as "a furious, rash young fellow," and assured both Oglethorpe and the Trustees that Thomas's opinions were not his.

Stephens did not approve of Whitefield's establishing the Bethesda Orphanage because it was not a Church of England project. He called the sponsors "a parcel of wild enthusiasts."

In 1741 the Trustees divided Georgia into two separate parishes; they made Stephens president of the one in Savannah and left Oglethorpe in command at Frederica. The General also was commander-in-chief of all the military matters in the colony, and for South Carolina as well.

Stephens had been given another job in Georgia several years before. He was appointed storekeeper in place of Thomas Causton. Causton, the uncle of Sophie Hopkey whom Wesley had almost married, was the colony's first storekeeper. He was paid forty pounds a year as salary, but he handled his accounts badly. Once when Oglethorpe was in England, Causton became so dictatorial that he gave credit only to his friends, and some colonists who opposed him went hungry because he would not let them have supplies. He became rich and bought a fine home, which he named "Oakstead." When Oglethorpe returned from England, he discharged Causton, who went before the Trustees. He died at sea on the voyage back, but Stephens had already been appointed in his place.

DR. PATRICK TAILFER LED THE MALCONTENTS: One of those who caused Oglethorpe trouble was Dr.Patrick Tailfer, an apothecary surgeon. He was the leader of a group of people who had various complaints against Oglethorpe and the Trustees. Some did not like the rules against slaves and rum. Another thing they resented was the land laws, which forbade larger land holdings and also made it impossible for a man to sell his land or to pass it down to his heirs. Later inheritance was permitted, but only to male heirs, and finally this too was changed. Others rebelled when supplies had to be cut down because Thomas Causton, the storekeeper, had done away with much of the colony's stores. Disappointed at the slow growth of Georgia, some moved to South Carolina.

Tailfer and his fellow malcontents wrote a pamphlet about their dissatisfactions. It was titled " 'A True & Historical Narrative of the Colony of Georgia in America' by Pat Tailfer, M. D., Hugh Anderson, M. A., Da. Douglas and Others." Tailfer undoubtedly influenced young Thomas Stephens, son of William Stephens, to join the group. Young Stephens went to England to present the complaints to the Trustees and to Parliament. He told them that the climate, soil, and other things in Georgia had been represented to the colonists in "false and flattering colors" and that they had been led to expect too much of the colony. The complaint charged that most of the five thousand colonists who had come to Georgia in its first six years had already left, and that the colony was in danger of becoming extinct. It was said that the people were especially angry at not being allowed to have slaves, inasmuch as South Carolinians were permitted to have them. Georgians had petitioned for slaves, but the Trustees had refused, though they later relented and allowed them. Oglethorpe had said that "if the petition is countenanced, the colony is ruined." He had held to this view despite the fact that such influential people as James Habersham and Reverend George Whitefield condoned slavery.

Young Stephens also said that the colonists wanted fee simple land holding, that is, the right to own their property outright. The House of Commons refused to interfere with the authority of the Trustees, though it did recommend that rum be allowed in Georgia. Egmont was indignant with the complainers. "Always a fling at Mr. Oglethorpe," he said.

Thomas Stephens was forced to apologize on his knees for his antagonistic attitude toward Oglethorpe and the Trustees. The Earl of Egmont wrote in his diary, "Tomorrow (June 29, 1742) Thomas Stephens is to be brought upon his Marrowbones and Reprimanded from the Chair."

Oglethorpe, who had left his comfortable home in England and spent ten years on the hard frontier trying to help the colonists get a start in a new land, was frequently troubled by this ingratitude and complaining.

Sometimes the colonists felt that the General was too harsh; there were even those who called him a dictator. Others felt that he had to be stern and enforce rules to get anything done at all in the frontier colony, but Tailfer and

165

his group called him "our perpetual dictator" and considered him a tyrant. Once there was even a plot to assassinate Oglethorpe and turn the colony over to the Spanish. Biographers of the General point out that only his determination and courage enabled Georgia to get through its hard beginnings and become a permanent part of the New World.

HOW OGLETHORPE GOT READY FOR THE SHOWDOWN WITH SPAIN:
From the first, Oglethorpe had foreseen that sooner or later England and Spain would clash here on the frontier in Georgia. The Spanish were in Florida, and had once had their forts and missions strung along the Georgia coast. They had been pushed by Indian attacks and the enmity of other nations down to St. Augustine, where they were then entrenched. The English had colonies all along the Atlantic seaboard, but it was the Georgia colony that was next to the Spaniards, and was a buffer state between them and the other English in the New World.

Oglethorpe started as soon as he could to prepare for the coming war. He set up forts and trading stations, and formed settlements at Augusta and Frederica. He sent families to set up homes and trading posts in the Indian country to keep the Indians friendly. One of these was Mount Venture, the trading post of Mary Musgrove on the Altamaha.

The General was so persuasive that once he had talked Sanchez, the Spanish governor of Florida, into pulling back the Spanish outposts to the lower side of the St. Johns River. This had so enraged the king of Spain that he ordered Sanchez back to Spain, had him hanged, and sent another governor to Florida.

In February, 1736, Oglethorpe sent Charles Dempsey with a letter to the Florida governor. Dempsey was accompanied by Major Richards of Purrysburg, the settlement just across the Savannah River from Georgia. The two were courteously received. Dempsey had trouble with his boat, and lingered to repair it, while Richards carried the Spanish governor's reply back to Oglethorpe. Later the General found that the Spanish were holding Dempsey a prisoner, and he sent Major William Horton, his military aide, to look for him. When the Spanish governor really found out how well Oglethorpe had fortified the Georgia

166

Dempsey Was Captured While Repairing His Boat.

coast, he released Dempsey and sent with him back to Georgia a delegation to talk with the General about peace between Georgia and Florida.

Oglethorpe received the delegation on board a ship called the *Hawk* in the harbor at Jekyll. He did not want them to get close enough to St. Simons to see the forts he had built there.

In late summer, Arredondo, the Spanish commander, came from Havana, Cuba, to talk with Oglethorpe. Despite the General's hospitality and the toasts that were drunk to both the British and Spanish kings, the Spanish soon afterward sent Oglethorpe a formal demand to get out of Georgia. The General reported to the Trustees that the danger was serious, and that he would need more men and more money to get ready for the war that was sure to come with Spain.

OGLETHORPE MADE A DANGEROUS JOURNEY ACROSS GEORGIA: It was important for Oglethorpe to keep the Indians on England's side in the coming war. Tomochichi had advised him to meet with the Indians at their great council at Coweta

167

Town, near the present Columbus but across the Chattahoochee River. That was a long and dangerous journey; Oglethorpe would have to cross rivers that had no bridges, and get through tangled swamps that had no paths, but he went.

The Indians were often stirred by the French who had moved down the Mississippi and settled in along the Gulf. The French King Louis claimed two-thirds of the land that Georgia claimed between the Atlantic and the Mississippi. The Spanish were also moving in from the south and the west. Both nations were seeking trade with the Indians; they gave them many gifts, and tried hard to alienate them from Oglethorpe and the British. Both Tomochichi and Mary Musgrove had felt that it was very important for Oglethorpe to journey to Coweta Town to renew and strengthen his ties and friendship with the Indians. Chiefs gathering at Coweta Town would represent twenty thousand Indians in the southeast.

The General, with a party of Scotch Highlanders and Indians, both of whom could travel through frontier country well, started out from Frederica. They slowly made the hard trip across Georgia, about three hundred miles the way they went. Finally they came near the Chattahoochee River, where they were met by a welcoming party about forty miles from Coweta Town, or Kawita, as the Indians called it. (Later, Fort Mitchell was built here.) At the site near which Oglethorpe crossed the Chattahoochee there is now a modern bridge, and a marker. Indian boys and girls gave the visitors watermelons, muscadines, venison, and wild turkey meat; and Oglethorpe's party brought many gifts for the Indians, too. He arrived at the council town on August 21, 1739.

The General sat with the Indians on logs covered with bearskins, drank their black cassena tea and smoked the peace pipe with them. The Indians called him "Tasanagi-Takke," which meant "White Chief." The presiding chief at the Coweta Council was Yahoo-Lakee. Among the Indian leaders there was Mary Musgrove's kinsman, Malatche. He was the son of her uncle, the Emperor Brim. Malatche's uncle Chigilly, the King of the Cowetas, was there, as was Queekachumpa, whose name meant "Long King." Some of the chiefs had come to Coweta Town from settlements as far as two hundred miles away. Besides the

Creeks, the Chickasaws, and the Choctaws, there were Cherokees with whom Oglethorpe talked. These Cherokees had been very angry with the British. Some English traders had gone among them, carrying rum and diseased with smallpox, which the Indians caught, and many died. Some, seeing their scarred faces mirrored in the streams of water, killed themselves.

"They did much damage to us. A thousand of our people died. We could not harvest our crops," the Cherokees told Oglethorpe.

"Were these traders from the Colony of Georgia?" he asked. They said no. Oglethorpe promised to give them fifteen thousand bushels of corn to feed their hungry people. At this news, the Indians whooped so loud it nearly deafened their white guests.

On August 21, 1739 — the same day the Georgia group arrived — the Indians ratified their old agreement to let the English colony have the land to the Altamaha, and they extended this to the St. Johns River. They reserved for themselves again the same hunting islands, St. Catherines, Ossabaw, and Sapelo, and the camping site near Savannah.

Oglethorpe felt that his long, hard journey had been very much worthwhile. After he had rested, he and his men started on their return trip. He came back by way of

Augusta, where he stayed for several weeks, ill with a fever and suffering from an infection in his side. He had fallen off his horse in a canebrake, and a sharp cane had pierced his side. The wound had become infected. In September a messenger sent by William Stephens reached him. There was important news: Spain had declared war on England. Oglethorpe was not surprised. There was other, and still sadder, news. The aged Tomochichi, so long a friend and a source of strength to Oglethorpe, was dying.

TOMOCHICHI'S DEATH HANDICAPPED OGLETHORPE: Tomochichi, who had been an old man past ninety when Oglethorpe first met him, died at ninety-seven. He had done so much to keep the Indians friendly and to help Oglethorpe get Georgia started, that the General felt a severe loss at his death. He knew that he would grievously miss the staunch old Indian in the coming trouble with Spain.

Tomochici had died on October 5, 1739. He had said that he wanted to be buried in Savannah, among his white friends. The *Gentleman's Magazine* reported it this way:

"He desired his Body might be buried among the English in the Town of Savannah, since it was he who had prevailed with the Creek Indians to give the land and assisted in the founding of the Town."

The old Indian's body was put on a boat and rowed from Yamacraw Village down to Savannah. Oglethorpe was one of the pallbearers. Guns were fired in salute to the memory of the faithful old Indian. A big stone marks Tomochichi's grave in Savannah today. On it are these words:

"In memory of Tomochichi, Mico of the Yamacraws, the companion of Oglethorpe and the friend and ally of the colony of Georgia."

After Oglethorpe had helped lay the body of his friend in the Georgia earth, he turned his attention to the war for which he must now get ready without the help of the loyal old chief. He sent friendly Indians speeding to the tribes to summon warriors, and sent Mary Musgrove to rouse the chiefs to the aid of Georgia. Then he went home to Frederica, where the coming war would focus.

THE PECULIAR WAR OF JENKINS' EAR   The oddest thing about the coming war was that it was the only one in history named for a man's ear. Churchill, writing about this ear centuries later, said, "The power of this shriveled object was immense!"

It happened like this:

In Europe, England and Spain were quarreling. The Treaty of Utrecht, signed by Spain and England in 1713, provided that England would send only one trading ship each year to the Spanish colonies in South America. But this agreement was not kept. British merchants began to send more ships, and this smuggling of goods angered Spain. Spanish ships often captured these British cargoes, and threatened the sailors roughly.

In 1731, the British ship named the *Rebecca* was captured by a Spanish ship. On the *Rebecca* was a seaman named Robert Jenkins. The Spanish captain, Fandino, tore off Jenkins' ear, handed it to him, and told him to take it to the king as a warning to stop his British ships from taking smuggled goods to Spanish colonies in South America. The poet Alexander Pope later wrote,

"The Spanish did a waggish thing;
They cropped his ear and sent it to the king!"

Jenkins put his ear in a bottle and appeared before the British Parliament with it. The ear captured the imagination of the public. A member of Parliament asked Jenkins, "What did you do when they tore off your ear?"

He answered, "I commended my soul to God and my cause to my country."

There were some who said that Jenkins really lost his ear in a tavern brawl in some port where the ship stopped, but his story stirred England and hastened a war that was already threatening the peace between the two countries. On October 9, 1739, Spain officially declared war on England, and the repercussions were felt in Georgia. The Spanish in Florida were sure to attack the English in Georgia. Some historians call this "King George's War,"

171

Jenkins Appeared Before Parliament.

but here it was better known as "the War of Jenkins' Ear."
Robert Walpole, the powerful British prime minister, did
not really approve of this war; he did not believe that England
was prepared to fight it. But England won this war, finally.
And in Georgia, Oglethorpe led the English to a spectacular
victory at Bloody Marsh.

HOW THE FIGHTING STARTED IN GEORGIA   Georgia was the
only one of the English colonies in America that was affected
very much by the actual fighting in this war, though all the
colonies remained under England because of it.

The fighting started here when Spaniards landed on
Amelia Island and killed two unarmed Scotch Highlanders
who were simply cutting wood. This was in the middle of
November, 1739. Captain Francis Brooks, in command of the
British fort on the island, heard the shots, rounded up his
soldiers and drove out the invading Spaniards. He reported
the occurrence to Oglethorpe, who was furious. The General
sent to Savannah and to the Indian settlements and to the

172

Scotch Highlander community at Darien for reinforcements. He wanted all the help he could get. Among the Indian warriors who came was Tooanahowi, the adopted son of old Tomochichi. The young Indian had gone with Oglethorpe to England when the General took the Indians to visit there.

Oglethorpe chased the Spaniards up the river and burned their ships. He forced them back to their headquarters at St. Augustine. He captured two forts: Fort Francis de Papa, twenty-five miles from St. Augustine, and Fort Diego, nine miles from St. Augustine. The Spanish also abandoned Fort Moosa as they returned to St. Augustine.

By spring of 1740, Oglethorpe decided to attack St. Augustine itself. This was the first of many attacks that would be made by Georgians on the strongly fortified Spanish city (which is the oldest city in America established by white settlers). Oglethorpe thought he could take it. He had nine hundred soldiers and eleven hundred Indians when he left Frederica in May. The Florida fort at St. Augustine was under the command of General Manuel de Monteano. He had fourteen hundred men, and was more strongly entrenched than Oglethorpe had thought.

The General put his own men at various strategic points around the section, telling them not to spend more than a night in any one place. The officer in command of his troops at Fort Moosa disobeyed this order, spent three nights there, and was routed by the Spaniards at daylight. Though his men fought like tigers, they were defeated.

Many of Oglethorpe's men were sick, and the weather was growing hot. After storming St. Augustine's fort for twenty days, he withdrew his siege and returned to Frederica in July, 1740. Oglethorpe had lost fifty men, and he had a fever that lasted two months.

He had failed to capture St. Augustine, but he had so awed the Spaniards that they did not come to attack him in Georgia for another two years. He knew, however, that they would come because the question had to be settled: who would control the land in the future, England or Spain?

THE SPECTACULAR LITTLE BATTLE OF BLOODY MARSH: On St. Simons Island is a white marble monument that marks the site of the Battle of Bloody Marsh. Here Oglethorpe and his men fought an important battle.

In June, 1742, the General heard that fifty-six Spanish ships with seven thousand men had left Havana, Cuba, headed for St. Augustine. He knew that this was the beginning of the war on Georgia. The Spaniards were getting ready for the final showdown with the English colony. They had already threatened to "wipe the English off the Atlantic coast." Horcasitas, the Spanish governor of Cuba, now sent Monteano back with instructions to get the English out.

On June 28, 1742, just at sunset, thirty-six ships with more than three thousand Spaniards aboard neared the shore of St. Simons Island off the Georgia coast. Oglethorpe at that time had only six hundred soldiers at Frederica. Quickly he sent again to Savannah, Darien, and other settlements for help. At most, he could muster about nine hundred men. But he said,

> "We are resolved not to suffer defeat. We will, rather, die like Leonidas and his Spartans in old Greece if we can but protect Georgia and Carolina and the rest of the American colonies from desolation."

The troops from St. Augustine itself were commanded by Monteano, and others, from Cuba, by Don Antonio de Rodondo. They had been ordered to destroy Frederica, and then to pillage and burn the rest of the settlements in Georgia and Carolina.

Among those who were helping Oglethorpe were Captain Noble Jones and his Georgia Rangers, Lieutenant Charles Mackay and his Scotch Highlanders, and the Indian leader, Tooanahowi and his Creek warriors. William McIntosh, the older brother of Lachlan McIntosh who was later to play a tragic role in Georgia's history, fought at Bloody Marsh with Oglethorpe, though he was only sixteen. Their father, John Mohr McIntosh, leader of the Scotch Highlander clan, was in a Spanish prison.

As the Spanish had approached St. Simons Island, Oglethorpe had pulled his men out of Fort St. Simon on the southern end of the island, destroyed the equipment and ammunition he could not move and concentrated his forces at Fort Frederica on the upper end of the island. He had already built a narrow road, just wide enough for two to

174

march, and planned to ambush the Spaniards.

The Spanish soldiers landed, and started their troops marching up that road, as Oglethorpe had known they would. The General and his men marched out to meet the enemy. In a battle, a hundred Spaniards were killed, and Oglethorpe himself took two prisoners. The Spanish were driven back to their ships. Oglethorpe left soldiers to guard the approaches to Frederica. When the Spaniards came back for another attack, these men had hidden behind bushes. Thinking that the Georgians had gone, the Spanish soldiers relaxed and started preparing for supper.

The Georgia officers had hidden their men all through the woods. Captain Mackay had told them, "When I hold up my cap on the end of my gun, that will be the signal for you to attack the Spaniards." He held up the cap; the English soldiers from Georgia, with their Indian allies, rushed to the attack. They caught the Spaniards by surprise, and the ground at the battle site was strewn with the wounded and the dead.

"What a bloody marsh!" somebody said. The site became known as "Bloody Marsh." Oglethorpe and his men had won the fight on July 7, 1742. Even though this battle was small, it was important to the future of America. Carlyle, the British essayist, said that it was one of the most momentous battles in history. Whitefield said that one would have to go back to the Old Testament to find anything like it. Many governors wrote to congratulate Oglethorpe on his victory, which also determined their future. But Oglethorpe knew that the Spanish were still on this island, and might attack again. The trouble was not over.

THE ODD LETTER THAT TRICKED THE SPANISH: The battle of Bloody Marsh alone did not settle the Spanish problem, nor rid Georgia of the invading Spaniards. It had only proved to the Spanish commander that Georgia would not be as easily conquered as he had thought. The Spanish soldiers were still on Georgia's coast, and a threat not only to Georgia's four thousand colonists, but also to the sixty thousand in South Carolina, eighty thousand in North Carolina, and more than a quarter of a million in Virginia. Georgia was at this moment, in deed and in truth, the "buffer colony" that the Trustees had told King George II it could be between the English colonists along the Atlantic seaboard and the menacing Spaniards in Florida.

A few days passed after the battle of Bloody Marsh. Oglethorpe thought that the Spanish would attack again, and he was ill-prepared to resist them. Then something unexpected happened.

A Frenchman who had been fighting with the soldiers under Oglethorpe deserted to the Spanish. Oglethorpe knew that he would tell the Spanish commander just how few soldiers Georgia really had. The General wrote a letter to the Frenchman, making it sound as if the deserter had been deliberately sent as a spy into the Spanish camp. He urged the Frenchman to "try to get the Spanish to stay until we get the heavy reinforcements that we are expecting here on St. Simons." Then he gave the letter to a Spanish prisoner whom he released, and naturally the Spaniard carried the letter directly to the Spanish commander. This officer did not know whether to believe it or not, but he took no chances. He sailed away from Georgia on July 14, 1742.

Now Georgia was safe from the Spaniards. So were the half-million other colonists along the Atlantic coast. The power of Spain in America had been broken forever. Later the French and Indian War, from 1754 to 1763, would drive the French out. In 1775-1783, the colonists would drive the British themselves out, and America would be a new nation in control of its own government. That, however, was far in the future just now when Oglethorpe and the colonists were jubilant over resisting the Spanish attempt to seize control of Georgia.

Frederica, its mission accomplished, would soon fall into decay, its cannon rusted, and its soldiers gone. Later it would be sold to Captain Charles Stevens, a native of Denmark who had a coastal sailing operation based there. He would build a home for his family here. In 1945, more than two centuries later, the Fort Frederica Association would buy seventy-eight acres and give it to the federal government to create a national park there, one of the few historic shrines in America dating back beyond the Revolution. But just after Bloody Marsh and the affair of the letter, the regiment disbanded, and only a small guard was kept there to keep pirates from stealing the property that remained.

GEORGIANS HELD THEIR FIRST THANKSGIVING IN JULY: Oglethorpe, jubilant at the victory over the Spaniards, proclaimed July 25, 1742, as a day of thanksgiving to God. So the first Thanksgiving Day was observed in Georgia not in November, as later set up nationally, but in July.

The first Thanksgiving proclamation issued in this state was worded by Oglethorpe like this:

> Truly God has done great things for us. Our salvation comes from the Lord. He has rescued us from the power of a great foe, who boasted that they would conquer and dispossess us. It is highly fitting, therefore, that we render thanks in His name Who had been our Deliverer. In regard to these considerations and for this purpose, I do herefore appoint this, the 25th day of July, one thousand seven hundred and forty-two, as a day of special thanksgiving to God for His Great Deliverance and the end He has brought to the Spanish invasion. And I enjoin everyone to observe this festival in a Christian and godly manner, abstaining from intemperance and excess, and extravagant signs of rejoicing.

OGLETHORPE LEFT GEORGIA FOREVER: Oglethorpe had been in Georgia for over ten years. He had left his comfortable home in England and come out to help a handful of poor people start a new life, and he had ended the Spanish threat. Now he could think of going back home to England. His little colony was safe; his work was done. But first, he made one final trip to the Georgia-Florida border. He had to be sure that the Spaniards had really cleared out, so he took his soldiers on a quick trip, marching them ninety-six miles in four days! When he felt sure that the border was safe, Oglethorpe began to get ready to leave Georgia, forever.

He recommended to the Trustees that William Stephens, who was already president of the Savannah area, be made president of all Georgia, and that Major William Horton take over the duties of military commander. Stephens, "the man with the diary," had come to Georgia in 1737 as a secretary to report to the Trustees more often than the General had time to do. Horton had come over with Oglethorpe in 1736, bringing sixteen servants. He had been given five hundred acres on Jekyll, and had built a house there. The tabby ruins are still standing. Besides his military duties, Horton was a planter. He grew barley, hops, and rye, and made beer for the soldiers on St. Simons. He also planted ten thousand orange trees. In England, he had been under-sheriff of Hertfordshire. Later, after Horton died in 1749, his lands were sold to the colorful Christopher Poulain du Bignon.

Oglethorpe bade his people goodbye. He took a ring from his finger and gave it to Mary Musgrove, the Indian who had been his interpreter, not aware that she would later cause much trouble to the little colony that she had helped him get started. When he boarded the ship *Success* he found in hiding two young Georgia boys, William and Lachlan McIntosh of the Scotch clan at Darien. The boys, their heads full of youthful dreams of adventure, had heard that Oglethorpe was returning to England to fight for young Prince Jaime, the youthful pretender to the British throne. Oglethorpe's own mother and sister favored this claimant, but he loyally supported the House of Hanover. He told the boys they must go back to their homes and grow up to be good citizens of Georgia. When they found that he did not intend to fight for the Stuart prince, they returned to

Darien. As it turned out, Oglethorpe would later be court-martialed by the British government for an occurrence in connection with this prince, an anxious moment in his life which was undreamed of when he boarded the *Success* and sailed over the sea to the home he had not lived in for a decade.

THE LATER YEARS OF OGLETHORPE

The General who had done the most to found Georgia returned to his home in England in July, 1742. Nine years later he married Elizabeth Wright, heiress of Cranham Hall. An old novel romantically, and erroneously, described the wedding this way:

> "The General wore his splendid uniform. The bride had bought her wedding dress in Paris, and in her trousseau was another gown of violet velvet. The church was decorated with moss and pine cones sent by the Indians from Georgia. The wedding was one of the most brilliant of the social season in England."

They lived quietly at her home, Cranham Hall, but occasionally they went up to London, where Oglethorpe also had a town house. (His country place had burned, and many of his records were lost in the fire.)

He still served as an officer in the king's army, and was also a member of Parliament. Oglethorpe became a member of the colorful circle that revolved around Dr. Sam Johnson, whose biography was written by Boswell. In that circle were David Garrick, the actor; Oliver Goldsmith, the writer (who sometimes sang for them songs from his play *She Stoops To Conquer*); Joshua Reynolds, the artist; and others.

Both Johnson and Boswell urged Oglethorpe to write his memoirs. He did not think they would be interesting. "The life of a private person is of no interest to the public," said the General. Boswell replied, "You just provide the bare facts, the skeleton, Dr. Johnson will put flesh upon

179

the bones." Oglethorpe said, "He will be a very good doctor indeed if he can do that!" He promised Boswell that he would find an almanac and try to fit the dates to the things that had happened in his life, but he never found the time to do this.

Johnson and Oglethorpe sometimes disagreed about things, including the subject of the colonies. Johnson was dictatorial and opinionated, though colorful and brilliant. Once he protested Boswell's inviting Oglethorpe to the house. "Oglethorpe never finishes anything he starts," complained the old doctor. One thing they disagreed about was the right of England to tax the American colonies. Johnson upheld this right. He had, in fact, written the pamphlet "Taxation Not Tyranny," for which King George III had given him a pension. Johnson, who had written scornfully of pensions, accepted it. (He was always pressed for money, and once had to write a play hurriedly to get money for his mother's funeral.) Oglethorpe protested that the American colonies would never stand for taxation by Parliament, in which they were not represented.

Oglethorpe helped Goldsmith establish the science collection and group that later became the British Academy of Science. The two also set up a medical fund for the poor.

Boswell writes of Oglethorpe in his famous *Life of Johnson.* The portrait of Oglethorpe which hangs high on the wall in the rotunda of the Georgia State Capitol in Atlanta, shows the aged Oglethorpe at the auction of the library of Johnson, reading without his spectacles!

The General had some serious difficulty with the government. He was still an officer in the army of King George II, and was put in command of royal troops that were putting down the rebellion of the Stuart forces. The young Pretender had rallied his friends and was trying again to regain the British throne, which he considered rightfully his.

Oglethorpe's force of six hundred men had marched all day. They were tired and badly outnumbered. The General let them rest before leading them to an encounter with an enemy troop of more than two thousand. His enemies charged him with deliberate delay, and he was suspected of secretly favoring the young Pretender because his family was close to the Stuarts. This was cruelly unfair because

180

Oglethorpe had defied his own family to support King George II. His sister Eleanor had become so furious with him that she had once slammed the door in his face when he refused to support the Stuarts. Even his mother, who had been lady-in-waiting to Queen Anne, was disappointed. But Oglethorpe believed it to be his duty to support the king who was on the throne, and this he did.

The young Duke of Cumberland, the same one who had given Tooanahowi a gold watch, had Oglethorpe court-martialed. It was a sad time for the great man; friends became cool and enemies worked against him. But he was cleared of all the charges. His wife said, "I told you everything would come out all right." He answered, "Your faith sustained me." He was very lonely after her death.

Oglethorpe's Court-Martial

Cumberland, who had put down the rebellion, was the hero of the hour. But even with all his power, he could not sustain against Oglethorpe the unfair charge of "lingering on the road." This was the same Cumberland for whom Oglethorpe had named Cumberland Island in Georgia, at the request of young Tooanahowi, to whom the English lad had given the watch.

There were many in England who loved and appreciated Oglethorpe, and knew him for the great man that he was. One was the witty and warm writer, Hannah More. She wrote to a friend,

> "I have a new admirer. He is the famous General
> Oglethorpe, perhaps the most remarkable man
> of his time. He is past ninety, and the finest figure
> of a man you ever saw. His literature is great,
> his knowledge of the world is extensive and
> his faculties as bright as ever. We flirt out-
> rageously."

Of course she was joking about the last, and she was wrong
about his age, too. He was only eighty-nine when he died on
July 1, 1786, after three weeks' illness.

The *Georgia Gazette* waited a whole year to
carry the news of his death, ran only three lines about it,
and got the date and his age wrong: "General Oglethorpe
died August last, aged 103." But it had been a long time
since the General had left Georgia.

OGLETHORPE'S GRAVE WAS LOST

Georgia's founder was buried in the little All Saints
Church at Cranham, beside his wife, Elizabeth. They were
laid in a crypt in the basement of the church, near the center.
The little building was later rebuilt, after damage in a war,
and the plaque that pointed out the graves was taken down
from the wall. By 1923, nobody remembered where General
James Edward Oglethorpe was buried!

The late Dr. Thornwell Jacob, then president of Oglethorpe University in Atlanta, found the grave. He got permission from the British authorities to have the bricks
removed from the floor of the little church. One by one,
the workmen removed the bricks. Then one workman was
lowered into the crypt. There, side by side, two black
coffins lay: the caskets of General Oglethorpe and his
wife! Outside, a gray autumn rain was falling, and a robin
sang in a rosebush. It was a solemn moment within the
little church: the grave of Georgia's founder had been
rediscovered after being lost for 138 years. Dr. Jacob
asked permission to move the casket to Georgia, but this
was refused. Plans were made to hold memorial services
in the little church each Georgia Day, February 12, and to
have flowers put on the graves of the General and his wife.

Edmund Burke, the great Irishman, said that Oglethorpe was the most remarkable man he had ever known. The historian Bancroft said that Oglethorpe was chivalrous in a commercial age, and risked his life for others. He was sometimes boastful and tinged with vanity, and now and then stern; but he was a man of great, unselfish concern for others, and of tremendous courage.

The poet Alexander Pope wrote of him:

"Hail, Oglethorpe, with triumphs crowned
That ever were in camps or sieges found, —
Thy great example shall through ages shine,
A favorite theme with poet and divine,
People unborn thy merits shall proclaim,
And add new luster to thy deathless name."

When Sherman went through Milledgeville in 1864, as the Civil War was ending, he was surprised not to find a portrait of Oglethorpe in the State House there.

Georgia has a county, a town, and a university named for him, besides many streets, hotels, and other things. In Savannah there is a $38,000 monument to his memory. High on a north Georgia mountain, Grassy Knob in Pickens County, is a monument to him. Fort Oglethorpe keeps his name alive, as does Mount Oglethorpe. There is a bust of him on the stair landing in the State Capitol, sculptured by an artist, that looks curiously like Voltaire. The finest portrait of him in Georgia hangs in Oglethorpe University.

There is an old story that Oglethorpe was offered command of the British forces in the American Revolution, but refused to fight against the colonies. This is not true. He was too old at the time, though he probably would have refused.

He welcomed the first American ambassador to England after the colonies won their independence. This was John Adams. Oglethorpe said, "I am very glad to see you here, sir."

Chapter 13

WHAT HAPPENED IN GEORGIA AFTER OGLETHORPE LEFT?

The Three Presidents Of Georgia

There were three presidents that served as heads of the government in Georgia between the time that Oglethorpe left and the coming of the first of the three royal governors.

WILLIAM STEPHENS, GEORGIA'S FIRST PENSIONER

William Stephens, the "man with the diary" who had come to Georgia in 1737 to report to the complaining Trustees, had already been appointed president of the Savannah area in 1741. That year the Trustees had divided Georgia into two parts: one centered at Frederica, under the direct supervision of Oglethorpe and the other at Savannah, under the supervision of Stephens.

When Oglethorpe left Georgia permanently in 1742, he had recommended that Stephens be made president of the entire colony, and the Trustees had appointed him to this position. Stephens had done very well in Georgia. He had come at a salary of one hundred pounds a year, guaranteed six years employment, plus five hundred acres. His sons were to get both his job and his land if he died before the six years were ended. One son, Newdigate, was a great comfort to him, but Tom had joined the group against Oglethorpe.

Stephens had troubles with the colony as well as

personal troubles. It was during his regime that Mary Musgrove and her third husband, Thomas Bosomworth (a former chaplain of Oglethorpe's regiment) had roused the Indians to a frightening march on Savannah, demanding that she be paid for services to the colony and for goods from her trading station. They had gone to pick up copy from England to press their claims before the Trustees and Parliament, then they had come back to rouse the Indians.

Bosomworth got the Indians to name Mary their empress. Her kinsman, Malatche, was their emperor. The Indians deeded to Mary all their hunting lands "from the fourth day of the wintry moon and so long as the waters run down to the ocean forever." She stamped her foot, and said to the colonists, "The very earth is mine. You Georgians do not own a foot of this land."

Then the Indians put on their war paint and marched menacingly on Savannah. Captain Noble Jones and his Rangers marched out to meet them, disarmed them, arrested Mary and Bosomworth, and brought President Stephens to talk with the others. He gave them a feast and some gifts.

Bosomworth was still angry with Stephens because the President had ordered that some slaves, which the Bosomworths had bought in the Carolinas and put on their Georgia plantation, be removed. It was against the law at that time in Georgia to own slaves.

Stephens talked calmly to the Indians, and finally the matter was quieted, though the claims were not to be settled until the time of the second royal governor, almost a decade later.

Calming the Indian menace about the Musgrove claims was only one of the tribulations that the aging Stephens had during his regime as president of the Georgia colony. He also had to resist the pressure of South Carolina, which wanted to absorb the Georgia colony.

Stephens did some other excellent things for Georgia. He was a well-educated man, and had been, like Oglethorpe, a member of Parliament. His parents had little money, but they had sent him to King's College at Cambridge so that he could get "the education of a gentleman." Though he was sixty-six when he came to Georgia, he was a good administrator. It was he who presided at the first venture into self-government that the Trustees had allowed the colonists. It was a representative assembly of sixteen members, which met in Savannah on January 15, 1751. The members elected Francis Harris speaker. President Stephens presided temporarily and had reported to them on the state of the colony.

In April, 1751, he was feeble with age. His eyes, once clear and the color of blue morning glories, were glazed with age, and his big, tall figure was now bent and weak. A committee, embarrassed at its mission, called on him, and offered him a pension of eighty pounds a year if he wanted to retire to his plantation, Beaulieu, which he called "Bewlie." It had been named for an estate in New Forest in England. It was on the Vernon River, twelve miles below Savannah. Here, in 1779, the Frenchman D'Estaing would land troops to help the Americans in the siege of Savannah.

Stephens accepted the offer. He thus became the first man in Georgia to be pensioned.

At Beaulieu he read, took walks, smoked cigars,

drank coffee, and every night before he went to bed promptly at nine o'clock, he downed a mug of brown ale. He had two years more to live. On an August day in 1753, his servant handed him a cup of tea. Stephens waved it away. "I am done with eating and drinking in this world," said he, tottering over to bed. By noon the next day he was dead. He was buried across the marshes of the Black River, about one and a half miles from Wormsloe, the plantation of Noble Jones. The exact site of his grave has been forgotten. He is the only member of the British Parliament ever buried in Georgia.

His journals, which were originally printed by the Trustees, have been reprinted in recent years in Georgia. The first were titled, "A Journal of the Proceedings in Georgia, Beginning October 20, 1737, by William Stephens, Esq., to Which Is Added a State of That Province as attested upon Oath in the Court of Savannah, November 10, 1740, is published in three volumes, being printed for W. Meadows, at the Angel, in Cornhill, MDCCLII."

His son Thomas wrote a biography of his father. It was published in London in 1759. Its title was *The Castlebuilders, or the History of William Stephens.* Another William Stephens, grandson of the first, later became mayor of Savannah, and a prominent person in Georgia. In the absence of a minister, he read the funeral service at the burial in Savannah of Revolutionary General Nathaniel Greene of Mulberry Grove Plantation, who had died of sunstroke.

HENRY PARKER, WHO WORE A PURPLE ROBE

Henry Parker, who had been Stephens' assistant, was made the second president of Georgia by the Trustees on April 8, 1751, when Stephens retired. He lived on the Isle of Hope. James Habersham was secretary of the colony. Parker, who had come to Georgia in 1733, was a linen draper and a bailiff. He had not been very successful and was often in debt. He wore a purple robe, edged with fur, on official occasions.

Parker organized Georgia's first militia, or home soldiers, in June, 1751. This was a company of 220 men, under the command of Captain Noble Jones. It later grew and the cavalry did also. A year and two months after he

187

took office on April 8, 1751, the Trustees gave up the charter, on June 23, 1752. Parker lived only a few months after he became the second president of Georgia.

It was during his regime that more Germans came and settled Bethany, five miles northwest of Ebenezer. They were relatives of the Salzburgers at Ebenezer, and they supplied cocoons for the Salzburgers to make silk. Bethany was destroyed in the clash with the British during the Revolution. Germans also settled Goshen, about ten miles below Ebenezer on the road to Savannah.

When Henry Parker died in 1752, soon after the Trustees gave the colony back to the king, Patrick Graham became Georgia's third president.

PATRICK GRAHAM WAS A DRUGGIST

Patrick Graham, the third president, was a dealer in medicines. Today he would be called a pharmacist or druggist. One day a rich woman named Ann Cuthbert came to him for medical advice. History does not record what medicines he sold her, but he fell in love with her and they were married. She inherited Mulberry Grove Plantation about twelve miles above Savannah. Here Graham grew mulberry trees for the colonists, and raised other crops.

It was Graham who was in charge of the government of Georgia when the king sent the first of the three royal governors. Graham turned the affairs of Georgia over to the new governor, and he and his assistants became members of the new governor's council. Graham was president from Parker's death in 1752 to the coming of Reynolds in 1754.

Some people are under the mistaken impression that Patrick Graham was the father of John Graham, Georgia's lieutenant governor who was assistant to the third royal governor, James Wright, and who lived at Mulberry Grove Plantation, but they were not related. It is just a coincidence that two early Georgians named Graham owned this same plantation. Because John Graham was a Tory, the plantation was confiscated by Georgia after the Revolution. It was later to be given to General Nathaniel Greene, and it was to be here in 1793 that a New Englander named Eli Whitney would invent the cotton gin.

Georgia was becoming prosperous again when Patrick Graham was president because many of the people who had moved away due to the trustees' harsh laws came back again. New settlers had also moved in. Among them were the Puritans, who first came in 1752. It was a much more prosperous and happy place that Graham was able to turn over to the first royal governor when he arrived in 1754. But there was a shadow over the land; the French and Indian War was rumbling through the colonies.

The Puritans Came To Georgia In 1752

The first group of Puritans in Georgia included 280 whites in 43 families. They brought with them 536 Negro slaves. The first group of these Puritans arrived May 16, 1752. Later, others came, increasing the total to 350, with 1,500 slaves. The leader of the move was a Puritan named Benjamin Baker who had come to Georgia some years before when he was quite young, to help Oglethorpe. Born in December, 1717, in South Carolina, he is buried in the churchyard at Midway in Georgia.

They had bought 22,500 acres of land in the vicinity of the Midway River, twelve miles from the sea, midway between Savannah and Darien, and here they settled. Because of its location, the Puritan settlement became known as "Midway." (Later they acquired another 10,000 acres.) These Puritans had come from their Carolina settlement of Dorchester, where descendants of some of the original Puritans had established a colony called Dorchester in 1695. The ones who had come to South Carolina were from the village of Dorchester in Massachusetts, which was settled by the first Puritans who came to America. The Carolina village of Dorchester was on the Ashley River about eighteen miles below Charleston. James Habersham wrote to Benjamin Martyn, secretary of the Trustees, about the coming of the Puritans. He said he thought they would be a valuable addition to the Georgia colony.

Dr. Lyman Hall, who was to become one of Georgia's three signers of the Declaration of Independence, had first gone to the Carolina colony from New England, and later came with the Puritans to Georgia to become their doctor.

The Puritans had a hard time the first year or so. They were ill of malaria and other swamp fevers, and many died. They set aside two acres, now across the road from their church, as a burial ground. Here are the graves of many

189

famous people. One, with a $10,000 monument erected by Congress, is that of General Daniel Stewart, an ancestor of President Theodore Roosevelt. The monument is in memory of Stewart and General Screven. Also buried here is John Le Conte, Sr., a brilliant botanist who studied with Louis Agassiz at Harvard. The two LeConte sons, John and Joseph, helped found the University of California. Alexander Stephens was once their tutor.

The Puritans planted rice and indigo and built up a prosperous community. Their Congregationalist church was burned by the British in 1778, but was rebuilt fourteen years later and still stands. Beside the church stands a museum which contains mementoes of Puritan life here. Here can be seen things once owned by Dr. Lyman Hall, and by his friend Button Gwinnett, who was not a Puritan but who worshiped in this church and lived on nearby St. Catherines Island.

The Puritans were Congregationalists, but most of their pastors were Presbyterian. Among them was Reverend Abiel Holmes, father of the poet Oliver Wendell Holmes, and grandfather of Justice Oliver Wendell Holmes of the

United States Supreme Court. Two other pastors were Reverend I. K. Axson, grandfather of the first Mrs. Woodrow Wilson, and Reverend Jedidiah Morse, the father of Samuel F.B. Morse, who invented the telegraph and was a well-known painter. Samuel Morse once visited Georgia and painted portraits of many people in and around Savannah. Among those he painted were the poet William Cullen Bryant, and General Lafayette. His portrait of Lafayette was loaned to the Atlanta Art Museum for exhibit in 1963.

About twelve miles down the road from the little Midway Church is old Sunbury. The Puritans opened it because they needed a port nearer than Savannah to ship their exports. It was established by Mark Carr, to whom the king gave a grant in 1757. His grant was five hundred acres, but he gave up three hundred acres for Sunbury. The little port was laid out in three squares, with 496 lots. Dr. Lyman Hall owned two.

By 1769, Sunbury would be an active little port with as much shipping as Savannah. It is now a ghost town, but was once the bustling, prosperous port of the Puritans. All three of the signers of the Declaration of Independence from Georgia were once at Sunbury at the same time. Dr. Hall, whose plantation on "Hall's Knoll" is above the Midway Church, owned a town house at Midway. Gwinnett was in and out on business from his home just across the water on St. Catherines. George Walton, captured by the British, was kept in prison here for a time. Two other Georgia governors, Richard Howley and Dr. Nathan Brownson, were residents here at the Puritan port.

By 1772, Sunbury had become so prosperous that people here owned a third of all the wealth in Georgia. In 1788, an academy was established here.

The Puritans were destined to lead Georgia into the Revolution about twenty-five years after they came, and with the Liberty Boys of Savannah, they wielded a powerful influence against Governor Wright and the Tories. "Those meddlesome Puritans at Midway," the Tories were to call them later. They were so active in the cause of liberty that later their county was named Liberty.

The Trustees Gave Up
Their Georgia Charter In 1752

On June 23, 1752, a year before their twenty-one-year charter, granted on June 9, 1732, was to have expired, the Trustees gave up the charter. A year before this they had asked to be relieved of their responsibilities for the colony of Georgia. Only six of the original trustees were still active. In all, seventy-two had served since 1732. One of those in the last group was another Earl of Egmont, grandson of the original earl who was Oglethorpe's friend.

The Trustees had found it hard to govern a colony that was three thousand miles away because they did not always understand conditions on the frontier. Their laws were sometimes ill-suited to conditions here and caused discontent. Some colonists had even moved away because of their dissatisfaction with the laws of the Trustees.

Parliament had been more and more reluctant to provide money for the Georgia colony. Oglethorpe, back in England, now rarely attended the meetings of the Trustees.

Before they gave up the charter, the Trustees had rescinded some of their harsher laws. An urgent letter, written by James Habersham, had told them that their laws were hurting the colony, and might even put an end to it. This was one of the reasons they changed them. They allowed colonists to own and sell lands and to buy rum. After July 1, 1749, they also allowed Georgians to buy slaves, but they had to register these Negroes, and they also had to have one white servant for every four slaves. They must see to it that the Negroes did not work on Sunday, but went to religious services. They were forbidden to educate them, but Habersham thought this nonsense was un-Christian, and he had his slaves taught to read and write. The agreement to allow slaves was ratified by the Georgia assembly on October 26, 1749.

The Trustees even tried a small venture in self-government in Georgia before they relinquished the colony. This was to be a hint to the king and his government that Georgians were capable of self-government, and could not be trusted with more and more of it. This Georgia government had little power, and could only voice opinions, but it was a beginning. As one of his last official acts, President

Stephens addressed the group when it met in Savannah on January 15, 1751. There were sixteen members, based on population, and Francis Harris was elected Speaker. They recommended for Georgia a pilot boat, a standard of weights and measures, a clerk for the market, officers for the military guard, and repairs for the courthouse.

The Trustees also specified that South Carolina was not to be allowed to gobble up Georgia!

The year 1752, when the Trustees gave up Georgia, was the year that the calendar was changed from Julian to Gregorian.

The Earl of Shaftesbury was appointed chairman of a committee to plan "proper means for supporting Georgia for the future and to take from time to time all such measures as they should find necessary for its well-being."

King George II decided that until the appointment of a royal governor, the officials in Georgia who were already in office should continue to handle the affairs in Georgia. These officials were Henry Parker, third of Georgia's presidents, and his four assistants, James Habersham, Noble Jones, Francis Harris, and Pickering Robinson.

Georgia now had 2,381 white people and 1,066 Negroes. There were also soldiers, Indians, and the just-arriving Puritans at Midway. In Georgia there were more Germans than English settlers.

The French And Indian
War Was A Coming Danger

Just as the government of Georgia was changing from the presidents to the royal governors, the French and Indian War broke out. Though it really affected Georgia very little, the colonists had to be prepared. The governors each in turn had to cope with it, and strengthen the defenses. Men even carried their guns to church. The old forts that Oglethorpe had built were in ruins. Defense was a big problem now.

The war was a fight between the French, with some of the Indians as allies, against the British for control of American territory. It was known in Europe as the Seven Years' War, or King George's War. While it was going on, another little war broke out, known in the southeast as the

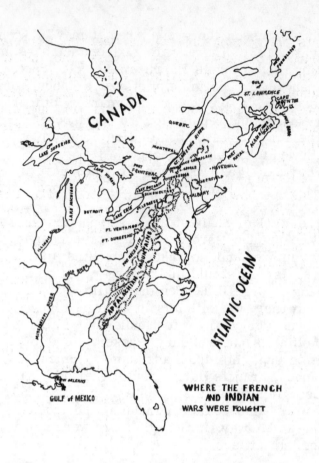

WHERE THE FRENCH
AND INDIAN
WARS WERE FOUGHT

Cherokee War. That was a savage fight between the Cherokee Indians and the Virginia and Carolina colonists. It happened like this: some of the Cherokees had gone to Virginia to help the British colonists fight against the French and their Indian allies. The Cherokees lost some of their horses while they were fighting, but on their way home, they saw some horses running loose, and took them in place of the ones they had lost. The white colonists objected, and young hotheads shot into the Indian group, killing about a dozen. The Indians attacked the white settlements. The governor of South Carolina, who refused to listen to the Indian chiefs, demanded that twenty-four Indians be sent him to be executed in turn. He also marched the chiefs along with his army as prisoners. Attakullakulla, always a friend to the British, helped calm the Indians, and kept the war from being even more destructive to the white colonists. The Creek Chief Oconostota was fiercely against the British because of the horses and the treatment accorded the chiefs by certain white officials. One white commander reported that he had destroyed fourteen hundred acres of Indian corn and bean fields, and had driven five thousand Indians into the swamps where they were likely to starve. The fighting crept close to Georgia, but never reached here. This Cherokee War, however, was only a part of the bigger French and Indian War.

This is how the war came about. The French had settled on the St. Lawrence River in 1608 and built forts and settlements down the Mississippi to New Orleans.

Frenchmen, who had begun to creep closer and closer eastward from the midwest to the English settlements on the coast, were worrisome to the colonies. They were trying to take over the whole Ohio Valley. One of their forts was Fort Pitt, the site of the present Pittsburgh, Pennsylvania. The English had settled the coast and moved westward; a clash was bound to come. Finally, the governor of Virginia sent George Washington, then a young officer, and some troops to tell the French to get out of the Ohio Valley. They refused, and began to fight back. This started the war of the British and the colonists against the French and Indians in America. That was in 1754, the year that the first royal governor came.

The English had settled along the coast and were gradually pushing across the mountains. The French had come down the Mississippi from the St. Lawrence, and were stringing out forts along the Gulf of Mexico, expanding their Indian trade through the Alabama area, and urging Indians to help them if they clashed with the English.

The French and Indian War was not over until 1763. Britain won, and the Treaty of Paris, which ended the war, doubled the territory of Georgia.

The southern boundary was proclaimed by the king to be the St. Marys River instead of the Altamaha. Four new parishes were created out of this and added to the eight already existing. The southern boundary of the state was a bone of contention for a long time, in spite of the king's proclamation. It was actually settled in 1795: the St. Marys River up to its source, then from a site known as Ellicott's Mound at the headwaters of the river, thence to the spot at the southeast corner where the Chattahoochee and the Flint River join to form the Apalachicola. That was, and still is, the southern boundary of Georgia.

The French and Indian War broke the power of France and Spain forever in North America. France lost Canada to England also. England got Florida, which had been in the possession of Spain, and divided it into east and west Florida. Spain had come into the war, on the French side, just in time to lose the Spanish possessions in this part of the New World, but it regained Cuba. England also got the lands around the Mississippi, except the New Orleans area and Louisiana, which went to Spain to make up for its losing Florida. Napoleon got it back in 1800 in a secret treaty. Spain got out of North America completely. Jefferson bought the Louisiana lands later from Napoleon, and English-speaking Americans were masters of the continent.

England had acquired a tremendous new territory, which would be expensive to administer. Besides, Britain still had to pay for the French and Indian War. This started the king and his ministers to thinking about how the American colonies of England could help pay for this war. After all, said the king, the colonies had benefited from the war, since the Spanish and Indian danger had lessened. But the colonies were not represented in the British Parliament, and had no voice in decisions that would determine their future. With their old enemies defeated, the colonists no longer needed the protection of the mother country as much.

After the close of the French and Indian War, King George III directed the royal governors of Georgia, Virginia and the Carolinas to meet with the Indians to talk about maintaining the peace. He wanted the Indians to understand clearly that England had defeated Spain and France and was now in control. But he also wanted to maintain peaceful future relations with the Indians. He forbade the colonists going any farther west into Indian country than the headwaters of the rivers that flowed to the Atlantic.

There were seven hundred Indians at the meeting, to talk about trade and peace with the English colonies along the Atlantic seacoast. Royal Governor James Wright of the Royal Province of Georgia was named chairman of the powwow. It was held at King's Fort.

CANADA
(GAINED FROM FRANCE)

LANDS GAINED FROM FRANCE

SPANISH LANDS

MAINE
(owned by Mass.)

NEW HAMPSHIRE

NEW YORK

MASS.

CONN. RHODE ISLAND

PENNSYLVANIA

MARYLAND

NEW JERSEY

DELAWARE

VIRGINIA

NORTH CAROLINA

SOUTH CAROLINA

GEORGIA

LAND GAINED FROM SPAIN

Atlantic Ocean

1763
The Thirteen
English Colonies In
America

Gulf of Mexico

Chapter 14

WHEN GEORGIA BECAME A ROYAL PROVINCE

The Three Royal Governors

By 1754, King George II and his ministers were ready to send the first of the three royal governors to the Province of Georgia. (After the Trustees had given up their charter, Georgia had come under the jurisdiction of the Lord Commissioners of Trade and Plantations.)

The royal government adopted a new seal of silver to replace the one which the Trustees had broken when they gave up the colony. On one side of the new seal was the figure of a young woman representing Georgia, and offering a skein of silk to the king. (England was still determined that Georgia should produce silk, even though it had been shown that the weather affected the mulberry trees and the cocoons and silkworms, and the crop had proven impractical.) The words on one side of the seal were "Hinc laudem sperate, coloni," meaning "Thus hope for praise, colonists!"

The king's plan for governing Georgia in the future was to have a royal governor, with a twelve-man advisory council named by the king. It would also serve as the upper house of the Assembly. The lower house, similar to the British House of Commons, would be composed of delegates elected by the people.

The Church of England (Episcopal) became the established church. Colonists were taxed to support it. In 1777, all parishes would be abolished and eight counties created instead.

THE FIRST ROYAL GOVERNOR:
CAPTAIN JOHN REYNOLDS OF THE KING'S NAVY

The first of the three royal governors who came to

Georgia was a navy captain named John Reynolds. He had been born in England in 1700. He arrived in Savannah on October 29, 1754. President Patrick Graham turned the government over to him.

Reynolds was used to commanding men, but not working with them. Though Georgians welcomed him with bonfires and kindness, his fussy ways and his bossy attitude soon made him unpopular. He was involved in bitter quarrels with his council. One of his first acts was to ask for a raise!

His official title was "Captain-General and Governor-in-Chief of His Majesty's Province of Georgia and Vice-Admiral of the Same." They addressed him as "Your Excellency," which is still the formal address for Georgia's governors today.

The new governor found the houses Oglethorpe and his first colonists had built growing old and dilapidated. In fact, one fell in on him! He wrote to the King,

> "The houses in Savannah are all wooden houses, very small, and old. The biggest was used for our Council meeting for a few days, but one end fell down while we were having the meeting. We had to move to a shed behind the courthouse."

He decided to move the capital away from Savannah, and picked a new site fourteen miles up the Ogeechee River. He wanted to name the place Hardwicke in honor of his kinsman, the Earl of Hardwicke, Lord Chancellor of England. But the king and the British Parliament would not give him money for new buildings and the moving of the capital. The only thing left of his dream of moving the capital is a marker on the highway below Savannah that points to the site where Hardwicke would have been if Reynolds had had his way.

He found the defenses of Georgia in bad condition. The fort at Frederica was in ruins. Savannah had only a few old rusty cannons. The fort at Augusta was falling down. He drew up a ten-year defense program. Reynolds wanted to build seven forts, to be manned by three thousand soldiers; he also wanted to draft all men from sixteen to sixty to serve in the state militia. His plan would cost $28,750. Parliament was reluctant to let him have the money.

Reynolds did one very good thing; he set up a new kind of government in Georgia, a bicameral legislature. His Council of twelve members, and the lower house that was elected by the people, met for the first time in January, 1755, in Savannah. Its first act was to pass a law to punish any citizen who questioned its decisions! The representatives elected to this body had to be over twenty-one and own five hundred acres of land. The only other representative government Georgians had before this was the timid venture in democracy which the Trustees had allowed, with sixteen delegates who could only recommend, but had no authority. Yet even that was better than no self-government.

Governor Reynolds had as little success with the Indians as he did with the colonists. He once summoned them to a meeting in Augusta, but after ten days they had not come, and he had to leave. He left gifts for them with his secretary. That secretary was the chief cause of his trouble in Georgia, though his own hot temper and domineering disposition hurt him too. The secretary was his former ship's surgeon, whom he had brought with him to Georgia. His name was William Little. He had so much influence with the governor and got so much power in his hands that the colonists resented him even more than they did Reynolds.

The Acadians came to Georgia while Reynolds was governor. Britain had gained Nova Scotia from France in the Treaty of Utrecht. The French Acadians who lived there had been driven out, and four hundred of them had come by boat to the Georgia shore in January, 1756. These people were Catholic, however, and Georgia law forbade Catholics from becoming citizens in Georgia. Some of these Acadians took the oath of allegiance to the king and remained in Georgia. At St. Marys is the grave of an Acadian named Margaret Comeau.

Governor Reynolds and his people generously cared for the Acadians at public expense through the winter and helped them to go in ships, when spring came, to other places like South Carolina and the bayou country of Louisiana. There the Acadians eventually became known as "Cajuns," and to this day form one of the most colorful groups in the nation. Nova Scotia had strange ties with Georgia; their people came here, and when the Revolution began many of the British in Georgia, including the governor, went to Nova Scotia.

200

Longfellow's poem "Evangeline" is a story of these Acadians. Greatly romanticized, it tells of an Acadian girl who had become separated, in the expulsion, from her sweetheart Gabriel, and spent her life searching for him. Robert Sallette, who was later to help the patriots defeat the British in Georgia, was said to be a descendant of the Acadians. This might have accounted for his hatred of the British. They had driven his people out of their homes in Nova Scotia.

Finally the governor and his secretary became so unpopular in Georgia that the people wanted to get rid of them. A group of Georgians had even hanged Little, the secretary, in effigy! He had distributed favors and offices to his friends, and had even got himself elected Speaker of the Assembly. One historian reports that "he gained so much ascendancy that he was disliked by the people."

Reynolds continued his dictatorial rule for three years. He did have many problems to solve. Among them was the strange case of Edmund Gray. He was a Quaker from Virginia who came with his followers to settle first at Brandon, above Augusta. Later he moved, with three hundred of them, to New Hanover on the Satilla. Unscrupulous and ambitious, he gained power by pretending to be close to various noblemen in England and saying that they were planning to turn Georgia's government over to him. He was ordered out of Georgia, but when he threatened to join forces with the Spanish in Florida, he was allowed to remain on Cumberland Island. Once he even got himself elected to the Georgia legislature.

Jonathan Bryan finally wrote to the Earl of Halifax and told him that the people of Georgia wanted him to use his influence to get Governor Reynolds recalled. The Council even sent a representative to England to complain about the governor. The man told the British government that Reynolds even changed the minutes of the Assembly and Council when they did not suit him!

Reynolds was summoned to England by a letter dated August 3, 1756, to answer fourteen complaints against him. A lieutenant governor, Henry Ellis, was sent to govern Georgia until the charges against Reynolds could be heard. The governor sailed from Georgia February 16 on a ship called *The Charming Martha*. It was captured by French privateers and Reynolds lost his possessions, including his records. It was a year before his case came up for a hearing. His defense was that he may have been "guilty of mistakes, but never of crimes." Nevertheless, he was finally dismissed from office, and he returned to the Navy, where he became an admiral. He died in 1776, just as the American Revolution was spreading through the country. Ellis was named governor.

THE SECOND ROYAL GOVERNOR:
HENRY ELLIS, SCIENTIST, EXPLORER, AND FRIEND OF VOLTAIRE

Georgians were so glad to have a change in government that they had warmly welcomed Lieutenant Governor Henry Ellis when he arrived on February 16, 1756, and they rejoiced when he was appointed their governor on May 17, 1757.

Ellis had been greeted with bonfires and a parade of

thirty-two schoolboys, led by their schoolmaster and playing in the band.

The new governor, described by one writer as "an odd and rather wonderful Englishman," had been born in 1721. His father was wealthy but stern, and Ellis had run away to sea when he was young. He had great curiosity and he explored many parts of the world, collecting science specimens of various kinds. He knew many famous people, and often visited his friend Voltaire, the controversial French writer.

Ellis was a delightful conversationalist and a charming host who served gourmet food to his guests. He thought Georgia was the hottest place on this earth, and he went about with a thermometer dangling from his umbrella so he could see exactly how hot it was at any minute.

Ellis had remarkable tact. He listened while Georgians told him their troubles. He got the quarreling factions together, and gave them all understanding, intelligent leadership.

The eight parishes were created during his administration, when the Church of England was the tax-supported church in Georgia. They were St. Matthew, St. Philip, St. John (the Midway parish of the Puritans, later to become famous as the hotbed of liberty during the Revolution),

St. Andrews, St. George, St. Paul, Christ Church, and St. James parishes. The four created out of the land below the Altamaha that was added to Georgia by the treaty that followed the French and Indian War were St. Patrick, St. David, St. Thomas and St. Marys. The only trace of the parishes today is the name St. Marys on a village and a river.

Ellis made a speech to the Assembly, asking them to forget their differences and work in harmony for the good of Georgia. But he firmly took back into his grasp the governmental duties that Reynolds had given over to the Council in a vain effort to curry favor with them. He was concerned with defense, and he built a boat at his own expense to protect the coast.

The Elbow Story is typical of this governor. It was important to keep the Indians friendly to Georgia because the French and Indian War was going on, and though it had not affected Georgia, nobody knew whether it eventually would. He met with the Indian chiefs, who had been escorted to Savannah by Georgia soldiers under the command of young Captain John Milledge.

Ellis entertained the Indians at a bountiful feast, then he talked to them. He knew that the French, trying to win their friendship, had told them many untrue things about him. The Indian chiefs were garbed in skins, with their war paint and feathers. He said to the Indians, "The French have told you that my arms are red with blood, up to the elbow. I will roll up my sleeve and you can see for yourself that my arm is white. The French have told you that anybody who shook my hand would be struck by disease and die. If you believe these foolish lies, do not touch me. If not, I am ready to embrace you."

He won the Indians over. He left presents with the chiefs, and gave them more to take back to their villages and distribute. He invited them to supper at his home. They agreed to oppose the French and the other Indians who were allied with the French, especially the Cherokees who were leaning toward the French in some places.

Chief Sustonagehoboys of the Tallahassees said, "The Cherokees are treacherous. We will wait until my people come in from hunting, and then we will go after the Cherokees." Ellis gave him a present of silver armor, and said, "Nothing can be more agreeable to us than the resolution of your people to go to war with your old and our new enemies, the Cherokees."

In 1930, a piece of this throat armor which Ellis had given to the old chief was returned to Georgia by the State of Alabama. It had been buried with the old Indian and had washed from his grave over two hundred years later, when the creeks flooded.

The Mary Musgrove claims against Georgia were finally settled by Ellis. He was authorized by the British government to pay her. He gave her a deed to St. Catherines Island (where she and her third husband and his second wife, who was her maid Sarah, are buried). He also paid her 2,100 pounds in cash, which he got from the sale of two other islands, Sapelo and Ossabaw. They actually were sold for more, and he put the rest in the treasury. Sapelo brought 1,350 pounds, Ossabaw brought 700 pounds, and the campsite near Pipemakers' Creek, which the Indians had always reserved near Savannah, brought 638 pounds. Later, the Bosomworths sold some land on St. Catherines to Button Gwinnett, who became one of Georgia's three signers of the Declaration of Independence. He built a house on the island.

Sunbury, the port established by the Puritans because Savannah was too far to haul their produce, was laid out during Ellis' regime. Fort Morris was near Sunbury, to guard it. By 1769, Sunbury would rival Savannah.

Ellis' health finally failed in the hot climate, and he asked to be relieved of his duties as governor. The Union Society of Savannah gave him a handsome gift of silver. He left Georgia in November, 1760, sailing on wintry seas by New York to ask the British commander, Sir Jeffrey Amherst, to send more troops to defend the Georgia frontier. This was his last act in behalf of the province he had governed. He had been in Georgia three years and nine months.

He went first to his estate in Ireland, but he spent the summers visiting friends in London and on the continent. The French Revolution marooned him on the Riviera in France, down by the warm Mediterranean. He could not get his favorite brand of tea from England. Every year he visited Voltaire. He was appointed governor of Nova Scotia, and governed "in absentia" for two and a half years. He died in Naples, Italy, January 21, 1800.

THE THIRD ROYAL GOVERNOR:
SIR JAMES WRIGHT, BARONET

Most historians agree that the ablest and best of the three royal governors was the last one, Sir James Wright.

They disagree about whether he was born in South Carolina, where his British father became chief justice, or in England. The younger Wright himself studied law at Grays Inn in London and was for twenty-five years attorney general of South Carolina. He later became the state's agent in England, and that's where he was when he was appointed royal governor of Georgia, May 13, 1760, by King George II, just six months before the king's death. He arrived in Georgia by way of South Carolina, where he still had a home, on October 11, 1760. The Wrights had stopped there in September to bury their little child, who died at sea. Mrs. Wright, whom the governor had married in 1740, was Sarah Maidman, daughter of an army officer. She was destined to drown on a voyage to England in 1762.

Georgia welcomed him. As soon as the mourning was over for his child, they had a brilliant ball in his honor, the biggest social affair that had been held in Savannah up to that time.

Wright would remain in Georgia thirty-two years, and leave it a broken and disappointed man. But he would accomplish much. His commission named him "Captain General, Governor, and Commander-in-Chief of the Province of Georgia."

Like the other two royal governors, he set about strengthening Georgia's defenses, and keeping the Indians friendly. He discouraged unscrupulous traders from preying on the Indians, and he paid the Indians' debts in exchange for lands they ceded to Georgia. Some of the old Indians were shrewd bargainers. The story is told of one Indian chief who said to a white trading post owner, "I dreamed last night that you gave me that red coat there on the shelf." The trader, who wished to keep the goodwill of the powerful chief, gave him the coat. "We must do what our dreams say," he told the Indian. A few days later, the white man said to the chief, "I dreamed that you Indians gave me that plot of land down by the creek." The old chief thought awhile and then he said, "All right. But we will dream no more!"

Once when the Indians met with the governor in Savannah, he warned them of the horrors of war. They called his talk "good and pleasing." The old men of the tribe told him that many of their wars were caused by the madness of a few young Indian hotheads. They admitted that the French gave gifts to the tribe, but they dismissed these as "trifles" and said the English were their strong reliance and support and that they intended to "hold them firmly by the hand."

The Galphin claims marked one episode of Wright's administration. He refused to pay Indian debts owed an Irish trader, George Galphin, because he thought Galphin was sympathetic with the patriots and against the king. Galphin's trading post, known as Galphintown, was on the Savannah River about fifty miles below Augusta. There he had also an elegant home at nearby Silver Bluff on the Carolina side of the river. These claims dragged on in the courts for years. They were finally settled in 1848, long after Galphin's death.

Wright had to cope with the tendency of Governor Boone of South Carolina to grant huge land tracts to his friends, to territory claimed by Georgia below the Altamaha. Once he granted 160,000 acres in one day.

Governor Wright's two brothers, Charles and Germyn, acquired land in Georgia, too. They were to cause much trouble when the Revolution came.

Since the strict land laws of the Trustees were relaxed, the plantation system began to grow up in Georgia. Wright himself acquired eleven plantations, with 25,578 acres, worked by 523 slaves. He shipped about three thousand barrels of rice abroad each year. His property in Georgia was worth about 160,000 English pounds. After the war, it was confiscated by Georgia, as was all Tory property. His assistant, John Graham, had even more land and slaves.

Many Georgia planters were growing so prosperous that they lived in fine style, ordered handsome clothes like chamois gloves, "Cherryderry jackets," and fine brocades and furniture from Europe. They sent abroad for gold and silver jewelry, ribbons, silver buckles for their shoes. They had tutors for their children.

The planters brought in slaves to work their fields after the law against slavery was repealed. At first, in 1751, there had been only a few, but by 1753 there were a thousand, and by 1773 there would be fifteen thousand. But on the upper frontier, small farmers often had a hard time, and children often grew up without knowing how to read or write.

Georgians had by now turned to more practical crops than silk and flax and indigo, though these were still produced to some extent. They were selling lumber and naval stores, growing livestock, shipping deer and beaver skins from the forests, and growing rice, corn, peas, tobacco and wheat. They also grew cotton. Some of the timber shipped from Georgia forests was being made into furniture in London, and some was going into ships built in the north. Georgia had 18,000 white people and 15,000 Negroes. By 1773 there would be 1,400 farms, with 120,000 acres under cultivation.

Wright worked hard at his duties. Even those who disagreed with him and did not like royal government respected him. He was the only one of the three royal governors really qualified for the job. He tried hard to convince Georgians that since England had invested much money in this thirteenth and youngest colony, it should stay loyal to the king. Besides, he said, it was exposed on a dangerous frontier, and needed the king's protection. Some listened; some did not. But he saw the dark shadow of the Revolution falling over the land.

John Bartram, naturalist from Philadelphia, who came with his son William from Philadelphia in September, 1765,

208

wrote, "Governor Wright is universally respected by all Georgians, and they can hardly say enough in his praise." Less than six months later Georgians, enraged by the Stamp Act, were not so unanimous in praise of him. In fact, some of the Liberty Boys were so aroused against him that they suggested he be hanged! But it would be another ten years before he was actually arrested. Quakers, who came to Georgia in 1768 from North Carolina, named their town, located above Augusta, Wrightsboro in honor of him. They settled here on fifteen thousand acres. Later, the modern town of Wrightsville was also named in memory of him.

The Mystery Of The Lost Flower

The two Bartrams studied the flowers and the animals in Georgia swamps. They found growing in the wild forest a beautiful flower that resembled the magnolia or camellia, known as the gordonia. He named it the *Franklinia altamaha*, for the river and his friend Benjamin Franklin. He sent some plants to Philadelphia to a kinsman. Nobody has ever been able to find the flower in Georgia since. It is known as "the lost gordonia."

William Bartram wrote a book about his travels that was widely read. It tells much about Georgia. It became a classic. Carlyle and Emerson liked to read it. The poet Coleridge is said to have found in it some of the beautiful imagery he used in his poems about Kubla Khan and the Ancient Mariner. He wrote of dark green swamps, deep red berries, pale gold fish, dark grey storm clouds, yellow corn, white birds flying, purple muscadines, and spreading live oaks.

Of Wright, Bartram wrote, "I arrived in Savannah, the capital, where acquainting the governor, J. Wright, with my business, His Excellency received me with great politeness and furnished me with letters to the principal inhabitants of Georgia, which were of great service to me."

One Indian tried to kill him but changed his mind. In the Cherokee country, Indians gave him "strawberries and fresh cream, excellent coffee, hot corn cakes, and excellent butter and cheese," he wrote.

The Shadow Of
The Revolution Falls

The little flower in the Georgia swamps was not the only thing lost in these years. A naturalist had lost a blossom, but a king far over the blue waters was soon to lose a whole new world, much to his surprise and sadness. For the American Revolution was gathering like a coming storm, and would break in fury over Georgia and the other colonies soon. When it was over, they would be free, and the king would be wandering in the darkness of insanity, like Shakespeare's troubled King Lear. But before that, there was a lot of fighting to be done, and many would die, and battlefields would be bloody. Some of them would be in Georgia.

Fathers and sons would quarrel still more bitterly and the shadow of old, sad quarrels would fall between neighbors who had shared the same plow, and borrowed cups of sugar from one another. There was a terrible sorrow coming upon the world, and Georgia would be a part of it. A new nation was about to be born.

UNIT 3

GEORGIA AND THE AMERICAN REVOLUTION

CHAPTER 15

HOW THE REVOLUTION
CAME ABOUT

The war which we know as the American Revolution began with the now-famous skirmish at Concord on April 19, 1775. Actually, the situation that brought about the fighting had started ten years before that. John Adams, the dumpy little Boston lawyer who became the second President of the United States, said, "The Revolution was effected before the War commenced. The Revolution was in the hearts and minds of the people."

There were three million people in the thirteen American colonies when the trouble with England began. In Georgia there were twenty thousand white residents and seventeen thousand Negroes. Those who were on the king's side were called Tories (the British called them "Loyalists"); and those who sided with the Patriots were called Whigs.

THE LITTLE BLUE STAMP THAT CAUSED THE TROUBLE

The first rumblings of trouble with England came when King George III and his Parliament passed the Stamp Act in 1765.

George III, the tall, blue-eyed grandson of King George II (who had signed the Georgia charter in 1732) had ascended the throne after his grandfather died in 1760. His father, Prince Frederick, for whom Oglethorpe named Frederica in Georgia, had died nine years before. After Frederick's death, his wife Augusta, for whom Oglethorpe had named Augusta in Georgia, began to train her son to be king. When he became king, Augusta, Princess of Wales, kept saying to her son, "Be king, George, be king!" He tried to be.

King George III

The French and Indian War was being fought in America. It started in 1754, and was ended in 1763. It doubled the American territory that belonged to England. However, the war also had doubled England's national debt. Administering the added territory would be expensive. Already Parliament had added twenty percent to the taxes on land owners in England. Now the king and his advisers decided to put new taxes on the colonists themselves to help pay for the war and the expenses of keeping British soldiers in America to protect the larger territory.

But the colonists objected. Led by Virginia's twenty-nine-year-old, red-haired Patrick Henry and others, they claimed that it was not fair to have taxes levied upon them by a Parliament in which they were not represented. "Taxation without representation is tyranny!" became the cry of protest all over the colonies.

CHAPTER 16

GEORGIA AND THE

AMERICAN REVOLUTION

Georgia was late joining the other twelve colonies in the American Revolution. There was a good reason for this, but it almost got Georgia in trouble with the other colonies. The Continental Congress, in which Georgia was the only colony not officially represented, put it under a non-intercourse ban until it sent official delegates. South Carolina actually passed a law decreeing death to any of its citizens who traded with Georgia, and it refused to allow the Georgia Puritans from the St. Johns Parish to join with it to send delegates to Philadelphia. The Puritans, who were relatives of New Englanders made hungry in Boston when the port was closed by Britain as punishment for the "Boston Tea Party," were impatient with the rest of Georgia for being slow to get into the Revolutionary movement.

But there were reasons for Georgia's being slow. Parliament and private Britons had invested a substantial sum of money to get the little colony of Georgia started. Its royal governor, when the trouble with England started, was Sir James Wright, able and well-liked. He exerted a powerful influence in keeping Georgia loyal to his master, King George III. His associates, and most of the other older and influential Georgians, had memories rooted deeply in England, where they had grown up and still had friends and relatives. It seemed to them disloyal to be against the king.

The Americans Began To Revolt

The colonists' protest against the Stamp Tax surprised King George III. " I only want what is best for my people,"

215

he said. "Whoever opposes me is a scoundrel." In America many colonists considered him a tyrant. They spoke bitterly about the Stamp Tax which Parliament had passed on March 22, 1765. It was to become effective November 1, 1765.

The little blue stamp was to be required for all documents, such as deeds, notes, contracts, bonds, marriage licenses, newspapers, mortgages, newspapers, almanacs, pamphlets, and even diplomas! The tax had to be paid in silver or gold, which would drain the colonies of coins.

This was not the first tax England had put on the colonies. There had been the 1734 Molasses Act, but that had been largely ignored. Then, in 1764, there had been a Sugar Tax, which affected mostly New England since that section carried on a rum trade with the West Indies.

The Stamp Tax, however, was different. It would affect all the colonies, and make a difference in the daily lives of the people. Colonists objected. In the House of Burgesses at Williamsburg, Virginia, Patrick Henry thundered, "Caesar had his Brutus, Charles the First his Cromwell, and George III. . . " When cries of "Treason! Treason!" interrupted him, he calmly finished, "and George III should profit by their example! If that be treason, make the most of it!"

In England, some advised the king that the colonies would never stand for this tax. One was the ailing William Pitt, Earl of Chatham, who dragged himself before Parliament, waved his crutch, and said, "They will never stand for it. I might as well talk of driving them before me with this crutch. Let us retreat now while we can and not wait until we must!" Georgia named Chatham County for Pitt. The great Irishman Edmund Burke, for whom Burke County is named, made an eloquent speech on conciliation with the American colonies. Benjamin Franklin, then in London, warned the British: "I judge the other Americans by myself. I have many debts due me there, but I would rather they would never be paid than to submit to this tax." In 1768 Georgia hired Franklin as its agent in England. He succeeded William Knox, who had angered them with his advice to submit to the British taxes.

Georgia was invited to send delegates to a Stamp Act Congress that met in New York on October 7, 1765, but sent only an unofficial observer to bring back a copy of the minutes. The Stamp Act Congress voted to send a man to England to explain the colonists' side.

In Georgia, rumors flew. The Liberty Boys, the local organization of the Sons of Liberty which had started in New England and spread throughout the colonies, were stirring up sentiment against the British. They held meetings at Tondee's Tavern, operated by Peter Tondee, where they would soon erect a Liberty Pole. Older residents called them "Liberty Bawlers." Governor Wright called them "Sons of Licentiousness." The king's friend James Habersham, whose own sons John, James, and Joseph, were among them, wrote a friend in England, "Thus we are almost deprived of thinking by those who miscall themselves 'Sons of Liberty.' " But even Habersham believed that the Stamp Tax was unfair. The Liberty Boys had determined that no stamps would be sold in Georgia.

Governor Wright was uneasy. The Liberty Boys were camped on the edge of Savannah, and he was daily expecting the stamps to arrive. He did not know what the Liberty Boys might do when they came. For four days and nights he did not even take off his clothes.

In October when the day came around for the annual celebration of the king's birthday, the Liberty Boys had a separate parade of their own. They had spiked the cannon so the governor's soldiers could not fire them for the birthday celebration. Then they paraded around Savannah while the Tories drank toasts to the king, shouting "Liberty, Property, and NO STAMPS!" They hanged the governor in effigy. They also hanged a dummy of the stampseller, who had not yet arrived in Georgia. Sailors on shore leave dressed up one of their group and hung a sign around his neck saying, "No stamps, no riot, gentlemen!" The *Georgia Gazette*, which had started publication in 1763 and was the first newspaper in the colony, had a report by its editor, James Johnston, calling all this "high jinks" and reporting that no real damage was done.

But the Liberty Boys were more determined than ever that no stamps should be sold in Georgia. The little blue stamps finally arrived on December 5, 1765, on board the ship *Speedwell*. The governor had them hidden on Cockspur Island.

Finally, on January 6, 1766, the stampseller himself arrived. He was named George Angus, and was frightened by the hostility he found. The governor took him to his home, which was guarded by forty British Rangers. In a few days he left, unharmed. Only seventy stamps were ever sold in Georgia. These were used for clearance papers on a ship that had a perishable cargo that needed to sail before it was ruined by the delay. This infuriated South Carolina, and some of their citizens threatened to burn the ship. On February 8, 1766, Governor Wright returned the unsold stamps to the *Speedwell*.

The *Gazette* was not only the first (and for a long time the only) paper in Georgia, but was the eighth in America, having begun publication on April 7, 1763. It was suspended May 2, 1765, when the editor said the Stamp Tax would make publication too expensive.

Johnston was also the state printer, and got a hundred pounds a year for official printing. He also sold books, like *Robinson Crusoe* and *Swiss Family Robinson* , and maps and legal forms.

On May 21, 1766, the little tabloid paper was published again. It reported that the Stamp Act would be repealed. In the cold gray dawn of July 16, 1766, a Parliament that had wrangled through the night in London voted 275 to 176 to repeal it. It was hurting British trade and merchants pressured for its repeal. Americans were boycotting British goods.

Georgia was as happy as the other colonies at the repeal. Like other colonies, it sent a thank-you note to King George III: "Most Gracious Sire: Your Majesty's loyal subjects of the Province of Georgia beg leave to thank you with hearts full of affection. May you long reign over us."

"Champagne Charlie" Put On More Taxes

In 1767, Charles Townshend, known as "Champagne Charlie," had become Chancellor of the Exchequer in England. He did much to persuade Parliament and the King to put other taxes on America: for glass, paint, paper, lead, and tea. He said, "These colonies are children of the mother country. They were planted by our care and nurtured by us. They will not grudge us their mite to help with the heavy burden we bear." Colonel John Barre scoffed, "Planted by our care indeed! They fled from our oppression, and thrive by our neglect!"

James Habersham saw the coming trouble. He warned the British, "If you persist in your right to tax the colonists, you will drive them to rebellion."

In September, 1769, led by Jonathan Bryan, people in Savannah voted to boycott British goods, and not to buy anything they could possibly do without, even black cloth for mourning. Governor Wright was furious. He made up his mind to dismiss Bryan from his Council. Before he could do this, Bryan walked out. "I will save you the trouble," he said. British exports had dropped fifty percent in America. Bryan was the son of Joseph Bryan, who came from South Carolina to help Oglethorpe start Georgia.

Finally, England repealed all taxes except the tax on tea. This was three cents a pound.

England also wanted to keep one tax on the colonists as a sign that they were subject to English law. In his proclamation repealing the other taxes, King George III said, "It is with the utmost astonishment that I find my subjects encouraging the rebellious disposition which unhappily exists in my colonies in America. Having confidence in Parliament, I support the measures they recommend for the commercial interests of my kingdom." Georgia objected to being taxed to keep British soldiers here. But the king's government threatened to withdraw them, and since Georgia had fewer than three thousand soldiers to protect its frontiers, the assembly reluctantly agreed.

THE BOSTON TEA PARTY MOVED THE WAR NEARER

In Boston harbor was a ship with British tea aboard. One night, December 17, 1773, 120 young men, including Paul Revere and John Hancock, disguised themselves as Mohawk Indians, boarded the ship and dumped the tea into the water. They did not know the sailors on board had smallpox! It took them about three hours to throw the tea overboard. The same thing was done in other ports. In Maryland, the patriots also burned the ships.

The furious British closed the Boston port June 1, 1774, and moved their shipping to Salem, Massachusetts.

The port, said England, would not open again until the tea was paid for. It never was paid for, though an old story says that Benjamin Franklin offered to pay for it himself.

In Boston, people grew hungry because no ships could go in or out. One man wrote, "We eat pork and beans one day and beans and pork the next! And a fish when we can catch it." They had no fruits or vegetables, and could not get enough firewood. There was much suffering.

The British took away Massachusetts' charter, and sent Governor Thomas Gage as military governor to occupy Boston with four regiments. They also decreed that colonists who committed crimes must be taken across the sea for trial in England.

All the colonies were full of angry people who resented these actions. Samuel Adams of Boston, who had a brother-in-law in Savannah, had started Committees of Correspondence so the colonies could keep in touch with one another. The Sons of Liberty, known in Georgia as Liberty Boys, kept anger alive against Britain in the youngest colony. The Midway Puritans in the St. Johns Parish were full of sorrow and sympathy for their kinsmen in Boston.

How The Patriots Took Over Georgia's Government

During the summer of 1774, following the closing of the Boston harbor by the British, two furious factions grew up in Georgia: one for the king, and one against him.

Practically nobody, in Georgia or any of the other colonies, had any thought at this time of separating from England. Even the rebellious ones simply wanted the king to stop his tyranny, and to redress their grievances. The idea of separating came later.

Leaders in Georgia who opposed the king were in touch with similar leaders in Boston. Samuel Adams, second cousin of future vice-president and president John Adams, was one of the masterminds of the Revolution. Another leader of the Boston group was John Hancock, probably the richest young man in New England, who had many shipping interests with which British laws interfered. Paul Revere, a silversmith, and James Otis, a lawyer, were others. In Virginia, Jefferson, Washington, and Patrick Henry and, in Philadelphia, Benjamin Franklin, were in the group that favored liberty, and all were known to Georgians.

THE ADVERTISEMENT THAT STIRRED GEORGIA

On July 20, 1774, this advertisement appeared in James Johnston's little tabloid newspaper, the *Georgia Gazette:*

The critical situation to which the British colonies in America are likely to be reduced, from the arbitrary and alarming imposition

221

of the late acts of the British Parliament respecting the town of Boston, as well as the acts that at present exist, tending to the raising of a perpetual revenue without the consent of the people or their representatives, is considered an object extremely important at this juncture, and particularly calculated to deprive the American subjects of their constitutional rights and liberties, as a part of the British empire. It is therefore requested that all persons within the limits of this Province do attend at Savannah, on Wednesday the 27th of July, in order that the said matters may be taken into consideration, and such other constitutional measures pursued as may appear most eligible.

It was signed by four Georgians: Noble Wymberly Jones, Archibald Bulloch, George Walton, and John Houstoun. Jones was a well-educated, wealthy doctor. He was about fifty years old. His father, Noble Jones, had come over with Oglethorpe.

Archibald Bulloch was born in Charleston, South Carolina in 1730. He had moved to Georgia to practice law, and lived in Savannah. He was a man of such ability and integrity that he was soon chosen a leader, but met sudden tragedy later. He was an ancestor of President Theodore Roosevelt, whose other Georgia great-grandfather was the Revolutionary General Daniel Stewart, who was fighting the British when he was only fifteen. British soldiers took over Stewart's home, and when he returned he found a scrawl on the wall saying, "This is a nest of rebels." Georgia named counties for both Bulloch and Stewart.

George Walton had come to Georgia from Virginia. He had been orphaned early, and his uncle had apprenticed him to a carpenter. He studied law, by firelight, when he could, and came to Georgia when his apprenticeship was over, first to be a surveyor, then to enter a law office at Savannah. He was later to be one of Georgia's three signers of the Declaration of Independence. He would also become governor.

John Houstoun, who was to be the second governor of Georgia, was the son of a British nobleman who had brought his wife and four sons to the colony some years before the Revolution. John Houstoun was destined to be governor of Georgia twice.

The meeting these four had called with their *Gazette* advertisement was held July 27. Governor Wright tried hard to keep people away. He even forbade the meeting, but it was held anyhow. However, not enough people were there, and they adjourned to meet again on August 10, 1774. They had elected John Glynn chairman of a thirty-one member committee to draw up some resolutions of protest against the king. They named another committee to gather up rice to send to the starving people in Boston. Then they sent messengers to the outlying districts to tell the people to come to the meeting on August 10.

On August 10, 1774, more people did come, in spite of Governor Wright. At this meeting, the patriots adopted strong resolutions, which had been drafted by John Glynn and his committee, condemning England's actions. Plans were made to collect more rice and money for Boston. They also set up plans to keep in touch with patriots in other colonies through the Committees of Correspondence.

DO NOT CATCH AT SHADOWS, WARNED GOVERNOR WRIGHT

The governor and the Tories, or Loyalists, who favored the king, were alarmed by what had happened at Tondee's Tavern.

Wright wrote, "The world will judge whether that meeting, held by a few persons in a tavern with the doors shut, can in truth and decency, be called a 'general meeting of the inhabitants of Georgia.'"

About three weeks later, the governor and the Loyalists published a resolution of their own in the *Georgia Gazette*. They had sent messengers through Georgia and obtained more than a hundred signatures. The Liberty Boys claimed that some of these were dead people, whose names had been forged! The resolution condemned the August 10 tavern meeting as "reflecting improperly on the King and Parliament." The Tories denounced the Liberty Boys and "those meddlesome Puritans at Midway." They said further that they did not see why Georgia should be concerned with New England's quarrels with the mother country.

Among the supporters of Wright and the king, who

disapproved of the action of the Liberty Boys and the Puritans and who signed a report of their own, were James Habersham, who had been Wright's assistant, Chief Justice Anthony Stokes, Lachlan McGillivray, father of Chief Alexander McGillivray who was to cause Georgia much trouble later, Edward Langworthy, Alexander Wylly, John Graham and Noble Jones. The Tories and Wright still had enough influence to keep Georgia from sending official delegates to the First Continental Congress, which met at Carpenters' Hall in Philadelphia in September, 1774, with fifty-six delegates from the other twelve colonies. The Congress met for a month and adjourned agreeing to reconvene in May, 1775. They little dreamed what would happen before then.

Wright, who said that the conditions in the other twelve colonies made him shudder, warned the Georgia Assembly, "Do not listen to voices and opinions of men of overheated ideas. Do not catch at shadows." On October 14, 1774, he was reporting to England that "the poison of rebellion has affected the whole province. There is hardly a shadow of government remaining." On December 13, 1774, he wrote

Queen Charlotte, Wife Of King George III

the Earl of Dartmouth that feeling in Georgia "has been raised to such a frenzy that God knows what the consequences may be."

GEORGIA ELECTED DELEGATES, BUT THEY WOULD NOT GO TO PHILADELPHIA

On January 18, 1775, Georgia held its first Provincial Congress. It remained in session only five days. This was four months after the first Continental Congress had met in Philadelphia without Georgia's being represented. The other colonies were resentful of Georgia's lagging, and Congress put Georgia under a ban of non-intercourse.

In Georgia, the January Provincial Congress in 1775 elected three delegates to go to Philadelphia. But they would not go! They pointed out that only five of Georgia's twelve parishes had sent representatives to the Provincial Congress that elected them, so how could they represent all of Georgia even if they did go to Philadelphia?

The three chosen, Noble Wymberly Jones, Archibald Bulloch, and John Houstoun, wrote a letter dated April 6, 1775, to the President of the Continental Congress in Philadelphia. They said,

> The Georgia Provincial Congress, convened at Savannah, did us the honor of choosing us delegates to meet your respectable body at Philadelphia on the 10th of next month. We are sensible of the honor and weight of the appointment and would gladly have rendered our country any service our poor abilities would have admitted of; but alas! with what face could we have appeared for a province whose inhabitants had refused to sacrifice the most trifling advantage to the public cause; and in whose behalf we did not think we could safely pledge ourselves for the execution of any measure whatsoever?

All three of them were re-elected later and became a part of the larger delegation from Georgia, but not one of these three would be there when the Declaration of Independence was signed.

Though the First Provincial Congress of Georgia

225

elected the three representatives, it did not adopt the resolutions that other colonies had adopted. So Georgia remained outside the organization of colonies, and was for a time increasingly unpopular with them, especially with South Carolina.

THE IMPATIENT PURITANS SENT THEIR DOCTOR

The Liberty Boys had done all they could, but Georgia still had no delegate in the Continental Congress.

The Puritans at Midway were especially impatient at this lag because of their kinsmen still hungry in Boston, and undergoing hardships because of the British closing the port and passing the Intolerable Acts. South Carolina, wanting to have nothing to do with anybody from Georgia, had refused to allow the Puritans to join with them in sending delegates.

The Puritans decided to send their own delegate, feeling that they could wait no longer for Georgia. On March 21, 1775, the people of the St. Johns Parish sent their physician, Dr. Lyman Hall. As it turned out, he would be one of the three who would be there to sign for Georgia when the Declaration of Independence was adopted the next year. He started on his long journey in the spring. He carried north with him sixty barrels of rice and fifty pounds sterling for the Boston people. Hall arrived in Philadelphia, where the delegates from the other colonies were in session at Independence Hall, formerly known as Carpenters' Hall. (The old courthouse in White County, at Cleveland, Georgia, was a replica of this famous building.) Dr. Hall arrived on May 13, 1775, three days after the Second Continental Congress opened. He sat in on the deliberations of this Congress, but he did not attempt to vote.

Congress named George Washington commander-in chief of the American armies. He was the only one there in uniform and the only member of the Congress who had any experience at all in frontier warfare in which the British were engaged. He had fought with them as allies in the French and Indian War. Now he would lead the fight against them as enemies, but he knew their tactics. John Adams of Boston recommended him. The tall, solemn, red-haired Virginian took command of the army on July 3, 1775. General Ethan Allen and his Green Mountain Boys

226

had already captured Fort Ticonderoga, and cut the British off from help in Canada.

Dr. Lyman Hall

Washington wrote his wife, Martha, "My dear Patsy, I did not ask for this job but I consider it my duty. I will be at home with you in the fall." He was wrong. So was King George III. They both expected it to be a short war. It would be a long time before Washington was back at his farm at Mount Vernon, which he had inherited from his brother Lawrence. And even when he did get there, seven long weary years later, his countrymen would not let him stay. They had another, and still bigger, job for him. Washington's wife was at Mount Vernon, with her children from a former marriage. A daughter, Patsy, was an epileptic who died young. The son Jackie married Nellie Calvert and became the father of Mrs. Robert E. Lee.

Dr. Hall, the first delegate from Georgia to the Continental Congress, knew Washington, and was there when he was named commander of America's raw troops. Later,

227

in 1791 when the war was over, Washington would come to visit Georgia.

He would have a long, hard struggle to defeat the British. There were about 282,000 men in the colonies capable of bearing arms, but never did he have more than 25,000 of them under arms at one time. And even for these, he would be unable to get enough food and clothes. It was a miracle that he won that war which was the beginning of a great nation.

The British General Thomas Gage had fought beside Washington in the French and Indian War. Now he was to fight against him. Former British General Horatio Gates had married a Virginia heiress and become Washington's neighbor. Another British-officer-turned-American was old Major Pierce Butler who married Polly Middleton of South Carolina and owned two Georgia coastal plantations at Butler Island near Darien and on St. Simons.

CHAPTER 17

HOW THE REVOLUTION
BECAME A SHOOTING WAR

The smouldering angers in and around Boston over the closing of the port and other things had broken into a shooting war on April 19, 1775, at a little place called Lexington, on the road to Concord. Both villages were outside of Boston about sixteen and twenty miles, respectively. This was fourteen months after the Boston Tea Party. For more than a year, emotions had been seething.

General Thomas Gage, the British commander, had heard that the patriots had hidden ammunition at Concord. He knew that the tensions were growing worse. As far back as March, 1770, there had been a riot when soldiers had fired after a snowball incident with saucy Boston youths on the Common. Three Americans had been killed and five wounded. Red-coated British soldiers with their tall black fur caps had been seen more and more since then, sent from England to keep down trouble. Bostonians called them "lobsters," and children sang "Burgoyne! Clinton! Howe! Bow! Wow! Wow!" Boston leaders of the movement against the king had stirred not only New England but the whole of colonial America. In North Carolina in 1771, farmers calling themselves "Regulators " had fought the king's men. Their leaders were hanged.

Gage sent eight hundred soldiers from Boston to get the ammunition he had heard was hidden at Concord, twenty miles from Boston, and also to bring back the ringleaders, if possible. But Boston patriots had keen ears; they heard of the plans. They had already made their plans. They had horsemen ready to ride at an instant's notice to alarm the countryside not only that the British were coming, but how they were traveling. They would hang lanterns in the tower of Boston's Old North Church, "one if by land, and two if by sea." When a single lantern gleamed, three horsemen were ready: Paul Revere, William Dawes, and Samuel

Prescott. The poet Longfellow wrote of the time in his poem "Paul Revere's Ride," which begins

> Listen, my children, and you shall hear,
> Of the midnight ride of Paul Revere;
> Hardly a man is now alive,
> Who remembers that famous day and year.

His poem has obscured the fact that two other riders galloped, too. Revere himself did not get through. Their horses flashed through the countryside arousing farmers who called themselves "Minute Men" because they could be ready at a minute's notice to defend their country.

When the British reached Lexington, on the road to Concord, seventy farmers awaited them with guns called muskets. Others came later. Captain Jonas Parker, their leader, said, "If they must have a war, let it begin here!" Parker was killed in the skirmish; so were seven other Americans. Only one Britisher was wounded. But the Minutemen swarmed to the road as the British marched back to Boston, killed 73, and wounded 174. To this day, there is argument about who fired the first shot there at Lexington that dawn. Emerson wrote a poem, "The Concord Hymn," many years later to be used at the dedication of a memorial bridge. In it, he describes the scene.

Samuel Adams' twenty-one-man Committee of Correspondence was spreading the word about how the British were treating Americans. News of the fighting at Lexington reached Georgia on May 10, 1775. This was the same day that the Second Continental Congress met in Philadelphia. Georgia did not have any official delegates there. The Puritan delegate arrived in Philadelphia three days later, but the three elected by Georgia's first Provincial Assembly in January, 1775, had already written letters to the Congress saying that they had been elected by representatives from only five of twelve parishes, and would not attend.

Back in Georgia, on May 10, patriots broke into Governor Wright's ammunition stores east of Savannah. They were twelve feet underground, and made of brick. He had thought them so safe that he had not even put guards there. Liberty Boys raided the store, took six hundred pounds of the king's ammunition, and sent part of it to Boston. Part of it is thought to have been used at the famous battle of Bunker Hill, which was really fought on Breed's Hill. (General Benjamin Lincoln, the hero of that battle, would be in Georgia five years later, fighting at Savannah.) Governor Wright offered 150 pounds reward for information about who took the ammunition. Many people knew or suspected that it was Joseph Habersham, John Milledge, James Jackson, and Edward Telfair, but nobody told the governor. Three of the four would later become governors of Georgia, and Habersham would be postmaster general in Washington's administration.

After Lexington and Concord, Britain got ready for war in America, though it was not until August 23, 1775, that King George III officially proclaimed the colonists "rebels." He hired professional Hessian soldiers from Germany, "renting" them from the Prince of Hesse. Eventually thirty thousand Hessians fought in America. Some of them found German girls in German communities in America, married them, and became Americans. In Georgia, so many Hessians deserted that their military commanders in Savannah offered rewards for each one returned, dead or alive.

One of these Hessian soldiers is depicted in Washington Irving's "Legend of Sleepy Hollow," a classic tale in American literature.

Britain asked the Empress Catherine of Russia, one of the most colorful personalities in the history of the world, for twenty thousand Cossack soldiers, but she refused. Later, she even loaned the colonies a little money to defeat Britain. Holland loaned America a great amount of money, thereby causing England to declare war on the little Dutch country.

Thomas Paine Stirred the Colonists With His Words

Benjamin Franklin, aware of the power of words to stir men's minds, sent Thomas Paine, an English writer, to America. He thought that Washington needed a man who could use words to rouse men to high deeds and keep them from the black brink of despair when things went wrong. He was right. Washington was so impressed with Paine's writings that he issued orders that one of his pamphlets must be read to all the troops.

Later, President Theodore Roosevelt was to label Paine "a dirty little atheist," and Eli Whitney, on his way to Georgia where he would invent the cotton gin and change history, met Paine and disliked him.

Paine had been a corset maker and a tax collector in England. When he and his fellow tax collectors wrote the king protesting their low pay and asking for a raise, they not only did not get the raise but Paine was fired because he had written the letter. Franklin read Paine's writings. "Go to America, Mr. Paine," he said. "We need your kind of writing there." Paine came to Philadelphia, started writing words that lit fires in people's minds and stirred their souls to new bravery. One, published in January, 1776, was called *Common Sense.* "There is something absurd in the idea of a continent being governed by an island. England belongs to Europe. America belongs to itself," he wrote. It sold 150,000 copies. People throughout America, including people in Georgia, read it. Another was called *The Crisis:* "These are the times that try men's souls." Paine left his sweetheart to be with Washington at Valley Forge. She married another man. Later, he left America to help France. "Where freedom is not, there is my country," he said.

Georgians Organized A Council Of Safety

On June 22, 1775, two months after war had started at Lexington, Georgians organized a Council of Safety. These were also being organized in the other colonies. This Council was to be the focus of government when legislative bodies were not in session during the coming years. William Ewen was chosen president of the first one. The historian C.C. Jones, Jr., lists these as members: William LeConte, Joseph Clay, Basil Cooper, Samuel Elbert, William Young, Elisha Butler, Edward Telfair, Francis Harris, John Smith, John Morel, John Glynn, John Houstoun, George Walton, Joseph Habersham and Seth John Cuthbert.

The Council was organized at Tondee's Tavern. The meeting was reported by the *Georgia Gazette* in this paragraph in June, 1775:

On Monday last (June 5, 1775) a considerable number of the Inhabitants met, and having erected a Liberty Pole, afterward dined at Tondee's Tavern in the Long Room. They spent the day with the utmost harmony, and concluded the evening with great decorum.

A Union flag had been hoisted on the Liberty Pole, and at the foot of it were two field pieces for shooting. At the dinner, thirteen toasts were drunk, one to each of the thirteen colonies in America.

When the Council of Safety was organized, it was given instructions to keep in touch with the other colonies. It was to meet at the Tavern every Monday.

George Walton

The Liberty Boys, who kept the colonists aroused with their activities for freedom, became more and more active. They were often at the Tavern, talking about what was going on in America, and urging Georgia to get into action. They tolerated no different sentiments. A sailor named John Hopkins made what they considered impertinent remarks about the colonies' revolt against the king. He was tarred and feathered and made to kiss the Liberty Pole and to apologize and say, "Damnation to all Tories and success to the cause of American liberty!" Others got the same treatment in these stirring days.

The Council of Safety, with the urging of the Liberty Boys in its ranks and outside, issued a call for the Second Provincial Congress of Georgia to meet July 4, 1775. The date was pure coincidence. The Declaration of Independence had not even been written at that time, and the date July 4 did not have the meaning it was to have thereafter.

All Twelve Parishes Sent Delegates
To Elect Men To Go To Philadelphia

When the Second Provincial Congress met in Savannah at Tondee's Tavern on July 4, 1775, all twelve Georgia parishes had sent over a hundred delegates. At the first one, in January, 1775, only five of the twelve had sent representatives.

This Second Provincial Congress, which stayed in session until August 20, 1775, was later to be called "Georgia's first secession convention." It indicated Georgia's secession from England, as the secession convention in 1860 would mark the state's secession from the United States to form the Confederate government.

Archibald Bulloch was elected president, and his salary set at three hundred pounds a year. He was also named as one of the five Georgia representatives to go to Philadelphia to the Second Continental Congress in session there. Lyman Hall was already there, but was not voting since he represented only the one parish of St. John. Hall was named one of Georgia's five to represent the whole colony. John Houstoun and Noble Wymberly Jones were also elected delegates.

The fifth delegate was a minister, Reverend Joachim Zubly. He was the scholarly pastor of the Calvinist Independent Presbyterian Church in Savannah. He was a fifty-one-year-old Swiss, born August 27, 1724; he spoke six languages, and had come to Georgia from South Carolina in 1760. It turned out that he was not for independence at all. He was only for resolving the differences between the colonists and the king. He was a Tory, and he was alarmed when he got to Philadelphia to find how strong was the sentiment for independence. He wrote his close friend, Governor Wright, "A republican government is little better than a government of devils." When the other delegates from Georgia, who had arrived in Philadelphia after the Congress adjourned for a few weeks, found out his true sentiments, they expelled him from the delegation. He returned to Georgia in November, 1775. John Houstoun also returned to Georgia at that time, and no doubt explained why Zubly had been ousted. Houstoun did not go back to Philadelphia.

Remaining in Georgia, he probably helped Governor Bulloch. John Adams expressed regret that he did not return. Houstoun had married Hannah, daughter of Jonathan Bryan. Rev. Zubly lost his church and most of his property and left Georgia. Though he returned briefly when the British got temporary control of Savannah during the Revolution, he later left again, and died old and poor and sick on July 27, 1781. Another pastor who found his church doors closed against him in Savannah was Reverend Haddon Smith, pastor of Christ Church, who escaped to a British ship at Tybee.

Jones had to stay in Georgia because his aged father, who had come over with Oglethorpe in 1733, and who was still loyal to the king, was ill and dying. On February 1, 1776, the vacancies thus caused by the absence of Jones, and the actions of Zubly, were filled by the appointment of Button Gwinnett and Lyman Hall. Since Bulloch was naturally too busy with his duties as president of Georgia, he could not be in Philadelphia. This resulted in the presence of Hall, Gwinnett, and Walton when the Declaration of Independence was ready to sign. They signed it for Georgia.

Georgia was now dividing into Whigs, those against the king, and Tories, those for the king. Some were neutral, but were finding it harder and harder to remain so. Even then, however, many of those against the king just wanted him to appease their grievances. They did not at first clamor for independence.

Governor Wright Was Arrested

The Patriots were now in control of Georgia.

In January, 1776, British ships appeared in the harbor at Savannah. The patriots feared that Wright would try to get in touch with them and strengthen the Tories in Georgia. The governor had already been in fear for his personal safety and had warned England that the government in Georgia was in danger. On September 23, 1775, he had written in a letter to the Earl of Dartmouth, "I have not the least means of protection, support, or even personal safety. It is a wretched state to be left in." The Georgians had already forced Chief Justice Andrew Stokes off the bench and had taken over the courts.

But the Liberty Boys had no intention of harming the governor. Georgia had prospered under him. He was the ablest of the three royal governors. Since land laws had been relaxed, the plantation era had started under him. This is what Oglethorpe and the Trustees had feared, that rich men would buy up great acreages of land, need slaves to work it, and the colony would no longer be a place of small farms and independent owners.

They wanted him to relinquish the government, but they were willing to make the transition in safety. On January 18, 1776, the Council of Safety had adopted a resolution: "Resolved, that the person of his Excellency, Sir James Wright, Baronet ... and his four aides ... be forthwith arrested."

As Wright sat in his home with members of his Council that day, twenty-four-year-old Major Joseph Habersham walked in. He laid his hand on the governor's shoulder

Joseph Habersham

237

and said, "Sir James, you are my prisoner." The Council members fled. Wright was allowed to remain in his own home. On February 11, 1776, he escaped. He went first to Bonaventure, where his friend Tattnall lived. He was rowed by boat over Tybee Creek to board the British ship "Scarborough" in the Savannah harbor. The captain received him on board at three o'clock in the morning, on February 12, 1776. He went to Nova Scotia, and was away from Georgia for three and a half years. His brothers, Charles and Germyn, were still at Scrubby Bluff where they had built Fort Tonyn, named for Florida's governor, and made it a hideout for Tories.

Georgians Elected Bulloch President

After Governor Wright was arrested and escaped, Georgians took over their government and elected Archibald Bulloch as its head. He had already been chosen as President of the Provincial Congress, and was once in charge of the Council of Safety. Now he was head of Georgia's government.

Bulloch was a very democratic man and, when General Lachlan McIntosh wanted to place guards at his door, he declined. He had faith in his people, he said, and did not believe anybody would want to harm him. He thought guards sounded as if he were trying to display his position.

John Glynn was named Chief Justice succeeding the deposed Briton, Anthony Stokes. The new government, which had been set up on April 15, 1775, wanted a state constitution.

President Bulloch called a constitutional convention, which was to meet in Savannah the next October. But before that date came, many exciting things had happened.

Georgia Strengthened Its Defense

The American colonies now had a flag of their own; it was red, white, and blue. Legend says it was designed by Washington and stitched by Betsy Ross. The flag was flown on January 1, 1776. The motto of the new nation was *E Pluribus Unum,* meaning "one from many."

The colonies were joining together to strengthen their defenses and to support the Continental Congress. The Liberty Boys had already organized a battalion commanded by Lachlan McIntosh. The Continental Congress let the various colonial governments name the commanders in their states, and Georgia's Provincial Congress named McIntosh as Continental Commander in Georgia, with the rank of brigadier general. This angered Button Gwinnett, and was to cause deadly trouble later.

Early in January, 1776, McIntosh headed a delegation sent by Georgia to Charleston to confer with the American commander in charge of the South. This was General Charles Lee, who was no relation to the Virginia Lees.

The Georgians pointed out to Lee that the Creeks, long-time allies of the British, were a danger to the Georgia colony. So was Florida. The Continental Congress finally sent money to help Georgia strengthen its defenses.

Lee also came to Savannah to review the troops and look at Georgia's defense plans and the forts on the coast.

General Lee though the Georgians were too optimistic about their ability to defend their part of America. This bitter and cynical man wrote,

> These Georgians would tackle anything. They propose to defend their frontier with Horse Rangers, and it turns out that they do not have there a single horse. Later, they planned to defend it by boats — and they had no boats! I would not be surprised to hear them propose to defend the coastal country with mermaids mounted on alligators!

Edward Telfair, who was later to be governor, became the foremost boat builder of the Revolution in this section.

Samuel Elbert was named chief aide to General Lachlan McIntosh, with the rank of lieutenant colonel, and Joseph Habersham was named major. Habersham was an officer in both the army and the navy. The Georgia Provincial Congress had commissioned him and Oliver Bowen to take charge of whatever ships and naval defenses Georgia could establish.

Georgia and the Declaration of Independence

Three of the men who had been named to represent Georgia at the Continental Congress in Philadelphia were there on July 4, 1776, when the Declaration of Independence was adopted. It was actually signed later. They were Dr. Lyman Hall, Button Gwinnett, and George Walton. Later, each of them became head of the government of Georgia. There is a county named for each of them. The counties join. Two signers, Hall and Walton, are buried under the Signer's Monument in Augusta, built in 1848 and designed like the Washington Monument in Washington, D. C. Gwinnett's body was lost to history for a long time. The Declaration, first proposed by Richard Henry Lee of Virginia, had been drafted by a committee composed of Jefferson, Franklin, John Adams, Roger Sherman, and Robert Livingston. Jefferson, who had a way with words, actually wrote most of it. They set forth twenty-eight grievances against King George III.

News of the Declaration reached Georgia in early August and a copy of it, with a letter to Georgia President Archibald Bulloch from President John Hancock of the Continental Congress, arrived in Georgia on August 8, 1776, brought by a messenger on horseback. John Hancock's signature was the biggest one on the document. To this day, people often refer to a signature as a "John Hancock."

The Declaration of Independence was read several times in Savannah: to the Assembly members in the Council House; to the public gathered around the Liberty Pole near Tondee's Tavern, and to another crowd in the Trustees' Garden. The Declaration of Independence set out in detail all the wrongs that King George III had done to the American colonies.

The crowds were very excited. They held a mock funeral service in Savannah and buried an effigy of King George III, whom Georgia had proclaimed as its king in 1760. They listened solemnly as a reader intoned these words:

> Forasmuch as George III of Great Britain hath most flagrantly violated his coronation oath and trampled upon our country and the sacred rights of mankind, we therefore commit his political

240

existence to the ground, corruption to corruption, tyranny to the grave, and oppression to eternal infamy, in sure and certain hope that he will never obtain a resurrection to rule again over this country. But let us not be sorrowful as men without hope, for tyrants that thus depart. Rather, let us remember that America is free and independent, that she is and will be, with the blessing of the Almighty, great among the nations of the earth. Let this encourage us in well-doing and in fighting for our rights and privileges, for our wives and children, and for all that is near and dear to us. May God give us His blessing and let all the people say AMEN!

The celebrating crowd rang bells and fired cannons. At Tondee's Tavern they had a feast, and drank toasts to the success of their new country, and to the three Georgians who had signed the Declaration of Independence. But not all Georgians were in favor of independence and, in the next few months, about two thousand moved away. Some went to Florida, some to Nova Scotia, some to Jamaica, and some, like the Tattnalls, to England. A son, Josiah Tattnall, returned and was later elected governor. He signed "with lively expressions of gratitude" a legislative bill restoring to him his family's confiscated property.

Vice-president John Adams, who was later to become the second president of the United States, and who was also a signer, wrote, "This day, I believe, will be celebrated by succeeding generations as the Great Anniversary Festival, with shows, games, sports, balls, bonfires, and illuminations from one end of this continent to the other, forevermore." Adams had liked the Georgia delegation. He wrote, "They are spirited, intelligent men, and will be a powerful addition to our phalanx."

July 4 is celebrated as Independence Day, though actually it is not the real anniversary of the signing of the Declaration of Independence. It was signed after it was inscribed on parchment, in August.

On September 9, 1776, the Continental Congress officially adopted the name "United States of America" to replace "United Colonies of America."

The portraits and white marble busts of Georgia's three signers are in the State Capitol in Atlanta.

Millions who go to the Archives in Washington, D.C. to view the Declaration of Independence see the signatures inscribed on it by the three who signed it for Georgia. Not one of them was a native Georgian.

Dr. Lyman Hall was the physician of the Puritans at Midway in the St. Johns Parish. He was from Connecticut, where he had been born April 12, 1734. He came first to join the Puritans in South Carolina, then moved to Georgia in 1754. When he signed the Declaration, he was fifty-two, the oldest of the three. He had first studied for the ministry at Yale, but later studied medicine. He was a large, likeable man. Dr. Hall treated the Puritans there in the malarial swamps for their ailments, was one of the congregation at Midway meeting house, and represented them in politics. He had two homes, one at Sunbury, and a plantation, Hall's Knoll, above the church. A sign on the highway points to it now. His pistols are in the Midway Museum near the church.

He came back home to Georgia from Philadelphia, but after the British burned his house, he moved his wife and son to Philadelphia for the rest of the war. Later, he came back to Savannah, and was elected governor.

Dr. Hall bought a plantation on Shell Bluff, on the Savannah River. Here he died October 19, 1791, at sixty-seven. Both his wife and son, an only child, died in Georgia and he has no living descendants.

George Walton had come from Virginia, where he was born in 1741, to work with Matthew Talbot as a surveyor. They both later became Georgia governors. Walton studied law. He joined the colonial army, was wounded, and had a limp that lasted the rest of his life. He was taken prisoner and was once in jail at Sunbury. His wife, Dorothy Camber, was the daughter of Tories who tried to persuade her to go to the West Indies with them when the war started, but she refused. She was once arrested by the British.

After the war, Walton became a judge and lived in Augusta. One of the main streets there now is Walton Way. His home, Meadow Garden in Augusta, is a historic shrine. His granddaughter, Octavia Walton LeVert, attained

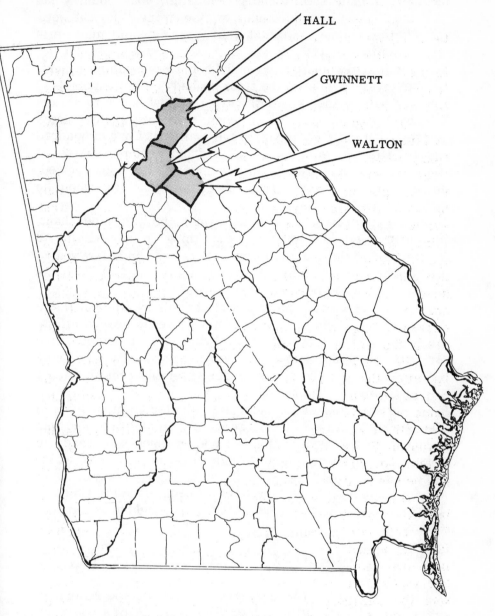

HALL

GWINNETT

WALTON

Counties Named For Georgia's Three Signers

world fame for her brilliance and charm. Washington Irving, author of "Rip Van Winkle," said of her, "Such a woman as that comes along only once in a century." Once when she was in Europe, where she knew kings and queens, a man said to her, "Madame, your country has the most precious document in the world, the one your grandfather signed. Do not your young people make pilgrimages to see it?"

Button Gwinnett, who had been a Savannah merchant, is the mystery man of the trio. He had come from England shortly before the Revolutionary shadow began to darken the land. But nobody knows when. Another mystery later arose about him when his grave was lost for two hundred years. His curious name came from a cousin, Barbara Button, who left him a small legacy. He had married, in England, the daughter of a tea merchant for whom he worked.

He came first to Savannah, where he was a merchant. He advertised his wares, every thing from medicine to silver and gold hats, in the *Gazette*. In a few years, he bought some land on St. Catherines Island from Thomas Bosomworth, and built a house there.

He was in and out the port of Sunbury, and became a friend of Dr. Lyman Hall, who may have influenced him to join the side of the colonists. Gwinnett was elected to the Assembly in 1769. Sometimes he had to pay a fine for being late or not attending, and once the Assembly sent an officer to bring him. He had been ill.

He was one of the delegates elected from Georgia to the Second Continental Congress in Philadelphia, and was there when the Declaration of Independence was ready to sign. His signature, small and cramped, is now worth fifty thousand dollars. The State of Georgia owns one of the few in existence. A new tomb has been placed in Colonial Park Cemetery in Savannah, with bones thought to be those of Gwinnett.

HOW GEORGIA GOT ITS FIRST CONSTITUTION

It was in 1776, the second year of the American Revolution, that Georgia leaders began to plan for a constitution that would change Georgia from a royal province to a state.

Georgia had already adopted something called Rules and Regulations. The Council of Safety and the Provincial Congress had already given evidence of Georgians' ability to handle their own government. Now they needed a state constitution. President Archibald Bulloch set up a committee to draft a constitution. Button Gwinnett, who had just come back from Philadelphia where he had signed the Declaration of Independence for Georgia (along with Lyman Hall and George Walton) was on the committee to work on this first state constitution. It was destined to be the basis of Georgia's government for the next twelve years.

The committee worked hard all through the winter of 1776-1777. The war was being fought bitterly in the North between British redcoats and colonists, but it had as yet scarcely touched Georgia. It would be nearly two years before Georgia would feel its terror and hardships. But there was tragedy that year, too; it was a star-crossed springtime.

By February, 1777, a constitution of sixty-three articles was ready to submit to the legislature. They adopted it without referring it to a vote of the people. One of the things it provided was that schools should be erected in each county, "supported at the general expense of the State."

The official church was disestablished. Georgians, who had been taxed to support it and fined if they did not go to church on Sunday, were free to worship as they pleased.

The constitution provided for eight counties instead of the twelve parishes of the Church of England that had existed. These eight counties were Chatham, Richmond, Burke, Effingham, Liberty, Glynn, Camden, and Wilkes. Liberty, one of Georgia's few counties not named for a place or a person, honored the Midway Puritans who had been so insistent and vigilant in the cause of liberty. The others were named for Britishers who had championed the cause of the colonies as the Revolution had loomed.

The first constitution provided for two members from each county to form an advisory council for the governor, who was to be the state's chief executive. Superior courts and "courts of conscience" were set up. The governor was to be elected by the legislature, and to serve for only one year. The first governor would serve only the remaining half of the year in which the constitution was being adopted; thereafter, each governor would have a one-year term, until

245

another constitution lengthened it. He would also be required to swear that he would not try to "hold over" in the office. Patriots were wary of too much power in government, and were fighting a war to get rid of British governors. The strict rule about governors not holding over was to cause trouble and leave Georgia without a governor when the British suddenly swooped down on Savannah, and the government had to flee.

The constitution was adopted on February 5, 1777. A Great Seal had on one side, "The Constitution of the State of Georgia" and the Latin motto, *Pro bono publico.* On the other side was the drawing of a house, fields, river, and ship, with the words, *Deus nobis haec otic fecit.* Georgia's Seal bears the date 1776 because this was the date of the colonies' independence from England, as adopted and signed in the Declaration of Independence.

President Archibald Bulloch set a date for the meeting of the first legislature under the new constitution: May 7, 1777.

The biggest task of the coming legislature was to elect Georgia's first constitutional governor. This would undoubtedly have been Bulloch himself. But by early in March he had died. An old rumor says he was poisoned. He was buried in Savannah's Colonial Park Cemetery. A strange mark is on his tomb: a figure carved in a circle.

Why Gwinnett Did Not Become
Georgia's First Governor

Even though Button Gwinnett had been somewhat late siding with the Patriots, he had achieved considerable eminence in the new state. He had worked on the first state constitution, and had been assistant to President Archibald Bulloch.

When Bulloch died, Gwinnett was named Acting President. The Commission issued to him on March 4, 1777 began with the quaint wording formerly used by King George: "To Our Trusty and Well-Beloved Button Gwinnett....We elect you in the name of the good people of Georgia, reposing special trust and confidence in the Prudence, Courage, Patriotism and integrity of you, the said Button Gwinnett."

246

But Gwinnett was not the well-beloved of all, nor was he trusted by all, despite his many staunch friends and admirers. He had incurred the enmity of the powerful Scotch Highlander clan of McIntoshes. There were two reasons for this. First, he had humiliated General Lachlan McIntosh. The general had been appointed by the Continental Congress in Philadelphia as commander of the military forces in Georgia, and worked hard at this job. Gwinnett had wanted the position, feeling perhaps that since he had been the one who served in Philadelphia and signed the Declaration, the Continental Congress should have preferred him.

So when Gwinnett became Acting President of Georgia and found himself automatically commander-in-chief of the state's soldiers, he planned an expedition to Florida without even consulting McIntosh. Samuel Elbert, second in command to McIntosh and a future governor of Georgia, was embarrassed by this and told General McIntosh so. The expedition was a failure. Then McIntosh also led a group of his own. Georgia's Council of Safety summoned both Gwinnett and McIntosh and inquired into it. They hurled charges at each other. McIntosh called Gwinnett, a "rotten-hearted, lying scoundrel." George Walton said that Gwinnett, like Alexander the Great, imagined himself to be lord of the earth.

The second reason the McIntoshes did not like Gwinnett was that he had arrested and had put into irons George McIntosh, their youngest brother. Gwinnett had received a letter from John Hancock, President of the Continental Congress, informing him that George McIntosh was suspected of trading with the British in Florida. Even though George McIntosh had been a member of the Council of Safety, Gwinnett refused to allow him out on bail. He finally got out, went to the Continental Congress to answer the charges, and was cleared. He had not been present when the Georgia Assembly elected Gwinnett Acting President, because of the funeral of his twenty-one-year-old wife, Nancy Houstoun McIntosh, sister of future governor John Houstoun. He later said that he would have voted for anybody before he would have voted for Gwinnett. The McIntoshes controlled enough votes to defeat Gwinnett.

After the legislature dissolved the Council of Safety

and named an Executive Council, it was ready to elect the first governor under the state's new constitution.

When the election for governor was held on May 8, 1777, the day after the first state legislature under the new Constitution convened, Gwinnett was defeated by John Adam Treutlen. Treutlen, a staunch, old Salzburger, was to serve six months as governor, achieve some fine things, and later to vanish from history.

Gwinnett was bitterly disappointed. Lachlan McIntosh was delighted and said so.

GWINNETT AND MCINTOSH FOUGHT A DEADLY DUEL

Now things had come to a crisis between Button Gwinnett and Lachlan McIntosh. Now the humiliated Gwinnett challenged McIntosh to a duel at dawn on May 15. "Dawn is earlier than I usually rise," said the General, flippantly, "but I will be there."

They met in the meadow of the house in which Royal Governor Wright had lived, within the present city limits of Savannah. Both men were shot, Gwinnett the more seriously. He had a bone shattered above his knee. As he fell, he called out, "My hip is broken." McIntosh, who was shot in the fleshy part of his leg, replied, "Do you want another shot?" Gwinnett said, "Yes, if somebody will help me up." But their seconds stopped the duel. The two men shook hands and each went to his own home. McIntosh recovered, but Gwinnett had gangrene in his wound, and died four days later. Nobody remembered where he was buried. In 1964, bones thought to be his were found and reburied in Savannah.

Mrs. Gwinnett moved to South Carolina where her only child lived, and both died soon after. Gwinnett has no living descendants.

Gwinnett County is named for Button Gwinnett. A a bust and portrait of him is in the State Capitol. Gwinnett's signature is the rarest of all those of the Signers of the Declaration of Independence. Only thirty-six are known to exist.

Some authorities say that the usual picture in the history books, and the marble bust in the State Capitol, are not authentic pictures of Gwinnett. They say the only authentic portrait of him in existence is the one that hangs in a bank in downtown Atlanta. It shows a thin-lipped man, solemn-

248

eyed, with dark, receding hair, and a rather grim look, wearing a green coat with bronze buttons, and a white neckerchief. His hand is thrust into his jacket.

Button Gwinnett

Feeling ran high against McIntosh. Lyman Hall and other friends of Gwinnett pressed authorities to arrest and try him. McIntosh claimed as his defense that the dueling was permissible, and that Gwinnett had died because he had not had proper medical attention. More than five hundred Georgians signed a petition asking that McIntosh be transferred out of Georgia. He was sent to Valley Forge just in time to spend the bitter winter there with Washington. When the fighting was transferred to Georgia he asked to be sent back here. Despite the opposition from Walton who sent a letter purported to be from the legislature and later proved a forgery, he came back and fought valiantly.

McIntosh's wife and family had been in Savannah when the terrible siege damaged that city in October, 1779. When McIntosh was released, he returned to Savannah. He entertained Washington at his home in Savannah in 1791. The patriot hero lived out his remaining years in Savannah. When he died, he was buried in Colonial Park Cemetary in Savannah. An odd round stone lies in the middle of his grave. The epitaph reads, "In 1784, the Continental Congress promoted McIntosh to Major General, vindicating him from unjust suspicion of four years before, as misrepresented to it by Governor Walton."

When McIntosh had been transferred out of Georgia, he left the Continental military forces in Georgia in charge of General Robert Howe. Howe set up headquarters in the area. But he was a very inept and incompetent officer, as was proved when he lost Savannah to the British in December, 1778, months after McIntosh left.

The First Governor Disappeared

John Adam Treutlen, the man who defeated Gwinnett to become the first governor of Georgia under the state's first constitution, was a Salzburger. He was born in 1733 near Berchtesgaden in Austria, a place to become infamous later as the retreat of Hitler. He and his family, members of a religious group being persecuted in Austria, started on their long journey toward a new home when Treutlen was six years old. One old story says that the ship was captured by pirates, who took his father prisoner but allowed the family to continue their journey. The boy John, his mother, and his brother came with the other Salzburgers to Georgia. His pastor and tutor was John Bolzius, who is buried in the old churchyard near the Jerusalem Church at old Ebenezer in Effingham County.

Treutlen grew up to be a prosperous farmer. Once he was a school teacher. His first political office was that of justice of the peace in St. Mathew's parish.

His people elected him to represent them in the Assembly of Georgia in Savannah. When the Revolution came, the Salzburgers were divided in opinion about what they should do. Some thought they should remain on the side of the British, since the Trustees had first allowed them to join the British colony when they needed a refuge. Others believed that since they were victims of British tyranny

250

John Adam Treutlen

like the others, they should join in the protest. Treutlen was on the side of the Patriots who protested Britain's tyrannies.

He was a member of the Council of Safety and later of Georgia's Provincial Congress. Then, after Archibald Bulloch died and Gwinnett's enemies were strong enough to keep him from changing from Acting President to the first governor of Georgia, Treutlen became governor. His term was very short, since he was elected on May 8, 1777, and the constitution provided that a new governor should begin his term each January.

Because of the dangerous times and the threat of trouble with England, the assembly was in session practically all of Treutlen's term.

He resisted the pressure of South Carolina to absorb Georgia. That state had tried to get this done during the time that Gwinnett was acting president but he too had opposed the idea. They tried again when Treutlen took office, and he opposed it even more vigorously. Moreover, on recommendation of his Council, July 14, 1777, he offered a reward of a hundred pounds for the arrest of William Drayton, the man they had sent to press their proposal. He fled back to South Carolina. From that safe haven, he ridiculed Treutlen, calling him a "buffoon."

Treutlen strengthened the defenses of Georgia, just in case the trouble broke into a war with England. After the war started, he mortgaged his home to help pay for it. This made the British angry and they burned his house. The British, with their allies from Florida and the Indians, were terrorizing the border of South Georgia, and Treutlen did what he could to protect the Georgians there.

When Treutlen's brief term as governor was finished, he took his family to visit relatives in South Carolina. He never came back; he disappeared and nobody knows to this day what happened to him. Somewhere in the vicinity of Orangeburg, South Carolina, he simply vanished. A marker in the area where he disappeared tells his story. In 1917, Georgia named a county for him. His bust and portrait are in the State Capitol in Atlanta.

When his short term was over, he was succeeded in office by John Houstoun, one of the four who had signed the advertisement in the *Gazette.*

CHAPTER 18

WHEN GEORGIA BECAME
A BATTLEGROUND

THE WAR MOVED SOUTH

The first three and one-half years of the war were fought in the north. Georgians hardly knew, except by rumor, that a war was going on.

England, losing to George Washington in the north, decided to move the war south. They believed that the king had many friends and supporters in the south, and they would rally to Britain and the Tory cause. Then, having won in the south, British troops could fight their way triumphantly back up the Atlantic coast and re-take the territory that had been wrested from them by George Washington.

By the end of 1778, the British held only New York and Newport. Washington had regained Philadelphia and many other sites from them.

King George III had problems. France, Spain, and Holland were all roused against Britain and he had to keep some soldiers in Europe because of this. He could not hire enough Hessians to help British soldiers fight in America. The king was still poring over maps and trying to tell his generals how to run the war in America, from his palace three thousand miles away! The war continued to go against the king in the north. "Gentleman Johnny" Burgoyne, the British general who also wrote plays, surrendered to Americans at Saratoga on October 17, 1777. This had impressed the French, who were still angry at having lost their American territory to England in the French and Indian War. After Burgoyne's defeat by the Americans, King Louis XVI, prodded by Franklin and

Lafayette, agreed to a treaty to help America, which he signed on February 6, 1778. King George III and his ministers wanted to regain control of the war before this French aid could reach the colonies.

The British king's ministers included Lord George Germain and, later, Lord Frederick North. North was a big, humorous man who liked to sleep through tiresome debates in Parliament.

Now the king told them that he wanted to move the war south. They figured that it would take about two thousand British soldiers to capture Savannah, and about five thousand to take Charleston, South Carolina. On March 8, 1778, the king appointed Sir Henry Clinton to put this plan into effect.

England's First Plan To Capture Georgia

The new British commander's strategy to capture the South did not at first succeed.

His idea was to move on Savannah first from Florida and then from New York. The attack from Florida was to be a two-pronged one, by land and by sea. General Augustine Prevost, the British commander in Florida, sent four hundred soldiers, under his brother Lieutenant Mark Prevost, plus three hundred refugees and Indians under turncoat Dan McGirth, an American who had gone over to the British. They led soldiers up through Georgia by land to take Savannah and Sunbury. They were to join forces at Sunbury with a sea force under the command of Lieutenant Colonel L.V. Fuser. Strong winds delayed this sea expedition and it did not keep this appointment.

The land forces entered Georgia from Florida on November 10, 1778, marching toward Midway and Sunbury. Colonel John Baker gathered Georgia soldiers hastily, near the Midway Church, and made a brave stand on November 24, 1778. The British outnumbered them. General James Screven (for whom Screven County was named) was killed by the British after he surrendered. He is buried in Midway cemetery, sharing a $10,000 monument erected to the memory of him and General Daniel Stewart by Congress. Young Lieutenant James Jackson, who had come to Savannah at fifteen and was not yet twenty, was also fighting here.

Colonel John White, another Georgia officer, dropped a letter in an effort to trick Prevost. The letter said help was on the way for the Americans. Prevost did not know whether to believe the letter or not. But he left anyway, after burning Midway Church, and destroying many homes and crops in the area. Then the British marched on back toward Florida, by way of Frederica.

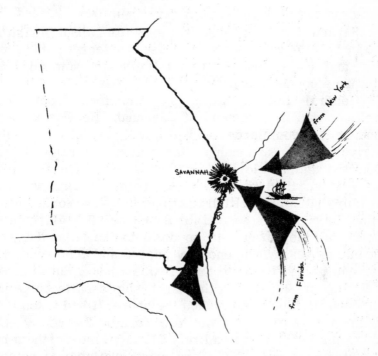

After they left, Fuser arrived by sea with five hundred men. He demanded the surrender of Fort Morris which guarded Sunbury. Colonel John McIntosh, of the Darien Scotch Highlander clan, was in command. He had only two hundred soldiers there, but he sent back a defiant retort to Fuser. "Come and take it!" he dared him. Fuser, having missed connections with Prevost and the land forces, decided not to fight for the fort. He left. Later, the Georgia legislature presented McIntosh a sword inscribed with his brave words, "Come and take it!"

This first effort of the British to move the war south, in November, 1778, failed, but a bigger British force was getting ready to sail from New York, under command of General Archibald Campbell.

Late in 1778, Governor John Houstoun, General Robert Howe, Naval Commander Oliver Bowen and troops from South Carolina had just come back from another futile expedition to conquer Florida. They returned to Georgia just in time to hear the bad news: the British were on their way to capture Savannah!

THE SECRET PATH AND THE FALL OF SAVANNAH

Savannah was captured by the British about Christmas time in 1778. It was captured because of a secret path, a gold piece, and a slave named Quash Dolly, who smoked a pipe and wore a coonskin cap.

General Robert Howe, an American from North Carolina, was in command at Savannah. He was a cousin of the British commander named Howe. He had just reached the river below Savannah on his return from the ill-fated expedition against Florida.

William Haslam, a deserter from the British Navy, told him that a big British fleet had left New York and was sailing the high seas headed for Savannah! This alarmed the people and they began to go down to the ocean daily and look out to sea. When one day passed and another, and no ships came, they began to think it was a hoax. But at sunset on December 23, 1778, the first ship's sails came into sight, and the fleet approached the shore. It had taken them seventeen days to come from New York on the wintry seas.

Commander Howe had only 672 men, most of them new and untrained; only 250 more were available to come to help him. On the British ships were 3,500 men.

Howe had even fewer men than usual because he had, on his way back from Florida, left some to guard the post of Sunbury.

He called his officers together to decide what to do. They voted to try to hold the city. George Walton and Samuel Elbert were among these officers. They warned Howe that he should set a guard over the jungle-like swamps near the river. But Howe was scornful. "Only a tiger could get through those jungles. There is no need to put a guard there," he said. That was his undoing.

Later, at Howe's court-martial, Walton said he

256

knew the place well because he had walked along the river there with young ladies of the town, picking jessamine.

General William Moultrie, for whom Moultrie, Georgia was named, did not believe that Savannah could be defended with only the handful of men Howe had. "It was absurd," he said later, "to suppose that 600 or 700 men, some of them very raw troops, could stand up against over 3,500 of the best troops the British had, under the command of an able officer like Major General Archibald Campbell. This was a rash and ill-advised decision Howe made to try to defend Savannah."

Washington had already ordered General Benjamin Lincoln south, but he had not had time to get to Savannah. Some officers had urged surrendering Savannah to the British, then joining Lincoln when he did reach the south, to take it back. Howe, however, had made his decision to defend the city and this he did. He sent his official papers to the home of Jonathan Bryan, father-in-law of Governor John Houstoun twelve miles away, and prepared to fight.

In the meantime, the British commander was coping with the problem of getting through the jungle-like swamp. He had landed his men, and now he had to get them into Savannah. "Surely there must be somebody around here who knows how to get through that swamp," said Campbell. Somebody had heard of an old slave named Quanimo ("Quash") Dolly, an expert woodsman who lived on the Giradeau plantation. He was a slave, captured on the coast of Guinea in Africa. Campbell sent men to find him. The old man, who was short and fat, was also sharp and shrewd. The British showed him a shining gold piece and asked him the way through the swamp. Dolly, who probably did not even know there was a war on, led the redcoats, under the command of Sir James Baird, through the swamp. Campbell had kept half of his men marching back and forth in sight of the Americans so they would not suspect that the others were crawling through the swamps.

Savannah was about to fall. Chief Justice Anthony Stokes, of the king's royal government in Georgia, had written that Savannah was "the Gibralter of the Gulf passage, the key to the conquest of the Southern provinces."

The British overpowered the small American force at Savannah on December 29, 1778. About three hundred

257

Quash Dolly Led The Way Through The Swamp.

Americans were killed. The British lost only fifteen. The battle was over so quickly that the town itself was not greatly damaged. About a hundred Americans tried to swim Musgrove Creek after the town fell; some forty were drowned. Two hundred Americans had to surrender to the British. Only four hundred of the nine hundred Americans who were fighting at Savannah escaped death or capture.

George Walton was captured by the British and put into prison at Sunbury. He wrote to Governor Houstoun, who was then in South Carolina, and Houstoun helped him get released in September 1779. After the fall of Savannah, some of those who escaped gathered about eight miles above the Savannah River and started toward South Carolina to join the American army there and continue their fight against the British.

Two future governors, who got lost from the rest, traveled by themselves to find the American army. The two were James Jackson, not yet out of his teens, and John Milledge. As soon as the war started, he enlisted and was quickly made an officer. When the two boys reached the

American army, they were thought to be British spies. This might have been because of Jackson's British accent. The Americans, their own army, were about to hang them when Major Peter Devaux, an American officer who knew them both, arrived just in the nick of time and identified them.

Washington named General Benjamin Lincoln to replace Howe as southern commander. Howe was later court-martialed. He was cleared, but he was never again given a responsible command after his loss of Savannah to the British. Howe was always sensitive about this, and once shot off the ear of General Chris Gadsden in a duel when Gadsden criticized him for losing this city.

The British in Savannah set up a government there and started exporting lumber, hides, rice and other crops. They subsidized the newspaper, the *Georgia Gazette,* and changed it to the *Royal Gazette.* In it, they offered amnesty to those who would take an oath of loyalty to the king, and a reward for the capture of those who would not. The British general, Sir Archibald Campbell, left Lieutenant Colonel Mark Prevost in charge of Savannah, and started on his conquest of the remainder of Georgia, going toward Augusta by way of Ebenezer. He sent his aides to take Sunbury.

GEORGIA'S GOVERNMENT HAD TO MOVE

Governor John Houstoun, who had succeeded Treutlen as governor, was just going out of office when the British captured Savannah. He could not "hold over" as governor because Georgia's constitution forbade it.

Houstoun had been one of the four patriots who had signed the ad in the *Gazette* that roused Georgians to support the Revolution. He was a son of Sir Patrick Houstoun, Baronet. Before he was twenty-one, he was practicing law. A report says he had many clients and was "comparable to any lawyer of his day, and born to lead." He had studied law with Henry Laurens, of South Carolina, the only American to have been imprisoned in the Tower of London. Houstoun married Hannah Bryan, daughter of Jonathan Bryan, and bought a plantation at White Bluff, November 15, 1769. He was twice governor.

Houstoun had just returned from the Florida expedition

259

when he heard news that the British were on their way to capture Savannah. He held his last Council meeting on December 26, 1778, and took Georgia's papers to the home of his father-in-law, Jonathan Bryan. Then he went to Retreat, the home of his brother George on the Vernon River. He escaped the British by climbing a tree and hiding.

In a few weeks, the British had taken not only Savannah, but Sunbury and Ebenezer, and were on their way to capture Augusta.

The Georgia government tarried in Augusta a while and then in February, 1780, moved briefly to Heard's Fort, eight miles from where the town of Washington stands now, then back to Augusta.

Two factions of Georgia's Patriot or Whig government developed in Augusta. One elected John Wereat head of the government, and the other elected George Walton. But by January 4, 1780, the two settled their differences and elected Richard Howley. He had also been elected to the Continental Congress, and in a few days he got on his horse and galloped off to Philadelphia. That left George Wells, president of the Council, as acting governor. He was soon killed in a duel with James Jackson. Stephen Heard, Council president, was then head of the Georgia government. Later, Heard went to North Carolina for a time, and Myrick Davis became acting head of the government. He was later murdered.

In Savannah, the civil government, temporarily headed by Lieutenant Colonel Mark Prevost, was headed by Royal Governor James Wright again. Wright had returned in July, 1779. When Wright returned to Savannah, he hanged many patriots, and confiscated the property of others. The British held Savannah for three and a half years, from December 29, 1779, to July 11, 1782. They were proclaiming news and orders through James Johnston's paper, which had now become the *Royal Georgia Gazette*.

THE BRITISH STABLED HORSES IN EBENEZER'S CHURCH

After General Augustine Prevost came up from Florida to take command in Savannah, Colonel Archibald Campbell was free to push into northern Georgia and capture the rest of the state if he could. By January 31, he would be in Augusta, and stay only two weeks.

His first stop was at Ebenezer, the spot where the

Salzburgers had settled, which he took on January 2, 1779. This village was in what is now Effingham County. It became an outpost from which the British conquered the remainder of Georgia after they had taken Savannah. Pastor John Triebner took the oath of allegiance to Britain, but all his people did not follow him.

First the British used the fine old Jerusalem Church, built in 1767, with its swan on the steeple, as a hospital. Later they used it as a stable for their horses. They moved into the homes of the people, and were often insulting and offensive to them. They brought to Ebenezer the prisoners they took in their skirmishes and battles in Upper Georgia. Sometimes they were very cruel to these prisoners. They kept them at Ebenezer for a time, and then sent them on to Savannah.

Sergeant William Jasper, already famous for saving the flag at a battle in South Carolina, decided that he would rescue a group of these prisoners. He and his friend, Sergeant Newton, surprised British guards who had stopped at a spring above Savannah for a drink of water. "Surrender or you are dead men!" Jasper freed the prisoners and took the guards away to be hanged. The spring, nine miles from Savannah on U.S. Highway 17, is named Jasper Springs.

HOW SUNBURY FELL TO THE BRITISH

Sunbury and Fort Morris were captured by the British on January 9, 1779. General Augustine Prevost marched his troops into the village, and rolled his guns into threatening position against the fort. Major Joseph Lane, with two hundred men, was in command. "Surrender!" demanded Prevost. "I have two thousand men and plenty of ammunition." The British guns almost destroyed the fort before the outnumbered little band of patriots surrendered it. The British renamed it Fort George. This site stands there by the water today, with its deep ditches under the old trees.

Sunbury, which had been a bustling little port, never recovered from this attack. It began then to become the ghost town that it is today: a few buildings in the sun, an old cemetery and markers that relate its history. The last big ship to dock at the port of Sunbury came in 1815.

Prevost went on to Savannah. He took command there, relieving its conqueror Campbell to fight on toward Augusta in upper Georgia.

By early February, Colonel Archibald Campbell had moved his troops into Augusta. He had taken Ebenezer, had put down the brave resistance of patriot troops in Burke County and other spots under Samuel Elbert, John Twiggs, and Benjamin and William Few. Now, by land and by the Savannah River, he put two thousand troops in Augusta, where Oglethorpe had built the old fort and put a trading station.

The American commander in charge of Augusta, Colonel Andrew Williamson, believing that the British controlled Georgia and would soon win the war, practically handed over Augusta to Campbell. He later joined the British Army.

Campbell, now entrenched in Augusta, and in control of most of Georgia, began sending out soldiers to terrorize the countryside, burn homes, destroy crops, and kill livestock, and often to murder people. He spared those who took the oath of allegiance to the king, and more than a thousand Georgians, many of them alarmed about their children, signed this. There was much distress in upper Georgia. The government had moved to Heard's Fort. Valiant men in Wilkes were carrying on such guerrilla warfare as they could, but the time was dark and despair gripped many.

Campbell now heard that Washington was sending General Benjamin Lincoln, the big, fat hero of Bunker Hill, and that Lincoln had set up headquarters at Smoking Camp near Purrysburg and was drilling troops.

General Lincoln Took Command in the South

General Benjamin Lincoln, who had come south to replace the discredited Howe who lost Savannah, was a very fat man. He kept two servants to get him into his uniform with its colorful sash and the sword that Congress had given him. It was a reward for his spectacular victories at Saratoga and his valiant service at Bunker Hill.

At first the soldiers of the Georgia militia hesitated to fight under the heavy, lumbering general. But they came to see his remarkable ability, and his fine personal traits. He was destined to meet defeat in Georgia, but

Washington would try to make it up to him later by letting him accept the British surrender. Many months, however, lay between his arrival in the south and the surrender of Cornwallis, the British general.

Lincoln's chief aide was General Lachlan McIntosh, who had requested to be sent back to his native Georgia which was in danger. Since he had to leave Georgia because of the high feeling against him after the duel that led to Button Gwinnett's death in 1777, he had been in the north. After the bitter Valley Forge winter with Washington, he had commanded soldiers in other places.

George Walton protested McIntosh's return. Walton had been elected governor. He sent to Congress a letter of protest said to have been signed by Speaker William Glascock of the Georgia House of Representatives. Glascock said he did not sign the letter. The mystery has never been cleared up. McIntosh returned, fought valiantly, and was elected to positions of honor by his fellow Georgians. He was host to Washington when the first President visited Savannah in 1791. McIntosh's grave, with a curious round stone in the center, is in Savannah's Colonial Park Cemetery, and his house still stands in Savannah.

He loyally supported General Lincoln, and together they planned the strategy for the recapturing of Georgia from the British. The first thing Lincoln did was to send out skirmishing parties over the Savannah into Georgia, where Tories were plaguing the people. Then he expected to bottle up the British in Savannah, and finally defeat them there. He brought with him four thousand troops, including some Hessian soldiers. He expected to recruit enough here to have a force of eight thousand when he got ready to recapture Savannah. In the meantime, he had asked the government to request that its ally, France, get seaside help for the Savannah attack from D'Estaing, whose ships were cruising in the West Indies at the time. Before Savannah there were other, smaller fights, sometimes won, sometimes lost.

THE PATRIOTS WON AT KETTLE CREEK

On War Hill, near Kettle Creek, about eight miles from Washington, Georgia, the Americans won a battle on February 14, 1779. It encouraged them, and broke the iron grip that the British had on Georgia.

British Colonel Thomas Boyd started from South Carolina with about eight hundred British soldiers to meet the traitor, Dan McGirth, at Little River. McGirth did not come. Nancy Hart, who often acted as a spy for American forces, had made a raft of grape vines and logs to cross the river and find out what was going on. She heard that Boyd was marching. She hastened back to Wilkes, where Colonel Elijah Clarke, her friend and neighbor, was recovering from battle wounds and smallpox at his home. Clarke sent a servant on his horse to round up his neighbors to waylay the British. About five hundred Continental soldiers were led by Clarke. General Andrew Pickens and Colonel John Dooly.

Boyd's men had been marching for three days, and were tired and hungry. They came to Kettle Creek, six miles from Little River, near a swamp and canebrake, with a high bluff nearby. There they stopped to rest, and to eat. They turned their horses loose to forage, and they caught a farmer's cow to roast, with some parched corn to go with the browned beef.

At daylight, the patriots launched a surprise attack. The American commanders divided their little forces into three parts, to attack from three sides. Clarke's fifty men went around the hill and attacked from the rear. The British troops were caught by surprise. The battle was short and furious. Clarke's horse was shot from under him. He was provided with another one by Austin Dabney, a free Negro who showed great heroism in this battle, and was wounded. He was nursed by white friends, whose son he afterward financed through college. The legislature, in a special act, later granted land to this Negro.

At Kettle Creek the British lost 145; of these, 70 were killed and 75 captured. Only nine Americans were killed and only 23 wounded or captured.

The British commander, Boyd, was fatally wounded. Roused from unconsciousness, he asked, "How is the battle going?" General Andrew Pickens, the American officer for whom Pickens County was named, told him that the battle was over and the British had lost. "It would have been different if I had not been shot and had been able to lead my men," said Boyd. Pickens also told the English general that he was dying.

"What can we do to make your last hours more comfortable?" asked Pickens.

"Leave two soldiers here to give me water through the night, and send my watch and other things to my wife in England, please," he answered. This Pickens did. When Mrs. Boyd died she left the watch to the Pickens family.

The defeated British soldiers scattered from Kettle Creek, leaving six hundred horses. This victory broke the Tory grip on Upper Georgia for a while. Patriots took heart again and many who had fled from their homes returned.

General Archibald Campbell, who had taken over at Augusta, decided to leave, even though he had been there only a few weeks. He got the bad news about Kettle Creek, and he had also heard that General Lincoln was planning to move into Georgia from South Carolina and cut the British supply and communication line from Savannah. Campbell evacuated Augusta without even taking time to destroy his ammunition. He went to Hudson's Ferry, twenty miles above Ebenezer. After he left Georgia, Campbell was knighted by the British government and became governor of Madras in India.

A gray stone shaft stands now on the hill above Kettle Creek, several miles out of Washington in Wilkes County, commemorating the Battle of Kettle Creek. Fighting in this furious battle on February 14, 1779, was a thirteen-year-old boy there with his father, General Elijah Clarke. He was John Clarke, who was later to be governor of Georgia and one of the state's most colorful leaders. He also fought so bravely at another battle that it was named for him: the battle of Jack's Creek.

Americans rejoiced at their Kettle Creek victory. Historians often refer to this area of old Wilkes County as "the Hornet's Nest." But the next month, the picture changed.

THE BRITISH WON AT BRIER CREEK

Soon after the victory at Kettle Creek, General Benjamin Lincoln located at Smoking Camp on the Carolina side of the Savannah River, sent Colonel John Ashe with 2,300 men to establish a camp on the Georgia side. General Samuel Elbert and Colonel John McIntosh led regular soldiers and militia. Lincoln was getting ready for the showdown. General Augustine Prevost was still in command at Savannah. Lincoln chose Smoking Camp for his headquarters so that he could protect South Carolina from the British, and also train and drill his troops for the coming battle.

Colonel Ashe crossed the Savannah with his 2,300 men, and set up a temporary camp on Brier Creek, in what is now Screven County. Sir Archibald Campbell heard of Ashe's presence and sent nine hundred regular troops under Colonel Mark Prevost to attack. The British surprised Ashe there about three o'clock in the afternoon, on March 3, 1779. The British won. About 340 Americans were killed or captured: some drowned as they attempted to swim the unfordable, sixty-yard-wide Brier Creek. The enemy lost only sixteen.

About this same time, the British ships *Comet* and *Hornet* defeated two U.S. ships, *Congress* and *Lee*, near Savannah.

Plans had been made for the Americans and the French to join forces to recapture Savannah from the British, who had held it since December 29, 1778. It was now early autumn of 1779, about ten months later. General Augustine Prevost, known as "Old Bullet Head," was in command at Savannah, with Royal Governor James Wright as head of His Majesty's Civil Government.

The French king, Louis XVI, having agreed to help America, was willing to have his men and ships help with this siege. Later, Georgia named a new capital Louisville in gratitude for the help of the French king in the Revolution. The young Lafayette, who had come to America at nineteen, had already become one of Washington's aides. Other Frenchmen were fighting in America, too. One who was in the French secret service was the Baron de Kalb, who was not a baron at all but was a very brave man. He was Johann deKalb, son of a Bohemian peasant. But he fought valiantly with the Americans, and was killed in the Carolinas, with nineteen wounds in his body. De Kalb County is named for him, and his likeness is in bas-relief in stone above the De Kalb Building in Decatur.

General Benjamin Lincoln had plans laid for the recapture of Savannah. He started southward from Smoking Camp across the Savannah River. Tories delayed him by burning bridges. It was raining heavily, too, as the huge general and his soldiers marched toward Savannah.

Count Charles Henri D'Estaing, the dashing French naval commander, was to bring his ships from the West Indies and meet Lincoln in Savannah. This Frenchman was a great admirer of George Washington. John Hancock gave him a picture of Washington. Lafayette said, "A young man was never gladder to get a picture of his sweetheart than D'Estaing was to get the one of his hero, Washington."

Lincoln was plodding on his way, with two aides, General Lachlan McIntosh and Polish Count Casimir Pulaski, commanding two sections of his soldiers.

D'Estaing reached Savannah before Lincoln. He landed at Beaulieu, the old home of William Stephens, on September 11, 1779, with twenty-two ships and 4,500 men. Then the Frenchmen did a very foolish thing. They demanded that Prevost, the British commander at Savannah, surrender

America Asked France For Aid In The War

the city in the name of the French king. Some said that D'Estaing's success in the West Indies had gone to his head. Others said that he wanted all the glory for himself and had determined not to share it with the Americans. One even commented, "I thought at first I saw a superior talent in D'Estaing, but he is a fool, and a dangerous one. He thinks he is the wonder of the age, and that Caesar and Alexander were nothing compared with him."

Prevost, commanding at Savannah, was anxious about the defense of the city. Governor Wright had said, "If Savannah goes, the king's cause is lost!" The people were anxious, too. Chief Justice Anthony Stokes said, "I never allow a word of fear to cross my lips for fear of alarming the people more."

The truth was that Savannah was not well defended.

One British officer said later, "They could have taken this pile of sand in ten minutes."

Instead of waiting for Lincoln, or attacking, D'Estaing sent the note demanding surrender. The British commander decided to make a desperate play for time. He wrote in return, "Sir: I am honored with Your Excellency's letter. The business we have in hand being of great importance, a just time is absolutely necessary to deliberate. I am therefore proposing a cessation of hostilities shall take place for twenty-four hours. You are to draw your columns back out of sight during that time."

D'Estaing should have seen through this trick, for it was evident that Prevost wanted him out of sight so that he could work through the night building up his defenses. But the Frenchman actually agreed to the truce. He wrote, "I consent to the truce you ask. It shall continue till the signal for retreat tomorrow night, September 17, 1779."

The British called for help from all the plantations near Savannah, and they worked feverishly all night long strengthening the defenses of the city. Moreover, they sent an urgent message to Colonel John Maitland in Carolina for help. Through a fog, he slipped in with his ships right under D'Estaing's nose, and reinforced Prevost's forces in Savannah, with eight hundred men, who walked in mud up to their knees, to land.

Maitland was the son of a Scottish nobleman, the Earl of Lauderdale. He had already lost an arm in the king's service, and now he was sick with malaria, but he had come, with his soldiers.

After he got there, they asked him if he thought it was really wise to try to defend Savannah. Maitland banged on the table, and said with his Scotch accent, "Any officer that utters a single syllable in favor of surrender becomes my enemy!" Another officer threatened to report to King George III any officer who suggested surrender.

Governor Wright, who had said that, "If Savannah goes, the British cause is lost," sent to his plantation and had five hundred slaves brought through the rain-soaked marshes to work all night on the defenses. The British also sank some ships in the Savannah River to keep out attacking American vessels.

Finally, Prevost had 2,500 men, and a stronger defense.

He was ready to write D'Estaing, "The King, my master, pays these men to fight, and they must fight. I decline your terms."

In the meantime, General Lincoln had arrived on September 16. He was astonished to find out what the French commander had done. The rains poured. Tempers were short. D'Estaing thought Lincoln dull, and made fun of him. Lincoln was perplexed at the Frenchman's impulsive action.

There were many women and children inside Savannah, and they hid in the damp cellars. One soldier reported, "The poor women and children have suffered beyond description. Some of them have already been put to death by our bombs and cannons, in their beds or the rain-soaked cellars." McIntosh's wife was there, and he sent Major John Jones to ask Prevost to let the women and children out. He refused. He believed that the Americans would not bombard the city so heavily if their own families were in danger. Later, Prevost asked the Americans to let the British women and children go to the ships in the harbor for safety. He wrote, "The houses in Savannah are occupied by women and children. Several have asked me to request the favor to allow them to embark on ships and go down the river. If you are so good as to grant this, my own wife and children, with a few servants, shall be the first to profit by this indulgence." The American commanders refused! Mrs. McIntosh finally got out, and made her way to Virginia, where Jefferson loaned her money.

On the American side was Pierre L'Enfant, who was later to design Washington, D.C., and was wounded so badly he was left for dead. Sam Davis, father of Jefferson Davis, who would be the Confederate president nearly a hundred years later, was also fighting here. He came down from his up-country farm with his horse and rifle. Sam Davis lived in Georgia then; later he moved to Kentucky. There his son Jefferson Davis was born, about a hundred miles from the site where Abraham Lincoln was born.

Savannah was still holding out, after three weeks. D'Estaing was growing impatient. The hurricane season was at hand, and his men were sick. They did not like American food, especially rice, and meat was becoming scarce. Once they captured a British ship, the *Experiment,* commanded by the forty-eight-year-old Sir James

Pierre L'Enfant

Waller, whose twenty-year old bride was on board. She was the daughter of Governor Wright. The ship carried 2,200 barrels of flour, oatmeal, beef, port, and 30,000 pounds of English sterling money! The French ate well and felt prosperous that night!

The French also suffered from the climate. They said the days were too hot and the nights too cold.

D'Estaing insisted on an all-out attack. Lincoln agreed. It was set for October 9, 1779. D'Estaing, who was brave, led his troops, with the Americans under their commanders, in a bloody, savage, all-day attack. The British lost 264 of their 2,500. The French lost 600 of their 4,500. The Americans, who had 2,500, lost 600. The siege of Savannah had failed.

JASPER BECAME A HERO: Sergeant William Jasper, who had already become a hero at Fort Moultrie, was killed that day. He was trying to save the flag. "I have got my furlough!" he said. There is a monument to him in Savannah, and a county named for him in Georgia.

271

On the Jasper monument on Bull Street in Savannah, placed there on February 2, 1888, is this inscription:

> To the memory of Sgt. W. Jasper, who, though mortally wounded, rescued the colors of his regiment, in the assault on the British lines about the city, Oct. 9, 1779. A century has not dimmed the glory of the Irish-American soldier whose last tribute to civil liberty was his life. Erected by the Jasper Monument Association.

Jasper County in Georgia has Monticello as its county seat. The town of Jasper in Pickens County, and Jasper Springs, where he rescued the six prisoners, two miles above Savannah, keep his name alive in Georgia.

COUNT PULASKI WAS KILLED AT SAVANNAH: Among the officers who died in the siege of Savannah was the young Polish commander, Count Casimir Pulaski, for whom Pulaski County and Fort Pulaski in Savannah were named.

He had come to America at the suggestion of Benjamin Franklin. Pulaski's father, County Joseph Pulaski, was once so rich that he owned over a hundred Polish towns. At twenty-one, young Pulaski had helped his father found the confederation of Barr to free Poland of foreign domination. His side lost, and he went to help the Turks fight Russia. In 1776, he went to Paris and met Franklin. Washington made him a brigadier general of cavalry. A book he wrote on cavalry drills was long used by the U. S. Army. Congress voted to equip a legion for Pulaski. When the money was slow in coming, he wrote his sister Anna, a nun, to sell some property and send him money for troops. With this money he outfitted his American troops in sky-blue uniforms, with linings of orange, red, and green. Their boots were of the finest leather. They marched under the special banner of Pulaski's Legion. Their flag had been made for them by the Moravians of Pennsylvania, whose ancestors once lived in Georgia. It had thirteen stars and the slogan "Union Makes for Valor."

Once Pulaski resigned from the Continental Army because he disagreed with General Anthony Wayne. But they

Count Casimir Pulaski

both came later to fight in Georgia. At Savannah, Pulaski charged into battle on his spirited black horse. In the thick of the fight, he was badly wounded. One of his men later described this fight: "For a half hour after the battle started, the guns roared and the blood flowed. Seeing an opening in the enemy line, Pulaski told General Lincoln that he would dash in with his men, confuse the enemy and cheer up the people of Savannah. Lincoln approved. We dashed in. At first, all went well. Then we were caught in a cross-fire. I looked around. Oh, sad moment ever to be remembered! Pulaski lay prostrate on the ground. I leaped toward him, thinking that possibly his wound was not dangerous, but a shot had pierced his thigh and blood was flowing from a wound in his breast. Falling on my knees, I tried to raise him, I heard him say faintly, 'Jesus! Mary! Joseph!' Further, I knew not for at that moment a shot grazing my scalp blinded me with blood and I fell to the ground insensible."

In the retreat, Pulaski was left where he fell, but a brave Georgia officer, Captain Thomas Glascock, for whom Glascock County is named, went back through gunfire and rescued his wounded leader. Pulaski was not dead. He was put on an American ship, the *Wasp,* and attended by French surgeons sent by D'Estaing. But a few days later, when the ship was on its way to Charleston, South Carolina, he died of gangrene on October 11, 1779. He was thirty-one. Some say his body was dropped into the ocean. Others say he died in a house near Thunderbolt and was buried in the dead of night. A memorial service, with an empty coffin, is said to have been held in Charleston, South Carolina.

In 1825, when the French Marquis de Lafayette was visiting Georgia and being entertained at a brilliant dinner in Milledgeville, General John Clarke made a mistake about Pulaski. In proposing the toasts, he said, "To that brave Frenchman, Count Casimir Pulaski, who fell at Savannah!" But Pulaski was no Frenchman.

Georgia named Pulaski County for the Count. A monument to his memory was erected in Savannah. On November 1, 1929, the 150th anniversary of Pulaski's death was observed in Savannah. Many famous Polish officials and members of the Pulaski family attended. The Polish king called Pulaski "the foe of tryants."

Fort Pulaski at Savannah was named for the Polish hero. It took brick masons twenty years to build its massive walls, in which there are 25,000,000 bricks. It was to play an important part in the Civil War in the next century.

THE MEMOIRS OF A TEEN-AGER: Betsy Lichenstein, a teen-aged Tory who lived in Savannah during the siege, wrote of it many years later in Nova Scotia. Many Tories fled after the Revolution to the same Nova Scotia from which the Acadians had once come to Georgia to escape the British. She had been born in Georgia. Her mother's father was born in Russia, and had come over with Oglethorpe; her father was the son of a schoolmaster there. Her memoirs, *Recollections of a Georgia Loyalist,* give the other side of the picture of the Revolution. At fifteen, she married young William Martin Johnston, whose father was a surgeon in the British Navy.

The Americans were surprised at the outcome of the battle. They had thought Savannah would be easy to take. On October 9, 1779, as the battle began, General Charles Cotesworth Pinckney of South Carolina had written his mother, "Hon'd Madam: This morning about daybreak, we made an assault on the enemy's line and were repulsed. It seems not to disspirit our men, as they are convinced that it was owing to mistake of ground. I have not the least doubt that we shall soon be in possession of Savannah." But he was wrong. The British still held Savannah when the battle was over. They held it from the day they captured it, on December 29, 1778, until July, 1782.

Count D'Estaing, humiliated at his defeat, and wounded, sailed away despite the urging of the American commanders. He said his men were sick, the food was bad, and the hurricane season was at hand. The disastrous failure of the siege of Savannah was largely his fault. But General Lincoln generously wrote an appreciative letter to Congress about the brave, quarrelsome Frenchman. In the letter he said:

> Count D'Estaing has undoubtedly the interest of America much at heart. This he has evidenced by coming to our assistance, by his constant attention during the siege, his undertaking to reduce the enemy by assault when he despaired of effecting it otherwise, and by bravely putting himself at the head of his troops and leading them to the attack. In our service he has freely bled. I feel much for him; for while he is suffering the distresses of painful wounds on a boisterous ocean, he has to combat chagrin. I hope he will be consoled by the assurance that although he has not succeeded according to his wishes and those of America, we regard with approbation his intentions to serve us, and that his want of success will not lessen our idea of his merit.

Georgia gave D'Estaing twenty thousand acres of land in the state. He was grateful. He wrote, "The mark of its satisfaction, which Georgia gave me after I was wounded, was the most healing balm that could have been applied to my pain."

General Lincoln and his troops retreated to Ebenezer, and then to Charleston, South Carolina, where smallpox broke out and weakened the armies. Outnumbered there, he surrendered to Cornwallis on May 12, 1780. In 1781, when the British were defeated, Lincoln would be given the satisfaction by George Washington of accepting the surrender of Cornwallis' army at Yorktown, but that time was not yet. Lincoln and General McIntosh were taken prisoners with their soldiers when Charleston fell. Georgia's official records, which had been sent to Charleston for safekeeping were sent to New Bern, North Carolina, and then to Baltimore, and finally back to Georgia.

The British moved back into Augusta. Colonel Thomas Browne was put in command. Then Congress sent General Horatio Gates to take command of the south. But he soon fled, riding his horse 180 miles in four days. He was greatly criticized, especially by Alexander Hamilton.

General Henry Clinton, the British commander, was jubilant over the success of his plan to capture and hold Savannah and Charleston. But it was not to be for long. He left Cornwallis to "mop up" in the south.

English soldiers were growing tired of a war being fought three thousand miles from their homes. Many soldiers married American girls and changed sides. The British never had more than 25,000 Tories in America.

The state was in the iron grip of the British, all but part of Wilkes County. Here fought Elijah Clarke and his son John along with others. Nancy Hart acted as a spy to bring them information. Sometimes she acted as a crazy woman, going to and fro in the streets of Augusta, but collecting news that would help the patriots to know where the British were and what they were planning. Across the border was General Francis Marion, called "The Swamp Fox," fighting with his little band, living off meager fare. Governor Wright was hanging patriots in Savannah and confiscating the property of Georgians.

ELIJAH CLARKE LED GEORGIANS THROUGH THE DARK DAYS
During the year 1780, the British held Georgia. The siege of Savannah had failed. People on the frontier were suffering incredible hardships. One was the Tyner family. While Richard Tyner was away fighting for the

"Noah's Ark"

patriots, the Indians killed and scalped his wife, killed their baby, and carried off their daughters Mary and Tamar to live in Indian country at Coweta Town. Later, one of the girls was rescued by a man who married her, and the other girl escaped in a canoe. The only one of the Tyners to escape was a small boy named Noah who hid in a hollow tree. It was for years after known as "Noah's Ark."

Major Micajah Williamson had left his family at home to go and fight. The Tories hanged his twelve-year-old son in his wife's presence. Mrs. Williamson took her older children and escaped to South Carolina.

Colonel John Dooly, who had come from the Carolinas and settled in Wilkes, was dragged out of bed and killed, with his wife and children looking on.

General Elijah Clarke, who had come into upper Georgia from Edgecomb County, North Carolina the same year that Georgia was founded, was fighting the British and the Tories. He had been with General Howe on the expedition to Florida. He was wounded, and had to go back to his home in Wilkes to recuperate. His wife and their eight children were there. Clarke's biographer says he never

277

learned to read or write, yet the rough old warrior almost single-handedly saved his section from the British. Louise Hayes has written his biography, titled *The Hero Of Hornet's Nest.*

Like the other settlers, the Clarkes had come into Upper Georgia, cleared land by hard work, built log cabins of the trees they cut down, planted their fields, put up grist mills along the streams and managed to eke out a hard frontier existence wherever they could find fertile soil and good trees. They set up forts in some places. Indian attacks at one time became so frequent and terrible that they had notified the government that unless they got protection, they would have to give up their frontier homes and go back where they came from. But no help came. They were fighting now to keep their homes.

Despite their hardships, there were times when they enjoyed fiddling parties, corn huskings, log rollings, house raisings, and quilting bees. They made rag dolls for their little girls and reed whistles for their boys. They were fiercely patriotic and were good fighters. British soldiers and their Georgia allies, the Tories, roamed and burned and pillaged the homes of these people who refused to take the oath of allegiance of the king. They sometimes took their clothes, even rings, and often beat and insulted the people. They sometimes tried to terrify the children into telling where the family possessions were hidden.

These were friends and neighbors of Clarke, and he was determined that all together they should keep fighting the enemy until they rid Georgia of the hated British. Among those who fought with him were Andrew Pickens, John Dooly, John Twiggs, Benjamin and William Few. William Few was later to become one of Georgia's signers of the U. S. Constitution.

General Clarke had smallpox, which left his face scarred for life, as it did George Washington's. But he got up and went galloping about on his horse to round up patriots to fight these enemies who were inflicting such suffering on his friends and neighbors. Sometimes he crossed over the river and fought in the guerrilla band led by General Francis Marion, who became known as "The Swamp Fox." Sometimes Clarke's wife Hannah would go to camp with him to see that he ate his favorite foods, buttermilk, sassafras and catnip tea, and apple pie, and that he gargled his throat with honey and garlic. She often dressed his wounds. Sometimes Clarke had three hundred soldiers; sometimes he was down to twenty. Once he managed the gigantic feat of taking four hundred women and children over the mountains, out of Georgia, to the safety of Watauga Valley in North Carolina. The British had driven Mrs. Clarke and her children out in the snow, and had even taken their last pony. They also burned his home. Clarke thought it was time to take his own family and the families of his neighbors to a safe place while the war was being fought in Georgia. Clarke was said to have captured a hundred redcoats and killed sixty-three at Musgrove Hill.

Clarke was to get into trouble after the war, but history would give him a secure place, and Georgia would grant him land and name for him the Clarke Dam near Augusta, Clarke County, and the town of Clarkesville. The evidence that these are named for the old warrior and not for his son the governor is that all these names have an "e" in them. Governor John Clark, who would later be the rough and able leader of the frontier men, dropped the "e" because he thought his followers would consider it too aristocratic!

General Elijah Clarke fought up and down Georgia, and all around the swamps. But what he really wanted to do was to take Augusta back from the terrible Tory turncoat, Thomas Browne, who had been put in charge after Campbell left.

The Indians usually helped the British, who could supply them with guns and provide them with gifts. Some of the Indians were also probably loyal to the British because of Oglethorpe, and some of the royal governors who had won their allegiance many years before.

By September, 1780, General Elijah Clarke had rounded up about three hundred fighting men. Their rendezvous had been at Spirit Creek above Augusta. He had trained and drilled them there and at Soap Creek, forty miles above Augusta, until they felt ready to attack Browne and his men.

They began the siege, and drove Browne and forty men into a building then called Seymour's Trading Post. It was later known as the White House, and it has recently been restored. It stands at 1822 Broad Street. Clarke and his men attacked fiercely for four days. Browne and his men barricaded themselves inside. Clarke had no cannon to shoot, so he cut off Browne's supplies. The men inside had no food and no water, and some of them were badly wounded. The Americans outside could hear their pitiful cries for water and for medicine. "Water! Water! they moaned. Their tongues were swollen with thirst, but Browne would not surrender. He himself was wounded in both thighs, but he sat in a chair and kept shooting out the window. He was as brave as he was cruel. His men grew nearly mad with pain, hunger, and thirst, but he made them keep fighting. Clarke and his soldiers besieged the house for four days. On the fifth day, Browne got reinforcements. Cruger, the British commander, sent soldiers from Ninety-Six, South Carolina, and Cherokee Indians sent fifty warriors across the river to help Browne.

THOMAS BROWNE, TORY, HANGED THIRTEEN ON A STAIR

Colonel Thomas Browne had been a Georgian, living in Augusta, when the war began. He was not in favor of independence. When he uttered these sentiments aloud, the Liberty Boys tarred and feathered him. This was a rough and cruel custom that had started in New England early in the Revolution and is reported in many diaries and histories of the war. It usually meant pouring hot tar over the body of a man and then rolling him in feathers from a feather pillow. This the Liberty Boys in Augusta had done to Thomas Browne. Then they put him in a wagon, drawn by three mules, and paraded him through the streets of the town and gave him twenty-four hours to leave Georgia. After Browne had scraped off the tar and feathers with the help of his servant, he fled to South Carolina, furiously swearing revenge on those who had humiliated him.

Governor James Wright at Savannah wrote to one of his friends in England on August 17, 1775, that a "young gentleman, one Mr. Browne, has been most cruelly treated by the 'Liberty people' for his utterances in the town of Augusta and has retired to South Carolina."

Browne joined the British, as did another such man named Thomas Grierson. The British made them lieutenant colonels. They helped the British take Charleston. Browne, aided by Grierson, was put in command of the forts at Augusta after Campbell left.

Clarke finally had to give up the siege. He took most of his men with him, but thirty were so badly wounded that he was forced to leave them behind, in the yard of the house where Browne was barricaded. He thought they would be treated as prisoners of war, but he was wrong. Browne had thirteen of them dragged inside the house, and hanged them, one for each of the thirteen colonies, from the stairway.

The other Americans left in the yard were turned over to the savage Indians, who tortured them. Among these prisoners were two teenage brothers named Glass, fifteen and seventeen. The older one was badly wounded, and when Clarke's soldiers left, his younger brother, refusing to leave him, stayed behind. They both died. A woman from Darien, a widow named McKay, whose son Daniel became a prisoner of Browne, traveled all the way from the coast to plead for his life. She brought baskets of food. Browne ate her food, and hanged her boy and four others whom he had imprisoned in a pig pen.

Clarke, defeated but not discouraged, kept his men fighting guerrilla fashion, swooping down on the British, doing what damage they could, and vanishing. The next May, in 1781, the tide would turn, and Thomas Browne would give up Augusta. Clarke and other brave Americans would have a part in it. And Augusta would be recaptured by America.

A HORSE NAMED "GRAY GOOSE" CAUSED TERROR IN GEORGIA

Much terror was spread in Georgia during the Revolution because of trouble that started about a horse named Gray Goose, a gray mare with a white-starred forehead. She belonged to an American soldier and woodsman named Dan McGirth. An officer wanted the horse, but McGirth refused to sell her. Trouble developed between the two men about this, and McGirth was court martialed for striking the officer. He was sentenced to be lashed with a cowhide whip, ten lashes a day for three days. Back in jail, he tore the bars off the window, whistled for his horse, mounted and rode away under their fire, shaking his fist and vowing revenge. He joined the British, was made a colonel, and spread terror throughout Georgia for the next few years. Creek Chief Alexander McGillivray supplied him with Creek soldiers to help his Tory troops. He galloped over the state, leading the troops from Florida to South Carolina. Americans offered a big reward for his capture, but his horse was so swift that he always eluded them. Once General Twiggs took three hundred soldiers into the swamps of Liberty County to capture him, but McGirth knew the swamps so well and had Gray Goose so expertly trained that he got away. After the war, he went to Florida. He committed some offense against the law there, and was put into prison for five years. When he got out, he was so broken in health that he could hardly travel back to his wife's home in his native South Carolina. There he lived out his years, and there he is buried.

GOVERNOR STEPHEN HEARD WAS RESCUED, BY HIS COOK, IN A CLOTHES BASKET.

During the dark years of the Revolution, the British captured Stephen Heard, who served briefly twice as temporary governor of Georgia and Council president. He was about to be hanged when an old family servant appeared at the jail with a clothes basket on her head. She was a giantess, about six feet tall, named Kate.

Born in Ireland, Heard had fought under General Elijah Clarke, and was one of twenty-three Americans wounded and captured at Kettle Creek. He had been in prison, and was condemned to be hanged. His brother, Major Bernard Heard, had been a British prisoner, and their father, John Heard, had been captured by the British and almost starved before he was rescued. The British had driven Mrs. Heard and her children out of their home and burned it. When Kate appeared at the prison, she asked to be allowed to give her master some clean clothes. "He won't need them. We will soon hang that rebel!" said the jailer. "Let him hang in clean clothes," begged Kate. The jailer let her in. She put Heard, a little man, into her basket, covered him over with clothes, and took him out of prison on her head. Outside, she had waiting his two fine Arab horses, Silver Heels and Lightfoot. They mounted the horses and rode to safety.

"You have saved my life, Kate. I free you," he said, "But I don't free you, Master Stephen," she said. She remained with the Heard family all her life, and is buried in the family graveyard at Heardmont, near Elberton. They

282

had given her a cottage in which she lived with her husband,
Daddy Jack, and their nine children. The Heards were descendants of William the Conqueror and, in Virginia, they
had been neighbors of George Washington and had bought

Arab horses from him. Stephen Heard had once fought under Washington.

The second wife of Heard was Elizabeth Darden, great-niece of George Washington.

ROBERT SALLETTE AND THE "PUMPKIN HEAD"

A mysterious man of the Revolution was named Robert Sallette, of Liberty County. No one knows where he came from, nor where he disappeared when the war was over. He became known as a terror to the Tories. One rich Tory farmer offered a hundred guineas to anybody who would bring him the head of Robert Sallette. One day a man appeared with a sack. He said to the farmer, "I hear that you have offered a reward for the head of Robert Sallette. I have it here." The farmer looked at the sack, then he counted out the money. The young man took the money, and then removed his hat and pointed to his own head.

"Here is the head of Robert Sallette," said the man. The farmer was so frightened to be face to face with this notorious fighter that he could not move. Sallette, with the money, ran from the room, got on his horse and left. In the sack was a pumpkin.

HOW NANCY HART CAPTURED THE TORIES

Nancy Hart was a rough old heroine who was six feet tall, had red hair, blue eyes, and a fiery temper. She did much to help save Georgia from the British. She and her husband Benjamin and their eight children had moved to Elbert County from Carolina. Benjamin Hart's niece married Henry Clay.

Nancy hated the Tories and the British, and helped General Elijah Clarke to get information about them. She could shoot as straight as any man, and when Clarke moved the women to safety across the Georgia border, she refused to go. "I will stay here and fight," she said. The Indians called her "the war woman." Once when she saw an Indian peering between the cracks of her log cabin, she threw a dipperful of the soap which she was stirring in his face. She like to hunt, and often killed deer; she had their antlers hanging all over her house.

When several Tories forced their way into her house, she told them to stack their guns in a corner while she got

A Replica Of Nancy Hart's Cabin

supper ready. To her daughter, she said, "Laura, go to the spring and get some fresh water." Laura blew a conch shell at the spring for help.

When the Tories sat down to eat, Nancy grabbed a gun, and said, "I will kill the first one that moves." She shot one and the others were hanged in her front yard. "They murdered John Dooly," she said. "Now let them hang for it."

After the war and the death of her husband, Nancy married a younger man. She later lived in Kentucky and in Brunswick, Georgia. She is the only woman for whom a county in Georgia is named. Near Elberton is a reproduction of Nancy Hart's cabin; nearby is the spring.

Many years later, the skeletons of the Tories were found in shallow graves, three feet deep. The Atlanta *Constitution,* on December 22, 1912, reported that the skeletons of the six Tories were unearthed by a squad of men at work grading the Elberton and Eastern Railroad. The site was thirteen miles from Elberton.

Washington Sent Greene South

A few weeks after the siege of Savannah had failed, Charleston also fell to the British. That was in May, 1780. They took as prisoners General Benjamin Lincoln, the American commander in charge of southern forces, his staff, and his soldiers. General Horatio Gates, who was sent to command the Patriot troops in the south, soon retreated before the enemy. Washington and Congress then sent his ablest general, Nathaniel Greene, to command the troops in the south. He was from Rhode Island, where he had been a blacksmith and an iron forger. His family were associates of Roger Williams, the famous Baptist preacher who had founded Rhode Island for religious freedom. When the Revolution came, he tried to enlist with his local militia. They rejected him because he had a limp. He was a Quaker and was turned out of the church because they did not favor war. He had no military experience whatsoever. He was, however, a natural military genius, and he found a way to get to General George Washington and offer his services. Greene wrote his wife, "Turn where you will, only widows, fatherless children, ruined houses, plantations laid waste, ruin and misery in every shape are what you will see."

Mrs. Greene was a very remarkable woman who was later to suggest the invention of the cotton gin to Eli Whitney. She and her husband were at Valley Forge with Washington during the dreadful winter. Mrs. Greene had been Catherine Littlefield. Orphaned early, she was adopted by her aunt, who was the wife of the governor of Rhode Island. Greene was also at Brandywine.

When he came south, Greene found troops poorly clothed, fed, and trained. One historian wrote, "It was the same old story, Americans, half-starved, and half-clad, marching, marching, marching." Greene himself said, "We fight, get beat, then get up and fight again." His courage was contagious. He knew that even if he did not win the battles, he could keep enough British soldiers in the south so that they could not go to fight Washington in Virginia.

Once Greene marched his men nine hundred miles in pursuit of Cornwallis. The British commander was so harassed that he burned his heavy baggage so he could

travel lighter and faster to get away from Greene and the American soldiers.

Gradually, the picture brightened.

In May, 1781, Greene ordered General Henry ("Light-horse Harry") Lee, father of Robert E. Lee, to help Clarke and others attack Augusta and try to take it back from the British.

Greene sent Dr. Nathan Brownson of Sunbury, a physician who was head of hospitals in the south during the war, to Augusta to take command of the Georgia government.

THE PATRIOTS TOOK AUGUSTA WITH A CURIOUS TOWER

General "Lighthorse Harry" Lee, with the help of General Andrew Pickens, General Elijah Clarke, General James Jackson and others, now began to concentrate on

287

taking Augusta. It was May 1781,

First the Americans took a fort at Silver Bluff, where the British had stored gifts for the Indians. Then they began their siege of Augusta.

There were two forts there. Fort Cornwallis, Oglethorpe's old Fort Augusta, was commanded by Browne. Fort Grierson was commanded by Grierson. Clarke wanted to cut off Browne's supply line from Galphin's fort.

An officer named Hezekiah Mayham, who had been fighting with Lee in the Carolina battle, remembered a curious device used by ancient warriors: a wooden tower raised so high that guns placed on it could fire down into a fort which could not be stormed any other way. This tower, which came to be known as Mayham's Tower, was used in one of the battles in South Carolina. The Americans built another one on the flat land around the Augusta fort. Browne tried desperately to destroy it, but could not. The fighting started, and with the advantage of the tower, the Americans won.

Browne delayed surrender a few hours, until June 5, because he did not want to surrender on the king's birthday. One of the conditions of his surrender was that he be escorted in safety to the British headquarters in Savannah. Later, he was exchanged and fought against the Americans again. But finally he went to England where, in 1812, he was jailed for forgery and died in prison.

Colonel Grierson, who was as cruel as Browne, was shot while in the fort. Some thought it was done by James or Samuel Alexander, sons of a seventy-eight-year-old Georgian whom Grierson had chained to a wagon and forced to walk many miles, beating him when he slowed down. Greene offered a reward for the name of the man who shot Grierson, but nobody ever told it.

Colonel James Jackson, now twenty-five years old, was left in charge of Augusta after the surrender. Some British sympathizers once threatened to murder Jackson and kidnap Governor Nathan Brownson, who had been elected in June, 1781. David Davis revealed this plot to Jackson, who ordered all troops to report at once. He arrested twenty, court-martialed the three leaders and hanged them. Davis was given a suit of clothes, a horse with a saddle and bridle, three hundred acres of land, and a slave. Sometimes Jackson's soldiers had little food. He wrote, "My men were for months without supplies and for more than forty-eight hours had no rice or bread nor anything like it."

Augusta was short of food and other supplies. Planters like John Wereat sent their servants on flatboats, poled up the Savannah River, with what rice and other food they could spare to feed the people. Some were starving.

But in the north, George Washington was winning and the next autumn the British army was ready to surrender.

"MAD ANTHONY" WAYNE CAME TO FINISH THE WAR

In January, 1782, Washington sent General Anthony Wayne of Pennsylvania to Georgia to finish getting the British out. He set up headquarters at Ebenezer. Even though Cornwallis had surrendered at Yorktown on October 19, 1781, there were still some British soldiers fighting in Georgia.

Wayne had been a successful commander in the north. In Georgia, his idea was to push all the remaining British back into Savannah, and then capture the city. The British were getting desperate. Governor James Wright had written the British commander, "The rebels hold Georgia from Augusta to Ebenezer. Here in Savannah we

Colonel "Lighthorse Harry" Lee

have no beef or pork and no money to buy any. Do not let any women and children be sent here."

The last battle of the Revolution fought in Georgia was at Ogeechee Ferry. The British and Tories were led by the notorious Colonel Thomas Browne, who had been allowed to rejoin the British after he had to surrender Augusta, despite the terrible cruelties he inflicted. Some Indians fought with them. Wayne surprised them in the night, took their horses and ammunition, and captured thirty prisoners. As Wayne pushed on toward Savannah, he met Creek Indians along the way. He treated them kindly, explaining to them that the British had been defeated and could no longer help them. He gave them presents. Many Indians pledged friendship to the Americans. One old chief named Guristersigo, however, took three hundred Indians and attacked Wayne's army about seven miles from Savannah, at three o'clock one morning. Wayne's horse was shot from under him. The old chief was killed and his braves were routed.

In February, 1782, Parliament negotiated for peace with the Americans. Once before, only one vote had kept the war going. Sir Henry Clinton wrote, "All has gone except Savannah." In the spring, Sir Guy Carleton notified Governor James Wright to get ready to leave Savannah.

"All is lost!" mourned King George III in England. "At last the fatal day has come." Lord North said, "Oh dear God, it is all over." The defeat of England brought the downfall of North's ministry. He resigned in March.

Wayne and Wright agreed on July 11, 1782, for the surrender of the British in Savannah. They had held the city since December 29, 1778, three years, six months, and thirteen days.

General Greene wrote Georgia's Governor John Martin to allow Tories another chance to be loyal citizens of Georgia. "Leave a door open for them to come back," Greene advised. "It is always dangerous to push people to the edge of desperation. It is better to save than to destroy. I wish the cause of liberty never to be tarnished with inhumanity, nor the morals of the people bartered in exchange for wealth."

On July 10, 1782, General Wayne wrote an official

order: "As the enemy may be expected daily to evacuate the town, the troops will take care to be provided with a clean shift of linen and to make themselves as respectable as possible for the occasion. Lieutenant Colonel James Jackson, in consideration of his severe and fatiguing service in the advance, is to receive the keys to Savannah and is allowed to enter the western gate." General Jackson was just twenty-six years old.

CHAPTER 19

HOW THE WAR ENDED

After Savannah had been surrendered, and the state government was back there, Governor John Martin gave the Tories time to get their affairs in order and leave. Some took the oath of allegiance and remained, but seven thousand left, starting on July 11, 1782. They took about five thousand slaves with them. Some went to Nova Scotia, some to the West Indies, and some to England. Georgia confiscated the property of many of them.

In the group waiting on Tybee for ships to take them away were Governor James Wright, who was going to England by way of South Carolina and sailed on the "Princess Caroline," and Chief Justice Anthony Stokes. Wright had been in Georgia for thirty-two years, except for a business trip to England (1771-1773) and the brief time after he fled in February. Stokes had never liked Georgia, and it seemed to him the final indignity to have to wait there on the hot beaches of Tybee with no shelter, the pestering sandflies, and the poisonous rattlesnakes. Another Tory who was leaving was the Scot, Lachlan McGillivray, father of the half-breed Creek chief Alexander McGillivray. His property was confiscated. This was one reason why the son hated Georgia and caused so much trouble later.

Governor Martin, who had brought the state government back to Savannah by way of Ebenezer, on July 13, 1781, called the legislature into session on the first Monday in August, 1782. On January 7, 1783, Dr. Lyman Hall was elected governor. George Walton was Chief Justice.

Governor John Martin was born in Rhode Island, where the Greenes also lived before they came to Georgia. He had been a member of the first Provincial Congress in 1775, as a delegate from Savannah, where he lived. He was a lieutenant colonel in the army during the Revolution. Governor

292

Wright called him "Black Jack from the Northward."

He became governor during a difficult time, and he knew it. He said, "I now have the arduous and unthankful office of Chief Magistrate. I sincerely wish that I may be able to conduct myself through this troublesome business with propriety to myself and satisfaction to the public. The moment a man is appointed to an elevated station in life, he that moment becomes a target for every fool to level his arrows at. I expect many rubs, anxieties, and unpleasant moments."

Governor Wright was still in Savannah when Martin was chosen governor, and he wrote sarcastically to the king, "The rebel Governor Martin, now at Ebenezer, has issued three proclamations, one to the king's troops, one to the Hessians, and another to the militia, inviting them all to revolt and join the virtuous Americans against the tyranny of the British government!"

One plantation confiscated by the Americans was that of the printer, James Johnston, whose paper had become the *Royal Gazette* while the British occupied Savannah. His excuse for going over to them was that he was a printer, not a politician. He later got back in the good graces of Georgia, and resumed printing his paper. His nephew, Nicholas, became his partner. When Johnston died in 1808, he was buried in Savannah's Colonial Park Cemetery. His epitaph says, "He knew the art and mystery of printing." In Savannah, the site of this first Georgia newspaper is marked.

Georgians got started with the rebuilding of their lives in a state that had been ravaged by war. Money and food were scarce, and there was almost a salt famine. The government could at first be of little help to them. It had to get started again, too. There were no courthouses; the jury sat on logs and the judge on a stump. The governor and his advisers had to decide which British property would be confiscated and sold. Some property was given to generals and soldiers who had fought for Georgia. Some was sold to provide necessities for the government and to start schools. The government helped the people in such ways as it could to start again with their homes and farms.

Few seeds were obtainable. Sometimes people walked fifty miles to get a handful of seeds to plant a little crop. Money was almost worthless. The old saying "not worth a Continental" comes from this year when the money issued by the Continental Congress lost most of its value. There were few wagons and horses. Many homes had been burned or plundered. Crops had been destroyed, fences burned or pulled down, barns pillaged, livestock killed or stolen or driven off. Half of Georgia's property was gone. Robbers roamed the roads. Legislators carried guns to assembly; the Council furnished ammunition.

Each patriot was now given 250 acres, free of tax for ten years. Many army officers were given plantations. People began to rebuild their state. Soon crops were growing. Tobacco was added to the other crops. Peddlers' wagons were rolling around the country roads. Women were cooking on the hearth, spinning, weaving, and quilting. New cabins were built in the upcountry. Better homes were rising in many places. The plantations were being developed in the coastal section. Georgia was a free state, and would soon be part of a new nation. "Tory" for a long time was a dirty word. Politicians screamed it at each other, and careers were destroyed by it.

The Treaty of Paris, which ended the war, was signed on November 30, 1782. A more detailed treaty, ratified by England, America, and France, was signed September 3, 1783. Benjamin Franklin and John Adams went to Paris to settle these terms. The United States got all the land below Canada, and west of the Mississippi, except for Florida, which went to Spain.

What Became of King George III?

King George III had a tragic end to his life. After the colonies had won the war, and driven the British out of America, King George III was so humiliated that he considered abdicating. Finally, he became insane. Thackeray, lecturing in Georgia in 1853 on "The Four Georges," said, "All the world knows the story of his malady. History presents no sadder picture than that of the old king, blind and deprived of reason, wandering through his palace, addressing imaginary troops that did not exist, holding ghostly court, in his purple gown and snowy beard."

William M. Thackeray

Now and then, he had clear moments, and once Queen Charlotte opened a door and found him playing the harpsichord and singing hymns. When he finished, he knelt and prayed, asking God to either remove his afflictions or resign him to them. As soon as he finished, his reason fled again, and he burst into tears and started babbling with senseless rage. Thackeray described his story as "too terrible for tears." He added, "There was something grand about his courage." His children rebelled against him; they neglected him, too. His colonies were lost. In 1810, he could no longer rule and a regent was appointed. George III, the great-grandfather of Queen Victoria, lived until 1830. Thackeray quoted Shakespeare's words about Lear, which also described King George III: "Vex not his ghost; O, let him pass; he hates him who would upon the rack of this rough world stretch him out longer." And the novelist added, "Fall, dark curtain, upon his pageant, his pride, his grief, his awful tragedy."

Churchill says of George III, "A more conscientious sovereign never sat upon the throne of England." Rip Van Winkle, in Washington Irving's story, was surprised when he came down from the mountain and his twenty-year sleep, to find that at the village tavern they pulled down the picture of King George III and put in its stead a picture of George Washington, the first President of the new United States of America.

How Georgia Rewarded the Generals

The new state of Georgia was so grateful to the generals who had helped rid them of the British that they rewarded many of them, and also made land available for many of the men who had fought under the generals.

Much of the land given to the generals was either confiscated Tory property or was bought with money appropriated by the legislature.

GENERAL GREENE WAS GIVEN MULBERRY GROVE

General Nathaniel Greene was the only general who had fought under Washington for the entire eight years of the Revolution. During the final months of the war, he had been sent to Georgia, replacing General Benjamin Lincoln.

Four of the generals who got land and homes in this way were General Nathaniel Greene, the Quaker from Rhode Island, "Mad Anthony" Wayne, General James Jackson, and General Elijah Clarke.

The Green family came to Mulberry Grove in 1785. The 2,170-acre plantation had belonged to John Graham, the assistant to the third royal governor, Sir James Wright.

It had later come into possession of Patrick Graham, the third president, through inheritance of his wife. Later, the Grahams demanded pay for the confiscated property.

Greene's wife Kitty was regarded as one of the most charming women of her time. When she went to Valley Forge to be with her husband, then Washington's quartermaster general, she was Washington's favorite dancing partner, when there was time for a little gaiety in that bitter winter. Once they had danced four hours without sitting down! When Washington came to Georgia in 1791, he stopped at Mulberry Grove to pay his respects to the widow of his old friend.

Greene enjoyed his Georgia home. He had only a year of life remaining. He lived it there. In October, 1785, he wrote to a friend:

> We found the house, situation and outbuildings
> more convenient and pleasing than we expected.
> The prospect is delightful, and the house mag-
> nificent! We have a coach house, a poultry house,
> a large out-kitchen, stables, a pigeon house that
> will contain a thousand pigeons, a fine smoke-
> house, and a garden that is now in ruins but still
> with a variety of shrubs and flowers.

By April, 1786, he was writing that he was busy planting corn and rice, growing fruit trees, and eating "green peas and as fine lettuce as you ever saw" from his gardens. He wrote of apples, pears, peaches, plums, apricots, nectarines, and "strawberries that measure 8 inches around."

He had some worries. General James Gunn, who was also back in Georgia after the war, challenged Greene to a duel because Greene had reprimanded him about some horses. He sent the challenge by General James Jackson. Greene wrote to ask Washington's advice. Washington told him to ignore it because an officer would forever be in trouble if he had to answer in civil life for every order or reprimand he had to give those under his command in time of war.

Greene was in debt, too. He had spent much of his own money to help with the Revolution. He laid plans to recoup his fortune by going into the lumber business on the coast. He planned to renovate Dungeness, a thirty-room house on Cumberland Island.

General and Mrs. Greene went to Savannah from Mulberry Grove in June, 1786. On the way home, he stopped at a neighbor's house and strolled out with him to look at his fields. The sun was hot and Greene suffered a sunstroke. They took him back to Mulberry Grove, where he died at 6 a.m. on June 16, 1786. He was forty-four years old.

His friend, General Anthony Wayne, was there from his own nearby plantation, Kew Gardens. Wayne wrote of Greene's death to James Jackson, their old war comrade: "Pardon this scrawl; my feelings are too much affected. I have just seen a good man die."

Greene's body was taken to Savannah for a Masonic burial. Presiding was a second William Stephens, grandson of the one who succeeded Oglethorpe. The funeral was paid for by the State of Georgia. Greene's body was buried in the old Graham vault, but everybody later forgot that, and for 114 years the location of his body was unknown. Then it was found, and moved with the body of his son to the plot on Johnson Square marked by a monument. It was dedicated by Lafayette when he was in Savannah in 1825. Greene's son, George Washington Greene, born at Valley Forge, was also buried here when he drowned in Savannah in 1794. Georgia named Greensboro and a county for General Greene.

WAYNE WAS GIVEN TWO PLANTATIONS

In addition to the Kew Gardens plantation, Georgia gave dashing General Anthony Wayne a second plantation, and he asked for a third! He was always disappointed because Greene's plantation was larger than his.

Wayne, a brilliant if erratic general, had been sent to Georgia by Greene, and had pushed the British into Savannah in the final weeks of the war. Gracefully, he had chosen James Jackson to receive the British surrender. Later, he and Wayne were to become political opponents. They ran for Congress, and Jackson demanded a re-election because he thought Wayne's supporters had used unfair tactics. He challenged Wayne's manager, Thomas Gibbon of Effingham County, to a duel. Neither was injured. When the voting was done again, John Milledge was elected.

Wayne was a Pennsylvanian. His daring exploits and

298

victories at Stony Point and elsewhere during the early days of the Revolution had attracted the attention of Washington and Greene. Congress voted him a gold medal. His home in Pennsylvania, like the Georgia town named in his honor, was Waynesboro. Wayne County is also named for him. His wife Polly remained in Pennsylvania, and eventually he left his Georgia home and returned there. He was also reassigned to military duty in the north. While in the south, just before the Georgia campaign, he became ill of swamp malaria, was delirious for many days and hovered between life and death. He was never again the dashing, fiery warrior that he had been. His debts also plagued him because he had little business judgment. His talents were those of the battlefield.

NEW IDEAS CAME OUT OF THE REVOLUTION

The colonists discovered that together they had a strength that none of the thirteen had alone. Together they had defeated the powerful England, which had itself defeated France and Spain.

The colonists also learned that a representative government suited them better than a monarchy. Jefferson had pointed out in the Declaration of Independence that power must come to a government through the consent of the governed. Americans had come to believe that the idea of the "divine right of kings" was nonsense.

But the colonists also learned a greater lesson: that there must be some kind of central government, with law and order, even in a democracy. After the war, they were thirteen separate states, only loosely held together. Their paper money had little value. There was no way to make the states pay their share of the war or for administering a central government. There were few roads, or means of communication. Some states were quarreling among themselves. For instance, Maryland would not let Virginians fish in the Potomac River, and Virginia would not let Maryland's ships through the Chesapeake Bay. Men from both states got together on George Washington's porch at Mt. Vernon and settled this in 1785. They decided that they should get together at Annapolis the next year and talk over their other problems. But few states sent anybody. Even

299

Maryland, the state in which the group met in 1786, would not send anybody. Maryland was aggrieved because it did not own western lands like other colonies. It contended that these lands would make the other states so rich and their taxes so low that colonists would move out of Maryland, so it held out for the other states' deeding their land beyond the Appalachian Mountains to the central government.

At the Annapolis meeting, however, were representatives from five states, and one of them, Alexander Hamilton of New York, suggested that the Continental Congress call a meeting to work out the problems that were troubling them, and strengthen the Articles of Confederation. It was a powerful idea.

When the men met, they drew up the Constitution of the United States of America, probably the most remarkable and powerful document in the world.

The colonists had learned that getting rid of a bad government, like that of George III, does not mean that no government at all is needed. They learned that any good government must be based on law and order, have responsible men at its head, and have some way to enforce its dictates for the good of all. American representative democracy was getting its start.

UNIT 4

GEORGIA, A NEW STATE IN A NEW NATION

CHAPTER 20

FROM WAR'S END
TO CENTURY'S END

The seventeen years between war's end and century's end were full of tremendous happenings and exciting events. Georgians, emerging from the dark and bloody days of the Revolution, had shaped a new state. They had a kindred feeling with the other twelve states that had been colonies, and having suffered with them through the war, now shared the feeling of triumph with them at victory over England. American colonies, free of the domination of a king who had tried to rule them from three thousand miles away across an ocean, had many problems brought by their new freedom. But they had found strength in unity. Now they looked toward a future that would weld them into a new nation. Some, just having cast off the domination of a strong and stubborn king, were reluctant to give too much power to a central government. But they soon found that the loose connection of the colonies through the weak Articles of Confederation would not work. They had to shape a nation that would have workable strength.

Georgia was growing. Though the Tories had taken hundreds of slaves when they left in 1783, the incoming of new settlers to the cheap lands soon increased the number of workers and settlers in Georgia. Soldiers who had fought in Georgia were given free land, whether they were Georgians or not. By 1790, the first official census would show 82,548 people living in Georgia. This was a far cry from the 114 first colonists who came with Oglethorpe, or the 518 listed by John Wesley when he took an unofficial census in Georgia in 1736.

Georgia allowed a newcomer to qualify as a citizen after a three-year residence and a certificate from a grand jury that he was an honest man and not an enemy of the government. But he had to live here seven years before he could hold an office. Because France had helped in the Revolution, Georgia allowed Frenchmen to become citizens, especially those who had married Americans.

With the incoming of new settlers and the opening up of new lands, Savannah was no longer the center of the state. In 1785, the legislature authorized the location of a new capital "within 20 miles of Galphin's old town." A committee appointed on January 26, 1786, to select the city included William Few, soon thereafter one of the two Georgia signers of the new U. S. Constitution, Dr. Nathan Brownson of Sunbury, a Yale graduate who was later governor of Georgia, and Hugh Lawson.

William Few

Before Louisville was laid out, an old slave market had been built at the crossroads for the convenience of planters in the area. It stands today in the center of Louisville, with its bell that was sent by King Louis to a convent in New Orleans, captured by pirates, and sold in Georgia.

It was some time before Louisville, the new capital, was ready. In the meantime, the government was located in Augusta, where it had been from time to time during the Revolution as it fled from Savannah to escape the British.

In 1796, the first meeting of the legislature in the new capital had momentous business on the agenda: the righting of a scandalous wrong from the last session held in 1795 in Augusta, and known in history as the Yazoo Fraud. It involved savage duels, bitter quarrels, golden bribes, a superstitious governor, and "fire from heaven" to burn some historic documents.

People were building homes, not just log cabins in the wilderness but some very beautiful homes over the state. Redman Thornton, a Virginian who came to Georgia, acquired 25,000 acres at Union Point in Greene County, and built a home there in 1785. He had a fine library, five carriages, and many slaves. His home has in recent years been transported to Atlanta and rebuilt in the yard of the Atlanta Art Association, as an example of the attractive homes which were built in this period of Georgia's history.

One of those starting new homes in Georgia after the Revolution was John Johnson, the great-great grandfather of President Lyndon Baines Johnson. He had fought at the Siege of Savannah. He married Ann Ealy in 1787, the year that the Constitutional Convention was held in Philadelphia. They started housekeeping on a tenant farm in Oglethorpe County, near the village of Maxeys. Their son, Jesse, (great-grandfather of the President) was a court officer in Henry County. He decided to go west later, and left Georgia by wagon train with his wife, slaves, cattle, and nine children. As they passed through Alabama, another child, Sam Ealy Johnson, Sr., was born. This was Lyndon Johnson's grandfather. Sam Ealy Johnson, Jr. was the father of Lyndon Baines Johnson, who in 1963 as Vice-President of the United States succeeded to the presidency when President John F. Kennedy was assassinated in Dallas, Texas.

Education was making headlines in this era. Important visitors were coming to the state and leaving an impact on Georgia. Some Frenchmen who lived through the Reign of Terror in France sped to the New World to save their necks from the guillotine. Some bought property on the Georgia coast.

304

Georgia had a state church, the Church of England, which had been set up during the time of the royal province, and any preacher who preached a different doctrine could be arrested. A Georgian invented a steamboat, and got the only patent Georgia ever granted. The first history of Georgia was written by an invalid who wrote from bed or wheel chair, often in pain.

The years between war's end and century's end were colorful and exciting. In them lay the seeds of future prosperity and coming woes and wars!

CHAPTER 21

HOW THE
GOVERNMENT
DEVELOPED

Americans, now free from England, were faced with a problem even harder than fighting a war: shaping a government that was practical and would work.

The New Constitutions: Federal And State

Georgia had adopted a state constitution in 1777, soon after the American Revolution started. In 1787 the new nation, having found that the Articles of Confederation would not work, adopted a national constitution. Georgia's constitution was changed to fit it.

Some states were slow ratifying the federal constitution, but Georgia unanimously did so, the fourth state to ratify. Thereafter, the state constitution had to be changed to be brought into line with the national constitution. The leaders later found that the state constitution could be improved still more; so it was changed more than once before the century ended. A curious thing about the national constitution was that although Georgia was prompt in ratifying the constitution itself, the state waited 148 years to ratify the first ten amendments to it, known as the Bill of Rights. Georgia signed the Bill of Rights on March 18, 1939.

GEORGIA VOTED ITS APPROVAL OF THE NEW U.S. CONSTITUTION

Some states had bitter fights that developed between those who were for the Constitution and those who were against it. Patrick Henry in Virginia, who was against any strong federal government, opposed the new Constitution. So did some other prominent Virginians. Alexander Hamilton, who was fighting for its adoption, knew that Virginia's vote would influence New Yorkers. He arranged for a rider on horseback to gallop to New York with the news when Virginia ratified. This was done, and it did influence New York. Hamilton, with his fellow authors, John Jay, later to be first Chief Justice of the U.S. Supreme Court, and James Madison, later to be president, had already done much to influence public opinion for the new Constitution by writing the Federalist Papers.

Georgia's Assembly was meeting in Augusta until the new capital at Louisville was ready. In February, 1787, it named delegates to go to Philadelphia to work with those from other states in writing the Constitution. The delegates were William Few, William Pierce, Abraham Baldwin, George Walton, William Houstoun, and Nathaniel Pendleton. Only four of these attended: Few, Baldwin, Houstoun, and Pierce. When the Constitution was ready for signing, only Abraham Baldwin and William Few were still there. Both signed it. Pierce said he would have signed it if he had been there. An interesting thing about Pierce is that he kept notes and wrote down his frank, sometimes astonishing, opinions of his colleagues!

Curiously, some of those who had led in the Declaration of Independence were not there when the Constitution was hammered out and signed. Some were out of the country. Thomas Jefferson was in France as U.S. minister. John Adams was in England. Others were absent because they were not in favor of it.

James Madison, later to be president, was there and kept notes, despite Washington's frowning disapproval. It is because he did keep notes that Americans were later to know what went on there in Philadelphia at the Constitutional Convention.

Franklin, who had once worked for Georgia, was there. He often calmed their hot quarrels and guided their actions. When it was all finished, he made a little speech. He said he did not like everything about it, and didn't think anybody did. They had to give a little, take a little, compromise here and there; but they had done their best.

Jefferson had written to Franklin from France, "Dear God, how little my countrymen know what precious blessings they have, which no other people on earth enjoy. I confess

Benjamin Franklin

I had no idea myself. Being over here makes me appreciate America!"

On September 17, 1787, thirty-nine of the fifty-five delegates actually signed the document, including Few and Baldwin. The fifty-five were from twelve states; Rhode Island had not sent any. Then they all went down to the tavern with Washington and Franklin and drank a toast.

Pierce brought a copy of the Constitution to Georgia when he returned south on October 10. It was printed in the *Georgia Gazette*.

The whole world, and posterity, would marvel at the document that these two Georgians and their colleagues from the other states had signed. William Gladstone, the British prime minister would later call it "the most remarkable document ever struck off a given time by the hand of man."

THE TWO WHO SIGNED THE U.S. CONSTITUTION FOR GEORGIA

Of the two men who signed the Constitution of the United States for Georgia, one was from Maryland and the other from Connecticut: William Few and Abraham Baldwin. Baldwin has been memorialized by Georgians. A college at Tifton and a county are named for him. Few remained almost unknown.

Abraham Baldwin may have saved the Constitution when he joined with his Connecticut friends to work out a compromise for the small states, who feared the power of the larger states over them. A personable bachelor who never married, Baldwin was born at Guilford, Connecticut, on November 2, 1754, the son of a New England blacksmith. His mother died when he was fourteen and his father remarried. Baldwin graduated from Yale, studied for the ministry and served as a chaplain in the Revolution. Later he studied law. He was thirty when he came to Georgia. On January 14, 1784, he applied to the legislature for a license to practice law. On October 22, 1784, he was granted two hundred acres of land in Wilkes County. On January 12, 1785, he was elected to the legislature from Wilkes. He served Georgia well as a state legislator. He helped design the University of Georgia and served as its head during the fifteen years when it was in the planning stage. Baldwin was a frugal man, and he helped send his brothers and nephews to college. He crusaded for good roads, and once said, "There is nothing of which we should be more ashamed than our public roads. Some of them are little better than original Indian tracks." Abraham Baldwin's portrait was painted by Robert Fulton, inventor of the steamboat.

Baldwin and his friend James Jackson served together in the U. S. Senate from Georgia for some time. It was a

Abraham Baldwin

wintry day in 1807 when Baldwin died and was buried in Washington. A colleague wrote: "We laid him by the side of his friend, James Jackson, whom he had followed to that place (the cemetery) the year before. It was a stormy day, and five miles from the Capitol, yet everybody who could go, went. Never did I see such solemnity and regret." The U. S. Senate paid for his funeral. In Georgia, members of the legislature wore mourning bands on their arms for him. Richard Malcolm Johnson, the poet, said, "Baldwin was the greatest man who ever lived in Georgia. In some respects, he was greater than Jefferson."

William Few, the other signer, moved away from Georgia after the Revolution. He is therefore not so well known as Baldwin. His ancestors, named Ffew, were Welsh, and came over with William Penn. Born June 3, 1748, in Baltimore, he came to Georgia in 1776, at twenty-eight. He and his brother Benjamin fought bravely during the Revolution. They lived in Wilkes County. He took his books to war with him. He went to the convention that worked on the Articles of Confederation. He represented Georgia in the Continental Congress, was a U. S. Senator, and had served in the Georgia legislature from Richmond County. He was also a judge. He served as a commissioner to settle disputes with the Indians. He lived in Augusta once, but later practiced

310

law in Savannah. He was a trustee of the University of Georgia. He had married Catherine Nicholson, daughter of a commander in the Navy. An old record says that "with her he lived in harmony and affection to the day of his death."

In 1796, he was appointed judge of the Second Judicial Circuit of Georgia. In 1799, after he had become ill, he moved to New York. There he was an alderman and a bank president. He died at the residence of his son-in-law at Fishkill-on-the-Hudson, July 16, 1828.

William Pierce's notes record that Few was about thirty-five years old when he went to the Constitutional Convention in Philadelphia, that he had been twice a member of Congress from Georgia, and had "served in that capacity with fidelity to his state." Pierce thought Few possessed a strong, natural genius and that he spoke "tolerably well."

GEORGIA CHANGED ITS STATE CONSTITUTION

Of Georgia's eight state constitutions adopted since 1776, three were adopted in the eighteenth century.

The first one, adopted in 1777, was the one that Button Gwinnett worked on during the winter after his return from Philadelphia, where he had been one of Georgia's three signers of the Declaration of Independence.

Georgia adopted a new state constitution, so that the state constitution would be in line with the federal Constitution. The governor's term was extended to two years. The Georgia House of Representatives chose three names and the Senate selected one of these for governor.

Each of the eight counties named three representatives to draw up a new constitution. Then, each county would name three more, and these twenty-four would review what the first had done. A third group of twenty-four would then meet later to ratify it. Georgians, who had cast off the rule of the king and his little group, were determined to have a democratic government!

One curious thing about the early state constitution was the little power that was given to the governor. With their bitter experience under the king's tyranny still fresh in the minds of the representatives, they would not entrust too much power to one man again.

Finally, the new constitution was ready in 1789.

311

In 1795, another convention met in Augusta to consider whether a new constitution was needed. This was probably due to the influence of Thomas Jefferson, who had advised the states to have meetings about every five years to look at their constitutions. It turned out that 1795 was a bad year to consider a constitution. The Yazoo matter was at its height, and tempers were flaring. They did, however, adopt eight amendments to the 1789 constitution. This was the year that seven new counties were created in Georgia too. One of the leading men in the 1795 meeting was Noble Wymberly Jones, who had been known as "the Morning Star of Liberty" in the early days.

The next constitution was the one adopted in 1798. By this time, the capital was Louisville. The president of this constitutional convention was Jared Irwin, an old Indian fighter who was twice governor of Georgia. The leading figure in adopting the new constitution was James Jackson, who was then governor.

The 1798 constitution also abolished the ban against ministers becoming legislators. It removed the fine that had been levied for not voting, but it provided that all of a man's taxes must have been paid before he could vote.

These men who devised the 1798 constitution chose for the Georgia seal the words from Plato's *Republic:* "Wisdom, Justice and Moderation." They appear on the Georgia seal today.

Gradually, the constitutions began to give the governor a little more power. They had found that he could not really carry out his duties efficiently with as little power as he had been allowed. One governor begged the legislators not to leave, because without a quorum he could not attend to any state business. At one time, legislators could be fined if they were late; 25¢ for the first ten minutes, and a penny a minute after that. They could not be seated until the fine was paid. They could also be arrested if they were absent without cause, as Button Gwinnett once was. He had been so busy with his own affairs that he had overlooked the date of the meeting. Another time, he had been sick.

The 1798 constitutional convention did its work so well that this constitution lasted with only twenty-three amendments until 1861, when Georgia pulled out of the Union to join the Confederacy and needed another constitution to suit this circumstance. The next constitution was in 1865, when the war was over.

A CONSTITUTIONAL QUESTION SOON AROSE: COULD A CITIZEN SUE A STATE?

That question came up in 1792 in Georgia. A South Carolina man named Chisholm sued the State of Georgia to recover money owed to him. The U. S. marshal served the papers on Georgia's governor and attorney general. Georgia maintained that states were sovereign and could not be sued by a citizen. The Georgia legislature passed a law imposing the death penalty on anybody trying to serve papers in a case such as this on the governor and attorney general. When the case was tried by the U. S. Supreme Court the state refused to defend itself. The Court nevertheless decided that a citizen could sue a state. But Chisholm could not enforce the judgment that he had obtained.

The opinion of the Georgia government was shared in most of the other states and, as a result, the Eleventh Amendment was passed, which denied the right of any citizen to sue a state. It reads:

ARTICLE XI: The judicial power of the United States shall not be construed to extend to any suit in law or equity, commenced or prosecuted against one of the United States by citizens of another state, or by citizens or subjects of any foreign state.

CHAPTER 22

WHAT WAS HAPPENING
IN EDUCATION
AND RELIGION

Schools, colleges, and churches were spreading across the state. Many churches started schools and, in the next century, would establish the beginnings of great colleges. The first college established in Georgia was the first state university to be chartered in the entire nation.

How The Schools Grew

Georgians had always been interested in the education of their children, and the first colonists brought books with them on the ships. The church sent teachers, and other teachers came. Whitefield had set up his orphanage and school and had dreamed of a college there, though it had not developed. Georgians had balked at sending their children to charity schools and the Trustees had to relent and remove the stigma. By 1752, a small budget was set up for the schools. The money for Georgia schools was actually a part of the appropriation of the British Parliament, and the teachers in Georgia were certified by the royal government of England. Colorful personalities came to Georgia to teach.

TUTORS, GOVERNESSES, AND ACADEMIES

The first public school in Savannah was taught by Charles Delamotte with the help of John Wesley. At Ebenezer, the Salzburgers had employed Christopher Ortman as the first teacher in Georgia, and then fired him when he did not please the preacher. The Moravians had set up their school "Irene."

As the planters along the coast grew wealthy, and the merchants in Savannah made money, they began to send their sons north to college. Tutors and governesses were employed to teach their children. Joseph Clay sent his children to school in England because he thought the Georgia schools poor.

The academies began to develop about this time. First was the Richmond Academy in Augusta, chartered by Georgia in 1783, and opened in 1785. In the same decade, academies in Chatham, Glynn, Waynesboro, Sunbury, and Louisville were started. By the time of the War Between the States, Georgia would have over five hundred academies.

In 1783, the legislature set aside a thousand acres of land in each county to provide for schools. Private schools were operating, too. James Cosgrove had a school in Chatham, and had girls as well as boys for pupils. Mrs. Cosgrove helped with the teaching and may have been Georgia's first woman teacher. They advertised that they taught languages grammatically! Some schools offered courses in needlework, embroidery, and manners.

An Old Field School

315

Serano Taylor, musician, artist, and Baptist preacher, started a girls' school at Sparta. He had taught at Richmond Academy in Augusta. At his Sparta school, he had four teachers, 130 pupils and a library of 800 books. The school failed because he paid his teachers too much, bought music and science equipment with his own money, and displeased the community with his violin playing!

THE OLD FIELD SCHOOLS: During the late eighteenth and early nineteenth centuries, old field schools were operated in Georgia, in abandoned fields that had been worn out by cotton. They were often on the edge of a wood, where a spring of water could be easily reached. School teachers often wandered from one community to another applying for jobs, teaching a short term, and moving on to another place. Some were good teachers and some were disreputable. Some were kind and some were cruel. They "boarded" with the families, the board being part of the pay. Each family also paid a small tuition fee.

One Irish schoolmaster, described by Richard Malcolm Johnston in *Early Education in Middle Georgia*, told his scholars:

> Boys, I suppose ye know that the races is to be
> in town tomorrow. Now I advise that ye don't go
> into town at all, and so keep yourselves out of
> temptation. But if ye parents let you go, don't go
> near the racetracks. That's no place for boys. But
> if ye just will go to the races, don't bet! Betting
> is a bad thing for grown people, to say nothing
> of boys. But if ye just will go to town, and if ye
> will go to the races, and if ye will bet, be sure
> to put your money on Abercrombie's mare.

On the other hand, there were gentlemen like Andrew Stephens, teacher-father of Alexander Stephens, who would also become a teacher. The elder Stephens loved children, patiently explained things to them, seldom scolded or raised his voice, and taught them good manners. On Friday afternoons he invited the parents to come share his pride in their children's achievements.

Many teachers in the early Georgia public schools had to have a second job to support their families.

316

THE MYSTERIOUS GEORGIA TEACHER WHO INVENTED A SUBMARINE

One of the most remarkable teachers in Georgia was a "Doctor Bush," who taught school in Columbia County and at Warrenton under an assumed name. He was really David Bushnell of Connecticut, who had invented a submarine. He had been a captain in the American army during the Revolution. He had contrived a submarine to destroy the British fleet in Delaware Bay below Philadelphia. It failed, but it caused the explosion of two or three hundred kegs of powder, and frightened the British. A ridiculous panic ensued. Francis Hopkinson of Philadelphia wrote a poem titled "The Battle of the Kegs," making fun of the submarine. Bushnell went to Europe, and later came to Georgia to visit his friend Abraham Baldwin, and got a job in Columbia County as a teacher under the name of "Doctor Bush." He later settled in Warrenton as a "doctor of physic." He lived in Georgia for about forty years. It was only when he died and his will was executed that his real identity was revealed. Peter Crawford was executor of the will. The doctor directed that a search be made in Seabrook, Connecticut for surviving relatives, and if none be found, the money he left should go to Franklin College, which later became the University of Georgia. But relatives were found and claimed their legacy.

GEORGIA'S UGLY SCHOOLMASTER

"Once when I was still living in my native Ireland, I was walking down the road when an old lady stopped me, stared, and said, 'You are the ugliest man I ever saw. Your face looks as if the devil had been threshing peas on it!' " That was the tale Reverend William McWhir, schoolmaster at Sunbury for thirty years, often told his students on himself. McWhir, who had been headmaster of a school in Virginia, was a friend of George Washington, whose nephews were his pupils. He came in 1793 to head Sunbury Academy, authorized by the legislature on February 14, 1786. He married the widow of Colonel John Baker, bought a plantation called Springfield, and started a private academy near Sunbury. His school attained such a wide reputation that he had to turn students away. Tuition and board had to be half paid in advance, and no student was accepted for less than a year. McWhir advertised in

317

European papers for good teachers, and once he went to Europe to interview some.

After seven years, a hurricane blew his school away. He became again head of the Puritans' academy, and also preached in southeast Georgia. He went to Florida and established churches there.

The University of Georgia, which was then Franklin College, conferred the degree of Doctor of Divinity on him. He lived past ninety, and often visited his former students. They always had for him his two favorite drinks: cold buttermilk and a glass of wine.

At the Midway museum may be seen his mug and one of his Irish blackthorn walking sticks. McWhir was one of the best of the Georgia schoolmasters of his time. He had had smallpox which left his face scarred, like the face of George Washington. McWhir had also lost an eye, and he prematurely became gray. But people who knew him said that the schoolmaster was such a remarkable character that people considered him one of the most attractive personalities in Georgia. He was never an eloquent preacher, but he was an excellent schoolmaster. He is buried at Sunbury.

GEORGIA CHARTERED THE NATION'S FIRST STATE UNIVERSITY

The state had, during the term of Governor John Houstoun, set aside forty thousand acres to be sold to raise money to charter the University of Georgia.

John Milledge, Georgia's eighth governor, gave a 633-acre tract for the actual college site. This was on the edge of the Indian territory on the Oconee River. The Indians watched in wonder, from the forest, as the college went up. The city of Athens began to grow up around it.

This was the first state university in the nation to be chartered. Harvard had been founded in 1636, the College of William and Mary in 1693, and Yale in 1703, but Georgia's was the first state university. Samuel Elbert had been governor when the first bill was passed to set up such a university: "to provide for the full and complete establishment of a public seat of learning in the state." Three Yale graduates, Lyman Hall, Abraham Baldwin, and Nathan Brownson, had a big part in planning the university. They saw it as the capstone of a complete educational system for the state.

318

The charter was lost, and later rescued by a janitor from a basement where the heat and damp had faded it. It is now at the University at Athens. There is also a historical marker on the campus proclaiming the date, 1785, when the university was chartered by the legislature, then meeting in Savannah.

The university did not actually get into operation until after 1800. Abraham Baldwin acted as president during the intervening years. By 1800, he had persuaded his friend, Dr. Josiah Meigs, also a Yale man, to come to Georgia and take the presidency. The legislature had in 1784 set aside 20,000 acres of land, tax exempt, in what was then Washington and Franklin counties, to be sold and put into the university fund. The General Assembly set up two boards, a board of visitors and a board of trustees, which together were called the Senate Academicus. This met in Louisville, July 2, 1779, and decided to get the university into operation.

President Meigs, a brother of Indian Agent Return Jonathan Meigs, left Georgia after a few years. His politics did not agree with that of the trustees, and they demoted and finally dismissed him. Said he, bitterly, on his demotion, "I suppose they will make me Professor of Turnips and Cabbages next." He said later that he had to put in a bill for work as bell ringer to support his family. His daughter married Governor John Forsyth, who later became Secretary of State, minister to Spain, and governor of Georgia. President Meigs later got a government position in Washington.

The University grew, and the first graduating class had ten members. Two were sons of Governor James Jackson. One was later Chief Justice of the Georgia Supreme Court. The sheriff led the first graduation procession, and the custom of the sheriff leading the procession at commencement is now traditional with the college.

Churches — And A Preacher Arrested On His Knees

At one time, Georgia had an official church. It was the Church of England, known now as the Episcopal Church. Georgians were taxed to support it and expected to attend it. The Church of England had been established in England when Henry VIII broke with the Catholic Church over his divorce. The Church was supported by public taxation. In

1758 Georgia was divided into eight "parishes." Under the constitution of the new state, these were changed to counties.

When the Scotch Highlanders came, they had brought with them their Presbyterian faith, for which John Knox had crusaded in Scotland. The first Presbyterian minister was ordained in Georgia on January 21, 1790, under a poplar tree that still stands in Washington, Georgia, and is known as the Presbyterian Oak. His name was John Springer, of Delaware. He weighed over four hundred pounds. He was a teacher as well as a preacher. His Walnut Hill Academy, four miles from Washington, had pupils who were to become famous: William Harris Crawford, ambassador to Napoleon's court, cabinet member, and almost President; John Forsyth, governor, Secretary of State and ambassador to Spain; and Reverend Jesse Mercer, the great Baptist preacher for whom Mercer University was named.

The Independent Presbyterian Church in Savannah stands on the site where a Presbyterian congregation was organized in 1755, about twenty years after the Scotch Highlanders had brought their staunch faith to Georgia. The present building, on the site of one which burned, was erected in 1890, a copy of the one burned in 1815. It has white granite walls, a steeple like those designed by London's famed architect Christopher Wren, and Doric columns. The annex replaces the Manse where Woodrow Wilson was married to Ellen Axson of Rome, by her grandfather, who was then pastor of the Savannah Presbyterian Church. This particular church has never been affiliated with the Scotch Presbyterian church's organization in America.

The first Methodist conference, with ten members, was held in Georgia in April, 1788. Some people believe that John and Charles Wesley introduced Methodism into Georgia but this is not true. They were not Methodists when they were here, but ministers of the Church of England. It was after they returned to England that they established the Methodist Church. Bishop Francis Asbury and Reverend Hope Hull, who rode the circuits on horseback and preached to Methodist congregations in Georgia and other parts of the nation really established this sect here. Bishop Asbury had come to the United States in 1771, and he rode over 300,000 miles on horseback, often studying his Latin and Greek while riding. But the trail in Georgia had been

320

blazed for Asbury and Hull by two preachers named John Major and Thomas Humphries, who began to hold cabin prayer meetings on the frontier about 1784. The first Methodist Church was "Grant's Meeting House" in Wilkes.

The Baptists were the first to protest being taxed to support the Church of England. There were more Baptists in upper Georgia than in any other part of the state. The first Baptist Church to be founded was at Kiokee, twenty miles above Augusta, where a Baptist congregation was started in 1772 by sixty-five-year-old Daniel Marshall, a preacher who went there from Augusta to baptize converts. A church, which still stands, was built there soon after. It was a square building of handmade brick and hand-hewn pews, with a gallery for slaves. The congregation was first known as "Anabaptists," followers of Zwingli, who had started the sect in Zurich, Switzerland, in 1526. The Church of England was still the official church in Georgia and it was against the law to preach any other doctrine. In 1779, Marshall was arrested while on his knees praying. The warrant was served on him by a court officer named James Cartledge. Marshall's wife gave Cartledge such a tongue lashing that he agreed to wait until Marshall was through with his prayer and sermon. Listening, he was converted to the Baptist faith. He arrested Marshall and took him to Augusta, where he was tried and cleared. Afterwards Marshall baptized Cartledge into the Baptist faith. He became a deacon in the church, and finally a Baptist preacher. Marshall's grave is in front of the courthouse of Columbia County, at Appling.

The Baptists were incorporated December 23, 1789. Georgians were not required to go to church. But if they disturbed others who did go, an act passed in 1792 provided that they would be fined five pounds, sentenced to ten days in prison, or get thirty-nine lashes on a bare back!

The first Catholics to set up a church came to Wilkes from Maryland at the end of the eighteenth century. The Spanish Catholics had really been the first religious sect in Georgia, when they set up missions along the Georgia coast to convert the Indians in the sixteenth and seventeenth centuries.

CHAPTER 23

HOW LAND PROBLEMS
MADE HISTORY INTERESTING

Land affected Georgia history, especially in the years after the Revolution. The state had confiscated the lands of the Tories, and much of this was made available to both Georgians and people who came in from other states and countries. Indians ceded more of their land, and this was sold at low rates. Eli Whitney invented the cotton gin, making cotton profitable, and farmers and plantation owners needed more land. (Cotton wore out the land quickly.) Some moved west, as other easterners did, and took slaves with them, hastening the states' rights question that developed into the Civil War.

Creek Indians were still on the rich and fertile land in middle Georgia but did not grow much on it. Georgians wanted it.

Land problems after the Revolution were at the center of many other things: Elijah Clarke and the Oconee uprising; George Washington's visit to Georgia, during which he talked with leaders about the Indian problem; the hatred of Georgia by Creek Chief Alexander McGillivray, who influenced his people not to honor their promises to cede land; the scandalous Yazoo Fraud in which the Georgia legislature sold Georgia's western lands; the incoming of settlers from Virginia and the Carolinas; and the buying of land in the coast country by French noblemen fleeing the guillotine in the French Revolution.

Land, cheaper than it would ever be again, was a problem that influenced Georgia history.

322

Indian Troubles Loomed

Some of the Indians, especially the Creeks, had been on the British side during the Revolution. This, added to the clashes that naturally occurred on the frontier between Indians and settlers, created a problem that Georgia had to settle in these years.

Tecumseh had tried hard to persuade the Indians in the southeast to join in an Indian confederacy to hold their lands against the encroachments of the white men. But they had not all followed him, and later he was defeated.

But the Creeks did listen to one leader, and this was a chief who hated Georgia; he was Alexander McGillivray. He believed he had two reasons to hate Georgia: first, that the white men were taking too much of the lands of his people; and second, the State of Georgia confiscated the property of his father, Lachlan McGillivray of Savannah, who had been on the side of the Tories during the Revolution.

Lachlan McGillivray went among the Creeks in Georgia and Alabama with his wares. He married Sehoy Marchand, daughter of a French captain at Fort Toulouse who had been killed by his own men. She was a member of the Tribe of the Winds.   Lachlan McGillivray settled in Savannah, acquired a great deal of property, and sent his ten-year-old son, Alexander, to school in Charleston. Here he learned the classics and Greek and Latin; more important, here he learned to write well and it was this that influenced his Indian people to make him a young chief. He was sickly and never led his people in battle, but he could present their case well and logically to high officials like George Washington.

Young McGillivray had gone back to his mother's people because he found it dull to work in his father's business in Savannah. After the Revolution, his father went back to Scotland, leaving with the other Tories. He left his wife and daughters in Savannah, hoping that the victors would let them keep his property.

Alexander was already a young chief of the Creeks, made so in 1783, when he was only twenty-three. His Indian name was Hobo-Hili-Miko, which means "the good child king." He had a plantation, many herds of livestock, and dozens of slaves. One of his aides was LeClerc Milford, who had been an officer on Napoleon's staff and had come to

America and married McGillivray's sister. He was a leader in several Indian attacks on Georgia.

McGillivray influenced the Indians, in Georgia especially, not to abide by the treaties which they had signed ceding their lands to the white men and their governments. He wrote Andrew Pickens, a general and later governor, "We want nothing from the white people but justice. We want our hunting grounds preserved from encroachment. They have been ours since the beginning of time. I trust that with the assistance of our friends, we shall be able to maintain them against any attempt to take them from us."

In December, 1787, the United States had sent Dr. James White to Cusseta to see what he could do about this prolonged discord between the Creeks and the State of Georgia.

White wrote a tactful letter from Cusseta to McGillivray, who by now had established one of his homes at Little Tallassee, in the vicinity of Rome. McGillivray answered the letter with a long list of the offenses that the State of Georgia had committed in "trying to take away the land of our people." He even said that Georgia had "assassins with guns employed for atrocious purposes." Finally, McGillivray came to Cusseta to meet White. White asked him to get his people to ratify the treaties of Augusta, Galphinton, and Shoulderbone Creek. They refused. They said, "These are our lands, and if we part with them, we part with our blood." They claimed that Georgia had compelled them to sign the treaties "by threats and the flourish of long knives." White suggested that Congress might set up a new government south of the Altamaha. McGillivray said he would "take the oath of allegiance first" to such a government, and would grant Georgia new lands on the Oconee if it would give up enough lands south of the Altamaha River for such a new government. The idea seemed preposterous to Georgia. Nothing ever came of it. Nothing came of the conference with White at all, unless it was his reporting to Congress that McGillivray was a hard man to handle.

Influenced by McGillivray, the Indians had repudiated treaties they signed at Augusta, at Galphinton and at Shoulderbone Creek in Hancock County. McGillivray had agreed to bring his Creeks to meet the white leaders again, at Rock Landing just below the present Milledgeville on the Oconee River. President George Washington thought this meeting was so important that he sent back to Georgia former General Benjamin Lincoln, who was now Secretary of War. Lincoln and his fellow commissioners met with McGillivray and his two thousand Creeks at Rock Landing on September 20, 1789.

General Lincoln told the Creeks and McGillivray, their leader: "We are now governed by a President, who is like the old King over the waters. He commands all the warriors of the thirteen great fires. He has regard for the welfare of all Indians, and when peace is established between us, he will be your father and you will be his children so that none can do you harm."

McGillivray listened. He was a commanding figure. No picture of him exists, but an old history book gives this description of him:

> General McGillivray was six feet high, spare made, and remarkably erect in person and carriage. His eyes were large, dark, and piercing. His forehead was so peculiarly shaped that the Indians often spoke of it. It commenced expanding at his eyes and widened considerably at the top of his head. It was a bold and lofty forehead, indicative of quick thought and much sagacity. Unless interested in the conversation, he was disposed to be taciturn. He had three uniforms, Spanish, British, and American. His usual dress was a mixture of the Indian and American garb. He always traveled with two Negro servants, David Francis, a half-breed and Paro, a Negro who was said to have saved the lives of a hundred Tories in 1781. He had good houses at Hickory and at Little Tallassee, where he entertained, free of charge, distinguished government agents and persons traveling through his extensive dominions.

The commissioners were amazed to wake up one morning and discover that the whole Indian camp at Rock Landing had vanished in the night. McGillivray sent a messenger with a note saying, "Your terms are not satisfactory and we have left to find forage for our horses."

Georgia had been plagued with a whole series of little wars known as the Oconee Wars. General Elijah Clarke, who had fought in the Revolution, led soldiers against these Indians and asked the federal government for help and troops to deal with the Indians. President Washington first thought of war against the Creeks, but it would be cruel and costly. He decided to try talking personally with McGillivray. He sent Colonel Marius Willett to invite the Creek chief to New York. Willett went to the chief's home, Little Tallassee on the Coosa, and McGillivray agreed to go back with him to New York to see the President. With their party, they left Stone Mountain June 9, 1790.

The Creek chief was royally welcomed to New York by Washington and his staff and by officials of the Tammany political organization. The most fashionable hostesses entertained him, including Abigail Adams, whose husband was vice-president and would later become the second president. Mrs. Adams wrote of the Indians, "We entertained them kindly and they behaved with much civility. McGillivray could talk politics, philosophy, art and literature — and in several languages."

McGillivray and Washington came to an understanding. The Creek did not tell the President that he was already on the Spanish payroll as a brigadier general. He had proposed to help Spain acquire lands between the Chattahoochee and the Mississippi, if they would help Creeks keep their lands in Georgia. He was once employed by England, Spain, and the United States. Washington put him on the payroll as an army officer; he also promised six other chiefs money for services. On August 6, McGillivray signed a treaty agreeing to restore to the State of Georgia the Oconee lands that had been fought over, but reserving for the Creeks the Tallassee country between the Altamaha and the St. Marys, which the Creeks had already ceded to Georgia. Washington sent the Indians back to Georgia on a chartered boat that landed near St. Marys.

McGillivray was astonished to find that he had angered everybody with his treaty. The Indians did not want to give up their Oconee lands. The Georgians were angry because the treaty took back the Tallassee country for the Indians. They also resented the federal government bypassing the state government in dealing with the Indians. This was the first states' rights issue in Georgia. The states' rights issue was later to be settled by the Civil War. Spain was angry because the Creek chief was planning to work with the United States when he was already on their payroll.

McGillivray had a personal enemy who was also a business rival in Indian trade. He was a curious white man named William Bowles, born in or near Baltimore, Maryland in 1763. He had been an actor, a portrait painter, a pirate, and a trader with the Indians. He was also a close friend of Lord Dunmore, governor of the Bahamas, but he had left those islands to make money in the upcountry in Indian trading. He married an Indian maiden and set up residence on the Upper Chattahoochee. Some called him "the prince of scoundrels." Once McGillivray ordered him to leave, saying that if he were not out in twenty-four hours, he would have his ears cut off. Bowles had a temper, too. Once in the U. S. Army, which he joined at sixteen, he became angered about something, took off his uniform, rolled it into a ball and threw it into the ocean!

Now he began to tell the Creeks that McGillivray had sold them out. Nobody profited by the New York treaty but McGillivray himself, said Bowles. The Creeks, already angry, turned against their chief. Saddened, he left the tribe and went to Pensacola where he died in 1793. Refused burial in the churchyard there, he was buried with Masonic rites in the garden of a friend. When he died, the Creeks felt an upsurge of their old affection for him and they mourned him throughout their land.

Their grief for McGillivray, and a reward which the Spanish had offered for the capture of Bowles, prompted them to tie up the white man with ropes and start with him to the Spanish country. They stopped to camp overnight in the swamps, and Bowles gnawed off the ropes and escaped. But he was sick and starving, and they soon found him again in the swamp. They took him to the dungeons of Morro Castle prison in Havana, where he languished and died.

Some thought that Benjamin Hawkins, agent to the Indians, had encouraged the Creeks to capture Bowles. Hawkins felt that with both McGillivray and Bowles out of the way and not influencing the Creeks, some satisfactory treaty could be worked out about the Georgia lands, but when it was signed at Coleraine, a village not far from St. Marys in 1795, it too would be unsatisfactory.

President George Washington was a little surprised to learn that the people of Georgia were very much displeased not only with the terms of the agreement he had made with McGillivray, but with the fact that the federal government would deal directly with an Indian chief and not go through the state government.

George Washington Visited Georgia

President George Washington left Philadelphia, then the capital, in a carriage drawn by four horses, at eleven o'clock on the morning of March 12, 1791, for a trip to the south. Georgia's General James Jackson was with him. There were several others. Behind the carriage was Washington's saddle horse. Traveling about thirty miles a day, the party came to Purrysburg. Washington's diary, now in the Library of Congress, notes: "May 12, 1791. By 5 o'clock we set out for Purrysburg, driving twenty-two miles to breakfast. I was met by a committee from Savannah, Mr. Jones, Colonel Habersham, Mr. John Houstoun, and Mr. Clay, to take me in a boat down the Savannah River. On the way down, I called on the widow of the deceased General Greene, at a place called Mulberry Grove. I asked her how she did." He also stopped to see her on his way back to Augusta. In Savannah, he was saluted with guns and lavishly entertained. He visited General Lachlan McIntosh, who had been with him at Valley Forge. With McIntosh and Anthony Wayne, he inspected the forts. He talked with Georgians about land and the schemes of land companies trying to buy up western lands, which Spain still claimed. Then he started by carriage to Augusta on Sunday, May 15. He conferred with the governor about the Indian problem and other matters, attended a brilliant ball given by Governor and Mrs. Telfair in his honor, and wrote in his diary about the well-dressed ladies he had met in Georgia. He also visited Richmond Academy and heard the pupils debate. Master Edmund Bacon made a speech. After his return to Mount Vernon, he sent each of the students a book. One, inscribed "a premium due to merits," was treasured for years by Judge Adam Smith Clayton of Athens.

Washington, who hated to shake hands even with his close friends because his hands were so large, bowed to each person. He wore elegant clothes, often with velvet and lace and silver buckles; he wore his sword in a white leather scabbard. He was over six feet tall, weighed about 220 pounds, and had blue eyes. His powdered red hair was caught up in a silk bag behind.

Gilbert Stuart's unfinished portrait of him has hung in Georgia schoolrooms for generations. It is one of two unfinished presidential portraits Georgians know. The other is of Franklin D. Roosevelt, who was stricken at Warm Springs in 1945 while an artist was painting his portrait. Nobody knows why Stuart never finished Washington's. The painter had finished several others of Washington. Stuart, who got remarkable expressions on the faces of people he painted by talking to them of what they were interested in, was talking with Washington about the horses at Mount Vernon. The artist's critics, who claimed that he "could not paint below the fifth button" admitted that he got warm skin tones and remarkable expressions on faces. The artist, son of Rhode Island Tories who had fled to England, returned chiefly to paint Washington. He had painted many other famous people in London, including King George III. Stuart was a curious character. He wore elegant clothes, usually of a brown color described as "the color of a crushed flea." He married a girl named Elizabeth, whom he had first noted because she was wearing a yellow satin dress. He was once in jail for debt.

While George Washington was on his visit to Georgia, a committee of the Puritans at Midway wrote him a letter, dated May 12, 1791. They thanked him for the treaty he had made with the Creek Nation, which had promoted more peaceful relations with these troublesome Indians in the Altamaha section. They wrote, "The hatchet is now buried and we smoke with our Indian neighbors the calumet of peace." They also told him that they were glad he had been elected president, and that they joined in welcoming him to Georgia. The letter was signed by a committee that included Reverend Abiel Holmes.

The President left Georgia very early on May 21,

crossing a new bridge, and going to Columbia, South Carolina.

The highway along much of which he rode when he visited in Georgia in 1791 bears the name of George Washington now. It goes from Augusta to Sylvania and Waynesboro, and connects with roads leading to Savannah.

Washington Oak At St. Marys, Planted The Day George Washington Died

Whitney's Gin Increased Demands For Cotton Land

The most far-reaching event that happened in these postwar years was the invention in Georgia of the cotton gin, by a New England school teacher named Eli Whitney.

Whitney, who had an inventive mind, had set up a nail-manufacturing business when he was only fourteen. It did so well that he had to hire an adult to help him. He was late getting to college, and was twenty-six when he graduated from Yale. He was interested in a job as tutor on a plantation in South Carolina. On the boat coming down, he had met the widow of General Nathaniel Greene. She and her

330

children had been to visit relatives in her native Rhode Island. She invited Whitney to visit them at Mulberry Grove, their home near Savannah. A Yale alumnus, Phineas Miller, whom she later married, was already there as farm boss and tutor to her children. He later became Whitney's business partner.

There at Mulberry Grove, Whitney heard Georgia planters talk about how difficult and expensive it was to separate cotton from its seeds. Mrs. Greene, whose watch and embroidery hoops Whitney had repaired, said, "Talk to Mr. Whitney about it. He can solve any problem."

He solved their problem by inventing the cotton gin. An old story says that Mrs. Greene herself put the finishing touch on the invention by handing him her hair brush when he could not find a way to pull the cotton lint through. The cotton engine, soon shortened to "gin," quickly did work that had taken a whole family an entire day to do. Whitney started manufacturing the gins. But he spent most of his profits on court suits against those who infringed on his patent rights. He came to hate Georgia because some of his cases dragged on in the courts for years.

He went back to his home in New England where he started a factory, which soon burned. Whitney later did something that had an even greater effect on American history than the cotton gin: he invented assembly line manufacturing. His product was guns. It occurred to him that instead of making one gun at a time, a factory could manufacture various parts and then these could be assembled into many guns. The United States government ordered his guns.

His cotton gin also had a powerful effect on the country. Up to this time, with hand labor involved, the raising and marketing of cotton had been so expensive that there was little money in it. Now that cotton had become a money crop, with the invention of the gin, men began to plant more cotton. They also needed more slaves to work in the hot cotton fields. This helped entrench the institution of slavery in the South, and gave it new importance. Besides that, there was a larger angle to the matter. Men began to move west in search of more land for cotton. They took their slaves. When there were enough people in a western territory to create a state, this

An Early Cotton Gin

gave them representation in Congress. The North, which had a growing group fiercely interested in the abolition of slavery, developed anxiety lest the slaveholders get more power and thus control the nation, shaping it to the interest of those who owned slaves. The hot question of the moment became, "Should a new state come in as a free state or a slave state?" This influenced politics for many years. Eventually, it would bring about the question of state's rights. It was unquestionably, however, the matter of slavery that brought the states' rights issue to a head. Eli Whitney's cotton gin was more important than anybody dreamed.

Elijah Clarke And The Troublesome Trans-Oconee Republic

A Frenchman named Edmond Charles Genet had come to America to stir up sympathy for the French Revolution. France had helped America fight its Revolution, and there was a great deal of sympathy in this country for France.

Genet landed in Charleston, South Carolina. He made

his way in triumph to Philadelphia and New York. Among the things he wanted to do in America was drive the Spanish out of Louisiana and set up a French republic there. France had owned Louisiana once, and would own it again when Napoleon came to power.

Genet hired General Elijah Clarke, and authorized him to raise an army. Many of the general's old Revolutionary soldiers came flocking to fight with him again. But George Washington disapproved of Genet's scheme, and America asked France to recall him. He never left; he remained in America and married the daughter of New York's Governor Clinton. But his mission failed.

When the plan failed, Clarke was left with his soldiers and no money to support them. He thought of the lands beyond the Oconee. In 1794, he marched them across the river, gave each man 640 acres and promised each 500 more. He designed the Trans-Oconee Republic that was 10 miles wide and stretched 120 miles along the Oconee. Clarke said Georgia owned this land because the Indians had ceded it to the state in the treaty of 1773 at Augusta. George Walton, now a judge, pointed out that it could not be taken for individual Georgians, and that Clarke's attempt might bring on a war.

Clarke and his soldiers started building forts and homes. But Governor George Mathews did not like the scheme. He said the land belonged to the Creeks. President George Washington did not like it. The governor sent for Clarke, who willingly came back to Wilkes County. There the matter was taken up in court. Four justices of the peace heard all the story. They decided that Clarke had broken no law, and the general went back to his Trans-Oconee Republic.

George Washington advised Governor Mathews to stop it; he said that it might bring on a war. Besides, he pointed out, the land belonged to all Georgians if it belonged to any, and Clarke could not give it away himself. Governor Mathews sent the Georgia militia under Jared Irwin, who later became a governor, to destroy the new settlements. They burned the forts, all three of them on the same day: Fort Defiance, near Milledgeville, and Fort Advance and Fort Winston. Clarke had planned to have his capitol at Rock Landing on the Oconee River, six miles from Milledgeville.

Clarke, now past sixty, went home to his wife Hannah, in Wilkes County. Scarred by smallpox, and limping from old battle wounds, he felt discouraged at the failure of his latest venture.

Elijah Clarke died December 15, 1799, one day after George Washington died. Hannah Clarke lived to be ninety. They were buried at Lincolnton, where his will was on file at the courthouse. When the waters of the new dam covered the territory, the Clarke graves were moved.

After the Trans-Oconee Republic matter was settled, Washington sent officials down to meet with the Indians and talk about the Treaty of Coleraine.

The Yazoo Scandal
And The Western Lands

The worst political scandal in Georgia's history occurred between the end of the Revolution and the end of the century. It was known as the Yazoo Fraud. The name came from the western river to which the claim extended.

Land speculators had been trying for years to buy Georgia's western territory, the land that is Alabama and Mississippi today. George Washington had warned the Georgia legislature about this, pointing out that the titles had never been really cleared, and that Spain claimed some of this Yazoo territory.

But the land schemers tried again and again. They attempted to bribe some legislators. Other legislators were convinced by the argument that it would be a good thing for the state to sell these unused western lands to get money to pay up debts to the Revolutionary soldiers. A United States Senator came back home to Georgia to try to convince legislators to sell these lands. His name was James Gunn. He was soundly condemned for his part in the fraud. One promoter came to Georgia to try to bribe men to vote for it. The speculators offered some influential men thousands of acres of the land, free. Some men, like Patrick Henry, genuinely believed the unused land should be sold to pay the debts of the Revolution, including back pay to soldiers.

Finally, the 1795 legislature, the last one to meet in Augusta, voted to sell the lands at a ridiculously low price. The vote in the House of Representatives was nineteen to nine; in the Senate, it was ten to nine. Four companies were involved: the Georgia Company, the Georgia-Mississippi Company, the Upper Mississippi Company, and the Tennessee Company.

THE GOVERNOR FROM GOOSE POND AND THE OILED PEN THAT WOULDN'T WRITE

Opponents of the sale, appalled at the legislature's act, hoped that Governor George Mathews, the Irish governor from Goose Pond, would not sign the bill.

He had come from Virginia in 1784, leading colonists to Broad River. Born in Virginia, August 30, 1739, he had gone at fifteen to fight Indians after they killed his neighbors. Once they shot off his hair, which he wore in a queue. He had fought ably with Washington at Brandywine. Taken prisoner, he suffered cruelly on a British prison ship until released near the end of the war. He had fought in Georgia in the Revolution, had liked the state, and later acquired a farm on Goose Pond in Wilkes County. Here he reared a large family. The girls slept in an attic, and the boys in a lean-to in the back. Though prosperous, Mathews continued to call the log cabin with a dirt floor home. He was a somewhat eccentric man, and was married three times. He divorced one wife, in that day when divorces were rare and could only be granted by an act of the legislature, because he was angry when she went to visit her relatives against his wishes. When she sent for him to get her, he refused. "I did not take her, and I will not go to bring her back," he said. Mathews spelled coffee "kaughy," dictated his speeches and sent them to an Irish schoolmaster, Francis Simmons, to be "grammared up."

Joel Chandler Harris, in *Stories of Georgia*, says that the governor was a superstitious man, and his secretary dipped his goose quill pen in oil so that it would not write. He thought the old governor might consider that a bad omen and refuse to sign the Yazoo bill. Mathews had vetoed a similar bill in 1794. He was an honest man, but the pressure on him, from very influential people, was too great, and he signed the Yazoo bill on January 7, 1795. Two of his sons bought western lands.

Later, when he realized how bitterly people resented his action, he moved out of the state he had served twice as governor and once as congressman, and went to Florida. Governor George Gilmer wrote of the colorful old man in his *Sketches Of The Early Settlers In Upper Georgia.* President John Adams nominated him for governor of the Mississippi Territory. He was an able man.

Despite this fine record, some senators refused to confirm President Adams' nomination of Mathews and the President withdrew it. Mathews was furious. He threatened to go to "lick the President." He went to Philadelphia, appeared at the White House door, and ordered a servant to tell Adams that a gentleman from Georgia was there to see him. When the servant protested that the President was busy, Mathews said, "He is not too busy to see me. Do you see this sword? Go tell him I am here, or I will use it to cut your head off." Adams came, calmed him down, and listened to him.

Mathews said, "I understand you nominated me for this office. If you did not know me, you should not have done it. If you did know me and did it, you should stick by it." He didn't get the job, but Adams did appoint Mathews' son John as supervisor of revenue. Said Mathews, "My son is about my inches, with the advantage of a liberal education. On his integrity, I pledge my head." Governor George Gilmer wrote in his book on his Wilkes County neighbors that Mathews was "a short, thick man who stood very straight on short legs. He had red hair, and fair complexion. He wore knee breeches, top boots, a three-cornered hat and a dangling sword. He admitted no superior but George Washington."

Later, President Madison appointed him to settle some territorial disputes with Spain in Florida. He made a treaty, but Spain said he made it with improperly constituted authority, and Madison repudiated it. Mathews was furious for the second time with a president, and was on his way to Washington to thrash Madison when he fell ill in Augusta. He had worked hard, and was exposed to malaria in the fever-ridden swamps. It was all too much strain on his poor old heart. He died of a stroke in Augusta, in his seventy-third year, in 1812. He is buried in St. Paul's churchyard. He had never got over his sadness at the way his neighbors in Georgia felt about his signing the Yazoo bill in 1795.

JACKSON FOUGHT THE YAZOO WITH PEN AND PISTOL

Fiery little James Jackson, with the king-size sense of honor, was in Washington representing Georgia in Congress when he heard that the Yazoo bill had become law. He was furious. The Yazoo men offered him a half million acres just for the use of his name. He scorned them.

Jackson was chosen governor but rejected the office because he thought he was too young. Ten years later, he accepted it. He had been given a house, "The Cedars," in Savannah, by a grateful Georgia because of his valor in the war. He married Mary Charlotte Young, with whom he was so happy that he did not like to leave home, even on matters of business. Once he wistfully wrote her from Washington, "I got no letter today. Two boats have arrived, and still no mail for me. What am I to think, darling?" He said in his will that he would like for his wife to marry again after his death if she could find "an honest, worthy man deserving her love."

Burning The Yazoo Fraud Papers

337

This was the hot-tempered, honorable little man who resigned from Congress and came charging home, indignant, to right the wrong of the Yazoo Fraud. He was elected to the 1796 legislature from Chatham County. He wrote letters to the newspapers, signed "Silicus." They were later published in a book, *The Letters Of Silicus to the Citizens of Georgia.* He went up and down the state telling the people that the Yazoo lands belonged to them. "I and my comrades fought for them in the Revolution. They belong to you and your children. The legislature has no right to vote them away. This dreadful wrong must be righted." The 1796 legislature, meeting in Louisville, voted to rescind the Yazoo law. Jackson was chairman of a committee named to reconsider the matter. The committee included two other future governors, David Brydie Mitchell and David Emanuel; and William Few, one of Georgia's two signers of the Constitution. The Act to Rescind passed the House forty-four to three, and the Senate fourteen to four.

Jared Irwin was governor. He signed this bill February 15, 1796. The legislators and state officers filed out of the new capitol, and burned the infamous papers the same day. An old story says that an old white-haired man rode up on a grey horse, and said, "We must call down fire from heaven to burn such vile papers as these," and held a sunglass over them to kindle flame from the sun. As the papers were burning, the Secretary of State prayed, "God save the State of Georgia, and preserve her rights, and may every attempt to injure them perish as these wicked and corrupt acts now do." A stone on the courthouse lawn in Louisville marks the site.

Jackson forbade any mention of these Acts in Georgia's legal reports. When a lawyer named Robert Watkins, appointed to edit and publish the reports, put in both the act and its repeal, Jackson literally tore the pages out, refused to sign the state pay warrant for the reports, and fought three duels with Watkins about it.

Reaction had set in now against the men who signed the Yazoo Act. Most were defeated. Some of them hid rather than brave the wrath of their neighbors. One was hanged, and one was followed to South Carolina and murdered. Many were boycotted by their neighbors, socially and in business.

When Jackson became governor, he led in the adoption of a new constitution, which decreed that any bill must mention in the title every matter that is contained in the body. He felt that one of the reasons for the passage of the Yazoo bill was that its title was simple, and the damage was down in the fine print which some legislators did not read carefully.

The Yazoo matter was really not ended until long after Jackson's death in 1806. The U. S. Supreme Court, of which John Marshall was then Chief Justice, handed down a decision in 1810 which denied Georgia's right to repeal the Yazoo Act because the repeal affected the validity of a contract. The case was Fletcher vs. Peck. George Walton, then a Georgia judge, had said the same thing. By this time the lands had passed into the hands of some people who were innocent of wrongdoing. The United States, to which Georgia sold its western lands in 1802, had to pay about four million dollars to the owners of Yazoo lands.

J. Harris Chappell, first president of the Woman's College of Georgia, wrote in his history, that "The Yazoo was the strangest instance of wholesale corruption of public officials in American history." Henry Adams wrote, "A more flagrant case of wholesale legislative corruption was never known."

Jackson went back to Washington as a Georgia senator after he had served as governor. He died there March 19, 1806, after three months' illness. John Quincy Adams noted in his diary, "Mr. Jackson, one of our senators from the State of Georgia, died at 4 o'clock this morning. His disorder was the dropsy. His colleague, Mr. Abraham Baldwin, told us of the event with tears in his eyes." Thomas Hart Benton said that Jackson's death was hastened by all the twenty-three duels he had fought. He was buried first in Rock Creek Park cemetery in Washington, and was later moved to the Congressional Cemetery. In Savannah, an empty coffin was put into the earth at a Masonic funeral for him.

Some called Jackson a "brawling pygmy." But Thomas Spalding of Sapelo called him "the noblest man I ever knew." Jackson himself said, "If you cut my heart open, you will find 'Georgia' engraved upon it." His courageous fight for the honor of Georgia, like his valiant deeds for the state in the Revolution, gave evidence that he did love the state which he had chosen above his native England. A very large portrait of him hangs in the Capitol in Atlanta.

SENATOR JAMES GUNN AND HIS STRANGE DEATH

The man who worked hardest to get the Yazoo Act passed was James Gunn. He always claimed that he sincerely believed it was the right thing to do, and that those who did not agree with that did him an injustice. He was sensitive about his honor.

Gunn died at Louisville, Georgia. On August 6, 1801, the *Gazette* reported, "Senator James Gunn arrived in Louisville last Sunday, and died about 11 p.m. after a short illness. Said death was due to a draught of cold water after taking medicine. What is strange to observe is that several gentlemen were in his room and not one of them observed his death until sometime after he had expired. He was buried with the honors of war."

His grave is in an old cemetery in Louisville, with this inscription: "Here lies the body of Brigadier General James Gunn, who died on the 30th day of July, 1801, aged 48 years, 4 mos. and 17 days."

CHAPTER 24

HAPPENINGS
THAT MADE
THE HEADLINES

The newspapers reflect many other important things that were happening as the eighteenth century drew to a close in Georgia. A Georgian invented a steamboat before Robert Fulton successfully demonstrated his *Clermont* on the Hudson River in New York. A Georgian wrote the history of the state.

Longstreet Invented A
Steamboat Before Robert Fulton Did

During the latter part of the eighteenth century, a Georgian named William Longstreet was working on a steamboat. He finished it before Robert Fulton patented one and ran it successfully in New York.

On September 20, 1790, the inventor wrote a wistful letter to Georgia's Governor Edward Telfair, who was also a boat builder. In the letter, he wrote, "I make no doubt that you have heard of my steamboat, and as often heard it laughed at."

Longstreet worked on his invention for ten years, suffering poverty, derision and neglect, but he finally had a steamboat that would actually run. It made a short trip up the Savannah River, and broke into pieces! He had obtained a patent for it, however, issued on February 1, 1788 to him

Stern View Of An Early Steamboat

and a partner named Isaac Briggs. This was the only patent ever granted by the State of Georgia. After this, the federal government took over the issuing of patents for inventions. When Longstreet heard that Fulton had patented and demonstrated a successful steamboat in New York, he gave up his dream, which he had no money to pursue further. He is buried in St. Paul's Churchyard in Augusta.

Captain Hugh McCall
Wrote Georgia's History

An invalid, Captain Hugh McCall, who sometimes wrote when he was in agonizing pain, was one of Georgia's first historians. Some discount his history because it was not documented. He relied much on the memory of men who had made history. Some people confuse him with his uncle, who fought in the Revolution, because they had the same name. McCall, the historian, was only eight years old when the Revolution began.

McCall was born in North Carolina on February 17, 1767. He heard the stories of the war, and knew the people who had fought. He himself was a member of the militia, and was interested in old battles and the soldiers who had fought to free Georgia from the British. Hugh McCall began his history because he felt that it should all be written down while people remembered, and he talked with the men that had fought the British and the Indians. He knew the people who had coped with the hardships at home. He felt that those that lived in later years should have a written record of earlier people and times, so that new generations might appreciate them.

McCall was a small man, a bachelor and sick most of his life. He often wore a huge overcoat, looking like a little boy dressed in his father's clothes. Someone who knew him described him as having "windblown hair, big nose, uncertain eyes, a thick mouth, and delicate hands." Sometimes he wrote in his wheelchair, sometimes in bed. But he kept on writing, and finally, he had two volumes of Georgia history completed.

His history was titled *The History of Georgia Containing Brief Sketches of the Most Remarkable Events Leading Up to the Present Day.* He began writing it soon after the British left in 1782. One volume was printed in 1784, the second volume in 1816. Some of the history is not quite accurate, but it is interesting. Both volumes were reprinted in 1822 and in 1909. One publisher prefaced a reprint with these words: "It will be helpful to Georgians of this day to read of what Georgians of that day did and suffered." There are few histories of unfaltering accuracy. Even with the most painstaking research, historians make some mistakes. The remarkable thing about McCall is not only that he thought of writing down Georgia's early history, but that he, an invalid, could have written a history at all.

Hugh McCall died June 10, 1824, and is buried in the Colonial Park Cemetery in Savannah. The epitaph on his grave has these words: "Sacred to the memory of Hugh McCall. Brevet Major in the U. S. Army, born in North Carolina, February 17, 1767, June 10, 1824."

The Savannah Historical Society owns an oil portrait of McCall.

The first official historian would not be appointed until 1824, the year of McCall's death. He was Joseph Vallence Bevan, born in Ireland in 1798.

Some colorful men had been chosen by the legislature as governors of Georgia since the first constitution was adopted in 1777. The first one, Salzburger John Treutlen, served only about six months. John Houstoun, the second governor, was just ending his term when the British captured Savannah in December, 1778, and was prevented by the constitution from attempting to "hold over" under any circumstance. In that crisis, Georgia had no governor; this led to confusion when the government in exile from Savannah broke into factions and chose both John Wereat and George Walton before they could agree on Richard Howley. Howley had also been named a delegate to the Continental Congress, and after two months he left Georgia and went to Philadelphia. That left George Wells, president of the Council, as acting governor. He was killed within a few weeks in a duel with James Jackson. Jackson explained that he had not liked Wells' "overbearing disposition." This led to a quarrel which they felt only a duel would settle. Humphrey Wells was acting head of Georgia for two days! Stephen Heard was governor for a brief time, and when he left for North Carolina, Myrick Davies held the government together until a new governor could be chosen. This was John Martin, who carried the government back to Savannah after the British left and America had won the war.

Dr. Lyman Hall was elected governor. In his gubernatorial message he urged the people to "set up seminaries of learning, to educate the young people, and to establish a university."

Dr. Nathan Brownson, who was a member of the Continental Congress from 1776 to 1778, was also president of Georgia's Executive Council. He was born in Connecticut, like Lyman Hall and Abraham Baldwin and, like them, he was a graduate of Yale. He also helped them design the charter for the University of Georgia. Brownson had a merry wife and, when she did not move fast enough to suit him, he would say, "I will come back in some form and haunt you if I die first." When she was an old, old lady, she would sit brushing away a buzzing fly and muttering, "Get away, Dr. Brownson, don't bother me!" The Brownsons, who were devoted to each other, are buried at Midway.

John Houstoun was governor again, the first one to serve for a second time. The son of Sir Patrick Houstoun, a British nobleman, John was born near Augusta, but centered his career around Savannah, where he was once mayor.

After his second term, he turned the governor's office over to former Revolutionary General Samuel Elbert, for whom Elbert County is named. He was born in South Carolina, the son of a Baptist preacher. After he was governor, he served as sheriff in Chatham County. He is buried in Savannah's Colonial Park Cemetery.

George Mathews, "the governor from Goose Pond," was the one who figured in the Yazoo land deal. Edward Telfair, a wealthy Savannah merchant and planter, was governor when George Washington came to visit Georgia. He served twice. The Telfair Academy of Art and Science in Savannah is his former residence. George Handley is the

Telfair Academy

345

governor of this era about whom the least is known. He was chosen governor when James Jackson declined the office. Handley was a former soldier with a valiant record, and was a dependable civil officer. Jared Irwin was governor in this era, and again when the capital was moved from Louisville. James Jackson was the governor who was in office when the century ended, but would soon go to the U. S. Senate.

When The Century Ended

By the end of the century, the end of life had come to several men who had been a part of Georgia's story. Oglethorpe, founder of the little colony of Georgia in 1733, had died in England at eighty-nine. George Washington, who had visited Georgia in 1791, died on December 14, 1799, at his home at Mount Vernon, of pneumonia which he contracted after he came in from a rainy, cold ride over his farm. His wife Martha, at his bedside, had said, " 'Tis well. I shall soon join him." John Wesley, the powerful little preacher who had stirred England and was sadly unhappy in Georgia, had died. So had Benjamin Franklin, who had been Georgia's agent in England, and for whom Georgia named a college, a county, and a town.

Thomas Jefferson of Virginia was president, having defeated the dumpy little New Englander, John Adams, whose son, John Quincy Adams would later defeat a great Georgian for the presidency in 1824. Georgia's two United States senators were Abraham Baldwin and James Gunn, who died that year.

Men were seeking new lands in the west. Where settlers went, states developed. The question of whether the states would be slave states or free states had to be decided.

But what kind of west, slave or free? The question, which was a big part of the whole state's rights question, had to be answered, and a terrible and bloody answer it would be. But before the guns started firing, there was a colorful half century and a decade intervening.

INTO THE 1800'S

UNIT 5

PLANTATIONS, POLITICS, AND PERSONALITIES

CHAPTER 25

PREVIEW OF THE

HUNDRED YEARS AHEAD

Introduction

The 1800's, the new nineteenth century, was to be a colorful, tempestuous era. There were 162,686 people in Georgia, according to the 1800 census. This was great growth, for the first official census, taken in 1790, listed only 82,000. Fiery little James Jackson was governor of Georgia. John Adams of New England was president of the United States; he was the first to occupy the White House, where his wife Abigail hung out the wash in the famed East Room. The national capital was moved to Washington, "the city of magnificent distances." The city was laid out by the Frenchman. Pierre L'Enfant.

In Georgia, the great plantation system was growing up. It had started during the regime of Royal Governor James Wright. The Trustees had lifted their ban on slaves and had also changed the rule against Georgians having complete title to their property, so men acquired great plantations. Slavery, which had appeared to be dying out, took on new vigor after Eli Whitney invented the cotton gin and made cotton a money crop with undreamed profits. Men who had money and made more acquired huge tracts of land, especially in the coast country. But up-country, there were small farmers and frontier settlers who had acquired little tracts of cheap or free land after the Revolution. They were often uneducated but intelligent, and fiercely independent. Later these two groups, the great planters and the frontier farmers, were to shape the pattern of Georgia politics into two bitterly feuding factions.

349

Visitors came and left their imprint: the great Lafayette; the British novelist Thackeray; Seward, who was later to buy Alaska; Vice-President Aaron Burr, fleeing the ghost of Alexander Hamilton, whom he had killed in a duel; and a brilliant British actress who would write here a bitter book that may years later have doomed the Confederacy. A lady-in-waiting to Queen Victoria came, and resigned when she returned to England to keep from embarassing the queen with views she had acquired in Georgia.

Georgians helped Texas fight for independence. Texas chose a Georgian for its second president, and erected a monument to a teenage Georgia girl.

Education made surprising strides, and colleges figured in curious stories. Involved with the colleges, and the churches which established them, would be China's Madame Chiang Kai-shek; Kitty, a slave girl who split the Methodists North and South; Sidney Lanier, Georgia's first great poet; the Baptist preacher Jesse Mercer; and a man buried standing up.

Georgia began to take care of its mentally ill, its blind and its deaf. Railroads spread over the state. Reluctantly, Georgia, which did not want one, established a state supreme court. Businessmen in Savannah sent the first steamship across the Atlantic Ocean and alarmed Europe, which thought it had come to rescue Napoleon from his island prison.

And all the time, during this first half of the century, the shadow of a great war was over the land.

Problems The Government Faced

The new century brought a number of problems for the governor and the General Assembly and the people. One was what to do with the western lands that had been sold to and then taken away from the land companies in the Yazoo Fraud matter. Another interest that developed was the exploring of western lands bought by the state and the federal government. The capital at Louisville was proving to be unhealthful, and a new capital was needed. New political factions were developing, but the War of 1812 with England came along and pushed this and the Indian problem into the background for awhile. States.

350

The court situation was in what some newspapers called a "dreadful muddle." There was no state supreme court. Each local court could interpret the law to suit itself; yet the legislature and the people were reluctant to invest power in one high court. These were some of the problems confronting Georgia as the new century began.

Georgia Sold Western Lands To The United States For $1,250,000 And A Promise

Nothing had caused more trouble in Georgia than the lands that the state claimed between the Chattahoochee and the Mississippi rivers. This is the area that is now Alabama and Mississippi, the lands sold in the infamous Yazoo Fraud. The 1796 legislature had rescinded the action, though lawyers like George Walton warned that it could not be done. The United States Supreme Court was later to prove him right.

Tired of the whole affair, the legislature voted to sell the western lands, which it thought the state now possessed again after rescinding the 1795 sale, to the United States government. In 1802, Georgia sold the land for $1,250,000 and the federal government's promise to remove the Indians, who still occupied over 30 million acres, from Georgia's remaining territory. This promise was to cause real trouble later. Twenty years afterward, it had not been kept.

Jefferson Chose A Former Georgian To Explore The Northwest

Western lands played a still more prominent part in the American story when President Thomas Jefferson bought from Napoleon the vast territory known later as the Louisiana Purchase. He had wanted to buy New Orleans because France was blocking the American ships that needed to use that port. He was surprised to find that Napoleon was willing to sell the whole territory.

It was ironic that Jefferson, who had disagreed with Hamilton on the federal government's having strong powers, was the president who used the authority of the national government to make this vast purchase. It was a wise investment, however, and doubled the size of the United

351

Thomas Jefferson

Jefferson wanted the new land explored, and a path charted to the Pacific Ocean. For this task, he chose his young Virginia neighbor who had lived for some years in Georgia, Meriwether Lewis, known as "Merne" Lewis. Lewis's father had been killed in the Revolution, and his mother had married Captain John Marks, who soon moved the family to land he owned on the Broad River in Georgia.

Gilmer, in his book about these early settlers in upper Georgia, writes of young Lewis. One anecdote he relates is the boy's quick thinking in dousing a campfire in the woods to keep the Indians from finding a group of white settlers that had fled before their savage fury.

Lewis went back to Virginia to go to college, and to tend land his father had left him there. When Jefferson became president, he named Lewis his private secretary and the young man moved into the White House. Then he met many famous men, like Thomas Paine, and the poet, Joel Barlow, brother-in-law of Georgia's Abraham Baldwin.

Lewis had had experience exploring and fighting in Indian country. He had fought under General Anthony Wayne, who had also once lived in Georgia. Jefferson asked Lewis to head the expedition to explore the West. He invited his friend, Captain William Clark, to share the leadership of the expedition with him. They led their men over eight thousand miles, with the help of a young Indian squaw called Sacejawea, known also as the Bird Woman. Many schools, rivers, streets, and other sites are named for them, and there are statues of the Indian maiden in many places in the West. A university is named for Lewis and Clark. Lewis never married. All his life, so an old story goes, he loved Theodosia Burr, the only daughter of Aaron Burr, but she married Governor Joseph Alston of South Carolina, and disappeared when the ship vanished as she journeyed to New York to visit her father. Later, Lewis was made governor of the territory he explored, and died mysteriously on his way to Washington to report on his administration of the territory.

The journals kept on the famed expedition are now classics. Lewis and Clark took twenty-nine men on the venture. They started in 1804, opening up the route to the Missouri River, then to the Pacific. Lewis wrote on May 26, 1805, "I behold the Rocky Mountains for the first time." On November 7, 1805, Clark wrote, "The fog has lifted; the ocean (Pacific) which we have been so anxious to see, is in view. Ah, the joy!" Their journey took them two and a half years. Once they were so near starvation that they ate a pony; another time, a whale. In 1806, the journey was over. On his thirty-first birthday, Lewis wrote, "This is my 31st birthday. I figure I am halfway through the years I have to spend on this earth." He was wrong. He was dead at thirty-five. Whether he was murdered or committed suicide, nobody really knows.

Jefferson wrote the epitaph on Lewis's lonely grave

in Tennessee: "Of courage undaunted, possessing a firmness and perseverance of purpose which nothing but impossibilities could divert from its direction."

The city of St. Louis has erected a tremendous arch, seventy-five feet higher than the Washington Monument, to commemorate the whole westward expansion, especially the Lewis and Clark Expedition. Many years after Lewis and Clark, John C. Fremont, the "Pathfinder of the West" who was born in Georgia, would also help open up the West. Many were the Georgians who went west in search of land and gold.

Meriwether Lewis

Back in Georgia, there was another small "westward movement"; the state capital, which had followed the center of population from Savannah to Augusta to Louisville, was making another move westward, to Milledgeville, where it

354

would remain until 1868.

James Jackson, who had been governor as the new century started, went to Washington as United States Senator. He was succeeded by Governor David Emanuel, who served only a short time. Emanuel was the only governor of the Jewish faith that Georgia has had. He was an able man. During the Revolution, he had been captured by the British. They had promised his clothes to a Negro orderly to execute him, but Emanuel escaped, hiding in a mudhole until he could reach American lines. Josiah Tattnall followed him as governor. He became ill, went to Nassau, and died. He was followed as governor by John Milledge.

The Capital Was Moved To Milledgeville

On May 11, 1803, the Georgia legislature, meeting at the capital in Louisville, appointed a committee to pick the site for a new capital. Louisville had become malarial, and they wanted a more healthful place closer to the center of the state's population. General John Clark was chairman of the committee. They had evidently already decided to name the new capital for the governor, John Milledge, when on September 27, 1804 Clark wrote the governor a letter from Milledgeville:

Dear Sir:
The business upon which I came here, we have found to be extremely troublesome. To do it with accuracy and to the best advantage required much time and labour. We have agreed upon a plan. Since my arrival here I have had a severe bilious attack so much as to be confined to my bed for eight or ten days; but being able to procure the constant attendance of a pretty good physician, I am now quite recovered and shall set out for Wilkes in the morning. I cannot ascribe any part of the cause of my sickness to this place. It is as well watered with good springs as any place I ever saw and every other appearances are in favor of its being a healthy situa-

tion. With much respect, I am, Your Excellencys Hble. Servant, John Clark.

Milledgeville was to remain the capital for more than sixty years, until after the War Between the States. John Clark himself was later to be one of the governors who would be elected there. It was to be the focus of great happenings: bitter political fights, hospitality to Lafayette, the momentous secession convention, the dramatic quarrels between Troup and the federal government, and between Joe Brown and the Confederate president Jefferson Davis.

THE GOVERNOR'S WIFE AND THE OXCART

On December 12, 1804, the General Assembly in Louisville officially proclaimed Milledgeville as the new capital. The governor issued a proclamation calling for the next meeting of the legislature in Milledgeville. Actually, it was three years later when the first legislative session was held in Milledgeville. The capital was not moved there until 1807.

On October 9, 1807, the Louisville *Gazette* noted, "Yesterday fifteen wagons left this place for Milledgeville with the Treasury and Public Records of this State. They were escorted by the troop of horse from Washington county, who had arrived here a few days hence for that purpose."

By this time, John Milledge, for whom the new capital was named, was no longer governor. He had been appointed United States Senator to succeed James Jackson, who died in 1806. The governor who went to Milledgeville was Jared Irwin, who had become famous fighting the Indians.

Irwin had already been governor once before, from January 17, 1796, to January 11, 1798. He was a man of fine character and good disposition, very hospitable and well liked. It was he who had signed the act that rescinded the Yazoo Fraud.

His wife refused to travel to the new capital by oxcart. She pointed out to her husband that this would not be in keeping with the dignity of the head of the state and his wife. The governor bought her a stylish carriage to make the journey. It was called a "gig." This was a light carriage with only two wheels, drawn by a horse.

However, misfortune awaited. When the governor and his lady stopped at an inn for lunch, Mrs. Irwin decided not to get out of her carriage. She asked that lunch be brought to her. On the hitching post where the horse was tied sat a rooster. He crowed. This frightened the horse and he plunged wildly, throwing the governor's wife out of the carriage. This upset her lunch tray and broke her leg. She had to be taken to Milledgeville on an oxcart.

CHAPTER 26

GEORGIA HELPED WITH
THE WAR OF 1812

Most Georgians were in favor of the War of 1812. One statesman said, "If all states were as ready as Georgia for this war, I should not be afraid for it to come." Troops were placed along the coast and on the frontier. There was as much to fear from the Indians, spurred on by the British in Canada and their Indian allies down the Mississippi, as from the British. The United States sent soldiers to aid Georgia when the Creeks in Alabama threatened to invade the state. General John B. Floyd, a famous Indian fighter, was sent to Savannah and was in command there until the war ended.

The United States got caught up in the war that was raging in Europe between Britain and France. This country was trading with both nations, and threatened to stop when its shipping was interfered with. Britain thought that certain laws passed about this favored France and its emperor Napoleon. British ships began to stop American ships on the high seas, claiming that some of the sailors were British and taking them off.

Some historians have felt that President Madison was pushed into this war. But whatever the facts are, the war came. This was the war in which the British burned the White House, and out of which we got the national anthem, "The Star Spangled Banner."

The war against the Creek Indians was actually fought

about this time because they were stirred up by the British and by Tecumseh and his brother, the Prophet.

British ships attacked the Georgia coast, and there were skirmishes within Georgia's territory. America won the war, mainly because Britain had to send its ablest armies against Napoleon, but also because this nation had the best ships. The American navy had deteriorated after the Revolution and this country had to prepare ships to fight in the War of 1812. One of the best was built of lumber grown in Georgia. John Randolph, Jefferson's cousin, opposed the War of 1812. Georgia had named a county for Randolph, but considered his views about this war unpatriotic and changed the county's name to Jasper. Many years later, another county in Georgia was named for this able, eccentric man.

Many places on the Georgia map are named for heroes of the War of 1812: Newnan, Perry, Clinch, and also Lawrenceville, which was named for James Lawrence, who said to his men as he lay dying after a naval battle, "Don't give up the ship!"

THE WAR GOVERNORS OF GEORGIA

Two governors served Georgia during the War of 1812. David Brydie Mitchell, a Scot, had become governor November 10, 1809, following Jared Irwin. He was defeated by Peter Early, who took office November 5, 1813. Mitchell defeated Early in 1815.

It is interesting to look at the personalities of these two governors.

GOVERNOR DAVID MITCHELL WAS IN FAVOR OF THE WAR:

David Brydie Mitchell, who was governor of Georgia for three terms, came to Savannah in 1783 when he was seventeen years old to inherit the estate of his uncle, a Georgia surgeon who served in the Revolution and died on a British prison ship. He studied law, opposed the Yazoo Fraud, and became a major general in the Georgia militia. He was elected governor in 1809, re-elected in 1811, was succeeded by Early in 1813, and elected again in 1815. Mitchell crusaded for good transportation on roads and rivers, and signed a bill outlawing dueling in Georgia. When he ended his first two terms in 1813, he wrote in his message to the

359

legislature: "Having served this state as its governor for 4 years in succession, with slender talents, it is true, but with a zeal inferior to no one's, and entertaining an opinion that in a government like ours, a rotation in office, particularly of the executive, should prevail at reasonable intervals, I take the liberty to decline being a candidate in the coming election."

Mitchell resigned as governor on November 4, 1817, to become Indian agent and dispenser of the Creek annual grants, succeeding Benjamin Hawkins, who died in 1816. John Clark, later governor of Georgia, brought charges against him for mishandling this money and he was fired by President Andrew Jackson, but the charges were never proved. Mitchell built a home on Mt. Nebo, later known as McComb's Mount, near Milledgeville. He tipped the lightning rods with five-dollar gold pieces. Long after his death and burial in the Milledgeville cemetery, his wife, a quaint figure in a Martha Washington gown and bonnet, who kept her snuff in an apron pocket, used to come into Milledgeville to trade. A monument, erected by the order of the legislature in honor of the old Scot governor, stands over his grave. He had died at seventy-one, on April 22, 1837.

GOVERNOR PETER EARLY LOANED U. S. MONEY: Peter Early, born in Virginia on June 20, 1773, was a Princeton graduate. He studied law in Philadelphia and came back to Georgia in 1795 to practice law at Greensboro. He was a close friend of William Harris Crawford. Early became the first judge of the Ocmulgee Superior Court Circuit. His most curious sentence was probably his decree that a sharp-tongued woman in Milledgeville be dipped in the Oconee River. She was placed in a sulky, driven out into the river and dunked three times!

Early went to Congress, where he helped impeach Supreme Court Justice Samuel Chase. He also voted to outlaw the African slave trade. Elected Georgia's governor in 1813, he lost his popularity when he vetoed a bill that would have suspended the payment of debts for a time, saying that this affected the legality of a contract. He had been one of those who warned that this was the reason why the Yazoo sale could not legally be rescinded. A captain marched soldiers threateningly around the governor's mansion to show Early they did not like his veto. He said to the captain, "I order you to march your men immediately to Fort Hawkins in Macon (thirty-four miles away). If you disobey this order, I will have you shot here and now, at the head of your company." The men marched, and that ended the first picketing in Georgia.

Early made one of the noblest utterances in the history of Georgia. Asked by the federal government for a loan of $80,000 to help with the War of 1812, Georgia, at his insistence, granted it. Asked by an opponent what would happen to the loan if the United States lost the war, he said, "I would not wish my state to survive the defeat of my country."

Historians have had varying comments on Early. One said, "His countenance reflected more sadness than cheer, yet indicated the deepest reflection. He measured out justice evenly. Seated on the bench as a judge, he was erect, commanding, with his arms usually folded across his breast, and one knee thrown over the other. He seldom altered this posture. He looked severe and haughty; yet he was dignified without the least affection. His mind never hesitated or faltered. There was nothing negative or vacillating about him. He was a modern judge." Another said he was "gentle, graceful, dignified."

Peter Early

Early's father, Joel Early, had come to Georgia from Virginia and settled first at Heard's Fort. Then in 1792 he bought a vast tract of land on the Oconee River near Greensboro. Here he built "Early's Manor" and lived like a British lord, requiring his family to dress for dinner every night. He was the first man to suggest sending the slaves back to Africa, offering not only to free his own, but pay their passage. He left his property to his favorite sons, after disinheriting two, one for disrespect and the other for extravagance.

Peter Early died August 15, 1817. He is probably the only Georgia governor ever to have three funerals. His widow was so grief-stricken that she was unable to attend the first funeral. A private service was held for her. She later married the minister, Reverend Adiel Sherwood, after a third funeral at Early's summer home, Skull Shoals, about twenty miles south of Athens. A hundred years later he was moved to Greensboro. Early County was named for him.

CHAPTER 27

NEW VENTURES

IN GEORGIA

Georgia Finally Established
A Supreme Court

In the white Georgia marble Judicial Building on Capitol Square in Atlanta is the room where the Supreme Court meets. Black-robed justices sit here to hand down their decisions on cases appealed to them from the lower courts. Above them is a Latin sentence: FIAT JUSTITIA RAUT CAELUM ("Let justice be done though the heavens fall.")

HOW GEORGIA'S SUPREME COURT ORIGINATED

Many Georgians at first opposed the creation of a supreme court. One argument was that it would be too expensive and was not really necessary. Another was that it would take too long to settle a case if it could be appealed to a supreme court. But it is possible that the people often associated the very words "supreme court" with the federal Supreme Court in Washington, from which Georgia was having adverse decisions in the Indian problems. The judges of the state's lower courts led the movement to establish a supreme court, beginning about 1823. The newspapers of the state supported them. In 1835, a constitutional amendment was prepared, providing for a court with three justices. In 1842, the people got a chance to vote on whether they wanted a supreme court. But the vote was so small that the governor thought it was not a fair picture of state opinion. In 1845, the legislature itself actually put into effect the court that had been authorized by the constitutional amendment ten years earlier.

The first chief justice was Joseph Henry Lumpkin (1799-1867) of Oglethorpe County. He wore his hair long, in the fashion of the day. His name is on a marker there. His brother was Governor Wilson Lumpkin. He graduated from the University of Georgia, which was about thirteen miles from his home, and he also graduated from Princeton. Lumpkin Law School at the University of Georgia is named for him. The other two justices were Hiram Warner (1801-1881), a Massachusetts native who came to Georgia when he was seventeen to teach school, and Eugenius Nisbet (1803-1871), who graduated from the University of Georgia and a Connecticut law school, and introduced the secession resolution in the legislature in 1861.

The first meeting of the Georgia Supreme Court was at Talbotton, Georgia, on January 26, 1846; a bronze plaque there marks the site. It reviewed seventy-two cases the first year, and decided that the lower courts had been wrong in forty-four of them.

Joseph Henry Lumpkin

In the foyer of the present Judicial Building in Atlanta are busts of all the chief justices of Georgia.

Public Health Was A Concern

The people of Georgia had been long concerned about public health. In the early colony, the Trustees had provided medicine and money to care for those who were ill on the voyage. Oglethorpe was careful to have medicines provided for the Savannah colony and for the soldiers on Frederica Island.

A number of other health measures were put into operation early in Georgia. One ruling regulated the quarantine of ships to prevent the introduction of disease into the colony. In 1817, laws in Georgia against the sale of impure foods were much like the present-day Pure Food and Drug Act. The state was second in the nation to require births to be registered.

In spite of Georgia's attention to health problems, disease continued to take high tolls in the state. During the first hundred years of Georgia's history, the average life span of a man was about twenty-eight years. The most common diseases were malaria, bilious fever, and pleurisy. Pellagra later developed, and smallpox was a great menace in the early part of the eighteenth century. Funds were provided, however, for smallpox vaccine by the state. Long jail sentences could be imposed on persons who concealed a case of smallpox. With other diseases, quarantine was often the only method used against them. As medical knowledge increased, aided by the founding of the Medical Academy in 1828 at Augusta, many false ideas about the cause and cure of disease began to disappear.

Many outstanding physicians lived in Georgia. Even in the early colony, there had been some. Noble Jones, a close friend of Oglethorpe, was skilled in medicine and carpentry, the old records say. Another early physician was Dr. Samuel Nunez, who had been a prominent doctor in Portugal. He was so good that even when the Jews were persecuted there during the infamous Spanish Inquisition, he had a large practice. He was physician to the Grand Inquisitor himself.

THE HOSPITAL FOR THE MENTALLY ILL WAS STARTED

The state opened the first wing of this hospital for mentally ill people on November 1, 1842, near Milledgeville. There were ten patients the first year. By 1844, 33 had been admitted; by 1846, there were 67. The first superintendent was Dr. Thomas Greene. Sherman sent four soldiers to guard this hospital when he marched through Milledgeville on his way to the sea in 1864.

The hospital, like those of its kind everywhere else, was first called the lunatic asylum. The word "lunatic" was coined because of the old superstition that people became mentally ill from sleeping in moonlight. "Luna" is the Latin word for "moon."

THE GEORGIA MEDICAL SOCIETY WAS ORGANIZED

In 1804 the Georgia Medical Society was incorporated in Savannah. Dr. Noble Wymberly Jones was elected president.

Epidemics had plagued Georgia at intervals for years. Malaria was always present. Yellow fever was brought in on a

The Davenport House In Savannah

vessel from the West Indies. It became so bad that Georgia built a crematory and quarantine on Blackbeard's Island, the ruins of which can be seen today. The culture of wet rice was also an unhealthful occupation, and fevers plagued the coast country. In the uplands, pellagra became a scourge, and hookworm was rampant.

In 1830, Georgia's first medical college was established by the state in Augusta.

State Banks Were
Started In Georgia

State banks were started in Savannah and Augusta in 1811. Most of the money came from the state treasury, but this was increased by private investors. Some were Georgians; some lived in other states; some lived as far away as Europe. The two banks were the Planters Bank in Savannah and the Bank of Augusta. There was in the state capital itself a branch of the State Bank of Georgia.

The state banks, usually backed by the conservative plantation owners, but not popular with the upcountry men, were not the first banks in Georgia. A branch of the United States Bank had been opened in Savannah in 1802, and there was much rivalry between the state banks and the federal banks.

The War of 1812 had decreased cotton production, but afterward, with cotton prices zooming, more settlers bought land in the interior of Georgia. With new settlements, more stores and banks were needed. In 1819, a branch was established at Milledgeville of a bank that had been started at Darien in 1818. Another branch was started in Twiggs County. The Darien bank failed, and for a while no new banks were started. Then, after 1850, new ones began to appear.

Many followers of John Clark in Georgia's upcountry did not trust banks. He wanted the state to handle the money, and in 1823, while he was governor, the Central Bank, set up in Milledgeville, was virtually the state treasury. Clark believed state control of such money would decrease the need for taxes, and might in time do away entirely with the state's need to tax.

Opposition to the Central Bank grew after 1840, following the 1837 depression. Some leaders did not think the state should be in the banking business; among these were

Governor George Crawford, Alexander Stephens, Robert Toombs, and Charles Jenkins. The Bank was ended in 1842.

Opposition to government's doing banking business was not confined to Georgia. President Andrew Jackson waged such an angry campaign against the federal government having an interest in banks that he was able to stop this for a time.

Later, the Federal Reserve Bank was organized by the millionaires who developed its plan while they were on their annual visit to their retreat at Jekyll Island.

Bitter Political Factions Developed: Planters Vs. Frontiersmen

Georgia's politics in the new century did not exactly follow the pattern of politics in the remainder of the nation. President George Washington had become chief executive with the support of most of the country. Though he had leanings toward a strong central government, he was not a party man. In his Cabinet, however, were the two men who became the focal points of two developing ideas of government. Alexander Hamilton, a brilliant New Yorker who had been born in the West Indies, favored a strong federal government with power. He was Secretary of the Treasury, and might have become president after Washington, except for a personal incident in which he became involved. His party then supported John Adams. The leader of the opposite group, which believed in the states' retaining most of the power of government, was Thomas Jefferson, Secretary of State, who was to become the third president.

Those who, like Hamilton, favored strong federal government were known as Federalists. Most of the nation's wealthy and conservative men were of this party. The other group was known as anti-Federalists. But in Georgia, the Federalists were believed to have been connected with the Yazoo Fraud. Conservatives like James Jackson, George Troup, and William Harris Crawford therefore were on the opposite side. They were anti-Federalists or States' Rights men. There were Federalists in Georgia, however; one of them was the able John McPherson Berrien. The Federalists were still powerful enough in Georgia in the second decade of the new century to force the resignation of the president of the University of Georgia, who was a Jeffersonian. One

The Capitol Dome

Peaches . . .
first the blossom,
then the fruit.

The Chattahoochee River
...first the land, then..

Opposite above: Where some of the mound Indians lived. (Excavation at Etowah Mounds.) Opposite below: Diorama of a council chamber interior. Below: Ft. Mountain fortifications.

The early settlers made buildings of "tabby," crushed shells mixed with sand and water. (Tabby ruins near St. Marys)

Ft. Hawkins

Top: *The Georgia coast where pirates lurked.*
Below: *Pirates' House of Robert Louis Stevenson's*
"Treasure Island" fame in Savannah.

Herb House —
Trustees' Garden...
blue shuttered to keep
the evil spirits out.

The Trustees' Bible...
Shown with beautiful silver and a
mahogony desk. All were in use at
the time of the Revolutionary War.

Opposite: Historic old Midway Church, on the coast of
Georgia... burned by the British Lieut. Col. Mark
Prevost during the Revolution but later rebuilt. Some
of Georgia's noted leaders before and during the Revo-
lutionary Period are buried in the cemetary near by.

A room in the Vann house...
The Indians liked the colors.

The home of Sidney Lanier

The Little White House
...The Georgia home of
Franklin D. Roosevelt.

The valleys...
(North side of Black Rock
Mountain overlooking the
Wolffork Valley.)

...and canyons...
(Providence Caverns, known as the Grand
Canyon of Georgia, are beautiful in their for-
mation and coloring, though an example of the
destruction of some 3,000 acres by erosion.

...and the swamps...

Autumn in Georgia

odd thing about politics is that Jefferson's party was known as Republican, and then as Democratic Republicans, but it is the party of Hamilton that is known as the Republican party today, having gone through many changes, of course, through the years. Jefferson's Republican party, its Georgia branch organized by James Jackson, became the States' Rights Party of Troup. Later, most Troup men joined the national Whig Party. Clark's followers, like Andrew Jackson's, were Union men, or Democrats. It was confusing.

Most Georgians were followers first of Jefferson, then the States' Rights party, and then the Whigs. The chief political differences in Georgia came to be due to personal allegiances. Many followed this leader or that. Quarrels were fierce and fights were frequent, but not often over issues. After 1829, the two colorful leaders, George Troup and John Clark, were out of Georgia. Troup was in Congress and Clark in Florida. Georgia politics fell more into line with national politics. Georgians became Whigs or Democrats.

The two groups pitted against each other in Georgia in the first two decades were the wealthy planters, who lived chiefly in the coast country, and the up-country frontier farmers. But the lines were not always sharply divided. There were men in upper Georgia who were wealthy and conservative. For the most part, the planters were the aristocrats, wealthy and well-educated. The frontiersmen of upper Georgia were intelligent, but often poorly educated, and sometimes illiterate. James Jackson was the first leader of the planter group, with William Harris Crawford, a brilliant lawyer later to become nationally known, as his chief follower in north Georgia, and George Michael Troup, later to be governor, in south Georgia.

Later, James Jackson went back to Congress as U.S. Senator from Georgia. He had already been governor and congressional representative. Soon William Harris Crawford was elected to Congress, appointed to the Cabinet, made ambassador to Napoleon's court, and was no longer active in Georgia politics. That left Troup as the chief leader, pitted against the able, tempestuous John Clark. For many exciting years, their followers quarreled and fought over politics. Crawford dueled with State Attorney General Peter Van Allen, a Clark follower, and killed

369

him. Clark and Crawford fought a duel, in which Crawford's wrist was shattered.

An old tavern keeper, who tried to be neutral, found his business falling off. He complained, "Whenever a Crawford man comes in, he asks whether I am a Crawford man. When I tell him I am neither for Crawford or Clark, he curses me for a Clarkite and refuses to buy a drop to drink. When the Clark men come in, they accuse me of being for Crawford. I sell not a drink to either. Faith, it pays to be a politician in Georgia!"

The Troup men fought many duels. On December 19, 1818, the legislature passed a law to fine duelists up to five hundred dollars and make them liable for a prison sentence of up to two years. But some still went across the state line to fight duels. Not even the legislature could stop the kind of fighting the Clark men often staged.

The Two Colorful Leaders

Small farmers in north Georgia, clearing their acres on the edge of the Indian country and living always in danger, were a sturdily independent crowd. They worked hard and played hard. Often they found their cabins burned and their families scalped by Indians. They had few schools and their children did not have much opportunity to be educated.

They were likely to follow a bold, daring leader with whom they had fought in the Revolution or against the Indians. These men followed John Clark as their political leader.

The planters gave their allegiance chiefly to one of their own. They lived mostly in the coast country, though many had built summer homes in upper Georgia to get away from the malarial country and the fog, or "miasma," which they then thought produced fevers. They planted rice, indigo, and cotton; shipped timber from the forests; and had many Negro slaves.

They often sent to Europe for their clothes and supplies. They entertained with a fabulous hospitality, served dinner at four o'clock, had boat races, collected libraries, and supported the church. These men made up most of the following of George Michael Troup.

John Clark was just the kind of man that frontiersmen would quickly follow. Rough, uneducated, brave, and able, he had lived with danger much of his life. His father was the Revolutionary General Elijah Clarke. John dropped the "e" from his name because he thought his political followers would think it pretentious and fancy. The younger Clark, born February 28, 1766, had started fighting at thirteen.

His critics said that he had considered himself "cock of the walk" ever since that time. But his followers said that it proved his courage and his ability as a leader. He had been living on the Indian frontier all his life, and he was so fearless that he could bravely fight either the British or the Indians. He was a friend and supporter of General Andrew Jackson, who later became president of the United States.

Clark spoke roughly and bluntly. He gave orders, but he did not know how to reason with men and he had no tact or diplomacy. He expected his word to be law and he thought that politics was simply a kind of "peacetime war." But he made strong and loyal friends. He was loyal to his friends and merciless to his enemies. As Andrew Jackson did in the nation, so Clark in Georgia brought in "the era of the common man." His followers were not satisfied to let the wealthy planters decide what should be done in Georgia. Under his leadership, they developed a powerful political group that was later to make him governor and give them control of the Georgia legislature for a time.

Clark's own brothers-in-law, however, were in the opposite political group. Reverend Jesse Mercer, whose first wife was a sister of Clark's sixteen-year-old first wife, was very much opposed to Clark politically. Mercer himself was at one time in the legislature. Clark's followers accused Mercer of preaching a political sermon against Clark when he delivered the funeral oration of Governor William Rabun, who died in office. People liked Rabun. His neighbors said, "Public office does not bloat him as it does some."

Clark's other brother-in-law was Judge Charles Tait. Clark was angry with him for witnessing some legal papers against him, which came to be known as "the dark lantern affidavits" because they were made at night. Riding up on his horse, on a Milledgeville street, Clark took his whip and savagely lashed the judge, who had one wooden leg. He was fined for this by Judge Peter Early; but later the fine was remitted by Governor Jared Irwin.

Clark had been a member of the committee that picked the new capital of Milledgeville. Here he was to become governor later. His daughter Nancy had one of the most fashionable weddings ever seen in the state while he lived in the Governor's Mansion.

Clark served two terms as governor, from 1819 to 1823. When he was not governor, he was throwing his powerful influence behind his candidates. He and Troup seesawed for power for many years in Georgia. Sometimes one won, sometimes the other. After his years as governor were over, Clark was appointed by his old friend President Andrew Jackson as governor of Florida. He was later to die of yellow fever, on October 12, 1832. He had contracted this disease when he made a trip to Cuba on his yacht. He and his wife, the former Polly Williamson, were first buried in Florida, and then moved to Marietta, Georgia. When he left Georgia, he had sold all of his Georgia property except a twenty-foot cemetery lot. He said he forgave all of his enemies except William Harris Crawford. Even Troup!

PROFILE OF GEORGE MICHAEL TROUP

George Michael Troup was born in 1780 in a part of Georgia that is now Alabama, but his father soon moved to the coastal country in Georgia. He went to Princeton University, finishing at nineteen. He was not quite twenty-one when his neighbors elected him to the Georgia legislature, and he was in politics for many years after that. It was Troup who first quarreled with the federal government over the removal of the Indians from Georgia.

He became a follower of James Jackson, who sought him out after reading newspaper articles Troup had written signed "Z." With Jackson's help, Troup went to Congress ten years, resigning in 1818 to run against John Clark for governor.

Troup, every inch the aristocrat, refused to campaign for anything. He would never ask any man to vote for him;

he was too proud. He had contempt for "electioneering" and he considered personal campaigning as "evidence of human depravity."

He was a first cousin of the Creek Indian Chief William McIntosh, who was later to meet such a tragic death in Georgia for signing away Indian lands. Troup was scrupulously honest and very able. He was a stubborn man who refused to compromise. He said, "If I am wrong in anything, I will surrender, but I will never compromise." Some people considered him stiff and proud and haughty, but his personal friends were deeply devoted to him. He was careless in his dress, but his pictures look very neat.

He and Clark made their political era very colorful. Troup was destined to have much trouble with the federal government over the removal of the Indians. After his retirement from politics, he went home to his farm "Val d'Osta" in Laurens County. He heard that his constituents were planning to re-elect him to Congress, and got in his buggy and drove as hard as he could to keep them from it. He arrived too late, and was persuaded to go back to Congress. But he developed serious throat trouble and soon retired again. He owned six plantations. His overseer in Montgomery County summoned him to come down and deal with a rebellious slave. He went, but died there five days later, at seventy-three. He was buried at Rosemont, near Soperton. Troup County was later named for him.

Some Of The Plantation Owners

The men of wealth usually built two homes: one in the coastal country, and another in the part of Georgia that was higher and healthier. They did not know that malaria was caused by mosquitoes. Finally, however, some suspected the mosquito and the Dents were the first to screen their homes. They had two, four miles apart. One was Hofwyl, which was part of a big rice plantation, in a low marsh. They spent the day there, but left before sunset to escape the fog. James T. Dent read of experiments conducted to show that mosquitoes caused malaria; then he had Hofwyl screened, and the family began to spend their summers there.

Thomas Spalding, who had been born in the St. Simon house that Oglethorpe owned, had a plantation on Sapelo and built a home there. He had a Mohammedan overseer named Bu Allah, who wore a red fez and had a prayer rug on which he knelt to pray to Allah. Joel Chandler Harris based a character in a novel he wrote on this Mohammedan. Spalding, a cultivated, well-educated man, served Georgia in the legislature, and helped draw up its constitution. He was a man of integrity and principle, and once left his home to go across the bay to Darien to protect a newspaper editor whom a mob was threatening for writing editorials with which they disagreed. Spalding believed in freedom of speech. He spoke to the crowd, and it dispersed. The editor went on editing his paper, and writing as he pleased.

John Couper and his friend James Hamilton had bought much land and developed it on the coast. Couper was a merry Scot, whose family was very prominent there. He remained on the island, but his friend and partner later moved to Philadelphia. Couper experimented with many plants, including olives which he planted at the suggestion of his friend Thomas Jefferson. He also planted dates from Persia. Later he sent his sons to study agriculture in other parts of the world. The Coupers were scientific farmers. They were also widely known for the lavish hospitality at their plantation, which was known as "Cannon's Point." One of his guests was the Honorable Amelia Murray, lady-in-waiting to Queen Victoria. She wrote many letters back to friends in England praising the life on the Georgia coast.

Major Pierce Butler had fought in the British army, and remained in America after the war. He married pretty Polly Middleton, a South Carolina heiress. He acquired two plantations on the Georgia coast, and ran them with military precision. He would not allow his slaves to mingle with those of other plantations, and everybody who came to visit his plantations had to give their names at the gate. One of his plantations was at Butler Point, just below Darien, and the other was on St. Simons.

A guest at Butler's plantation on St. Simons was his friend, Vice-President Aaron Burr. Burr fled to Georgia after he killed Alexander Hamilton in a duel in New York. Since duelling was an accepted way of settling quarrels in those days, Burr was welcomed in Georgia. He had been

374

in Savannah before, visiting his niece there. He stayed on the coast for several weeks, writing his daughter Theodosia about how kind people were to him, and how they sent him wines and vegetables and fruit. He "sipped his wine and fished for trout," one report says. He stayed in Georgia until he had to go to Washington to preside over the Senate. Later, he was to be carried across Georgia in chains as a prisoner charged with treason, though he was acquitted at his trial in Richmond. Jefferson believed that Burr, who had wanted to be president, tried to set up an independent nation in the West.

Aaron Burr

The old major left his Georgia property to his grandsons with the requirement that they take the name of Butler. They were his daughter's sons and their own name was Mease, but they took the Butler name. One of them, young Pierce Mease became the second Pierce Butler. He married the brilliant British Shakespearian actress, Fannie Kemble, a friend of the Brownings and Tennyson. She came from a stage family; her parents were actors. Her father owned Covent Garden Theater in London, and her aunt was the great actress Sarah Siddons. Miss Kemble came to America to make enough money to save her father's theater in London. She was received at the White House, and her tour through America was a triumph. She remained here as the wife of young Butler, and came with him to spend a few weeks on the Georgia plantations. She was horrified by slavery, and wrote angry letters about it to a school teacher friend, Elizabeth Sedgewick in New England. She loved the scenery in Georgia, and enjoyed riding her horses, Miss Kate and Montreal, around the island. "I would like to meet my death in a fall from a galloping horse on a fine day," said this strange young woman. She liked the Coupers, who were kind to her, but she hated slavery and had many bitter quarrels with her husband about it. They were divorced in 1848.

Many years later, when she went to England and found that some statesmen favored the South, she published the letters. They caused a sensation in London. They are said to have influenced powerful men in the government not to support the South in the Civil War. Her book is *Journal Of A Residence On A Georgia Plantation.*

Fannie Kemble

After the war, Frances, one of her two daughters, came back with her father to farm the Georgia land. They had sold the Negroes before the war to pay up debts. Butler gave them each a silver coin, and promised to gather them up again when he could. They were freed in the war, but some came back to work for wages. Frances Butler wrote a book Ten Years' Residence on a Georgia Plantation Since the War. It was exactly opposite to the one her mother had written. She later married her cousin, Reverend James Butler Leigh, who came to Georgia to visit. Her sister Sarah married a doctor in Philadelphia. Sarah's son was Owen Wister, the novelist whose book The Virginian is the basis of a modern television series of that name.

CHAPTER 28

GEORGIANS BECAME
NATIONALLY PROMINENT

Crawford Was Almost
Elected President

William Harris Crawford of Oglethorpe County, Georgia, came within a hair's breadth of being president of the United States instead of John Quincy Adams in 1824.

Crawford was born in Virginia. He came with his family to Appling County, Georgia, in 1783. In 1788, his father died of smallpox and Crawford had to help his mother care for the family. He had studied at the famous school of Moses Waddell, brother-in-law of John C. Calhoun of South Carolina and later president of the University of Georgia. Calhoun also attended Waddell's school, which had been moved to Georgia from South Carolina. The two boys disliked each other and the animosity that developed there carried over into national politics later when both were nationally prominent political figures. Crawford later attended Richmond Academy in Augusta, and taught there for a while. He studied law and went to Lexington, a small town near Athens, to practice. He married a girl whom he had met at Richmond Academy. She was Susannah Giradin, the daughter of a French Huguenot who had a plantation on the Savannah River and had been a professor at the College of William and Mary in Virginia.

Crawford's law practice prospered. He became a very prominent member of the group known as "the gentlemen of the green bags." These were the lawyers who rode horseback or in buggies around the court circuit carrying their papers in green bags.

When Abraham Baldwin died in 1807, Crawford was

named to succeed him as United States Senator from Georgia. Crawford rose rapidly to prominence in Washington. He became president pro tempore of the Senate. From 1816 to 1825 he served in the Cabinets of two presidents, Buchanan and Monroe, as Secretary of War and then as Secretary of the Treasury. In 1813, he had been sent to France as America's ambassador to the Court of Napoleon. The little Emperor said that the tall, handsome Georgian was the only man to whom he ever felt inclined to bow. Monroe came to Georgia and visited Crawford at Woodlawn. It is said that they talked over the terms of the famous Monroe Doctrine there. Monroe issued this remarkable doctrine in 1823. Much of Crawford's thinking is said to have gone into it. Later, Monroe and Crawford quarreled so bitterly that they threatened each other with a walking cane and a fire poker, and Monroe ordered Crawford to leave his office. Politics could be violent in those days!

Crawford, who had seemed a logical candidate for president but had stood aside for Monroe, became one of four candidates for the presidency in 1824. The others were Henry Clay, Andrew Jackson, and John Quincy Adams. But just as his prospects seemed brightest, Crawford was stricken with some kind of paralysis. It temporarily crippled him, and made him almost deaf and blind. His family and friends were shocked. Rumor reported that the malady grew worse when an inept doctor gave him the wrong medicine. His friends tried hard to keep his condition a secret. They felt that he would rally enough to make a fine campaign, and they did not want the public to get the idea that he was not to be in the running. But the secret leaked out. The newspapers termed his condition "pitiable." Still his friends hoped. A caucus showed that he was the most popular candidate.

When the showdown came, he did not get the nomination. Even his most loyal supporters were convinced by that time that the disease would keep him from being able to discharge the duties of President of the United States. When the election came, Jackson got the most votes, but not a majority. When the election went to the House of Representatives, it chose John Quincy Adams, whose father, John, had been the second president, following Washington. Jackson was furious. He felt that Clay had betrayed him by teaming up with Adams to cheat him out of the office. Jackson did become president in 1829.

But Crawford was calmer about the outcome. His faithful Georgia friend, T.W. Cobb, went to the Crawford home in Washington to break the news. A daughter answered the door. "May I see your father?" Cobb asked. Crawford listened quietly. Then he said only, "I thought it would be Jackson." The beloved Susannah said, "But for my husband's tragedy, it would have been a different story." She started to take the children off to bed, but he said, "Don't take them yet. I need them now." His daughter said, "Father, I dreamed last night I was back home in Georgia picking strawberries. Now my dream will come true."

Adams offered Crawford a place in his Cabinet, but the Georgian declined. So the Crawfords came home to Woodlawn, the rambling old house on the hill, which he had built in 1804. It had two stories, and two wings, with fourteen rooms. It had a separate kitchen with a fireplace so big that it could burn an eight-foot log. Outside the window of his room Crawford had planted a cherry tree given him by Napoleon. Once, when Crawford wanted to build a porch on Woodlawn, he built it around the tree. A village nearby was named Crawford in his honor. A monument stands there today. The William H. Crawford Highway also honors him.

After he decided to come home, the neighbors gathered to welcome him. They were aghast at the sight of the broken, old and sick man; they remembered him as their tall, handsome, energetic neighbor. They were very kind to him.

When Judge John Dooly died, Governor Peter Early appointed Crawford to the judgeship of the circuit. Crawford was slow, a little impatient now and then, but he was still a man of great ability. Once he said to a tiresome lawyer, "Mr. X, you go around and around, like a blind horse in a gin." Once, when a Clarkite was introduced to him by a man who said, "There ARE some good Clark men, sir," Crawford answered, "Mighty few, mighty few."

Around and around the circuit went Crawford, holding court in all the county seats. On one trip around the circuit, he had stopped to visit his daughter and see his new grandchild. Then he spent the night with a friend in Elbert County. He became ill in the night and died there the next day, September 15, 1834.

He was buried on the hill behind his home at Wood-lawn, which burned in 1936. His epitaph reads, "Sacred to the memory of William Harris Crawford, born 24th February in Nelson County, Virginia. Died 15th September 1834, in Oglethorpe County, Georgia (now Elbert). In the Legislature of Georgia, as Minister to the Court of France, in the Cabinet, and on the Bench, he was alike independent, energetic, fearless, and able. He died as he lived, in the service of his country and left behind him the unimpeach-able fame of an honest name." A magnolia tree shades the lonely grave and in the spring, yellow jonquils make a small patch of sunshine there.

Thousands of travelers zoom by the highway at the bottom of the hill, never realizing that a few feet from the grey pavement lies the great Georgian whom Napoleon delighted to honor, the Georgian who came nearer than any other to being president of the United States.

Crawford was the nephew of Mrs. Nathan Barnett, wife of a man who was later to be secretary of state for Georgia. She, who had been Susannah Crawford, was the one who hid the Seal of State under the pigpen in Milledgeville during the War Between the States.

The uniform in which Crawford was presented to Napoleon is at the Department of Archives in Atlanta. The towns of Crawford and Crawfordville and the county of Crawford keep his name alive on the Georgia map. His bust stands in the hall of statuary at the State Capitol. Sev-eral books have been written about him. John Quincy Adams, the dour old president who kept a diary faithfully from the age of twelve to his death at eighty-one, wrote much in it about William Crawford of Georgia.

John Forsyth Became
Jackson's Secretary Of State

Until President John F. Kennedy appointed Dean Rusk as Secretary of State in 1960, the only Georgian to have held this office was John Forsyth. The town of Forsyth and the county of Forsyth are named for him. There is also Forsyth Park, named in his honor, in Savannah. In 1960, Dr. Alvin Leroy Duckett wrote the Forsyth story in a new book titled *John Forsyth, Political Tactician.*

Forsyth also served as governor of Georgia, elected in 1827. As American Minister to Spain, he handled the deal in which the nation bought Florida from Spain. In Congress, he voted to outlaw the slave trade and to impeach Judge Samuel Chase.

He had married Clara Meigs, the daughter of President Josiah Meigs of the University of Georgia. She did not like the South, and it was largely for her sake that he sought office elsewhere. But she was devoted to him and she wrote a girl friend just after she married, "I am proud to have caught myself so handsome, good, and genteel a husband."

Forsyth, who had been born in Virginia in 1780, came with his parents to Augusta when he was only five. He was a cousin of Joe Johnston, later a Confederate general.

His father Robert, a United States marshal, was killed

John Forsyth

in attempting to arrest a Methodist preacher, Reverend Beverly Allen. Robert Forsyth had fought under Colonel "Lighthorse Harry" Lee who saved Augusta. Georgia granted the elder Forsyth land.

Young John graduated from Princeton and came back to practice law in Augusta; there he entered politics. He became Secretary of State under President Andrew Jackson. Van Buren retained him but Forsyth resigned. He came back to Georgia, spoke in Milledgeville, and was being considered again for election to the United States Senate when he died unexpectedly at his home in Washington, D.C., October 21,1834. He was buried at the Congressional Cemetery in Washington.

Berrien Became
Attorney General

In the beginning of party government, when Jefferson and Hamilton diverged from the no-party policy of George Washington, most Georgians were Jeffersonians.

John McPherson Berrien belonged to a family that supported Alexander Hamilton, Jefferson's opponent. Berrien was born August 23, 1781, in the New Jersey house from which Washington bade farewell to his soldiers. His father had fought in Georgia in the Continental Army under General Anthony Wayne. Berrien's mother was a sister of an aide of British General Montgomery, who attained fame through the battle of Quebec.

After the Revolution, the Berriens came to live in Georgia when John Berrien was two years old. His father lived in Savannah but owned land in Bulloch and Burke counties. Berrien went to Princeton, and started practicing law in Savannah. He became a judge but resigned in 1822. He entered the legislature just as his friend George M. Troup became governor. In 1824, Troup influenced the legislature to name the forty-three-year-old Berrien U. S. Senator. Berrien supported Troup in his fight against President John Quincy Adams over the Indian Springs Treaty and the removal of the Creek Indians from Georgia. When Troup's cousin, Creek Chief William McIntosh, was murdered for signing the removal treaty, Berrien got Congress to vote reimbursement to the family for the home that was burned.

Berrien's eloquence in Congress attracted attention and he became known as "the American Cicero" and "the honey-tongued Georgian." President Andrew Jackson appointed Berrien attorney general.

Berrien also backed Troup in removing the Creeks from Georgia, but he urged him to temper down his belligerent attitude toward the federal government. Berrien was always in favor of a two-party state, and became the leader of the States' Rights party. He presided at the Milledgeville convention on June 1, 1840, when that party adopted the name "Whigs." This was regarded as a radical group, opposed to the conservatives of which John Forsyth was once leader.

Berrien supported the policies of Henry Clay, who wanted to be president but never was. Clay once visited Berrien when he was on a speech-making trip to Georgia. Some Georgians criticized Berrien for not consulting his constituents about his votes in Congress. He said that a public official was elected to use his own judgment, and he intended to use his. He voted as he saw fit. He had the courage of his convictions; he even opposed President Jackson on the national bank issue.

When the clamor over the Peggy O'Neill Eaton matter split the Jackson Cabinet, Berrien resigned. John Eaton, member of Jackson's Cabinet, had married a Washington girl whose reputation was not spotless, and who had been married before with some question about her divorce. Jackson, who had married his wife Rachel before her divorce became final, always felt that Rachel's death had been hastened by the cruel gossip about the matter. He therefore gallantly championed Mrs. Eaton, and demanded that the members of his Cabinet and their wives accept her. Some wives refused, especially the wife of Vice-President John Calhoun of South Carolina. Many historians believe that this action, which incurred the wrath of Jackson, resulted in the presidency going to Martin Van Buren, who had no wife and could support the Eaton cause, instead of to Calhoun.

Berrien, who differed with Jackson over the Eaton affair and other things, resigned from the Cabinet. He returned to Georgia and, when the Whig party disintegrated, he became the leader of the Know-Nothing party, and presided at a session of this strange group in 1855. Wearied

Peggy O'Neill Eaton

by his exertions, he died on New Year's Day, 1856.

Berrien was one of the first crusaders for a two-party system in this state. He was also very much interested in history, and was the first president of the Georgia Historical Society.

CHAPTER 29

PERSONALITIES ON
THE GEORGIA SCENE

Dr. Crawford Long
Discovered Anesthesia

It was not only in the realm of government and politics and business that Georgians were achieving prominence. Professional men were having their triumphs, too.

Dr. Crawford Long, a physician who practiced in the quiet little town of Jefferson, discovered that sulphuric ether could be used as an anesthetic for pain. The record shows that he was the first to publish what he had done. Counter-claims clashed, and Congress never awarded the $100,000 which it had offered for this achievement. Dr. Long's statue has been placed in the Statuary Hall in Washington as one of the state's two distinguished sons to be honored there. The other is his friend and University of Georgia classmate, Alexander Stephens, later vice-president of the Confederacy and governor of Georgia.

Long's office at Jefferson, where he made his great discovery, has been set up as a historic shrine. There are dioramas showing scenes of his life and work, and his discovery.

Long was born November 1, 1815, not far from Jefferson, in the little town of Danielsville, where he later taught school. A statue of him stands in front of the courthouse there. After he finished the University of Georgia, he went on to the medical school at the University of Pennsylvania.

386

He studied abroad, too; then he returned to his native state to practice.

Dr. Crawford Long

He had noticed that young people in the little town had developed the habit of sniffing nitrous oxide, which they called "laughing gas," at their parties. It made them merry. He noticed that it had another result, too. When they were under its influence, they scarcely noticed bruises they might get from falling or bumping into the furniture. They seemed to feel no pain. Long thought about this.

One day, some of them came to his office to get some nitrous oxide. He had none, but he gave them sulphuric ether, which produced the same results. He began to wonder if he could use this to deaden the pain of his patients.

On March 30, 1842, he tried this. He put some on a towel and let James Venable, who had a tumor on his neck that had to be removed, sniff it. Then, as Dr. Long operated, Venable felt no pain. He had been putting off this operation because he dreaded the pain. The doctor operated near the window of his little office so that he could have the sunlight.

Nobody knows why this Georgia doctor did not put his discovery into print. It may have been that Long, a careful physician, wanted to do more experimenting just to be sure. Or it may be that he knew that relief of pain, strange as it seems to us now, was not always welcomed. Some people believed pain to be decreed by God and regarded any attempts to alleviate it as interference with divine plans. When Joseph Priestly experimented with pain-killing drugs in England in 1772, a mob wrecked his house. Paracelsus, a sixteenth century Swiss doctor, had experimented with methods to relieve pain.

By the time he reported his discovery, Dr. Long found that others claimed to have discovered it first. But records show that it was not until September 30, 1846 that Dr. William Morton, a Boston dentist, used anesthesia with his patients. The name "anesthesia" was suggested by Dr. Oliver Wendell Holmes, New England physician and poet.

Dr. Long and his wife moved to Athens to educate their twelve children. He has been honored in many ways. The U. S. government issued a postage stamp in his honor. Statues of him are in many places. Some bear the words that were his creed: "My profession is to me a ministry of God."

He died on June 16, 1878. Records about his discovery are in the Library of Congress in Washington.

Georgia-Born Fremont Was The
First Republican Candidate For President

National politics took on new patterns in the era between the Revolution and the Civil War, and Georgians had a part in it. The old Federalist party had lost its strength, and the anti-Federalist movement had focused on states' rights. Union parties still believed in strong national government, as Hamilton had.

The Republican party, which Lincoln was later to bring to fame, had been organized just before the Civil War. But its first candidate for president of the United States was not Lincoln; it was a Georgian-born explorer named John C. Fremont. He was born in Savannah, educated in South Carolina, and had married petite Jessie Benton. She was the daughter of the powerful Senator Thomas Hart Benton. Fremont's own father had been a French dancing master who had wandered into the South.

Fremont became known as "the Pathfinder of the West." Brave and able, he explored western lands and blazed new trails for his country. He was hot-headed and impulsive, but he rendered great service to his people.

In 1856, he moved west. He knew the value of new territory for this growing country, and though he was a southerner, he wanted the newly settled areas to come into the Union as free states, not slave states. Georgia's Howell Cobb and Herschel V. Jenkins, who both served as governors, recommended seceding if Fremont was elected, but he was defeated.

The secession idea was quiet for a little while after that, but not for long. Soon Abraham Lincoln would be nominated as the second presidential candidate of the Republican party, and he would be elected. And then would come a bloody war.

Longstreet Won National
Fame As An Author

Augustus Baldwin Longstreet of Georgia was the first Georgian to become nationally famous as an author. Strangely enough, writing was not really his profession, and he later became somewhat embarrassed by what he had written.

He was born September 22, 1790, the son of William Longstreet, who had invented the steamboat. He grew up in Augusta, became a lawyer, and later was presiding judge of the Ocmulgee Superior Court.

Longstreet wrote *Georgia Scenes,* a humorous book that is said to have delighted, and perhaps influenced, Mark Twain, Bret Harte, and Joel Chandler Harris. It was widely read over the nation. He later wrote a novel about school teachers.

He married Frances Eliza Park of Greensboro. After the death of a son, Judge Longstreet decided to enter the Methodist ministry. He was elected president of Emory-at-Oxford when the Methodists started that college. The students, who liked him and were often in his home, nick-named him "Old Bullet." He was later president of three other colleges: the University of South Carolina, Centennial College in Louisiana, and the University of Mississippi. When he moved to Oxford, Mississippi, to head that college, his daughter and son-in-law, Lucius Quintus Cincinnatus Lamar, later a justice of the United States Supreme Court, moved to Mississippi also. Lamar was a United States Senator from that state. It was Lamar who gave to the Long-streets the handsome curtains which had been originally made for the German emperor, were bought for President Buchanan, and rejected by him as "too expensive."

Longstreet was still so active when the Civil War broke out that he offered to spy for the Confederacy! But his offer was rejected.

He and his wife celebrated their golden wedding anniversary in 1887. After her death, a little Negro named Prince slept in the room with Longstreet, and got up and made a fire whenever Longstreet felt like writing.

He kept writing until his death at eighty, but he felt that *Georgia Scenes* somehow lacked the dignity that the writings of a minister and a college president should have had.

Visitors Georgia Welcomed

Not only were Georgians going outside of the state and

winning wide acclaim, but people from outside were coming to Georgia. They brought new ideas, made friends here, and often opened windows on a larger world. Georgia was becoming more interested in things cultural. During this century, the chautauqua, visiting lecturers, and a theater circuit which would bring Sarah Bernhardt and other great dramatists to the state, would make life more interesting for Georgians.

Four of the most interesting personalities who left their imprint briefly on Georgia during these years were Seward, who later bought Alaska; Lafayette, the great Frenchman who had helped America win its independence; General "Lighthorse Harry" Lee, who had helped free Augusta from the British during the Revolution; and Thackeray, the British novelist.

Seward, Who Bought Alaska, Taught School At Eatonton

William H. Seward, who was responsible for the purchase of Alaska from Russia in 1867 for $7,200,000, came to teach school at new Union Academy, nine miles from Eatonton in Putnam County, when he was only seventeen years old. He came after leaving Union College in New York because his father had refused to pay for a pair of pants he had bought. Seward's college classmates had made fun of his homespun clothes, and he had ordered new and more fashionable ones from a tailor.

In his diary, he writes of his trip to Georgia: "On Jan. 1, 1819, I left Union College as I thought forever, and proceeded by stage with a classmate who was going to take charge of an academy in Georgia." Seven days later, he arrived by boat at Tybee near Savannah, delighted with the sunshine after New York's snow. Though his money was giving out, he took a stagecoach to Augusta. There his companion got a teaching job. Seward got his clothes mended, and then started walking to Eatonton. Sometimes farmers would give him a ride on their wagons. In Eatonton, he learned that the academy was still ten miles in the country.

He writes, "I had only 9 shillings and sixpence. My

William H. Seward

shirt was soiled by travel. My light cravat was even worse. I invested 8 shillings in a neck clothe which covered my shirt bosom, and with one and six shillings left, I resumed my journey."

In a log cabin near Eatonton, he found a New York doctor and his family, and stayed with them. The next day, he got in touch with the school trustees. They hired Seward, even though his father wrote them threatening letters. Since school was not ready to start for six weeks, he borrowed a horse and buggy and traveled to Milledgeville, Sparta, and other places.

He had one assistant in the school, Miss Martha Spalding. This was the curriculum: Latin, Greek, Theoretical and Practical Mathematics, Logic, Rhetoric, Natural and Moral Philosophy, Chemistry, Geography, English Grammar, Reading, Writing, Spelling, "and such other subjects as are taught in northern colleges!"

Soon his sister wrote him that their mother was very

392

ill. He opened the academy with sixty-five pupils, thirty-one girls and thirty-four boys, and Miss Martha Spalding to assist him. Seward then asked the trustees if he might be relieved so that he could go home to his mother. They agreed. He writes, "My successor came and was accepted. I took leave of my generous patrons and affectionate scholars and departed with a sadness I have seldom experienced."

Later Seward hoped to be president instead of Lincoln. But he served in Lincoln's Cabinet as Secretary of State. He bought Alaska, which was a very unpopular thing to do. They called it "Seward's Folly" and "Seward's Ice Box." They could not have foreseen the time when it would become our fiftieth state.

The same crowd that plotted the assassination of Lincoln also planned to kill Seward. He was in bed, recovering from injuries he got when a horse ran away with him, and one of the plotters got inside his house, stabbed him about the throat and face but did not kill him. His wife Frances, who was an invalid, never got over the shock. She died two months later. This story has been all but forgotten because of the greater tragedy of Lincoln's assassination.

LAFAYETTE WAS GEORGIA'S GUEST

All America was excited when the news came that the Marquis de Lafayette was coming on his second visit to this country in 1825. The French nobleman, whose name was Marie Joseph Paul Yves Roch Gilbert du Montier de Lafayette, was just nineteen when he came to help the colonists fight for their freedom from England.

Benjamin Franklin, who was then America's representative in France, had suggested that he come. George Washington and Congress had scarcely known what to do with a red-headed, blue-eyed, rich teenager from France who suddenly appeared expecting to be made an officer in the Revolutionary army. But they gave him a commission, and he turned out to be a brave and able leader.

Lafayette was a member of one of the richest families in France. He had been so interested in helping America gain its freedom that he had left his young wife and baby at his vast estate in France to come to this country.

After the war, he came back in 1784 for a visit. He was a guest of George Washington at Mount Vernon. Mrs. Washington had sent Madame Lafayette a barrel of Virginia hams and George Washington had written her a letter.

Later, when France suffered its own terrible Revolution, Lafayette sent Washington the key to the Bastille, the infamous prison which the people had stormed. It still hangs in the hall at Mount Vernon.

Lafayette himself had been imprisoned by the French people during the Reign of Terror. They had beheaded their king and queen, Louis XVI and Marie Antoinette, and guillotined many of the noblemen. Some of Lafayette's wife's family were among those killed. The Lafayettes escaped very narrowly.

Lafayette had suffered much since he had left America. In 1825 he was sixty, and aged by his sad experiences. He had lost much of his money and property.

Georgians wanted him to include Georgia in the American tour he was making. Governor George Troup sent a letter to be delivered to him when his ship, the "Cadmus," docked in New York, on September 1, 1824, inviting him to come to Georgia.

On January 19, 1825, Lafayette notified Troup that he would come to Georgia during his four-thousand-mile journey. The governor and his aides and many Georgians were awaiting him when he arrived in Savannah on March 19. In greeting Lafayette, Troup said, "Ninety years after Oglethorpe stood right on the spot where you are standing, 400,000 Georgians welcome you to Georgia."

In Savannah, Lafayette laid the cornerstone on the monuments for two of his old war comrades, General Nathaniel Greene, and the Polish nobleman, Count Casimir Pulaski. Both had died in Georgia.

In Milledgeville, then the capital, Lafayette was royally entertained. Guns boomed in salute.

Troup had invited Georgia's veterans of the Revolution to Milledgeville to greet Lafayette. Seeing Father Duffell, a Catholic priest from Twiggs County, Lafayette embraced him. He said, "I remember you. You helped carry me off the battlefield when I was wounded at Brandywine."

Georgians honored Lafayette not only for what he had done for their country, but for the courage with which he

Lafayette

Portrait by Samuel F. B. Morse

had endured his own imprisonment and suffering in the French Revolution. Carlyle called him "the hero of two continents." Though Lafayette did not dwell on his past sorrows, there were Georgians who knew that in one hour, on July 22, 1794, the French populace had beheaded three of his wife's family: her mother, her grandmother, and her sister. His wife Adrienne, whom he had married when she was sixteen, was spared only because Robespierre, who had imprisoned her, had died before she could be executed.

In Milledgeville, Lafayette attended the Masonic lodge, went to church with the governor, saw little girls scatter flowers in his path, and attended a vast barbecue on the grounds of the old State House. He was guest of honor at a ball, which was open to "all persons of respectable character." A band played "Hail to the Chief."

He also visited Augusta. He spent a night at the old Creek agency on the Flint. Then he went on to Alabama on his twenty-four-state tour.

On the one hundredth anniversary of his birth, Congress approved a stamp in his honor. Georgians named Fayette County and the towns of Lafayette and Fayetteville for him, and LaGrange for his farm in France.

A GEORGIA GIRL MADE THE TEXAS FLAG

Joanna Troutman, a sixteen-year-old Georgia girl who lived in Crawford County, became a Texas heroine by making the Lone Star State Flag, which is the emblem of the State of Texas today. There is a monument including her statue in the Texas capital city of Austin. She was buried beneath it after her body was moved by Texas from her native county of Crawford, Georgia.

Georgians, who had volunteered to go to help Texas fight for its independence from Mexico, were marching from Macon to Columbus in November, 1835. When they passed through the little town of Knoxville, Joanna gave them a beautiful white silk flag which she had made, with one lone blue star in its center. This became the Texas state flag. Its colors were later reversed, with a white star on a blue field. On one side of the flag are the words, "Liberty or Death," on the other side, the Latin phrase

Joanna Troutman

for "where Liberty dwells, there is my country."

Lieutenant Hugh McLeod wrote Joanna a letter from Columbus, on November 23, 1835:

Miss Joanna:
Colonel William Ward brought your handsome and appropriate flag as a present to the Georgia Volunteers in the cause of Texas and Liberty. I was fearful from the shortness of the time that you would not be able to finish it as tastefully as you would wish, but I assure you...without flattery...it is beautiful, and with us its value is enhanced by recollection of the donor....Your flag will wave over the field of victory in defiance of despotism.

When General Sam Houston defeated Santa Anna in

April, 1836, at San Jacinto, grateful soldiers sent Joanna a silver spoon and fork from the Mexican commander's possessions. Houston became the first president of Texas. The second was a Georgian, Mirabeau Lamar. He was founder of the *Columbus Enquirer,* a Georgia newspaper. He had gone to Texas in 1834, after the death of his young wife and his defeat for Congress.

Colonel J. W. Fannin, who had gone to Texas with Lamar, was leader of a brave band of 500 soldiers who were murdered by the Mexicans at Goliad, in what came to be known as Fannin's Massacre. A county in north Georgia was later named for Fannin.

Many Georgians had moved to Texas in search of fresh land for cotton. Others had gone for various other reasons. Mexico had won its independence from Spain, and had claimed all the land in America that Spain had once owned. This included Texas. Soon thereafter, Mexicans and Texans clashed.

Men in Texas began to think of seeking independence for Texas from Mexico. Georgians, like others from the East, volunteered to go help Texas fight for its independence.

Sam Houston, a brave Indian fighter who had been governor of Tennessee, and who had gone to live among the Cherokee Indians, helped the Texans fight. Some were slaughtered by the Mexicans at the famous battle of the Alamo. Among those killed at the Alamo were Davy Crockett, the picturesque warrior and Congressman, and Jim Bowie, inventor of the Bowie knife. Bowie had been born in Burke County, Georgia, and moved with his parents to the West when he was young. He had been very ill and was lying on a cot when he was slain by the Mexicans at the Alamo.

What Was Happening In Education

Courses in Georgia schools varied. As early as 1763, John Poythress, a schoolmaster near Savannah, had advertised that at his plantation school he would teach writing, mathematics, and surveying, sounding a vocational education note with the traditional academic education.

Students at the academies boarded with families in the community or in a dormitory. Many academies were located in rural areas "far from the temptations of the city."

After the Civil War, the academies gradually gave way to high schools. But it was a long time before the high schools got state financial support. Many felt that it was enough to provide elementary education for children. Some even objected to that. Governor John Clark was one who did not give his support in 1822 when there was a strong fight made in the legislature for free schools.

CHAPTER 30

GEORGIA WAS
PROMOTING TRAVEL

TRANSPORTATION WAS MAKING PROGRESS

This was the era in which progress was made in roads, canals, and rivers for transportation.

Many governors recommended better transportation in Georgia. New roads began to be built, and old ones improved. A road from Tennessee through the Cherokee country was opened in 1805. The War of 1812 had shown how much roads were needed. When the Creeks began their uprising, a road was built from Gwinnett County to the Chattahoochee River, so that soldiers could move more easily to keep the Creeks in line. This was known as Peachtree Road, and part of it is now Peachtree Street in Atlanta. Three Notch Road was one over which General Andrew Jackson traveled on his way to Florida to fight the Seminole Indians.

The federal government put a road through Georgia going from the Carolinas to Alabama. Turnpikes and toll stations helped pay for the roads through Georgia. Some roads were kept up by the people who lived near them. Once all able-bodied men except teachers and doctors were required to give a certain amount of time to working on roads.

In 1821, a road from Augusta through Wilkes County to Athens opened up that section. Carriage travel increased. Travelers stopped at inns like Travelers' Rest, or Jarrett Manor, near Toccoa. A trip from Milledgeville to Washington,

D.C., in 1837 took seven days and nineteen hours!

Some commercial companies asked for rights to build canals, but few new ones were built. Rivers were cleared where possible so that produce could be sent to the seaports on boats.

Georgians Sent The First Steamship Across The Atlantic

In 1819, businessmen from Savannah sent the first steamship across the Atlantic Ocean. It was named the *Savannah*. Europe needed Georgia cotton. During the War of 1812, England, which had much manufacturing, had been unable to get cotton, and it was now paying twenty-five cents a pound for it. Creek lands, the fertile area in middle and south Georgia, were being farmed by Georgians who were growing more cotton on them. In other sections, rice, tobacco, and timber were marketable crops. Fast ocean transportation was needed. It was thought, too, that ships might develop paying passenger service to and from Europe if they could provide faster travel.

The Savannah men bought a steamship that had been built in New York. They brought it to Georgia, and held excursions on it up and down the Savannah to attract passengers for the coming European voyage. President Monroe, visiting Georgia, was a passenger on one of these excursions. But they did not attract passengers for the trip to Europe. People were afraid to travel on a steamship. Not even glowing advertisements in the newspapers attracted any passengers. So when the ship sailed out of the harbor at Savannah on May 22, 1819, it carried only the crew.

The vessel was something really new in ships. Governor William Rabun of Georgia had signed the charter for the company on December 10, 1818. The ship had thirty-two staterooms, with no passengers! It had sails which could be used when the wind was blowing; it also had paddle-wheels that could be folded up and put on deck. For fuel, it carried seventy-five tons of coal and twenty-five cords of wood, but had to stop in Ireland for more fuel. As it neared the coast, a British ship, the *Kite*, was near. The British crew thought the American ship was on fire and hastened to aid her. The trip across had taken twenty-nine days and eleven hours.

S.S. Savannah, First Steamship To Cross The Atlantic

N.S. Savannah, First Nuclear-Powered Merchant Ship

In Europe, the ship was a sensation. Sweden offered to buy it, but wanted to pay in hemp and iron. The owners wanted cash. They thought they could sell it for cash to Czar Alexander I. The Czar did not want to buy the ship but he gave the captain a gold watch. Some Europeans were hostile to the *Savannah* and its crew because they thought the ship's purpose was to rescue Napoleon, who had been imprisoned again on the lonely island of Helena. Napoleon's brother Jerome had offered a reward for his rescue.

The return trip from Europe to America took six weeks.

The men of the *Savannah* had strange endings to their lives. The ship itself had run aground in a storm on Fire Island, in sight of New York's harbor, November 4, 1821. No newspaper explained it. One member of the crew fell off the gangplank and drowned. Captain Moses Rogers, who commanded the ship, had been on Robert Fulton's first steamboat, the *Clermont.* He later died of yellow fever, and was buried at David's Churchyard in Cheraw, South Carolina. His cousin and brother-in-law, Steve Rogers, also a partner in the venture, died at seventy-nine at New London, Connecticut. A picture of the *Savannah* was put on his tomb. William Scarborough, who arranged the financing of the ship, had moved from South Carolina to Savannah in 1789 and bought one of the beautiful houses that the famous English architect William Jay designed. But after the loss of the ship and fire and other business reverses, he had to sell it to pay his debts. Educated in England and Scotland, Scarborough was of distinguished ancestry. He died of yellow fever.

National Maritime Day in the United States, May 22, commemorates the historic day when the *Savannah* started its voyage across the Atlantic. On National Maritime Day in 1958, the keel of another *Savannah* was laid. This one, too, made history. It was the first atomic-powered merchant ship in the world, a streamlined 600-foot vessel that can carry 60 passengers and 9,000 tons of cargo. It can travel for three years without refueling. The glistening-white, newly-built *Savannah* was launched and christened with flags flying on July 21, 1959, just 140 years after the *Savannah* left Georgia on its historic trip across the Atlantic. The new nuclear ship *Savannah* dramatically demonstrated peace-time use of atomic power.

Georgia built more railroads in this era than any other southern state.

The first railroad to be chartered was the Georgia Railroad in 1832. It was a venture undertaken by Athens citizens and others in that area. They named James Camak president. Work on it was delayed, and did not get really started until 1835. The road went from Augusta to Eatonton; it was later extended to Athens, and finally west of the Chattahoochee.

Savannah citizens had a survey made for the Central of Georgia Railroad, which was to run for two hundred miles, up to Macon.

In 1836, the state chartered the Western and Atlantic, which was to figure in politics for years to come. The 1837 depression delayed its completion. In 1858, the legislature earmarked rentals of $100,000 from this road for free elementary education. The road ran from Rossville on the Tennessee line to a point on the Chattahoochee River known as Terminus. This name was later changed to Marthasville, in honor of the daughter of Governor Wilson Lumpkin.

By mid-century Georgia had more than five hundred miles of railroad. Some communities objected to the railroad coming through. It made noise, was dirty, and frightened horses, chickens, and children, they said. Some of these towns later disapproved when businesses moved away to be near the railroads. One of these places was Troupville in Lowndes County, named in honor of Governor George

EARLY AMERICAN RAILROAD TRAIN.

Troup. They named the new center that grew up a few miles away near a new railroad, Valdosta, for his Laurens County plantation, Val d'Osta, which he had named for a beautiful valley in the Italian Alps.

The Indian Problem Had Yet To Be Solved

The most serious question the Georgia government had to deal with during the half century was the vexing problem of the Indians. The Creeks still occupied the fertile cotton lands of middle and south Georgia. Though they had ceded the territory, the land still could not be distributed to Georgians because the Indians often refused to give it up. They felt that they had been wronged.

When gold was discovered in the region around Dahlonega, thousands of gold-seekers swarmed into the region. The discovery was to be a part of the story of the removal of the Cherokee Indians to the west. The government set up a mint at Auraria to coin money.

Georgia miners from Auraria went west after the mines here began to give out, and settled Auraria in Colorado, which later became Denver. Some went on to California. They had learned how to mine and pan gold in Georgia, and they used these methods in the west.

The old mines and the panning methods can still be seen at Dahlonega today. The Indians called the gold "yellow money." The first gold is said to have been found on Duke's Creek in what was then Habersham County.

THE INDIAN STORY

UNIT 6

HOW THE INDIANS DISAPPEARED FROM GEORGIA

CHAPTER 31

THE INDIAN STORY

Introduction

Once the only people who lived in Georgia were Indians. DeSoto saw them in 1540. Oglethorpe, with Tomochichi's help, became friends with them in 1733. A little over a hundred years after the colony of Georgia was founded, the Indians had gone west.

How did this happen, and why?

It finally became clear to many leaders of both whites and Indians that the two races could not live here together in peace. Though there was kindness on both sides, there was also cruelty on both sides. The story is complicated and it came to a climax in the second and third decades of the nineteenth century. The U. S. government had promised in 1802, when it bought Georgia's western lands, to move the Indians; but in 1824, the Georgia congressional delegation was protesting that this had not been done. As late as 1825, Governor George Troup was urging the legislature to demand that the 1802 promise be kept.

Who Were The Indians And
Where Did They Come From?

The Indians are believed to have come to America from Asia by way of the Bering Strait, probably 25,000 years ago. The Indians, both the early Mound Builders and the later Indians, are men of mystery. They filtered down through the two American continents. Some half million of them remained in North America, and of those about 200,000 were between the Mississippi River and the Atlantic Ocean.

The Aztecs went to Mexico and the Incas to Peru. Both were later conquered and their treasures looted by the Spanish. They had attained remarkable degrees of civilization. The Mayas, who went on to Central America, especially Yucatan, are thought by some historians to have stopped briefly in what is now Georgia.

The chief tribes in Georgia were the Cherokees and the Creeks. There were several groups of the Creeks; they were a Muscogean group. Those in the southeast lived mostly by the little creeks so the British called them "Creeks." Among the smaller tribes of Creeks were the Yamacraws, to which Tomochichi had belonged. The Lower Creeks were the ones who lived in middle and south Georgia, usually along the Flint and Chattahoochee rivers. They were friendly to the whites. The Upper Creeks lived in Alabama on the Coosa and the Tallapoosa. They were called Red Sticks and were hostile. An old story says that this name grew out of the fact that Tecumseh, the great Shawnee Indian leader who came south trying to weld the Indians into one group powerful enough to resist the white men, gave them a bundle of red sticks to count off the days before a council or a battle. These red sticks came also to be used to set the dates of wars and other events in their lives. A red stick was also supposed to point in the direction of one's enemies.

The Cherokees, an Iroquois tribe, lived among the north Georgia mountains. They achieved a higher degree of civilization than the Creeks. They resisted removal longer, and carried their case to the higher courts, but they, too, lost in the end and moved west to new homes.

The Indians rarely called themselves "Indians." As

everybody now knows, the name was a mistake. Columbus, who was searching for India, thought he had found it, and named the red-skinned people he found here "Indians." The name lasted.

Alexis DeToqueville, the European who wrote a book about America, said, "The Indians have unquestionably displayed...much natural genius. But they have been ruined by a competition which they did not have the means of sustaining."

In 1924 Congress conferred citizenship on all Indians born in the United States. In 1960, the U.S. Census listed 552,228 Indians in the nation.

In 1965, the U. S. Commissioner of Indian affairs estimated that there are now about 200,000 Indians in the country who live off reservations and 380,000 living on or near Indian reservations.

Trouble Arose Between Whites And Indians

Clashes and trouble were bound to come where two very different races lived together. There were good men and greedy men on both sides.

Indians said white men who brought them the horse and wheel also brought them whiskey, guns, smallpox and other ills. Chief Bloody Fellow said some white traders put prices too high on their wares. The white men said many Indians were lazy and would not pay their debts, though some, like Tomochichi, were friendly and honorable. Now and then Indians swooped down on white settlements or isolated homes, ruined crops, and left smoking chimneys, death, and despair where they had been, but whites had attacked Indian villages too.

Sometimes Indians ceded lands to the whites willingly. At other times, they had to cede land to pay the big debts they ran up at trading stations and compensate white settlers for damages. Indian leaders resented seeing the white men come into their lands. One Cherokee chief reproached a young warrior for making a wagon. "Wagons mean roads, and roads bring the white man. Then our land will be gone, and the ways of our fathers will be changed," he said. Once the Creeks stopped all white travel through their territory.

411

Both Indians and white men could be cruel. In 1732, just as Oglethorpe was starting from England toward Georgia, where he made friends with the Indians, British General Jeffrey Amherst in New England was writing to an aide: "You will do well to try to inoculate the Indians by blankets in which smallpox patients have slept, as well as by every other method that can serve to extirpate this execrable race. I should be very glad if your scheme of hunting them down with dogs could take effect."

In Georgia, an old story says that soldiers drew lots to see which would kill the last Indian who fled for refuge into the Okefenokee Swamp. Legend says the Indian's screams can be heard on a dark and stormy night. But in Georgia also, the U. S. agent to the Indians, Return Jonathan Meigs, who was eighty-two, died of pneumonia that he contracted when he gave up his bed to an old chief on a bitter winter's night in 1823. Meigs, who lived at Marietta, got his strange name from his father, Return Jonathan Meigs, Sr. The elder Meigs was so named because his mother at first refused his father when he proposed to her, but before her rejected suitor reached the door she said, "Return, Jonathan!" They married and later gave this name to their son. Meigs, the Indian agent, was the brother of Dr. Josiah Meigs, first president of the University of Georgia.

Georgians on the frontier begged the government to send them protection from the dangerous Indians. On May 31, 1787, Creeks scalped two residents of Greene County, stole two slaves and fourteen horses. Georgia soldiers stalked them and killed twelve Indians. Indian leaders demanded twelve white lives in return. Governor George Mathews said, "We will deliver up none of our people, and if the Indians spill a drop of blood, we will lay their towns in ashes and sprinkle their land with blood."

At Jarrett Manor near Toccoa can be seen today the dark bloodstains and the scars where Indians besieged Jesse Walton and those who were in his house. Indians had threatened any who built another house in the Blue Ridge. Walton, an Englishman, built in 1782 his big house with twenty-seven doors, clocks and keys from England, four stairways, and a secret room to hide women and children if Indians attacked. The room did not save them. The slain are buried in the front yard. In the back yard is a small museum with

412

Indian relics. On the Tugaloo River nearby, when the Hartwell Dam was built, a mound was uncovered that was part of Estatoe, a village there eighteen hundred years before Christ.

Jarrett Manor

It is true that white settlers did often suffer from Indian savagery, but it is also true that some white men, who wanted the rich cotton lands of the Creeks in middle Georgia and the gold lands of the Cherokees in the north Georgia mountains, wanted the Indians removed.

What was justice in the Indian problem? Could the crisis have been resolved in another way?

Who Were The Creeks?

The Muscogean Indians who came to be known in Georgia and Alabama as "Creeks" never achieved as high a civilization as did the Cherokees, the other chief tribe in the southeast.

The Creeks were a hunting people. Agriculture was not as important to them as to some other tribes though they had

413

become acquainted with the plow. They hunted, fished, and traded their deerskins and such things with the whites.

Their most colorful festival was the Boos-ke-taus or Green Corn Dance, which began a new year for them. They held their general councils in the public square of their principal town. The cabin of their great chief always faced the sun. All of the cabins were painted red except those of the old men; these were painted white to symbolize age and virtue. In the center of the square a fire always burned.

The chief of each town was called the "mico." He was appointed for life, and was always succeeded by a nephew. The military chief was called the "Great Warrior." During the days of the Green Corn dance, the Creeks pardoned all crimes except murder. They made a canoe by burying a big log for three years, then digging it up and burning out the center and pointing the ends.

These Indians never called themselves the "Creeks"; that was the white man's name for them. And like the other red men, they never referred to themselves as "Indians" either. The Creeks had white (peace) towns, and red (war) towns. Coweta was the leading war town, and Cusseta, the leading peace town.

TECUMSEH AND "THE PROPHET" STIRRED THE CREEKS TO REBELLION

Tecumseh, great chief of the Shawnees in the north, came to the southeast to get the Indians here to join in his confederacy against the whites. He came to Georgia and tried to persuade the Creeks, but they would not listen to him. He joined the Indians in their festivals, taught them "the Dance of the Lakes" and tried hard to get them to join him. He wanted Indians to reject the white man's ways and return to Indian customs.

The Upper Creeks in Alabama were greatly stirred by his words. He urged them not to cede any more of their lands to the white men who were, he said, trying to crowd them out of the lands of their fathers. "Sell our land?" he asked. "You might as well sell air and water. The Great Spirit gives the land and air and water, and they belong in common to us all. Do not sell the lands of our fathers. The dead will be grieved if you do. I can hear their voices wailing on the winds. They cannot rest in their graves." Nature itself helped Tecumseh. Comets, meteors, and even an earthquake oc-

414

curred. The superstitious Creeks thought he caused them. When he left, he said, "When I get home (to Ohio) I will stamp my foot and the earth will tremble." It did, but from an earthquake.

In Georgia, the Lower Creeks had already repudiated

"The Prophet"

many treaties they made with the whites, such as those at Augusta and Bone Creek. They were influenced by the Creek Chief McGillivray.

Tecumseh's brother Elkswatawa or Sikabos, known as "The Prophet," was a wild man. He shrieked and called to the Indians, urging them toward attacks of terror. He roused them to a frenzy. This was later to climax in the bloody massacre at Fort Mims, which Georgians and their Indian allies went to help General Andrew Jackson avenge at Horseshoe Bend.

Georgians Asked For
More Protection

The trouble between the Indians and whites on the Georgia frontier grew so dangerous that as long ago as 1793, Governor Edward Telfair had proposed raising an army of five thousand to crush the Creeks. But President George Washington, who had been in Georgia just two years before and had discussed the Indian problem, protested. Washington had believed that he could help solve Georgia's Indian problem by summoning Chief McGillivray to New York to confer with him, but this did not solve the problem. Washington, disappointed at this, told Telfair that he would send commissioners to try to work out some solution.

THE TREATY OF COLERAINE HAD NOT PLEASED ANYBODY

The commissioners had in 1796 met with both whites and Indians at a place called Coleraine, in an oak grove forty-five miles up the St. Marys river, six miles from the present Folkston. About four hundred chiefs were there. Mico Fushatchee was their spokesman.

Head of the U. S. delegation Washington sent was Colonel Benjamin Hawkins, who would later become permanent U. S. Indian agent in Georgia. As the Treaty of Coleraine was being worked out, General James Jackson, later Georgia's governor, presented a list of grievances of the white men against the Creeks, for which he demanded money in damages. An old Creek chief replied, "I could fill many pages with ten times that amount which the whites owe the Creeks." But finally, the Treaty of Coleraine was signed in 1796.

416

The treaty established lines between the whites and Indians to run "from the Currahee mountain to the source of the main south branch of the Oconee, called by the whites the Apalatchee and by the Creeks, Tulapolka." It also established a trading post at Beard's Bluff. The U. S. gave the Indians six thousand dollars, and provided them with blacksmiths and tools. Georgia's representatives there were James Jackson, James Hendricks, and James Seagraves.

Georgians had not been satisfied with this treaty made with the Creeks. The lands they got were too poor for farming, and too far out on the frontier. It left the Creeks still in possession of much of the most fertile farm land in the state, between the Ocmulgee and the Chattahoochee rivers. Each Indian was also granted a square mile to live on. This, too, added to the discontent of the whites.

On May 24, 1802, federal commissioners headed by General James Wilkinson met the Creeks at Fort Wilkinson below Milledgeville and got more land cessions from them.

In 1805, Creek leaders went to Washington and signed another of their many treaties. One of the signers of this treaty was a young Indian named William McIntosh. Twenty years later he was to be savagely murdered for signing still another treaty at Indian Springs.

HAWKINS BECAME U. S. AGENT TO THE CREEKS

When Colonel Benjamin Hawkins returned from Georgia to report to Washington on the Coleraine Treaty, he told Washington that a permanent agent should be sent to live among the Indians in Georgia. Washington already believed this and had asked Congress as early as November 6, 1792 (the year after he returned from his presidential visit to Georgia), to send an agent. But it had not yet been done. Now he listened while Hawkins advised him:

"The Creeks and the other Indians can be controlled but it would take a man of talent, and he would have to make the sacrifice of giving up his home and living permanently there in the wilderness among them," said Hawkins.

Washington asked Hawkins himself to do this. He was a North Carolinian who had graduated from Princeton, served five times in Congress, and had once been Washington's interpreter. He had written Chief Alexander McGillivray

417

urging the Indian to accept the President's invitation to New York in 1790.

Hawkins moved to Georgia, with his fine library and his other possessions. He traveled among both Creeks and Cherokees for a time, learning about the Indians. Then he established the Creek Agency on the Flint River, on the stagecoach route between the present Columbus and Macon. Here he entertained some of the great men who came this way. Moreau, the Frenchman, said that Hawkins was the most remarkable man he met in America.

Hawkins spent most of his time helping the Creeks to farm better, to raise livestock, to have better homes, and to care for their children more intelligently. He planted 5,000 peach trees, and experimented with new crops. He grew the biggest strawberries ever seen here. He taught Indian women to weave, much to their husbands' displeasure. The Indian men thought their wives would no longer obey them if they became too smart. Hawkins was stern with the Indians, but he was fair and considerate. He compiled a grammar for them.

The agent carried on a tremendous correspondence with people all over the world, especially Thomas Jefferson. He sent the Empress of Russia a report on Indian dialects because she was interested in languages. He met Tecumseh at Tookabatcha in 1811.

One friend of the agent said, "Hawkins knows more about the Indians than any other man who ever scraped pen to paper." He looked out for the interest of the Indians. The white people sometimes resented Hawkins because they wanted the Indians removed, and they felt he was helping them put down roots to stay forever.

He worked on quietly, however, trying to keep peace between the two races, reading his books, writing his letters, entertaining his guests, enjoying his family. Hawkins had married his white housekeeper, Lavinia Downs, and they had three daughters whom they named Georgia, Cherokee, and Jeffersonia, and a son named James Madison Hawkins.

Hawkins was saddened when the Georgia Creek Indians became angry at him because he had advised them to be neutral in the Creek wars in Alabama. He had done much to keep peace between white men and red men. Then something happened in Alabama, where the more savage Upper Creeks had been stirred up, that brought the Creek question to a climax and caused more trouble in Georgia. It was the Fort Mims massacre.

The Situation
Reached A Bloody Climax

The War of 1812 pushed the Indian problem to the background for a little while, but it was during this war that the Red Sticks of Alabama, the Upper Creeks, who were supporting the British, attacked Fort Mims. Stirred to a frenzy by the fanatical oratory of "The Prophet," set against the whites by Tecumseh, and encouraged by the British to oppose all Americans, the Alabama Indians were ready for a fight.

GEORGIA AND THE MASSACRE AT FORT MIMS

At noon one day more than a thousand Creek Indians swooped down on Fort Mims, near Mobile, attacking five hundred whites, including women and children who had taken refuge there. The leader of the Indians was William Weatherford, a follower of Tecumseh and a nephew of Chief Alexander McGillivray. In three hours of terror they killed nearly all the people in the fort. Only twelve escaped. About four hundred Indians were killed or wounded. It was August 30, 1813, the second year of the War of 1812.

When news of the Fort Mims massacre spread, there was anger all over the country. The United States sent General Andrew Jackson from Tennessee to quell the Creeks and to punish them for the Fort Mims massacre. Georgia sent three thousand to help. The Georgians assembled at Fort Hawkins, near the present Macon. Their commander was General John Floyd. Friendly Lower Creek Indians from Georgia under the leadership of the halfbreed Creek Chief William McIntosh went to help Floyd and his Georgians.

Though lacking food and equipment, Floyd captured the Indian villages of Atasi and Tallassee in a daring daylight raid, on November 29, 1813. He and his men killed the Indian leaders and two hundred of their followers, and burned two hundred dwellings. He kept fighting even though he was badly wounded in the knee. The famous Indian fighter Davy Crockett fought in this battle. He said later, "We shot the Red Sticks down like dogs." Later, however, he made a speech in Congress favoring Indians. Floyd sent Indian peace pipes he had captured to Georgia's governor.

JACKSON DEFEATED THE UPPER CREEKS AT HORSESHOE BEND

General Andrew Jackson picked Horseshoe Bend as the site for the chief battle he waged to defeat the Upper Creeks who had slaughtered the whites at Fort Mims.

In a seven-hour battle on the Tallapoosa River on March 27, 1814, the Red Sticks were finally defeated. A friendly chief, Junaluska, saved Jackson's life there. (Later, when Jackson refused to help the Indians keep their lands, he was to regret this.) The wounded Menewa, who was leading the hostile Creeks, escaped disguised as a squaw. Only seventy escaped.

After he defeated the Upper Creeks, Jackson forced them to sign a treaty ceding more of their lands, on August 9, 1814. Benjamin Hawkins, the Indian agent, was sad over this treaty because he said that friendly Creeks as well as hostile Creeks were forced to give up more land.

In this treaty which Jackson required them to sign at Fort Jackson, near the present city of Montgomery, Alabama, the Creeks ceded territory that included a ninety-mile strip in Georgia. This had belonged to Creeks friendly to Georgia. Jackson demanded a total of 23 million acres. This treaty turned some of the friendly Georgia Creeks into enemies. Some Creeks even fled from the region and joined the hostile Seminoles in upper Florida. After Horseshoe Bend, the Creeks were a broken and disspirited people.

Georgians felt that the treaty Jackson made with the Creeks should have included the removal of the Creeks from Georgia, in accordance with the promise the United States had made to the state when it bought Georgia's western lands in 1802. The Georgia legislature even protested this treaty. They wanted the federal government to have a new treaty signed. Another one was signed on January 22, 1818, at the Old Creek Agency on the Flint in Georgia. It gave Georgians two more tracts on the Ocmulgee and the Altamaha rivers, totaling one and a half million acres, but it said nothing about moving the Creeks out of Georgia.

The Creeks were sad over the treaty at Cusseta; Mico Yahola had said, "Our lands are our life and breath; if we part with them, we part with our blood."

THE REMOVAL MOVEMENT

Governor Troup Insisted That
the U. S. Remove the Indians

After the war, cotton prices went up, and men looked with eager eyes on all that fertile land in middle Georgia that the Creeks still occupied but did not farm. The white settlers were also frightened by the fearful massacre in Alabama. It could happen in Georgia, they told one another. Governor Troup pressed the federal government to carry out its 1802 promise to remove the Indians.

Two Factions Grew Up
Among the Creeks

As the problem of whether the Indians would be removed became more acute, two factions grew up among the Creeks.

The leader of the group that favored removal was a halfbreed, part Scotch, Creek Chief William McIntosh, a first cousin to Georgia's Governor George Troup. His Indian name was Tusunugee Hutkee.

McIntosh was a wealthy Indian. He had a two-story home of hewn logs in Carroll County. His plantation was called Lockchau Talafau. McIntosh Trail, starting at Fort Hawkins in Macon and passing the Creek Agency on the Flint, led to it. Here lived his two Indian wives, Peggy and Susannah. In another home, about fifty miles away, on the Tallapoosa River lived his white wife Eliza and her children. Her son, Chilly, became clerk of the Creeks.

McIntosh controlled the distribution of the annuities, or annual payments, which the government made to the Creek Indians. He had been a Creek warrior since he was twenty, and had great influence. He had been born in 1778 at Coweta Town, below Columbus, on the Alabama side of the Chattahoochee River.

His influence grew even greater after his cousin was elected governor. He often went to Milledgeville to visit, attended the Methodist Church, and impressed people with his intelligence and polished manners. He had once visited Jefferson and talked about better roads for Georgia, but there were Indians and whites who did not trust him and who felt that he was using the Indian people and their cause for his own enrichment. The Cherokees, whom he was trying to persuade to sign away their Georgia lands and move west, forbade him to set foot on their land.

The leader of the faction that at first bitterly opposed the removal of the Creeks from the lands of their fathers was Menewa, who was also known as Big Warrior. His Indian name was Tustunegee Thlucco. He was a huge, strangely light-footed, scarfaced Indian who was wealthy, owned 50 slaves, huge herds of livestock, and trading station, and lived at a big plantation at Tuckabatchee. He was the voice of the Upper Creeks. He was very close to the ninety-year-old "Little Prince," who was the head chief of all the Creeks. He was also a close friend of U.S. Indian Agent John Crowell, who detested both McIntosh and his cousin, Governor Troup. Crowell had succeeded David Mitchell as agent. Mitchell was a Georgia governor who had resigned the governorship to become Indian agent in 1817 after Hawkins died.

THE CREEKS SIGNED MORE TREATIES

At Indian Springs in 1821, Creeks, influenced by McIntosh, had signed another treaty. Georgia said that the Creeks owed a half million dollars in old debts that had been piling up at the trading stations since the Revolution. The state proposed that the Creeks cede enough of their land now to put Georgia's western boundary at the Flint instead of the Ocmulgee River. For this, they would be paid $200,000 and have their debts paid by Georgia. The debts were scaled down by the U. S. commissioners to $25,000. Then the treaty was signed. But when it was claimed that undue influence, including whiskey and bribes, was used trouble arose.

In 1823, Monroe appointed two Georgians, James Meriwether, and Duncan Campbell, to arrange another treaty with the Creeks. They set up a meeting at Broken Arrow in Alabama on December 7, 1824. But the Upper Creeks refused to agree to sell another foot of the tribal lands. There was a tribal law that forbade it. McIntosh himself read this law to a Creek crowd assembled for a ball game. Later McIntosh lost his life because of this law.

The two commissioners, seeing that they could never talk Big Warrior into another treaty, or get Agent John Crowell to agree to one, decided on another plan. They would arrange a meeting with the Lower Creeks only, at Indian Springs. They knew that McIntosh and his faction would sign and sell.

On January 11, 1825, Colonel Campbell told the Secretary of War that he believed the Creeks were ready to go west. On February 7, 1825, he invited all Creek chiefs to Indian Springs. Crowell reported that only eight of the fifty-six Creek settlements sent representatives.

AT INDIAN SPRINGS McINTOSH SIGNED THE FATAL TREATY

The meeting was arranged to be held at Indian Springs. McIntosh and his aides were there, having agreed to sign the treaty. Some historians believe that McIntosh signed the Indian Springs treaty because he got much money and land. Some even say he got the other Indians drunk and bribed them to sign. Others pointed out that the Creeks signed because they believed in McIntosh. He had stood up for their rights in many cases. He had been a spectacularly successful leader in war. He had practically forced the United States to pay indemnity to the survivors of a small Creek Indian village in Georgia burned by mistake by Captain Obed Wright of the Georgia militia on April 23, 1818, who did not know that the Creeks there were friendly. General Andrew Jackson, who was at this time coming back and forth through Georgia on his way to put down Seminole uprisings in Florida, and Georgia's governor William Rabun had angry correspondence about the burning of this town. Congress paid an indemnity. A sign put up by Georgia on the site (in Lee County) says, "Chehaw, large Indian town, home of the Chehaws, a friendly agricultural people of the Creeks."

423

McIntosh, who had played a big part in getting this indemnity for the Creeks, now agreed to sign the second removal treaty at Indian Springs. It granted the last of the Creek lands in Georgia to the white men.

William McIntosh

As McIntosh bent over the desk, one of his enemies,

Big Warrior, the Upper Creek leader, warned him that if he signed the treaty, he would die by "the Law Of Pole Cat Spring." His enemy shrieked at him through the window, "You snake. You will die for this." To the Indians around him, the man standing on the big rock, warning against the treaty, said, "Brothers, the Great Spirit has met here with his painted children of the woods and with our pale-face brethren. I see His golden locks in the sunbeams. You have been charmed and deceived by the double tongue of the snake McIntosh and by the pale face. You are drunk with the fire-water of the pale face. Brothers, the grounds of our fathers have been stolen by our chief and sold by him to the pale face. Their gold is in his pouch. Brothers, the grounds are gone from us, and the plows of the pale face will soon upturn the bones of our fathers."

But McIntosh signed the treaty that was to cost him his life soon afterward. So did a few other chiefs. McIntosh got lands and money for signing the treaty. This treaty provided that in return for ceding 4,700,000 acres of Georgia land, the Creeks would get the same amount west of the Mississippi River, plus a large sum of money, then more money when removal began.

McINTOSH WAS MURDERED BY THE CREEKS FOR SIGNING THE TREATY

Chief William McIntosh went back to his home in Carroll County after he had signed the Indian Springs Treaty.

Big Warrior left Indian Springs after McIntosh signed the treaty and went back to report to the Upper Creeks what had been done. Soon after this, he died.

The Indian agent John Crowell told the President that the Indian Springs Treaty had been obtained by fraud, and that it was not valid. In March, John Quincy Adams succeeded James Monroe as president. Adams decided that the treaty was not valid, and a new treaty with the Creeks should be made. He ordered Georgia's Governor Troup to stop surveying the Indian lands. But Troup was up for re-election. This was the first governor's election that was to be decided by the people. Many of the people wanted those lands that had been obtained from the Indians. They rallied around Troup in his contention that the Indian Springs Treaty was legal and that Georgia would insist on its terms.

The campaign cry of the Troup people became "Troup and the Treaty." Troup even went so far in defying the federal government as to threaten fighting. "Having exhausted our argument, we must stand by our arms," he said. Troup called Secretary of War John C. Calhoun "the unblushing ally of savages" and warned him that if the federal government sent soldiers, Georgia would fight them as enemies and invaders.

Adams called the Creek chiefs to Washington and had them sign another treaty on January 1, 1827. This treaty allowed the Creeks to keep a strip of land along the Chattahoochee, but Georgia did not recognize this treaty. The state went on with the surveying of the Creek lands that had been ceded under the treaty of Indian Springs, including the strip. The lands were distributed to the white men. Out of this land the counties of Fayette, Henry, Monroe, and Dooly were eventually created. President Adams had still another treaty signed on March 4, 1828. In this one the Creeks relinquished even the little strip.

The Upper Creeks, grieving for Big Warrior, decided to execute McIntosh. They met, formally heard the case against him, and condemned him to death under their Law of Pole Cat Springs. Menewa took 170 Indians with him to carry out this sentence. They crept stealthily into the woods near McIntosh's inn, which was also his home, and waited through most of the night. They told James Hutton, an interpreter, to reassure any guests who might be there that they would not kill them. One was there. Badly frightened, he escaped unharmed. About three o'clock on the morning of May 1, they set fire to the house. McIntosh fought as bravely as he could. His son-in-law, Samuel Hawkins, was also killed.

A bloodstained letter was written by one of the Indian wives. Nobody knows whether it was Peggy or Susannah. It was signed by both of them. The letter reads like this:

When you see this letter, stained with blood
of my husband, the last drop of which is now spilt
for the friendship he has shown for your people, I
know you will remember your pledge to us in behalf of your nation, that in the worst of events, you
would assist and protect us. And when I tell you

426

that at daylight on Saturday last, hundreds of the hostiles surrounded our home and instantly murdered Gen. McIntosh.... Chilly escaped by the window... Indians commenced plundering. I was driven from the ashes of my smoking dwelling, left with nothing but my poor little naked, hungry children. I need some immediate aid from my white friends. The same morning, the Creeks caught and tied Col. Samuel Hawkins, kept him tied until 3 p.m. when their chiefs returned and ordered his execution. They refused to cover his body, which is exposed to the fowls and beasts of the forest.... If you do not assist us, God help us.

Chilly McIntosh lived with his mother fifty miles away, but he happened to be at his father's Carroll County house the morning of the attack. He jumped out the window, and went to Milledgeville as fast as he could to tell their cousin, the governor, what had happened.

Help got to them finally. Later Judge John Berrien, a Georgia representative in Congress, got the family payment for the property they had lost.

By this gesture, Berrien did much to heal the breach between himself and his friend Troup, who had resented Berrien's berating him for his fighting attitude toward the federal government. "You are making it hard for the Georgia delegation to help you with the Indian problem," Berrien had warned.

McIntosh's house, containing the desk on which he signed the treaty, is now a museum at Indian Springs. In front is the marker telling the story. The big rock from which the Indian shouted his warning is in front.

MORE TROUBLE FROM THE RED STICKS

Long after the Creeks in Georgia had deeded their last remaining lands to the white governments and gone west, Georgians continued to have trouble with the Upper Creeks from Alabama. These were the Red Sticks, who had always been unfriendly to Georgia. They had been influenced by Alexander McGillivray and by Tecumseh.

Border incidents became so frequent that in 1828 the Georgia legislature passed an act to protect the frontier settlements. The act made it unlawful for any Creek Indian to cross the Chattahoochee River from Alabama for any reason whatever without a written permit from the United States government. Even then, he could stay only three days. The 1964 Georgia legislature revoked this act.

The Alabama Creeks continued to swoop down now and then and attack the settlements. One quiet Sunday morning, May 15, 1836, they attacked the little village of Roanoke in Stewart County, and killed its people. White men in the section later followed three hundred into the Chickasaw-hatchee Swamp, and in a bloody half-hour battle on July 3, 1836, killed many of them. Fourteen whites were also killed.

A Creek Indian Drawing

When the Creeks Left

After the last treaties were signed, the Creeks sent a delegation to explore the western lands that were to be their new homes. Some settled in Arkansas and some in Oklahoma. Andrew Jackson became President in 1828 with the avowed intention of moving the Indians across the Mississippi River. Even the Upper Creeks signed the Removal Treaty of March 24, 1832, in Washington. The federal government guaranteed

428

their safety there in the West. The Creeks were cleared from the path of the whites in the southeast. About 23,000 had moved West.

Many had carried their little possessions tied up in bundles. The leaders had their aides carry the council fire which, they said, should never go out in the West, and conch shells out of which they drank the official "black drink" at their councils and festivals.

The Creek power in the southeast was broken. Some were sad about it. One old Indian said, "Now our people are on the road to disappearance; we are at the end of our trail."

But they built new lives in the West, lighted there their ancient council fires, and recovered much of their old status and dignity as a people.

CHAPTER 32

HOW THE SEMINOLES
WERE DEFEATED

Between the time of the defeat of the Upper Creeks at Horseshoe Bend and the 1820's when the Georgia Creeks began signing the series of treaties under which they eventually gave up their lands and went West, there was trouble with the Seminoles in Florida. Georgia was concerned in this, too. The Seminoles were mostly Creeks who had left other tribes. They were a remnant of the old Creek Confederacy.

Many Creeks had fled to the Florida swamps after the defeat at Horseshoe Bend. Some Creeks in Georgia who had been friendly to the whites were disheartened when Andrew Jackson forced them to sign a treaty giving to the government some land that belonged to friendly Indians who had actually helped the government defeat the Red Sticks or Upper Creeks. These Creeks had gone to Florida and joined the Seminoles. Also with the Florida hostiles were fugitive slaves from Georgia who found refuge there.

In 1815, General Daniel Clinch, for whom Clinch County was named, was sent to demolish the Indian fort. His plantation, Auld Ange Syne in Camden County, had been attacked. McIntosh and two hundred Indians from Georgia helped him. Clinch built Fort Scott where the Chattahoochee joins the Flint River. A hot cannon ball fell into the ammunition at the Indian fort, and exploded, killing three hundred. This angered the Creeks and Seminoles even more. They determined never to cede another inch of their land to the whites. They also refused to vacate lands they had already ceded.

Once the Indians waylaid a mailman and killed him,

430

claiming that it was in revenge for the murder of a Seminole. They later killed Colonel Wiley Thompson of Georgia, an officer who had walked out of the stockade with a friend after dinner for a stroll. They ambushed and killed Major Francis Dade (for whom are named Georgia's Dade County and the Florida county in which Miami is located). With him they killed eight officers and a hundred enlisted men. The country was so enraged over the Dade massacre that scores of volunteers went to fight.

The Seminoles, whose name means "wild ones," began to cause so much trouble that on December 12, 1818, Secretary of War John C. Calhoun ordered General Andrew Jackson to go to Florida and quell the Seminoles and their Creek allies.

Jackson had gone back to his home in Tennessee after Horseshoe Bend and the Battle of New Orleans. He came marching through Georgia on his way to

Florida. Once he stopped at Herod Town near Dawson, where old Creek Chief Herod gave him food and soldiers. On January 22, 1818, Jackson was also at Fort Hawkins in Macon, the fort that had been built there in 1806 and named for Benjamin Hawkins, the Indian agent. A blockhouse of this old fort stands today on the banks of the Ocmulgee just outside Macon. Two days later he was marching through Pulaski County. He put three notches in the trees where he went along. This road came to be known as "Three Notch Trail." Indians who lived in a village called Chehaw also cared for his sick soldiers, and sent along with him forty of their best warriors to help the United States forces defeat the hostile Indians. About this time Governor William Rabun of Georgia had sent Georgia soldiers to the south Georgia country where unfriendly Indians had been attacking Georgians, burning their houses and destroying their crops. Captain Obed Wright was in charge of them. He had orders to stop these depredations and to burn Felemma and Hopaunee, the towns of the hostile Indians. By mistake he burned the village of Chehaw and his men killed some of the Indians there. This led to an angry protest by Andrew Jackson to Governor Rabun. They quarreled vehemently through the mail for some time. Jackson had Captain Wright arrested, but he was released by military authorities. Later

Governor Rabun had him arrested. The President of the United States ordered Georgia to turn him over to the federal marshal, but Wright escaped.

Osceola Was A Seminole Leader

One of the Seminole chiefs was Osceola, for whom Georgia's town of Ocilla was named. His father was a white Georgian who is said to have returned to Florida with a group of Indians who came trading to Harris County, where he lived. In Florida he married an Indian woman named Sally. Osceola was born in the corner of Alabama that is nearest to Georgia, in 1804. He grew up around the camps of white soldiers, and learned many things about war. Later, Americans said that he could not have learned more about strategy if he had studied at West Point. After the death of Osceola's father, his mother took him to live with the Seminoles at Peace Creek.

He became a warrior and a young chief. He was intelligent and, in some ways, he was humane. He forbade his warriors to kill women and children. "We are not making war on them," he said. But he was fierce and merciless to his enemies. His Indian name was As-se-seha-ho-lar. His fellow chiefs among the Seminoles were Jumper, Black Dirt, Prince Philip, Billy Bowlegs, Micanopy, and Wild Cat.

Finally, Osceola was captured, and taken in chains to prison at Fort Moultrie, South Carolina, after he had gone under a flag of truce to negotiate. He had malaria. As he lay dying, he suddenly rose, put on his war regalia and paint, bade goodbye to prison officials and to his family there with him, and died. Osceola was buried at Fort Moultrie.

Jackson had pushed on into Florida and quelled the Seminoles. He had hanged two British subjects whom he accused of inciting the Seminoles to war. One was Arbuthnot, an aged Scot from Nassau who sold guns to the Indians. The other was Armbruster, a Briton who had fought at Waterloo and had later guarded the exiled and imprisoned Napoleon. These hangings caused trouble between the United States and the British government. Federal officials in Washington severely reprimanded Jackson. He never forgot or forgave this.

Chief Osceola

Andrew Jackson Defeated
the Seminoles

The Seminoles were finally quelled, though they claim to this day that they never actually surrendered, and that they were the only ones that did not. The Seminole war, the most costly of all the Indian wars, lasted seven years. The government wanted the Seminoles to move west. But many of them refused.

Jackson wrote: "If you listen to the voice of friendship and truth, you will go quietly and voluntarily. But should you listen to the bad birds that are always flying around you and refuse to move, I have directed the commander to remove you by force. I pray that the Great Spirit will incline you to do what is right." In 1819, John Forsyth of Georgia, then U. S. Ambassador to Spain, had helped buy Florida from Spain. As U. S. property, it was no longer as dangerous to Georgia.

The Seminole matter was not finally settled until after another clash that lasted from 1837 to 1842. Florida became a state in 1845. By that time, 11,700 Seminoles had been sent west. But the small band that fled to the swamp was still there.

The U. S. and the Seminoles had come to an agreement: a twenty-year treaty had been signed at Fort Moultrie on September 18, 1823. They were to give up Florida and get a five-million acre reservation. They got money for moving, to buy tools and stock, to pay a blacksmith, and to educate their children. There was later another treaty at Payne's Landing on the Ocklawaha River May 8, 1832, signed by Chief Holata Amathla and fourteen other chiefs. General Thompson said, "Your father, the President, will compel you to go. The land will be yours while the grass grows and the water runs. If you stay here, you won't have a piece of land as big as a blanket." Some went; others fled to the swamps.

Their descendants boast that they never surrendered. Many of their descendants live there today. They grow most of the palms used in American churches on Palm Sunday. They also make totem poles and canoes. They live much as their ancestors lived. They are said to be the healthiest Indian tribe living today.

CHAPTER 33

THE CHEROKEES

OF GEORGIA

The Cherokees and Their
"Trail of Tears"

The Cherokees, who lived in upper Georgia in what they called the "Enchanted Land," stayed about a decade after the Creeks had left. Then they too left, on their famous "Trail of Tears." North Georgia is often referred to, even today, as "Cherokee country." There is a Cherokee County in north Georgia. Georgia's official state flower is the Cherokee rose, a native of China.

How did it happen that they stayed longer? Whatever the reason the Cherokees held on to their homes longer. They took their case to the president and the Supreme Court, but to no avail. The old prediction of the Jesuit Gottlieb Priber, who lived with the Cherokees and was arrested by Oglethorpe, did not come true. He had prophesied that white men would be driven out by the end of the 1700's. But it was the Indians who had to leave.

This is the story of the Cherokees and how they finally left Georgia for new homes in the West.

Who Were the Cherokees?

The Cherokees were a primitive people when DeSoto moved among them in 1540. Related to the Iroquois nations of northern New York, the Cherokees lived in the Great

Smokies and the Blue Ridge foothills of the southeast, in what are now the states of Virginia, North Carolina, Georgia, and Tennessee.

The word "Cherokee" is said by some to mean "Mountain or cave people." Others say it comes from "chera-log-hoja" which means "men of fire." Their capital, Echota in Tennessee, was burned. For five years their council met at New Town; in 1825 at New Echota, which they called "Oothcaloga." They called themselves "The Principal People," or Ani-yun-wiya.

They were one of a group known as "The Five Civilized Tribes": Cherokees, Choctaws, Chickasaws, Creeks, and Seminoles.

At first the Cherokees lived in caves or rock shelters. After the white men came among them, the Cherokees began to build log cabins, and they had fires inside them. They also got new ideas of government.

Missionaries who came to the Cherokees found many bright children to teach. At first the missionaries only set up missions to convert the Indians. But the Cherokees insisted on schools for their children. At Spring Place in Murray County was a Moravian mission. Not far away was Oothcaloga where John Gambold and his wife had a mission school and a thirty-five acre farm. The teachers sent the brightest of the Indian lads to Cornwall, Connecticut, for further education.

The Cherokees gave surprisingly important place to women. They had a group of "War Women," Nancy Ward, for example, who advised them about battles. Property passed through the female line, and there was provision for divorce. The women had the greatest control over the children. William Bartram described Cherokee women as tall, slender, erect, delicate, with cheerful, friendly faces and with grace and dignity in their movements. He found the Cherokee people grave, dignified and, when not busy with war, gentle and hospitable.

Women tended the gardens, made bread from chestnuts, and stew of possum, of ground hogs, and even of yellow jackets! Cherokees knew more than eight hundred plants and herbs. They made medications of peach leaves or rabbit tobacco. They grew potatoes, squash, pumpkins, corn (which they called maize) and beans. They caught fish and hunted the white-tailed deer, bear, and other game. They gathered berries, persimmons, nuts, crabapples, and grapes. In time of famine, they sometimes ate horsemeat. They had never seen horses before DeSoto brought them; but they would never eat dogs or cats, no matter how great a famine became. They liked broiled venison and corn meal mush. They always threw a piece of meat in the flames for "Grandfather Fire." The men ate first. They drank sassafras tea and a drink called "qualoga," made from sumac berries. They sometimes ate raw fish as a cure for whooping cough. They thought that eating live fish would make them good swimmers. Smallpox ravaged the tribe in 1738, 1783, and 1809, brought by the white men, and they never learned to cure that.

Their name for the Great Spirit was U-ha-lo-te-ga or Setalycate: "He that sitteth above." They believed in a kind of immortality. They believed their priests could talk with the dead. Seven was their magic number, and they had seven clans: Wolf, Deer, Bird, Red Paint, Sky Blue, Potato, and Twisted. Their sacred color was bright yellow.

Their aged men were to them "the old beloved men." They had a saying, "The great chief is longest remembered for the time he helps the lame man across the stream."

The Cherokees had been spread out in about 200 villages over the Appalachian range from Virginia to Florida. Each village had about 100 lodgings, but their territory diminished as the years went by. There were about 20,000 Cherokees in Georgia spread over 40,000 square miles in the Blue Ridge section, later 23 Georgia counties.

They had three groups of settlements which they called the Over Hill Towns, the Middle Towns, and the Lower Towns. Some of their local chiefs were Dragging Canoe, Junaluska, and Hanging Man. There were many half-breeds among them, the sons of white traders who had married Indian women. Many of these became leaders of ability and influence. Some became rich.

The Cherokee half-breeds most prominent in the story are George Guess (known to history as Sequoyah) who invented the alphabet; John Ross, who opposed removal; and the three who favored removal, and were killed for it: Elias Boudinot, who edited the Cherokee newspaper, the *Phoenix*, his cousin, John Ridge, and John's father, known as Major Ridge. Many Cherokees had sided with England against the colonists in the American Revolution. This was a disaster for them.

Indian loyalties shifted. Sometimes they were friendly to the white settlers, but the Cherokees and white men sometimes fought fiercely, and the Indians were at times friend to one white nation and then to another. Once, during a battle between the Cherokees and the English, Captain James Grant reported that he and his soldiers drove 5,000 Cherokees into the woods to starve, and destroyed 1,400 acres of their crops. Sometimes savage Cherokees swooped down on frontier settlements and murdered the white men. Like the Creeks, most Cherokees sided with the British during the war. But Chief Attakullakulla, "Little Carpenter," raised a troop of 500 to help the colonists.

The early Cherokees had been very warlike. A chief said, "If we make peace with the Tuscaroras, we will have to find somebody else to fight, for we cannot live without war. It is our favorite occupation." Their chief path to war was known as "the Warrior's Trace."

They liked fierce games, and one ball game they played with the Creeks was rather brutal. They called it "the little brother of war." Sometimes, they wagered land on the outcome of the game. An old story recounts that a thousand acres around Ball Ground, Georgia, got its name because it passed from one tribe to another after a fierce, three-day ball game in 1818.

The last fight between whites and Indians on Georgia soil was in 1793. Georgians did not fight in it. It was a battle between Tennesseeans and Cherokees. They had attacked a Tennessee settlement, and Colonel John Sevier, a frontier fighter, led his men across the Georgia border, where the Cherokees had fled, and fought a battle with them near the forks of the Oostanaula and Etowah rivers, in the Rome area, in October, 1793. The site, near the city cemetery, is now marked. The Indians dug foxholes along the river bank, but Sevier and his men defeated them badly, and broke much of the fighting spirit of the Cherokees.

Some Cherokees were wealthy, and owned big plantations and slaves. One was James Vann, whose home on a hill near Chatsworth has been restored. (President James Monroe once spent a night here.) He built his home here in

438

1804. He owned many taverns and ferries. He imported fine furniture from Europe for his house. Will Rogers, the late Oklahoma humorist, was a descendant of Vann.

Vann gave the missionaries land. Spring Place, where the Moravians had a school and mission, is within sight of the Vann House. But he did not agree with their teachings, and they did not approve of his actions. He had three wives, and he worked his slaves on Sunday. He was murdered by his brother-in-law in a family quarrel in 1809. His son Joseph, who lived in the house, was evicted three years before the Trail of Tears began. He went west in 1835. He had fought with Andrew Jackson at Horseshoe Bend, and had served in the Cherokee legislature.

His house, now restored, had a fire scar on the stair. Indian colors are in the mantel: blue for the sky, red for the earth, green for the trees, and gold for the autumn harvests.

James Vann's widow, Margaret, who later married her overseer, was the first convert of the missionaries at Spring Place. She was baptized nine years after the mission opened.

The Vann House

Like most peoples of the world, the Indians, especially the Cherokees, had legends, myths, and folklore that they passed down from one generation to another. They had developed as the early Indians tried to explain the mysteries of nature to themselves and their children.

They thought that bears were men who had wandered off to live in the forest. They had a saying, "Don't be too friendly with the bears. You may become one."

Their name for the big sky was "Ga-lun-tali." They thought that the mountains were made by a great buzzard that pulled up the earth with his claws.

The old tales said that Walasiyi, the Big Frog, at Neel's Gap, was once the marshal or leader of the Council, and that the Rabbit was the messenger and mischief maker.

Old men in the Council Room told these tales. They recounted the secret lore of the tribe and retold the old legends. The Old Beloved Men sat, because the Council Room was not high enough for them to stand. They told the youths the old tales.

Instead of beginning his stories "Once upon a time," the Cherokee storyteller always said, "This is what the Old Beloved Men told to me when I was a boy. Ha-you! Ha-You!" ("Ha-you" meant "It is true!")

They believed in kindly guardian spirits: the Yun-Wee-Chuns-Dee, small fairies who lived in caves and looked after the lost among the mountain, especially children, and the Nunnehi, an invincible race of spirits, mortal size. They believed that there had once been a great flood among the mountains and that the people who had drowned returned to dance among the moonbeams when the nights were ashine with silver. They also believed in evil spirits.

The Cherokees Had Many Myths and Legends

TRAHLYTA AND THE WITCH OF CEDAR MOUNTAIN

Nine miles above Dahlonega in the golden hills of Georgia there is a great pile of rocks. This cairn has a strange story.

It is the grave of Trahlyta, a Cherokee Indian princess. But it is there because of the Witch of Cedar Mountain. The

Storytelling In The Council House

witch knew a secret, so the legend goes. The secret was of a spring whose waters would bring eternal youth. She had told this secret to the tribe to which Trahlyta belonged. She showed them the spring, at the foot of Cedar Mountain. The warriors bathed in it and kept their bodies strong and fit for war. Trahlyta, the princess of the tribe, bathed in the waters daily and remained young and beautiful. Many suitors courted her. Wahsega, a young warrior, loved her with a great devotion, but she rejected him. He kidnapped her and took her far from the spot where the crystal spring flowed. Away from the magic waters that could keep her young and beautiful, Trahlyta soon became old-looking and ugly and ill. Before she died, she made Wahsega promise to carry her body back and bury it near the eternal spring.

The Indians put stones from her beloved mountains on her grave. Whenever they passed, they dropped another one there. Soon the legend grew up that it was good fortune to put another rock on the grave of Trahlyta. The legend also said that the Witch of Cedar Mountain would put a curse upon a mortal who took a stone away, or molested the grave of Trahlyta in any way.

The "magic springs" later became known as Porter Springs, and when the white men came, they flocked to the place to bathe there. The waters were supposed to have the power to heal. Porter Springs became, for a time, a popular health center. Lake Trahlyta is not far away from the cairn.

The place is known also as Stone Pile Gap, but that mundane name is rejected by those who like much better the romantic, legend-haunted name of Trahlyta's Cairn. Above the place, the superstitious say, broods the dark spirit of the Witch of Cedar Mountain. She knew the secret, the old tale says, of the fountain of eternal youth for which Ponce de Leon looked in vain.

HOW THE MILKY WAY BEGAN

The Milky Way in the heavens puzzled the Cherokees. They accounted for its origin like this: all the people had a big grinding mill to which they brought their corn, back in the beginning of time. Here they ground the corn into white

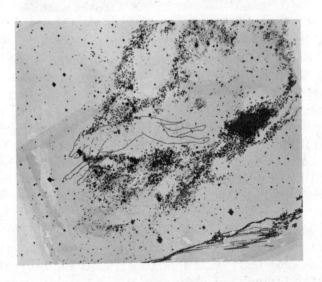

meal. One morning, they came to the mill and found that somebody had stolen most of the meal in the night. They set a watch the next night. The watchman fell asleep. When he was wakened by a noise, he saw that a great dog had eaten most of the meal. He chased and beat the big dog as far as he could reach him, but the dog ran up into the sky. As the dog ran through the heavens to his home in the north, some of the meal he had eaten fell from his mouth, leaving a white trail. The Cherokees called the Milky Way "Gi-li-utsun-stanun-yi," which means "where the dog ran."

THE GHOST OF YAHULA

Yahula was a young Indian trader. He always had bells around his pony's neck so that his customers would hear him coming. Once, after he had been on a hunt, he did not appear on his trading route. They thought he had been killed. They mourned for him, but he came back. He said that he had been cared for in the mountains by the Nunnehi. Yahula told his people that he could not remain with them, for he had eaten the bread of the Nunnehis and had to return to them.

He just stood up and vanished. He came back often, like a ghost. He talked with them, as he always had. But he would suddenly vanish like a phantom. Once he vanished and returned no more. There was a square stone house without an entrance, about ten miles from Dahlonega, known as Yahula's Place. There was also a little stream named for him. At night there, it was said that one could hear him singing his old songs, cracking the whip over his pony, as the bells tinkled, but some thought he went West.

LOVER'S LEAP

On the lower Chattahoochee River were two Creek tribes, the Cussetas and the Cowetas. They were constantly at war with each other. The Cusseta chief was very old. He had outlived all his sons. All that he had left was his only daughter, Mohina. She had once been engaged to a Cusseta, but when the war came, they were not allowed to see each other. They managed to meet in secret in the woods. The Cussetas saw them and chased them. The two lovers ran and leaped from a mountain. They were killed. The old chief listened to the news in silence. Then he let his campfires die. He sat in the quietness and dark and grieved for his child. Soon he was dead.

LEGEND OF THE SWEETWATER BRANCH

Near St. Marys River, there was a small stream that looked like liquid silver. Near it one day sat Chief Withlacoochee, trying to get a thorn out of his foot. Mary Jones, a white girl, came by. She got the thorn out. He told her that if she ever needed a favor, she should let him know. Soon a ship called the "Smashing Nancy," a U.S. recruiting vessel, came by. All the white youths enlisted, including Mary's sweetheart, Ben Johnson. She never expected to see him again and was very sorrowful. She met the old Indian and told him about it. He picked some red and green berries and scattered them on the liquid silver stream, which was called Sweetwater Branch. He told Mary that he had cast a spell here, and that whoever drank the waters of his little silver stream would return. She brought Ben there before he went away, and they drank the waters. He came back safely and they were married.

UTSUTLI, THE SNAKE OF COHUTTA MOUNTAIN

Cohutta means "Frog Mountain," but the Cherokees told the story of a huge snake that lived there. It had feet at each end of its body. It could throw itself across the hollows, from one mountain to another. It bleated like a little deer. When there was danger, the Cherokees said they could see its footprints. When hunters heard its sound, they fled. Finally, not a hunter would hunt on Cohutta Mountain. They had no meat. A man came who wanted meat. He offered to kill the snake. He had heard that it could not move sideways. He set fire to the grass and leaves and encircled the snake. Heat cracked its scales, and the snake died

THE STORY OF HIAWASSEE

When the Cherokees and the Catawbas had a bitter war, a young chief captured a Catawba town. Among the

444

prisoners was Hiawassee, whose name means "beautiful fawn." A lad named Notteley loved her, but the Cherokees refused him permission to marry her unless he could find the place where the waters of the east meet the waters of the west. He found it in the Blue Ridge, near Clayton. But the chief still would not consent to the marriage. The two ran away. The boy became Cherokee chief, and the two made peace between their tribes.

THE RABBIT AND THE TERRAPIN, CHEROKEE VERSION

Many of the old animal tales, told later by Joel Chandler Harris in the Uncle Remus stories, were told long before by the Indians here and elsewhere. The Rabbit was the great mischief maker and bragger in the Cherokee tales as well as the later versions.

The famous story of how the slow turtoise or turtle won a race over the too-confident rabbit by plodding steadily and overtaking the sleeping hare, was also told by the Cherokees. But their version was different: the rabbit did not go to

This was their story: The terrapin and the rabbit had a dispute about who was the fastest runner. The rabbit, always a show-off, laughed at the idea that the slow, plodding tortoise could outrun him.

"You are foolish," said the rabbit. "Everybody knows

445

that I am the swiftest runner in all the world. We will run across four mountain ridges, and I will even give you the first one, just to show you that you have not a chance in the world of beating me in the race.''

Each of them went home to get ready for the race that would begin the next morning. The terrapin called a meeting of his friends. He told them that he needed their help.

''I know I cannot win a race with a rabbit, but at least we can stop his boasting,'' he told them. He explained his plan. His friends agreed to help him, for they, too, were tired of the rabbit's incessant boasting.

Since most terrapins look alike, three friends offered to help. Each one appeared over the top of a ridge — one was there when the rabbit arrived.

WHERE STRAWBERRIES CAME FROM

The Cherokees, who knew over eight hundred different plants, had this story about how strawberries began to grow upon the earth. When the first man and the first woman were created, they lived together happily for a time, and then they had a quarrel. The woman left her husband, telling him that she was going to The Land of the Sun, or Nundagun-yi. He followed behind her, lonely and full of grief.

The Sun, Une-lanun-hi, took pity on him, and asked him if he loved his wife, and wanted her back. He did. The Sun then started planting berries by the road so that she would stop. First, there was a patch of huckleberries. She passed right by them. Then there a clump of blackberries, but she had seen these before, and they did not attract her. One after another, the Sun put berries in her path. But she passed them all. Then the Sun created strawberries, big, red, ripe, luscious. There they nestled in their dewy green leaves. She had never seen strawberries. They were beautiful and tempting. She stopped to pick some. Then she thought of her husband and how they shared good and beautiful things. She began to be sorry she had left him. She made a basket of leaves, filled them with the biggest red strawberries in the patch. Then she turned back, and carried this gift to her husband.

CHAPTER 34

HOW THE CHEROKEES

BUILT A NATION

Sequoyah Invented A

Cherokee Alphabet

A crippled Indian who never learned to read or write the English language gave the Cherokees an alphabet he invented. He is known as "Sequoyah." His alphabet was actually an 86-symbol syllabary. It was an almost miraculous achievement; yet it was to hasten the departure of the Cherokees from their lands in Georgia.

It enabled them to have a printing press, a written constitution, a newspaper and, thus unified and informed, a bicameral legislature and a civilization much like that of the white man. They set up a Cherokee Nation within the bounds of Georgia, but the Georgia legislature refused to tolerate this.

Sequoyah, who invented the Cherokee alphabet, was really never named Sequoyah, though that name is emblazoned on the United States map from California to Georgia. The Sequoia trees in California are named for him. Oklahoma has put his statue in Statuary Hall in Washington as one of the two great men from that state. Many roads, motels, schools, mountains and communities are named for this strange half-breed Indian. His name was actually George Guess or Gist. The word "Sequoyah," which means "possum in a poke," was the term of derision shrieked at him by his superstitious and angry neighbors who did not understand what

447

Sequoyah

he was doing in his cabin, working on pieces of bark, day after day, scratching curious markings. They remembered that his mother Wurteh had belonged to the clan famed for its magic. They thought that crop failures and lost battles were being caused by spells he was weaving against them.

Sequoyah had been a crippled child, and his mother had gathered berries and cured skins for the medicine man in return for his treating the child. Though Sequoyah became able to serve in war, he was always a little lame. He became a silversmith, and he noticed that white men signed the things they made. He believed he could devise written symbols to sign his silver wares. It occurred to him that he could even make an alphabet so that his people would be able to write down their words, or "make the leaves talk" as the white people did. College graduates among the missionaries had tried to devise a written language and failed. It was almost a miracle that this unlettered Indian did it. Some of the symbols are letters of the English alphabet turned upside down, and others are Greek letters.

The Cherokee Council members, especially the "Old

Beloved Men" of the tribe, did not want this written language. They did not welcome the white man's ways. They were not at first convinced that Sequoyah even had the means to provide a Cherokee written language. He took his small daughter, Ay-yo-ka and she helped him convince the elders that their language could be written down, and so easily that a child could understand it. This turned the Cherokee country into one vast schoolroom overnight. The Indians sat around on stumps and fallen trees and learned the new alphabet. A spectacle salesman happened to travel through the country just then selling eyeglasses. The Indians took a fancy to them, and many bought spectacles, and sat around looking like owls as they studied the new alphabet. Some learned it in one day. Scholars marveled at Sequoyah's achievement. Later he was to go back west, and would die in 1843 pushing on farther and farther, with his son Teky and an Indian called The Worm, to find Indians to whom he could teach his alphabet. His grave is in Mexican territory.

In the meantime, here in Georgia, trouble was looming.

The Cherokees Published A Newspaper

After the Cherokees had a written language, they voted to invest in a printing press. The office in which they printed their newspaper, the *Cherokee Phoenix,* is one of the buildings that has been restored at New Echota near Calhoun. Elias Boudinot was appointed editor.

The newspaper was printed in two languages, Cherokee and English. The first issue appeared February 21, 1828. Accounts of the manners and customs of the Cherokees, their progress in education, their religion, the arts of civilized life, and notices of other Indian tribes, plus interesting news of the day were printed. The press and type were sent by ship from Boston to Savannah and hauled by wagon and oxen to New Echota. A printer came from Boston to show them how to install it. They forgot to order paper on which to print the first issue, and had to hurriedly import it from over the mountains in Tennessee.

There were two printers, both white, and an assistant editor named John Candy. One of his duties was to interpret the editor's handwriting for the printers.

The editor, Elias Boudinot, was a bright young Cherokee who was originally named Buck Watie. When he was sent north to school by the missionaries he had taken the name of a Congressman in whose home he had lived. In New England, the Georgia Indian fell in love with a white girl named Harriet Ruggles Gold. She was the daughter of Colonel Benjamin Gold of Cornwall, Connecticut, where the school was located. When Harriet decided to marry the Cherokee, it caused a commotion that closed the school, disrupted the town, and created great anxiety in her family. Her parents warned her that life on an Indian frontier would be hard, especially so far from home. Her sisters, married to young ministers, pled with her to change her mind, largely because they feared their husbands would find it hard to get a pastorate once it became known that they had an Indian as a brother-in-law. Her own brother Stephen and her neighbors burned Harriet in effigy as she watched in terror from the neighbor's home in which she was hiding. The shocked trustees closed the school.

But she stuck to her decision. Boudinot, who had gone to the ministerial school at Andover, came back and they were married. They came to New Echota, and lived in a house much like that of their close friends, Reverend Samuel Worcester and his wife Ann. The Worcester home, from

The Office Of The "Cherokee Phoenix"

450

whence Worcester went to trial in Gwinnett County and then to jail in Milledgeville for being in the Indian country without a license, has been restored at New Echota.

Harriet Boudinot started a Sunday School in her new home, and was greatly loved by the Cherokee people. She wrote letters home telling her family there about her new life, what they had to eat, and how they fared. She always signed her letters "Your Cherokee Sister." Her parents came by carriage to visit her and were delighted with what they found in Georgia.

The Boudinots saw that trouble was coming between the whites and the Cherokees. "I know not what will happen," wrote Harriet.

She was living through the days that her husband was editing the *Cherokee Phoenix,* and she helped and encouraged him in his editing troubles. He had many. First, the printer was getting a higher salary than the editor. So the Cherokees raised Boudinot's salary. Sometimes he found it hard to get ink and paper. He wrote editorials about everything from the wisdom of the Cherokees moving west, which he favored, to the evils of snuff-dipping. In a "warning to snuff-dippers," he wrote of an old woman who took a dip of snuff, sneezed, and got her neck out of joint! An early issue reports the murder of an Indian named Bear's Paw. In his columns are anecdotes about Washington and Jefferson, news of Washington occurrences, and comments on what he liked or disliked about the happenings of his time. He complained that he was not always free to print the truth. The Cherokee Council once warned him to stop writing quarrelsome editorials. The Georgia government seized his presses in 1835.

Gold Was Discovered In the Cherokee Land

When gold was discovered in 1829 on Duke's Creek in what was then a part of Habersham County (now White County), ten thousand goldseekers came swarming in. This aggravated the already existing conflict between white men and Indians. This brought about the nation's first gold rush twenty years before the forty-niners swarmed to Sutter's Mill in California. It also sealed the fate of the Cherokees.

A mint was set up in Dahlonega. The name "Dahlonega" means "yellow metal." The town Auraria became the center

Harriet Boudinot

of the gold rush. About six million dollars worth of gold coins, 1,381,748 pieces of gold, worth $6,115,569, were eventually minted at the U.S. mint in that section. It was taken over by the Confederacy in 1861. Later, the buildings became a part of North Georgia College. Tourists still stop to "pan gold" at the old mines at Dahlonega. Gold was brought in 1960 by covered wagon to Atlanta from Dahlonega to be put on the dome of Georgia's Capitol.

The "gold fever" made many Georgians look with longing at the Cherokee lands. This song was sung in Georgia:

All I want in this creation
Is a pretty little wife and a big plantation
Way up yonder in the Cherokee Nation.

Georgia law decreed that everybody who wanted to dig for

gold must have a license to do it. Indians could be arrested even for digging on their own land, though a judge at Lawrenceville refused to jail an Indian named Cunatoo for digging for gold on his own farm.

When gold was later discovered in California, a geologist stood on the steps of the courthouse at Dahlonega and said to two hundred miners, "Stay here in Georgia. Don't go west. There are millions right here in these hills." Some of these miners went anyhow, and repeated these words, which Mark Twain heard there, and later used for his character, Colonel Mulberry Sellers.

Georgia Extended Its Laws
Over the Cherokee Nation

Georgia authorities did not approve of the existence of a separate nation within the borders of their state. In 1827, the Cherokee Nation had adopted a constitution, which provided for a bicameral legislature and other things similar to the white men's government. Pathkiller was their chief, though he was something of a figurehead. The real power was held by younger, stronger men. Finally, they elected John Ross chief and it was he who fought the desperate fight to keep the Georgia mountain country for the Cherokees.

In 1828, Georgia, which had been waiting in vain since 1802 for the federal government to remove the Indians from its borders, enacted a law that extended Georgia's authority over the Cherokee Nation. This was to become effective June 2, 1830.

The U. S. Supreme Court Finally
Decided Against Cherokees

The Cherokees had several cases that were taken to the highest court in the land. Sometimes Chief Justice John Marshall and his associates decided for the Indians, and sometimes against them. The trouble was that when the decisions were against Georgia, the state ignored them, backed up by President Andrew Jackson himself. "Marshall has made his decision. Now let him enforce it!" said Jackson.

453

The two cases that the court decided for the Indians were these:

The Case of Corn Tassel was a murder case. An Indian named Corn Tassel was sentenced to death in Hall County for killing a man. The case went up on appeal to the United States Supreme Court. William Wirt of Philadelphia was the lawyer for the Cherokees. The Supreme Court ruled that Georgia was in the wrong, but Governor George Gilmer ordered the Hall County authorities to go ahead and execute the sentence. The Charleston, South Carolina "Mercury" summed up the matter like this: "The United States says, 'You, State of Georgia, shall not hang the Indian.' The State of Georgia says, 'We will hang the Indian.' Well, the Indian is hung." This took place in Gainesville, Georgia, earlier called Mule Camp Springs by the Indians.

The case of the arrested missionaries was the second case in which Georgia and the United States Supreme Court were at odds. In 1828, Georgia passed a law requiring all white men in Cherokee territory to have a permit to be there after June, 1830. Those that had no permits had to leave. Eleven of the missionaries who were there were arrested because they had no permits. Governor Gilmer offered to free them if they would leave. Nine of them did. Two, Reverend Samuel Worcester and Dr. Elizur Butler, refused. They were sentenced in the court of Gwinnett County to four years in prison and were taken to the state penitentiary in Milledgeville. The governor went to visit the missionaries. When the two missionaries saw that Georgia did not intend to be bound by the decisions of the Supreme Court, they accepted the offer of the State of Georgia for a pardon. This was granted by Governor Wilson Lumpkin, then the chief executive, and they left Georgia.

The Removal Bill passed Congress on May 24, 1830. Cherokees appealed to the Supreme Court, having hired the famous William Wirt of Philadelphia as lawyer. But on March 5, 1831, that court handed down the decision saying that they were not a separate nation in the meaning of the legal term, and could not bring a suit in the court.

In 1830, the Cherokee chiefs met in their last Council. Georgia laws decreed that no further Council meetings could be held on Georgia soil. (They moved to Red Clay near Dalton after this.) By 1832, New Echota was deserted. Colonel

454

John Lowry, sent by the federal government, told them that Georgia was about to survey their lands, and the white men would draw lots to buy them. The federal government would not interfere. The U. S. government planned to pay annuities to each individual Indian and not to the national treasury, since the Cherokee Nation was no longer recognized. The U. S. began to give them a chance to sign up for new homes in the West.

Elias Boudinot

Two Bitter Factions Grew Up
Under Cherokee Leaders

Just as they had among the Creeks, two bitter factions grew up among the Cherokees. One led by Chief John Ross was against the removal of the Cherokees to the West and fought it to the bitter end. The other, known as the Treaty

455

Party, believed that removal was inevitable and favored ceding the lands to the whites under the best terms they could get. This group was led by Chief Major Ridge, supported by his son John and his nephews, Buck Watie (Elias Boudinot) Cherokee editor, and Stan Watie, later to be a Confederate general.

John Ross was a brown-haired, blue-eyed man who was only one-eighth Cherokee. He had been born at Turkey Town in Alabama in 1791. His parents, Dan and Mollie McDonald Ross, had brought him to Georgia when he was a child. John Ross was the grandson of a Scotch trader, John McDonald, who had grown rich trading with the Indians. McDonald's wife was Ann Shorey. The Cherokee chief was an educated man, and read a great deal. His father had hired a private tutor for him and the other children in the neighborhood. He grew up in Rossville, a town named for him on the Georgia-Tennessee border. His childhood home has been restored in recent years. He fought in the Creek Civil War, helping General Andrew Jackson defeat the Red Sticks or Upper Creeks. He became the business partner of John Timothy Meigs, son of U. S. Indian Agent Return Jonathan Meigs, Jr. Ross acquired much property, including a large plantation at the Head of Coosa and many slaves. His house was just fifteen miles from the home of Joseph Vann, near Chatsworth. Ross married a sixteen-year old Indian girl named Quatie, known for her excellent cookery. Many of her recipes have been preserved. She had gone to the Moravian school and adopted their religion. She was later to die on the Trail of Tears, after giving her coat to a sick child on a wintry night.

Ross was an avid reader of Jefferson's writings and he had helped design the Cherokee Nation and constitution on the principles of Jefferson.

The Treaty Party's leader, Major Ridge, was a full-blooded Cherokee of great charm. He was born at Hiawassee in 1773. His Indian name was Kahmungdahegah, which means "the man who walks the mountain tops." He was known as "The Ridge." He always rode a white horse. He was elected to the Cherokee Council at twenty-three. Many tribal meetings were held at his home, "The Chieftains" on the Oustanaula River. His son John was one of the bright lads who had gone to the school operated in north Georgia by the Moravian missionaries. John had once complained that the courses were being made too easy so that the duller students could learn. He demanded harder lessons to sharpen his mind. Like his cousin, Elias Boudinot, he was sent to the school at Cornwall, Connecticut, and like his cousin, he too married a New England girl. Her name was Sarah Northrup.

Ridge and his Treaty Party members said, "We cannot exist under the laws of the white man. Let us go West."

On October 24, 1835, both groups met at Red Clay near Dalton, after they could no longer meet at New Echota, and signed an agreement to stop quarreling among themselves. Among the chiefs were Rattling Gourd and Rain-in-the-Face. The Indians instructed the Treaty Party to get the best removal terms possible.

Many of the Treaty Party had once been against removal. In 1805, Major Ridge himself was said to have been the executioner when the Cherokees sentenced Chief Doublehead to death for making a secret agreement to cede tribal lands. Boudinot had written in his paper, the *Cherokee Phoenix* on September 7, 1833, "The Cherokees will never give up their land. Georgia might as well try to empty the Atlantic Ocean into the Pacific." But he too had come to believe that removal was inevitable.

John Ross went to Washington in 1834 to seek Jackson's help for the Cherokees' keeping their lands in Georgia. He carried with him Chief White Path, head of an Indian town called Ellija. It stood where the present Ellijay now stands. Jackson was polite to them even though he did not help. He gave White Path a silver watch, which the old chief kept as a precious treasure all the days of his life. At his death, it was sold to erect a monument to him. He became sick at Hopkinsville, Kentucky, and the white people there were very kind to him.

Why the Author Of "Home, Sweet Home" Was Arrested In the Cherokee Country

During the long disagreement between Georgia and the Cherokees, John Howard Payne came into the southeast to get some material for a magazine. He was the songwriter whose song, "Home, Sweet Home," was to become one of the world's most beloved tunes.

457

In Georgia he saw Tallulah Falls, Toccoa Falls, Amicalola, Mount Yonah and the gold mining country. He also went to interview Indian Chief John Ross. Suddenly, Payne was arrested by Georgia officers for being in the territory without a permit. For a while he was held at the Vann House near Chatsworth. Later, his account of his arrest by Georgia authorities was published under the title "John Howard Payne to His Countrymen." He said that he was kept in a small log hut with one door and no window, and that an Indian, the son of Going Snake, was in the same room, chained. Payne was released about two weeks later, and the Georgia Legislature apologized to him.

While he was in Georgia, the songwriter was a guest of Colonel Edward Harden in Athens. He fell in love with pretty Mary Harden, but her father opposed the romance. Neither of the young people ever married.

Jackson Refused To
Help the Indians

In their desperation, the Cherokees appealed to their old war comrade, Andrew Jackson, who had become President of the United States. They had helped him defeat the hostile Creeks and the Seminoles. One of their Cherokee chiefs had even saved Jackson's life at Horseshoe Bend.

The Indians had many friends who did try to help them: Sam Houston, John C. Calhoun, David Crockett, and Edward Everett. A man from Savannah wrote a letter to the *Cherokee Phoenix* reminding the public that the Cherokees had helped save Georgia from hostile Indians and should be protected in their lands. He compared the eviction plans to the partition of Poland in Europe.

However President Jackson was not to be moved by the pleas of the Indians or their friends. He said, "You are not my friends. I have no friends. A curse upon all Indians. If my enemies had not kept me in the South so many years fighting Indians, they would not have been able to defeat me for the presidency in 1824 when I had the most votes." Jackson had received 99 electoral votes, but since there were several in

458

the race, that was not a majority and the election went to the House of Representatives, which elected John Quincy Adams.

Jackson said to Chief John Ross, "Removal is best. We will guarantee your safety and peace in the West." Ross answered, "How can you protect us in the West when you can't even protect us now in our homes in Georgia?"

Chief Junaluska, the one who had saved Jackson's life at Horseshoe Bend, said, "If I had known that Chicken Snake (Jackson) would turn against our people, I would have let him die that day." Jackson appointed a friend from Tennessee, named Benjamin Curry, as "Superintendent" of rounding up the Georgia Cherokees for removal to the West.

Andrew Jackson

Two Governors Worked To Remove the Cherokees

The two Georgia governors who were in office during the Cherokee Removal crisis were, oddly enough, men who had been neighbors in Oglethorpe County. They had both lived near Lexington, Georgia. They were Wilson Lumpkin and George Gilmer. They both wrote books later explaining their part in the removal of the Indians, and why they

thought it necessary that the Indians go to new homes in the
west. They had both been in Congress and had there urged
the removal of the Indians from Georgia.

GOVERNOR LUMPKIN HAD INTRODUCED

THE REMOVAL BILL IN CONGRESS

Wilson Lumpkin worked hard as congressman and as
governor to get the Indians moved to the West. He had been
a teacher, a surveyor, railroad pioneer, and congressman.
But most people remember him mainly for the role he
played in the Indian drama. When he was over seventy
years old, he wrote his memoirs about this, attempting to
show that it was the wisest thing to do. He said at one time
that he valued his work in the Indian removal as the most
important service that he rendered during his life.

Wilson Lumpkin, born in Virginia January 14, 1783,
was brought to Oglethorpe County before he was a year old.
He never went to formal school, though his father taught
him to read the classics and to develop an inquiring mind.
When he was eighteen, he married fourteen-year-old
Elizabeth Walker. He was hired to teach a one-room school
at Long Creek before he was twenty-one.

He went west, on a four-month trip, to see if he would
like to live there. He liked Georgia better. But he had seen
the Indians on his journey, and he had come to believe that
all of them should be moved out of Georgia to the West. He
ran for Congress, got on the Indian affairs committee, and
persuaded them to set up a fund to make plans to
remove the Indians. President Monroe appointed him to
settle some Indian boundaries. He was not re-elected to
Congress, but his defeat had nothing to do with his views
about the Indians. The country was angry with Congress
because it had voted to raise its own salary. Lumpkin had
voted against this, but the country swept out most Congressmen, no matter how they had voted.

In Georgia, he was in the legislature. He was appointed
one of a six-man board to help engineer Hamilton Fulton
survey the state for better transportation, both railway and
waterway. More than ever, he wanted to clear out the
Indians. The Creeks would not let travelers go through

460

some of their territory, and the Cherokees did not want wagons because they would bring in the unwanted white men. Young Indians organized the Pony Club, a gang that attacked, robbed, and killed travelers from Tennessee to Augusta and Savannah.

Lumpkin, back in Congress in 1827, served on many committees that considered Indian affairs. He was appointed by President Andrew Jackson, whom he had supported in 1824 when Jackson lost to John Quincy Adams, to negotiate treaties and work on boundaries.

He talked often with Jackson about the Indians. In 1829, Jackson included in his first message to Congress his views about the removal of the Indians from Georgia and the rest of the southeast to the West. Finally he introduced a removal bill in Congress. There was much spirited debate about it because there was great sympathy all over the nation for the Cherokees.

GILMER WAS GOVERNOR WHEN THE CHEROKEES LEFT

George Rockingham Gilmer would be serving his second term as governor when the Cherokees finally left Georgia. He had been governor in 1829 and 1830, had gone to Congress in the meantime, and was re-elected governor and served from 1837 to 1839. The new Governor's Mansion in Milledgeville was completed during his second term, and he became the first of the eight governors who lived in the Mansion. Gilmer appealed to President Andrew Jackson to remove the federal troops from the Cherokee country so that he could send in Georgia troops. This Jackson did. Gilmer did not run again in 1839. He retired in 1840, bought a home, The Cedars, at Lexington, which is still there. It had been built in 1800. Around it were crepe myrtle, jasmine, and rose bushes.

Nearby are Shaking Rock and Coon Hollow. He was ill and, to pass the time, he wrote a book in which he told many things about the Cherokees. The book, which also included his opinions and some gossipy reports of his neighbors, was titled *Sketches of Some of the First Settlers of Upper Georgia, of the Cherokees and of the Author*. He sent several copies to his aristocratic relatives in Virginia. Gilmer's family was one of the original families that came from Virginia and settled at Goose Pond after the

461

Revolution. Visiting his relatives in Virginia some years later, he was surprised to find that they were ashamed of his book and had hidden it in the attic. He came home, bought every copy he could find and burned them. A rare collector's item, it has recently been reprinted.

When he died in 1859, Gilmer left a fund at the University of Georgia, which he served as trustee for thirty years, to be used for the education of teachers. Gilmer Hall on the University campus was named for him. So was Gilmer County, one of the counties made from the Cherokee lands. His tombstone at Bethsalem cemetery in Lexington does not mention the fact that he was governor.

CHAPTER 35

THE FINAL DEPARTURE
OF THE CHEROKEES

There had been about 25,000 Cherokees in Georgia. But some of them had started going west as early as 1795. By 1817, two thousand had crossed the Mississippi River. Sequoyah was with a group that had gone west in 1818. When the crisis came, there were about 20,000 still here.

As early as 1833, the federal soldiers began rounding up the Cherokees to take them to their new home in the West. The first group was scheduled to go in 1834. The government expected 1,200 Indians to sign up for this, but only 475 did. They were housed in 28 log shelters built at Hiawassee. The journey was delayed because there was a cholera epidemic in the West. The camp where the Indians were kept was the center of fighting and brawling. The Indians, not used to being kept in a camp, often got sick and died. The food was not very good. Lieutenant Joseph Harris was the army officer in charge. He was assisted by a man named John Mills, who had married a Cherokee girl and kept a diary of the Indian removal. The first expedition started down the river in March, 1834. By April it had reached the Arkansas River, but 81 had died, 50 of them of cholera.

The Ridges and Boudinot Signed
the Final Removal Treaty

On December 29, 1835, the United States government met with some of the Cherokee leaders at their capital,

New Echota, near the present town of Calhoun, Georgia, and made a treaty with them about their removal to the West. The Treaty Party leaders, Elias Boudinot, Major and John Ridge, signed the agreement to give up their lands and move west.

For a large sum, the Cherokees gave up all their claims to lands east of the Mississippi River which, of course, included all their lands in Georgia. "Our gold alone is worth more than this," Ross had protested. They were to get seven million acres beyond the Mississippi. This land was never to be included in any state. If they needed more land, the U. S. government agreed to sell it to them. The government was to protect them from foreign enemies and civil strife. The United States was also to convey them free to their new home and to maintain them for one year. This treaty was ratified by the U. S. Senate on May 23, 1836.

They were given two years to leave Georgia, until May 23, 1838. The lands in the ten counties created were distributed by lottery. Even before the final treaty had been signed, white settlers were pushing into the lands; the lotteries had begun in 1834.

Spring Place, near Chatsworth, where there was a mission school, was taken over by a newcomer. The house that James Vann had built was taken. A man knocked at its door one day and told the owner, "You can pay the rent to me now." At first the missionaries bolted the door. Later, they left. John Ross came home one day to his beautiful house with its imported French furniture, and its big library, there at the Head of Coosa. He found a stranger in the yard, calling to his strutting peacocks. It was the new owner. Now the stage was set for the well-known "Trail of Tears."

On Friday, May 18, 1838, Georgia took possession of the Cherokee land. On that day, Georgia's soldiers met at New Echota, organized and elected officers. On May 24, 1838, they started helping the U.S. Army men round up the Indians, and they continued until June 3, 1838. The Indians were taken to Ross' landing.

General Scott Was Sent With the
Army To Remove the Indians

General Winfield Scott, commander-in-chief of the U.S.

464

Army, rounded up the Cherokees and moved them from their Georgia mountains. He was on the border of Canada when he was ordered to Georgia. He had two regiments and five hundred guns from Georgia. The Georgia Volunteers helped him round up the Cherokees.

He later helped remove the Seminoles from lower Georgia and upper Florida. He was also later to fight with brilliance in the Mexican War. A lake in north Georgia is now named for him. Between Dahlonega and Auraria, in Lumpkin County, is a bronze marker pointing to "The Station," where he had chief headquarters while superintending the Cherokee removal on their "Trail of Tears." He was known as "Old Fuss and Feathers."

Scott was fond of games like whist, but he always liked to win. When he lost, he could always give a reason. He read much, especially Shakespeare and Gibbon. He disliked eating alone, and would pay for another person's dinner in order to have company. He prided himself on his ability to cook, especially to make bread. Sometimes when he had to stay at a hotel or inn, he would try to teach the cook how to make bread that he liked. He liked soup, but since soup was then considered a very "sissy" dish, this is thought by some to have helped defeat him for President later. His part in the removal also lost him votes.

When he was out of uniform, he liked to carry a gold-headed cane. He was Episcopalian, and often attended church. He had dropsy, and was also so big that it was almost impossible for him to kneel, but he sat with his head bowed in prayer when he was in church.

He was so tactless that he made many enemies, some in high places. But some of his enemies also became his friends when they saw him closely and realized that he was a man of integrity who never swerved from what he considered his duty. One of these was Nicholas Trist, the husband of Jefferson's granddaughter, who was sent to Mexico to negotiate the peace treaty. Filled with tales against Scott by enemies in Washington who did not want the old general to become a national hero and perhaps get to be president, Trist wrote him sharp letters. Scott replied even more sharply. But when they met they became fast friends and Trist defended Scott against the charges later brought against him.

Winfield Scott

Scott was careless about keeping vouchers for the money he spent. He was stern about punishing officers or men, and was more than once brought before a court of inquiry. Twice nominated for president, he never was elected, but he played an important role in history. Without him, Georgia most likely could not have removed the Cherokees. Without him, the United States could not have defeated Mexico's Santa Anna. He and General Zachary Taylor became heroes in the Mexican War.

He was terribly strict with his officers, never allowing them to appear without regulation attire when they were in uniform. One night an aide tiptoed out of Scott's sickroom in his shirtsleeves to get some water, thinking the old man asleep. When he returned, Scott said to an officer, "Take that man to the guardhouse!" He did not hesitate to arrest or punish the highest officers who were derelict in their duties.

GENERAL SCOTT'S ADDRESS TO
HIS SOLDIERS MAY 17, 1838

Scott, a former lawyer, issued two official proclamations. To his soldiers, he said:

"Considering the number and temper of the masses to be removed, together with the extent and vastness of the country occupied, simple indiscretions, acts of harshness and cruelty on the part of the troops may lead step by step to delays to impatience and exasperation, and in the end to general war and carnage — a result, in the case of these particular Indians utterly abhorrent to the generous sympathies of the whole American people. Every possible kindness, compatible with necessity of removal, must therefore be shown by the troops; and if a despicable individual should be found capable of inflicting a wanton injury or insult on any Cherokee man, woman or child, it is hereby made the special duty of the nearest good officer or man instantly to interpose, and to seize and consign the guilty wretch to the severest penalty of the law. The major general is fully persuaded that this injunction will not be neglected by the brave men under his command, who cannot be otherwise than jealous of their own honor and that of their country.

"By early and persevering acts of kindness and humanity, it is impossible to doubt that the Indians may soon be induced to confide in the army, and instead of fleeing to the mountains and forests, flock to us for food and clothing. If, however, through false apprehensions, individuals, or a party here and there, should seek to hide themselves, they must be pursued and invited to surrender, but not fired upon, unless they should make a stand to resist. Even in such cases, mild remedies may sometimes better succeed than violence; and it cannot be doubted if we get possession of women and children first, or first capture the men, in either case the outstanding members of the same families may readily come in on the assurance of forgiveness and kind treatment.

"Every captured man, as well as all who surrender themselves, must be disarmed, with the assurance that their weapons will be carefully preserved and restored at or beyond the Mississippi. In either case, the men will be guarded and escorted, except it may be where their women and children are safely secured as hostages; but in general, families in our possession will not be separated unless it be to send men as runners to invite others to come in.

"It may happen that Indians will be found too sick, in

the opinion of the nearest surgeon, to be removed to one of the depots indicated above. In every such case, one or more of the family or the friends of the sick person will be left in attendance, with ample subsistence and remedies, and the remainder of the family moved by the troops. Infants, superannuated persons, lunatics, and women in helpless condition will all, in the removal, require peculiar attention, which the brave and humane will seek to adapt to the necessities of the several cases."

GENERAL SCOTT'S ORDER TO THE CHEROKEES
ABOUT REMOVAL, MAY 17, 1838

"CHEROKEES: The President of the U.S. has sent me, with a powerful army, to cause you, in obedience to the treaty of 1835, to join that part of your people who are already established in prosperity on the other side of the Mississippi. Unhappily, the two years which were allowed for the purpose, you have suffered to pass away without following, and without making any preparation to follow, and now, or by the time that this solemn address shall reach your distant settlements, the emigration must be commenced in haste, but I hope, without disorder. I have no power, by granting a further delay, to correct the error that you have committed. The full moon of May is already on the wane, and before another shall have passed away, every Cherokee man, woman, and child, in these states, must be in motion to join their brethren in the far west.

"My friends, this is no sudden determination on the part of the President, whom you and I must now obey. By the treaty, the emigration was to have commenced on or before the 23rd of this month, and the President has constantly kept you warned, during the two years, that this treaty would be enforced. I am come to carry out that determination. My troops already occupy many positions in the country that you are to abandon, and thousands are approaching from every quarter, to render assistance and escape hopeless. These troops are your friends. Receive them and confide in them. Obey them when they tell you that you can no longer remain in this country. Soldiers are as kindhearted as brave, and the desire of every one of us is to execute our painful duty in mercy. We are commanded by the President to act toward

468

you in that spirit, and such is the wish of the whole people of America.

"Chiefs, head men, and warriors — Will you then, by resistance, compel us to resort to arms? God forbid! Or will you, by flight, seek to hide yourselves in mountains and forest and thus oblige us to hunt you down? Remember that in pursuit it may be impossible to avoid conflict. The blood of the red men may be spilt, and if spilt, however accidentally, it may be impossible for the discreet and humane among you, or us, to prevent a general war and carnage. Think of this, my Cherokee brethren! I am an old warrior, and have been present at many a scene of slaughter; but spare me, I beseech you, the horror of witnessing the destruction of the troops; but make such preparation for the emigration as you can, and hasten to this place, to Ross' Landing, or to Gunter's Landing, where you will be received in all kindness by officers. You will find food for all, and clothing for the destitute, and thence at your ease and in comfort, be transported to your new homes in accordance

The Trail Of Tears

with the terms of the treaty. This is the address of a warrior to warriors. May his entreaties be kindly received and may the God of both prosper the Americans and Cherokees and preserve them long in peace and friendship with each other.''

Many Died On The Trail Of Tears

The Cherokees were sad at leaving their beautiful mountain country in north Georgia, which they had called the ''Enchanted Land.''

The army took the men from the fields, the women from their cabins, and the children from their play. It was hot summer weather when the round-up began. John Ross begged General Scott to let them wait until cooler weather, promising that they would go peacefully then. Scott agreed, provided that these Cherokees would leave on their 700-mile journey by October 20. About 5,000 Cherokees had already gone West by this time.

In October, some 14,000 more Cherokees gathered at Ross' Landing on the Tennessee line. Others left from Rattlesnake Spring near Hiawassee.

They had waited too long. The weather, cool at first, became freezing wintry weather. They did not have enough blankets. There was much suffering. One Georgia officer said many years later that he had seen nothing in war as sad as this exodus of the Indians from Georgia. About 4,000 died on this westward journey.

There was so much misery on this journey that it became known in history as The Trail of Tears.

WHY TSALI DID NOT GO WEST

As the Indians started out on the Trail of Tears, many of them looked back at their little homes there among the mountains. One Indian woman, the wife of Tsali, walked too slowly along the road. A soldier prodded her with his bayonet. Suddenly Tsali and his friends jumped the soldier and killed him. Then they all escaped into the mountains. They lived on berries and roots and fish.

The United States soldiers hunted and hunted for them. There were other Cherokees who were still in the mountains also. Finally, the American commander sent a message to

Tsali. He said that if the old Indian would come down with his sons and be shot, the government would let the remaining Cherokees stay on in the hills undisturbed. Tsali thought this over, and he came down, with his sons. They were shot by members of their own race, at the order of the commander, near the Tuckaseegee River. All but one of the sons died. The commander spared the youngest son, Watisunia, who was only a child. Many of the descendants of this remaining son of Tsali live at Cherokee, North Carolina, on the Cherokee Indian reservation there now.

The dramatic story of Tsali and his people has been told in the play "Unto These Hills" by Kermit Hunter. This starlit story is enacted in an amphitheater on the summer nights there at Cherokee. Money from it has sent many Indians to college. About 3,500 Indians live at Cherokee. A fair held each October exhibits their ways and wares to the world.

Alum, the cave where Tsali hid, is near Mt. LeConte, a peak named for Georgia's famous scientist, Joseph LeConte, of Liberty County.

These Cherokees have adopted modern ways, but they still re-enact their old tribal dances, like the Bear Dance, the Green Corn Dance, and the Ground Hog Dance, at festival time in the Great Smokies.

Boudinot And The Ridges Were Killed By Their People

The Cherokees did the same thing the Creeks had done; they killed their leaders who had signed the treaty that ceded away their Georgia lands.

Major Ridge and his son John Ridge, and their kinsman, Elias Boudinot, had moved with the Cherokees to Oklahoma after they signed the Removal Treaty at New Echota. They had taken up new homes there in June, 1839. The Cherokees sent a party of warriors to kill them. They had decreed death for these three, under the ancient laws of the tribe.

Boudinot was living with his second wife and their six children. He was helping a neighbor build a house. Three men came up and asked him for some medicine. Boudinot was in charge of the supplies. He started with the three men toward the house three hundred yards away, where the medicines were kept. Halfway there, they killed him. The Ridges were also killed. Major Ridge was dragged out of his house and shot. John was ambushed, killed, and left dead on the roadside. It was June 22, 1839.

There were stories that John Ross had a hand in plotting these murders, and a guard of six hundred Indians was placed around his home in the West to keep friends of the Treaty Party from murdering Ross in revenge.

What Became Of John Ross?

John Ross was a leader of the Indians in the West. He helped heal the old factionalism, and signed a treaty of friendship with the other group. They chose Tallequah for their western capital on September 6, 1839. New Echota and the days in Georgia had became just memories. He lacked the warmth and charm of John Ridge. His talk was dull, low-keyed, but sensible. He did not have the education or the eloquence of the Ridges, but he had done his best for his people. He married a seventeen-year-old Quaker girl after the death of his wife Quatie.

He was still alive in the West when the War Between the States divided the North and the South. He tried to keep the Indians neutral, but in spite of him, some of them signed a treaty with the Confederacy, which he would not repudiate, even when Union troops invaded the West. He went to Philadelphia and stayed until the war was over.

And so at last the Indians were gone. The red men who had hunted in the Georgia swamps, fished in its waters, and crossed the old trails to make war or to trade had gone to the West.

But there were still on Georgia's earth and Georgia's map reminders that once they had been the sole occupants of this land. There were Indians sites, like Rock Eagle Mound and Track Rock Gap, Indian names like Tallapoosa, "Golden Waters," Ellijay, "the place of green things growing," and Chestatee, "place of the lights," and a thousand and one more. Never as long as there is a Georgia will men forget that the Indians had been in this place.

Indians Filed Claims Against U.S.

In modern times, many Indian tribes have sought payment for old wrongs they felt were done them by white men.

On August 13, 1946, Congress set up the Indian Claims Commission to act as a court to "settle all just and equitable Indian tribal claims against the U. S." The Indians were given a five-year deadline to do this. By the deadline, groups representing 350,000 Indians had filed claims. In 370 cases, they asked payment for one and a half-billion acres which they said were taken from them by white men.

Descendants of Georgia and Alabama Creeks sued for payment for the lands Andrew Jackson took from the friendly Creeks after Horseshoe Bend. The seven hundred descendants were awarded $3,573,810.

THE CIVIL WAR

UNIT 7

AMERICA'S DEADLIEST FIGHT

SHERMAN'S MARCH THROUGH GEORGIA

CHAPTER 36

BACKGROUND OF THE WAR

Introduction: A Hundred Years Ago

What was the Civil War? How did Georgia get into it? What happened here, and what difference did it make? Why did the Confederate flag have thirteen stars when there were only eleven Confederate states? And why did the South sing "The Bonnie Blue Flag" when its flag was not blue?

This war is often called "The War Between the States." That term came from a book Alexander Stephens wrote, titled *A Constitutional View Of The Late War Between The States.* Some southerners like that name better because they point out that the term "Civil War" refers to war between the people of the organized state or nation, and that this was a war between two separate nations: the United States and the Confederate States of America. But war was fought to decide whether states could secede from the United States and form a separate nation — and the answer was "No." Thus it became a Civil War between people of two sections of the same nation. Lee himself referred to it as the Civil War, and the term has now become almost universally accepted. In 1961, there began a four-year observance of the Centennial. Georgians and others took a long look at this tragic four years in a time long past.

Why was it fought? Was slavery or were states' rights the cause? The historian Bruce Catton says, "Slavery was not the only cause of the Civil War, but it was unquestionably the one cause without which the war would not have taken place."

It settled the question of whether the state could secede. It ended slavery. Could the war have been avoided? Some think it could have been. Churchill said this was the least avoidable war in all history. The poet Longfellow thought it as inevitable as the Revolution.

The South was not the first section to think of seceding from the Union. The New England states had threatened to secede as early as 1814 and as late as 1857.

Many think also that Ulysses S. Grant in the North and Robert E. Lee in the South were in command from the first day of war to the last. Actually, both came very late to their high commands, though they had been fighting in lesser positions before. Lincoln had tried six generals before he put Grant in command in 1864. Davis made Lee commander on February 6, 1865.

This was not only a war of Americans against Americans, but of friends, neighbors, and sometimes families against their dearest ones. Lee resigned from the United States Army to fight for his native Virginia. Some northern men, like General John C. Pemberton of Pennsylvania, chose to fight with the South. Mrs. Abraham Lincoln herself had brothers fighting for the Confederacy; some were wounded in Georgia. Her brother-in-law was a Confederate general. Most Georgians, even those who were slow to favor secession, were for the Confederacy after it was established. But there were in north Georgia, especially in mountainous Union County and in Pickens, those who kept the United States flag flying throughout the war. And some families were like that of Wilkes County Union man, Judge Garnett Andrews, whose children were all passionately for the Confederacy.

Why It Was Deadly

More men died in this war than in all the other seven wars the nation has fought combined. In the Civil War, 618,000 Americans died. In the other seven wars, 589,511 died; 4,435 in the American Revolution; 2,260 in the War of 1812; 1,733 in the Mexican War; 2,446 in the Spanish-American War; 116,563 in the first World War; 407,828 in the second World War; and 54,246 in Korea. In the Civil War, the North sent in 2,500,000 soldiers and lost 360,000. The South had a million fighting and lost 258,000. Georgia sent 125,000 and lost more than 25,000. Over one out of ten of the South's soldiers were Georgians. Georgia sent more and lost more than any other state in the Confederacy. The 3,500,000 men who fought in the Civil War made other wars seem small. In one battle alone, the Battle of Fredericksburg, 200,000 men were fighting. Even at Waterloo, where Napoleon was defeated, only 170,000 men fought. During the four years of the Civil War, there were over 6,000 combat engagements, of one kind or another. About 300 were fought in Georgia, where some of the bloodiest battles of the entire war were fought.

Why It Was Different

This was the first war covered so well by newspaper reporters. One even came from London, and covered both sides. He was William Russell, whose reports were later published in the book: *My Diary, North and South.*   Some generals objected, especially Sherman.   He threatened to hang a reporter, probably because newspapers had called him insane. But he said that he objected because the enemy could read about his plans in the papers. Some generals jailed reporters.

Matthew Brady, a photographer, made this the best-photographed war up to that time. But he invested so much in cameras and equipment that he died in poverty.

THIS WAS A SINGING WAR

More songs came out of it than any other; Julia Ward Howe's "Battle Hymn of the Republic" was one. Soldiers also sang "Tenting Tonight," "Just Before the Battle, Mother," "Dixie," "Bonnie Blue Flag," and many others.

People are often puzzled about the song "Bonnie Blue Flag." The first Confederate flag adopted, the "Bonnie Blue Flag" was one with blue two-thirds of the way down, background for a circle of white stars, and in the middle third, a red field with a white stripe. This is the flag that was unfurled in Montgomery on March 4, 1861. When it became apparent that it looked too much like the Stars and Stripes and caused confusion in the first battle, it was changed. The later flag, designed by General Beauregard, is the one we know today as representative of the Confederacy: red field with blue diagonal cross bars and the thirteen white stars, even though only eleven states were actually in the Confederacy.

MANY FAMOUS MEN FOUGHT IN THIS WAR

Lew Wallace, who later wrote *Ben Hur,* was a Union general. Justice Oliver Wendell Holmes, the United States Supreme Court's "Yankee from Olympus" was wounded. General Ambrose Burnside, a famous Federal officer, wore his hair cut in a fashion that prompted the word "sideburns" as a hair style for men afterwards. Two poets were in the war: Walt Whitman for the North, and Sidney Lanier for the South. Both spent much of their time caring for the sick and wounded. More men died of disease and privations in the Civil War than from bullets.

Sidney Lanier

MORE BOOKS HAVE BEEN WRITTEN ABOUT THIS WAR THAN ANY OTHER

There are already more than 100,000. There are clubs devoted to the discussion of this Civil War. Two books written before the war started had tremendous impact.

In 1852 Harriet Beecher Stowe wrote *Uncle Tom's Cabin*, a book that many southerners considered a sentimental and unfair picture of slavery. It roused great opposition in the North and in England to slavery. Fannie Kemble put her bitter, anti-slavery letters from a Georgia plantation into a book.

The Events That Led Up To Secession

There was no one thing that caused the war. Many events, one after another, increased the bitterness and the differences between the North and the South. At first it was possible to compromise some of the differences, but that only delayed the inevitable conflict.

The crux of the secession situation was, of course, slavery. The South thought that a state should have the right to decide about that. Thus it was the states' rights question, sharpened by the opening of the West and provoked by the differences over the tariff, that contributed most to the final outcome: war.

What The Slavery Situation Was

Slavery had long existed in the world. The old Greeks and Romans had had slaves. Many of them were very well-educated people who had been conquered in war. Some acted as tutors to the children of their owners.

After the fall of Greece and Rome, other civilizations had slavery. In 1685, King Louis XIV of France issued a slave code protecting the slaves from cruel treatment. England and Spain did likewise. Later many southern states, including Georgia, had slave codes that protected the slaves. Georgia had been the only original colony to forbid slavery. Slavery had started among the American settlements when a ship landed in 1619 at Captain John Smith's Jamestown (founded in 1607) with twenty slaves for sale.

But slavery began to die out in the world. In the United States, the Constitution itself authorized Congress after 1808 to forbid slave trade. Parliament decreed its ending in the British Empire at this same time. The Northwest Ordinance of 1787 forbade slavery in that territory.

Slavery did not pay. It cost a great deal to buy slaves,

The Old Slave Market In Louisville

and it was expensive to maintain them. In the United States, northern factory owners found that it was cheaper for them to hire the incoming European labor for wages than to own slaves, and the slaves did not take well to factory work. Thus slavery became a dying institution. George Washington had said he wished some way could be found to abolish it. In his will, he had freed his own slaves.

Jefferson and Lee were among the southerners who later freed theirs. Grant still owned slaves when the Civil War began.

Wealthy Indians, like Joseph Vann at Spring Place, owned slaves. So did Chang and Eng Bunker, the famous Siamese twins who left P.T. Barnum's Circus, married, and bought farms in North Carolina.

Most of the slaves brought into the United States were in the South because they worked best in the cotton, rice, and indigo fields. (Indian slaves had been tried unsuccessfully.) But the southerners found slavery expensive; it took one slave all day to separate a little cotton from the seeds. Then Eli Whitney invented the cotton gin. Cotton became a money-making crop, and more land and more slaves were needed. About 70,000 slaves were imported each year.

By 1860, southerners owned four million slaves. Some southerners moved west to get more land. The northerners feared that slavery would spread throughout the West. One result might be that slaveholders would then control Congress, and it could never be ended.

Many southerners had begun to feel that slavery was morally wrong. But they were caught up in an economic system. They could not afford to lose the great amount of money they had invested in slaves, and no way could be found to reimburse them for the loss. Besides, what would happen to four million black people freed and uneducated and unprepared for freedom?

Some had suggested that the slaves be freed and established in a colony somewhere. Lincoln himself had once suggested that a colony in the Caribbean be started for them. Some slaves were sent to a new colony in Africa named Liberia. Alfred Cuthbert, a Georgia slave owner, for whom Cuthbert, Georgia, was named, not only freed slaves but paid their way to Liberia. He was chairman of a group of slave owners that did this.

The Missouri Compromise Delayed War

The slavery question of the West first clamored for national attention when Missouri wanted to come in as a slave state. This was about 1820. By this time, a group of radical anti-slavery people, known as Abolitionists, were making concentrated efforts to abolish slavery. The North and South became more and more divided on the subject, though there were slaveholders in the North and there were southerners who were against slavery.

There were now eleven slave states and eleven free states. Missouri wanted to come in as a slave state. Naturally, the North objected. Henry Clay proposed a compromise that said Missouri could come in as a slave state, but that there could be no more slave states above her southern border, or a line that ran across the whole Louisiana Territory at 36° 30′ latitude. It was just at this time too, too, that Maine, which had been a part of Massachusetts since 1677, wanted to separate and come in as a free state. That kept the balance at twelve-twelve and enabled the Missouri Compromise to be accepted. But later, it would be made null and void.

The aging Jefferson, at Monticello, read about the Missouri Compromise and foresaw that the nation was heading toward a conflict. He said, just a little while before he died, "It is like a firebell clanging in the night!" John Quincy Adams, who became president four years after the Missouri Compromise was reached, said that it was but the preface to a tragic story.

The Missouri Compromise delayed the Civil War. But in the meantime, there were other issues besides slavery that were dividing the North and the South. One was the tariff, the threat of "nullification."

Nullification And The Tariff Provoked A Quarrel

Nullification and the tariff were other sore spots between the North and the South. The factory owners in New England and other parts of the North, found that the factory owners in England, who paid their workers less, could ship their products over here and sell them cheaper than the products made in this country. So they wanted a protective tariff put on these goods. The tariff, which means a tax paid on things imported into this country, had at first been just another source of revenue for the young American government. Now the factory owners wanted it for protection. The southerners, who had to buy these products, did not want high tariffs.

The northern men used their power in Congress to get tariffs set so high in 1828 that one became known as 'The Tariff of Abomination."

Some states, notably South Carolina influenced by Calhoun, threatened to pay no attention to this tariff law. They said they would nullify it within the state boundaries. President Andrew Jackson said if they tried this, he would send soldiers down to force them to obey the law. Some states threatened to secede over nullification. Finally, Henry Clay proposed a compromise by which the tariff was gradually reduced. So this sore spot was eased somewhat, until the panic of 1857 brought new pressure for higher tariffs.

The tariff was not the first law that had caused states

to threaten nullification. As early as 1798, Virginia and Kentucky had threatened to nullify the Alien and Sedition laws.

Why Georgia Agreed To The Compromise Of 1850

In 1848, twenty years after the discovery of gold in Georgia, gold was discovered in California, and thousands swarmed in. California wanted to come into the Union as a free state. Georgia-born John C. Fremont was governor. Clay again worked out a compromise that had so many things in it that it became known as the Omnibus Bill. In general, it was favorable to the South, though some southerners opposed it. It provided that (1) California enter as a free state, (2) all the rest of the land the United States had acquired from Mexico be divided into two territories, north and south, and each be allowed to decide by "squatter sovereignty" (vote of the people there) whether the state should be free or slave, (3) part of Texas should be taken to create the state of New Mexico, and Texas be paid for it,

Stephen A. Douglas

(4) slave trade should be forbidden in the District of Columbia, though the slaves already there or brought there by their owners would still be slaves, and (5) a stronger Fugitive Slave Law would enable slave owners to recover their runaway slaves more easily.

Henry Clay, known as "the Great Compromiser" had visited in Georgia and knew well the Georgians in Congress and other leaders in the state. Once when speaking in Milledgeville, he was given a red rose for his lapel by a tiny girl who wrote of it later in her diary.

Some Georgians disliked Clay because he had supported John Quincy Adams for President in 1824 instead of Georgia's William H. Crawford. Adams named Clay Secretary of State. Clay so wanted to be president himself that he twice declined to run for vice-president, though both times he would have become president by the death of the man in that office. Many Georgians did like Clay, and some listened to his proposal that the states compromise their differences in 1850.

The North did not like the 1850 Compromise because it opened up all the rest of the territory, except California,

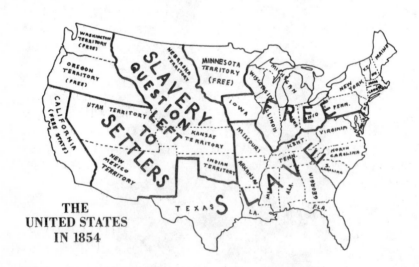

**THE
UNITED STATES
IN 1854**

to slavery if the people there so voted. The Missouri Compromise of 1820 had said no slave states could be created above 36° 30′ latitude. This Compromise said they could.

It was Georgia that practically saved Clay's 1850

Compromise. It was championed in Georgia by three Georgians then in Congress: Alexander Stephens, Robert Toombs, and Howell Cobb. Governor George Towns was the first in Georgia itself to support it. Georgia and the other slave states sent 157 men to a conference in Nashville, Tennessee, to discuss it. Georgia's support became known in Congress as "The Georgia Platform." It said, "We do not like all the terms of this 1850 Compromise, but to keep the nation intact, we will go along with it. However, if the North continues to be aggressive, we will rescind our approval and the Union could possibly be dissolved."

Georgia's attitude had great influence. The nation rejoiced, and many felt that Georgia had made the 1850 Compromise possible.

But The Trouble Increased

The very things that Georgia had warned the North about happened.

The Abolitionists became more furious than ever about slavery. William Lloyd Garrison was publishing a paper called *The Liberator* which constantly crusaded for freeing the slaves. Georgia offered a $5,000 reward for his capture, enacted a death penalty for any who circulated abolitionist literature and asked Congress to deny the mails to Garrison. Once he burned, on Boston Common, a copy of the United States Constitution because it did not forbid slavery. The bitterness increased. Young Preston Brooks, angry over Congressman Sumner's attack on his kinsman, a congressman from South Carolina, took his walking stick and beat him. It was three and a half years before Sumner returned to Congress.

Reverend Henry Ward Beecher "auctioned off" a slave from his pulpit in a Boston Church to dramatize his opposition to slavery. His sister, Harriet Beecher Stowe, in 1852 wrote *Uncle Tom's Cabin,* a novel about slavery. The South felt that it was unfair. It depicted a cruel slave owner who was merciless to his slaves. There were some like that, but not many, the South said. However, in America and in Europe millions read the book and were influenced against slavery.

It helped hasten the Civil War. When Lincoln met Mrs. Stowe, he said, "So this is the little woman who started a big war." But when Georgia's Robert Toombs met her, he told her she did not know the facts or understand the situation.

Harriet Beecher Stowe

The Kansas-Nebraska Situation Made Things Worse

One of the provisions of the 1850 Compromise was that part of the remaining territory in the Louisiana Purchase would be divided into a northern and southern territory, where people would be free to decide for themselves whether they wanted slaves. It was thought that those people who were against slavery would naturally settle in the northern half, known as Nebraska, and the slaveholders would gravitate into the southern half, known as Kansas. What happened was that the Abolitionists and others were determined that there would be enough anti-slavery people in Kansas so that when the time came to vote, they, as well as Nebraskans, would vote against slavery. Fights followed, and much conflict and trouble arose. Kansas came to be known as "bleeding Kansas." One of the leaders who was fanatically anti-slavery was a strange old man named John Brown, who was to play the leading role in a macabre drama a little later.

The Dred Scott Decision:

Never did the name of such an obscure person become so important to so many people. Dred Scott was a simple man who hardly knew what all the excitement was about. A decision about him made the Missouri Compromise void.

For some time, many people had wanted a decision from the United States Supreme Court about the issue of slavery, and whether slave owners could take their slaves into free states without those slaves thereby becoming free.

The case finally got to court. Dred Scott, a slave who had been taken by his original owner from Virginia to St. Louis, Missouri, ended up as the property of a surgeon. The doctor took Scott into free territory, where he lived for some years. After he went back to Missouri, which was a slave state, the son of his original owner got Scott interested in making his mark, since he could not sign his name, on a petition to the court to declare him free. The theory was that he had become a free man by being so long a resident in free territory. The court said Dred Scott was right; he was a free man. The case was appealed. In 1857, the United States Supreme Court said the decision was wrong; Scott was not a free man because he was a slave and not a citizen; therefore he could not even bring a legal suit in court! On the Supreme Court at that time was a judge from Georgia, Justice James Wayne. The Chief Justice was Roger B. Taney. This case added fuel to the fire that was blazing into a war. It spurred the "Underground Railway."

The Underground Railway

This was a plan whereby those who opposed slavery helped runaway slaves to escape to Canada or other places where they would be free. There were secret "stations" where the slaves could hide in the daytime and be helped to travel to the next station at night.

There had been laws as early as 1793 that decreed that fugitive slaves must be returned to their owners, who had money invested in them. But anti-slavery persons ignored this.

489

The northern Abolitionists were so angry over the Dred Scott decision that they stepped up their efforts to help slaves escape. Many escaped each year, representing a huge loss of money to the South.

Mark Twain in his novel *Huckleberry Finn* tells of the emotional struggle of the boy Huck in trying to decide whether to turn in his Negro friend Jim, who was the property of a slave owner, or to let him go free.

The New Republican Party Came Out Against Slavery

The old party alignments had gradually changed. The Whigs had split over the issue of slavery. A new party, known as the Republican party, now came into being. It had the same name that Jefferson's party once had, but it was really the successor to Hamilton's old Federalist party. The new Republican party immediately angered the South by coming out against slavery.

Fremont From Georgia Was The New Republican Party's First Candidate for President

The Georgian who was the new Republican party's first candidate for President, four years before Lincoln, was the son of a French royalist. His father had once been imprisoned by the British.

Fremont was governor of Arizona, was twice governor of California, and later went to the United States Senate. The newly organized Republicans nominated him for President in 1856, and one faction nominated him again in 1864 when the other Republicans nominated Lincoln. He was a tiny man, able, arrogant, colorful. Once he kept Grant waiting six hours to see him. Again, he arrogantly defied Lincoln by freeing 77,000 slaves on his own without even consulting the President. Fremont had by that time been made commander of the Union forces in the West. Lincoln countermanded the order, and fired Fremont. But all that was ahead of him in 1856 when he was nominated by the Republicans as their very first candidate for president of the United States. Their slogan was "Free soil, free speech and Fremont." Some Georgians suggested secession if Fremont got elected.

The Republicans
Elected Lincoln

In 1859, the new Republican party nominated its second presidential candidate; he was Abraham Lincoln, a lanky backwoodsman from Illinois. Lincoln was tall and awkward and plain-spoken. He had appeal to the common people. He was against slavery and had said so. But he did not believe that he had the right, except in war, to try to abolish it where it already existed, as in the South. Later he was to say, "If I could preserve the Union by freeing all the slaves, I would do it. If I could preserve the Union by freeing none, I would do that." And to southerners who went to see him, he said, "You do not have an oath registered in heaven to preserve this Union, and I do." On January 1, 1863, right in the middle of the war, he would issue the Emancipation Proclamation freeing four million slaves. But since the states in which most slaves lived were not at that time, according to them, even in the Union, not many were actually set free then.

John Brown

Lincoln was elected over three other presidential candidates. That was in November, 1869. In Augusta, a four-year-old boy named Tommy Wilson was playing on the street in front of his home. His father, Reverend Joseph R. Wilson, was pastor of an Augusta church. He was surprised that men were so excited about a man named Abraham Lincoln being elected. He heard them say that war was sure to follow. Little did he dream that one day he himself would be elected president, and guide the nation through another war, as President Woodrow Wilson.

Mary Boykin Chesnut, wife of a wealthy South Carolina planter, was on a railroad train riding through Georgia to visit relatives in Florida. In her diary, she wrote that she heard people calling to each other that Lincoln had been elected. "That settles the hash!" she said.

John Brown's Raid On Harper's Ferry

One of the matches that lighted the fires of war was John Brown's raid on Harper's Ferry in October of 1859. He wanted to get the guns and ammunition there, give them to the slaves, and destroy the slave owners. He came unknown, out of the shadows, and struck the match that set men's minds on fire.

Brown, fifty-nine, had been born in Connecticut, lived in Kansas, and bought a farm at Lake Placid, New York. He was fanatically opposed to slavery. He had a notion that if he could just start southward on his mission to free the slaves, the people would rise up and join him, and the people in the South who opposed slavery would join him too. This did not happen.

He started his march into Harper's Ferry, Virginia, on October 16, 1859 with thirty followers, including several of his sons. (He had twenty children.) There was a skirmish in which the first casualty was a Negro in the village. Eleven of Brown's group were killed, including two of his sons. Robert E. Lee, an officer in the United States Army, was sent with a group of marines to put down the disturbance.

Brown was tried for treason and murder. He and six of his followers were hanged. Brown rode to the gallows

492

sitting on his coffin. He said, "This is a beautiful country, and this is a fine day." Brown's second wife waited nine miles away, and took his body to the New York farm for burial. Brown became a martyr in the North. A song, "John Brown's body lies a-mouldering in the ground" was sung everywhere there. The South sang "We'll hang John Brown to a sour apple tree." Julia Ward Howe was in Washington some years later, with friends. They heard soldiers singing this song. A friend said to her, "Why don't you write new words to this stirring tune?" She wrote "The Battle Hymn of the Republic."

A professor named Thomas J. Jackson, thinking about the John Brown story, said to students he was teaching at The Virginia Military Institute, "The time for war has not yet come, but it will come soon." When it came, Jackson would die, shot by mistake by his own men. He would be known to history as "Stonewall" Jackson because somebody would say, "Look at Jackson there, standing like a stone wall."

The North and The South As War Approached

There were 33 states in the United States when the Civil War loomed. In them were 31,443,321 people, according to the 1860 census. This included 3,953,780 Negro slaves and 487,690 free Negroes.

Now these states and their people were dividing into two sections, the North, with 22 states and 21,955,513 people, and the South, with 11 states and 8,907,678 people, of whom 3,500,000 million were Negro slaves, and 260,000 were free Negroes. There were also 429,501 slaves in the Union states.

The North had most of the factories, but the South had some too. The South was mostly a farming section, but there were also farms in the North.

Both sides thought the war would be short. Lincoln just asked soldiers to volunteer for three months. Seward said, "If I don't settle things in sixty days, I will give you my head for a football!" A southern leader said he would mop up with his handkerchief all the blood that would be spilled. Both sides were wrong; it was to be a long, costly, bloody war.

The South, though outnumbered, would be fighting on home ground, near its supplies, near its homes. They had cotton and their leaders were convinced that European nations, especially England, would support the Confederacy because they wanted southern cotton.

The North had four white men, from whose numbers could come soldiers, to every one in the South. But the South had some excellent officers. At least three hundred of them were West Point graduates. Lee had been commander at West Point.

The North planned, as it gradually became clear, to blockade the South, to split the Confederacy in two, destroy its supplies, and to wear its armies down. Northern commanders would be at a disadvantage so far from their supply bases, but they had enough reserve soldiers to keep pouring them in, whereas the South soon depleted its human reserves and had to call up sixteen-year-old boys and old men. Once Grant lost 12,000 men in 30 minutes, at Cold Harbor. Ten days later, he lost 8,000 more. At Petersburg, a Maine company of 900 lost 700 in 7 minutes. The North could always get more, but the South could not. Once Grant, trying to wear Lee down in the last years of the war said, "I will fight it out on this line if it takes all summer." Grant had said, "Get control of the railroads and the rivers. Then face 'em and fight. Wear 'em down."

Railroads and The Telegraph
Had Brought People Closer

It was a curious fact that just as the nation was being torn apart by its differences over slavery and states' rights, it was being brought into closer communication by railroads and the newly invented telegraph.

Canals and rivers and wagon roads had been the "highways" over which the hardy pioneers and traders had bravely traveled west. Now railroads were beginning to span the continent. The idea of a transcontinental railroad was said by some to have been the idea of Thomas Butler King, who held a government post for some months in

California. When the first railroad to span the continent was completed, a golden spike was nailed down to mark the site where the roads met. By 1860, the North had over 20,000 miles of railroads, and the South had less than 10,000. King was from Sea Island, Georgia.

Samuel Morse had invented the telegraph in 1844, completing it with money that Congress had appropriated. The first message sent over the newly invented telegraph was from the Bible, "What hath God wrought?" It was sent from Washington to Baltimore. In 1866, words would travel by cable across the Atlantic, by the marvelous invention of Morse. The United States President would send greetings to Queen Victoria.

But as the nation acquired these new inventions and became able to keep in closer touch through travel and communication, it was growing farther apart in its ideas about slavery and states' rights. The dreadful Civil War was about to burst upon the nation, leaving hundreds of thousands of Americans dead, with their dreams unfinished and their work undone.

Georgia Got Into The Civil War

Georgia, one of the original thirteen colonies, had become a part of the new United States of America after the American Revolution. Now it faced the question of whether to secede from that nation and become a part of a new nation the South was attempting to form of the seceded states. The new nation was to be the Confederate States of America.

Some Georgians wanted to do this; others opposed it. The times were tight with tension as Georgia came to the end of the haunted decade between 1850 and 1860. Some wise leaders could see that dark days were ahead.

When the Civil War actually came, Georgia had a total population of 1,057,286 people, and half of them were slaves. On the coast where the big plantations were, eighty percent of the population were Negro slaves.

Georgia was prosperous when the war began. Its fertile fields, its bountiful harvest of cotton and other crops, its growing industry, its state-owned property, such as the W & A railroad, made it one of the most promising of all the Confederate states. The war would take a terrible toll: the state would lose three-fourths of its property in the conflict. The slaves, valued at a great sum, would be lost. Many homes would be ruined, and fields devastated. Sherman's March to the Sea would destroy over a hundred million dollars worth of property.

Georgia had always been an agricultural state, and one of the astonishing things about the war was the vigor and will that increased the state's ability to manufacture what was needed. War supplies were produced at Confederate arsenals located at Augusta, Macon, Atlanta, Columbus, Savannah, and Macon. Atlanta, in fact, became a supply center for the Confederacy and disbursed supplies through the southeast. Not only were things like ammunition and guns made in Georgia, but the state also produced shoes, uniforms, saddles, wagons, cloth for uniforms, and even gunboats! Textile mills located in various places over the state turned out cloth for sheets, pants, and shirts. Prisoners at the state prison in Milledgeville made weapons of war.

Georgia And Slavery

Georgia had been the only one of the original thirteen colonies that forbade slavery. Many colonists became so dissatisfied because of this that they left Georgia. Finally in 1749, the Trustees decided to allow slaves.

In 1798, Georgia passed a law forbidding importation of slaves for sale. After 1808, federal law forbade the importing of any more slaves. Many were smuggled in after that. One record in 1817 says that 20,000 a year were still coming in, some into Georgia.

But most Georgia farms were small. Only five thousand farms in Georgia were larger than five hundred acres. Fewer than a thousand had more than one thousand acres. In 1860, only three thousand people in Georgia owned more than twenty slaves. Only forty thousand Georgians owned any slaves at all. A few slave owners who had several plantations owned hundreds of slaves. Howell Cobb, who had ten plantations, owned a thousand slaves to work them. The slaves were divided into three groups: the house slaves (who felt

Old Governor's Mansion At Milledgeville

themselves superior), the field hands, and the mechanics.
Under the slave code, they had to be provided for, could not
be overworked, could not carry guns, or leave the plantation
after dark without a permit, could not be taught to read and
write (though many owners did teach them), could not work
in printing offices where they might come into contact with
incoming abolitionist literature, and could not assemble in
groups of more than seven. They had to be taken care of in
sickness and in old age. Few Georgia owners ever divided
families by selling them. Benjamin Braswell, of Madison,
in 1817 sold thirteen of his slaves to educate poor children
there. In Georgia, Savannah residents who had suffered
disaster in a terrible fire refused supplies and cash
from the North because they had been directed to "distribute
it without regard to color." They felt it was an insult to them
to assume that they would not be fair to all. Governor George
Troup was angered when a congressman proposed selling
free public lands and using the money to free slaves.

THE LAST SLAVE SHIP IN GEORGIA

The slave trade had been banned for nearly a half

497

century when the last slave ship was smuggled into Jekyll Island, flying the colors of the New York Yacht Club! It was November 28, 1858, and the ship brought a load of young boys in their teens.

The ship had previously smuggled a load of slaves from the Congo up the Ogeechee River and sold them for a fabulous profit. On this last journey, the ship had started from Africa with 490, but 81 had died on the way over. The mess kettle of this ship, named the *Wanderer,* stands in front of Jekyll Museum, with this inscription: "This kettle from Slave Yacht Wanderer used for feeding the slaves landed on Jekyll Island, November 28, 1858. Yacht owned by Charles A.L. Lamar of Savannah." Lamar was not on the *Wanderer* and was later acquitted. He became a colonel in the Confederate Army, and ran the blockade for the South. He was shot by a Federal officer. What became of the *Wanderer* and last slave ship? Charles Lamar's father asked President Andrew Johnson for the return of the ship to him, and actually got it! It had Brussels carpets on its floors, and rosewood furniture. It was sold and finally wrecked off the coast of Cuba in 1874.

A vivid description of a slave ship, one not as luxurious as the *Wanderer,* however, is in the beginning of the powerful novel in poetry, *John Brown's Body* by Stephen Vincent Benet.

How Joe Brown
Became War Governor In 1857

Joseph Emerson Brown had become governor of Georgia in 1857. He defeated Benjamin Harvey Hill, one of the South's great orators. Brown, a "dark horse" of whom few people had ever heard, was nominated when the nominating convention could not agree on any of five candidates. He was cutting wheat on his farm near Canton when he was told of his nomination. Robert Toombs, traveling in Texas, asked "Who's Joe Brown?" He was a pale, awkward, able "mountaineer of the silent solitudes." He was to be elected governor of Georgia four times.

Brown had been such a poor boy that he plowed with oxen until he was twenty, with little chance to go to

Mess Kettle From The "Wanderer"

school. Barefoot, he peddled vegetables and splinters in Dahlonega. He was born near Pickens, South Carolina, April 15, 1821. His family moved to Georgia and eked out a bare living on a tiny farm near Gaddistown. He was the oldest of eleven children. When he was nearly twenty, his father, Mackey Brown, gave him the oxen to swap for an education. He borrowed the rest of the money he needed to go to school in South Carolina, and later to Yale. Brown taught school at Cherokee Academy for a while, then started to practice law. He married Elizabeth Grisham, and soon became a judge. Brown bought a farm near Canton on which copper was later discovered. He made wise investments, and later became a wealthy man, with a fortune in seven figures. For forty years he was to dominate Georgia politics.

Few people thought he had a chance to be elected governor. Benjamin Hill was well-known and popular. He spoke eloquently. Brown had a flat, harsh voice and a plain speech. But people liked and remembered what he said. Governor

Northen called Brown "a homespun mountaineer, hero of the ploughing bull, who became the genius of a great commonwealth in its fiery ordeal, with his cool sense and iron nerve."

The mountain people, especially proud to have one of their own honored, backed him up. An old story tells of mountain women trudging over the hills to a neighbor's cabin to make a quilt to be sold for the campaign fund. Hill is reported to have spoken slightingly of this quilt. A newspaper in Milledgeville stated, "All we have to say is 'Go ahead, gals, give Joe Brown as many calico quilts as you please.' It will be a compliment to the Mountain Boy. Hurrah for the girls of Cherokee, the plough boy judge, and the calico quilt!"

"Hill is a fine orator and good man, but has no judgment," said Brown. The people began to call Brown "Old Judge-ment."

So the tall, raw-boned, pale, awkward Brown became governor. His son "Little Joe" Brown later became a governor too. The elder Brown served four terms. Georgians relied on his blazing courage and his steady nerves to get them through a terrible war. After it was over, they would be angry at him for a while, and then come around to liking him again.

Henry Grady visited him in the Governor's Mansion at Milledgeville during the war and found him sick, with lawbooks piled all over his bed. An old Negro told the visitor, who tiptoed out when Brown fell asleep, "You don't have to tiptoe. You could shoot your pistol off right under his ear and he wouldn't wake up less'n he wanted to." It was this ability to sleep and relax that enabled him to carry the terrible burdens of the war. He disagreed with President Jefferson Davis about many things. He was against conscription and suspending the writ of habeas corpus, for instance. He was a courageous war leader for Georgia.

BROWN AND THE LEGISLATURE PREPARED FOR WAR

The Georgia legislature was in session in Milledgeville, then the capital, when news came that Lincoln had been elected President of the United States. They were alarmed.

Even though a special convention had to decide whether Georgia would actually secede, most people felt that the outcome was already certain. Former Governor Herschel V. Johnson went into Milledgeville to talk with the legislators. He later said, "They were for secession. I felt that the State of Georgia would soon be launched upon a dark, uncertain and dangerous sea. I never felt so sad before."

The legislature appropriated a million dollars to get Georgia prepared for the war that seemed sure to come. They did this on Governor Brown's recommendation.

The Governor, with their approval, called a special convention to meet in Milledgeville on January 16, 1861, to decide whether Georgia would secede from the Union. On December 20, fiery little South Carolina seceded. General Francis Bartow, who was soon to become the first Confederate general killed in the Civil War, spoke to an audience in Atlanta, and said, "Shall this noble, gallant little state of South Carolina stand alone?" The audience roared, "No! Never!"

Georgians began to choose delegates to send to the convention in Milledgeville that would decide on secession. About 50,000 voters chose delegates who were for secession, but 37,000 chose representatives who opposed it.

On January 2, 1861, Governor Brown ordered that Fort Pulaski, on Cockspur Island near Savannah, be seized. The Georgia government delivered it to the Confederacy on March 20, 1861. The Union forces would recapture it on April 11, 1862. It was badly damaged by the Union forces, destroying the belief that forts like this were impregnable. It thus changed military history.

Georgia began to prepare for war in many other ways. For instance, Mrs. Joe Brown, the governor's wife, made plans to have twelve hundred yards of cloth made into garments for the soldiers. Soon there was a military company that called itself "Mrs. Joe Brown's Boys." Her statue is on Capitol Square, with that of her husband.

When The Secession Convention Met

It was a cold January day when the 297 delegates elected to decide the future of Georgia began arriving in Milledgeville, there on the banks of the Oconee. They drove their horses up to the little inns around Capitol Square, gathered in the lobbies or on the streets, and began to talk of the danger they thought loomed since the election of Abraham

Fort Pulaski

Lincoln. A few urged that Georgia think long and carefully before seceding. But most of the men and their leaders were excited over the prospect of secession, and undaunted by the threat that it might bring war.

How did the leaders stand on the question of secession? It was an odd alignment. Alexander Stephens was against secession. His closest friend, Robert Toombs, was an ardent secessionist. "We can whip the Yankees with cornstalks." Both Stephens and Toombs had been in Congress, and had come home when the situation darkened.

Benjamin Hill, with whom Stephens had often disagreed (the two had once almost fought a duel) were together on this issue. They were against secession. With them stood Stephens' beloved half-brother, Judge Linton Stephens. With them also was former Governor Herschel V. Johnson, who had been a candidate for vice-president on the 1857 Democratic ticket with Stephen A. Douglas, the "little giant" whom Lincoln defeated. Thomas R. R. Cobb was for secession. Howell Cobb, who had a thousand slaves, was once a strong Union man. He had resigned his position as Secretary of the Treasury in the Cabinet of President

Buchanan, however, to stand loyally by Georgia.

Governor Joe Brown was urgently for secession. He was a strong states' rights man. But his deep belief in the right of a state as opposed to the right of a central government would soon make him just as dissatisfied with the Confederate government. He and the Confederate president would often be at odds.

The chairman of the secession convention was former Governor George Crawford. Crawford had once engaged in a curious duel. When a woman wrote a scathing attack on his father, Peter Crawford, he demanded that someone from that political faction answer for it in a duel. One of his friends, Thomas Burnside, who was in the opposite political camp, offered to fight the duel. Dueling had been outlawed in Georgia, so they rode together in a buggy to Alabama to fight. Burnside was killed the next morning. Crawford sent money anonymously to his family for years. Crawford was one of the lawyers who finally settled the old Galphin Indian claim. Crawford was an able man, and presided with great dignity and fairness over the secession convention.

Georgia Voted To Secede
From The United States

The delegates to the Secession Convention assembled at the old State House in Milledgeville, then the state capital, for the decisive vote on January 19, 1861, at two o'clock in the afternoon. They had been in Milledgeville anxiously discussing the matter for three days.

It was a tense moment. There was excitement everywhere. Men from South Carolina and other states that had already seceded were in Milledgeville to observe the proceedings, and incidentally to urge Georgians to vote for

secession. Robert Toombs demanded that the proposed Ordinance of Secession be read twice.

The vote was 208 to 89. Judge Eugenius Nisbet, who had introduced the resolution, asked that even those who had voted against it sign it after the majority had voted for it. All of them did this, though six signed under protest. Alexander Stephens, who had opposed secession, stood loyally by his state once the vote had been taken.

Actually, what the convention did was simply to rescind

the 1788 action that had ratified the Constitution of the United States after the American Revolution.

This was the wording of the Ordinance of Secession:

AN ORDINANCE TO DISSOLVE THE UNION BETWEEN THE STATE OF GEORGIA AND OTHER STATES UNITED WITH HER UNDER A COMPACT OF GOVERNMENT ENTITLED "THE CONSTITUTION OF THE UNITED STATES."

We, the people of the State of Georgia, in convention assembled, do declare and ordain

That the ordinance adopted by the people of the state of Georgia, in convention assembled, on the 2nd day of January, in the Year of Our Lord 1788, whereby the Constitution of the United States was assented to, ratified, and adopted, and also all Acts of the General Assembly ratifying and adopting amendments of the said Constitution, are hereby repealed.

We do further declare and ordain that the union now subsisting between the State of Georgia and other states, under the name of the United States of America, is hereby dissolved and that the state of Georgia is in full possession and exercise of all those rights of sovereignty which belong and appertain to free and individual states.

Bells rang, cannons boomed. Men held torchlight parades. Candles lit the Mansion windows. But some said, as once a Britisher prophesied before another war, "They ring the bells now, but they will be wringing their hands before it is over."

When Georgia seceded, Joe Brown had already served two terms and said he did not want to run again. But early in 1861, a newspaper ran a story "The Man for the Times" urging his re-election. Even some of his enemies considered

504

him remarkable, but domineering. He had, said a friend, "wisdom with patriotism, prudence with nerve, and boldness with justice and deliberation. He is the man for the times."

A convention met in Milledgeville on September 11, 1861, and elected him over Eugenius Nisbet, with 49,493 of the 79,295 votes cast. He was inaugurated again on November 8, wearing a suit of made-in-Georgia jeans!

CHAPTER 37
GEORGIA IN
THE CONFEDERACY

Georgia Was One Of Six States
That Organized The Confederacy

By February 1, 1861, six states had seceded from the
Union: South Carolina, Georgia, Alabama, Mississippi,
Louisiana and Florida. Texas came in on February 23. These
six sent delegates to Montgomery, Alabama to organize the
Confederate States of America. They elected Jefferson Davis
of Mississippi president. He would have preferred to be
Secretary of War, a position which he had already held in
the Cabinet of President Buchanan. He was United States
Senator from Mississippi when war approached. Leaving, he
said, "Gentlemen of the North, a war is to be inaugurated,
the like of which men have not seen." Davis had been born
in Kentucky. His parents died when he was quite young.
His father, Sam Davis, who was born on a farm near Macon,
and had grown up in Georgia, had fought at the Siege of
Savannah during the American Revolution, then in 1793
moved to Kentucky. An older brother of Jefferson Davis,
named Joseph Davis, had moved to Mississippi, acquired a
plantation and become wealthy. He took a fatherly interest
in the boy after their parents died, and carried him to
Mississippi to his own home at Briarfield. Later, when he
was seven, the boy was sent back to Kentucky to attend a
Catholic school.

Davis went to West Point. He was an able soldier, and

Jefferson Davis

fought in Indian wars and in the war against Mexico. He married Sarah Knox Taylor, daughter of General Zachary Taylor who afterward became President. But she died of malaria within three months, and Davis remained unmarried for ten years. When he was thirty-five, he married lively, bright seventeen-year-old Varina Howell of Mississippi. When she met him at a Christmas party in 1843, she wrote her mother, "I can't tell whether he is young or old, and he just takes it for granted when he talks that everybody will agree with him." She was later to go through all the glory and the terror of the Presidency and the war years with him. Like the Lincolns, the Davises lost a little son while they lived in a presidential mansion. His name was Joe, and he died from a fall off the porch.

When Davis was Secretary of War, he was highly successful. He had advanced the idea of buying Arabian camels for the United States Army to use in the West. He was so accustomed to military operations that he found it hard, during the Confederacy, to leave decisions to his generals. He had three: Lee in Virginia, Joe Johnston in the West, and Kirby Smith west of the Mississippi. He was always telling them how to run the war. It was only in the last few months, when hope was almost gone, that he gave Lee the position and power of commander-in-chief.

Oddly enough, there was another Jefferson Davis in the Civil War. He was General Jefferson C. Davis, a Union officer from Indiana. He was with Anderson at the surrender of Fort Sumter.

FRAIL, THIN ALEXANDER
STEPHENS BECAME VICE-PRESIDENT

Alexander Stephens of Georgia was elected vice-president. He had been in Congress and had known Lincoln there. He had begged Georgia not to rush into secession, but to wait to see whether Lincoln would abide by the Constitution.

Stephens, whose father had been a teacher, had taught at Madison and in Liberty County, after graduating from the University of Georgia. He left Madison after he fell in love with one of his students. He was so poor and sick that he felt he had no right to ask a girl to share his life, so he never even told her. He went to Liberty County and became tutor

Alexander Stephens

508

to the sons of the LeConte family. The two boys later helped develop the University of California.

Stephens went back to Crawfordville and became a lawyer. He bought Liberty Hall, where many people came to consult him. It is now a historic shrine. In the backyard are the cabins where his Negro servants lived. Upstairs is the "Tramp's Room," where any dusty wanderer could come in and get a night's rest. Stephens was lame after a gate fell on him, and he spent much time in a wheel chair. He never weighed a hundred pounds in his entire life, though he was tall. He was elected to the state legislature and to Congress. His closest friend was bluff, hearty Robert Toombs, who lived at Washington, not far away. They were on opposite sides on the secession question, however. Later, when he was very old, Stephens became governor of Georgia. He and his college roommate, Dr. Crawford W. Long, were chosen as the two representative men of Georgia whose statues were placed in Statuary Hall in Washington, D. C.

Robert Toombs of Washington, in Wilkes County, was named Secretary of War in Davis' Cabinet. Toombs, who was a financial genius, would have preferred being Secretary of the Treasury. He was bored with a Cabinet job and soon resigned to get into an active command on the battlefield. Longstreet, who once had him arrested, said that all Toombs lacked was discipline, to have been one of history's greatest generals. Toombs was a colorful personality, accustomed to saying exactly what he thought and, like Governor Joe Brown, he would be critical of Davis' war policies.

Toombs was the son of a plantation owner, and he himself was a lawyer and a planter. He owned slaves, and lived in a white-columned mansion in Washington that still stands today. He was a proud patrician. Once when his home town wanted to build a hotel, he said, "We do not need a hotel here. If a gentleman comes to town, he can stay at my house. If he is not a gentleman, we do not want him here."

He was for secession, but he did not believe it was a good idea to fire on Fort Sumter. He foresaw that this action would catapult the South into a war.

JUDAH P. BENJAMIN, A STRANGE PERSONALITY

Judah P. Benjamin, a Louisiana man of the Jewish

faith, who was born in the West Indies, was to hold three positions, one after another, in the Davis Cabinet: Attorney General, Secretary of State, and Secretary of War. He had two sisters who lived in LaGrange. He sent them gold during the war, when money and provisions grew scarce. Benjamin's young Creole wife lived in France and remained there. Some people have called Benjamin "the brains of the Confederacy." (He had entered Yale at fourteen.) Others have been sharply critical of him. He would, after the war, escape in an open boat to the Bahamas, then to Europe, and become one of England's most famous lawyers.

The officers elected at Montgomery were only provisional officers. On February 22, 1861, an icy Washington's birthday, they would be inaugurated for six-year terms. A Constitution, which was in some ways an improvement on the United States Constitution and very similar to it, was adopted. Stephens was sent to help persuade Virginia to secede. He promised that the capital would be located in Richmond, though Davis felt this was dangerously near Washington.

After Virginia seceded, the Confederacy moved its capital to Richmond. Georgia offered ten square miles for it, but the offer was rejected. One by one, the other southern states seceded and joined the original six. Texas had seceded, despite the efforts of Sam Houston, who had been first president of Texas, but now became very unpopular. Arkansas, Tennessee, Virginia, and North Carolina brought the Confederacy up to eleven states.

When the Confederacy was established, Lincoln was not even President of the United States. He had been elected in November, but he did not take office until March, 1861.

Three slave states, Maryland, Missouri, and Kentucky, remained in the Union. Many men from two of these states fought with the South, so the Confederate flag had thirteen stars, though only eleven states ever officially seceded. Some counties in the western part of Virginia had neither slaves nor southern sympathies, and they refused to join Virginia in seceding from the Union. These counties seceded from Virginia instead, and became the state of West Virginia.

Though there had been some in the South who were opposed to secession, once it was decided upon, most southerners joined with loyalty and enthusiasm in the war.

By August 1, 1861, more than 200,000 men had volunteered, and the Secretary of War said that almost that many more would volunteer if the South had guns and uniforms for them. Each state had a quota, and single volunteers were also taken.

The general belief at first was that with the fighting skill of southerners ("A southerner can lick five Yankees!"

The Second Confederate Flag

they said, half seriously), and with three and a half-million slaves to grow the crops needed to back up the army and keep the home front going, the war would be short. The South had more than three hundred West Point graduates among its leaders, and many were among the institution's most brilliant alumni. Churchill has said that Lee was the noblest American who ever lived and one of the greatest commanders known to the annals of war.

Though President Jefferson Davis said that the South only wanted to be independent, and would not attack unless invaded or attacked, many southerners believed that since the North had more available war resources, the sensible thing would be to invade and attack the North quickly before it could rally these resources.

The same clamor for states' rights that had made Georgia seek its release from the United States would later cause a disturbance between Georgia and the Confederate government. Governor Joe Brown, together with Confederate Vice-President Alexander Stephens and General Robert Toombs, both Georgians, objected to Davis' war decisions, and kept up a constant disagreement with him for most of the war.

At the same time, northerners were disagreeing with Lincoln. Practically all of his aides thought they knew better how to run the Union than he did. They called him every ugly name they could think of, and made fun of him as a "gorilla." The newspapers called him an imbecile. Once he said, sadly and patiently, "All of our best generals seem to be newspaper editors. They tell me every morning in their papers how to run the war."

Some Of Georgia's Generals

Some of the South's most brilliant generals were either native Georgians or had been connected with the state in some way.

GENERAL JOHN B. GORDON AND THE "RACCOON ROUGHS"

Probably the best known of the generals Georgia sent to the Civil War was General John B. Gordon. His statue, on his horse Marye (which ran riderless across from Federal lines and became his favorite mount), stands on Capitol Square outside the office of the governor. He was the first governor to serve in that capitol when it was opened in 1889.

Gordon was just twenty-nine years old when he came down from the mountains, the brand-new captain of a company of mountaineers known as "the Raccoon Roughs." They called themselves that because they had no uniforms. No two men were dressed alike, and the only thing that made them look alike was that every man wore a coonskin cap with the tail hanging down his back.

Gordon was a preacher's son, born February 6, 1832, in the Black Ankle district of Upson County, six miles from Thomaston. The Gordons had moved to the Cherokee country, but the elder Gordon didn't like the schools there. He hired a tutor from Princeton, Reverend Richard Baker, to teach his own twelve children and the other children thereabouts. Young Gordon liked him, but he had never forgotten a cruel Irish teacher who had flogged him mercilessly. Gordon went to the University, then left to study law privately. But he didn't like law, and he worked as a newspaper correspondent for a while. He was managing coal mines in Dade County when the war came. In Atlanta, he met Fannie Haralson, a seventeen-year-old girl from LaGrange who had a gardenia in her hair. Three weeks later, on September 18, 1854, he married her. She stayed as close to the battlefield as she could get when he went to war, saw him wounded one day and fainted.

A Negro servant named Jim went with Gordon to war. Later, Gordon sent Jim's sons to college. Jim's grandson later became governor-general of the Virgin Islands.

Though Gordon had never had a day's military training, he became a general in two years. The soldiers loved him. One said, "Hit would put spirit into a whupped chicken just to look at him fight!" He led a charge at Gettysburg, and was in many other battles. At Spotsylvania on May 12, 1864, he stemmed a break in the Confederate lines and prevailed on Lee to go to the rear. People later said he saved the general's life.

When the battles of the war were over, Gordon would have a spectacular part in other battles of peace, known as political campaigns.

GENERAL JOE WHEELER, THE TINY GIANT, WAS APPOINTED

Joseph Wheeler was the smallest general in the Confederate Army, maybe in the whole nation. He was only five feet five inches tall, and weighed just 120 pounds, but he fought like a bantam rooster. A soldier who admired him said, "He warn't afeared of nothing, Joe Wheeler warn't, and you shoulda seen him fight!" They said he had no sense of humor whatsoever and that he took himself and life and other people too seriously. He was a curious mixture of gentleness and fire.

Wheeler was born in Georgia. His father had moved to Augusta from Connecticut, and he was sent to relatives in that state for his education after his mother died. He was

Joe Wheeler

appointed to West Point from New York. He was the lowest
in his class there, and the only one to gain fame! He was
sent to New Mexico, and on the way he got into a fierce fight
with Indians and won the name "Fighting Joe."

When the Civil War broke out, he returned to Georgia,
and his brother got him a Confederate commission. He
fought brilliantly, with the tactics he had been taught at
West Point. General Nathan Bedford Forrest, a natural-
born fighter with no military training, was so scornful of
"book soldiers" that he once said he would prefer being in
his coffin to fighting under Wheeler, and he never did again.

Toombs was no admirer of Wheeler, either, and when
Wheeler's soldiers began to forage off the Georgia countryside, like enemy soldiers, Toombs said he hoped Wheeler
left Georgia and never came back. But many others developed
deep admiration of the little general.

It was during the war that Wheeler met his future wife.
Her father owned a big plantation, and the general had sent
an aide to get permission to camp on his land. The daughter
of the family, a pretty young widow, heard them talking. She
said, "I would like to see General Joe Wheeler." The aide
said, "He's so little that you won't see much when you see
him." The army camped there for a while. Wheeler and the
young widow fell in love and later married.

514

Few Georgians know about General Benning, the Columbus lawyer for whom Fort Benning was named. Yet his name, because of the great infantry school there, is known all over the world.

Benning was a native of Virginia, where he was born April 2, 1814. His father, Pleasant Moon Benning, moved to Georgia and bought a farm near Pine Mountain in Harris County in 1832.

Henry Benning went to the University of Georgia, and graduated when he was twenty with first honors. He became a lawyer, and opened an office in Talbotton. He later became a judge. He was a man of great integrity and fairness. But he was so candid and direct that his bluntness sometimes angered people.

He was very much in favor of secession, and was chosen as the temporary chairman of the Secession Convention in Milledgeville in 1861. He fought in many battles of the Civil War, and was wounded at Chickamauga. His wife, who was from Milledgeville, twice made the long journey to battlefields in Virginia, once to bring him home, and again to bring her wounded son home. The Bennings had lost four of their children, and their son died of his war wounds.

Mrs. Benning's niece was the novelist Augusta J. Evans, who wrote the popular novel *St. Elmo.* Much of the writing was done at the Benning home in Columbus. The house was then called El Dorado, but it had gradually become known as "St. Elmo," which was the name of the hero of the novel.

The War Years

The Civil War started one April day and the fighting was over on an April day four years later.

Many bloody battles and many colorful personalities were involved in the story of these war years. Some of the battles were fought in Georgia. Many Georgia soldiers fought in battles outside of Georgia, and strangers came to fight in Georgia now and then.

The capsule story of the war is simply that the South fought valiantly for its homes and its beliefs and its way of life. Only twice did the South invade Northern territory: at Antietam and Gettysburg. For the rest of the war, the Confederates were fighting on their own soil. The North aimed at control of the rivers and roads. Their final strategy was to split the Confederacy in two, which Sherman did by marching through Georgia, and to wear it down by ceaseless fighting in the area of the upper South. This Grant did against Lee. There were many other angles to the strategy in which the South lost the war, and the Union was preserved and slavery was ended, but this was the main story.

For four long, heartbreaking years, the fight went on until hope was gone in the South.

CHAPTER 38

WHAT HAPPENED IN 1861

In this first year of the war, southern hopes were high. The five other states in the South joined the six that had started the Confederacy. The Confederacy fired on Fort Sumter, opening the war, in April. The North blockaded the southern ports especially to keep cotton (on which the South founded its hopes that Europe would support the Confederacy) from being shipped, and other supplies from coming in. Queen Victoria and Napoleon III stayed neutral. The North got a shock when the South won the first big battle, Bull Run or the first Battle of Manassas, and Lincoln called for 75,000 volunteers. Lee spent three months in Georgia strengthening the coast for defense. He had been in Georgia before, assigned to Cockspur Island soon after he graduated from West Point. Then he married Mary Custis, great-granddaughter of Mrs. George Washington, and lived at her ancestral home, Arlington, which the United States took from them in the war.

The Shooting Started At
Fort Sumter April 12, 1861

Of the year's events, the opening of the war at Fort Sumter was the nearest to Georgia.

The Civil War started and ended in April, which T.S. Eliot in his poetry calls "the cruelest month." From the moment at 4:30 a.m. on April 12, 1861, when the first shot was fired by the Confederates on the Federal Fort Sumter

517

in Charleston Harbor, to the minute when Lee surrendered his jeweled sword to Grant on April 9, 1865, four tragic years had passed, and 618,152 Americans had died.

The shot at Fort Sumter was one of the three most important in American history and American wars. The other two were "the shot heard 'round the world," fired at Lexington on April 19, 1775, and the Japanese attack on Pearl Harbor on December 7, 1941.

Major Robert Anderson, a Kentuckian, was the Federal officer in charge of the Union forts in the Charleston Harbor. His father had fought the British here at Charleston and had been taken prisoner, along with General Benjamin Lincoln, Georgia's General Lachlan McIntosh, and their men, when it fell. Anderson, who had once sworn in a private named Abraham Lincoln during the Black Hawk Indian War, was fifty-five. He had taken command of the Charleston forts on November 21, 1860, about a month before South Carolina became the first southern state to secede from the Union. He was a graduate of West Point, where he had been a classmate of Jefferson Davis, and had later taught General Pierre T. Beauregard, who would soon fire on Fort Sumter.

Anderson's wife was the daughter of General Daniel Clinch, the Revolutionary general for whom Georgia named Clinch County. Her father had willed Mrs. Anderson some slaves but she had sold them.

The government had tried to send reinforcements to Sumter in a ship called *Star of the West* on January 9, 1861. But the ship had been fired upon and had gone back without delivering its cargo.

Eliza Clinch Anderson, who was an invalid and the mother of four children, went to the White House to plead anxiously with President Buchanan to send more reinforcements to her husband. The President would not do this, but he assured her that Major Anderson was in no danger. Many northern papers bitterly attacked Buchanan for not sending reinforcements. He was very glad to turn this, along with his other problems, over to the incoming president, Abraham Lincoln.

On December 26, 1860, just six days after South Carolina had seceded, Anderson had evacuated Fort Moultrie and moved his small forces to the one fort he thought he could hold longest: Fort Sumter. Sumter was named for the last surviving general on George Washington's staff, General Thomas Sumter, for whom Georgia's Sumter County was also named. Governor Pickens and other South Carolinians were furious at Anderson's moving to Sumter. They considered this an act of aggression!

When the Confederate government got organized in Montgomery in February, 1861, the first general it had appointed was Pierre T. Beauregard, the dark little Creole

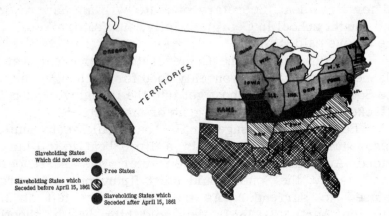

Slaveholding States
Which did not secede

Free States

Slaveholding States which
Seceded before April 15, 1861

Slaveholding States which
Seceded after April 15, 1861

from Louisiana. Beauregard himself had been appointed commander of West Point, but served only one day. He was an interesting but controversial figure. The little Creole general had been in love with Virginia Scott, daughter of General Winfield Scott, who opposed it because his daughter was so young. She entered a convent, and died a few years later. Beauregard married another girl, but he was so devoted to his military career that when she died, she asked to have put on her tombstone, "The country came before me." Beauregard, when he took charge of Fort Sumter, was forty-two years old, five feet seven inches tall, gravely courteous, aloof, and possessed a French accent. Women liked him and found him interesting; many men did not. He had been sent to Charleston in command of seven thousand troops. He had resigned from the United States Army to go with the Confederacy just a month before he went to Charleston.

Anderson notified Lincoln, who had become president on March 4, 1861, that the South had demanded the surrender of Sumter, and that if the United States expected him to hold it, a boat would have to bring him food. He had sixty-eight men, an eight-man band, and forty-three civilian employees who were busy repairing the fort.

Lincoln asked his Cabinet what they thought about holding Sumter. General Winfield Scott, United States commander-in-chief, who was now very old and had gout, said, "Yes." Scott had once been in Georgia to round up the Cherokees for removal. He had since that time been defeated for President. Secretary of State William Seward, who had taught school in Georgia briefly, also said, "Yes." But the others said, "No."

Lincoln notified the Confederate government that he planned to send Anderson only food for his hungry men, if the South would let the boat get into the island without being attacked. He would not send guns or ammunition.

Before this message, or the boat, could get to Sumter, Beauregard had sent men in a little boat to tell his old friend Anderson that unless Sumter was surrendered immediately, the South would start firing on it. Anderson refused to surrender. As the messengers left at 3:30 a.m. on April 12, 1861, they told him that the shooting would begin within an hour.

Said Anderson, "Goodbye. If we do not meet again in this world, may we meet in the next." To Lincoln he wrote, "My heart is not in this war which is about to begin."

Georgia's Robert Toombs, though an ardent secessionist, had warned the Confederacy that firing on Sumter would be fatal. "It will unloose on us a swarm of hornets that would sting us to death, and start such a war as the world has never seen," he said.

Beauregard ordered the firing to start at 4:30 that morning. Edmund Ruffin, a Virginia politician who had grown impatient with his own state at its delay in seceding, had moved to South Carolina, and asked to be allowed to fire the first shot. Later, Ruffin wrapped himself in the Confederate flag and committed suicide.

Anderson told his men in Sumter not to return the fire until daylight. They had very little ammunition, and they did not want to waste any of it by missing the target.

The firing kept up all day long, and through the next night: thirty-three hours. The Confederates fired three thousand shells. They blasted the twelve-foot wall at Sumter.

The heat at the fort was so intense that Anderson's men had to wrap wet rags around their faces to survive. But not a man on either side was killed in the firing.

Anderson surrendered Fort Sumter at 2:30 on Saturday afternoon, April 13, 1861. The Confederates allowed him to fire a fifty-gun salute to the United States flag. Two of his gunners were killed in an explosion in this salute. Anderson tucked his flag under his arm, and marched out with his men, as his band played. They got into little boats and left the island. The long, bloody war had started. It would end in April four years later, and Anderson would run up his flag again over this same fort. But in the meantime many men would die, and much sorrow would befall the nation.

Anderson went to his home in Kentucky, which was still undecided about whether to secede. Sumter had ruined his health and would help hasten his death. But he would still be alive to put his flag back up and to insist that there be no rejoicing, but a religious ceremony of thankfulness that the war was ending.

Beauregard was launched on a turbulent career with the Confederacy. He and President Jefferson Davis did not like each other, and Davis would later demote the proud Creole.

When the news of the surrender of Fort Sumter spread over the nation, there was much rejoicing. Bells rang and torchlight parades were held. In Atlanta, they burned Lincoln in effigy.

Lee Came To Georgia Again

General Robert E. Lee knew the Georgia coast well. The trip that he made to Savannah to look over the coastal defenses was not his first trip to Georgia.

Lee had been assigned to Cockspur Island, eighteen miles below Savannah, when he was a twenty-two-year-old lieutenant, just out of West Point. He arrived there November 10, 1830. The island was a lonely spot, but his good friend and West Point roommate, Jack Mackay, was in Savannah. Mackay, a native Georgian, had been assigned to Savannah, his home town. His home in Savannah had his four attractive sisters there.

Lee's favorite among the four sisters was pretty Eliza Mackay, but he wrote to all of them, and got letters

Robert E. Lee

from them in return. Lee was at Cockspur Island while Fort Pulaski was being built. When he could leave the island and his work there, he went to Savannah and the bright home of the Mackays.

Later, Eliza married William Henry Stiles of Savannah. Lee had left his own heart in Virginia in the keeping of Martha Washington's granddaughter, Mary Custis. He went back to Virginia and married her.

Lee's correspondence with Jack Mackay was a source of information for Lee's biographer, Dr. Douglas Southall Freeman.

Lee had a hard decision to make when the Civil War started. He was still an officer in the United States Army when Fort Sumter was fired on. His state of Virginia had not then seceded. When it did secede, he had to decide whether he would remain with the United States, which had offered him the position of commander of its forces, or go with his native state. He walked in the rose garden at Arlington all night, trying to decide. Next morning, he wrote two letters, resigning and also offering his service to his native state.

The South had believed that European nations would readily support the Confederacy, chiefly because of their dependence on its cotton. In England, especially, but also in France, the factories used millions of pounds of cotton for its factories, as New England factories did.

"Cotton is king!" cried the South. A newspaper reporter from England, William Howard Russell, who traveled through America writing about the war for his paper, heard this time and again. "Your country will have to recognize our government because your looms will be empty, your factories will close, your workers will starve without our cotton."

When Lincoln blockaded the southern coast from Virginia to Texas early in the war, it was a weak blockade at first, but it grew stronger. The South looked to England and France to break the blockade so that cotton would be shipped, but it did not happen. In the first place, England had a good supply of the South's cotton already on hand from the bumper crops of the two preceding years. So when the Confederacy asked its planters to hold back their cotton to pressure England to break the blockade and recognize the South's government, it was not effective. Moreover, England's workers, even when they became hungry, did not rise up against their government and pressure it to recognize the Confederacy. The workers were bitterly against slavery and, moreover, they had been told by their leaders that if the South won, slavery would be spread. The upper classes in England were inclined to sympathize with the South, not only because they owned the factories that depended on cotton, but because there was much that was alike about the way of life among the landed gentry of England and of the South. Even Gladstone expressed his belief that Davis had made a nation.

But Queen Victoria, when the blockade was at its height, proclaimed England's neutrality "between the two belligerents." Although that did not give recognition to the Confederate government, it did acknowledge that two separate powers were at war, and thereafter British merchants could buy and sell to the South as well as the North. But it was not recognition. European monarchs were not inclined to favor a democracy that had once rebelled against royalty.

523

They also felt that a divided America would never more be a serious threat to them.

France would not support the Confederacy, either. Napoleon III said he could not act, without England, in the matter. Although he kept repeating pleasant platitudes to the Confederate ambassadors, he would give the South no help.

Actually, Napoleon III was sympathetic with the Confederacy. But his advisers warned him that he had best be neutral, because if the North won they would speedily drive him out of Mexico. Napoleon had taken advantage of the civil war in Mexico (1858–1861) to try to set up a branch of his empire there. On the throne of Mexico he put Maximilian, brother of Austrian Emperor Franz Joseph, and Maximilian's wife, Carlotta, daughter of King Leopold of the Belgians. French troops defeated the armies of Juarez, but the Mexican venture of Napoleon was a failure. Maximilian was shot by a firing squad on June 19, 1867. Carlotta, who became insane, lived until 1927. After the North won the Civil War, General U. S. Grant took 100,000 soldiers, stationed them along the Rio Grande, and ordered the French to get out. Mexican troops under Diaz, who would later be dictator of Mexico, also fought to rid their land of French intruders. But the Mexican empire proposed by Napoleon III, who wanted the fabulous silver mines there, was the chief reason why he did not openly support the Confederacy.

Once the North came dangerously near war with England when a Union ship, the *San Jacinto* removed the Confederate ambassadors Mason and Slidell from an English ship. Britain demanded an apology and Lincoln made it. The United States had, in 1812, gone to war with England for stopping American ships and removing sailors.

CHAPTER 39

WHAT HAPPENED IN 1862

This was the year in which Lincoln found U. S. Grant, a general who would really fight. General Winfield Scott, commander-in-chief of the United States when the war started, remained in his position, against his native Virginia. But he was old and he did not like amateur soldiers, which he considered the state militia to be. He had only sixteen thousand professional soldiers, and he wanted to delay fighting until he could train new soldiers. Lincoln put in

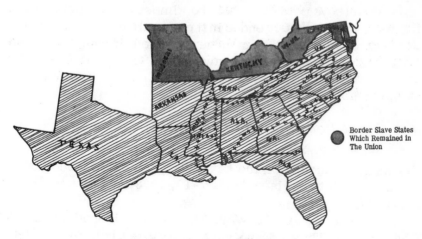

Border Slave States
Which Remained in
The Union

THE CONFEDERATE STATES

McClellan, but he was slow, too. He did not always agree with Lincoln, and he actually ran against him for the presidency later on in the war. Halleck was put in, but still the fighting was not going as fast or hard as Lincoln thought it should. In 1862, a West Point graduate who had left the army, and failed at several other things in civil life, got back into the army. His name was Ulysses S. Grant. He had only wanted to teach mathematics, and he had never really found himself. He was an odd and silent man, who liked cucumbers for breakfast, drank too much, and wore plain, rough Army clothes instead of the splendid military regalia that many generals wore. But when he captured Fort Donelson and Fort Henry, Lincoln said, "I can't spare this man. He fights."

This year, at Shiloh in April, the South lost its brilliant General Albert Sidney Johnson, who bled to death of battle wounds.

The battle of the famous ships, the *Merrimac* and the *Monitor*, which made naval history, was also in 1862.

The Federals captured Fort Pulaski in Georgia, Corinth in Mississippi, and Memphis in Tennessee. The South won the Seven Days' Battle near Richmond, the second Battle of Bull Run or Manassas, and Fredericksburg. At the terrible Battle of Antietam, where one Maine regiment lost 700 of its 900 in seven minutes, and a North Carolina regiment was completely wiped out, neither side won.

In this year was one of the almost comic incidents of the war, except that it ended in the tragedy of hanging, which was not comic at all for those involved. It was The Great Locomotive Chase at Kennesaw or Big Shanty.

The Great Locomotive Chase

Walt Disney has made a film of one of the most dramatic incidents of the Civil War, the Great Locomotive Chase, which took place April 7-12, 1862, at Kennesaw near Marietta.

During the Civil War, the North planned to attack Chattanooga. They did not want the city to get help or supplies from Atlanta during the attack. The Western and Atlantic Railroad was a main line of supply. A daring Union spy named James R. Andrews, of Flemington, Kentucky, said he could come to Atlanta, capture a train and drive it to Chattanooga, burning bridges and cutting telegraph wires, and twisting the rails behind him so that the railroad would be ruined and the Confederates could not use it to help Chattanooga. "I'll succeed or leave my bones in Dixie," he said. Andrews was to be paid $60,000 if his plan was successful. He posed as a peddler smuggling quinine for malaria.

Andrews and his twenty-four Raiders wearing civilian clothes came to Atlanta. On April 12, 1862, the anniversary of the firing on Fort Sumter, they put their plan into action. "The General," a locomotive, pulled out of Atlanta before daylight, hauling three freight cars, a baggage car, and several passenger coaches. By daylight, it had reached Marietta. At a stop called Big Shanty, seven miles north of Marietta, the train stopped for twenty minutes so that passengers and crew could have breakfast. While others were having breakfast, Andrews' men started the engine, with only the three freight cars attached, and headed north. Captain William A. Fuller was conductor. He always ate by the window of the dining room, and he saw the engine start off. In amazement, he ran out, and started up the track on foot after it. The others followed.

Andrews and his men stopped every now and then to burn the bridge they had just crossed or to cut the wire or twist the rails behind them. The Resaca River was so crooked that there were eleven bridges to cross and burn over it. Then the bridges over the Chickamauga River were next. But they had trouble getting the wood to burn.

They had to stop at Cassville because wood and water ran low. The agent there asked why the train had only three cars. Andrews told him they were rushing three cars of gunpowder to Confederate General Beauregard. The man believed this story.

Seven miles further at Kingston, Andrews knew he would meet another train. He put the General on the siding. But when the other train came, it bore a red flag, meaning that another train was behind it. Then came a third. Andrews was delayed more than an hour.

Then he went on to Adairsville and to Calhoun, taking a chance on not meeting a passenger train that was due any minute. They tricked a seventeen-year-old telegraph operator into sending a message for them. They made the nine miles from Adairsville to Calhoun in seven and a half minutes!   Then they heard the whistle of a locomotive in pursuit of them.

Conductor Fuller chased the train three miles. He met some section hands who had been repairing the railroad and were puzzled because Andrews had told them to tear it up. They began to suspect that he was not a Confederate officer rushing gunpowder to Beauregard, but a northern spy, which he was.

The workers had a small hand car at Moon Station. Fuller took this and got as far as he could. At Etowah Station, Fuller got a rickety old locomotive, the "Yonah." It made the trip to Kingston, thirteen miles from Etowah, in twelve minutes. Kingston was where Andrews had to wait an hour. He had just gone ten minutes when Fuller arrived.

Andrews' men filled up their box cars with cross-ties and rails and threw them out to obstruct the pursuing locomotive of Fuller. When Fuller, who had been removing the rails and cross-ties thrown out, came to the places where the railroad was torn up, his locomotive was useless. He and his crew ran on foot toward Adairsville. Three miles from there they got an engine from a freight train. It was named the "Texas." He had not time to turn it around; so he ran it backward all the way back to Adairsville, which it had just left. Beyond Calhoun, Fuller came in sight of Andrews. There was a hot race for a few miles. Andrews dropped more cross-ties and rails. He even uncoupled his freight cars to block Fuller. But Fuller's men removed the obstructions in their path, and at Resaca the "Texas" drove the "General" onto a siding.

Both engines left this place and raced on toward Ringgold. There Andrews' Raiders, knowing they would be captured, jumped off the train and fled into the woods, but were recaptured. Andrews and seven of his men were hanged in Atlanta on June 7, 1862, at the corner of Peachtree and Ponce de Leon. Six others escaped from prison and made their way to Federal lines. The other six were later exchanged in March, 1863, in Richmond for southerners who had been put in prison in the North.

Today, the "General" is in Chattanooga, but the "Texas" is in the Cyclorama Building in Atlanta.

After the raid, Governor Joe Brown put guards on the railroad. But the next spring, Colonel A.D. Streight tried to get into Georgia to cut the railroad that carried supplies to Confederate General Braxton Bragg in Tennessee. He came up the Coosa River to Rome in 1863. A Georgia-born teen-age girl named Emma Sansom helped a southern general to thwart this plan.

CHAPTER 40

WHAT HAPPENED IN 1863

This was the year that Lincoln issued the Emancipation Proclamation designed to free the slaves in the Confederate states. He had surprised his Cabinet by telling them on July 22, 1862, that he planned to have the Emancipation proclaimed and made effective January 1, 1863.

In this year, the Federals burned Darien, Georgia's Scotch Highlander town on the Altamaha. The South won at Chancellorsville, but paid the terrible price of the death of Stonewall Jackson, who was mistakenly shot by his own men. The Federals took Vicksburg, Mississippi.

This year marked the beginning of the end for the Confederacy. Two events of the year especially concerned Georgia. At Chickamauga in northwest Georgia, there was fought a deadly and bloody battle. A young soldier from Tennessee inspired a Georgia doctor to write a ballad that became famous. In this year Lee had been driven back from Gettysburg, and an argument would go on for years about whether Georgia's General James Longstreet had caused it by his delay in bringing up troops.

Lincoln made a five-minute speech which he said few people would notice and nobody would remember. But he was wrong. It was the Gettysburg Address, and though many of his own people and the press made fun of it, those who came after thought it was one of the finest collections of words ever uttered. It is now inscribed not only in thousands of history books, but on the Lincoln Memorial, back of the Lincoln statue, which Daniel Chester French carved in Washington, out of Georgia marble.

General Joseph Johnston replaced General Braxton Bragg, who had won at Chickamauga but faltered afterward. The Confederate Army wintered at Dalton. There was tragedy ahead. In a few months, a schoolteacher named Sherman would step over the Georgia line from Tennessee, and Georgia would never be the same again.

A Teen-ager Helped A General Save Rome

Emma Sansom, a girl who was born near Social Circle, climbed up on a horse behind General Nathan Bedford Forrest and helped him save Rome from destruction on May 2, 1863 and kept the Federals from destroying the railroad that carried supplies to Confederate troops in Tennessee. A hotel is named for the general in Rome now. On the street is the first statue honoring the women of the Confederacy. That includes Emma Sansom. A statue of her is in Gadsden, Alabama.

General Forrest was a Tennessean. He never had much education. "Nobody knows how embarrassed I feel in the company of educated people," he said. He couldn't even spell. There are misspelled words even in the thank-you note he wrote to Emma. He didn't like to write, and once said, "I never see a pen that I don't think of a snake."

He had never been to West Point. He enlisted as a private, and had had no military training whatever. Yet Lee, who had never seen him, was said to have considered him his best general. Sherman feared him so much that he offered to promote any officer who would kill or capture "that devil Forrest." European military men made his strategy required study in their schools. He was one of the first to use psychology in warfare. Joe Johnston said if Forrest had had military training, he would have been the central figure of the war. Forrest had twenty-nine horses shot from under him, killed thirty men in hand-to-hand combat, and with four hundred men, he captured sixteen hundred of the enemy.

Emma Sansom, her sister, and their widowed mother were outdoors on their farm, on Black Warrior Creek, looking at the bridge across the river. The Federals had just set fire to it, and the fire was about to burn their fence. General Forrest rode up and saw the burned bridge. He asked if there was any other way to get across. He had to hurry to save Rome from the enemy, commanded by Colonel Abel Streight.

"There is a place where the water is low enough for our cows to walk across," said Emma. "Saddle my horse and I will show you."

"There is not time," said General Forrest. "Climb up here on my horse behind me." He told her mother he would bring Emma back safely, and he did. She showed him a way that saved him three hours, and made it possible for him to save Rome.

John Wisdom, a rural mail carrier who rode sixty-seven miles, up through Vann's Valley, in eight and a half hours to warn the countryside, started at 3:30 p.m. on May 2, 1863, and reached Rome at four minutes before midnight. He wore out four horses, a mule, loaned him by the widow Hanks, and a lame pony. His ride was much longer than that of Paul Revere. Later, Rome gave him $400 and a silver service, and sent $400 to the widow.

Rome built a monument to Forrest. The inscription says: "On Sunday, May 3, 1863, General Nathan Bedford Forrest, by his indomitable will, after a running fight of three days and nights, with 410 men captured Colonel A. D.

Streight's raiders, numbering 1,600 men, thereby saving Rome from destruction.''

Dr. John Wyeth, biographer who fought with Forrest and wrote the book *That Devil Forrest* dedicated it ''To Emma Sansom, a woman worthy of being remembered by her countrymen as long as courage is deemed a virtue, who rode with General Forrest at Black Warrior Creek, May 2, 1863, and by guiding his men to an unguarded ford, enabled him to capture Colonel A. D. Streight.''

Forrest became known for a sentence he never said, ''Git thar fustest with the mostest.''

The Bitter, Bloody Battle of Chickamauga

The most terrible battle ever fought on Georgia soil, and one of the worst in the Civil War, was fought at Chickamauga in northwest Georgia on September 19 and 20, 1863.

''Chickamauga'' is an old Indian word. It is said to mean ''the place of death.'' It was the place of death for 34,000 American soldiers. That many died of the 124,000 who fought there those two days. More were wounded.

The South won this battle, and it gave them hope again after the defeats of Gettysburg and Vicksburg. Not much good came of it, however, for Confederate General Braxton Bragg strangely failed to follow it up. Much of the worst fighting was done there on the Lafayette Road, which came to be known as ''Bloody Lane.'' General John B. Hood, who would be in command at the Battle of Atlanta a year later, lost his leg there. So did many another soldier.

Both sides fought hard and savagely here at Chickamauga. The tide turned for the South when Rosecrans, a Union general, gave an order based on poor information. It left a gap in the Union lines and Confederates poured in. The South won, but it cost them a terrible price.

Bragg commanded the Confederate army there. Plagued with boils and loneliness, Bragg was a stooped, harsh, cadaverous-looking man who was almost friendless. But he had more real devotion to his men than almost any other Confederate general. Once when Jefferson Davis himself came to a battlefield to talk with him, Bragg sent the president word that he could not see him until after he had looked after his wounded men.

533

It was Georgia's General James Longstreet who suggested that more troops be sent to Bragg just before Chickamauga so that he could defeat the Union soldiers under the command of General W.S. Rosecrans. Lee was reluctant to send so many of his troops away from Virginia, but Davis and his Cabinet insisted. Some thought that Longstreet had ambitions to replace Bragg as commander in the western section where the Battle of Chickamauga loomed. Because of inadequate railroads, it took a mighty effort to get more troops to Bragg and many did not get there in time.

The two great companies of military men who faced each other here in the top of Georgia were the Union Army of the Cumberland, commanded by Major General William S. Rosecrans, and the Confederate Army of Tennessee led by Lieutenant General Braxton Bragg. It was fought largely in the woods along the banks of Chickamauga Creek. Both commanders were soon to be replaced because of their bungling of this battle. The man who attained most fame from this battle was General George Thomas, who came to be known as "the Rock of Chickamauga." Thomas was a native of Virginia who had chosen to remain as an officer in the United States Army when the Civil War began. His decision was exactly the opposite of that made by his fellow Virginian, General Robert E. Lee. Thomas had graduated from West Point, where he had roomed with General William Tecumseh Sherman. Sherman thought Thomas a great general, and once in a speech said that some day southerners would make pilgrimages to honor the statue of Thomas that stands on Thomas Circle in Washington, D.C. But this did not come true. Moreover, Thomas' sisters, Fannie and Judith in Virginia, rarely spoke his name again. They even wanted him to change his name, feeling that he had disgraced the family and shown himself a traitor to his state.

A brother-in-law of President Lincoln fought here, and was wounded. He was a Confederate officer, only thirty-two years old. His wife was Emily Todd, Mrs. Lincoln's sister. The wounded man was carried to Atlanta, died there and is buried at Oakland Cemetery. His wife came to the funeral service at St. Phillip's Episcopal Church. Lincoln had genuinely liked him and was greatly grieved by his death. Mrs. Lincoln lost three other brothers, Sam, Alex, and

David Todd, in this war. They all fought in the Confederate Army.

A writer who later became famous for his bitter short stories fought in this battle too. He was Ambrose Bierce, who later disappeared in Mexico. Bierce wrote a story of a little deaf boy wandering by chance onto the battlefield at Chickamauga and mistaking the dreadful battle for a game. The story is titled *In The Midst Of Life*. Later, Bierce, who developed a real affection for his Confederate enemies, said of them, "What glorious fellows they were, these my later antagonists of the dark days when, God forgive us, we were trying to cut one another's throats in the criminal insanity we call battle." After he had shot an enemy soldier, he once said, "Poor devil! I wonder who he was."

From Chattanooga, on that Sunday morning, the church bells sounded, over the dead and the dying, and those still able to fight. Then when the fighting was all over, a great stillness came.

The Georgians who died at Chickamauga are honored in the monument which Georgia erected there with this inscription: "To the lasting memory of all her sons who fought on this field — those who fought and died and those who

The Cabin Of The Widow Snodgrass At The Chickamauga Battleground

fought and lived, those who gave much and those who

535

gave all — Georgia erects this monument." It stands, as do many other monuments from many other states, on the Chickamauga Battlefield which is now part of the Chickamauga-Chattanooga National Military Park. When the Park was dedicated, the chief address was made by United States Vice-President Adlai Stevenson. The park is the nation's oldest and largest; it is three times as big as the one at Gettysburg. A museum there and the Adolph Ochs Observatory and Museum at Chattanooga have maps, pictures, and charts that make these battles of the Civil War much easier to understand.

"LITTLE GIFFEN," A
SIXTEEN-YEAR-OLD CASUALTY FROM CHICKAMAUGA

After the terrible two-day fight at Chickamauga, every building that was available was full of the wounded. Some were taken as far as Columbus, where hospitals and private homes were opened to them.

A teen-age boy who had been wounded was in a Columbus hospital, being treated by Dr. Francis O. Ticknor. The doctor's wife took a special interest in the boy, and asked to have him moved to her home, Torch Hill, about five miles below Columbus in the beautiful Chattahoochee Valley. The hospital authorities agreed because they thought the boy was going to die anyhow. But with the loving care he got, he recovered. Dr. Ticknor, who was also a poet, wrote a ballad about the boy, who was known as "Little Giffen of Tennessee." His real name was Newton Giffen, and he was from East Tennessee. He could neither read nor write. This worried him because he wanted to let his mother know where and how he was, and he wanted to let his captain know that he would get back to fighting just as soon as he could. He learned to read and write while he was at Torch Hill. He wrote to his captain, who replied that all the company was dead except himself and Little Giffen and urged the boy to come back as soon as he could, so reluctantly he left the Ticknors. He had become attached to them, especially to their son, young Douglas Ticknor, later a prominent physician in Columbus, too.

The Ticknors let Little Giffen have a horse to rejoin

his company. Young Douglas rode behind him a little way, on the back of an old grey horse. When they got to Bull Creek Bridge, they found that flooding rains had covered it. They couldn't find the bridge. They were almost drowned when the horse lost his footing. But they got to shore, and a Negro with a four-mule team, on his way to Columbus, offered Little Giffen a lift. The last time Douglas saw him, he was standing up in the wagon waving goodbye. He had stayed with the Ticknors from September, 1863, to March 1864. He told them he would write if he lived. He didn't live. No letter ever came.

This is the ballad the Georgia doctor wrote about him:

LITTLE GIFFEN OF TENNESSEE
by Francis Ticknor

Out of the focal and foremost fire
Out of the hospital's walls as dire
Smitten of grape shot and gangrene —
Eighteenth battle and he sixteen —
Specter! — such as you seldom see
Little Giffen of Tennessee.

"Take him and welcome!" the surgeons said,
"Little the doctor can help the dead!"
So we took him and brought him where
The balm was sweet in the summer air,
And we laid him down in a wholesome bed,
Utter Lazarus, head to head!

And we watched the war with bated breath
Skeleton boy against skeleton Death!
Months of torture, how many such!
Weary weeks of the stick and the crutch;
And still a glint in the steel-blue eye
Told of a spirit that wouldn't die.

And didn't! — Nay, more! in Death's despite
The crippled skeleton learned to write —
"Dear Mother" at first, of course, and then
"Dear Captain" — inquiring about the men.
Captain's answer: "Of eighty and five,
Giffen and I are left alive."

537

Word of gloom from the war, one day:
Johnston pressed at the front they say,
Little Giffen was up and away!
A tear, his first, as he bade goodbye,
Dimmed the glint of his steel-blue eye:
"I'll write, if spared!" — there was news of the
    fight
But none of Giffen. He did not write.

I sometimes fancy that were I king
Of the princely knights of the Golden Ring
With the song of the minstrel in mine ear
And the tender legend that trembles here,
I'd give the best on his bended knee,
The whitest soul of my chivalry
For Little Giffen of Tennessee.

What Happened After Chickamauga

Everybody expected Bragg to follow the defeated
Federal soldiers on to Chattanooga and keep pounding them
until he made his victory complete. But he seemed not to be
able to believe that he had won a victory at Chattanooga and
he did not do this. Rosecrans, the Federal commander, was
in despair at his mistake at Chickamauga that had given the
South a victory. He sent Thomas with the Federal army to
Rossville and thence to Chattanooga. They expected Bragg
to pursue them, and were amazed that he did not. So were
his own officers and men. Nobody ever fully understood why
he failed to do this. His officers almost mutinied; some refused to continue to serve under his inept leadership any
longer. But President Jefferson Davis still supported him.

Though Bragg did not continue to pound the Union
armies, he dug in at Missionary Ridge and Lookout Mountain.
The Confederate troops, though they did not assault the
Union army, had it bottled up in Chattanooga, and in such
a condition that it had to be rescued.

538

CHAPTER 41

WHAT HAPPENED IN 1864

Andersonville Prison Opened

This was the year that Andersonville Prison, near Americus, was opened and the first prisoners brought there. Besides the conferences Grant and Sherman were having about how to take Georgia, other things were going on in this war. The Battle of the Wilderness was being fought as Grant, who had now been made commander-in-chief of the Union armies, was trying to wear Lee down and take Richmond.

Between The Lines During A Truce

539

But the thing of most concern to Georgians, and of dark doom for the Confederate cause, was Sherman's push down into Georgia to take and burn Atlanta, and his March to the Sea, destroying Georgia homes and fields and possessions as he went. On the way to Atlanta, his enemy generals were first General Joseph Johnston, and then, just before the battle for Atlanta, General John Bell Hood, who had been wounded so badly that he had to be strapped in his saddle on his favorite horse, which he had named "Jeff Davis" for his close friend, the Confederate president.

Grant And Sherman Moved
To Split The Southeast

Though Bragg did not follow up his costly victory at Chickamauga, Rosecrans was still bottled up here, and without supplies for his Union soldiers. He was completely surrounded, and his troops almost starved. He did not even have forage for his mules and horses; 10,000 of them died because there was nothing to feed them.

General Ulysses S. Grant was sent to rescue the Union Army at Chattanooga. Some called him "Unconditional Surrender" Grant. He brought in reinforcements from Virginia and Mississippi, and in late November things looked better for the North, but not for the South.

Grant knew that Chattanooga was an important railroad center. Railroads branched out to Atlanta, Richmond, Nashville, and Memphis. Chattanooga was in the Cumberland Mountains and on the navigable Tennessee River. Grant did not want to leave it in the hands of the Confederates because he knew they could use it as a gateway to conquer the West. Lincoln had said that he considered it as important for the North to capture Chattanooga as to take Richmond. Grant had already split the Confederate states apart by clearing the rivers, while Admiral Farragut captured New Orleans.

Gradually Grant, with the reinforcements he had brought in, was able to push the Confederates around Chattanooga down from their positions on Missionary Ridge, Lookout Mountain and Orchard Knob. He drove them back into Georgia. He opened up more supply routes to bring in food for the hungry Union soldiers in Chattanooga. The

Battle of Chattanooga had lasted three days, from November 23 through November 25, 1863. Bragg was defeated, and Davis transferred him to Richmond as chief of staff there.

Grant went down to Ringgold, Georgia, to see what the situation was. He was now commander-in-chief of the Union force. He had been succeeded in his old command by General William Tecumseh Sherman, whom the northern papers had once called "insane." Now Grant and Sherman sat down and talked about how they could most effectively conquer the South.

Grant, like Sherman, was a West Point graduate. But he did not like army life, and had resigned his commission and left. He married five-foot-tall Julia Dent, first cousin of Georgia's General James ("Pete") Longstreet, who was best man at their wedding. Grant, a strange, silent man, had failed at several businesses and when the Civil War started, he applied for an army assignment again. He had fought well in the Mexican War, but nobody knew he was the able general that he turned out to be. Classmates at West Point later said he was the last one among them for whom they would have predicted a future as commander-in-chief of the United States Army, and President of the United States.

Sherman proposed that he split the Confederacy in two by marching through Georgia to the Atlantic Ocean. This would also cut off the "breadbasket" of the southern army, and drastically limit their food supply. But Grant thought it might be better if Sherman left Chattanooga and followed up the Union victories around Knoxville. However, he listened as Sherman outlined his plan. He wondered how Sherman proposed to feed and supply his troops. Grant thought the Union army would be too far from its base of supplies. What would they do if the Confederates got around behind them and cut off their food supplies? Sherman thought he could live off the country he was passing through. The crops were ripe, and they could take enough food for the men and the mules and horses. Grant was finally persuaded that it might work. But he did not think the war department would be in favor of it.

Lincoln was not enthusiastic about it. He pointed out that Sherman would have only one thin, single-track railroad line to Chattanooga and five hundred miles beyond it, over which to bring in supplies for his army of a hundred thousand men. Lincoln did not want a disaster now, for he was facing re-election. General McClellan was running against him for President. Lincoln knew how valiantly the men of the South were fighting for their homeland and their beliefs, and he knew it would be no easy victory.

Grant told Sherman he would talk the plan over with the Washington officials, and send him a telegram later.

Grant departed for Virginia to fight Lee, and left Sherman in command of the forces poised on the doorstep of north Georgia. Bragg sent Longstreet to drive out Burnside with fifteen thousand soldiers from Tennessee. Longstreet was defeated near Knoxville on November 29. Bragg himself was defeated on November 25, in a battle at Chattanooga. He was replaced by General Joe Johnston. Johnston took his troops to Dalton, where he set up winter quarters, during the last month of 1863 and early spring of 1864. A soldier wrote, "I am mity tired of this here war!" In Virginia, Lee and Grant battled wearily through the long, hot summer in the Wilderness Campaign. Grant lost thirty-four thousand men in sixteen days.

Sherman In Georgia

Early in May, Grant sat down on a log in Virginia, took a pencil, and wrote a telegram to Sherman at Chattanooga, right at the door of Georgia. The telegram gave Sherman permission to march through Georgia, establish connections with the Federal ships in the Atlantic, get around behind Lee's armies in Virginia while Grant fought Lee from the front, and split the Confederacy in two.

Sherman, tall, nervous, red-haired, chain-smoker of cigars, read the telegram, looked down from the mountains over the Georgia country he had once painted with his brushes, and got ready to battle General Joe Johnston toward Atlanta. It was May 5, 1864, when he stepped across the Georgia line.

In his memoirs, Sherman said that he knew if he failed in this venture, the public would call it "the wild notion of a crazy fool."

A mystery of history is why Sherman, coming down from Chattanooga to stalk through Georgia found the Snake Creek Gap pass unguarded by the Confederates. This made it possible for him to move into Dalton and later to win the battle at Resaca. This failure to guard Snake Creek Gap, which he mentions in his memoirs, has never been explained.

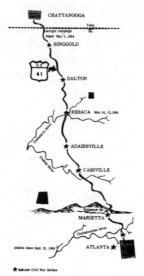

CHATTANOOGA

Tenn.
Ga.
Georgia campaign
began May 5, 1864

★ RINGGOLD

41

★ DALTON

★ RESACA   May 14, 15, 1864

★ ADAIRSVILLE

★ CASSVILLE

Kennesaw Mt.
MARIETTA ★

Chattahoochee River

Atlanta taken Sept. 21, 1864   ATLANTA ★

★ Indicate Civil War Battles

Civil War Battles In North Georgia

The Three Commanders Who Battled Toward Atlanta

Since personalities illuminate history, including wars, it is helpful to look at the three commanders who battled from the Georgia border to Peachtree Creek, and on toward the prize: Atlanta.

First it was Sherman against General Joe Johnston, cautious and capable. But when the public, desperate at the approach of Sherman, began to fear that Johnston delayed and retreated too much, President Davis replaced him with General John B. Hood.

What were these three men like?

SHERMAN HAD BEEN A SCHOOLMASTER

William Tecumseh Sherman, a West Point graduate, was a schoolmaster in Louisiana when the Civil War came. There were Georgia boys in his school. Some were sons of officers he would soon be fighting. Sherman had been a good schoolmaster. He encouraged his teachers to teach simply.

543

To one he said, "Everything you say goes right over their heads." When he told the boys goodbye, he put his hand over his heart, and said, with emotion, "You are all there!" Through the influence of his brother, Senator John Sherman, he regained an army commission.

Sherman was born in Ohio. His father died when Sherman was nine, and he was adopted somewhat informally by a Catholic family down the street. Finding that he had never been baptized, they asked the priest to remedy this. They required that he add another name to "the name of a heathen Indian."

He added William, and associates later called him Billy. But his wife Ellen, daughter of the family who adopted him, called him "Cump," and wished he would settle down in one place.

Remembering West Point, he said, "I was never chosen for anything at West Point. I remained a private the whole 4 years."

When he left West Point, he was sent South, first to Charleston and later to Augusta briefly. This was in 1845. He was sent to northwest Georgia to look for some horses the Army had lost. His hobby was painting, and he painted the Allatoona country. "I hate to put my brushes down," he said. Having painted it, he knew the terrain well when he came back to Georgia to destroy it.

At West Point, he had met a Georgia girl named Cecilia Stovall. He courted her but she came back South and married Charles Shellman. Coming through Georgia, he happened to find out that he was at her door, though she was gone. He heard a Negro woman moaning, "What will Miss Cecilia do if they burn her house." Discovering that it was the Cecilia he had known, he ordered his soldiers not to harm the house. Then he scribbled a note to her: "Madame, You once said that you would hate to be my enemy. I replied that I would protect you even if you were. This I have done. Forgive all else. I am but a soldier."

Sherman, starting his Georgia campaign, boasted that he would "bring every Georgia woman to the washtub." He was one of the first generals to use the scorched earth policy later made more horrible by Russia. Sherman planned to create such havoc and destruction in Georgia that leaders would end the war. Georgia newspapers called him "a thousand fiends incarnate."

This was the man who had stepped across the Georgia line on May 5, 1864. Georgia would be blighted with fire and torch and death from Dalton to the sea when he left Savannah a few months later.

CONFEDERATE GENERAL JOE
JOHNSTON, WHO WAS REPLACED

Both Grant and Sherman considered Johnston the ablest of the southern generals. General J.E.B. Stuart said that Johnston was head and shoulders above all the other generals of the war.

He was thoughtful, kind, had a sense of humor, and always tried to protect his men. Often he slept in a blanket roll on the hard, cold ground, just as they did.

Jefferson Davis and Joseph Johnston had never liked each other. Some said they had courted the same girl at West Point.

Johnston's great-uncle was Patrick Henry, hero of the Revolutionary era. Joe Johnston was a small man, but so impressive in his bearing that once Grant's staff officers had asked to be introduced to him. After he graduated from West Point, he married a girl named Lydia, and stayed in the United States Army. They had no children, and were devoted to each other. She followed him around from one war to another, staying as close to the battlefield as she could to take care of him. He had been so badly wounded at the Battle of Seven Pines that Lee, his West Point classmate, had to take over his command.

When the war started, United States General Scott asked Lydia to persuade Johnston to remain as an officer in the Union Army, where he was Quartermaster General, though he was a southerner. "Not when his state is about to be invaded," she replied. "Then don't let him join the Confederate Army." She answered, "He has no other profession and no other source of income." He joined the Confederacy, the highest ranking United States officer to do so. Davis made him fourth in rank in the Confederacy.

This was the man who, after a few weeks of battling with Sherman in northeast Georgia, would be replaced by another general who, Davis thought, could do better. He and his wife, who had come to Atlanta, had just celebrated their fourteenth wedding anniversary a week before he was fired. Lydia Johnston would not forgive Davis to the day she died for the hurt he had inflicted on her husband. She thought it unfair, and it cut the little general to the depths of his heart.

After the war, leaders on both sides wrote their memoirs; Jefferson Davis and John B. Gordon were among the Confederate authors. Sherman wrote his, explaining especially why he burned Atlanta and marched through Georgia. Grant, later President and then dying of cancer, wrote his, which were published by Mark Twain and brought his family a half million dollars. Many women kept diaries. Among them were Fannie Andrews, Emma LeConte, and Dolly Burge in Georgia, and Mary Boykin Chesnut in South Carolina. In modern times, two of the most widely read books about the war are the novel *Gone With The Wind*, a world-wide bestseller written by Margaret Mitchell of Atlanta, and a novel in poetry, called "John Brown's Body," written by Stephen Vincent Benet. Yet Walt Whitman had said, "The real war will never get into the history books."

GALLANT GENERAL JOHN B. HOOD
HAD TO BE STRAPPED IN THE SADDLE

The tall, sad-eyed, thirty-three year-old general who replaced Johnston was John Bell Hood of Tennessee. He stood six feet, two inches high, and had reddish hair. He had lost a leg at Chickamauga, and his left arm had dangled useless by his side since Gettysburg. He had to be strapped into his saddle. His men gave him a cork leg. He bought others, sending to Europe for them. He wore one and had one dangling from his saddle.

Hood had never been poor. He was the son of a doctor who said when the boy left for West Point, "If you can't behave yourself, don't come home. Go to the nearest post and butt your brains out."

Hood was a close friend of President and Mrs. Jefferson Davis, and had been their guest frequently in Richmond. He was very popular with the ladies. He loved a girl called "Buck." Her name was really Sally Buchanan Preston, and she liked to tease him. When he left he said, "Remember, I am engaged to you." She tossed her head and said, "But I am not engaged to you." Yet she went to church and prayed earnestly for him when he was in danger. She asked the convent nuns to pray for "Poor Sam." Why she called him Sam, nobody knows.

The war was not the greatest tragedy that lay ahead of Hood. In fact, he liked war and was a brave soldier. But as the other officers and the men themselves feared, he was no better or braver than "Little Joe" Johnston. Nevertheless, he battled Sherman around the mountains and over the bloody creeks that yet stood between the ᵀᵃderals and Atlanta.

THE FIGHT FROM DALTON TOWARD ATLANTA

Sherman was determined to fight his way to Atlanta, destroy the city, and march to the sea, destroying Georgia as he went.

By Christmas he would be in Savannah, giving Lincoln a strange Christmas present. But he had a fight on his hands all the way!

Sherman's Army Entering Savannah

Sherman had 97,987 men, 257 cannons, and scores of wagons, mules, and ambulances as he entered Georgia. Just twenty-five miles down into Georgia ahead of him was

547

General Joe Johnston with 50,000 men. After General
Leonidas Polk joined Johnston at Resaca, the Confederates
had 74,000 men under Johnston. In the campaign for Atlanta,
each side would lose over 30,000 men.

Johnston knew he was badly outnumbered. He believed
the best thing to do was to retreat slowly, making Sherman's
advance as costly as possible to the Federals. There were
some who said that Johnston could not make up his mind.
Mary Boykin Chesnut in her famous *Diary From Dixie,*
wrote, "He could never make up his mind. He came here to
our plantation in South Carolina to hunt. But the birds were
too high or too low, he said. The dogs too far or too near.
He feared to shoot and miss lest it ruin his reputation as a
crack shot. Johnston was a very brave man, but he was too
particular. He never could go ahead."

But Johnston's men were devoted to him, and appreciated his not being willing to risk their lives unnecessarily.
The little man had a genuinely warm smile, courtly manners,
and a deep concern for those under his command. His
superiors said, "If anybody can stop Sherman, Joe Johnston
can."

General John B. Hood, who would replace Johnston in
a few weeks, had finally joined Johnston in winter quarters
at Dalton in February. Hood, still courting Lucy ("Buck")
Preston in Richmond and going to dinner with President
and Mrs. Jefferson Davis, had delayed his departure from
the Confederate capital for several weeks. When he finally
took up his position as corps commander under Johnston,
he started immediately trying to change Johnston's mind
about the best way to fight this part of the war. Moreover,
he said that his idea was also the idea of Jefferson Davis,
and of General Braxton Bragg, who had become since
Chickamauga Davis' chief of staff. Their idea, said Hood,
was to concentrate all the forces in this area and march
into Tennessee, recapturing it and Kentucky from the
Federals. Johnston thought the best thing to do was to wait
at Dalton until Sherman advanced into Georgia, defeat the
Federals here, and then march into Tennessee and Kentucky.
Hood, ignoring protocol, wrote directly to Davis and Bragg,
and also to Robert E. Lee that he could not change Johnston's
mind. This is the way things stood as Sherman's army, nearly
a hundred thousand men, walked down the mountain into

Georgia, heading toward Atlanta and the sea.

Johnston moved to Resaca, where Polk had brought more men to aid him. After three days of skirmishing there, he moved on to Cassville. It was just at this time that Lee's men were fighting at Spotsylvania in the Second Battle of the Wilderness. It was at this battle that Georgia's General John B. Gordon saved Lee's life. In Georgia, the army of Johnston fell back behind the Etowah River at Allatoona Pass. Sherman struck out for Atlanta. Johnston intercepted him, and the armies, which had marched down roads so dusty that the dust all but blinded and choked them, soon clashed at Pumpkin Vine Creek and New Hope Church near Dallas in Paulding County, Georgia.

The skies darkened and it began to rain. It rained and rained and rained, for seventeen days. Men trudged through mud and wagons bogged up in the mire. The terrible two-day battle was fought in the rain, on May 25-26, 1864. It was like a spectacle out of some grim old drama. The lightning flashed and the thunder roared. The woods were lighted with such pine torches as would flame in the rain. In the kitchens of the little houses around the battlefield, the amber glow of lamplight shone as surgeons flashed silver knives amputating limbs of men whose lives they hoped to save. Through the wet woods, the moans and groans of the wounded and the dying could be heard between the awful claps of thunder. Sherman himself rode over the battlefield. A private soldier, Sam Watkins, writing his memoirs later in a book titled *Co. Aitch,* said, "We marched next day back to fortify ourselves in the little church, the battle scene of the day before...The stench and the sickening odor of dead men and horses were terrible... I ate dinner with the boys and filled my haversack with hardtack and bacon."

Next came the battles around Kennesaw, with the armies stretched along Noonday Creek, Brush Mountain, Pine Mountain, and Kennesaw. One of the peaks was called Lost Mountain. Sherman was pushing toward his objective, but there was hard fighting to do around Marietta and the Kennesaw region. The three mountains that centered the terrain were fortified by the Confederates. Both sides spent about two weeks, from June 8 to June 21, getting into position.

It was during the "getting ready" here that the only bishop who was also a general of the Confederacy was killed. He was Leonidas Polk, a cousin of President James K. Polk. The general, a graduate of West Point, was a bishop in the Episcopal Church. He baptized many officers during the war. In the weeks just before his death, he had baptized Hood, Johnston, Hardee and others. He was on Pine Mountain, looking over his lines for the coming battle. Federal artillerymen spotted him, fired, and killed him. Sherman gave the order to fire. In Polk's pocket was a copy of the Book of Common Prayer, and several little pamphlets titled "Balm for the Weary and Wounded." Each was inscribed with the name of an officer to whom he meant to give it.

Polk was fifty-five. He was one of the few officers without beard or mustache, since he was a clergyman. Born in North Carolina, he had graduated from West Point in 1827. His roommate was Albert Sidney Johnston. It was in his third year there that he had been converted. Leaving the military life after graduation, he entered Virginia Theological Seminary in 1830, and was ordained. He was sent to the Deep South, and in 1841 he was made Bishop of Louisiana. His wife inherited some slaves and they bought more. They had four hundred on their Louisiana plantation. The bishop started a Sunday School for Negro children, and tried to educate the whites, too. He helped establish the University of the South at Sewanee, Tennessee, and laid its cornerstone in 1860. He was a conservative southerner who believed in the gradual emancipation of the slaves. His old classmate, Jefferson Davis, called him back to army service when the Civil War broke out and made him a general.

Polk's body lay in state at St. Luke's Church in Atlanta, with magnolias banked on the altar. He was buried in the basement, directly under the altar, of St. Paul's Church in Augusta, Georgia. Many years later, Louisiana claimed his body and moved it back home. The original grave can still be seen in the church basement, where his wife was also buried for a time.

550

The Leonidas Polk Memorial Carillon at the University of the South at Sewanee, Tennessee has fifty-six bells,

Cyclorama, Giant Painting Of The Battle Of Atlanta

weighs twenty-three tons, and is the third largest in the world.

A tale that was a favorite of the soldiers was one about how the bishop survived in the midst of war's profanities. When General Cheatham and General Polk rode along the ranks, Cheatham called to the men, "Give'em hell, boys." The bishop added. "Do as he says, boys."

KENNESAW MOUNTAIN, THE
BATTLE THAT LASTED A MONTH

Most Civil War battles just lasted a few days, but the Battle of Kennesaw Mountain in Georgia lasted a month.

It was May of 1864 when Sherman moved his armies out of Chattanooga, pushed the Confederates out of their winter quarters at Dalton, and began to press toward Atlanta and the sea. Sherman had three armies. One was in command of General George Thomas, the Army of the Cumberland, named, like all Union armies, for a river.

The Confederate armies were named for states. Another was the Army of the Tennessee, commanded by General James B. McPherson. The third was the Army of the Ohio, under General John M. Schofield.

Sherman used the three in various positions to push General Joseph Johnston this way and that way as they fought savagely toward Atlanta. After bloody fighting around Dallas, at the Battle of Ezra Church, they moved east to the mountains near Marietta. Here were Pine Mountain, Lost Mountain, and Kennesaw Mountain.

HOW DAVIS REPLACED JOHNSTON WITH HOOD

Sherman kept attacking Hood's forces around Kennesaw, and lost many men there. The mountain paths were piled with the bodies of blue-clad soldiers who died. Sherman finally withdrew, and Johnston moved to the north bank of the Chattahoochee River. Sherman sent troops around him, and got between the Confederates and Atlanta. In his memoirs, Sherman wrote later, "I always thought that Johnston missed his chance here. He lay comparatively idle while we got control of both banks of the river above him."

Georgia was alarmed. Beyond the river lay Atlanta, in mortal danger. The newspapers and the people wanted Johnston to fight. When he would not, they began to beg Davis to replace him. Davis did not move hastily. He asked Johnston what his plans were. Johnston replied that since he was badly outnumbered, he thought defense best, and that his plans depended on what Sherman did. Davis sent General Braxton Bragg, chief of staff, to Georgia to talk with Johnston. Bragg reported that he could not find out what Johnston's plans were. Benjamin Hill, close Georgia friend of Davis, asked the Confederate president to replace Johnston. "But whom would you put in his place?" Davis asked. Hill did not know. Davis asked Lee what he thought of replacing Johnston with Hood. Lee was alarmed at the idea of changing commanders at such a strategic time. He said Hood was a bold fighter, but careless, and that Hardee had more experience.

Finally, perhaps on Bragg's recommendation, Davis decided to replace Johnston with Hood. "He is not a genius,

552

but he is the best available," said Bragg. Sherman was delighted. It helped him more than two divisions, he said. But he could never tell what the unpredictable Hood might do. "I could predict Johnston's plans, for he is a sensible man and does the sensible things," said Sherman.

Johnston was in his tent on the Marietta road, about three miles above Atlanta when he got the shocking news that he had been fired. He was handed a telegram. This is what it said:

> Richmond, July 17, 1864. General J. E. Johnston: Lieut. Gen. J. B. Hood has been commissioned to the temporary rank of general...I am directed by the Secretary of War to inform you that as you have failed to arrest the advance of the enemy to the vicinity of Atlanta...and express no confidence that you can defeat or repel him, you are hereby relieved from the command of the Army and Department of Tennessee, which you will immediately turn over to General Hood.

The soldiers at first refused to believe it. A Yankee told one who was down at the river bank, "Johnston has been taken out of command," he said. The Georgia boy replied, "You are a liar, and if you come down here, I will whip you for telling such as that." Another soldier said, "If that is so, I am going home. I am not going to shoot another gun. Give my regards to Jeff Davis and tell him I quit."

Johnston was amazed at the telegram. So were his aides. Even those who liked and admired Hood could not at first believe that this badly crippled man, noted for bravery and rashness, could command the army that had to defend Atlanta. He had the reputation of being a fighting man, but most fellow officers doubted his ability to command this army successfully at this tragic time.

Hood heard the news just before midnight in his tent not far from Johnston's. He could not sleep. He dressed at dawn, and went to see the man he was appointed to replace. With him were other officers. They all begged Johnston to put the telegram in his pocket and forget about it until after the coming battle, at least. Johnston had directed the movements of the army for seventy-nine days, and the showdown for Atlanta was now at hand.

553

But Johnston refused to ignore the telegram. He turned over his command to Hood at once, and left for South Carolina. He was deeply hurt. He thought he had done a better job in Georgia than Lee had done in Virginia. It was 1865 before he was appointed to command again, and then by Lee, who would at that late date have been made commander of all the Confederate forces.

Hood had to think of how he would save Atlanta, if that were possible. The two armies had been resting for a few days, after Kennesaw and the fighting from Dalton to Peachtree Creek. But the big battle was at hand for the prize, Atlanta. Could Hood save it, or would Sherman capture it? In the meantime, the country was busy with a presidential election. Lincoln was again the candidate. But opposing him was his own general, McClellan. A victory, like the capture of Atlanta, would assure Lincoln's re-election. Sherman, who would have preferred Seward as president to either of them, nevertheless knew how much depended on his victory. Besides, if his Georgia campaign failed, and Grant himself had only reluctantly approved of it, he knew it would be called the idiotic adventure of a crazy fool.

The incredible bravery of Confederate soldiers in the face of overwhelming odds is described by a Union officer, Captain George Pepper, writing of the desperate fight Hood's men waged to save Atlanta on July 22, 1864:

"The Rebels fought with a fierceness seldom if ever equalled. They stood firm as a rock though our artillery cut them down. No life was worth a farthing now. Whole heaps of corpses lay on the bloody ground. and fixed eyes had the awful stare of death. Now came the climax. Two Rebel lines came on, exultant and sure of victory. All our artillery opened upon them: 17,000 rifles, several batteries of artillery fired simultaneously. The whole center of the Rebel line was crushed down like a field of wheat through which a tornado had passed."

Atlanta Was Taken

On September 2, 1864, Sherman was in Atlanta, and the city had surrendered. The band played "Yankee Doodle." One soldier said, "People peek out their windows at us, surprised that we don't have horns and claws." From a brick house that later became the Peachtree Golf Club, on July 18, 1864 Sherman had written, "A sick Negro, the only human being left on these premises, says we are eleven miles from Atlanta, five miles from Buckhead." In this campaign, Sherman lost General James McPherson, shot as he left a conference with the commander. A soldier said, "The best general in our army has been killed." Fort McPherson near Atlanta was named for him. His portrait is there.

Davis still felt that Sherman could be defeated. He came to Jonesboro, where Hood was headquartered, to talk to the troops.

In Atlanta, they were asking Sherman to show mercy to the people. But Sherman felt that the worse one could make war, the more quickly it would be over. "My orders are not designed to meet the humanities of the case," he said. He gave the people time to get out. A ten-year-old named Carrie Berry was writing in her diary, "We could not sleep because we were afraid the soldiers might set fire to our house. They behaved very badly, I thought,

Battle Of Atlanta

going round setting people's houses on fire. Wish I could go to school. We are having all hollowdays. I wirk at home and sleep if mosquitoes don't bite too much. Soldiers pace back and forth but orderly. We are all in so much trouble. Mamma is so worried. Papa does not know where to go. We had stewed chicken. It is a dark rainy day. The last train has left. We are erbliged to stay now."

Some people fled to Camp Rough and Ready below Atlanta. Others went to Camp Exile near Dawson. Sherman gave orders to set fire to the city on November 15, 1864. Hood had blown up his ammunition and left, going north via Alabama, in the hope that he would lead Sherman to follow. "If Hood will go north, I will give him rations to travel on," said the grim general. He sent troops after Hood for a little while, and then turned back to burn Atlanta, cut loose from his Allatoona supply lines, and headed toward Savannah, living off the country until he could get to supply ships at the seashore.

The burning of Atlanta was spectacularly filmed in the movie version of Margaret Mitchell's *Gone With The Wind*, the story of Georgia's part in the Civil War and the hard days of Reconstruction.

Sherman wired President Lincoln: "Atlanta is ours and fairly won."

The capture of Atlanta actually helped Lincoln to get re-elected president. His general, George B. McClellan, was opposing him for the presidency in 1864 and criticizing his conduct of the war. Sherman's victory in Georgia came just in time to give the North renewed confidence in Lincoln.

Hood crossed Muscle Shoals, and went to Nashville. There he was defeated by his old West Point teacher, General George Thomas, who had stood like a rock at Chickamauga, Georgia.

The March To The Sea

The North did not hear from or of Sherman for weeks after he burned Atlanta and turned south. Nobody knew whether he would go to Augusta or to Mobile or to Savannah. Georgia had few soldiers to bar his way. General Howell Cobb with about three thousand soldiers awaited him in Macon.

General Braxton Bragg, with very few soldiers, was sent to Augusta in case he went there. Near Savannah, General W. J. Hardee waited with ten thousand soldiers, to meet Sherman's sixty thousand!

Sherman divided his marching men into two lines, and each of them sometimes divided for foraging or off-path destruction. The two lines of march were planned to go by Milledgeville, then the state capital, and by Macon. He had cut himself off from his supply line to Tennessee, planning to forage and live off the land he went through. His men ate what they could, and destroyed the rest. They poured out syrup, ruined the meat in the smokehouses, often burned the cotton in the field, and set fire to many houses. They often destroyed fine furniture, looted homes, frightened women and children, tore down fences, ripped open pillows and mattresses and scattered feathers over the sixty-mile-wide path. Only a fifth of the hundred million dollars' worth of property which he took was actually used by his soldiers. They destroyed two thousand miles of Confederate railroads. He had boasted that he would make Georgia howl cruelly. He wrote General Halleck, "If the people raise a howl against my barbarity and cruelty, I will answer that this is war and not a popularity contest. If they want peace, they and their relatives must stop the war."

Sherman was one of the first generals in the world to wage "total war" and use the "scorched earth" policy.

Many leaders urged Georgians to new hope, even as Sherman was marching to the sea from Atlanta. On November 18, 1864, Beauregard wrote: "To the People of Georgia: Arise for the defense of your native soil! Rally round your patriotic governor and gallant soldiers. Obstruct and destroy all the roads in Sherman's front, flank, and rear, and his army will soon starve in your midst. Be confident. Be resolute. Trust in an overruling Providence, and success will soon crown your efforts. I hasten to join you in the defense of your home and firesides."

Senator Benjamin H. Hill did what he could to encourage his fellow Georgians, by writing: "To the People of Georgia: You now have the best opportunity ever yet presented to destroy the enemy. Every citizen with his gun and every Negro with his spade and axe can do the work of a soldier. You can destroy the enemy by retarding his march. Georgians, be firm, act promptly, and fear not."

Governor Brown was desperately trying to rally enough soldiers to defeat Sherman. He paroled prisoners from the state penitentiary in Milledgeville to fight. Boys from military academies, including his own teen-age son, were fighting. Old men did what they could. Georgia's best

Sherman Enters Atlanta

soldiers and their brilliant leaders were in Virginia helping Lee protect Richmond from Grant. Brown felt that some of them should be sent to Georgia to protect their own state from Sherman. Georgians did all they could, but Sherman had sixty thousand soldiers, marching in four columns thirteen miles apart, destroying everything over a sixty-mile-wide march, as if locusts had come through the middle of Georgia.

He burned homes and public buildings, though he spared the State House and Capitol in Milledgeville. His soldiers held a mock secession convention in the old Capitol, repealed Georgia's Ordinance of Secession, stabled their horses in the church nearby, and poured syrup into the organ, "to make the music sweeter," they said. The legislature had fled, and the official records had been sent to a place of safety.

Through the countryside, the soldiers went, killing

livestock. Some families saved a few things, burying their silver, driving their livestock deep into the swamps. Most of the slaves were faithful; some left to follow Sherman, which he considered a nuisance. Where this army went along, black, smoking chimneys were left, and hungry people scratched in the potato hills and the horse troughs to get a few mouthfuls of food, and dug up the salty dirt in the smokehouses where once hams and sausages had hung in abundance. They had no salt.

An old Negro woman panted hastily into town to find her mistress. "Lawdy, Missy," she said, "they didn't leave us one rooster to crow for day." Sherman spied a little trunk in a house near Milledgeville, marked with the name of Howell Cobb. He destroyed the place. He considered Cobb one of the chief rebels who led the South into secession.

Governor Brown had called the legislature into session for forty days in Macon to talk over the situation. He ordered into service all Georgia men, from sixteen to fifty-five. The governor said, "Our cities are being burned, our fields laid waste, and our wives and children driven from their homes. We must strike like men for freedom. Death is preferable to loss of liberty."

Some Confederate leaders thought that the Federal prisoners at Andersonville should be moved, probably to Florida, to keep Sherman from releasing them when he marched through Georgia. They were not taken to Florida. But some were marched to another prison at Millen, and then taken back to Andersonville when Sherman had left the state. In his memoirs Sherman wrote that some prisoners escaped from this prison and joined him in Atlanta.

Andersonville had been made a prison and received its first prisoners in February, 1864, a few months before Sherman's march through the state. There were some 37,000 prisoners there in all. Many died. The South did not have enough medicine even for its own soldiers. The prisoners got the same food rations that the Confederates did. The trouble was that while a Georgia boy could eat cornbread and fatback, the Northerners could not. It gave them digestive troubles. There are 13,259 graves at Andersonville; 483 are marked "Unknown." The place is now a national cemetery and park. Many states have erected monuments there. MacKinlay Kantor wrote a novel about it. It was commanded by a Swiss officer named Captain Henry Wirz. He was the only Confederate officer hanged after the war.

Fort McAllister on the Ogeechee had been attacked more than once by federal forces, but the attacks had always been repulsed. The fort had been built by Confederates in 1861 and enlarged in 1862. It was a part of the surrounding defense of Savannah. It guarded the Ogeechee River from invading ships, and protected King's Bridge two miles north of the fort, and also the railroad bridge two miles down the river. Twice during July, 1862, the fort was attacked by Union gunboats, but repulsed them. In November, 1852, an ironclad called the *Wissahicken* fired on the fort, but without much damage. On January 27, 1863 another ship, the *"Montauk,* fired heavily on it, but the damage was surprisingly small. The 230 men who defended it were commended "for gallantry and endurance" by the Confederate Congress.

Sherman was headed toward Savannah, and a junction with Federal ships on the coast. He had to take Fort McAllister because ships needed to get up the river to bring supplies to the Union forces. He attacked the fort December 13, 1864. Major George Anderson, fort commander, refused to surrender, but he and 196 of his men who survived the attack, were overwhelmed and taken prisoners. Sherman built a wharf and depot at nearby King's Bridge, where his ships unloaded ammunition and food. The fall of Fort McAllister spelled Savannah's doom.

Fort McAllister is now a historic shrine. It was part of the Richmond Hill Plantation of the automobile magnate Henry Ford, who partially restored the fort. After Ford sold his Georgia properties, the International Paper Company, which bought it, gave to the State of Georgia the old fort and thirty acres surrounding it. The Georgia Historical Commission restored the site, now a Confederate shrine on the east bank of the Great Ogeechee River, a few miles from Savannah.

*Savannah Became
Lincoln's Christmas Present*

On December 21, 1864, Sherman sent a telegram from

Savannah to President Lincoln: "I beg to present to you as a Christmas present the City of Savannah with 150 guns and plenty of ammunition, also about 25,000 bales of cotton." (Actually, there were 38,500 bales of cotton.)

Sherman had got stuck in the mud near Wassaw Island on his way to the Ogeechee and Savannah, but he did get there. He went first to the Pulaski House, where he had once stayed as a young lieutenant. Later, he moved to an elegant house offered him by a rich British merchant named Charles Green.

His soldiers were feasting on oysters, broiled shad, turtle soup and other delicacies that they had been looking forward to. His officers were toasting him with fine wines, and calling him "a combination of Caesar, Hannibal and Napoleon." He wrote later in his memoirs that he looked back over his march through Georgia "like a man who had walked a narrow plank, and wonder if I really did it."

He was lonesome and homesick. "My children are growing up strangers to me," he said.

Christmas In Savannah

561

As it became apparent, following the fall of Atlanta and the capture of Savannah, that the Confederacy was tottering toward its fall, Davis tried desperate measures.

Lincoln and Seward met representatives of the Confederacy, including Confederate vice-president Alexander Stephens of Georgia, on a boat at Hampton Roads to talk about peace. But Lincoln would not hear of any peace on grounds less than total surrender and the maintenance of the Union. He greeted Stephens with special interest. They had known each other in the days before the War. He promised to set free from prison Stephens' nephew and he afterwards did.

When this peace effort failed, Davis held a mass meeting on a snowy day, February 6, in Richmond, at a church, and told his people that it had failed. But he still urged them to keep up their hopes that the South could win. There was no studied rhetoric in this speech; his whole heart was in it, and he spoke with deep feeling. Stephen Vincent Benet suggests in his novel-in-poetry of the Civil War that Davis lacked the power to warm men's hearts, brilliant though he was. At this last, desperate meeting, Davis may have come nearest to kindling a fire in the spirits of those who listened. The South even had plans for arming the slaves, with promise of emancipation when the war was won.

There was bitter opposition in the South to the proposal to arm and later to free the slaves. Former Governor Howell Cobb, a loyal Confederate, thought it was an outrageous proposal. Cobb owned more than a thousand slaves, but he honestly believed the proposal bad. Eventually the Confederate Congress authorized arming some slaves, but did not agree to emancipate them. None of the slaves were actually sent into combat.

On March 18, 1865, the Confederate legislature adjourned. Most of them knew in their hearts that they would never convene again. But Davis' Cabinet continued to meet. Davis believed that if Lee and his forces could have rallied enough soldiers to defeat first Grant, who was fighting them around Richmond, and then Sherman, who was coming up from Georgia and the Carolinas, there was still hope for the Confederacy. Only Judah P. Benjamin sustained him in this belief.

But Lee's dispatches grew darker. He could hold the lines only a few days longer. Davis had sent his family away. At St. Paul's Episcopal Church an usher brought Davis a note. It was from Lee. The fall of Richmond was a matter of hours. He got up and walked out of the church. Davis and his Cabinet left Richmond. They would hold their last session in Georgia, in the town of Washington.

CHAPTER 42

WOMEN IN WAR YEARS

When Queen Victoria's
Lady-in-Waiting Visited Georgia

In the early spring of 1865, the James Hamilton Couper family, who lived at Hopeton Plantation just above Brunswick on the Darien road, had a guest. She was Miss Amelia Murray, known as "Honorable Amelia" at her home in England. She was a lady-in-waiting to Queen Victoria. After she visited Georgia, she no longer had that position.

James Hamilton Couper, the son of the Scotchman John Couper, plantation owner on St. Simon's, was a well-known planter himself. He managed the plantations of his father's best friend, James Hamilton, for whom he was named. He went all over the world to study good methods of farming, and to get new and different plants and seeds. His plantation at Hopeton was a sort of experiment station for agriculture. He had slaves there who worked in the house and the fields.

The Honorable Amelia got a very different view of slavery from that which her fellow Englishwoman, Fannie Kemble, had received in 1838 on St. Simons and at Butler Island, below Darien. They visited in almost the same section of Georgia, but their views were vastly different.

The Honorable Amelia wrote to her friends back in England:

A canoe, with four oars, came down to meet us from Mr. Couper's plantation on the Altamaha, near Darien. After a very pleasant trip of above five miles on the river, Mr. Couper brought us to his house, which on the interior is like English houses. It is an interesting home, and was my first introduction to plantation life. A happy Negro population surrounds the house and is attached to it. I never saw servants in any old English family more comfortable or more devoted. It is quite a relief to see anything so patriarchal, after the apparently uncomfortable relationships of masters and servants in the North. I should much prefer being a slave here to being one of the saucy grumbling help which I saw there, but every one to his own taste.

She described the life of the rice plantations and in the green country lanes of the Georgia coast. Her letters were very interesting. Her friends urged her to publish them. She knew that the kindly view she had of slavery,

Miss Winnie Davis,

which she had found very different from the stories she had heard about the cruelty and abuse slaves endured in America, would embarrass the Queen. Victoria was vehemently opposed to slavery. So the Honorable Amelia resigned her position as lady-in-waiting to the Queen after her trip to Georgia.

Women Helped The Confederacy

In Rome, Georgia, is a monument to the women of the Confederacy. The inscription on it was written by Woodrow Wilson:

"To the women of the Confederacy, whose fidelity, courage and gentle genius in love and in counsel kept the home secure, the family a school of virtue, the state a court of honor, who made of war a season of heroism, of peace a time of healing, the guardians of our tranquillity and of our strength." One scene on the monument shows women ministering to the wounded. Another, a woman reading to her child the news of her father who died on the battlefield. This monument was unveiled on Jefferson Davis' birthday, June 3, in 1910.

Women often looked after the plantations or farms while their husbands and sons were at the front. They sewed, nursed the wounded and the sick, and showed a fierce patriotism that supported their men. At the end of the war, some wrote pitiful letters of hunger and loneliness, and some even begged their men to come home. But most women showed an endurance of hardship and hurt that make up a wonderful story.

Women devised all sorts of "make-do" things, like using thorns for pins they no longer could get, and taking down draperies to make dresses, tearing up household linens for bandages, making soap from lye, and dyes from berries.

Confederate money was becoming almost worthless. Bacon was $20 a pound, a live hen cost $50, two fish were $50, and butter was $20 a pound.

The War Diaries
That Women Kept

Hundreds of diaries kept by women in Dixie tell much about the war years, and what life was like during that time.

The most famous of them is *Diary From Dixie* by South Carolina's Mary Boykin Chesnut, edited and republished with a foreword by Ben Ames Williams in 1945. It contains interesting observations about Georgians whom she knew. Her husband was one of Beauregard's officers. Captain Chesnut once came to Georgia as an aide to Jefferson Davis. He was in the United States Senate when the war began.

Mrs. Chesnut's diary shows the whole range of the war from the gay days in Richmond to the hungry times when she was glad to get bread. In Richmond, early in the war, she wrote: "... such breakfasts, dinners, and suppers as we go to ... terrapin stew, gumbo, fish, oysters in every shape, game, such hams as these Virginia people cure, fine wines, claret cups, mint juices ... homemade bread ... there is no such bread in the world."

At the end, she was writing, "How grateful I was today when a friend sent me a piece of chicken... my pantry is empty... I have no wood to burn... and cannot afford sackcloth to wail in ... Enough! I will write no more!"

TEEN-AGE GIRL KEPT A WAR DIARY

Emma LeConte, of the famous LeConte family that lived down at Midway below Savannah, was living in Columbia, South Carolina during the war. She was thirteen when the war started.

Emma's father was a professor at the University of South Carolina when she was writing the diary, which is a slender little volume with the title *When The World Ended*. Emma married Farish Carter of Scottsboro.

Her diary, which students who study the war should read, is a very graphic and interesting account of the fears and the daily life of a teen-age girl who lived through these trying, desperate last days of the Confederacy.

She started her diary just before the last bleak Christmas before the Confederacy fell. It started December 21, 1864. She wrote of her fears that Sherman would do even worse in South Carolina than he had in Georgia, because that fiery little state had started the whole thing.

The hardships of the war days are gently suggested in this sentence: "After the war, when Christmas came, my little sister Carrie looked at her toys and said 'Why didn't Santa Claus come in South Carolina?' I looked up and saw the eyes of my father and mother filled with tears."

The diary tells about her father making the long and dangerous journey back to Georgia to be sure that his relatives in Liberty County were safe. He was almost captured there. Like others, he had lost all he owned.

YANKEE SCHOOL TEACHER IN THE SOUTH

Another woman who wrote of Civil War days was Dolly Sumner Lunt, a school teacher who had come from Maine and married Thomas Burge of Covington. He had died three years before the war, and she was left with her nine-year-old daughter, Sadai, and her slaves on the plantation. She had grown up among abolitionists in New England.

When Sherman approached, in November, 1864, she hid her silver and some food. Neighbors, passing in a wagon en route to Eatonton, stopped with her. The man had been wounded at Missionary Ridge.

When the Yankee soldiers stopped at her gate, one said to her, "Ever see Yankees before?" This former northern woman said, "Not for a long time, and never any like you."

They took her mules, tore down her garden fence, killed chickens and turkeys, plundered her smokehouse, and left her so poor that she had not a thing to put in small Sadai's stocking at Christmas. The Burge diaries so enchanted writer Julian Street that he wrote the foreword for them when they were published under the title, *A Woman's War Time Journal,* in 1918.

FANNIE ANDREWS AND HER SPARKLING STORY

Over at Washington in Wilkes County lived a lively redhead named Frances Eliza Andrews. Her father was Judge

Garnett Andrews, who was a Union man. But she and all his other children were avowed Confederates. Fannie kept a diary during the last year of the war. Fannie wrote of the Federal soldiers who came in and out of her town, of her neighbor, big Robert Toombs, of Governor Joe Brown, and of many others who played a role in the Confederacy.

Frances told of the hardships of travel, and of how she and her sister were sent to relatives near Albany to get them out of Sherman's path, though he did not go through Washington, and of how expensive things were during the last days of the war.

This young Confederate wrote vividly, and sometimes with sparkling malice. After the war she became a teacher. Frances was interested especially in science, including botany, and wrote a textbook that was widely used throughout the nation. Frances attained such a reputation in her field that she was the only American woman invited to Italy to an international conference on botany; but she could not go.

She taught at Wesleyan, and delighted the students by riding to class on her bicycle. She taught in Rome and, in her will, left the children money for a playground.

Her account of the war is remarkably interesting. Her diary, *Journal Of A Georgia Girl In Wartime* was reprinted in recent years.

CHAPTER 43

THE WAR ENDS

1865: How The War Ended

Sherman left Savannah and went on through South Carolina. Many people wanted him to punish the little state of South Carolina because, they said, "This is the state that started the war!" Grant was battering at Lee from the Virginia side. Lee had put General Joe Johnston in command of the forces that he hoped would stop Sherman and prevent the northern soldiers from pressing in upon him while he was trying to withstand Grant.

In April it was clear to most southern leaders that the South, which was outnumbered four to one, and blockaded so that it could not sell its cotton or get medical and other needed supplies from England, was about to be defeated. The gallant men and their officers had fought their best, but their cause was hopeless.

Lee Surrendered To Grant

On April 8, Grant was at a farmhouse in Virginia, ready to talk terms of surrender with Lee. Grant was out suffering with a terrific headache and soaking his tired feet in hot water. He was putting mustard plasters on the back of his neck to relieve his headache. But he still had a headache the next day when he went to meet Lee at Appomattox Courthouse. Lee was there to give Grant his jeweled sword, in token of surrender. Grant allowed the southern men to keep their horses and mules to make their spring crops. He also sent Lee's hungry men food. After the surrender had been signed, Lee mounted his horse Traveller and went home.

Johnston Surrendered To Sherman

General Joe Johnston had gathered up the remnants of Hood's army and tried to block Sherman as he marched up from Georgia through the Carolinas. But Johnston, too, was outnumbered. Near Durham, he had to surrender to Sherman.

Sherman gave Johnston easy terms that angered the bitter men in Washington. Secretary of War Stanton sent Grant to North Carolina to tell Sherman that he must make them harder and stronger. When Sherman got to Washington, he shook hands with everybody waiting for him there — except Stanton!

Mrs. Jefferson Davis

At West Point, Georgia, on April 16, 1865, sixty-four Confederates held a fort until their ammunition was gone, their commander killed, and somebody told them that the war had been over for a week.

Lincoln Was Assassinated

Five days after Lee surrendered, John Wilkes Booth, an actor, shot Abraham Lincoln in Ford's theater where the President, his wife, and some friends had gone to see a play titled "Our American Cousin." The next morning Lincoln died, on a bed in a house across the street from the theater. Mrs. Lincoln later lost her sanity for a time. Major Henry Rathbone, who sat in the box with them that night, later went berserk, killed his wife and committed suicide.

Lincoln, who had been disliked by the South, emerged from the shadows as a great man, revered by history. Many remembered his human qualities, his kindness; and they remembered his sadness. He had had a terrible burden during the war. Even his little boys, Willie and Tad (short for "Tadpole" which was Lincoln's nickname for him), could only lighten it now and then. Once, playing at war games, they tried a soldier doll and condemned him to death. Lincoln wrote a pardon that read, "The doll Jack is pardoned. A. Lincoln."

Fanatics in the North immediately charged Jefferson Davis and the South with conspiring in the murder of Lincoln. Men like Thaddeus Stevens and Charles Sumner urged the issuance of posters offering reward for Davis and the others who, they said, had plotted with the actor Booth to assassinate Lincoln.

Copies of these may now be seen. There is one at the Museum in the Cyclorama Building in Atlanta.

It reads like this:

Headquarters, U.S. Forces
Athens, May 7, 1865
$360,000 Reward

The President of the United States has issued his proclamation announcing that the Bureau of Military Justice has reported upon indubitable evidence that Jefferson Davis, Clement Clay, George N. Sanders, Jacob Thompson, Beverly Tucker, and W.C. Cleary incited the assassination of Mr. Lincoln and the attempt on Mr. Seward. He therefore offers for the arrest of Davis, Clay, and Thompson $100,000 each, for Sanders and Tucker, $25,000 each and for Cleary, $25,000.

Brevet Brigadier General Wm. J. Palmer.

$100,000

REWARD!

IN GOLD.

Headquarters Cav. Corp.,
Military Division Mississippi,
Macon, Ga., May 6, 1865.

One Hundred Thousand Dollars Reward in Gold, will be paid to any person or persons who will apprehend and deliver **JEFFERSON DAVIS** to any of the Military authorities of the United States.

Several millions of specie, reported to be with him, will become the property of the captors.

J. H. WILSON,
Major-General, U. S. Army,
Commanding.

The reference to Mr. Seward was because of the fact that Secretary of State William Seward was stabbed on the same night Lincoln was murdered by John Wilkes Booth.

Booth had once played in Columbus, and had been wounded in an accidental shooting there. Nobody in the South had wanted Lincoln killed, or had conspired with the actor who dramatically shot the President, screaming the words "Sic Semper Tyrannis" as he jumped to the stage below.

Lincoln's death was a tragedy for the South; he had compassionate plans for its treatment. His theory was that they had never really been out of the Union. As early as 1863, he had offered to recognize any state in which ten percent of the 1860 voters petitioned for it, and to pardon any southerner who took the oath of allegiance to the United States. He said to his aides, "Let 'em up easy!" Tennessee had been thus admitted in 1864, and its governor elected vice-president of the United States.

Georgia At War's End

The South was prostrate after the war. Georgia was desolate, and had a sixty-mile wide streak of utter ruin through its middle, Sherman's path from Atlanta to the sea.

Georgia had lost over a half million slaves, valued at a quarter of a billion dollars. A hundred million dollars worth of damage had been done by Sherman. Two thousand miles of railroad had been destroyed, the rails twisted, the tracks ruined. Land was down to half its value. There was no money, no schools to educate the children, little food to eat, and few seeds with which to plant crops.

It is an abiding tribute to the valiant courage of Georgians that they did not sit down in the ashes and weep as those without hope. They began to build a new Georgia in a new South. But first there were the bitter days of the Reconstruction to be lived through.

Jefferson Davis Was Arrested In Georgia

Confederate President Jefferson Davis had sent his family, with an aide, to safety. He wanted them to get to the Florida coast where they could take a ship for England or to some other safe destination. With Mrs. Davis were her children, Jeff, seven; Billy, four; Margaret, nine; and Baby Winnie, nine months old. They came through the Carolinas, and stopped overnight in Washington, Georgia.

President Davis came on to Washington, Georgia, after his family had been there and gone. In Washington, Georgia, on May 5, he met with the members of his Cabinet who still remained, and then they separated. His idea once had been to try to get across the Mississippi, rally southern soldiers and continue to fight. But his aides persuaded him that this was hopeless. He went on through Georgia on horseback. At Abbeville, he heard that his family had gone on ahead. He found them near Irwinville, Georgia. He had been concerned for their safety, for the roads were plagued with hoodlums wandering about. He planned to rest with them a few hours and go on. But he decided to spend the night there at the camp in the pine woods. Before daylight, on May 10, Federal officers arrested him.

At first the Federal soldiers who arrested Davis did not recognize their famous prisoner. Mrs. Davis, worried because her husband — whom she called "Banny" — had been ill, threw a shawl over him as he left. This gave rise to the false rumors and the cruel cartoons depicting Davis as attempting to escape disguised in woman's clothes. But Postmaster General John H. Reagan, said, "I saw Davis a few minutes after he was arrested. He was wearing his accustomed suit of Confederate gray." Davis himself later said he thought that he had picked up his wife's raincoat by mistake, and that this probably caused the hurtful stories.

The Davises were brought to Macon, where they spent the night. They had met with so much ingratitude and coldness by this time that they were grateful when a waiter put a flower on their supper tray. They went on to Augusta, from whence Alexander Stephens was also being taken by ship to Savannah. Davis and Stephens had disagreed, but they were polite to each other on this journey. Mrs. Davis had a mattress put on deck for the ill Stephens.

She and her children were taken to Savannah, where they remained for some time. Davis was sent to prison at Fort Monroe, Virginia, where he was put in chains. Within two years, powerful friends got him released. The Davises then went to England for some time. Later they settled at Beauvoir, Mississippi, where Davis wrote his memoirs. When Oscar Wilde, the British author, was in America he said he had rather see Davis than any other American, and he was a guest at Beauvoir. Another guest there was Fred Wilkinson, a northerner with whom Winnie Davis, then grown up, had fallen in love. "I did well to get in the door," he said. Davis reluctantly gave his consent to this engagement, but southerners rose in wild protest. A man from Americus wrote, "If you let her marry a Yankee, the very dead will rise in their graves." They never married, and Winnie went abroad. When she died, one of those at her funeral was Wilkinson.

Winnie Davis came to Georgia several times. Once

she came with her aged father to dedicate a monument to his friend, Benjamin H. Hill. She was introduced as the "original daughter of the Confederacy."

Davis died in 1889 in New Orleans. His body was brought through Georgia on the way to be buried in Richmond. It lay in state under the rotunda at the State Capitol in Atlanta. His birthday, June 3, is a legal holiday in Georgia.

The Jefferson Davis shrine at Irwinville, Georgia, is on the site where Davis was arrested that May morning. A portrait of Winnie Davis is in the Museum there.

Alexander Stephens Went To Prison

Alexander Stephens was back at his home, Liberty Hall in Crawfordville, playing a card game called casino with his friends on May 11, 1865. Jefferson Davis had been arrested in south Georgia the day before. Stephens said when he heard that Federal officers had arrived in Crawfordville, "I expect they have come for me."

Quietly, he had his servant pack his bags. In fifteen minutes, he was on his way to prison in Fort Warren, Boston Harbor. They let him take a servant. The frail little Georgian was a sick man. They took him by train to Atlanta and then to Augusta. The train had to pass again through Crawfordville. His family and neighbors were out to see him there. He was allowed to get some more clothes when the train stopped. He carried what gold he had.

His beloved brother Linton came to visit Stephens at the prison in Boston. Linton's wife had died, and while he was in Boston he met a lovely girl named Mary, who had come with her mother to visit Alexander Stephens. Linton and Mary fell in love and married. After they came back to Georgia, they lived in Sparta. Linton bought her a piano, which is in the museum next to Alexander Stephens' home, Liberty Hall, at Crawfordville, today.

Stephens' statue is in the front yard of Liberty Hall, where he is buried. On the statue is his favorite saying, "I am afraid of nothing...but to do wrong." The war did not end his career. There awaited him more service in

Congress, and a brief time as governor of Georgia.

On June 9, Stephens had applied for a pardon. Grant had spoken in his behalf. He was released from prison October 12, 1865, after a six-month stay, and started home to Georgia. Crowds greeted him in New York. In Washington he called on President Johnson. He was just fifty-three, but his hair had turned gray.

At Liberty Hall, many of his servants were still there. Harry, and his wife, the faithful Eliza, still took care of him.

He was elected United States Senator. At first he was not allowed to take his seat in Congress, for the bitter radicals of the Republican party were angered when Georgia refused to accept some of the terms imposed upon her. Stephens stayed in Washington. He called on Grant, whom he had always liked.

Later — when he was very old — he would be elected governor.

Benjamin Hill Was Imprisoned, Too

Benjamin Harvey Hill, "the silver-tongued orator of Georgia," was also sent to prison. People were amazed when he was defeated for governor by plainspoken, awkward Joe Brown. But Hill, though never governor, had served his state in many ways. He was one of the state's representatives to the Confederate Congress. Once he became so enraged during an argument there that he threw an inkwell at William Yancey. They later became friends.

Hill was a brilliant man who had the courage of his convictions. Sometimes this led him into fiery arguments. One was with small Alexander Stephens, over whom the tall Hill towered. Stephens challenged him to a duel; Hill declined to fight the small invalid. Hill was an ardent Unionist and anti-secessionist, but he was loyal to his state once it had seceded. During the war he went on a speaking tour, using his eloquence to keep heart in the people, and encourage them to fight on. After the war was lost, Hill was arrested by the Federals at his beautiful home in LaGrange. He was imprisoned briefly at Fort Lafayette in New York Harbor. He came home to find his native Georgia in the throes of

577

Reconstruction. Outraged at this, he made a speech in Atlanta advising Georgia to defy the conquerors. People were amazed at his brash courage. Later he changed his mind when he saw that there was nothing for them to do but submit with as much grace as they could. When he was sent to Congress, he did outstanding work there. In a speech he said, "There is no more Confederacy! We are back in the house of our fathers, and we are at home to stay, thank God."

It is ironic that this eloquent man should have died with cancer of the tongue. Stephens and Brown went to see him just before he died on August 16, 1883. Jefferson Davis, who came from Mississippi to unveil a statue to his memory, said, "If I had to choose the three greatest Georgians, I would choose Oglethorpe the benevolent, Troup the dauntless, and Hill the faithful."

Hill had owned two beautiful homes in Georgia. His home at LaGrange is now the Woman's Club. His home in Athens, one of the most beautiful of the ante-bellum mansions, is now the Corinthian-columned, boxwood-gardened home of the president of the University of Georgia.

What Became Of The Other War Leaders?

The men who had been in the limelight during the war soon scattered to many parts of the world. Some had sad days ahead; and some went on to surprising postwar destinies.

General John B. Gordon, who was with Lee at Appomattox, and Confederate Vice-President Alexander Stephens would be colorful figures in Georgia politics for many years. Joe Brown would be hated by the people who had elected him; then loved again and elected by them. But he would always be a controversial figure in Georgia.

Grant became President of the United States, served eight years in that office and was a victim of corrupt aides who discredited his administration. He is buried on Riverside Drive, near the Hudson, in New York City, in a tomb designed like that of Napoleon in Paris. Sherman, who had moved to New York and befriended Mrs. Grant after her husband's death, thought the tomb was far too fancy for a plain man like Grant.

Perhaps the most astonishing post-war career was that of the despised Sherman, who actually became a champion of the South which he had ruined, and who was invited, and came, back to Georgia later as a guest!

SHERMAN'S AFTER-WAR YEARS

Sherman was invited back to Atlanta when Henry Grady, who had referred to Sherman in a New York speech as a man regarded by southerners as "careless with fire," promoted an exposition after the war. He and other leaders thought Sherman might come to see the country he destroyed rising out of the ashes like a phoenix, and on its way toward a new prosperity. (The official seal of Atlanta has a phoenix on it.)

Sherman not only visited Atlanta, he lectured all over the country, and was in great demand. He hated to shake hands. "I'd like to hire a man to do my handshaking for me," he said. A friend, speaking for Sherman's last years, when he made so many speeches, said, "His last twenty-five years was just one long chicken dinner." He also wrote his memoirs.

The government bought Sherman a house in Washington, where his wife's father and his own brother had been powerful political figures.

Though the house was expensive, Sherman threatened to decline the gift unless taxes were paid on it! In 1874 he sold it. Sherman's son, a Jesuit priest, known as Father Tom Sherman, wanted to make a pilgrimage of peace along his father's route of destruction. He got as far as Cartersville, then his trip was canceled.

Once Sherman wrote:

> I confess without shame that I am sick and tired of fighting. Its glory is all moonshine. Fighting men want peace. Only those who never heard shot nor shriek nor groan of the wounded and dying, cry aloud for more blood, more vengeance, more desolation. I know the rebels are whipped to death and I declare before God that as a man and soldier, I will not strike a foe who stands un-

579

armed before me. Brave men never attack the conquered, nor mutilate the dead. Cowards always do, like Falstaff, that prince of scoundrels, stabbing again the dead Percy.

He opposed the imprisonment of Jefferson Davis. He despised the adulation of crowds. "Read history. Read Coriolanus," he said, "You will see the true measure of popular applause. Vox populi, vox humbug."

His wife died soon after they moved to New York. He liked the theater and often went. It was after a theater party one very cold night in February, 1891, that he took pneumonia, and soon died. He was seventy-one years old. His son, Father Tom, was on the British Isle of Jersey and arrived too late, but another priest had given Sherman the last rites of the church which his wife had long prayed he would turn to.

To this day the song "Marching Through Georgia" rouses Georgians to resentment, even though the old hatreds are over, and the hot passions cooled. Sherman himself came to detest this song, which was played everywhere he went.

GENERAL HENRY BENNING PRACTICED LAW

General Henry Benning, for whom Fort Benning was named, came home to Columbus to find his home burned. The general lost his wife in 1867. With the help of relatives, however, he reared not only his own children, but those of his widowed sister Caroline, and also helped his sister-in-law and her children. He had been defeated for a judgeship, but Governor James M. Smith offered him the position of Chief Justice of the Georgia Supreme Court. Benning declined it, probably because the salary was too small to support all of those who were dependent on him.

Benning had earned a reputation for great bravery during the Civil War. He had two horses shot from under him at Chickamauga, but he cut a third loose from a wagon and rode bareback into the thick of the fight. One man said that "Benning was one of the bravest men who ever lived." Another said "There is no war leader in Homer's *Iliad* whose record is braver." After Benning died, his daughter

580

Anna Caroline was asked for some facts for Governor William Northern's book about famous Georgians. Looking over her father's record, she wrote, "His life can be summed up like this: Benning the judge asked only 'What is the law?' Benning the general said, 'Boys, follow me.' "

When Benning died, on his way to the courthouse, a fellow lawyer said, "His death is a public calamity." A portrait of him hangs in the officers' club at Fort Benning. A little trunk he carried through the war is at the Confederate Museum in Crawfordville, Georgia.

GENERAL JOHN B. HOOD
WENT TO NEW ORLEANS

After the war, General John Bell Hood, with whom Davis had replaced General Joe Johnston just before the Battle of Atlanta, went to New Orleans. The general, who was in several kinds of businesses at various times, married a beautiful woman named Anna Marie Hennen. They had eleven children, including three sets of twins.

The yellow fever epidemic struck New Orleans in 1878. The doctor who had amputated Hood's leg at Chickamauga, and had been his close personal friend through all the years, lived across the street from him in New Orleans. He advised the former general to take his family out of the stricken city until the epidemic subsided. But Hood did not have the money either to move away or to take his family on a vacation. His wife died August 24, 1879, and their small daughter Lydia, who was ten years old, died two days later. In a few days, Hood himself was dead. He was only forty-eight years old. The ten remaining children were left with their grandmother, who had lost her fortune during the war. Friends of Hood raised money for the children. After the grandmother died, the children were adopted by several different families, and separated. Hood's last remaining daughter died in New Orleans in 1960.

The valiant general's story was over. He had been a good warrior, like his grandfather, who had once fought Indians with General Anthony Wayne.

GENERAL JOE
JOHNSTON LIVED IN SAVANNAH

General and Mrs. Joe Johnston were living in Savannah in 1870 when Lee came to Georgia on a visit to his father's grave on Cumberland. Johnston went about the city with his former chief, and the crowds applauded them. Lee died a few months later. Johnston had gone first to Richmond and then to Selma, Alabama, in transportation ventures that failed. He had also gone to Europe. Finally, he became agent for New York and English insurance companies and had his headquarters in Savannah.

He wrote his memoirs, titled *Narrative Of Military Operations Directed During The Late War Between The States*, a long and clumsy title. He attempted to explain his part in the war, and his side of the misunderstanding with Jefferson Davis. But Johnston refused to write his memoirs while Davis was in prison. Later, Johnston also wrote many magazine articles about the war. The old Johnston-Davis controversy flared anew in 1881. They had disliked each other ever since their West Point days. Once Lydia Johnston had said to her husband, "Davis hates you and when he has the power, he will ruin you." In 1881, Johnston was quoted in an interview with a newspaper reporter as saying that Davis was linked with the disappearance of Confederate funds after the fall of Richmond. The newspaper misquoted him, said Johnston, but Davis was angry. He refused to make the main address at the dedication of a memorial honoring Lee at Lexington in 1883 because he knew that Johnston would be there.

In 1876, Johnston moved his business to Richmond. He and his wife had many friends there. Johnston got into politics, and was elected to Congress, where he went on March 4, 1879. Two Georgians who had served under him were there in the Senate, General John B. Gordon from Atlanta, and L.Q.C. Lamar, who was living in Mississippi. Other Confederates were also there. Johnston served one term, and did not run again. President Cleveland appointed Johnston Commissioner of Railroads in 1885.

He went to the funerals, sometimes as a pallbearer, of former generals, including those of his enemies. He rode from Portland, Oregon to New York to be a pallbearer for former General and later President U. S. Grant. He went to the funeral of General George McClellan.

When Sherman died in New York it was a cold, chilling day with snow deep on the ground. Johnston stood bareheaded by the grave, a pallbearer, with his head uncovered.

582

"Put on your hat," they said to him.

He refused. "Sherman would not put on his hat if this were my funeral," he said. He became chilled, and when he got home to Washington, he took pneumonia. His beloved wife had died some years before. Having no children, they had been devoted to each other and he was lonely after her death. In 1890, he had returned to Atlanta, where old soldiers went wild with joy at the sight of this little cock sparrow of a general whom they had loved and followed. They had unhitched the horses of his carriage, and pulled it themselves. He remembered all that as he grew delirious with pneumonia. He is buried in Greenmount Cemetery in Baltimore.

ROBERT TOOMBS BECAME AN EXILE FOR A TIME

Big, colorful Bob Toombs went to his white-columned home in Washington, Georgia, where one day Federal General Wilde came to arrest him. Mrs. Toombs invited the officer and his soldiers into the parlor and kept them talking while her husband escaped out the back door. Finally suspicious, the Federals threatened to burn the house unless Toombs appeared and submitted to arrest.

"Then you will have to burn it," said Mrs. Toombs. They searched the whole house. Fannie Andrews, a neighbor who was keeping her "Journal of a Georgia Girl in War-Time" wrote scornfully that they even pulled up the mattresses on the beds looking for big Bob Toombs, "as if he had been a paper doll!"

The son of a neighbor, young Lieutenant Irvin, took Toombs' horse, Lady Alice, to him in the woods. Toombs rode off with the young lieutenant and spent some weeks riding over Georgia, hidden by friends. He visited his plantation in Stewart County, and stayed for a while near Toccoa at Stagecoach Inn, recently restored as Traveler's Rest. Then he sailed for Cuba and to Europe in July. He sold his lands in Texas because he needed money in his exile. "I eat an acre a day," he wrote. His daughter died, and he grew lonely and sad. He wrote his wife, who had been with him during part of his exile but had come home to her ailing child, "When I think of you, I believe that Antony was right to give up the world for the woman he loved." Sad and lonely, and grieving for their lost child,

583

Robert Toombs

Toombs came home. He went to Washington to talk with President Andrew Johnson. He was allowed to return to Georgia unmolested and he never took the oath of allegiance. Yet he became a power in Georgia politics again. He was to be the guiding genius in the 1877 revision of the Georgia Constitution. He expressed his opinions as loudly as before.

"Listen to Toombs talking," said a friend, "and him with no more vote than a chicken." His civil rights had been taken away until he swore allegiance again to the United States, which he never did.

"Have you asked them for a pardon?" inquired a friend.

"A pardon? I've done nothing to ask forgiveness for and I haven't pardoned them yet!" he shouted.

He was to outlive his close friend "Little Aleck" Stephens, but he would be nearly blind and old and sick. His sense of humor would remain to the end, however, and he once said, " I hope the Lord will let me go to heaven like a gentleman. There are some Georgia politicians I would not want to associate with, but I would like to talk with Socrates and Shakespeare there."

To this day he is known as Georgia's "Unreconstructed Rebel."

During the years after the war, General James Longstreet, one of Lee's generals, came to live at Gainesville. He is buried there in Alta Vista Cemetery.

Brave as he was, there were still people who blamed him for the defeat at Gettysburg. They said that he delayed too long in bringing up troops to aid Lee. Some said he ignored Lee's orders because he disagreed with them. But he fought valiantly at such battles as the Wilderness, where he was wounded by his own soldiers through mistake, and at Antietam and at both first and second Manassas. He sped like a silver arrow from Virginia to Georgia to bring reinforcements to Bragg's army and help him to win the battle at Chickamauga.

After the war, Longstreet urged the South to accept the terms imposed by the North as the easiest path through hard days of survival. When Longstreet rode up on his horse, just as the program was about to begin at the unveiling of Benjamin Hill's statue, he was invited onto the stage, and there he and Gordon and Jefferson Davis had a touching reunion that set the Confederate veterans in the audience to giving the Rebel yell and throwing their hats in the air.

When Longstreet died at eighty-three, on January 2, 1904, an aged veteran walked slowly from the Gainesville Court House to Alta Vista cemetery to the grave with his old gray army jacket and enlistment papers and said, "They were enlisted under his command, and as I don't ever want to be mustered out again, I'd just like to leave them with him always, if you don't mind."

Longstreet first married Marie Louise Garland and they had five children. They lived on a street in Gainesville that is now named for him. It was a place called Woods' Mill, noted for its huge grape arbor. Mrs. Longstreet died in 1889.

Later the general met a Brenau student at a ball at the Governor's Mansion in Atlanta. Her name was Helen Dortch, and she had worshiped him as a hero ever since she had been in high school. They married September 8, 1897. He was seventy-six, but still a powerful, tall figure, with fierce gray eyes and a commanding presence. After his death, Mrs. Longstreet lectured and wrote books about his career. She died in a hospital in Milledgeville in 1961.

The United States In 1865

LEE CAME ONCE MORE TO GEORGIA

Robert E. Lee and his wife lost their beautiful home, Arlington, which had been taken over by the federal government when the war broke out. It is now a national shrine, and its grounds are a national cemetery where many military heroes and famous people such as the assassinated President John F. Kennedy are buried.

Mrs. Lee, the granddaughter of Mrs. George Washington, was badly crippled with arthritis, but she and her daughters left Arlington and went to live in Richmond. The three Lee sons, Custis, Rooney, and Robert, Jr., were fighting in the war.

Lee became president of little Washington College, in Lexington, Virginia. The college is now Washington and Lee University.

Gray-haired and sad-eyed, Lee worked hard at his college duties. The trustees furnished a house for his family. He said to the students, "The only rule we have here is that each boy must be a gentleman."

Lee had been worn down by the war, and in March, 1870, the trustees insisted that he take a two-month leave of absence. With his daughter Agnes, he came southward. He planned to rest a few days in Savannah, but everybody wanted to see the beloved man. Crowds gathered, bands

586

played. People even stood long in the rain waiting to catch a glimpse of him. He wrote on April 18, 1870:

> My daughter Agnes and I visited my father's grave on Cumberland Island, where Agnes put fresh flowers. I presume it will be the last time I will be able to pay it my tribute of respect. The cemetery is unharmed but the house at Dungeness has been burned and the island devastated. I hope I am better.

After he returned to Lexington, he opened another term of college in September. In October, he presided at a meeting of the executive board at his church. They raised the preacher's salary. But it was a long meeting and the church was cold. It was raining and he got soaked going home. He took pneumonia, and was ill two weeks. The doctor said, "You must get well. Your horse Traveller is standing in the barn and wants you to give her some exercise." But Lee was never to ride his beloved horse again.

In his delirium, he fought old battles over. "Tell Hill he MUST come up!" he said, or "Strike the tent." On October 15, the great hero of the South died. His biography has been best written by Douglas Southall Freeman.

Lee is buried in the crypt of Washington and Lee. Next to him is the body of his father, moved from Georgia. They were two heroes who came to Georgia in two wars and helped the state cope with its enemies.

Robert E. Lee's birthday, January 19, is observed throughout the South.

ONLY ONE CONFEDERATE OFFICER WAS HANGED: WIRTZ

Captain Henry Wirz never understood why he was singled out for trial and hanging.

After the Civil War was over, the United States government tried and hanged the little Swiss doctor, Captain Henry Wirz, who had been commander of the notorious prison at Andersonville, Georgia. Some 37,000 prisoners had been kept there, without shelter and with little food and no medicine, in a 2,700-acre prison designed for 10,000. Whose fault was it? The South said they had no medicine for their own men, because of the blockade, and not enough food.

587

"What about no shelters from broiling sun and winter cold when there were millions of pine trees growing all around?" the North asked. There were few tools, said the South, and nobody left to use the few there were.

The argument about the prison goes on forever. So does the argument about the infamous prisons where southern prisoners were kept in the North. Thousands died in southern prisons; still more in northern prisons.

But Wirz was hanged. He was tried and convicted simply of the murder of eleven. He was sentenced to death and he was hanged on the morning of November 10, 1865. He was buried in the Arsenal Ground at Washington. But there is a monument to Wirz in the little village of Andersonville, near the cemetery and prison site.

Many of the northern states have erected monuments to their dead at the old cemetery at Andersonville. Some come on May 30 each year to decorate them with flowers.

One of the most well-known stories of Andersonville is of Providence Spring, said to have suddenly appeared after a storm, when the soldiers were dying of thirst. The site is thus marked: "The prisoners' cry of thirst rang up to heaven — God heard and with his thunder cleft the earth — And poured his sweetest water gushing here."

Thousands have read McKinlay Kantor's novel, titled *Andersonville,* which was awarded the Pulitzer Prize in 1956.

In 1963, a drama about the trial of Wirz attracted hundreds nightly to a Broadway theater in New York.

CHAPTER 44

GEORGIA IN THE DARK
DAYS OF RECONSTRUCTION

When the fighting was ended in April, 1865, Georgia found itself almost prostrate. Land was half its pre-war value. Most of the railroads had been destroyed. Sherman had torn up over three hundred miles of them. There was little money and no credit. The state cancelled taxes for the years 1864 and 1865. There was so little food that Kentucky sent Georgia a hundred thousand bushels of corn in 1866. People had few seeds to plant for new crops and hardly enough food to keep from starving. Cotton, once a dollar a pound, was four cents. There were few farm tools, no slaves to work the land, and little machinery. They had to set up new patterns for farming, wages, sharecropping, and tenancy. The towns and cities were swarming with people who had fled from farm to factory, seeking jobs that did not exist. Lee advised them to work with the North, do the best they could, and co-operate with the inevitable.

President Andrew Johnson vetoed a civil rights bill, but it was passed over his veto by a two-thirds vote in Congress.

Georgia's New State
Government Took Over

Lincoln had not wanted to add to the suffering of the

Statue Of General Nathan Bedford Forrest

South. After he was assassinated, President Andrew Johnson, the Tennessee tailor who succeeded him, felt almost the same way. Both took the position that the southern states had never really been out of the Union because they could not secede. The war had proved that. The nation was one, indivisible.

On June 17, 1865, Johnson appointed James Johnson as provisional governor of the state. He was a Columbus lawyer who had graduated from the University of Georgia, served in Congress, fought against secession, and taken little part in the war. Johnson took office in July, and at once ordered elections for delegates to a constitutional convention to meet in Milledgeville in October. The convention was to meet the requirements for readmission to the

Union, adopt a new constitution, and elect a governor.

On June 29, 1865, Governor Joe Brown, who had been arrested but soon paroled, resigned. He had issued a call for the legislature to meet in Milledgeville, but the federal government forbade the legislators to assemble, and arrested Brown at his home in the Governor's Mansion on May 11. He advised his people to cooperate with their conquerors. He accepted a high position with the federal government, saying he felt that in this way he could be of most help to his people. He had made a strong and able governor through the war years, though his quarrels with Confederate President Jefferson Davis had annoyed many people.

Provisional Governor Johnson told Georgia leaders that they must abolish slavery and repudiate their war debt. This was necessary to re-establish the state's credit and because Georgians held many Confederate bonds. Georgia thought it was ready for readmission to the Union. The state elected Alexander Stephens and H. V. Johnson as United States Senators, but they were not allowed to take their seats. There were three constitutional amendments Georgia must eventually accept: the Thirteenth, which abolished slavery; the Fourteenth, which made the Negroes citizens; and the Fifteenth, which gave Negroes the right to vote.

It became clear by the end of 1865 that the fanatical abolitionists in Congress, such as Senator Charles Sumner of Massachusetts and Congressman Thaddeus Stevens of Pennsylvania, were determined to overrule President Johnson and punish the South. They refused to agree to his milder policy for the conquered South. They pointed out that by trying to secede, the states had returned to the status of territories, which placed them under the jurisdiction of Congress. They insisted that military rule be established. They decreed that no state could re-enter the Union until it gave Negroes the right to vote.

The South was divided into five military districts and Georgia was in the third, with Florida and Alabama. On March 30, 1867, General John Pope arrived to take command. The military commanders were directed to register those who were to be allowed to vote. Many Negroes could, though they had little preparation; few white people were allowed to vote, and no one who had been a Confederate leader or owned $20,000 worth of property could register. In May,

591

Pope closed the University of Georgia when a student at graduation annoyed him with a speech. Benjamin Hill shook hands with the boy.

Congress set up a committee of fifteen to investigate the situation in the South and to decide what should be done. Johnson vetoed the harsh measures that resulted, but Congress passed them over his veto. Congress impeached him. He had broken their 1867 Tenure Law that forbade a president from firing even the members of his own cabinet. He fired Secretary of War Edwin Stanton on August 5, 1867. For this he was impeached, and only one vote saved him from being convicted. The trial lasted from March 13 to May 26. He was cleared of the charge against him, but his power was gone.

Governor Jenkins
Saved Georgia's Money

Governor Charles Jenkins was in office when the convention met to adopt the new 1868 constitution. The convention had worked from December 9, 1867, to March 11, 1868. One of the provisions of the new Constitution was that it finally abolished imprisonment for debt in Georgia. This was a strange law to have existed in a state that had been colonized in the first place for debtors freed from prison in Britain.

The convention cost $40,000. When General Pope, Commander of the Third Military District, demanded this money, Governor Jenkins refused to pay it. General George Meade, who succeeded Pope, also demanded the money, then removed Jenkins from office. On January 13, 1868, General Thomas Kruger, the last governor to live in Milledgeville, was appointed to the office. Jenkins hid the state seal, took the $400,000 from the state treasury to a bank in New York for safekeeping, and went to Nova Scotia. Later, when he returned this money, the Georgia legislature gave him a replica of the seal with the words, "*In arduis fidelis*" (faithful under difficulties) inscribed thereon. The seal is visible in a big painting of Jenkins that hangs in the State Capitol in Atlanta.

Bullock Elected Governor

General Meade set April 20-24, 1868 for voting on the new constitution and electing a new governor. The constitution was approved, and Rufus Bullock was elected governor. Bullock was from Augusta. He had come to Georgia from New York nine years before, and had served with the quartermaster corps in the Confederacy. General Meade left Georgia, leaving Bullock in charge. Bullock's regime was notoriously extravagant and corrupt. He persuaded Congress that Georgia was not abiding by its harsh rules, and had military government established again with General Alfred Terry in command. The state had ejected Negroes from its legislature. Georgia, however, finally adopted the Fourteenth and Fifteenth amendments to the United States Constitution.

Bullock resigned and left Georgia in October, 1871, leaving his associate Benjamin Conley, president of the Senate, in charge. The legislature ordered a special election in December, 1871, and chose James Smith, another lawyer, to be governor. Bullock was later indicted and returned to face trial, but he was never convicted. He remained in Georgia, and died in 1907.

Georgia was finally readmitted to the Union on July 15, 1870, and obtained control of her own government again. In 1877, President Rutherford B. Hayes removed the last of the Federal troops from the South.

The Negroes After The War

During the War Between the States, most Negroes stayed faithfully on the farms carrying on their work. Their situation changed after the war was over. Many of the plantations had been destroyed and others neglected. The presence of Union troops attracted many of the released slaves and many simply began to work for wages or a share of the crops. Some, influenced by carpetbaggers, joined in the political organizations that began to grow up in each state.

The Freedmen's Bureau was set up by the North to help the Negroes.

The fidelity of many fine Negroes in Georgia has been the subject of books and stories such as Harry Stillwell Edwards' famous short story "Eneas Africanus." A case of real life was the story of Neptune, the slave of the King family at Retreat Plantation, who managed to bring the body of his young master all the way from a battlefield in Virginia to Saint Simons Island so that he could be buried with his family in Christ Churchyard. Austin Dabney, who fought in the Revolution, educated the sons of his master's family with money he had made and saved. The child of a slave, George Washington Carver, of Tuskegee in neighboring Alabama, became one of the great scientists of the world and received many honors. His research with the sweet potato and the peanut helped to advance southern agriculture. Carver had once been traded for a horse by his owner.

Hosts of Negroes, however, were so elated with the idea of their freedom that they spent their time in idleness, taking food and supplies wherever they found them, and creating a real problem both for their former employers and the federal authorities. Unscrupulous men, both the Carpet-baggers from the North and the Scalawags in Georgia, took advantage of the ignorant and the shiftless. Some Negroes

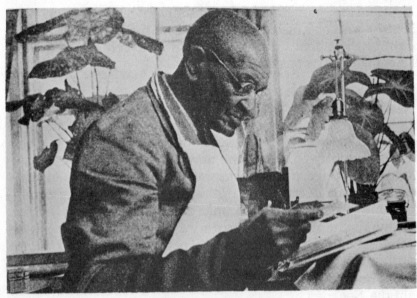

George Washington Carver

paid five dollars for a bundle of four red, white, and blue sticks which they had been told they could use to mark off for themselves any square mile of land not already taken.

They were told they would all get forty acres and a mule on New Year's Day. They called this "The Great Jubilee Day."

How The Ku Klux Klan Arose

Trouble arose from idle, mischievous Negroes who had been incited to lawlessness by Carpetbaggers and local Scalawags who preyed upon them, causing fear and anger in the South. Many organizations of Negroes and their new supporters arose to cause trouble.

The Ku Klux Klan came into existence almost by accident. Six young veterans near Pulaski, Tennessee, had been attending a masked revelry just before Christmas and were returning home. They and their horses were disguised in white bedsheets. Negroes whom they met on the road were frightened by these apparent apparitions, thinking them to be the ghosts of Confederate dead. Immediately southern leaders believed that they had found an effective way to control troublesome Negroes.

The name "Ku Klux" originated from the Greek word "Kuklos" which means circle. Soon the Ku Klux Klan was organized and spread over the southern states. General Nathan Bedford Forrest was said to have become Grand Wizard, though this was never proved at the 1871 congressional investigation of the Klan. Lee himself had declined to be the Klan's leader. Forrest, who had been quite wealthy before the war, had entered the war as a private. After the war Forrest moved to Memphis and went into the railroad business. He began organizing Klan units throughout the South at the same time. In Georgia, General John B. Gordon was the reputed head of the Klan.

Finally the power of the Klan was diminished by ridicule of men parading in bedsheets, burning crosses, and attempting to regulate the lives of people of whom they disapproved, and it became unacceptable to most Georgians.

Improved education slowly reduced the. Klan's power. The original Klan was formally dissolved in March, 1869.

One of the most notorious occurrences connected with the Ku Klux Klan during the Reconstruction years was the Ashburn murder case at Columbus. G. W. Ashburn, white overseer on a plantation, had become a leader and confidant of the Negroes. He was murdered after he had first received a warning from the Klan. Nine young men alleged to be Klan members were tried in a military court for Ashburn's murder. General George Meade, then military commander, had offered $2,000 reward for the apprehension of the killers. Columbus also had offered $500. The government hired Joe Brown, the "war governor," to help prosecute them after they were captured. The nine young men were defended by a brilliant battery of lawyers, including Alexander Stephens. But before the case could be finally concluded, military rule had been replaced by civil government again, and the prosecution ended.

After the federal government withdrew from Georgia in 1872, the state's legislature passed a poll tax and other measures which limited the number of Negroes who could vote. As the influences from outside the state subsided, the Negroes took up the jobs open to them. Most of them settled down and became wage hands, sharecroppers, or tenant farmers. Many became excellent citizens and active church members.

Atlanta: The New Capital

At the same time they ratified their new Constitution, the people of Georgia voted to keep their capital in Atlanta, where it had been during the Reconstruction era. As a railroad center, Atlanta was becoming more and more the center of the economic life of the state, and a gateway to the Southwest as well. By a vote of 99,147 to 55,201 on December 5, 1877, Atlanta officially became the permanent capital.

In 1883, the Legislature authorized the construction of a new capitol building. The government had been housed in temporary locations. When the bids were opened, the lowest bid designated Indiana limestone as the building material; the next bid specified Georgia marble. Many Georgians were later to lament that the exterior of the capitol was not built of Georgia marble!

Inside the building, completed in 1889, there are the offices of the governor and several other state officials. Still others have their offices in nearby state office buildings. There are the two legislative chambers in which the General Assembly meets, one for the Senate and one for the House of Representatives. On the **fourth floor** is an interesting museum with displays depicting the life and products of the state.

In the rotunda under the golden dome is Statuary Hall. Here are found white marble busts of many great Georgians of the past: Archibald Bulloch, John Adam Treutlen, Benjamin Hawkins, Button Gwinnett, Dr. Lyman Hall, George Walton, Abraham Baldwin, William Few, Dr. Crawford W. Long, William Harris Crawford, George Troup, and many others. A bust of Alexander Stephens is standing by the huge statue of the eloquent Benjamin H. Hill, whom Stephens once challenged to a duel.

On the stair landing is the curious bust of Oglethorpe

The State Capitol In Atlanta

which resembles Voltaire, the sardonic French writer. Around the walls are dozens of portraits of the great of yesterday and today. One shows Oglethorpe when he was very old, looking at a book during the auction of the library of his friend, Dr. Samuel Johnson. One of the portraits is that of Lafayette, painted by Samuel Morse. In the basement, there are equestrian statues of generals Lee, Gordon, Forrest, Hood, and Johnson. There are many other statues on the outside grounds.

The statue on top of the golden dome is called "Miss Freedom." It was one of many such statues made in the latter part of the nineteenth century. Some mistake her for a replica of the Statue of Liberty. The steel statue on the dome is fifteen feet tall, holds a torch in one hand and a sword in the other. Beneath her feet is the gold-washed dome that has glistened since 1959 with gold from Georgia's hills, near Dahlonega.

Atlanta was destined to become not only the leading city in the New Georgia, but a great city in the New South.

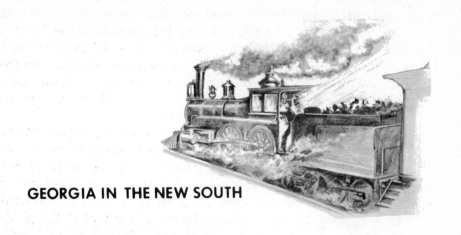

GEORGIA IN THE NEW SOUTH

UNIT 8

CHAPTER 45

GEORGIA IN

THE NEW SOUTH

There were nearly 50,000 fewer people in Georgia than when the war began. Many had been killed; some had moved to other states, and a few had even gone to South America or Europe to start life over there.

Between 1870 and the end of the century, many important things were happening. Georgians had a hard time making a living, and the era is sometimes referred to as a thirty-year depression. But things were taking new shape in the state, and in the South. Georgia's population doubled in those thirty years. In 1870, it was 1,184,068. By 1900, it would be 2,216,331. Factories would double, and their output triple, but at first this era was very dark.

The big plantations were gone; there was no labor to work them. Small farms grew up. Factories came in. More railroads were built. Schools, colleges, and churches increased. Northern men with money were induced to invest in Georgia.

Benjamin Hill described this era as "one of those rare junctures in human affairs where one civilization ends and another begins."

Georgia became important as a source of the nation's food and fiber. The products of field and farm and forest were more important than ever. In 1874, Georgia set up the first state department of agriculture in the nation.

Manufacturing became increasingly important. A state that made only seven million dollars' worth of products at mid-century was manufacturing a hundred million dollars' worth by the century's end.

Plantation owners had been accustomed to look with disfavor on factories, but now they began to consider the wisdom of manufacturing for their state. The war had shown them the danger of an agricultural economy dependent on a one-crop system. They had also seen the advantages of machinery and factories. They had yet to learn its dangers.

Northerners became interested in investing their money in factories in Georgia. The number of mills and factories doubled and their output tripled between 1870 and 1900. The break-up of the plantation system brought many workers to town, and the establishment of factories encouraged the growth of towns and cities; sometimes whole families worked in the factories. Along the Fall Line, where the rivers created water power, Augusta, Macon, and Columbus became centers for the manufacture of cotton textiles. Swiss immigrants, led by J. Staub, settled at Mt. Airy, after declining offers in Florida and in the West.

Georgia farmers began to use commercial fertilizers on their crops. By 1870, the state was producing 726,406 bales of cotton and was on its way to a new farm prosperity, too.

Railroads were repaired and more were built. In the decade after 1865, almost a thousand miles of railroads had been built. Georgia had more than any other state except Texas. They connected the state with other roads running to the North and the West by now-transcontinental railroads. The work on the railroads, like the work in northern factories, had brought many white laborers from other countries.

Men seeking ways to make a living took to the gold mines again. More than two dozen gold mining companies were organized and active in the north Georgia hills, where, in 1880, more than a million dollars' worth of gold came out of Georgia.

There was more than gold in the hills. Former Governor Joe Brown added coal mining to his many other business enterprises. Others had begun to see the value of clay for bricks, and Georgia timbers for fine furniture and for naval stores. The state also had stone, especially granite and limestone. It was just beginning to discover that its marble was beautiful enough to provide many of the world's finest buildings and statues.

Sawmills were being located along the coast and elsewhere in the state. There was a growing market for Georgia lumber. Textiles were bringing more money now.

Georgians became aware of the remarkable resources of their state. Dr. George Little, state geologist, wrote about them in his report in 1875: "Every variety of climate is afforded, as illustrated in my own experience during the present month, when leaving one party on the southern border sleeping in the open air on the islands of the Okefenokee, with oranges and bananas hanging in the gardens on its borders, I joined the same week another party on the Cohutta mountains covered with snow; while in passing through Atlanta, balmy breezes were blowing as if it were springtime."

Henry Grady Led The Way

Many people worked to build a better Georgia on the ruins that followed the Civil War. The clearest voice that sounded in the postwar South was that of a newspaper editor named Henry Grady. His voice was heard over the nation, and did much to inspire action that helped to heal the old hurts and unite the country again.

Henry Woodfin Grady's ancestors were originally named O'Grady and came from Ireland in the 1700's. His grandfather came to Georgia with his two little boys after his wife had died at their North Carolina home. He settled at Mountain Town, near Ellijay. Later they moved to Athens. Henry Grady was born in a four-room cottage in Athens on May 24, 1850. As he grew up, one of his playmates was a little girl named Julia King. Later, writing about her, he said, "I fell out of my baby carriage trying to reach out to Julia in hers. When she was 12 and I was 14, I asked her to marry me. I said, 'If you will say "Yes," wear a yellow dress to the picnic and wave a handkerchief at me.' "

When they grew up, they married. Their home was in Atlanta, where Grady became editor of the *Atlanta Constitution*. A member of his staff was Joel Chandler Harris, the creator of the Uncle Remus tales.

After Grady had graduated from the University of

Georgia and become a newspaper man, he attracted the attention of the nation with his stories about the earthquake that shook the South and almost demolished Charleston, South Carolina. Later, a nation that had read his words about that tragedy listened to him as he wrote and made speeches on what the South should do about rebuilding its section into prosperity and greatness. He urged his people not to sit mourning about the past, but to face the future, which could be bright. He believed that the state should develop its resources, bring industry in, start factories, and make the most of its products.

His speech about a dead man dramatically focused attention on Georgia's need to manufacture its own products, and not let its raw materials be sent out of the state to make richer the owners of factories in the North. This is what he said: "I attended a funeral in a Georgia county. It was a poor, one-gallused fellow. They buried him in the midst of a marble quarry; they cut through solid marble to make his grave; yet the little tombstone they put above him was from Vermont. They buried him in the midst of a pine forest, but his pine coffin was imported from Cincinnati. They buried him within touch of an iron mine, but the nails in his coffin and the iron in the shovel that dug his grave were from Pittsburgh. They buried him near the best sheep-grazing country in the world, yet the wool in the coffin bands was brought from the North. They buried him in a New York coat, a Boston pair of shoes, a pair of breeches from Chicago, and a shirt from Cincinnati. Georgia furnished only the corpse and a hole in the ground."

He promoted expositions in Georgia, to show off its products and its possibilities. He wrote editorials about the opportunities in the South, especially in Georgia. Day after day, he worked on his paper in downtown Atlanta, going back and forth on the horse carriage to his home out on Peachtree, where his beloved Julia and their children lived. Despite his long hours of work, he had time for his family. One day he took an armful of gifts home in July, and said, "I have decided that this year the Gradys will have TWO Christmases." Like Dickens, he loved Christmas. However, it was on Christmas, some years later, that tragedy struck.

People in the North heard about Grady. They began to invite him to come to speak to them. He spoke to the men of

603

New England and New York about the rich possibilities in the South. He painted for them in glowing colors what the South could be like, and what the nation could be like when all sections worked together toward a new prosperity and a new understanding.

On December 13, 1886, he went to New York to speak to the New England Society there at a banquet at old Delmonico's restaurant. One of the guests was General William Tecumseh Sherman, who once laid Georgia in ruins and who had himself become an after-dinner speaker in the postwar years. Grady, speaking of his experiences in talking before these audiences, said, "When I rose, every nerve in my body was strung tight as a fiddle string, and all tingling. But I knew that I had a message for these people. As soon as I opened my mouth, it came tumbling out." He said, "I want to say to General Sherman, who is considered an able man in our parts, but kind of careless with fire, that from the ashes he left us in 1864, we have built a brave and beautiful city in Atlanta, that we have caught the sunshine in the brick and mortar of our homes, and have builded therein not one ignoble prejudice or memory." A news report said that his speech "rang 'round the world."

He came back from one of his speaking trips to the North one year just at Christmas with a bad cold. He died on December 23, 1889, and was buried on Christmas Day. One editor wrote that "he died literally loving a nation into peace." He was thirty-nine years old.

Seven thousand people came to his funeral. The *New York Tribune* said, "Never was a private person so universally mourned."

The Grady monument on Henry Grady Square in downtown Atlanta was unveiled October 21, 1891. Alexander Doyle, a New York sculptor, designed it. People from many parts of the nation sent money to help build it. The New England businessmen to whom he had spoken of "The New South" just before he died, sent a thousand dollars. Andrew Carnegie, the little Scottish steel magnate who financed America's libraries, sent a check for $250. Five days after the movement to build the monument was launched, more than $12,000 had been received and within a few weeks, over $20,000. His daughter Gussie, later Mrs. Eugene Black of Atlanta, unveiled the statue. Her son Eugene Black became a banker who was even more famous around the world than his grandfather.

After Grady died, somebody said to his mother in Athens, "What a pity he could not have lived until his work was done." She replied gently, "Perhaps his work is done." Perhaps it was.

Many things in Georgia were named for Grady; among them are Grady County, Henry Grady High School in Atlanta, the Henry Grady School of Journalism at the University of Georgia in Athens, and Grady Hospital in Atlanta.

Grady Square in downtown Atlanta was officially dedicated on May 24, 1960, the 110th anniversary of his birth. It is near the office of the *Atlanta Constitution,* the newspaper he edited.

Georgia Held Expositions

Georgia leaders, including Henry Grady, believed that it would be a good thing if the state held expositions in Atlanta to show the nation and the world what it had accomplished and what it could do. Many people did not realize the rich resources that the state possessed, and were not aware of the talents of its people to use them. The federal government gave $200,000 to help stage these exhibitions.

In 1881, there began the first of expositions that brought more than a million visitors to see Georgia products and talents. In some of these, Georgia invited the other southern states to cooperate. The Liberty Bell was brought from Philadelphia. A replica of it now stands on Capitol Square.

Presidents came. President Grover Cleveland accepted an invitation engraved in Georgia gold. Once he and his pretty young wife were guests of Governor John B. Gordon, whom they had known when Gordon was in Congress. Once they went on to Savannah, where they were present when a statue to Sergeant Jasper, a hero of the Revolution, was unveiled.

Both whites and Negroes helped in the expositions. President Booker T. Washington of Tuskegee Institute in Alabama made a speech. Washington, born a slave in Virginia, got an education with the greatest difficulty. He graduated from Hampton and came to build a college for Negroes in the South. Once he traveled two thousand miles

to and from Boston to make a five-minute speech in Atlanta.
But it was that speech that led southern leaders to invite
him to go with them to Washington to get aid in putting on the
exposition. This he did. A whole building was devoted to
exhibits created by Negroes, and Washington was one of the
main speakers.

The achievements in farming and industry were tremendous. One of the persons who helped farmers was Dr.
George Washington Carver, Negro scientist who was teaching

Booker T. Washington

606

at Tuskegee. He graduated from college at Ames, Iowa, and took a job teaching at Tuskegee, though Thomas Edison offered him much more money.

When men in the North and elsewhere saw what was possible in Georgia, they began to invest more money in industry and agriculture in this state. The expositions had paid off. These expositions did more than merely display the wares of Georgia's farms and forests and factories. They brought people face to face with people, and deepened their understanding and strengthened their belief that the country was united again and that old hurts were healing. In 1895, old soldiers from both the northern and the southern armies met together at the exhibition in Atlanta.

At the very first exposition in 1881, there were more than two thousand exhibits. At one exhibition, visitors were amazed to see a demonstration of cotton picked, processed, and made into a suit all in one day!

Georgia Was
Beginning To Market Its Marble

Indians had known a little about the marble here. Marble bowls they made have been found in the earth. Their marble figures are now in museums.

The first crude quarrying had begun in the early nineteenth century when a wandering Irish marble cutter named Henry Fitzsimmons saw the white Georgia marble. Later great quarries were established here. One problem, besides digging it out of the earth, was how to move it out of Long Swamp Valley to the world that could build beautiful things with it. Gradually that was solved,first with oxcarts and later with trains. As the century neared an end, the world was learning about the beauty of Georgia marble. Daniel Chester French, the sculptor, used twenty-eight blocks (some weighing forty tons) to carve the brooding statue of Lincoln in the Memorial at Washington, D.C. In the capital, too, the Folger Shakespearian Library, the Pan American Building and the Corcoran Art Gallery are among the structures built of Georgia marble. The "Civic Virtue" monument in New York City, the Bok Tower at Lake Wales, Florida, and the Field Museum of Natural History in Chicago, are only a few of the buildings that have Georgia marble.

CHAPTER 46

WHAT WERE THE NEW
PATTERNS IN GOVERNMENT

The United States Congress, which impeached President Andrew Johnson and came within one vote of convicting him, kept troops in some parts of the South for ten years. When Georgians got their state government back, and the federal soldiers and officials had departed, they were not all in accord with one another.

There were divided opinions about many things. Some Georgians had wanted to cooperate with the conquerors, believing this was not only inevitable but best for the state.

There were also divisions between those who wanted the monied men from the North and East to come down and invest in Georgia. The farmers especially felt that these men, and the Georgia leaders who worked with them, devised benefits for the factory owners but not for the farmers. This later led to a revolt of the farmers, and the growth of farm groups and political parties strong enough to change the situation.

But first Georgia wanted a new constitution.

Robert Toombs And
The Constitution Of 1877

Exactly a hundred years after Georgia adopted its first constitution, the one which Button Gwinnett had worked on,

Georgians were meeting to work on the state's new constitution.

Georgians had never liked the 1868 constitution. It had been adopted while the Carpetbaggers and the Scalawags were in control.

After the last of the troops were removed, Georgia leaders assembled to draw up a constitution more to their liking. Former Governor Charles Jenkins was named chairman, but Robert Toombs, the colorful old Georgian who was now back from exile but had never taken the oath of allegiance to the United States, was the central figure in this assembly. He was chairman of the committee on revision, one of thirteen committees named. When money ran out in the state treasury before the members of the Constitutional Convention could be paid, he offered to pay them himself. The convention gave Toombs a rousing ovation that brought tears to his eyes. He was sixty-three years old; Jenkins was seventy. The young men marveled at the agile minds and the dedicated spirits of the men who had lived through Georgia's times of terror and times of triumph. Toombs sat with his unlighted cigar, his linen duster, and sometimes his brown straw hat, and spoke his mind. He was proud and happy to be in the midst of things again after his long, lonely exile. He put constitutional safeguards on the treasury because he remembered the wasteful corruption of the Bullock regime. "I have locked up the treasury and thrown the key away," he said. But many constitutional amendments were necessary before a new constitution was adopted in 1945.

This 1877 constitution forbade the creation of any more counties. Georgia then had 137. But the constitution was changed many times, and in the years that followed the total became at one time 161. Some consolidated.

When the people voted to ratify the constitution, they also voted to keep the capital permanently in Atlanta, where it had been during the Reconstruction, instead of returning it to Milledgeville.

Georgia Rejected Joe Brown — And Then Elected Him Again

The "Bourbon Triumvirate" led to the Farmers' Revolt. Three men, Joe Brown, John B. Gordon, and Alfred

Colquitt, wielded great influence after the war. They were dubbed the "Bourbon Triumvirate."

Joe Brown had been arrested after the South lost the war, and sent off to prison. After he came back, he advised Georgians to work with the northerners. He himself joined the Republican party. "I didn't leave the Democratic party; it left me," he said.

He went to the Republican national convention when Grant was nominated for President of the United States. Back in Georgia, Governor James Johnson, the Columbus lawyer whom the federal authorities had appointed, made Brown Chief Justice of the Georgia Supreme Court. He was appointed to a twelve-year term, but he soon resigned to become president of a railroad.

He was relatively quiet during the eighteen-seventies, attending to his many business interests. He became a rich man, this poor boy of the mountains, and had investments in mining, farming, and railroading. Behind the scenes, he cooperated with Colquitt and Gordon to wield tremendous political power.

But deep in his heart, Brown keenly felt his repudiation by the people of Georgia whom he had led through the war. It was always his ambition to be politically accepted by his people again.

When Gordon suddenly and unexpectedly resigned from the United States Senate in 1880 after having just been re-elected to a second term, Governor Alfred Colquitt appointed Brown to fill the vacancy. He had run for it and had been defeated earlier. Many Georgians were indignant. One city tolled the bells, as if mourning for the dead. Many people charged the "Bourbon Triumvirate" with "trading," particularly when Gordon got a $14,000 job with Brown's railroad. But all three denied it.

Yet many Georgians remained bitter toward Brown. They called him a turncoat and an opportunist. When they threatened to defeat Governor Colquitt at re-election time because he had appointed Joe Brown, the old war governor came to speak to an audience in Atlanta. Many audiences would not even listen to him. But finally, to this one, he read a letter from Lee that had counseled cooperation as the only way for the South. The next day, Colquitt was elected by a 51,000-vote majority.

Brown himself was later re-elected to the U.S. Senate

by the state that had disdained him so bitterly after the war. He stayed in the U.S Senate twelve years. In 1890, he voluntarily retired from public life. He had been accepted again by his people.

But during the time when Brown was out of favor with most Georgians, the feeling against him was so bitter that it even included his family. While one of his sons was at the University of Georgia, a group of students who were angry at Brown came to the boy's room, muttering threats. Nat Harris, who had fought in the Confederate Army at sixteen and was later to be governor, was also studying there. He said to them, "You know me, boys. I have heard the bullets whistle. I went through the war. If one of you puts his foot over the sill of this boy's room, I will shoot!" They knew he meant it, and they left young Brown in peace.

Later Joe Brown set up a $50,000 fund at the University to educate poor boys. It was a memorial to another one of his sons, Charles McDonald Brown, who had died very young. It was money the boy would have received if he had lived to be twenty-one.

Joe Brown died a millionaire on November 30, 1894. He is buried in Oakland Cemetery in Atlanta. On his tomb are these words: "His history is written in the annals of Georgia."

A historian says of the tempestuous Joe Brown, "For forty years you could not write any history of Georgia without his name being at the center."

General Gordon Became First Governor In The New Capitol

On Capitol Square stands the statue of General John B. Gordon, just outside the window of the governor's office. Gordon was the first Georgia governor to occupy these offices in the new State Capitol when it was opened in 1889. He had been elected governor in 1886; and a strange election it was, too.

Gordon had been defeated once before for governor, during the Carpetbagger Regime, when Rufus Bulloch was elected. Georgia loved and admired Gordon and elected him to various offices from the time he left the Confederate army until his death in 1904.

611

He had defeated Alexander Stephens for the U.S. Senate in 1874. He went to the Senate more than once, resigned, and then went back again when Joe Brown retired. Gordon was one of the "Bourbon Triumvirate" and there was a revolt against that during this era, but the personal popularity of the dashing General Gordon endured. Some thought he had been part of the "trade" made with Brown and Colquitt when Brown became unpopular because of working with the northerners, and could not get elected to the Senate. Gordon had been elected, had resigned, and accepted a job with Brown's railroad. Some said Brown's appointment by Colquitt to the Senate was in return for Brown's support of Colquitt politically. They all denied this. Gordon said he needed to make more money for his family than he could make in public office.

In 1886, A. O. Bacon seemed sure to be the next governor of Georgia, but strange things happened to change this.

Benjamin Hill had died and a statue of him was to be unveiled in Atlanta. (This statue now stands in the Capitol, but it was first in downtown Atlanta.) The aging Confederate President Jefferson Davis was persuaded to come from his home at Beauvoir, Mississippi, to attend the ceremonies.

Henry Grady, who was in charge of arrangements,had Gordon meet the Davises in Alabama and ride on the train with them to Atlanta. Davis, whom crowds swarmed to see, was too feeble to speak. He let Gordon speak for him. In Atlanta, he rode in a coach drawn by six white horses with 1,000 old soldiers marching behind, and 6,000 school children throwing flowers in his path, as the band played "Dixie."

Thousands came to the unveiling of the statue. The many Confederate veterans who were there were touched at the sight of their old leaders, Davis and Gordon. As the ceremonies began, General James Longstreet arrived from his home at Gainesville, and the three leaders had a touching reunion. The crowd went wild.

Though it was not mentioned there, this seemed to be the launching of a campaign for governor which Gordon won. Confederate veterans, some of them with one arm or leg, helped at the polls.

Gordon made a good governor. Among the guests he entertained was President Grover Cleveland. The Clevelands wanted to see a typical "Negro mammy" of that day. Gordon sent out to his farm to bring in the family's beloved old servant, who had been with them in Washington. But, much to the President's amusement, she told the boy who went to bring her that she had seen presidents in Washington, that she had a "misery in the leg," and was not coming into the Mansion to see Cleveland. Later she apologized to the President, who was delighted with her.

After Gordon finished his term as governor, he went to the U.S. Senate again. He had interests in coal mines and railroads, and he also made a great deal of money with a lecture on "The Last Days of the Confederacy." One reporter said, "His voice had the clarity of a trumpet, and the charm of the flute. He used no useless gestures."

In New England, his persuasiveness had been such that a northerner who had lost a son in the war told him, "I have hated you all these years because of my dead boy. But when I heard you tell about the sufferings of the Southern boys, and their dying, I realized that they too were fighting for what they thought was right." The ability to speak like this helped make Gordon governor.

Gordon had just been walking over his Florida farm with his grandson one day when he became ill. He died January 9, 1904. When his body was brought back to Atlanta, a newspaper story said, "Hats off! Gordon comes home today." This was only a week after the death of Longstreet and newspapers over the nation reviewed many of the old stories of these two illustrious Georgians.

Colquitt Was The Third
Of The "Bourbon Triumvirate"

The third man in the trio of power was Alfred Colquitt. He was less widely known than Civil War Governor Joe Brown or Confederate General John B. Gordon. He was the son of a wealthy Georgia planter, Walter Colquitt. Both father and son were also preachers, though neither was ever a pastor.

Alfred Colquitt was elected president of the International Sunday School Association when its convention was held in Atlanta. He was a graduate of Princeton University and had studied law there. He served as a soldier in the Mexican War and as a major general in the Confederate Army.

He entered the governor's race to succeed Governor James Smith.

In 1877, Alfred Colquitt had defeated Jonathan Norcross for governor by 111,000 to 33,000. This was the biggest majority that Georgia voters had ever given a governor. Colquitt was elected again in 1879. He was a very popular governor, but many turned against him, at least temporarily, when he appointed Joe Brown. Despite the clamor against Colquitt, he was re-elected. He later served his state in Congress also.

CHAPTER 47

SURPRISING CHANGES THAT
CAME TO THE STATE

A Husband-And-Wife Team Led A
Revolt Against The Democrats

The first real revolt against the power of Brown-Gordon-Colquitt was in a Congressional race. It foreshadowed the rise of the farmers' revolt in the 1890's. Later, the farmers' efforts to improve farm life also turned into a political movement.

The Independents were led by Dr. and Mrs. William H. Felton of Cartersville in northwest Georgia, and for awhile by Emory Speer in northeast Georgia. This Independent movement was a revolt against the regular Democrats.

The initial warnings of political discontent came when Felton, a doctor-lawyer-farmer, opposed the regular Democratic nominee for Congress in the district known as "the Bloody Seventh." He won this election and the next two before he was defeated. Felton had the help of a remarkable wife who was to become, for one day, the nation's first woman in the United States Senate.

Rebecca Latimer Felton grew up in Decatur. Her father, who entertained many famous and interesting people at his home, helped her develop an interest in public affairs. He was postmaster in Decatur, and read the news to neighbors who could not read. Rebecca listened too. She later wrote, "After the stagecoach left, my father read the news aloud to the eager people....I can look backward, through a long vista, and see a little girl as she listened to the wonderful

615

things going on in the busy outside world." She little dreamed that all over Georgia one day people would wait eagerly for the newspaper to read what she had written in it.

Rebecca attended the academy at Madison, where she graduated at seventeen with first honors. The commencement speaker was Dr. W. H. Felton. A year later, they were married. Settling on their farm in the Etowah Valley near Cartersville, they became a powerful team in Georgia life and politics. They wrote letters, edited a paper and made political speeches. They buried a son and daughter before the war came, left their home when Sherman swept across their valley, and buried two more sons from a shack near Macon where they had taken refuge. After the war, they had two more sons, but one died early. Mrs. Felton always said, "Politics caused the war that brought ruin, misery, and death to our common country."

The Feltons were strongly opposed to the iniquitous convict lease system, which had grown up in the state. After the war, the restlessness and difficult conditions increased crime, and the state was burdened with prisoners. Since the prison at Milledgeville had been burned, there were not adequate facilities for them. The convict leasing system grew out of this situation. Under the system, farmers and manufacturers and others could lease human beings from the state, sometimes for less than a dime a day, to work in forests, sawmills, mines, and fields. The leased convicts were frequently starved, overworked, and badly housed. Many became ill and died.

The Feltons were outraged by this situation and worked publicly against it. Later, Tom Watson raised his powerful voice in opposition to the degrading system.

During the period, three companies, partially owned by Joe Brown, John. B. Gordon and their associates, leased large numbers of convicts from the state for twenty years. In return, the companies agreed to pay Georgia a half million dollars in twenty annual installments for their hire. The state did have regulations that forbade working the convicts on Sunday and requiring proper food, clothing, shelter, and medical care. Without regulation, things got so bad that investigations were held by Governor Gordon. As a result two companies were fined $2,500 for mistreatment of convicts. But under such an evil system,

616

mistreatment was bound to continue.

Mrs. Felton nursed her sick husband faithfully through his last years. She had helped him in his political campaigns, despite the fun that many poked at her. One jingle went like this:

Some parsons hide behind their coat
To save their precious life;
But Parson Felton beats them all,
He hides behind his wife.

But one newspaper editor wrote, "Thank heaven for her. We need more wives who are willing to help their husbands bear the burdens of life." She literally wrote millions of words, in letters and newspaper articles including two books: *Country Life In Georgia* and *Memoirs Of Georgia Politics.* She kept a horse and servant at the door, to post a late letter by train when necessary.

After her husband died, she kept up her activities, and lent her talents to politicans whom she favored, among them her friend Tom Watson. By the late century she was crusading for women's rights. Until 1879, a woman who worked had no legal right to her own pay. Any employer who refused to turn it over to her husband or father, if asked, could be made to pay double!

In 1899, when she was sixty-five, Hoke Smith hired Mrs. Felton to write for his *Atlanta Journal.* For twenty years, thereafter, rural readers were powerfully influenced by her advice about how to improve their homes, rear their children, and vote. Politicians feared her and courted her favor. When Rebecca Felton's favor was withheld, they belittled or denounced her. Many called her the smartest woman in Georgia. She received thousands of letters asking her advice about everything under the sun. Young people asked her about their love affairs, wives asked about homemaking, men asked about farming, politicians asked about legislative bills. Reports came to her of cruelties and injustices that existed. She blasted those responsible, both in her speeches and newspaper columns. She was equally sarcastic about the "ring of rich Bourbon politicians in Atlanta, and the courthouse ring in the rural counties."

In 1922, when her friend Tom Watson died, Governor Tom Hardwick, as a gesture of deference and courtesy to the eighty-seven-year-old woman, appointed her United States Senator for one day. Mrs. Felton's name goes down in history as the nation's first woman senator.

The Aging Stephens
Was Governor Briefly

The agrarian or farm group which wanted to unseat the Bourbons had developed a strong core of Independents rallying around Judge and Mrs. W.H. Felton and Emory Speer. Speer, like Felton, had been a congressman from Georgia.

The Independents, in 1881, prodded by the Feltons, began to consider the aging Alexander Stephens as a candidate for governor. He had served his state for many years, and the people loved him. He had sent nearly 100 boys through college. Hundreds of influential people had visited him at Liberty Hall in Crawfordville. He said, "I named it Liberty Hall because I do as I please here and expect my guests to do

The Kitchen At Liberty Hall

the same." His name was known all over Georgia. Even his peculiarities were talked about with understanding affection. He had a curious notion that pie was good for children, and whether they liked it or not, every child who came to his house had to eat pie.

Stephens was about seventy years old when Emory Speer asked him to run for governor. He was confined to a wheelchair which he had used since a heavy iron gate fell on him. In his reply to the invitation Stephens said, "No man has a right to refuse that office unless he lacks the health, and I am very well, thank you." Speer sent a telegram to party officials saying that Stephens would accept the nomination. But Stephens accepted the Democratic, not the Independent, nomination for governor. The Feltons and the other Independents were furious. Mrs. Felton, who had corresponded frequently with him, had gone with her husband to visit him at Liberty Hall, and exchanged Christmas presents with him, never wrote to him again.

Robert Toombs was aghast when he heard that his aging friend had agreed to run for governor. "Mr. Stephens is in his dotage," he said. Actually their friendship never wavered, because they were too close. Once when Stephens was deeply in debt because he had signed many notes to run a newspaper in Atlanta, Toombs came to Atlanta, paid up all the notes, took them to Liberty Hall, threw them on the table with a flourish and said, "Aleck, you can use these to light your fires." Their pictures hang side by side today in Stephens' bedroom.

Stephens defeated the Independent candidate Lucius Gartrell by 107,253 to 44,896, carrying 130 of the 137 counties that then existed in Georgia. This defeat, coupled with the defeat of both Felton and Speer in their congressional districts, proved to be a blow from which the Independents never recovered. But they had by that time forced the regular Democrats to absorb most of their platform for reform, and had broken the real power of the Bourbons.

Stephens, who was actually too old to be burdened with the cares of governor, carried on as best he could. In February, 1883, he went to Savannah to make a speech about Oglethorpe at the observance of Georgia's becoming 150 years old. He caught a cold, riding in a carriage with a broken window in a chilling wind and rain. Back in Atlanta, he rapidly grew worse. They knew he was dying. He imagined he was on the train, nearing his beloved Liberty Hall. The last thing he said was, "Get ready. We are nearly home."

He died March 3, 1883. Twenty thousand people came to pay their respects as his body lay in state at the Capitol, and a hundred thousand lined the streets to Oakland Cemetery where he was first buried. He had once said, " I would like to be buried at midnight, with the Negroes marching around my grave, as they do, with flaming torches that they throw away and never use again, no matter how badly they need wood."

Toombs was so shaken that he wept for five minutes before he could speak a word. Linton Stephens had once said, "My brother was the best man I ever knew."

A year later, Stephens was removed to his own front yard at Crawfordville, where he now lies near his statue, which was erected in 1893. It shows him making a speech. One one side are his words: "I fear nothing...but to do wrong." In 1914, the body of his beloved half-brother, Linton, was brought there from Sparta.

Henry McDaniel of Walton County, who was elected governor in the special election held after Stephens' death, had been the youngest member of the Secession Convention.

The Farmers Elected
Northen Governor

The Bourbon triumvirate and their supporters had rescued Georgia from the Carpetbaggers and the Scalawags. But they had dominated Georgia politics for so long that many began to feel that the state needed a party that would free Georgia from them.

There was a tremendous power in the farm vote in Georgia, and the revolt of the Independents had helped make this clear. In 1888, Georgians organized a branch of the Farmers' Alliance, which had started in the West earlier. In just a few months, there were fifty thousand members here, and within two years, a hundred thousand. It was an organization dedicated not to politics but to improving life on the farm. Yet the farmers came to realize that in politics lay the power to make these improvements.

In Georgia, they rallied to the support of a former teacher who had become a farmer and had been president of the farm group in this state; he was W. J. Northen of Hancock County. So strong was the farm support that Northen did not even have an opponent for the race. The farmers and their friends elected him governor. They also elected a number of congressmen in the same year, 1890.

Northen had been for twenty years a schoolteacher. He was once headmaster of Mt. Zion Academy at Sparta. He was a strict disciplinarian and whipped or expelled boys who did not study or who misbehaved. One boy was very resentful. He said, "Professor, I will get even with you some day." Later, he became such a staunch supporter of Northen that he worked hard to make his former teacher the governor of Georgia. He said, "Professor, I rode fifteen miles to round up for you as many votes as you gave me licks when I was in school. That should elect you."

Northen was re-elected in 1892. He promoted education, as was natural for a former school teacher, and advocated free textbooks for elementary school children. He became the author of several volumes called *Men of Mark in Georgia.* It was during his term that a college for teachers was started in Athens, and the State Industrial College for Negroes was opened in Savannah. He urged farmers to diversify their crops. He sought to abolish lynching, the vicious convict leasing system, and the giving of free passes to state officials by railroads. He worked hard to improve farm life throughout Georgia.

Governor Northen Helped Northern Soldiers Come To Live In Georgia

After the War Between the States, a group of Federal soldiers who had fought for the Union came to live in Georgia. They started a colony at Fitzgerald. Two of them had marched with Sherman to the sea in his famous March through Georgia. One had been a prisoner at Andersonville, and one had been present when the Confederate president, Jefferson Davis, was captured at Irwinville, Georgia, on May 10, 1865.

In the 1890's, drought dried up the fields of the great northwest. A depression added to the troubles in the farmlands. Dust storms, freezing cold winters, and poor harvests brought hunger and hardships to the people there. They knew heartache and despair.

People in the South had little money after the war, but they soon had food. Led by their governor they began to send part of their harvests to the hungry people of the midwest in 1894. Georgia sent two trainloads of food — flour, corn, meat — to the people of Nebraska, and some food for their cattle. Nebraska, the country that Willa Cather was later to make famous in her novels, had been the hardest hit of all by the droughts.

An Indiana editor named P.H. Fitzgerald, who had been a drummer boy in the Union Army, began after the war to write in his newspaper, the *American Tribune,* that it might be a good idea to start a colony in a warmer climate where crops would grow better. He wanted a place where the climate was good, the weather was free of blizzards and bleakness, and the people were friendly. He wrote to Georgia's Governor W. J. Northen, who liked the idea and said he would do all he could to help.

The governor went with Fitzgerald and others who came with him to look over prospective sites. They decided to buy land between the Ocmulgee and the Altamaha rivers. Fitzgerald organized "The Soldiers Colony" and sold shares for ten dollars each. No veteran could buy more than ten shares. Veterans from all over the North bought shares. In 1895, the colony bought 34,000 acres in south Georgia, and more later. Some Georgians were reluctant to sell land to their former enemies. But the governor assured them that the newcomers would make good Georgians.

The town of Fitzgerald was incorporated in 1896. The new settlers came by train, boat, buggy, covered wagon, horseback, fringed surrey, and foot. One family floated on a raft down the Mississippi River and then came overland. It took them three months!

The little settlement, which at first was called "Swan," mushroomed almost overnight. At first there was not enough shelter, but soon they built homes and laid out streets. The streets that ran north and south were named for Union and Confederate generals. Those running east and west were named for trees and rivers. Three streets, Merrimac, Monitor, and Roanoke, were named for ships. They first named the hotel the Grant-Lee, but decided it would be more tactful to call it the Lee-Grant, since it was in the South. The park was named "The Blue and the Gray."

They encountered problems.Many of them had trouble learning to like southern food such as cornbread, sweet potatoes, turnip greens, and buttermilk. Before they could get crops grown and harvested, their food became scarce, but the neighbors were good to them.

Fevers and other illnesses plagued them, as they had the Puritans at Midway in the 1750's. There was illness and death. Mosquitoes and sandflies pestered them. But by year's end, nearly three thousand people had come. Gradually, they put their roots down. Young people married native Georgians. Southerners moved in among the newcomers. Fitzgerald became an asset to Georgia. In modern days, their story has been retold in an annual pageant titled "Our Friends, the Enemy."

Tom Watson And The Populist Party in Georgia

The legislature elected by the Farmers' Alliance men had not been able to effect all the reforms they had planned. It had criticized the Democratic party, but its own state appropriation had been bigger, and its leaders had found that actual problems of government were more difficult than they had imagined them to be.

They did, however, achieve much: better education, pensions for Confederate widows, and improvements that aided agriculture. The greatest achievement was their forcing the old Democratic party to adopt many of their proposals and put them into the regular party platform.

Many of the farmers joined a new national party that was arising as they realized that some of their state problems were also national problems. Things like railroad monopolies were plaguing the entire nation, and one state could not cure the evils by itself. This was the era of great fortunes, of ruthless power by men who sought wealth and position. A new movement called the Populist party, or the People's party, was coming to the front just now. It was organized in 1892; by 1896 it controlled a million votes. Many Democrats and Independents and

Alliance men joined the new party, and the old solid ranks of the Democratic party were splitting for the first time since the Civil War. The Populists advocated free coinage of silver, a postage savings bank, a graduated income tax, and government ownership of railroads, telegraph and telephone lines.

In Georgia this party wanted to nominate Thomas E. Watson for governor, but he wanted to run for re-election to Congress, and declined their offer. For president, they nominated James Weaver. He came to speak in Georgia, but hoodlums threw rotten eggs and old cabbages at him, and he cut short his campaigning here. Grover Cleveland, the Democratic party nominee, was elected President. Georgia voted for him. A Democrat was in the White House for the first time since the Civil War. But the Populist people were not happy with the Democratic program. Watson had been elected to Congress in 1890, with Populist backing. They put him on the national ticket for vice-president, and later for president. He lost, but he remained a power in state politics in Georgia for many years, and was a potent force in Congress.

He did not like the idea of Georgia's powerful Democratic leaders, headed by the Bourbon Triumvirate, collaborating with the monied industrialists of the North. He believed that these men from the North would exploit Georgians and Georgia resources for their own profit. He believed that the natural alliance of Southern farmers was with the farming West and not with the manufacturing East. He also had something of a personal grudge against the aristocrats. When poverty haunted his family after the war, they had a hard time making a living. His brother worked as a sharecropper on a farm. He was whipped by the wealthy planter on whose land he farmed. Tom Watson, in turn, waited one Sunday morning until this planter rode into town on his horse, then took the man's own whip and horsewhipped him in punishment for his brother's humiliation.

The statue of Tom Watson which stands on Capitol Square in Atlanta shows him making one of his fiery speeches, but it records on the base that he is "the father of the R.F.D." Though his thousands of followers were pas-

624

sionately devoted to him and he wielded as much power as any politician who ever lived in Georgia, it is likely that he will be longest remembered for launching the Rural Free Delivery of mail. The original R.F.D. is marked in Georgia. It was in Warren County near Norwood, on Georgia road 12, U.S. Highway 278.

Hoke Smith Was In President Cleveland's Cabinet

A rising political personality before the century's end was Hoke Smith, who became Secretary of the Interior in the Cleveland Cabinet and was powerful in Georgia politics from 1890 to 1920.

Smith, born September 2, 1855 in the family of a North Carolina college professor, was a lawyer at seventeen. He studied law in Atlanta where his family had moved, and opened an office in the same building with Woodrow Wilson. When he was only twenty, he held his first political office, chairman of the Fulton County Democratic Executive Committee. He was once president of the Atlanta Board of Education. He bought the *Atlanta Journal* in 1887, and supported Cleveland for president. Smith was for tariff reform and was bitterly against the vicious state system of leasing convicts to private employers. During Cleveland's second term as president, Smith became Secretary of the Interior. He opposed the Democratic nominee William Jennings Bryan in 1896, and resigned from the Cabinet.

In the next century, he was to be governor of Georgia twice.

CHAPTER 48

WHAT WAS

HAPPENING

IN EDUCATION

Nothing in the postwar story is more thrilling than what was happening in education after the Civil War. Most schools and colleges had closed. Teachers and the older students had gone to war. In the last days of the Confederacy, sixteen-year-old boys were fighting.

These "missed years" of education became one of the real tragedies of the war and the years thereafter. Young men who came back from the war, if they were not sick or wounded, had to make a living, and had little time to make up the schooling they had missed. Georgia did provide scholarships, however, for returned soldiers who wanted to or could go back to school. Little children had been growing up with no schools to go to.

Education was a real problem of the postwar years. Wealthy plantation owners who had once sent their sons to big colleges up North and brought in tutors for their smaller children could no longer afford this. Parents who had sent their children to private academies in Georgia now rarely had the money for their tuition and board. Confederate money was worthless and there was little credit.

Orr Became "The Father Of The Public Schools"

The Federals had named J. R. Lewis, a one-armed Tennessee dentist, the first state school commissioner. He had done his best, but he was not a teacher and knew little about school affairs. A system of public school education was designed in 1866, but it had not gone into effect after the state returned to military rule by order of Congress.

The 1870 legislature set up a system of free schools for the children of both races, but the Bullock regime had substituted worthless bonds for the school money and it could not be financed.

Finally, after Bullock left the state and Governor James M. Smith took office, he appointed in 1872 a new state school commissioner. This was Gustavus J. Orr, who had taught at Emory-at-Oxford. He was a graduate of the University of Georgia, where he had roomed with Benjamin Harvey Hill. They had tied for first honors there.

Orr put the public schools on a sound footing and became known as "the father of the public school system of Georgia."

In 1872, the state legislature voted that half of the Western and Atlantic Railroad rentals should go to finance the public schools, but the money was diverted to other purposes. The records in the State Department of Education show that although the public school system was actually set up in 1871, there were no schools and no state appropriation in 1872.

Finally, in 1873, the Georgia public school system was actually launched. The Constitution of 1877 provided for elementary schools, but not high schools. Since private academies often disbanded for lack of students whose parents could afford to send them, many local communities started their own high schools. Many had also become tired of waiting for the state to start elementary schools and had set up their own.

There was interest now in practical additions to the curriculum, and vocational education began to appear. Up to now, the curriculum had largely followed the pattern of the old Latin grammar schools. It was Benjamin Franklin in Philadelphia who had given a push to more practical education. In Georgia it was supported by many, including Henry Grady and Benjamin Hill. Some Georgians opposed the idea because they thought it had come from the North.

The Negro children benefited by the schools supported

by the Freedmen's Bureau. Private funds from northern sources were also given to some Negro schools. Often the Bureau provided the buildings, and churches and philanthropists sent the teachers.

About 30,000 Negro children went to these schools during the years of the Reconstruction. Georgia also began to provide schools for Negro children as well as white.

The Colleges Were Making Progress Too

The colleges also found it necessary to broaden their educational offering. In the beginning, colleges in this country were launched to educate ministers. But gradually they expanded to include other professions and then they opened to those who wanted to go into farming or trades.

Confederate veterans were helped to go back to college, and those who could leave their fields and workshops often did. Many who were crippled by the war went to the University. The state provided $300 a year for each veteran under thirty, but he had to promise to teach in Georgia a year for each $300 he received.

Colleges that had closed when professors and students went off to war opened again. Some new colleges were started.

What The Morrill Land-Grant Act Meant to Georgia

Georgia just barely did get in before the deadline on the act that Congress had passed to open college careers to those students interested in agricultural and mechanical pursuits.

This had been introduced into Congress on July 2, 1862 by Congressman Justin Morrill of Connecticut. It passed, and was signed into law by President Abraham Lincoln. But in that year Georgia and the other Confederate states were in a war. In 1866, the legislature appropriated $2,000 to put up a "mechanical and agricultural college" which could get funds under the federal law.

Morrill's idea was to set aside federally-owned lands to support "agricultural and mechanical" colleges. For each state there would be at least 30,000 acres of government-owned land for each congressional representative that

628

state had. This land was to be sold "to promote the liberal and practical education of the industrial classes in the several pursuits and professions of life." If there was not enough federally owned land within the boundary of a state itself, then some of the land in U.S. territories in the West would be sold for this purpose. The state was allowed to sell the land and use the interest on the money. All the states together would receive 11,383,082 acres of these free lands. This was sold for a total of $13,478,946.

Georgia was back in the Union before the deadline expired. The state applied for its share of this money and got 270,000 acres. It was sold to a westerner named Gleason F. Lewis for ninety cents an acre, or a total of $243,000, to be paid $50,000 down and the rest within eighteen months.

Many Georgia communities wanted the land-grant college to be located within their boundaries. It was finally set up in Athens, where the University of Georgia was already in operation. It was then known as "The Georgia State College of Agriculture and the Mechanical Arts." The Trustees also set up a branch of it at Dahlonega, where the old U.S. Mint building had been given the state for educational purposes by the federal government in 1871. This eventually became the North Georgia College. The main land-grant college at Athens was eventually absorbed into the University. Some of the Morrill money also went into an industrial college for Negroes located in Savannah.

There had long been an interest in the University's teaching courses in agriculture. Before the Civil War, William Terrell had given the University $20,000 to add these courses to the curriculum.

The colleges established throughout the nation under the Morrill Act were known as "land grant colleges." In 1962, when the hundredth anniversary of their establishment was observed, there were sixty-eight. They had become the largest single source of trained manpower in the nation.

Colleges Opened And Re-Opened in Georgia

The University at Athens, which had closed soon

after the war began, opened again in 1866 with seventy-eight students.

Mercer University, which had been started at Penfield in Green County, was moved to Macon in 1871. A law school was added in 1873. Emory-at-Oxford, also closed for the war, was reopened in 1867. Five hundred men pledged $20 a year to help the little college named for Bishop John Emory. In 1867, Atlanta University, planned especially for Negroes, opened with 62 men and 27 women students. It became the nucleus of the world's largest educational center for Negroes, aided by the Rockefellers and others.

The Georgia Institute of Technology was opened in Atlanta in 1885 as a branch of the University of Georgia. Later it became an independent university. One of its champions was Governor Nat Harris, who had introduced the bill for its beginning and served as chairman of its board of trustees for many years.

Oglethorpe College, which had been near Milledgeville, was moved to Atlanta, where it became Oglethorpe University. Shorter College in Rome (1873) and Brenau College at Gainesville (1878) were also opened in this era. Agnes Scott opened at Decatur in 1891. Fort Valley State College had five hundred students by 1899. Paine College in Augusta opened in 1884. The old state capitol building in Milledgeville became the center of a military and agricultural college. The old Governor's Mansion became part of a college for women.

In 1887, Richard B. Russell, Sr., who later became Chief Justice of the Supreme Court, introduced into the Georgia legislature a bill to establish a college for women as a branch of the University. Though the bill did not pass at that time, it was enacted when it was again introduced by W. Y. Atkinson. Mrs. Atkinson became ardently interested in the matter and helped her husband write many letters. A half century later, she came by plane from her home in Newnan to Milledgeville, where the college was located, and rode from the airport in a horse and carriage as part of the fiftieth anniversary celebration of the college. She said, "My husband and I were riding down a country road after the War Between the States and we saw girls who had been well-born but were poverty-stricken by the war, like so many Southerners, hoeing cotton. They pulled their hats down over their faces, ashamed of their menial labor. We knew that it was important to keep on pressing for a college that would educate the women of Georgia."

These friends of education, the Russells and the Atkinsons and others, persevered, and the college was soon established. It was first named the Georgia Normal and Industrial College, later the Georgia State College for Women, and now is the Woman's College of Georgia. It is located on one of the four big squares left in the original design of Milledgeville when the town was laid out for a capital in 1807. Its presidents lived in the old Governor's Mansion.

Other colleges and schools were getting a start. It was a long and painful struggle to find money and teachers. But Georgia was doing its best. By 1920, Georgia would have 8,447 schools, some good, many just fair, and some very poor. But education was becoming more and more important, as people saw that it enabled human beings to make the most of themselves and their resources and brought prosperity to the states and nations that gave it top priority.

A Georgia Woman Founded The PTA

Mrs. Alice McClellan Birney with the help of a rich patron, founded the PTA, which is officially known as the National Congress of Parents and Teachers.

Mrs. Birney was living in Washington, D.C. when her third child, a daughter, was born. She thought how little she really knew about children, and how urgently parents needed to know more, and to band together to help all children. "All children are our children" was later to become a PTA theme.

Mrs. Birney went on her vacation that year to Chautauqua, New York. Her husband had gone with his brothers on a hunting trip. At Chautauqua, some kindergarten teachers were having a meeting. They invited her to present to their audience an idea she had talked over with them. Later, she met Mrs. Phoebe Randolph Hearst, the very wealthy mother of newspaper tycoon William Randolph Hearst. Mrs. Hearst was interested in her ideas. Born on a Missouri farm December 3, 1842, Mrs. Hearst was the daughter of pioneers who had gone west from Virginia and the Carolinas, over the rugged mountains in covered wagons. She had gone to St. James College and graduated at seventeen. This school offered her a teaching job, young though she was, and she took it. She was always interested in children.

These two women launched what is now the National Congress of Parents and Teachers. It has millions of members. They joined together with mountain-moving power to help make the world a more comfortable and happy place in which children could grow up. They wanted better health conditions, better education, and a better chance for a happier childhood for all children.

This was an era of great fortunes, but it was also an era of child labor. This was the era when little children still worked ten and twelve hours in factories, and poverty and prison were the lot of many. Slums bred crime. Education was not available for all. Records show that a small girl named Helen worked twelve hours at night for three cents an hour! Sometimes the laboring children had to be kept awake by a special inspector who walked through the factory seeing that they did not drowse or slow down in their work!

In a school yard at Marietta, Alice Birney's home town, is the national shrine to her memory. At Oglethorpe University in Atlanta is Phoebe Hearst Hall. Mrs. Hearst's son, the late William Randolph Hearst, had one of his immense chain of newspapers in Atlanta. He gave money to the University, and the hall was named to honor his mother. Each year on February 17 these two women are honored by millions as the PTA celebrates Founders Day. The national headquarters of the PTA is in Chicago. Georgia's state PTA headquarters are in Atlanta.

CHAPTER 49

GEORGIA WRITERS AND

MUSICIANS BECAME FAMOUS

Almost the only Georgia writers who had become known beyond the bounds of the state in prewar days were Judge Augustus Baldwin Longstreet, who wrote *Georgia Scenes;* Dr. Francis Goulding, author of *Young Marooners;* and a physician, Dr. Thomas Holley Chivers who was one of Georgia's first poets.

After the Civil War years, Georgia writers achieved more fame. Sidney Lanier became a first-rate poet. Joel Chandler Harris, who created the character of "Uncle Remus" and retold ancient animal tales, brought Georgia new fame in letters. There were other writers, too.

A Negro musician, who could not read a note of music, became so famous that he played before royalty in Europe. He was slave-born Thomas Bethune.

SIDNEY LANIER WAS GEORGIA'S FIRST GREAT POET

Sidney Lanier was Georgia's first top-ranking poet, often spoken of as "the Poet of the South."

Lanier was born February 3, 1842, in a house that is still standing in Macon. Later, he clerked in the Lanier Hotel in Macon, which belonged to his family.

He was a student at Oglethorpe University near Milledgeville. Lanier often sat in the window there and played his flute. The college closed when students and professors went to war.

Lanier was taken prisoner when the ship *Lucy* was

633

running through the blockade to try to get medical supplies from Bermuda for sick southern soldiers. He was carried to the prison at Point Lookout, Maryland. He smuggled a $5 gold piece into the prison under his tongue. He also took his flute. Another poet, John Bannister Tabb, heard his music and sought him out. Released, he walked most of the way home. But he had contracted tuberculosis and had not many years to live.

He married Mary Day, a student at Wesleyan. They moved to Baltimore, where he taught literature at Johns Hopkins, played his flute with the symphony orchestra, and wrote poems.

He went to North Carolina when he became too ill to work. He had been there only a few weeks when he died, September 7, 1881, at thirty-nine. Somebody had just brought him a handful of morning glories, a flower that he loved.

His poems that Georgians know best are two about Georgia: "The Song of the Chattahoochee," and "The Marshes of Glynn."

A plaque on the farmhouse near Lynn, North Carolina, where he died, has these lines:

Night slipped to dawn, and pain merged into beauty,
Bright grew the road his weary feet had trod;
He gave his salutation to the morning,
And found himself before the face of God.

On his tomb in Baltimore, Maryland, is this line from his poem "Sunrise": "I am lit with the sun." Lanier County and Lake Sidney Lanier were named for him. The actor, Richard LeGallienne called Lanier "the greatest master of melody among American poets."

JOEL CHANDLER HARRIS AND HIS "UNCLE REMUS" TALES

A writer who became world-famous in this era was Joel Chandler Harris, who wrote the stories of the old Negro Uncle Remus and the little boy to whom he told the tales about the animals who could talk. These stories came out of the morning of the world and have appeared, in various versions, in the folklore of many people. But Harris, a shy genius who worked with Henry Grady on the

"Brer Rabbit And The Tar Baby"

Constitution, gave them his own special touch and made them unique.

Born in Eatonton December 9, 1848, he worked in the print shop of a planter named Joseph Addison Turner, who published a paper rather like Addison and Steele's *Spectator* papers in London. Turner's paper was called *The Countryman.* It was the only paper in Georgia published on a plantation, and may have been the only such paper in the nation.

Harris married a Canadian named Esther LaRose, and moved to Atlanta from Savannah, where he had been working as a reporter. Grady had read some of his writings and asked Harris to come by to see him the next time he was in Atlanta. Harris found Grady riding with his children on the merry-go-round at the Fair. They met and became fast friends.

While associated with the paper, Harris wrote, besides his regular articles, the whimsical stories of "Brer Rabbit" and "Brer Fox" and the other animals. His home in Atlanta, formerly Snap Bean Farm, is now known as The Wren's Nest. He once refused to let the postman put mail in the mail box because a wren was nesting there and he did not want her disturbed. Many famous people came to Snap Bean Farm to visit Harris. His daughter-in-law, Julia Collier Harris, a noted newspaper woman, wrote one of his biographies. A highway in Georgia named The Uncle Remus Highway commemorates the stories of Harris. Walt Disney filmed the Uncle Remus tales under the title "Song of the South."

GEORGIA HAD OTHER WRITERS AT WORK

In middle Georgia, Harry Stillwell Edwards, who was born in Appling County April 23, 1855, was writing about the New South. His father, a prosperous planter, had lost his money during the War. Edwards' godparents were President and Mrs. Jefferson Davis. The boy sold papers on the streets of Macon when he was ten to help support his family. He understood the South and its struggles, and would write about them with feeling.

His most famous short story, "Eneas Africanus," was reprinted in book form and had worldwide circulation. Among Edwards' writings was a tribute to his friend Sidney Lanier. He won a $10,000 first prize offered by a Chicago paper for a story titled "Fathers and Sons." He had promised the neighborhood children he would buy them all bicycles if he won, and he bought thirteen. For years he lived at Kingfisher Cabin on Holly Bluff and wrote a column for the *Macon Telegraph* titled "Coming Down My Creek."

Charles Colcoch Jones, Jr. wrote a two-volume history of Georgia during this era. Richard Malcolm Johnston, a schoolmaster and lawyer, was writing his famed *Dukes-Borough Tales.* Georgians were still reading the strange poetry of Thomas Holley Chivers. Richard Henry Wilde became most widely known for one beautiful poem among many, "My Life Is Like the Summer Rose." Henry Rootes Jackson of Augusta, American minister to Austria and Mexico, attained fame among Georgians for a poem titled "The Red Old Hills of Georgia." He was for twenty years president of the Georgia Historical Society. Dr. Francis R. Goulding, who invented a sewing machine, wrote an adventure story, *The Young Marooners,* that was as exciting as *Robinson Crusoe* or *Treasure Island.* Thomas

E. Watson, who became better known as a politician than as a writer, was writing a biography of Napoleon, a history of France, and a novel titled *Bethany*.

Frank L. Stanton, a *Constitution* writer in Atlanta, was writing such lyrical poetry that some of it was set to music. One was the song "Mighty Lak a Rose." Paul Hamilton Hayne published his *Legends And Lyrics* in 1872. James Ryder Randall became famous for his "Maryland, My Maryland" and a Catholic priest and Confederate poet wrote *The Conquered Banner* and *The Sword Of Lee*. He was Father Ryan.

BLIND TOM BETHUNE, A GEORGIA PIANIST, BECAME WORLD FAMOUS

Outside Columbus, on the Macon road, there is a grave with an astounding story behind it. It is the burial place of Thomas Greene Bethune, known also as Thomas Wiggins.

A blind Georgia Negro possessed a genius that no mortal has ever explained. When he was a baby, he and his family became the slaves of General James N. Bethune of Columbus. The child seemed almost imbecilic, but the Bethune girls noticed that sometimes when they were singing, the tiny boy would sing along with them in perfect harmony. Even when he was a toddler, his strange sense of sound made it possible for him to reproduce any sound he heard: a bird song, a politician's way of speaking, a dog's mournful hunting noises, animal cries from the woodland, and the mew of a cat.

The big surprise came when Tom was four. The Bethune sisters, who were musical, had been playing for guests. After the party was over, they heard melodies from the piano. The child, scarcely big enough to reach the keyboard, was playing like Mozart. The Bethunes took him to a music teacher in Columbus. It could have been the brother of Adelina Patti, the great singer, for he was then teaching there. Whoever the teacher was, he refused to take Tom as a pupil. "You cannot teach genius," he said. "This world has never seen anything like that blind Negro child."

Tom began giving concerts when he was eight. He also began composing music. Once, during a terrible storm, he ran to the window, exultant. After it was over, he began to play a composition of his own. He called it "The Rain Storm." For twenty years, he played to amazed and appreciative audiences throughout America, and in Europe. During the Civil War, he played for both sides. He could easily change hands, and play the left hand melody with his right hand, and vice-versa. Once, during a concert, he needed an extra note, and simply leaned over and struck it with his nose!

General Bethune's son John was named Tom's legal guardian. Later, a daughter-in-law of General Bethune brought suit for Tom's guardianship and, for the last fifteen years of his life, he lived in New York and was known as Thomas Wiggins. When he died in 1908, he was buried in Evergreen Cemetery at Brooklyn, New York. But Miss Fannie Bethune, the youngest of the Bethune daughters, got permission to have his body brought back and buried on the old plantation.

Willa Cather put him into her book *My Antonia,* in which he is called Blind d'Arnault.

CHAPTER 50

AS THE CENTURY

MOVED TOWARD ITS END

The century that had seen the Indians removed from Georgia and had brought the terrible Civil War moved toward its close. Queen Victoria was still on the throne of England. The Democrats had twice elected Grover Cleveland president and a Georgian had served in his Cabinet.

The last decade of the century was known in America as "the Gay Nineties." But there were many things that were far from gay, and the world would soon be moving into a century that would bring many new problems. Up from Mexico across the Rio Grande River was crawling a tiny insect called the boll weevil. And in Europe were gathering clouds for a war that would re-shape the world.

The "One-Eyed Plow Boy From Pigeon Roost" Became Governor

Allen D. Candler, born November 4, 1832 at Pigeon Roost in Lumpkin County, not far from Dahlonega, was governor as the century ended. He was born just after gold was discovered in the Cherokee country, and was one of the first white children born in the Indian territory. When he was four years old, the last of the Cherokees left on the Trail of Tears for their new home in the West. Thousands of gold seekers were swarming into the country where the Candlers lived on their farm. The boy who was later to be governor worked hard in the

639

fields. He called himself "the one-eyed plowboy of Pigeon Roost." He had lost an eye in a Civil War battle at Jonesboro.

He was graduated from Mercer in 1859, and taught school at Jonesboro. Then he fought for the Confederacy. Later he said, "When the war was over, I found myself with one dollar, one eye, one wife and one baby." After he moved to Gainesville he supervised the building of the Gainesville-Jefferson railroad. He was elected to Congress, and was once Georgia's secretary of state.

He won the governorship in 1898 as a Democratic candidate, defeating the Populist candidate J. R. Hogan by more than two to one. The Populists had tried again to get Tom Watson for their candidate, but he had refused.

Governor Candler served as governor from 1898 to 1902. Though his accomplishments were many, he is best remembered for his editing of Georgia's early records. In his message to the legislators, he reminded them that Georgia had been part of a great deal of remarkable history which should be preserved. Later the legislature asked him to go to London to see about getting the state's colonial records. He also preserved many records of the American Revolution and the Confederacy that might have been lost. There were so many that they filled 37 volumes! A historical marker commemorates his burial in the Alta Vista cemetery at Gainesville, Georgia.

Georgia In The Spanish-American War

The United States went to war with Spain, which had been guilty of incredible atrocities in Cuba. The lives and property of many Americans there were endangered. President McKinley had tried to keep America neutral in the conflict between Cubans and their Spanish rulers. But when the battleship *Maine* was blown up near Morro Castle in the harbor at Havana, on February 15, 1898, killing 260 of its crew, the United States, naturally indignant and further aroused by the Hearst press, went to war. The fighting, which began May 1, 1898, was over in less than three months. The mystery of the explosion has never been cleared up. Winston Churchill came over to report on this war.

Theodore Roosevelt, later to be president, led the

The Battleship Maine

"Rough Riders" in a charge up San Juan Hill. Georgia's General Joe Wheeler, of Civil War fame, also fought in the Spanish-American War. He had moved to Alabama after the war. His two sons and a daughter, Miss Annie Wheeler, who was a nurse, also went to this war.

The President had sent his war message to Congress April 11, 1898, and had called for 125,000 volunteers, Congress had officially declared war on April 25. The War Department added 182,000 men to the Regular Army, and one of the corps was at Chickamauga in north Georgia.

Georgia was asked for 3,000 volunteers, and quickly raised them. The Georgians complained because they saw too little action. The U.S. refunded the $30,000 it cost to furnish the state's quota.

Camp Chickamauga, on Georgia's old Civil War battle-field near Chattanooga, was used by the U.S. as a central place of mobilization and supplies. Camp Thomas there was named for General George H. Thomas, the Civil War general from Virginia. Georgia became a "mustering out center" for soldiers of this war.

When America defeated Spain, Georgia held a victory celebration, a "Jubilee" attended by President McKinley. A Georgian, Thomas Brumby, who had aided Admiral George Dewey in his famous victory at Manila Bay, was given a sword by Georgia, presented by Governor Allen D. Candler.

The country learned some valuable lessons from the Spanish-American War. One was how to handle its health

641

problems better. Yellow fever, sometimes called "yellow jack," had long plagued armies and civilian populations. Because of courageous experiments done by Dr. Walter Reed and others, this plague was eventually conquered. Because yellow fever and malaria were under better control. it was possible for the U.S. to build the Panama Canal.

Admiral Dewey, the hero of Manila, came to visit Georgia. Some of his chief aides in his brilliant achievements had been from Georgia.

Brass mortars, captured in the Spanish-American War at Santiago, Cuba, on July 17, 1898, are on Capitol Square in Atlanta now.

McKinley's Assassination Put Grandson Of Georgians In The White House

Early in the year 1895, powerful men in the Republican party had been planning to make Governor William McKinley of Ohio president of the United States.

Mark Hanna, a rich and influential man, rented a house in Thomasville, Georgia, where he planned much of the strategy that made McKinley president. The idea was for McKinley and his wife to come there to visit the Hannas, and while there to talk with prominent people in the South who could help in the presidential campaign if they were impressed with McKinley. He referred to his trip as "a little rest and outing" and did not admit that he was seeking the nomination. But much of the success of the coming campaign was later attributed to the plans that had been laid in Thomasville. Later, the McKinleys visited one of the millionaires who owned Jekyll Island, off the coast of Georgia.

McKinley was president during the war with Spain over Cuba, as the century drew to a close. Then, in September, 1901, he was assassinated by a guest at a public reception: a young man named Leon Czolgosz, who concealed a pistol in his bandaged hand. In his confession he said, "I killed President McKinley because I done my duty. I didn't believe one man should have so much and another man should have nothing."

The President said two things: "Be careful how you tell my wife," and of the assassin, "Go easy with

642

him, boys." The President seemed to know that he would die there. He said to the doctors, "It is useless, gentlemen; I think we ought to have prayer." A little later, he lapsed into a coma, softly sang, "Nearer, My God to Thee," and died.

Theodore Roosevelt, who had two ancestors in Georgia — Archibald Bulloch, first president of the Provincial Congress, and General Daniel Stewart, who went at thirteen to fight the British in the Revolution, became president.

Georgia In The Twentieth Century:
Wars, Woes, And Wonders

Nobody could foresee that this would be the bloodiest century the world had ever known. It would also be a century of marvels, with faster travel, life longer and more comfortable, and drudgery diminished.

Germany would be the explosion point for two terrible world wars and the United States, including Georgia, would be caught up in both of them. An old man with a withered arm and a terrible will to power would bid for world control. He was Kaiser Wilhelm, a grandson, like King George V of England, of Queen Victoria. An Austrian housepainter named Schickelgruber, known to history as Adolph Hitler, would engulf the earth in an even more destructive war.

State politics would be stormy. A murder trial would end one brilliant political career and start another. The death of a governor just elected to a fourth term would start a three-cornered battle for the office. The U.S. Supreme Court would hand down a decision that would end a whole way of life.

This was to be the century of technical miracles: the telephone, radio, television, airplanes, automobiles, and many other marvels. Men would soar into outer space, and the first dozen astronauts would include a boy from Cartersville, Georgia.

There would be a renaissance of writing and art in the state. Pulitzer Prizes would draw attention to the talent in Georgia, and one tiny Georgian would write a book that would sell millions and be translated into nearly all the languages of the earth.

Education would spread in this century, and millionaires such as Henry Ford and the Rockefellers would provide money for Georgia colleges to prosper.

Tourists, as well as native Georgians, would discover the beauties of the state and the uniqueness of its climate. A Supreme Court judge would come climb its mountains, loving them best of all the mountains in the world.

Industry and business, lured here by the remarkable resources of Georgia, would make Atlanta the gateway not only to the Southeast but to South America as well. Farming would undergo great changes. Already a tiny insect called the boll weevil was slowly crawling up from Mexico to topple powerful King Cotton from his throne. Georgia would change from a rural to an urban state in a half century.

The 1900 census showed that 2,216,331 people were then living in the state. Experts predicted that by 1965, this would increase to well over four million. More than a million and a half would be living in the Atlanta area alone.

When the century opened, Georgia was still a rural state, but this would change greatly.

It was to be a fascinating century.

BEFORE THE FIRST WORLD WAR

UNIT 9

CHAPTER 51

WHAT HAPPENED
BEFORE WORLD WAR I

The fourteen years before a shot crackled in Europe and plunged the world into war were part of the quiet time when soft winds blew across the world. Cataclysmic struggles were beginning, and deep stirrings were going on in labor, government, economics and other areas of life. But on the surface, things seemed relatively peaceful. Most Georgians were living on farms. Cotton was the main money crop, though headed for trouble. The dark days of Reconstruction were behind them. Industry was coming in, providing more prosperity for Georgia. Textiles, the oldest of the industries, was well established but was due for changes.

State politics were turbulent. Men struggled for the office of governor, and their followers waged colorful campaigns.

Education was making progress, and high schools were soon to be added to the state plan. Schools in the mountains were making a difference to children whose families had never had the advantages of education.

Roads were getting better and railroads were increasing their business. Favoritism in freight rates was beginning to cause trouble.

Georgia was discovering its natural resources and finding out what could be done with the riches that were here in the land. A Georgia-born chemist was working in his laboratory to find out what could be made out of pine trees, and a Negro genius was quietly laboring at

Tuskegee to help farmers in the South make more money with peanuts and sweet potatoes.

Governor Allen Candler, head of the state when the century began, was about to go to England to collect thirty-seven volumes of the state's earliest records.

What Was Happening In Government

Georgians were involved in these early years of the century in colorful happenings in government, both nationally and in the state. When the dynamic and controversial Teddy Roosevelt became president, he inaugurated a vigorous national pattern of politics.

In these days before radio and television, politics, as it reverberated through rousing political rallies and the newspapers, was one of the chief interests of Georgians, both in the cities and throughout the rural areas.

THEODORE ROOSEVELT, DESCENDANT OF GEORGIANS, BECAME PRESIDENT

Vigorous Teddy Roosevelt, who became president when an assassin's bullet killed President McKinley, had close ties with Georgia. Two of his great-grandfathers were Georgia heroes.

Theodore Roosevelt once came to Roswell, Georgia to visit the former home of his mother, Martha ("Mittie") Bulloch, who had there married Theodore Roosevelt, Sr., by candlelight on a chill December night in 1853. While visiting there, the President sent word by an aide that if an old friend of his mother wished to call upon him, he would be glad to see her. But this Georgia gentlewoman, reared in a tradition where ladies were the ones who received callers, retorted, "If Mittie Bulloch's son wishes to call on me, I will be at home to him."

Roosevelt, a devotee of the strenuous life, was a very active president. It was during his administration that the Panama Canal was built. His niece, Eleanor Roosevelt, married her cousin, Franklin Delano Roosevelt, another Georgia-connected president, some years later. President Theodore Roosevelt attended the wedding and gave the bride away. He attracted so much attention that the bride and groom were overshadowed at their own wedding.

648

From the time Thomas E. Watson was sent by his friends and neighbors in McDuffie County to the Georgia Legislature for the first time, to the time of his death in Washington, D.C., in 1922, this red-headed, fiery Georgian was a power to be respected in Georgia politics.

He changed his allegiances as it suited him, often for reasons clear to him, but not to others. He might support a man in one election, and be violently against him the next time. He at first championed the rights of Negroes, but later turned on them viciously. He was against foreigners, Jews, Catholics, Negroes and, late in his life, the American Legion. His bitterness, some people thought, kept him from greatness; but his power was not to be denied.

He set up newspapers and a magazine that influenced the thinking and voting of Georgia, especially in the rural areas, for decades.

Watson was the national candidate for president twice on the ticket of the Populist party. He had a hard core of about 25,000 followers in Georgia whom he could sway long after the Populists declined. Candidates for any office knew that Watson might hold the balance of power that could decide their political fates.

At times during his political years he withdrew from the arena of active politics and devoted himself to writing his biographies and histories, and practicing law. But always, behind the scenes, he was a skilled "kingmaker," and to his Monticello-like home, "Hickory Hill," in Thomson, politicians went constantly to seek his favor and win his support.

He believed that Woodrow Wilson was too conservative, and was not enough concerned with the interests of the common man. He opposed him, and led Georgia to vote for Oscar Underwood of Alabama in the Presidential primary of 1912. Watson was in the Georgia Legislature and in Congress, but he was never governor. In 1920, he was elected United States Senator by a state that, like many others, was indulging in a postwar reaction against Wilson and the League of Nations. But he lived only a little while after his election. In 1922, he died in Washington. Possessed of a bright mind and a great skill at swaying men, Watson ranks in history as one of the most puzzling figures of his time. He is remembered more for his launching of the Rural Free Delivery of mail than for his chameleon-like powerful political campaigns.

SENATOR WALTER GEORGE BEGAN HIS BRILLIANT CAREER

A Georgian who was to gain fame as a statesman was launching his congressional career in this early part of the century. Born in a pine house in the piney woods of Webster County near Preston, January 29, 1878, Walter Franklin George was the son of a farmer. His family, like other families in that section just after the War Between the States, knew poverty and hardship. George worked on the farm, and later went to Mercer University. The law school there now is named in his memory, the Walter F. George Law School.

He went to Vienna in Dooly County to practice law, and there married Lucy Heard. He was first solicitor, then judge, of the judicial circuit, and from 1917 to 1922 was a justice of the Georgia Supreme Court.

In 1922, when Tom Watson died, George was chosen to become United States Senator from Georgia. He rapidly rose to eminence in Congress, especially as chairman of the powerful Finance Committee and of the Foreign Relations Committee. Once when he opposed President Franklin Roosevelt in some of the New Deal measures such as packing the Supreme Court, President Roosevelt tried to "purge" him as too conservative. The President came to Georgia and spoke at Barnesville, urging voters to elect George's opponent, the late Lawrence Camp. Senator George was seated on the platform, and at the end of his speech, the President said, "God bless you, Walter." The courtly George replied, "I accept your challenge in this campaign." The people of Georgia refused to let anybody, even a President, tell them how to vote. They sent George back to the Senate. He retired in April, 1956. His health was failing, and he was threatened in the upcoming election by the increasing stature of young Herman Talmadge, who had made Georgia an excellent governor, and was then eyeing the Senate.

President Dwight Eisenhower, a Republican, named Democrat Walter George his personal representative to the

650

North Atlantic Treaty Organization. George was known and respected by men in many parts of the world. He had transcended party and loaned his wisdom and maturity to the counsel of nations. "America should be big enough to talk to anyone in the interest of world peace," he said. He had not been enthusiastic about the League of Nations, but after his son was killed in World War I, his heart reached out to understand a bigger world. He made moving and eloquent speeches in support of the United Nations. Before his death, August 4, 1957, he said to his Georgia neighbors, "You are today a part of the world. You cannot separate yourself from the rest of Georgia, the rest of the nation, from the rest of the world."

SMITH-BROWN CAMPAIGNS FOR GOVERNOR

The Hoke Smith–Joe Brown campaigns for governor divided Georgia into two excited factions for a decade. The governorship passed back and forth from one to the other more than once.

Hoke Smith, owner of the *Atlanta Journal,* had been Secretary of the Interior in President Grover Cleveland's Cabinet. Born in North Carolina, he had moved to Georgia with his family when he was sixteen. He was a young lawyer in Atlanta about the same time that Woodrow Wilson hung out his shingle as a beginning lawyer there.

Brown, known as "Little Joe" Brown, was the son of Joseph Emerson Brown, who had been elected four times governor of Georgia during the crucial years of the War Between the States. Brown, who had been born at Canton where his father owned a farm, lived during the war years in the Governor's Mansion at Milledgeville. He was a brilliant student, graduating with first honors from Oglethorpe. Because of poor eyesight he gave up his law studies and took a $40 a month job on the railroad his father owned. In 1904 Governor Terrell appointed him railroad commissioner. Governor Hoke Smith fired him from that job, and Brown then defeated Smith for governor. A depression was haunting the state and nation, and Brown's slogan was "Hoke and Hunger—or Brown and Bread." He won the election by 12,000 votes. He had the support of Tom Watson, who had supported Smith in 1906 and opposed him in 1908.

Smith and Brown opposed each other again in 1910 for the governorship; Smith won. When former Governor Joseph Terrell, who had become a United States Senator, died in Washington, Smith was named to take his place.

John M. Slaton, president of the Georgia Senate, who was to be elected governor later, held the governor's office temporarily, but in 1912, "Little Joe" Brown was re-elected governor of Georgia.

Not since the old days of Governor George Troup and Governor John Clark nearly a hundred years before, had there been such fierce political battles for the office as those of Hoke Smith and Joe Brown.

VINSON STARTED RECORD-BREAKING CAREER IN CONGRESS

In 1914, as a world war was threatening, a judge in Milledgeville was starting on a congressional career which was to be the longest in U.S. history.

Carl Vinson of Milledgeville defeated Tom Watson in 1914, and was destined to serve until he retired at eighty, in 1965.

Looking back across the busy years, he said, "When I first came to Congress, the chief question was the tariff; when I left, it was the problem of survival. I have watched man progress from the horse and buggy days to orbiting the earth at more than 17,000 miles an hour." Vinson had served as chairman of the powerful Armed Services Committee, and had been a strategic figure in keeping America prepared for survival in perilous times. He was to become known as "the father of the modern navy." Looking ahead, he said that world disarmament was no idle dream. He thought that it might be possible some time in the future, when people became more educated, and communication and travel facilities brought mankind closer. But the danger of Communist China, which he deemed more threatening than that of the Soviet Union, made it important to keep America prepared.

As Carl Vinson left Georgia to begin his congressional career in 1914, he little dreamed that he would set a record by being re-elected twenty-five times and serving more than a half century in Congress.

Carl Vinson

The People And Their Daily Lives And Work

Georgia was still a rural state early in this century. Most people lived and worked on the farms. The modern cities had not yet grown up. It would be mid-century before the state would change from a rural to an urban economy, and balance its agriculture with industry.

Many things affected the lives and health and jobs of the people. They had struggled past the postwar poverty, and had a better life than those Georgians who endured the hardships just after the South had lost the Civil War.

GEORGIA ENACTED HEALTH LAWS

Certain diseases had plagued Georgia from the beginning. Oglethorpe's colonists had malaria and, later, smallpox. Yellow fever was a plague along the coast.

When poverty beset the sharecroppers and their diet was meal, meat, and molasses, another disease weakened Georgians: pellagra. Hookworm was also a plague to the South.

By 1903, Georgia was aware of the need for a state board of health and local boards. In 1914, the laws were made stronger. The legislature, which had been urged by

653

Governor Allen Candler in 1900 to set up such measures, actually did. The State Board of Health had twelve members, one from each congressional district, usually a doctor. Local boards of health were set up.

Regulations pertaining to health became more stringent: water was analyzed, slaughter houses inspected, drugs restricted to prescriptions, nurses registered, mosquito-breeding lands drained, contagious illnesses quarantined, and strict sanitary rules about the removal of dead animals enforced.

THE CONVICT LEASE SYSTEM WAS ABOLISHED IN 1908

The convict leasing system was one of the evils that the Populists had been protesting. Many other people had been dissatisfied with it, too.

In 1819, Georgia had built a penitentiary at Milledgeville, which was then the capital. After the War Between the States when the freed slaves were uncertain and unsettled and Georgia contained also some lawless whites, the prison at Milledgeville could not hold all the prisoners. The state then started the convict leasing system. It leased convicts to certain companies; they were hired out to work in fields, mines, and forests, and in building railroads. By 1877, there were over a thousand convicts working for these companies. The state required that the convicts get medical attention. The state could not prevent all cruelty, and sometimes the convicts were very inhumanely treated by those who were sent to boss them in their work. They could be lashed.

More and more people in the state grew concerned and even angry about the situation. In 1880, the legislature appointed a committee to investigate the convict camps. They found that nothing was being done to reform or rehabilitate the prisoners, and that many became even worse criminals because of their association with other criminals. In some camps men, women, and boys were chained together.

Governor John B. Gordon fined two of the companies in 1887 because of cruelty to convicts. He did not condone it. Governor W.Y. Atkinson also fined a coal mining company for the same thing.

The chairman of the committee to investigate the

654

prisons, Robert Alston, a legislator from DeKalb, was shot and killed in the state capitol by Edward Cox, who managed the plantations of John B. Gordon, where convicts worked. He was given a life sentence, and later pardoned.

In 1897, the laws had been made a little better. A prison commission was set up and directed to build a prison farm where the very old, the very young and the sick could be kept. Of the other prisoners, those who were in for five years were distributed to the counties to build roads. The others were hired out first for $100 each, and later to the highest bidder. The state got about a quarter of a million dollars a year under this system. But the old evils were still there, and people renewed their clamor against it.

In 1908, the state passed a law that forbade any private hiring of the state's convicts. Those who were not sent to the prison farm near Milledgeville were sent to the counties to do road work. But the chain gangs that grew up, even under this system, became in many instances very bad. Later in the century, more improvement would be made in Georgia's prisons, and plans for the rehabilitation of prisoners would make things better.

In 1893 a law that put a stop to public hangings was passed.

GEORGIA WAS DEVELOPING ITS NATURAL RESOURCES

By 1900, Georgia had only begun to develop its mineral resources. From about twenty-five different minerals, about one hundred million dollars would flow into the state.

More than seventeen million dollars worth of gold was mined in Georgia after gold was discovered near Duke's Creek about 1829. By the time the U.S. established the branch mint at Dahlonega, the section was recognized as having one of the richest gold deposits then known. It was a belt about fifteen to twenty miles wide. The gold out of which the shining coins were minted came largely from placer deposits, with some vein mining. The mining and treatment of refractory ores, however, was done largely when gold mining was resumed, as the mint had been closed in 1861 because of the Civil War. It was resumed to a still greater extent about 1891, when some $80,000 worth of gold was mined. By 1927, though, very little gold was being found.

During the 1930's there was renewed interest in the mines. Companies were organized to work them, but little results came. Graham Dugas, who had his car plated with gold from the mines, leased the John C. Calhoun mines and made a strike. He later abandoned them to the ghosts of Calhoun and the slaves.

The chief interest now is for tourists and Georgians who like to pan for gold in the picturesque setting.

Some other minerals which had assumed a greater importance were marble, coal, flagstone, manganese, copper, chromite, bauxite, granite, and limestone. Georgia's clays had been exported since early days.

Georgia marble early attracted the attention of artists and builders. It had been known to the Indians. The great marble quarry around Tate in Pickens County is quite famous.

After 1900, manufacturing as well as natural resource development grew. Considerable money began to come to Georgia as a result of manufacturing progress.

One product developed in Georgia exceeded all expectations in popularity and worldwide sales volume. This was Coca-Cola.

HIGH FREIGHT RATES HANDICAPPED GEORGIA

Freight rates in the South were so high in the first half of the century that they put a burden on those who had to ship their products, and it kept some manufacturers from locating their industrial plants in Georgia. In Hoke Smith's time, the legislature had set up the Railroad Commission to tighten control over railroads, but it was the railroads outside of Georgia, over which it had no control, that caused the most trouble. The railroads had what they called a "density formula" that claimed it cost more to handle the freight in the South than in the North and East.

The Bullwinkle Bill that passed Congress in 1948 allowed railroads to get together and plan their rate schedules, even though the anti-trust legislation had been passed earlier that barred great corporations from too-close cooperation.

Governor Arnall entered suit in 1944 against twenty-one railroads asking fifty-six million dollars in damages to Georgia because of the high freight rates. But it was 1951 before the state got relief. In that year, the Interstate Commerce Commission ordered equalization of freight rates on all railroads east of the Rocky Mountains.

THE BOLL WEEVIL TOPPLED KING COTTON OFF HIS THRONE

Georgia sea island cotton had been sent here by a Tory exile, who had fled to the Bahamas, to a friend in Georgia, with the suggestion that it was a better and cleaner crop than the nasty purple indigo, which was dying out anyhow. This kind of cotton could be grown only along the coast. But when Whitney invented the cotton gin, even the short staple upland variety that could be grown anywhere had become profitable. They could not grow enough. Long before this, in Philadelphia, Ben Franklin had advertised for the return of his wife's "valuable cotton dress which has been stolen." Cotton pushed the Creek Indians out of Georgia and Alabama, as gold was later to push the Cherokees. Men needed the fertile lands to grow cotton. Cotton mills came South after the Civil War in greater numbers.

A tiny insect began crawling up over the Mexican border into Texas and across the states at the end of the nineteenth century. This tiny creature multiplied by the millions and left misery and poverty in its path, but it taught farmers what the agricultural colleges had been proclaiming: dependence on just one crop is unsound.

The South was shipping millions of bales of cotton to Europe, and selling cotton to the North and West. The crop was valuable. However the picture would soon change. The three million bales produced in 1916 would shrink to less than a half million in 1921.

Then came the Mexican boll weevil. By 1897, some wandering minstrel had written a ballad:

"The farmer say to the weevil,
What you doin' on the square,
The weevil say to the farmer,
'Got a nice big family there.
Gotta have a home, gotta have a home."

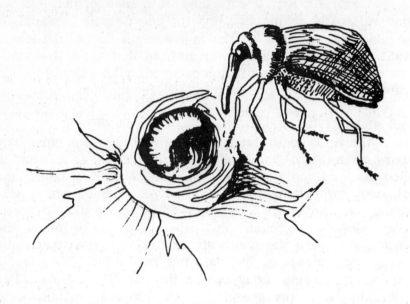

Carl Sandburg, in "The American Songbag," explained that
two boll weevils could arrive in a cotton field in spring
and have twelve million descendants by the end of summer,
to carry on the family traditions of tragedy.

The boll weevil changed farming. Farmers learned
to grow more of other crops: corn, peanuts, soybeans,
truck crops for the vegetable markets, tobacco and others.

Cotton had long been king in the South, since Eli
Whitney invented the cotton gin in Georgia in 1793. The
South had built a whole culture on it, and slaves had
been bought and brought to work in the cotton fields.

Cotton is still important. In 1963, Georgia was producing 605,000 bales. You can reach out your hand wherever
you are and touch cotton. More cotton can now be grown
with more mechanized and less human labor. By the century's end, there will be no cotton surpluses, say the experts.
The value of the by-products of cotton, such as cottonseed
oil, will increase. Good cotton land will find a quick market.

The tragedy of the boll weevil had a brighter ending
than the farmers could have imagined early in this century.

In Enterprise, Alabama, which had been in the cotton
belt and suffered the damage from the boll weevil, the people
erected on December 11, 1919, a monument to the boll

weevil, "In profound appreciation of the Boll Weevil and what it has done as the herald of prosperity."

PEANUTS PAID OFF IN GEORGIA

The boll weevil taught Georgia farmers not to depend on a one-crop economy; peanuts became a paying crop. Southwest Georgia became a major peanut-producing area. At Tuskegee Institute in Alabama, Dr. George Washington Carver, the Negro scientist who was born a slave, had already found over 300 uses for the peanut, as well as 118 for the sweet potato. Another scientist, at the Birmingham Research Institute of the South, found a way to keep the oil from collecting on the top of a jar of peanut butter, thus making this a more marketable product. Peanuts covered many fields, and brought more money into Georgia farm budgets. Factories were set up to roast and toast them; assembly lines turned out jars of peanut butter to be marketed over the nation and throughout the world. Soon the peanut industry became a multi-million dollar business.

Half of all the peanuts grown in the United States were, by 1963, being made into peanut butter. Americans were eating 16,400,000 peanut butter sandwiches every day!

HERTY AND THE PINE TREE

Charles Herty was born in Milledgeville in 1867 and attended Georgia Military College. He received degrees from two universities, and studied in Europe as well. In 1902, Dr. Herty gave up teaching at the University of Georgia for laboratory research. He experimented with Georgia pine trees and developed the Herty Turpentine Cup. Herty attracted nationwide attention and eventually became president of the American Chemical Society. President Wilson sent him to Paris in 1919 to confer with other chemists about postwar scientific matters.

Dr. Herty's chief contributions concern the paper industry. For some time he had been searching to find a method to make paper out of pine tree pulp. Up to that time, most paper made of pine pulp was too sticky to print newspapers. Dr. Herty's experiments were successful and soon worn-out Georgia cotton lands were being planted with pine seedlings.

Charles Herty was honored with degrees from universities. Medals, postage stamps, and banquets were a few signs of the appreciation he received. His real reward was seeing wasted Georgia acres productive again, and Georgia farmers with money in their pockets. Dr. Herty died in 1938 and was buried at Milledgeville. The pine tree and pulp business in Georgia is a multi-million-dollar industry now. Georgians owe Dr. Herty and the tree growers a great debt.

The Herty Medal presented each year at the Woman's College in Milledgeville honors him. The site of his birthplace is marked on college square with three pine trees. He is buried in the cemetery at Milledgeville. A likeness of him in the State Capitol in Atlanta has an inscription testifying to his genius:

"The spark of his genius and energy
touched Georgia's pines, and forests
of smokestacks began growing in the South."

660

By mid-century, the South's income from forestry products would be in the billions. Georgia would rank second only to California in lumber products. Paper companies would be moving into the state buying pulpwood and shipping products to the world. In pulpwood, Georgia was leading the nation.

Pine was not the only important tree. Gum, oak and pine were the principal woods for furniture. Naval stores were providing the raw materials for over three hundred products, including paint, varnishes, synthetic rubber, adhesives, soaps and disinfectants, inks, dyes, plastics, paper, and many others.

What Was Happening In Education

There were still many Georgians who were not getting a chance to go to school. But more and more schools were being started in Georgia. Among them were schools for children in the mountains.

THE SUNDAY LADY OF POSSUM TROT STARTED BERRY SCHOOLS

Miss Martha Berry, whose family had wealth and culture, started in 1902 the remarkable Berry schools near Rome. She became interested in the mountain children when a few of them happened to come by her little log cabin, built for a play house, where she was reading the Bible. Miss Berry began to read Bible stories to them, and they came back again and again, bringing other children from around Lavender Mountain, Trap Hollow, and Possum Trot. She began to visit their families, and set up a Sunday School for the children, gathering up many in her pony cart. Soon she came to be known as "The Sunday Lady of Possum Trot."

Miss Berry decided to use her own money to start a school for the mountain children. Then she began to go out from Rome, her home town, to talk with wealthy and influential people in other parts of the world, about her school. She talked with Mr. and Mrs. Henry Ford, who began to visit the school and eventually gave much money for buildings and equipment. Mr. Ford, who developed the Ford automobile, liked old-fashioned dances, and he taught the Berry students these dances. When he and Mrs. Ford came to visit, students lined up on both sides of "The Gates of Opportunity" at the entrance of their school, holding lighted candles to welcome them.

Once Miss Berry invited the governor to speak at commencement. "How many are graduating?" he asked. "Only one," she said, "but he's such a fine boy!" Later thousands were to graduate from the Berry School, and the Berry College that was established later.

Miss Berry required the boys and girls to work for their education. To show her feeling that work is a part of worship, she had steeples put on the chicken houses!

The Berry schools became famous all over the world. Miss Berry was known to millions, and books have been written about her. She is buried on the campus of the school to which she devoted her life.

OTHER MOUNTAIN SCHOOLS WERE STARTED

Two other excellent schools that began to educate mountain children and later drew students from all over the state are Tallulah Falls, in Habersham County, sponsored by the General Federation of Women's Clubs, and Rabun Gap-Nacoochee in Rabun County, a unique institution where the whole family can go to school. Pupils learn not only about America's history and the beauty of poetry, but the value of work. A limited number of families can carry on home and farm programs there. Both of these schools are located in the beautiful north Georgia mountain country. Tallulah Falls School is not far from the stupendous Tallulah Gorge. On the campus of the college is the old Council Chair in which the Indian chief Gray Eagle sat to preside over his councils. Nearby is a mountain peak from which one can see three states. A library building erected in recent years has an architectural pattern so unusual that it won a national award.

Toccoa Falls Bible Institute, in this section of the state, has been befriended by the industrialist R. G. Le-Tourneau, who makes earth-moving machinery, and who established a branch of his business in nearby Toccoa.

SCHOOLS IN SOUTH GEORGIA

Norman Park Institute, founded in 1901 "in the piney woods of south Georgia" came to be regarded somewhat as "the Berry school of south Georgia." Often the farmers swapped chickens and vegetables and kindling wood for learning for their children. They came in wagons drawn by mules. The sons and daughters they brought sometimes lived with families in the area until dormitories were built. The students often worked their way. They had a campus garden that the president helped them tend.

The college had been planned in 1897 by the Baptists, but did not get started until the century had begun. In 1927, it was the first junior college in the nation to receive a Freedom Foundation Award for its excellent program to help American students understand democracy. It became a junior college in 1928 and Norman College in 1951.

HIGH SCHOOLS WERE ADDED TO STATE PLAN

In 1912, the high schools were added to the state's educational program. Some children had attended private academies. Even as late as 1905, Georgia had only seven four-year public high schools, from which about a hundred pupils were graduating. The 1877 Constitution had authorized elementary schools and colleges, but not high schools. As an encouragement for the expansion of schools, the legislature passed the Barrett-Rogers Act, authorizing the payment of $1,000 to each school system that set up a four-year accredited high school. In 1900, Georgia was investing only $1.5 million of state money in education.

In 1916 Georgia passed its first compulsory attendance law requiring children between eight and fourteen to attend school. The spread of education was slow, but it was evident. In the first year after free schools were set up, following the War Between the States, only fifty thousand children attended. In Georgia in 1870, nine out of every ten Negroes were unable to read or write, and one out of every four white Georgians was illiterate. By 1930, only one out of five Negroes was still without basic education, and only one out of every thirty-five whites. By 1966, one million of more than four million Georgians would be in school.

"A & M" SCHOOLS WERE PROMOTED BY GOVERNOR TERRELL

The new agricultural and mechanical schools were a strong interest of Governor Joseph Meriwether Terrell, son of a doctor from Meriwether County, who was elected governor in 1902 to succeed Candler. He had been Attorney General from 1892 to 1902. He defeated the Populist party candidate for governor, who got only 5,000 votes. This showed that the strength of the Populist party in Georgia was nearing its end; once it had numbered 100,000 voters. It still had strength in the nation, however. In 1904, Tom Watson of Georgia was its presidential candidate. But that year, the Populists in Georgia did not run a candidate against Terrell, who was re-elected.

Governor Terrell is remembered especially for his crusade to get district agricultural and mechanical schools established. Georgia had only sixty-four accredited high schools in 1906, and only twelve of these had four years of education to offer. The academies were disappearing. There was need for schools to bridge the gap between the elementary schools and the colleges. The ten A & M schools set up at first got an appropriation of $100,000. Eventually, there were twelve, with $10,000 each set up in the budget for them. These were considered a part of the College of Agriculture which was established in Athens. As agricultural education in the college grew stronger, eventually becoming a part of the university itself, and as vocational agriculture courses were set up in the high schools, the A & M schools began to disappear from the scene.

The Georgia Court of Appeals was set up during the Terrell administration. Just before he left office, he presided at the dedication of the equestrian statue of General John B. Gordon on the grounds of the capitol.

Terrell, appointed United States Senator by Governor Joseph M. Brown, died in Washington in 1912. His scrapbooks and the silver service given him by the legislature are in the old Terrell home in Greenville.

NEGROES WERE GETTING BETTER OPPORTUNITIES FOR EDUCATION

Just after the War Between the States, many northern people and organizations took a special interest in educating the Negro children and young people of the South, and gave considerable money for this purpose. The Farmers' Alliance had set up a Negro college in Savannah. As the new century got underway, Atlanta was beginning to be recognized as a center of higher education for Negroes. Atlanta University (1867), Morehouse College (1867), Clark University

(1869), Morris Brown College (1881), and Gammon Theological Seminary (1883) became units in this great educational center. Spelman College (1888) was the special interest of the Rockefeller family, who gave money in memory of their mother Laura Spelman Rockefeller. A School of Social Work would later develop. Music and drama would become the special phases of education here that attracted national attention. Negro leaders educated here, and at Tuskegee and other Negro colleges in the Southeast, would some decades later take an active part in the drive for recognition and rights for their race.

Many Georgia Negroes went to Tuskegee Institute in Alabama, where Booker T. Washington was president. Harvard conferred a degree on him in 1896. He was later succeeded by Dr. Robert Russa Moton, a Georgia-born Negro educator.

Paine College in Augusta, and state colleges for Negroes in Savannah, Albany and Fort Valley were to be of increasing importance in Georgia as the century went on. Paine was founded in 1883, and named for Moses Paine of Iowa, who gave the first $25,000.

The Julius Rosenwald Fund, set up with Sears-Roebuck funds in 1932, had spent $22,000,000 on Negro education in the South before it was closed out in 1948. The will of Rosenwald specified that it should be spent within 25 years of his death, and "solely for the welfare of mankind." The fund built some 6,000 schools for Negroes in the South; 300 of these in Georgia. It also improved the education of teachers, library programs, and health services and did much to reduce illiteracy.

The Southern Education Foundation merged several agencies and funds and continued to improve education for Negroes, especially in rural sections.

The state set up means by which Negroes could get state funds to go to colleges outside of Georgia if there were none within the state offering the special education that they wished.

CHAPTER 52
GEORGIA AND GEORGIANS
IN THE HEADLINES

Many other things were making news in and about Georgia during these early years of the century. The interests of the state and its citizens ranged far and wide.

A Georgia Woman Founded The Girl Scouts

Juliette Gordon Low, whose nickname was "Daisy," founded the Girl Scouts of America. She was four years old when Sherman gave Savannah, her home town, to Lincoln for a Christmas present. She was born October 31, 1860. Her father was a Confederate officer, and her mother was from Chicago. Sherman brought her messages from her kinfolks there. Daisy sat in his lap and told him how her papa was off shooting Yankees.

Juliette Low had been presented at the Court of St. James in London, wearing the traditional three ostrich plumes in her hair, diamonds, and a beautiful dress. She went fishing at midnight once with Rudyard Kipling, wearing a Paris dress worth $1,500. When she died in Savannah, she was buried in a Girl Scout uniform. One of her cherished possessions was a telegram that said: "You are not only the first Girl Scout, but the best."

She had married an Englishman, Willy Low, a friend of the Prince of Wales who became King Edward VII. After his death, she became interested in founding the Girl Scouts when she met Sir Robert Baden-Powell who had founded the Boy Scouts. His sister had founded the Girl Guides. When Mrs. Low returned from England to Savannah, she started the Girl Scouts. There she organized a troop on March 12, 1912.

She devoted her life to this organization which became world wide and brought her international fame.

Juliette Gordon Lowe

Writers And Artists Were Making Georgia Famous

Joel Chandler Harris, who worked on the *Atlanta Constitution* from the days of Henry Grady through the first decades of this century, was bringing world wide fame to Georgia with his Uncle Remus tales.

Don Marquis, a reporter and friend of Joel Chandler Harris, went from Atlanta to New York to work on the New York *Sun* and to become famous for his creation of "archy the cockroach." The small bug, a character in Marquis's column, "The Sun Dial," became as famous in his way as Harris's Brer Rabbit. Archy was supposed to come into the deserted newspaper office at night, jump off a pile of books down to the typewriter keys and leave a column of his thoughts for print next day. He also reported on the doings of his disreputable friend "mehitable the alley cat." Since the cockroach could not handle the capital letter key, all of his typing was done in small letters. Grantland Rice in his memoirs *The Tumult and the Shouting* says, "How Marquis could write!"

Poets of Georgia were singing the songs of the South. Frank L. Stanton's verses, such as "Mighty Lak a Rose" and "Just a Wearyin' for You" were set to music. Poets laureate like Dr. W. F. Melton, Ernest Neal, and Ollie Reeves, one after another, were writing verses that lodged in mind and memory. Their portraits are in the State Capitol.

Corra Harris was the first Georgia woman writer to gain national fame. The wife of a Methodist circuit rider preacher, she lived at Rydal, Georgia, at her home which she named "In the Valley." Her frank impressions of the life of a minister's wife were published under the title *A Circuit Rider's Wife.* In recent years, they were made into a movie "I'd Climb the Highest Mountain." It was filmed in north Georgia. Susan Hayward, who played the role of Mrs. Harris, later became a Georgia housewife herself, and lived in Carrollton, between her assignments in Hollywood. Mrs. Harris wrote twenty-three books. The longhand manuscripts of these books are owned today by the University of Georgia. They are properly displayed in a special room in the Ila Dunlap Memorial Library in Athens. In her will, Mrs. Harris left small legacies to her neighbors for quaint reasons: money for a purple silk dress to an unselfish woman and funds for instruments for a country doctor. Mrs. Harris, having known the two, believed they would spend the money on other people if not legally limited.

Roland Hayes gave concerts for the world. A Negro woman who had been a slave in Georgia was freed soon after the Confederacy fell, and walked 123 miles with a group of other slaves to Chattanooga, Tenn. One night, when they were camping along the road, a man who was part Indian came into camp. He met the young Negro woman and later married her. They became the parents of Roland Hayes, who is known throughout the world as a singer, and gave a concert on his seventy-fifth birthday in 1962 in Carnegie Hall. After Hayes became rich, he bought the farm in Georgia where his mother had been a slave, though later he sold it. He came to know Joseph Mann, the son of the man who had once owned Hayes' mother. Mrs. Mann and the singer befriended each other. Mann told Hayes the history of his mother and his grandparents and his great-grandfather who was a tribal leader, and a composer of songs. Hayes provided a home for Mr. and Mrs. Mann in their latter days, after they had become ill and not as well off financially as they had been.

One of the songs that Hayes sang in Carnegie Hall, and before kings and queens in Europe, was one which his great-grandfather had composed about the death of Christ on the cross.

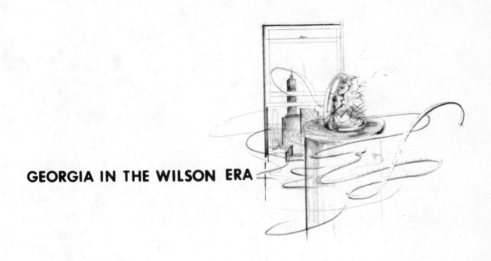

GEORGIA IN THE WILSON ERA

UNIT 10

CHAPTER 53

GEORGIA THROUGH THE

WOODROW WILSON ERA

The years from 1912 through 1929 are often called the Wilson Era, though President Woodrow Wilson had died before they were over. His career had also begun before 1912. But these two dates often mark the Wilson Era because he became President of the United States in 1912, and because the world-wide financial crash of 1929 seemed to mark the end of the postwar frenzy.

Wilson, believed by many to be one of America's great presidents, had close ties with Georgia. He had lived in Augusta as a little boy, had an uncle who taught in a Georgia college, had married a Georgia girl, and had opened a law office in Atlanta. Not all Georgia leaders agreed with Wilson, but nearly all of them respected his ability and admired his courage.

He was elected and re-elected, and guided the nation through the terrible years of World War I. This war brought Georgia and the rest of the nation into closer contact with the rest of the world. However, after the war, reaction set in, and Wilson's dream of a League of Nations was defeated. A postwar frenzy of installment buying and other financial episodes came about. The 1929 crash, five years after Wilson had died, put a spectacular end to the era, and another era began what was to include an even more dreadful world war. But both eras had many new things that brought hope and better ways of living to the people of Georgia and the rest of the world.

673

Woodrow Wilson And Georgia

Born at Staunton, Virginia, in December, 1858, President Woodrow Wilson was the son of Dr. Joseph Ruggles Wilson, an Ohio-born Presbyterian minister, and his wife, the former Jessie Woodrow, who was born in Scotland. Dr. Thomas Woodrow, who taught at old Oglethorpe University, was President Wilson's uncle.

Wilson's father was pastor of the First Presbyterian Church in Augusta. He lived in that city for several years. During most of that time, Woodrow was being tutored at home. He did not attend school until he reached the age of twelve. Shortly thereafter the family moved to Columbia, South Carolina.

After graduating from Princeton, Wilson opened law offices in Atlanta, but soon discovered that he did not like practicing law. He was more interested in government and politics. One important thing happened while he was waiting for clients in his office on Marietta Street in Atlanta; Walter Hines Page, the brilliant writer and statesman, came by his office. They met, liked each other, and were friends and colleagues as long as they both lived. Wilson later sent Page as United States Ambassador to London, England.

On June 24, 1885, Wilson married Ellen Louise Axson, daughter of a Rome clergyman. Wilson is thought of as a cold man, but toward his family, his wife and their three daughters, Margaret, Jessie, and Eleanor, he was warm and tender. At home he read the classics aloud to his family.

While in Georgia he vacationed at an old Indian settlement, White Sulphur Springs near Gainesville. Two of his daughters were born in Gainesville, verified by the unpublished records of Lester Hosch.

He had taught at Bryn Mawr, and then at Princeton; and eventually he became president of that great university. While a professor of political science and government, he wrote numerous books and articles about constitutional law and government. These impressed men in many places, and established Wilson as a man with original ideas.

In 1910, politicians in New Jersey convinced Wilson that he should run for governor, and he was elected. His outstanding record in office led to the Democratic nomination for President of the United States in 1912. After an exciting campaign, he defeated both President William Howard Taft and Theodore Roosevelt.

President Woodrow Wilson
675

The first Mrs. Wilson had planned to visit Rome, her old home town, in the autumn of 1914. The townspeople had planted shrubbery near the depot to spell out "Welcome" to her. But she died in August in the White House, and her husband brought her on a rainy day back to Rome where she is buried. The words on her grave are these: "Sacred to the memory of Ellen Louise Axson, beloved wife of Woodrow Wilson. Born 15 May, 1860, at Savannah. Died 6 August 1914, Washington, D.C. A traveler between life and death, the reason firm, the temperate will, endurance, foresight, strength and skill; a noble woman, nobly planned to warm and comfort and command; and yet a spirit still and bright, with something of angelic light."

In December, 1915, Wilson married Edith Bolling Galt, descendant of Pocahontas, and widow of a Washington jeweler. Later she was to be accused of trying to act as president during an illness of her husband. In her own published memoirs she tells her story. Others have also written biographies of her. Wilson was deeply in love with the beautiful woman. He had been very lonely in the White House after the death of the Georgia girl who was his first wife.

The First Mrs. Wilson

National politics was becoming increasingly interesting to Georgians as the 1912 election approached. The state, like most of the South, was always in the ranks of the Democratic party, and was to remain so until 1964. This was primarily due to the fact that Georgians and other southerners blamed the Republican party for their troubles of the Reconstruction years.

As 1912 approached, it looked more and more as if the Democrats had a good chance to elect a president. The Republican party was split. Theodore Roosevelt had picked William Howard Taft, a huge, jolly man who had often been to Georgia, as the president to follow him in the White House. Taft had been elected in 1908. Roosevelt had gone off to Africa to hunt big game.

But differences developed between Roosevelt and Taft and, on his return, Roosevelt became the candidate of a third party known as the Bull Moose party. The Republicans nominated President Taft again. Taft came to Augusta during his campaigns, ostensibly to play golf, but also to confer with his advisers in an attempt to break the "Solid South."

When the Democratic convention met in Baltimore, Wilson seemed to have a good chance to be nominated.

In the popular vote, Wilson carried 40 of the then 48 states.

In the 1916 election, he was re-elected. His campaign slogan had been "He kept us out of war." But circumstances were soon to make it necessary for America to enter the war. Wilson's opponent in the 1916 election was Charles Evans Hughes, who later became Chief Justice of the U.S. Supreme Court, as did Taft. The election was so close that Wilson had virtually conceded defeat. Only California had not been heard from, and it was expected to go Republican. It surprised everybody by voting Democratic and Wilson was in. The upset was said to be due to Hughes having unintentionally offended Senator Hiram Johnson, a powerful Republican leader in California. Hughes was reported to have gone to bed on election night believing that he had been elected. A reporter came to the door and was told, "The President-elect has retired. Is there any message?" The reporter answered, "When he wakes up, tell him that he is not President-elect."

677

In the second election, though Watson and his followers were still bitterly against him, Wilson carried Georgia with 125,845 votes to Hughes' 11,225. In the national election, Wilson got 8,563,713 votes to Hughes' 8,160,401, or 277 electoral votes to Hughes' 254, a very close margin of victory.

WHAT WILSON DID WHEN HE WAS PRESIDENT

This President who had such close ties with Georgia was regarded by many as one of the great leaders the nation had had. During his term, the income tax amendment to the Constitution was passed by Congress and ratified. Another was the change to election of U.S. Senators by the people instead of by the legislature. The Democrats also claimed that they enacted the best tariff law in fifty years. The Federal Trade Commission was created, and an anti-trust law enacted. Child labor laws were passed, and an eight-hour day for workmen. The amendment granting women suffrage was passed, though Wilson himself was not in favor of this.

World War I came during the second Wilson administration after which America was never the same again.

Wilson wanted especially to change four things. He thought taxes were not fairly apportioned. He wanted labor laws made more fair to workers. He believed the banking system was too rigid. He thought the tariff was too high. He went back to Jefferson's way of going directly to Congress and talking to them about it instead of sending a written message to be read. Congress set these things more nearly right, though there was much disagreement about how this should be done.

On June 28, 1914, when Wilson had been president about two years, a fanatic in Sarajevo, Bosnia shot and killed an Austrian archduke, the heir to the throne, and his wife. This triggered off the greatest war that the world had seen up to that time. Germany and Austria and their ally Turkey, went to war against England, France, Italy, and their ally Russia. Wilson tried hard to keep America out of it, even after 1915 when the Germans sank a British ship called the *Lusitania,* with 124 Americans among the 1,198 passengers. Theodore Roosevelt bitterly criticized Wilson for this, but the President spoke of being "too proud to fight."

678

He had already been plagued with a small fight with Mexico. There had been trouble there for some time. When Pancho Villa crossed the U.S. border in 1916 and killed seventeen people and set fire to an American town, the government sent General John J. Pershing to capture him.

Pershing found out how unprepared the country was for war. Suddenly it was confronted with the war in Europe. Wilson issued a proclamation of neutrality, but neutrality wouldn't work now. On January 31, 1917, Germany announced its intention to sink on sight all ships that entered European war zones. In 1917, four American ships were sunk off the Dutch coast. Wilson asked Congress to declare war on Germany, in a speech he made to them on April 2, 1917. He said, "The world must be made safe for democracy. We have no selfish ends to serve. But the day has come when America is privileged to spend her blood and her might for the principles that gave her birth and happiness and the peace which she has treasured. God helping her, she can do no other." Georgia's delegation in the U. S. House of Representatives backed Wilson, but Senators Hoke Smith and Thomas Hardwick disagreed with him. On April 6, war was declared. German submarines were already near Georgia's coast. The millionaires had to desert their Jekyll retreat because of them.

Jeanette Rankin, first woman in Congress, voted against war. Years later, she moved to Georgia and bought a farm near Athens.

Americans rallied to the war effort. Though the U. S. was just in the war for nineteen months, it made all the difference. The Allies in Europe had all but exhausted their resources, money, and men in fighting the Central Powers. The U. S. had four million men in arms, and sent two million of them across the ocean. Pershing insisted that they fight as an American army and not be put under European officers or into foreign units.

In this war, 126,000 soldiers died and 234,000 others were wounded, some crippled for life. The war cost the U. S. $50,000,000,000.

The Panama Canal was opened in 1914, as the war broke over the world. The canal later made it easier for the U. S. to move its ships from the Atlantic to the Pacific. In 1898 when America was fighting Spain, the battleship

Oregon had to travel 15,000 miles to join the fleet in the West Indies.

McAdoo, A Georgian, Was In The Wilson Cabinet

William Gibbs McAdoo, who was born at Marietta and grew up in Milledgeville, was made Secretary of the Treasury in the Wilson Cabinet.

McAdoo, who had grown up in the time of poverty after the Civil War, had a hard time getting his education, but afterward, he had moved to New York and become wealthy. He was president of the corporation that built the first tunnels under the river there. When the government took over the railroads during World War I, he became director of them.

He married Eleanor Wilson, the President's daughter.

Eleanor McAdoo has in recent years edited for publication the love letters of her parents, Woodrow and Ellen Wilson. The book is titled *The Priceless Gift.* The original letters were given to the library of Princeton University.

CHAPTER 54

WHAT WAS GOING
ON IN GEORGIA

Many things were happening in Georgia. Some of them concerned America's war effort and others were only within the state, but it is hard to separate them. Like ripples in a pool, one thing affects another.

A murder case that affected Georgia politics eventually put into the governor's chair a man who supported Wilson. But there were those who bitterly assailed Wilson and believed in neither his ideas on how to conduct the war, nor how to plan for world peace afterward.

The Leo Frank Murder Case Affected Georgia Politics

It was during this era that a spectacular murder case in Georgia had a curious effect on politics in the state. It ended the brilliant political career of one governor, and was the springboard that put an able solicitor in the governor's chair. It almost resulted in the lynching of a governor by a mob.

The governor whose career it ended was John M. Slaton. He had been born in Meriwether County on Christmas Day, 1866. He went to school in Atlanta, then worked his way through the University in Athens, graduating with top honors and membership in Phi Beta Kappa. He started practicing law in Atlanta in 1896, and was soon elected to the legislature, where he served seventeen years, thirteen in the House and four in the Senate. He served briefly as governor President of the Senate when Hoke Smith was appointed to the U.S. Senate, and before Joseph M. Brown was elected for a second term in 1912. Slaton had served twice as Senate president and also as Speaker of the House.

Slaton himself was elected governor and took office June 28, 1913. He supported Woodrow Wilson. In state government he wanted a county unit system of voting, a pay-as-you-go finance plan and a permanent voter registry, so the once-registered voters did not have to register again and could continue voting unless disqualified for some reason. He also advocated a tax equalization plan, which was enacted.

The big news of his administration was the Leo Frank murder case. Leo Frank, a New York man of the Jewish faith who had been born in Texas, had come to Atlanta as manager of a pencil factory. On Memorial Day, 1913, a fourteen-year-old girl named Mary Phagan, who worked there, went by to get her pay and never came out again. She was found murdered in the basement. Frank was tried and convicted of her murder, though the evidence against him was mostly circumstantial. The case was headlined in newspapers all over the nation, and noted in other parts of the world. There was much doubt of Frank's guilt. Judge Arthur M. Roan, the presiding jurist in the case, who had said that Frank's innocence "had been proven to a mathematical certainty," became insane and was put in a mental hospital.

Feeling was so intense that Frank was not in the courtroom when the jury brought in its verdict against him. There was danger that a mob would kill him. He was sentenced to be hanged; and his lawyers appealed the case. Governor Slaton, himself a lawyer, was not convinced that Frank's guilt had been proven, and commuted the death sentence to life imprisonment. He knew the danger he would encounter, but he did it anyhow. His wife, a prominent Atlanta socialite, agreed with his decision. They were living at their beautiful home Wingfield, in Atlanta, while the Governor's mansion was being repaired. A mob of 3,000 quickly gathered around the home in Buckhead, six miles north of the city. Slaton's friends went to protect him, and state police were called out. Later the Slatons left on a trip around the world.

Frank was taken to the state prison, then in Milledgeville, and there an old convict named Frank Creen tried to kill him. A mob took him out of prison one midnight, and hanged him as near as they could get to the grave of Mary Phagan in Cobb County. Many books and ballads were

682

written about the Leo Frank case. Tom Watson was convinced of his guilt and wrote editorials against him in his newspaper. One was seventeen columns long; it ran on February 11, 1915. When Slaton ran for the U.S. Senate, he was defeated. The solicitor who tried Leo Frank, Hugh Dorsey, was later elected governor.

Vocational Education Got A Boost

In 1917, two Georgians sponsored the congressional act that really launched vocational education in this nation. They were Hoke Smith, who had been governor and United States Senator, and Congressman Dudley M. Hughes of Twiggs County. (His home at Danville has a bronze marker in front of it.)

The Morrill Act of 1862, which Georgia began to share in 1872, set up new patterns of "mechanical and agricultural" education at the colleges, but the vocational education program as we know it today in the high schools of the nation was made possible by the Smith-Hughes Act of 1917. That has since been expanded and varied by other such acts, many of which bore the name of other Georgians such as Senator Walter F. George and Congressman Braswell Dean. The Dudley M. Hughes Vocational School at Macon and the Smith-Hughes Vocational School in Atlanta are two of the many things that honor Georgians for their part in this nationwide program.

Nat Harris Was The Last Confederate
Soldier To Be Governor

Nathaniel Edwin Harris, who liked to be called "Nat," was Governor of Georgia when the United States entered World War I. Governor Harris had been born in 1846, in the beautiful East Tennessee Valley. He attended the old field schools and the academy. After the war, he moved to Georgia to a town named Pine Log. He joined the Confederate Army at the age of sixteen. Later, he entered the University of Georgia with money borrowed from Alexander Stephens.

Harris was a classmate of Henry W. Grady at the

683

University. After he had graduated from the University, he taught for a time, and then went to Macon and started practicing law.

Harris eventually got into politics. When he ran for governor in 1915 he was elected largely because he had the backing of his fellow Confederate veterans. This proved to be the last election in which the veterans held the balance of political power, and Harris was the last Confederate veteran to serve as governor of Georgia. He was able to establish a pension for Confederate veterans, led in the passage of the state's first compulsory education law, and gained higher pay for teachers.

A great interest of his, both as a legislator and as governor, was the crusade to end the sale of liquor, usually called "Prohibition." He would probably have been elected governor again in 1917 had it not been that Hugh Dorsey was catapulted to fame as prosecutor in the Leo Frank case.

Though Harris was over seventy years old when the United States entered the war, he offered to go overseas. However, officials in Washington told him that he was past the age for war and that he could do more good for America at home.

Among the accomplishments for which he is remembered was his part in the founding of Georgia Technical University. He served as Chairman of the school's Board of Trustees for more than thirty years. He signed more than 15,000 diplomas.

Georgians Helped
In The War Effort

Georgia civilians joined with the military to support the war. Where there had been about 300 Red Cross chapters in the state before, there were soon over 3,000. They sent thirty million surgical dressings to Europe. Georgians were buying bonds in the Liberty Loan drives. Atlanta was the bond headquarters for eight southeastern states. Former Governor John Slaton was a tireless leader in this bond drive.

Schools were closed sometimes during the war years, once because of the influenza epidemic and once because of an acute shortage of coal.

Farmers grew food crops, and bankers loaned many the money to stock their farms with cattle and hogs. Many people had gardens. Georgians canned and conserved great quantities of food. They offered to share their food with people in parts of the country where the crops had failed. The government provided three million cans for this food. School pupils planted gardens on the campus or on vacant lots around town.

Georgians helped build ships, made bandages, bought bonds and stamps, worked in hospitals, sent their sons abroad to fight, and shared their homes with soldiers stationed in Georgia. There were camps in many places, including Atlanta, Macon, Augusta, and Columbus.

Fort Oglethorpe and Fort McPherson in Georgia were two of the fourteen sites in the nation that Secretary of War Newton D. Baker chose early for training camps. The government had also bought Fort Benning near Columbus, Camp Gordon, and Camp Wheeler.

The state sent almost 100,000 men to serve in the conflict. Back home, Governor Nat Harris was encouraging Georgians to do without, or to make, products they had been getting from the outside markets. Most Georgians responded loyally. In a proclamation on April 10, 1917, the Governor called on all Georgians to remain staunch and faithful through the crisis and, by April 18, Georgia stood fourth in the nation in the number of men who had been recruited for Army duty.

The war itself strongly affected life in Georgia. Cotton fell in price from 15¢ to 6¢ a pound. People who had worked in the cotton fields and factories were often idle. Because of the war in Europe, the market for naval stores and other exports which Georgia had been sending to Europe grew smaller.

FORT BENNING WAS ESTABLISHED

Fort Benning, which spreads over many acres in Chattahoochee and Muscogee counties, became an important part of Georgia during World War I. It is the world's largest infantry school, made permanent in 1922, after having served as a camp during the war. Officers continued to come to the fort from all over the world. It was named for Judge Henry Benning, a Confederate general.

General George C. Marshall, later Secretary of State, was once commandant there. The story of his years at Fort Benning have been told in the book *Together,* by his second wife, who was a Georgian. She was Katherine Tupper Brown, whose family lived at Washington, Georgia, where their beautiful old home is still a showplace. She was a widow visiting friends in Columbus when she met the General. Thousands of visitors come to Fort Benning annually. One of the sites that interests them is the monument to a crippled dog named Calculator because he "put down three and carried one."

What Happened During
Hugh Dorsey's Term As Governor

Hugh Dorsey was born at Fayetteville, just a year before Georgia regained its own government from the carpetbaggers after the War Between the States. He went to school in Atlanta and also in Hart County and, after graduating from the University of Georgia, studied law for a time at the University of Virginia. After opening law offices in Atlanta, he was appointed solicitor of the Atlanta judicial circuit, and was later elected to that office. While there he prosecuted Leo Frank.

In the 1916 campaign for governor, Dorsey defeated the aging Nat Harris, as well as Dr. L.G. Hardman of Commerce, and Colonel Joe Pottle of Milledgeville. Dorsey talked a lot during his campaign about the importance of upholding the verdict of courts. He said that Governor Nat Harris had pardoned too many people convicted by the courts. He probably was referring also to the Slaton commutation of the court sentence for Leo Frank to hang, after a jury had found him guilty of murder. Dr. Hardman, who was to become governor of Georgia later, declared that Georgia had had enough lawyers as governors, and needed a physician in this service.

The state was still aflame with the repercussions of the Frank case, and Dorsey was elected. He too supported the war effort, and urged every Georgian to work to the utmost of his ability. He recommended to the legislature a compulsory work law to be used if labor shortages became acute.

Perhaps the most important measure passed by the Legislature during Dorsey's administration was the Neill Primary Act. Its coming had really been foreshadowed by Henry Grady, who defied the politicians and put John B. Gordon in the governor's chair in 1886. Grady had asked the people to choose their own representatives to come to the State Convention to cast their votes.

The Neill plan provided a primary election in each county, and made it obligatory for whoever represented that county at the convention to cast his vote for the candidate preferred by the county, as indicated by the preferential primary. The Act, introduced by Cecil Neill, had been passed by the Legislature in 1916, but was vetoed by Governor Nat Harris. A similar bill passed the next year and Dorsey signed it. The County-Unit system, as established in 1920, was destined to last until the Federal Supreme Court doomed it in 1962. The system gave the eight largest counties three representatives and six unit votes; the next thirty had two representatives and four unit votes; and the remainder, one representative and two unit votes. Shifts in population could change this as the census changed. As a result, the Georgia government was dominated by the rural areas. Three small counties, with two unit votes each, could offset a big county like Fulton, with Atlanta in it, which had only six. The candidates made their overtures to the few people in the small counties. The urban centers did not gain equal power for their residents at the ballot box until 1962. By then thousands of Georgians would have moved from farm to city, and political power would move with the people.

Dorsey was re-elected in 1918, and served as governor for four years, from 1917 to 1921. Then he was succeeded by Thomas W. Hardwick, an opponent of Wilson elected in the resurgence of a feeling of weariness with the war and a desire of the people to return to isolationism.

Georgians Died In Influenza Epidemic

A strange and macabre part of the history of World War I was the influenza epidemic that suddenly swooped across the world, killing more than a half million people in the United States and twenty million in the world. It was like some plague out of the Middle Ages. It was known as the

Spanish influenza. In many communities no doctors or nurses were available. In other places, doctors and nurses worked themselves weary trying to care for the sick and the dying. Coffins piled up all over Georgia faster than they could be buried. People tried every desperate remedy they heard of. Little white gauze masks were worn over the face, even at offices and on the streets. Everybody tried to avoid crowds. In army camps, the disease killed thousands. More died from flu than war wounds. In many communities, whole families died. The plague disappeared as suddenly as it had come, and though there is a disease known as "flu" now, it is either not the killing kind or medical science and the new drugs counteract it. Katherine Ann Porter's short story "Pale Horse, Pale Rider" deals with people in this dreadful time.

CHAPTER 55

WHEN THE WAR ENDED

Finally, after a mighty effort, Germany and its allies were defeated. The entrance of America into the war had made the difference, coming as it did when the valiant people of Europe had all but come to the end of their resources.

Kaiser Wilhelm, the German emperor and grandson of the late Queen Victoria of England, fled to Holland for refuge. He, who set out to rule the world, had brought about tragedy for his own people and for the whole world.

On November 11, 1918, the Armistice was signed. There had been a false report four days earlier, and when the real Armistice came, people were slow to believe it. When it finally was made official, Georgia joined the rest of the world in jubilation over victory. Crowds in New York burned the Kaiser in effigy.

Wilson And The Plan For Peace

Woodrow Wilson had already been thinking about a peace for the world. He had outlined the famous "Fourteen Points" which he thought important as the basis for peace. The foundation of them was an idea that Thomas Jefferson had set forth in the Declaration of Independence: that governments should derive their just powers from the consent of the governed. Wilson wanted an end to imperialism; he wanted every nation, little or big, to decide for itself what kind of government it would have.

Instead of leaving the details of the peace treaty to Secretary of State Robert Lansing, Wilson decided to go to Europe himself. On December 4, 1918, he sailed from New York on a ship named *George Washington.* Mrs. Wilson went with him. He wanted to be sure that the peace treaty included a League of Nations that would, he thought, prevent future wars. He was wildly acclaimed all over Europe by the people in a triumphal tour. Wilson had a noble idealism. He knew that his own country did not want any territory out of the war. But other countries did. They also wanted Germany to be punished. The "Big Four," Clemenceau of France, Lloyd George of England, and Orlando of Italy who became offended and later withdrew, and Wilson, worked on the treaty.

Back home, opposition to Wilson's ideas was growing. Wilson had not talked things over with enough people. Senator Henry Cabot Lodge, grandfather of the future Ambassador, made a speech in which he reminded Congress and the nation that the Senate as well as the President had Constitutional powers in treaty making, and that no treaty could be conducted without its consent. Others who were in what Wilson was later to term "a little group of willful men," but who often honestly differed from him, were Borah of Idaho, Lafollette of Wisconsin, and George Norris of Nebraska. There were also others.

Wilson stayed in Europe for six months, and returned to America in June, 1919. He was shocked and saddened when his own nation rejected the treaty and the peace plan he had devised for the world.

Already exhausted by his tremendous labors in Europe, he decided to carry his case to the people. Against his doctor's advice, he started on a speaking tour of the nation.

There was no radio or television, and few public address systems to take the strain off his voice, but he made many eloquent speeches. In Colorado, he collapsed. Thereafter, he lay stricken and ill in the White House for many weeks. Only Mrs. Wilson and the doctors saw him regularly. The League of Nations was organized without the United States as a member. Wilson came to realize that the world was not ready for his advanced ideas, but he saw too that without some sort of league another and even more

President Wilson Took His Plea To The People

terrible world war would come. He was right.

As he convalesced, the 1920 election was approaching, time to choose a president again.

Franklin D. Roosevelt Came Into The National Picture

A young man named Franklin Delano Roosevelt from Hyde Park, New York, now came upon the national political scene. He was a son of wealth, and married his cousin, Eleanor Roosevelt, who was Teddy Roosevelt's niece. He had studied law and started to practice in New York. President Wilson appointed him Assistant Secretary of the Navy.

The 1920 Democratic Convention was held in San Francisco. Wilson did not endorse any candidate. If he had, his son-in-law and Cabinet member, Georgian William G. McAdoo might have become President.

The convention finally nominated Governor James M. Cox of Ohio, who was later to become the owner of the *Atlanta Journal,* the *Atlanta Constitution,* and WSB television and radio in Atlanta. His running mate as candidate for the vice-presidency was Franklin D. Roosevelt, who was nominated by acclamation.

Cox and Roosevelt went to Washington to see the stricken President. They campaigned on Wilson's record and they championed the League of Nations. The opponent nominated by the Republicans was a little-known senator from Ohio, Warren G. Harding, who campaigned on the odd slogan, "A return to normalcy." It appealed to a war-weary nation, and he defeated Cox and Roosevelt. Georgia's vote: 107,162 for Cox and Roosevelt; 43,720 for Harding and his vice-president, Calvin Coolidge. Coolidge was a New Englander who became president when Harding died in 1923.

Tom Hardwick, Opponent Of Wilson, Gained Political Office

Thomas William Hardwick had been born in Thomasville on December 9, 1872. After he left Mercer University, he opened law offices in Sandersville in Washington County. He was a brilliant man and an able lawyer, and he was soon elected to the Legislature. Then Georgians sent him to Congress in 1903, and kept him there sixteen years, eleven as Representative and five as Senator, before he was defeated in 1918.

In 1921 he became governor of Georgia for one term. In the middle of the term Tom Watson, then serving as United States Senator, died in Washington. Eight men became candidates to succeed him. One was Governor Hardwick himself, who was defeated by Walter F. George of Vienna. But Hardwick was appointed as special assistant to the United States Attorney General. He resigned after a year and returned to his Georgia law practice, with his main office in Atlanta.

Hardwick had fought Wilson's program and he was elected governor largely on the wave of reaction against the Wilson policies. He fought the revived Ku Klux Klan, set in motion a tax reform program for Georgia, and set up the Public Service Commission. A one cent tax on gasoline provided for roads. But the boll weevil had brought ruin to much of Georgia and Hardwick's popularity declined, as that of governors and presidents always does when times are hard. Labor was also against him because he used troops to quell labor disturbances. Watson had turned from him too. Clifford Walker defeated him in 1922. The village of Hardwick in Baldwin County was named for him.

Walker Wanted All Georgia Children To Be Educated

Clifford Walker of Monroe in Walton County became governor in 1922, defeating Thomas Hardwick, and was reelected without opposition in 1924.

His election was the first in which women voted. Georgia had opposed the Nineteenth Amendment, giving women the right to vote, but the nation had passed it anyhow, and it became a law.

Walker had been born in Walton County, July 4, 1877. After graduation from the University of Georgia in 1897, Walker had been mayor of Monroe, solicitor of the Western judicial circuit, and Georgia's Attorney-General from 1915-1920.

He had the support of Tom Watson, who was still powerful in Georgia politics. Walker in his campaigning hit hard at the "Kimball House Lobby" in Atlanta, and charged that the people's rights had been taken away from them by a group of powerful bosses who met there and decided what would be done (or not done) in Georgia.

One appealing plank in Walker's platform had been his urging of the right of all Georgia children to an education, regardless of their race or color. He also wanted them to have free textbooks.

Wilson Died In 1924

Former President Wilson and his wife moved to a home in Washington, D.C. There, as long as he lived, his friends and admirers went to get a glimpse of him. Occasionally he was able to go riding. Some talked with him when he was feeling better. One was Claudius B. McCullar of Milledgeville, editor of the *National University Law Review* and president of the Woodrow Wilson Club. Judge McCullar believed that Wilson foresaw the eventual organization of the United Nations, which was launched in San Francisco in 1945.

On a snowy February day in 1924, as hundreds knelt in the street praying, Wilson died. An era passed with him. Many books have been written about him. One titled *When the Cheering Stopped* tells of the years after he was no longer in the limelight on the stage of the world.

He was buried in the Crypt of the National Cathedral in Washington, D.C. The minister at this cathedral is his grandson, the Very Reverend Francis Wilson Syre, son of Wilson's daughter Jessie.

In Georgia there are four sites which make people think especially of Wilson: his former home in Augusta, the site of his law office in Atlanta, the grave of his first wife Ellen, in Rome, and the inscription that he wrote on the monument built in Rome to the women of the Confederacy. There is also a Woodrow Wilson Law School in Atlanta.

A Doctor-Farmer Governed Georgia

Dr. Lamartine G. Hardman of Commerce was the first doctor to become governor of Georgia since Dr. Lyman

Hall.   Born in 1856, he was seventy years old when he was elected governor over four other candidates in 1926.

Hardman graduated at twenty from the University of Georgia, and went on to further medical studies at universities in Pennsylvania, New York, and London. He was also a scientific farmer, a drug merchant, and a banker, and had served in the legislature. There he had helped draft the prohibition law of the state and sponsored many health measures. He was especially interested in good roads. He and others in the legislature had pushed plans for the setting up of a modern highway department in state government.

When he became governor, he appointed a commission to look into the reorganization of the unwieldy machinery of state government. His successor, Richard B. Russell, Jr., made this reorganization a reality when he came to office.

One of the four candidates that Hardman defeated for governor was his neighbor, John Holder, from the same county, who headed the highway department for many years.

The Crash That Ended The Era

In 1929 came the financial crash that ended this era. The nation was on a wild jag of prosperity. Installment buying had beguiled many into debts they could not pay, obligations they could not meet. The nation's businessmen were selling to Europe on credit. Economic experts were warning that the debts could not be paid because there was not enough gold in the world to pay them. America already had half of the world's gold, even then.

But few people paid any attention to the economists. It was the F. Scott Fitzgerald era of loud music and louder voices, and a generation was reacting against the hard days of war. Farmers were recovering from the boll weevil's blight with diversified crops of tobacco, sugar cane, pecans, lumber, turpentine, vegetables for trucking, dairy products, and other such things. They had money again, or credit.

Then, in 1929, the crash came. In Georgia, where at least the people on the farms could kill another chicken to eat and pick butterbeans off the garden fences, the depression was not quite so bad as in the cities. Men with gray faces

695

"Starvation"

walked the city's paved streets, looking for work that did not exist. People lost their jobs, their savings, their homes, and almost their hope. A darkness seemed to come down upon the world.

Millionaires saw their fortunes vanish overnight. In despair, some jumped out of the windows of skyscrapers to their deaths. Some sold apples on the street, proud men stood in breadlines, and women made over old clothes for their families. The era of jazz and gin and gaiety gave way to a time of hunger and despair.

The Meaning Of The Wilson Years

Many of those who looked back at the years marked with the Wilson imprint found in them great meaning for their country. With the advent of the first world war, the United States had to emerge from her isolation from the world. The nation had been busy looking within, trying to put itself together again after the painful tearing-apart of the North and the South in the Civil War. They had had neither the time nor the inclination to consider how this country was concerned with the rest of the world. It is true that all Americans had come, at one time or another, to this country from Europe. They were still coming, especially in the latter nineteenth century, to help build railroads, to find a better life. But they were quickly absorbed, and most of them were alienated from the country from which they had come, and Americanized.

After the war was over, the nation closed in upon itself again, or tried to. Rejecting Wilson's idea for a world League of Nations and weary of war, they tried to settle down to a country closed off from the rest of the world. They were to find that this could not be done. Better travel, better communication, better education, all this was bringing the countries of the world closer together, making a smaller and more compact world. Never again could the United States be unconcerned with the rest of mankind. In tragically few years, a still more terrible war would engulf the world, and Germany, led by another madman, would set out again to conquer the earth. Again it would fail, but not before a bitter price was paid.

THE ROOSEVELT IMPACT

UNIT 11

CHAPTER 56

THE ROOSEVELT IMPACT
ON GEORGIA

The years from the 1929 crash up to 1950, five years after he had died at the Little White House in Warm Springs, are often referred to in Georgia as the years of the Roosevelt impact.

Actually, Georgians had known Franklin Delano Roosevelt long before he came to the state in search of relief from the polio that had stricken him in 1921. They had known him as Assistant Secretary of the Navy during the Wilson administration. They had voted for him for Vice-President in 1920 when he was running mate of the Democratic presidential candidate, James M. Cox.

Roosevelt was in Georgia when the call came from Governor Al Smith of New York that really started the crippled man on his way to the White House. Destiny decreed that for the second time a president who had close ties with Georgia should guide the nation through a world war.

Several things are memorable about these Roosevelt years. Georgians once resisted his interference when he tried to defeat U.S. Senator Walter F. George. But the tremendous impact of his prestige and personality was felt in the state in many ways. Some governors agreed with him and his New Deal; others opposed him and his policies and programs.

Roosevelt. Georgia, And The Presidential Election

Franklin Delano Roosevelt came to Warm Springs, Georgia, the same year that Woodrow Wilson died in

Washington, D.C.

From 1924, when he first came to Georgia, to his death at Warm Springs in 1945, Roosevelt was a vital part of Georgia life and politics. The new vitalities that he set in motion during his years as president had such momentum that they continued to influence the state in the decade after his death, and are still affecting Georgia and the rest of the world.

Many other things were happening here during all these years. The state was becoming more urban than rural, manufacturing was employing more workers than farms were, writers were gaining national acclaim, the state was developing its resources and strengthening its schools. Much of the life of the people and the daily concerns that affected them were influenced by Roosevelt and his impact on his day.

HOW ROOSEVELT BECAME A PART-TIME GEORGIAN

A boy named Louis Joseph was actually the key that set momentous happenings in motion in history. He was a boy afflicted with polio. His doctor had found that exercising in the warm waters of a Georgia spring helped the boy walk better. George Foster Peabody, a friend

The "Little White House" At Warm Springs

of Roosevelt, had bought the springs. When he learned that the waters helped the Joseph boy, he wrote Roosevelt.

On August 19, 1921, Roosevelt had taken his wife Eleanor and their children for a sail at their summer home at Campobello. On their return, he and the boys helped fight a forest fire; then he took a swim to cool off. The water was icy cold. Roosevelt was stricken with polio. Three years later, he came to Warm Springs to bathe in the waters. Later he and his friends founded the Warms Springs Foundation. For years, the annual "March of Dimes," on his birthday, January 31, would bring funds to it. His friends built "Georgia Hall." He insured his life for $100,000 in favor of the Warm Springs Foundation.

He drove around Meriwether County in his little hand-operated automobile, and often went to the top of Pine Mountain, to sit quietly on Dowdell's Knob. He designed a swimming pool, now in Roosevelt Park, in the shape of the Liberty Bell. He built a little white house that would in later years take on new meaning after he became President and world leader.

HIS START TOWARD THE WHITE HOUSE

Roosevelt was sitting on the stage of the Manchester High School when he got another telephone call from Governor Alfred Smith of New York, who wanted him to run for governor of New York while Smith himself ran for President on the Democratic ticket. Smith had been calling all that day. Finally he said he would stay on the phone until Roosevelt agreed to talk to him. Roosevelt was reluctant to re-enter politics but, encouraged by his wife, his friend Louis Howe and others, he finally agreed. Smith, whom Roosevelt had twice nominated for President, lost but Roosevelt won. He went on to become President of the United States for four terms. He became the recognized leader of the world through perilous internal times and later through the worst world war mankind has ever known. All during these years, Roosevelt came back to Warm Springs when he could, to rest, to get away from his heavy burdens, and to swim in the warm waters.

In the 1932 presidential campaign, the first of four he was to make, Roosevelt got 22,821,857 votes, defeating President Herbert Hoover, who received only 15,761,443. Four years later, Roosevelt was to get 27,751,597 (his biggest vote) to Alf Landon's 16,-679,583. Landon got only eight electoral votes to Roosevelt's 523. In an unprecedented third term, in 1940 Roosevelt defeated Wendell Willkie by 27,243,466 to 22.304,755. In 1944 Roosevelt was elected for the fourth time, defeating Thomas E. Dewey by a vote of 25,602,505 to 22,066,278.

Georgia's record in these four elections is as follows: 1932 — Roosevelt: 234,118 (Georgia's largest presidential vote in history); Hoover: 19,836. A Georgia congressman named William D. Upshaw was the Prohibition party nominee and got 1,125 votes in Georgia.

1936 — Roosevelt: 255,364; Landon: 36,942

1940 — Roosevelt: 265,194; Willkie: 23,934

1944 — Roosevelt: 268,187; Dewey: 56,506

CHAPTER 57

THE NEW DEAL BEGAN

In his acceptance speech for which he set a precedent by flying to Chicago to the convention, Roosevelt said, "I pledge you, I pledge myself, to a new deal for the American people. Let us all here assembled constitute ourselves prophets of a new order of competence and of courage. This is more than a political campaign. It is a call to arms. Give me your help, not to win votes alone, but to win in this crusade to restore America to its own people."

At Oglethorpe University in Georgia, Roosevelt said, "This country needs bold, persistent experimentation. It is common sense to take a method and try it; if it fails, admit it frankly, and try another. But above all, try something!"

Americans, to whom the future looked black and who had lost the hope that prosperity was "just around the corner" as the Hoover Administration had kept saying, looked to Roosevelt for experiments that would change the situation. They would not agree with all he tried, and the courts would squelch his plans sometimes by declaring them illegal. But the main thing that matters to most people was that he was trying to lead them out of despair.

In 1933, the year he first became President, Georgia observed on February 12 the two hundredth anniversary of its founding.

705

Roosevelt's words "new deal" caught the imagination of press and public, and his administration was thereafter known as the "New Deal." He came to the presidency during a national depression. The nation had not yet emerged from the 1929 crash. Many people had lost their homes and their businesses. Banks were closing their doors, and people were losing the savings of a lifetime.

In his first inaugural address, Roosevelt spoke words that gave heart to the nation, "There is nothing to fear but fear itself." He closed the banks for ten days, until they could open with a sound financial structure. He took other measures, some of them drastic and sure to alarm and infuriate many people, that he thought necessary to the security and renewed vigor of the nation.

He instituted the famous "Fireside Chats," on national radio broadcasts, in which he calmly and reassuringly told the people what he was doing and why he was doing it. They took heart again, and the nation was on its way to a new strength and prosperity.

But people disagreed vehemently about the measures he took, and the way he did things. Some said he saved the country; some said he ruined it. In Georgia, some people admired him, and some people sincerely disagreed with him. In Milledgeville, the Georgia State College for Women helped the town celebrate the one hundredth anniversary of the completion of the beautiful old Governor's Mansion, opened in 1838. After the celebration, programs, and papers, and other things were collected to be kept for those who would celebrate the two hundredth anniversary in 2038. Dr. Guy Wells, then president of the college, wrote a letter to the man or woman, yet unborn, who would be president of the college in that year. After telling the future president that some trees had been planted that should be beautiful by that time, Dr. Wells added, "We have a president named Franklin Delano Roosevelt. Some consider him one of our greatest Presidents; others consider him a demagogue. By the time you are here, history will have decided."

Roosevelt set in motion many innovations. Some of his Hyde Park neighbors turned against him when he began to tax the rich to feed the poor. He took despairing people from the city streets and put them to work. Congress was called into the famous "Hundred Days" session to pass laws to chart new directions. He set up the "Brain Trust," the finest minds he could find who could advise him about what could and should be done. He asked the advice of many Georgians during these years.

Roosevelt came to Warm Springs whenever he could find time from the great burdens of the war and international involvements. Many famous figures came there to talk with him in the Little White House. When he noted that his electric bill in Georgia was four times as high as that of his New York home, he began to think about a plan that resulted in cheaper electricity for rural areas, and eventually brought about the Rural Electrification Administration, known as the REA. He often drove up the mountain to look out on one of the new cooperative villages set up there, where King's Gap had once led to an old Indian settlement. He sometimes bought from the neighboring farmers chickens, vegetables, buttermilk and pigs' feet. He liked pigs' feet boiled in salt water, split, browned to crackly crispness and buttered. Sometimes a neighbor brought him a possum to eat with Georgia yams.

The President returned to Georgia at Thanksgiving to share turkey with the patients in the Warm Springs Foundation which he and his friend had founded. Often Mrs. Roosevelt came with him. The Little White House was to bring Georgia into the national and international picture for a quarter of a century.

CHAPTER 58

IN THE STATE:

GOVERNORS OF THE ERA

The governor in office in Georgia and his relationship with the part-time Georgian who was President in Washington was of vital concern to people in Georgia. The young governor who was to streamline the state government and set in motion many changes of his own took office two years before Roosevelt was elected President.

This was a period of vast social and economic change in the state as well as the nation. These governors saw both gradual and explosive social, economic, and political forces at work in Georgia. Their problems were largely in helping their people to plan changes in social structures, economic bases, and political ideals.

Georgia Lost Two Congressmen

In 1930, Georgia lost two congressional places after the census figures were totaled. Since that time the state has had ten representatives in the lower house of Congress. After the first Constitution was adopted in 1789, Georgia had three representatives; when the first census was taken in 1790, the state had two. The figures from 1800 are as follows: 1800-1810, four; 1810-1820, six; 1820-1830, nine; 1840-1860, eight; 1860-1870, seven; 1870-1880, nine; 1880-1890, ten; 1890-1910, eleven; 1910-1930, twelve; 1930-present, ten.

Russell Streamlined Georgia's Government

Richard B. Russell, Jr., son of Chief Justice Richard B. Russell, Sr., of the Georgia Supreme Court, had become governor in 1931, two years before Roosevelt became president. He was one of thirteen children, and had grown up in Winder, and graduated from the University of Georgia at nearby Athens. He was elected to the legislature in 1921.

In the Georgia legislature, he soon became Speaker of the House of Representatives, and began to eye the governorship. He was elected on a platform of "the 3 R's": Reorganization, Redistricting, and Refinancing. He was thirty-one years old, the youngest governor in the nation. Many problems confronted him. The twelve congressional districts had to be reduced to ten because Georgia had lost population. This was largely due to Negroes moving North. The refinancing was helped by discounting for eight years the rentals of the Western and Atlantic Railroad, a railroad that Georgia owned.

Richard B. Russell

But most important of all was Russell's reorganization of the dated government machinery. The Reorganization Bill passed. Russell had said to the legislature: "One of the crying needs of Georgia is a complete and thorough over-hauling and rebuilding of our present structure of State government. We have Boards, Bureaus, Departments and Commissions almost too numerous to name. The average citizen of Georgia has little knowledge of the actual workings of the government he is taxed to support. The modern trend in government is toward a co-ordinated and simplified administrative system, and if I know the public mind of Georgia, I would say that the citizens of this state are more interested in your efforts to reorganize our administrative machinery than in any other measure that will be before you for consideration."

Other governors had recommended reorganization, but this was the first time it was actually done. Russell named a five-man committee to study and report on ways in which the cumbersome state machinery could be streamlined for more efficiency and economy. With the help of the legislature, he reduced the 102 bureaus, departments, and commissions of state government to 18, and streamlined the cumbersome governmental machinery in other ways. The trustees of all the separate colleges were abolished, and a board of regents named for the whole university system.

In 1933, after the death of Senator William J. Harris, Russell was elected to the United States Senate, defeating Charles R. Crisp. Crisp, an Americus man, had served long and honorably in the national House of Representatives, where his father had been Speaker for many years. Russell was one of the first to have the advantage of radio for reaching the people. In Congress, he went on to national fame as a statesman. He launched the national school lunch bill, and he became chairman of the powerful Armed Forces Committee of the Senate. He achieved a reputation as a brilliant orator and a skillful parliamentarian, and was once seriously considered for nomination by the Democrats for President.

The Man From Sugar Creek:
Governor Eugene Talmadge

"I may surprise you, but I will never deceive you." These words are carved in stone on the monument to

Eugene Talmadge, which stands on Capitol Square. The full-length figure of Talmadge, who dominated Georgia politics for two decades, stands in his familiar speech-making posture, finger pointed, and lock of dark hair falling over his forehead. When he spoke, he usually took off his coat, showing the red suspenders which came to be his political trade mark. He paid special attention to the rural voters, for during his administration the county unit system was most effective. Talmadge often said that he did not care about getting the vote of any county where a street car ran. When he was elected governor, he brought his cow and let her graze on the lawn in front of the Governor's Mansion. Yet this well-educated man could also enlist the aid of urban leaders and corporations.

Eugene Talmadge first came to public notice when he ran for commissioner of agriculture. His ancestors had come to Georgia from New Jersey generations before him. He was born at Forsyth in Monroe County on September 23, 1884. He graduated from the University in 1907 and opened law offices in McRae in Telfair County. Soon he married a widow, Mrs. Mattie Peterson. Together they ran their farm at Sugar Creek, campaigned, and kept up friendships with people all over Georgia. "Miss Mitt" was to see both her husband and son become governors of Georgia. Only one other father-and-son gubernatorial team ever was elected in Georgia: Joseph Emerson Brown and Joseph Mackay Brown. By coincidence, the stone monuments to the two men whose sons became governors stand at opposite corners of Capitol Square.

Talmadge was city attorney and solicitor in McRae; then he decided to run against J.J. Brown for the office of commissioner of agriculture. He won and served from 1927 to 1933. He got more than twice as many unit votes as all the other five combined. In 1932 he was elected governor. One of his campaign promises that appealed to many voters was $3 tags for automobiles. He wanted lower taxes, lower freight rates, cheaper electricity, prompt payment of teachers' salaries and Confederate pensions, and reorganization of the highway department.

Talmadge became governor of Georgia in 1933, the

711

Governor Eugene Talmadge

same year that Roosevelt became President. He had a turbulent career as governor. He did not agree with President Roosevelt's New Deal's paying workers 40¢ an hour to build roads, nor the way the relief funds were being administered in Georgia. Roosevelt and Harry Hopkins, his relief chief, put Miss Gay Shepperson in Georgia to handle the New Deal welfare program directly. Twice Washington cut off federal highway funds from Georgia. Talmadge and Harold Ickes, Secretary of the Interior, were often at odds. In 1936, Talmadge was re-elected governor, carrying all but three of Georgia's 159 counties against his opponent, Judge Claude Pittman of Cartersville.

Talmadge also had spectacular battles within the state. The legislature adjourned in 1936 without passing an appropriation bill. When the treasurer and the comptroller refused to pay out any money without specific

712

legislative authorization, Talmadge fired them, and ran the state by executive decree. He called out the National Guard to protect the state treasury, which had ten million dollars in it. He also used soldiers during a 1934 textile strike to "protect men in their right to work," he said. Some strike leaders were put in barbed wire stockades. This caused him trouble with labor. Talmadge believed in free enterprise. Having been a practical and successful farmer himself, he did not agree with the agricultural policies of Henry Wallace, then Secretary of Labor. He denounced the cotton contracts and the corn and hog programs as set up from Washington. When the federal authorities cut off highway money to Georgia, Talmadge stopped work on some of the road projects in the state.

Yet through all his difficulties with Roosevelt and the New Deal, he kept his hold on the hearts of Georgia's rural supporters. They flocked in droves wherever he spoke, called from the audience or from trees, "You tell 'em, Gene," and swarmed to shake his hand. Even though Georgia supported Roosevelt and greatly benefited by New Deal measures, it also gave Talmadge enough support to be elected governor four times.

He was finally defeated not by Roosevelt forces but by Georgia students, their parents, and their friends who did not like it when Talmadge's action resulted in the University's losing its accredited status. At that time, students could not vote, but their parents could and did; so did many of their friends. Talmadge was defeated for governor in 1942 by Ellis Gibbs Arnall of Newnan. Talmadge had been succeeded by Eurith D. Rivers after the completion of his first two terms, because he was ineligible to run again after two two-year terms. Then after Rivers' terms were ended, Talmadge was elected governor for another two-year term. During that term, the law was changed to give the governor a four-year term and make him ineligible to succeed himself. Talmadge ran again for the fourth time, was elected, and died before he could take office.

His opponent in 1946 was thirty-six year-old James V. Carmichael, of Marietta, lawyer and industrialist. In the primary, Carmichael, backed by Arnall, got the largest popular vote ever recorded in Georgia. But Talmadge got

713

Election of	Elected
1932	Eugene Talmadge
1934	Eugene Talmadge (could not run in 1936)
1936	E. D. Rivers
1938	E. D. Rivers
1940 (law changed to make governor's term four years)	Eugene Talmadge
1942	Ellis Arnall
1946	Eugene Talmadge (died before he could take office)

the greatest number of unit votes for a fourth term he would never live to serve.

He ran for the United States Senate, but did not succeed in defeating either Walter F. George or Richard B. Russell, Jr. Talmadge was also proposed for President once by a "Grass Roots" organization launched in Macon to oppose Roosevelt; it was not successful.

E. D. Rivers, The Governor From Arkansas And His "Little New Deal"

Eurith Dickinson Rivers was born at Center Point, Arkansas. He came to Young Harris College in Georgia, and married a fellow student, Lucile Lashley. For a while, they both taught school in Georgia. He became a lawyer in Lakeland, Georgia, and was elected to the legislature from Lanier County. One of Georgia's most persuasive orators, he was elected Speaker of the House, then later Governor in 1936.

He supported Roosevelt's New Deal, which his predecessor Eugene Talmadge had opposed. Rivers' own administration in Georgia became known as "The Little New Deal." He was re-elected in 1938. He had trouble financing many programs he wanted for Georgia. He pro-

714

posed a five-cent sales tax, but it was not passed. He did succeed in getting a free textbook law passed in 1937, and a seven-month school term.

To pay for his program, he attempted to divert funds from highways to other public services. The state highway board chairman objected, and the matter went into the federal courts. Rivers built many new buildings, and when his administration ended with the state 22 million dollars in debt, his supporters maintained that the progress he achieved had been worth the money.

It was also during this time that the live oak replaced the pine as Georgia's official tree.

Rivers served as Georgia's governor from January 12, 1937, when he succeeded Talmadge, to January 14, 1941, when Talmadge succeeded him, taking office for his third two-year term.

Arnall And The 1945 Constitution

Talmadge ran for the new four-year term that began in 1943, but was surprisingly defeated by his young attorney-general, Ellis Gibbs Arnall of Newnan.

A student from Georgia Tech, coming by the governor's office to congratulate him and bid him goodbye before leaving for the army, said, "I'm not old enough to vote, but I am old enough to fight." Arnall said to Georgians, "If our youngsters are old enough to fight and die for their country, they are old enough to vote." During his administration, the eighteen-year-olds were given the right to vote, first by his executive order, and later by the 1945 constitution. Georgia became the first state to do this. In 1955, Kentucky followed. Later, Congressman Charles Weltner of Georgia proposed it to the nation.

In 1914, Georgia's legislature had passed a law regulating child labor but it was somewhat weak, and was not enforced well. A better one was passed in 1925, but it still had weaknesses so, in 1946, the law tightened up, and children were protected against dangerous or unsuitable labor. The bill provided for such things as children working at home or on the farms of their parents, and for

715

those that had newspaper routes.

The Teacher Retirement Law was passed, and the legislature set up a million dollars to get it started.

The 1945 Georgia constitution was adopted during the Arnall administration. He appointed twenty-three Georgians to draft a new constitution. It replaced the 1877 constitution which had been amended 301 times. The 1945 constitution was later to be amended even more, and the need would become acute for further revision.

The poll tax was abolished. "No man should have to pay to vote," said the governor. Arnall brought a suit in federal court to establish fairer freight rates. He sued twenty-one railroads for $56 million in damages to Georgia. The South had long felt that it was discriminated against in this matter. The "density" rates favored the Northern industries, and worked an unfair hardship on southern farmers. The 1948 Bullwinkle Bill allowed railroads to get together and plan rate schedules. In 1952, action was taken on this by the Interstate Commerce Commission, and railroads equalized freight rates east of the Rocky Mountains. This saved Georgia over $20 million and gave meaning to the federal anti-trust laws.

There had been much talk of cruelties in Georgia prisons. During these four years, prison reform was a concern of the administration and a state board of corrections was established.

After Arnall went out of office, he became an attorney for film producers in Hollywood. He kept his home at Newnan. He wrote books, the most widely read being *The Shore Dimly Seen*. In 1965, he announced his intention of running again.

But before he left the governor's office in 1947, Arnall was to take part in one of the most spectacular political battles in the history of Georgia. Eugene Talmadge, elected for the fourth time, died before he could take over the governorship from Arnall. This event posed a problem.

The Three-Cornered Fight For Governor

Twice Georgia has had a three-cornered skirmish for the office of governor. The first time was in 1779, after the patriot government fled from Savannah, which had fallen to the British, to Augusta. In Augusta, factions of the patriot group met and elected George Walton, one of the three Georgia signers of the Declaration of Independence, as governor. The other elected John Wereat. In Savannah, the Royalist governor, Sir James Wright, still claimed to be the lawful governor of Georgia.

Nearly two hundred years later, after the death of governor-elect Eugene Talmadge, another three-cornered fight arose. Two men, Herman Talmadge and M.E. Thompson, each claimed the office of governor. Arnall, the incumbent, was determined to turn over the office of governor only to a duly chosen successor.

Eugene Talmadge had been ill during his campaign. Some of his supporters had foreseen the possibility of his death, and 675 of them had written on the ballot the name of his son, Herman Talmadge. In the general election of November 5, 1946, Eugene Talmadge received 143,279 votes, Herman Talmadge 675 write-in votes, and Carmichael 669 write-in votes. The new constitution, which had provided for the election of a lieutenant-governor, was vague in this contingency. It specified that the lieutenant-governor could succeed a governor but said nothing at all about whether he could succeed a governor-elect. The matter went to the legislature. On January 15, 1947, the legislature voted 161 to 87 that Herman Talmadge was the rightful governor of Georgia. But Governor Ellis Arnall, disagreeing with that decision, refused to turn the governor's office over to Talmadge. Then the Talmadge supporters, led by Adjutant General Marvin Griffin, later to become governor himself, took over the governor's office and executive mansion, barring Arnall from both. Arnall called this a "coup d'etat."

On January 18, 1947, when Thompson was sworn in as lieutenant-governor, Arnall resigned the office of governor. He believed that Thompson was his duly qualified successor. The matter went to the courts, while Talmadge held the office of governor for 67 days. On March 19, 1947, the Georgia Supreme Court, in a five to two decision, decreed that Melvin Thompson was the legal governor of Georgia. The legislature, said the court, had exceeded its authority in electing Herman Talmadge. Talmadge deferred to their decision, and Thompson became governor.

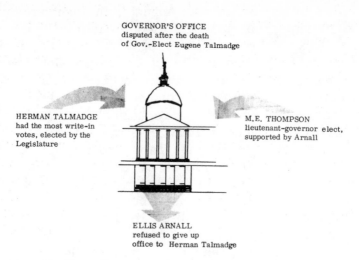

GOVERNOR'S OFFICE
disputed after the death
of Gov.-Elect Eugene Talmadge

HERMAN TALMADGE
had the most write-in
votes, elected by the
Legislature

M.E. THOMPSON
lieutenant-governor elect,
supported by Arnall

ELLIS ARNALL
refused to give up
office to Herman Talmadge

The Three-Cornered Battle For The Governorship

The two were to run against each other for the office again soon thereafter.

The election that named Eugene Talmadge governor for the fourth term was the first one in which Georgia Negroes had been allowed to vote in the primary. A primary is the pre-election in which a political party chooses its candidate to run in the general election. During the years in which Georgia was a one-party state, election in the primary was the same as in the general election, for there was rarely a candidate to oppose the Democratic nominee. Negroes had voted in the general election, but not until this election in the primary. The U.S. Supreme Court had decreed that they must be allowed to vote also in the primary election. The matter had reached the Supreme Court through a case brought by Primus King, a Columbus Negro in 1945.

Melvin Thompson Bought
Jekyll Island For The State

Melvin Ernest Thompson spent his boyhood in Millen, where he was born in 1903. His father died when he was a boy. He was reared by his mother and his grandfather, who was a Baptist minister. He had to work hard to get his education, and went up to the little mountain town of Demorest

718

in Habersham County and attended Piedmont College. Then he waited on tables and worked at other jobs to put himself through Emory University in Atlanta. After he got a bachelor's degree in liberal arts there, he went to the University of Georgia and obtained a master's degree. He became an educator, and was superintendent of the schools in Hawkinsville in 1933 when Governor Ed Rivers appointed him to a state supervisory job in education. He worked in the State Department of Education under the leadership of State School Superintendent M.D. Collins.

Thompson served as executive secretary to Governor Ellis Arnall. Then he became State Revenue Commissioner. In 1946, he was elected as the first lieutenant-governor under the new constitution of 1945 that had revived that office.

He did all he could for education. He also promoted Georgia's highway program. He backed a conservation program to "Keep Georgia Green." Thompson bought Jekyll Island for the state. It caused much argument at the time, but turned out to be a great benefit to the state, which adopted it as a favorite resort. The millionaires who had bought it from Christopher duBignon's heirs in 1886 and kept it as a retreat to use a few weeks each year, had virtually stopped using it. They sold it to Georgia for $650,000, though experts agreed that it was worth at least $20,-000,000. A bridge has been built over the river to connect the island with the mainland. During the time when it was one of *The Last Resorts,* described by Cleveland Amory in his book of that title, millionaires arrived there by yacht, and needed no bridge.

Many new buildings and recreation centers have been developed on the island, and many conferences are held there. Vacationers from this and many other states go there to relax and enjoy the beauty of the sand and surf and sunshine. It is now valued at $50,000,000.

Herman Talmadge And The Minimum
Foundation Program of Education

Herman Talmadge ran against M. E. Thompson in the general election of 1948 for the remaining two years of the unexpired term of Eugene Talmadge. Talmadge, who got most of the state's unit votes, received 357,865 popular votes to Thompson's 312,035. He likewise defeated Thompson for the full four-year term that came next. He served as governor for six years, from January, 1948, to January, 1955.

Herman Talmadge was born August 9, 1913, at the Talmadge farm at Sugar Creek. After graduating from the University of Georgia, he practiced law with his father in Atlanta before going into the Navy as a volunteer in 1941. Talmadge served in the Pacific at Guadalcanal, Okinawa, and Tokyo Bay, during some of the most spectacular battles against the Japanese. He was in the service 52 months, emerging as a lieutenant-commander.

During his administration, the Minimum Foundation Program of Education was put into effect, financed by a three-cent sales tax. This was a far-reaching thing, and the greatest single boost that education had had in Georgia. Schools and colleges were greatly strengthened. Better teacher salaries, a state school-building program, a nine-month school term, better bus service for country children, and other advances brought within reach of every Georgia child the opportunity to get a good education.

Government services in many areas expanded and improved during the six years that Herman Talmadge was governor. When he left office, he spent the next few months in private law practice. With his wife, the former Betty Shingler of Ashburn, and their two sons, he lived on his farm at Lovejoy, near Atlanta. In 1956, he decided to become a candidate for United States Senator. Senator Walter F. George, who held the office, decided not to run again because of poor health that would handicap him in a race against the popular Talmadge. Talmadge was elected and joined Senator Richard B. Russell of Winder in representing Georgia in the United States Senate. Both their fathers had served Georgia with distinction, one as governor and the other as chief justice of the Georgia Supreme Court. Both of the sons had served as Georgia governors, and had been young governors with progressive ideas. Both left distinguished records. Talmadge had won the place his father never obtained: U.S. Senator from Georgia. He carried every county against former Governor M. E. Thompson, and got 376,000 votes.

Both Russell and Talmadge were in Congress, to counsel the South and help guide the country as the nation moved toward change in race relations and in the shift from rural to an urban civilization.

CHAPTER 59

HOW WORLD WAR II
INVOLVED GEORGIA

Georgians began to read of an Austrian house painter named Schickelgruber, later known as Adolph Hitler, who dreamed of even greater conquests than Kaiser Wilhelm.

Germany, still resentful of the Versailles peace treaty that laid a heavy burden on them for their war guilt, paid little attention to Hitler at first. With his little mustache, and his emotional rantings, he was a rather comic figure. He served a time in jail, and wrote his book *Mein Kampf,* "My Struggle." His infamous Nazi party started with only seven men. But gradually he gained power in Germany, rebuilt the army, and persuaded Germans that they should build their nation into new strength and conquer the world.

When he felt strong enough, he marched into small nations and took them over. In 1939, he and Stalin of Russia divided little Poland; but Poland had been guaranteed protection by England and France, so they went to war against Germany.

America tried, as in World War I, to remain neutral, but on December 7, 1941, Japan bombed the U.S. fleet at Pearl Harbor in Hawaii. Instantly Roosevelt was on the radio condemning Japan's treachery and calling December 7 "a day of infamy," and America was at war. Georgia was a part of it.

Georgians turned to war work, as they had in the First World War. Shipyards in Savannah and Brunswick made Liberty Ships; war factories turned out bombers.

More than 300,000 Georgians served in World War II;

6,754 of these lost their lives. Georgia furnished many leaders: General Edward P. King, leader of the forces on Bataan; Colonel Robert Lee Scott of the China air forces, who later wrote *God Is My Co-Pilot;* General Courtney Hodges, who led the forces across the Rhine; Admiral J.H. Towns, who commanded the Pacific Fleet's air force; Rear Admiral W. A. Ashford, commander of the carrier *Midway;* General Lucius Clay, military governor of the Occupation Zone in Germany after the war, and many others. Congressman Carl Vinson was chairman of the Naval Affairs Committee of the House. (He was later to be chairman of the Armed Services Committee of the House, while Senator Richard B. Russell became chairman of the Armed Services Committee of the Senate.) A nineteen-year-old bomber pilot named Carl Sanders serving in this war would, at thirty-six, become governor of Georgia.

Military installations were placed in Georgia, and officers and soldiers were trained at those already here. An important site was Fort Benning, the world's largest infantry school, which had been set up as Camp Benning in World War I. Fort MacPherson in Atlanta was also already a permanent post. So were Camp Gordon at Augusta, and Camp Stewart at Hinesville. The Navy set up some of its training operations at the University of Georgia. The army had more training fields in Georgia than in any other state except Texas.

Georgia buzzed with the activity of workers getting planes and other things ready for the fighters in Europe and elsewhere. The Bell Bomber Plant at Marietta brought 20,000 workers to the site; in Macon, another 15,000 were working at Warner-Robins.

President Roosevelt had been elected for an unprecedented fourth term in 1944. No president had ever run
even for three terms before. He was widely loved and fiercely
hated; few were neutral about Roosevelt.

He had been to Yalta on the Black Sea to a conference
with Churchill and Stalin, accompanied by his daughter Anna.
When he returned to this country, he came to Warm Springs
to rest. His friends and neighbors there were shocked to see
how haggard he looked. But he worked doggedly on his speech
that was to open the United Nations, to be organized in San
Francisco within a few weeks.

He was sitting for his portrait which was being painted
by Madame Elizabeth Shoumatoff, on April 12, 1945, when
suddenly he put his hand to his head and said he had a
headache. In a few hours, he was dead.

On a green hillside less than a mile away, Warm
Springs friends were getting a barbecue ready for him at
the home of Mayor Frank W. Allcorn, Jr. In charge
was Ruth Stevens, who managed the Warm Springs hotel
and sometimes baked a nut cake for the President. Later,
she wrote a book about him titled *Hi Ya Neighbor,*
and still later became curator of the Warm Springs Museum
on the grounds of the Little White House. Newsmen came
with the tragic news that FDR was dead.

The nation mourned. Graham Jackson, an excellent
Negro musician who had often played for the President,
mournfully attuned his accordion to Dvorak's "Going

Home," as the long train pulled out of the Warm Springs station. Roosevelt was buried in his rose garden at Hyde Park. Vice-President Harry S. Truman of Missouri became president.

The Little White House Is Now A Shrine
In Memory Of FDR

Thousands of people from every state and from many foreign countries visit Warm Springs each year to see the Little White House and the nearby Warm Springs Foundation, both associated with the memory of President Franklin Delano Roosevelt.

Here, in the simple white cottage where he died, are his ship models, the wheel chair in which he sat, the leash for his little Scotch terrier, Fala, and the unfinished portrait for which he was sitting when he was fatally stricken. The artist presented it to the Little White House.

In the garage is the hand-driven car in which he drove himself around the country lanes of Meriweather County, up to Dowdell's Knob, and over the mountains. On the kitchen wall is the scrawl of Daisy Bonner, who cooked for him there in the simple, old-fashioned kitchen with its ice box and its old stove. She had penciled, "In this room Daisy Bonner cooked the first and last meals for the President Roosevelt." The last tray from which he ate breakfast, with the copy of the morning's *Atlanta Constitution* tucked into the side, is there in the Museum on the hill, among hundreds of other things associated with his years here. Scores of walking canes sent him by people from all over the nation and world are here. Stones from every state are along the walk up the hill. Former Mayor Frank W. Allcorn, Jr., who was host at the never-held barbecue, became manager of the Little White House.

Here have come many people, the famous and the unknown. Ralph Bellamy, the actor who starred in the play "Sunrise at Campobello," was here. John F. Kennedy, when he was a candidate for president, spoke from the front steps. Here, too, many a polio-crippled patient has found new hope. "If he could become President when he could not walk one step, I can manage my life, too," they think.

725

Warm Springs Rehabilitation Center

CHAPTER 61

WHAT ELSE WAS

HAPPENING IN GEORGIA ?

So much was going on during these years in Georgia! In 1936, a tornado struck Gainesville killing 200 people and doing millions of dollars worth of damage. Destructive storms hit other places, too, but Gainesville suffered the worst tragedy.

Many good books were being written by Georgians. Creative and talented people in many fields were winning national acclaim. Henry Sopkin was bringing the Atlanta Symphony Orchestra to great heights of distinction. Max Noah was developing an unsurpassed a capella choir at the Woman's College in Milledgeville. Hugh Hodgson of Athens was helping young people appreciate good music. The Emory Glee Club was singing before presidents and touring Europe. Drama was becoming more exciting, and little theaters were developing. Art was a real focus of interest, with Lamar Dodd of Athens, Marshall Daugherty of Macon and the talented artists and sculptors like George Beatie, Julian Harris and Steffen Thomas in Atlanta and others elsewhere drawing attention. Also beginning were local art shows, like that in the north Georgia mountains at Plum Nelly ("plum outa Tennessee and nelly outa Georgia") by Miss Fannie Mennen, a retired artist and teacher.

Art had a long history in Georgia. Raphael and Rembrandt Peale had a studio in Savannah. Edward Malbone, painter of miniatures, is buried in Colonial Park Cemetery. Samuel F.B. Morse, inventor of the telegraph and grandson of a Midway pastor, painted excellent portraits of wealthy planters in Charleston and Savannah. Savannah is a favorite haunt of many creative artists now, perhaps because of its picturesque waterfront and its interest in the cultural arts.

Tremendous changes were being made in economics, sociology, and education, but the most striking would be in where people lived: they were moving in off the farms by the thousands.

There Was A Renaissance In Writing

Georgia had some good writers from the first, but the entire nation was astonished when, during this era, the South began to blossom with writers whose writing was praised throughout the country, and often in Europe and elsewhere as well.

Georgia produced many of these, and among them were writers who won the Pulitzer Prize. This is a series of awards for excellence set up through the will of Joseph Pulitzer, the blind newspaper millionaire who was one of the men that owned Jekyll.

In 1934, Caroline Miller, then the wife of a high school principal at Baxley, won the Pulitzer fiction prize for her novel *Lamb In His Bosom,* a story of early settlers in south Georgia. Putting her three small boys in the back of a car, she rode around the countryside learning about the details of the region, and listening to the tales of the old settlers. By October her book — now in paperback — had sold 50,000 copies. Many more have been sold since. She later moved to North Carolina.

Gone with the Wind PUT GEORGIA IN WORLD HEADLINES

One of Georgia's best-selling writers of this era, curiously unfamiliar to many Georgians, was Frank Yerby, the Negro novelist who now lives abroad. Flannery O'Connor, whose short stories and novels of the grotesque in mankind had catapulted her to the ranks of the world-acclaimed, continued to write startlingly gripping literature. Her books *Wise Blood,* and *The Violent Bear It Away,* and her short stories in *A Good Man Is Hard To Find* drew consistently excellent reviews by the most perceptive literary critics. She lived at Andalusia, a farm near Milledgeville, and died there in 1964. Some consider her the greatest of Georgia's writers.

Carson McCullers, a Georgian from Columbus who now lives outside the state, already had many readers for her *The Heart Is a Lonely Hunter, Reflections In A*

Golden Eye, Clock Without Hands and *The Square Root of Wonderful.* She won a whole new Georgia audience with her short story that became a drama, *The Member Of The Wedding.* If there were Georgians who could not identify with the characters in *Ballad Of A Sad Cafe,* there were few in the state who did not feel a warm response to the twelve-year-old Frankie Adams and her little boy cousin John Henry, and the cook Bernice, played magnificently on Broadway and in the film by the Negro actress Ethel Waters. When the cook, sensing loneliness ahead and the growing up of her little charge, sang "His Eye Is On the Sparrow," Georgians knew the song because they had sung it in a thousand little churches.

Davenport Steward, a former newspaper reporter, was writing interesting historical fiction. Maggie Davis, a city girl who came from the North to live on a Georgia farm wrote *The Winter Serpent,* a Viking tale, and then *The Far Side Of Home,* a Civil War story that became the Book-of-the-Month of the Literary Guild in July, 1963.

Margaret Mitchell, the tiny, Georgia-born author of *Gone with the Wind,* wrote the big novel that made the War Between the States real to the world. Published in 1936 by Macmillan, it became an immediate best-seller and brought her the Pulitzer Prize. The world premiere in Atlanta drew huge crowds to see the picture, its author, and stars, the British actress Vivian Leigh, and the late Clark Gable. Miss Mitchell, a reporter for the *Atlanta Journal,* who was Mrs. John Marsh in private life, grew up listening to her family and their friends tell stories of the war and the days of the Reconstruction.

In 1963, a 25-year anniversary edition was published of the book that had been translated into 25 languages, had sold by millions all over the world, and had been made into a film. Ben Stahl, illustrating the anniversary edition, depicted Scarlett O'Hara as not beautiful but magnetic. Her driving will, her love of the land, her determination to survive seemed to explain much about why the South was indestructible. Southerners usually felt, however, that the gentler Melanie was more typical of the Southern woman of the war time. Tourists by the thousands came through

729

Atlanta wanting to see the author and to find Tara, the O'Hara home which never existed except in the book. Miss Mitchell herself died from injuries sustained on August 11, 1943, when she was hit by an off-duty taxi driver in his cab as she and her husband walked across her beloved Peachtree Street in Atlanta on their way to a movie. She died five days later at Grady Hospital, and was buried at Oakland Cemetery.

The Margaret Mitchell pavilion at Grady Hospital is named for her. An exhibit of her book, her portrait, and her typewriter are at the downtown library in Atlanta. A new biography of her was published in 1965. Her home has been torn down, but a marker on Peachtree Street in Atlanta tells where she lived in her youth.

GEORGIANS HAD LONG-RUN PLAYS ON BROADWAY

Of the four plays on Broadway in New York that have had the longest runs, two were written by Georgians. "Tobacco Road" by Erskine Caldwell ran for 3,182 performances, second only to Clarence Day's "Life With Father" which ran for 3,213, making it the longest run of all time there. The fourth longest-run play was also written by a Georgian. It was "Abie's Irish Rose," a comedy about the marriage of a Jewish boy and an Irish girl. It ran for 2,327 performances, and was written by Ann Nichols.

Lillian Smith of Clayton, who for years ran a girls' camp in Rabun County, was the author of the play "Strange Fruit," which ran for a time on Broadway. Miss Smith's books, including *Strange Fruit, Killers Of The Dream,* and others, were about the race problem, and this sometimes made her a controversial figure in her native state.

So was Erskine Caldwell, who grew up at Wrens, where his father was a minister and his mother a teacher of English. Caldwell had written *Tobacco Road, God's Little Acre,* and other books about the people who were sometimes derisively referred to as "po' white trash." Though appreciation of his work was slow to grow in Georgia, Caldwell attained world fame from his novels and plays.

730

The great playwright Eugene O'Neill took some of the money from his play "Mourning Becomes Electra" and built his first real home on Sea Island, on the Georgia coast. The house was green and white because those were cool colors on the hot sands by the sea. The house was designed by his wife, Carlotta, and they named it Casa Genotta, a combination of both of their nicknames: Gene and Lotta. They lived at the Cloisters until their house was ready.

Ilka Chase, the actress and writer, had suggested to O'Neill that he would like the Georgia coast. He was tired of the busy pressures of New York, and he wanted a place that was restful and beautiful. Mrs. O'Neill wrote to the O'Neill children, including Oona who had married the comedian Charlie Chaplin and lived in Switzerland, that they found Georgia's island warm and lovely. They liked the beautiful scenery of the island, as the British actress Fannie Kemble had liked it a hundred years before.

O'Neill worked on his plays in his study in the mornings at Sea Island, from 8:30 to 1:30, seven days a week. His study was designed like the captain's quarters of an old sailing vessel, with hand-hewn timbers. After lunch, he went driving around the island or down to the beach. He sent Ilka Chase a copy of "Mourning Becomes Electra" with the inscription, "To Ilka — who found our Blessed Isle for us — with profoundest gratitude. Eugene O'Neill." He wrote her that he and Carlotta had "become Georgia crackers and are going to remain so for the rest of our days, we hope." He said that he liked the Georgia people. It was here at Sea Island that he wrote his play "Days Without End."

But the restless O'Neill, who had never been long at home anywhere, finally decided to move away from Georgia. The summer of 1936 was very hot, and he disliked the hot weather as much as did Georgia's second royal governor, Henry Ellis. O'Neill did not like the snakes either, so he had all the shrubbery clipped close to the ground so that no snakes could hide under it.

His sons visited him at the island, but found him preoccupied and moody, as he was all his life. When he left Georgia in November, 1936, he and his wife went to Seattle,

Washington. He had swapped the Atlantic Ocean for the Pacific. There on the fir-treed slopes of the Olympic Mountains near Puget Sound not far from Mount Rainier, he built an English-style house. Later he built another near San Francisco. But no matter whether O'Neill was living in New York, on the quiet Georgia coast, in Washington, or in California, his heart was perpetually haunted and he never found a home for his restless spirit while he was alive upon this earth. He died November 27, 1953.

GEORGIA'S POETS WON ACCLAIM

Conrad Aiken, Byron Reece, and others were poets of whom the nation was becoming aware in this era. Young Ernest Hartsock, whom critics called a young Keats, died early, as did Keats, before all his 'songs' were written. Aiken, a native of Savannah, won a Pulitzer Prize in 1930. In recent years, he moved back to Savannah.

Reece, a shy north Georgia farmer, wrote quietly some of the greatest poems being written, but ahead of him lay a dark doom: he killed himself at forty years of age. Reece has been called "the Robert Frost of the South."

Georgia has had five poets laureate: Frank Stanton, Ernest Neal, Wightman Melton, Ollie Reeves, and Agnes Cochran Bramblett.

NEWSPAPER WRITERS GAINED NATIONAL READING

Ralph McGill, editor and later publisher of the *Atlanta Constitution*, won the Pulitzer Prize for editorial writing. After the Atlanta papers were acquired by the Cox organization, his column was run in other papers, and his readership became national. His stories about the South appeared in magazines such as the *Atlantic Monthly*, and his book on the South and Southerners was featured therein, besides being on the bookstands.

Mark Etheridge, a Mississippian who had edited the *Macon Telegraph* and married a reporter and author, Willie Snow of Guyton, also attained national stature. He went to Louisville as an editor and publisher, and later to edit other papers and teach journalism. Mrs. Etheridge wrote numerous books, both novels and books of humor. One of her novels, *Summer Thunder*, was about Oglethorpe, the founder of Georgia.

732

Don Carter of Plains, later of Atlanta, went to New York to work with the *Wall Street Journal*. He and his wife Caroline, a well-known photographer, built a home at Jekyll Island.

Medora Field Perkerson, who for years assisted her husband Angus in editing the *Atlanta Journal Magazine,* wrote books. One was filmed by Hollywood. Her various stories with Georgia settings and interesting old homes were titled *White Columns in Georgia,* and *Blood On Her Shoe* and *Who Killed Aunt Maggie?*

THERE WERE MANY OTHER GOOD WRITERS

There were so many writers producing interesting work during these years that it would be impossible to name them all. Georgia was rich in good writers. Edison Marshall and Berry Fleming were writing novels. Elizabeth Stephenson, an Atlanta librarian, was winning awards for her excellent biographies of Henry Adams, Henry James, and Lafcadio Hearn.

Vinnie Williams, who had moved to Thomson while her husband was in the army, was attaining prominence in the literary world with *Fruit Tramp, Walk Egypt,* and others. Nedra Tyre wrote strange and compelling mysteries of the human spirit. Genevieve Holden, whose husband, Charles Pou was political editor of the *Atlanta Journal,* wrote murder stories. Celestine Sibley, columnist for the *Atlanta Constitution,* was also writing good books. One was a murder mystery with a newspaper setting. Tommy Wadelton, an "army brat" flashed into fame for a time with *My Mother Is A Violent Woman* and *My Father Is A Quiet Man,* two charming volumes about two interesting people. They were stationed at Fort Oglethorpe, Georgia.

Dr. Lucian Lamar Knight, Georgia's official historian and founder of the Department of Archives and History, died in 1933. At his request, he was buried in Christ Churchyard on St. Simons. His daughter Mary became a newspaper reporter, and author of the book *On My Own.* She recounted many interesting experiences, and sometimes startling ones, which she had in the course of her duties. One was witnessing death on the guillotine in Paris.

Besides the epic filming of Margaret Mitchell's *Gone With The Wind,* with its spectacular burning of Atlanta, other Georgia books were made into movies by Hollywood. Directors, writers, actors and actresses from Georgia were there doing other productions. Nunnally Johnson of Columbus and Lamar Trotti of Macon were well-known writers and directors. Charles Coburn of Savannah, Miriam Hopkins of Bainbridge, Joanne Woodward of Thomasville, and Melvin Douglas of Macon were only some of the Georgians acting in Hollywood films.

A ROBERT BURNS COTTAGE WAS IN ATLANTA

Atlantans who appreciate the poetry of Robert Burns of Scotland built a granite replica of his birthplace at Alloway Place, Atlanta, near the Confederate Memorial Home. The Burns Club meets there.

The cornerstone was laid on the poet's birthday. Burns was born on January 25, 1759. This date is always celebrated with a dinner by the Burns Club at the Burns Cottage, which was opened on that date in 1911. A heavy oak door in the center opens into the banquet room. In the original cottage, there was a stall for the cows! The Atlanta cottage had a thatched roof at first, but mice gnawed it, and a slate roof was put on. A marble bust of the poet is in a fireplace niche, and pictures of him at his desk are there. There are scenes of "Brig O'Doon" and a plaque of the Burns cottage in Ayrshire. Framed there are two copies, one written in Celtic and the other printed, of the Scottish Declaration of Independence. Carlyle's essay on Burns lies on a table. There is pressed heather, and daisies from the grave of Burns' beloved "Highland Mary."

The Burns lovers read or sing his lively songs and poems. They begin their dinners with the familiar Scots' grace:

"Some hae meat and cannot eat,
Some hae nain that want it,
We hae meat and we can eat
And sae the Laird be thankit."

They end with his "Auld Lang Syne."

734

Georgians Became Famous In Sports

Georgia took much pride through these years in many national and worldwide records being attained by Georgians in the various sports. They reflected credit on the state and brought Georgia into world headlines.

ROBERT TYRE JONES, JR., BECAME THE WORLD'S GREATEST GOLFER

By the time Bob Jones of Georgia was twenty-eight years old, he had won all the world's golf titles that were important to win and become the greatest golfer the world had ever known.

It was fitting that such a champion should come from Georgia because it was Georgia's Scotch Highlanders at Darien who brought golf to the New World in 1734. The first golf course was in Savannah.

Jones was even more popular in England and Scotland than in his native Georgia. The whole world called him "Bobby," a name he hated. He won the four great golf championships of the world: the United States amateur and open and the British amateur and open, all by 1930. He came home and married his longtime sweetheart, and settled down to practice law in Atlanta. He discovered that he had an old spinal injury, and he became a crippled man who learned to live with pain.

He has been for years the focus of the Master's Tournament and the great golf center in Augusta. Here his

friend President Dwight Eisenhower, whose candidacy he did much to promote, came to play golf often. Here was built "Mamie's Cabin," named in honor of Mrs. Eisenhower. Eisenhower painted a portrait of Bob Jones, the greatest golfer. Another portrait is in New York's Hall of Golf.

Alexa Stirling of Georgia also attained fame as a golfer. Among her records were the winning of the Women's National Amateur Golf Championship annually during the years 1916 through 1920. She later married a Canadian and moved to Canada, returning to visit Georgia relatives sometimes. Her sister, Nora Stirling, became a well-known playwright and author in New York.

THE BASEBALL CHAMPIONS WERE ACCLAIMED

Baseball, long the nation's favorite sport, had Georgia champions. Among them were Ty Cobb and Jackie Robinson. "Babe" Ruth, though not a Georgian, had married a Georgia girl from Athens, and Georgians therefore took an added pride in his world fame.

TY COBB OF GEORGIA BECAME FAMOUS IN BASEBALL

Tyrus Raymond Cobb of Royston, Georgia, became one of the sports world's most famous personalities. He is in baseball's Hall of Fame. He was the son of Professor William Herschel Cobb, mathematics teacher, school principal, landowner, newspaper editor, and state senator. Professor Cobb did not want his son to become a professional baseball player; he wanted him to go to West Point. But after young Cobb seemed so determined about it, his father supported him in his efforts to become one of baseball's greats. The boy tramped sometimes 20 to 30 miles through Georgia woods and along country roads to help keep in good physical condition for the game he wanted to play.

While he was playing with a team at Anniston, Alabama, he attracted the attention of the sports reporter, Grantland Rice, who began to write about him. Cobb went up in baseball until he was earning $50,000 a year. This was the highest salary paid in the big leagues at that time. He bought Coca-Cola stock and General Motors stock, and eventually became a millionaire.

He played 2,805 games, and was noted as a "stealer" of bases. In his career he "stole" 866 bases, "stealing" 96 in a single season. He became manager of the Detroit team. He had a running feud with Babe Ruth. After he retired, he moved to the West Coast.

Many regard Cobb as the greatest baseball player who ever lived. When he died, he left funds for the Cobb Educational Foundation, to provide scholarships for young people in Georgia who needed college money. He also built a hospital at Royston in memory of his parents.

In June, 1964, Fred Haney, general manager of the Los Angeles Angels baseball team, wrote of Cobb in the series "My Most Unforgettable Character" in *Readers Digest*.

Jackie Robinson, who was born at Cairo, Georgia, on January 13, 1919, became the first Negro to win fame as a player in the big leagues. He was first with the Kansas City Monarchs, a Negro team, but manager Branch Rickey hired him for the Brooklyn Dodgers. He was traded in 1956 to the New York Giants, and was named to the Hall of Fame in 1962.

The Man From Choestoe

Dr. Mauney D. Collins, a native of the Choestoe region of Union County near Blairsville, became state superintendent of schools the year Roosevelt became president. He was to serve in that office twenty-five years, longer than any other man. He resigned in 1958, because of the serious illness of his wife, who died shortly thereafter. Dr. Claude Purcell was named as his successor.

Dr. Collins had worked hard for his education. He graduated from Mercer, and had degrees or honorary degrees from many other colleges. He started his teaching career in his native county, teaching eighty-one children in a one-room school.

Once he taught thirteen months in one year. The school month was twenty days, and the school term sometimes, in some places, only two or three months. When he ended the school term in one place, he started it in another, teaching also on Saturday. Between July, 1905, and July, 1906, he had taught thirteen school months. He was also a minister, preaching every Sunday. Once he married eight couples in one day. This event was reported by Margaret

Mitchell, then a reporter on the *Atlanta Journal*.

Many things were achieved during his years in the office: better salaries for teachers, more school buildings, the free textbook program, expansion of vocational education, the school lunch program, the longer school term, and the beginning of Georgia's educational television network.

His resignation came on January 13, 1958. He had always jested that thirteen was his lucky number. He had made thirteen successful races in politics. He had also been a farmer, newspaper editor, and merchant. He was Georgia's thirteenth chief state school officer.

Two state trade and vocational schools were set up to train Georgians for jobs. At Clarkesville, the North Georgia Trade and Technical School was established at the site of the old "A & M" school, which was one of those established by legislation of Governor Terrell's administration early in the century. Later Columbia University in New York

Dr. M.D. Collins

carried on experiments in rural education at this school and, during the Roosevelt days, the National Youth Administration had been there. In 1944, this became the site for the state school and new buildings and dormitories and shops began to make this an important place for Georgians who wanted to learn how to get and hold good jobs.

The South Georgia Trade and Vocational School was put at the site of old Souther Field near Americus, an air school where Charles Lindbergh, first pilot to solo non-stop across the Atlantic, had once been stationed. This school, like the one at Clarkesville, offered many courses, but became well known especially for its courses in diesel engines and auto mechanics. Both schools were operated by the State Department of Education through its division of vocational education.

What Was Happening
In Higher Education

Colleges established in the nineteenth century, Mercer, Emory, Wesleyan, Agnes Scott, Women's College, Tift, Brenau, Shorter, Lagrange Tech and Oglethorpe among them, increased and prospered. Georgia was becoming a more educated state. The University, with many branches, was reorganized into one system in 1931, as Abraham Baldwin and his colleagues had had in mind when the charter was granted in 1785, and had a single board of regents instead of trustees for each school. Columbia Theological Seminary, organized at Lexington in 1828, was moved to Columbia, South Carolina, in 1850, and back to Decatur, Georgia in 1927. Emory, aided with $8,000,000 of Coca-Cola money from the Candlers, spread out from Oxford to Decatur in 1915, and began in 1953 to admit women. Junior colleges spread over the state; some became four-year colleges. A Science Center for the University and a nuclear reactor for Tech helped gear Georgia to the space age.

More graduate work was going on throughout the state. Better research was surging out of the laboratories into action in utilitarian products that improved living standards. Georgia State College, started in an old downtown garage in Atlanta, was increasing with dynamic energy and spreading over a big area. It promised to become one of America's great city colleges.

739

Most important of all, the Southern Regional Education Board was linking together the southeastern states in an effort to provide stronger and better education throughout the South. What one state could not provide, another state could, and interstate cooperation and financing was making the South a strong educational center. Atlanta University, a cluster of Negro colleges that also admitted white students, was strengthened by well-wishers with money, such as the Rockefellers, and was commanding increased respect for its curriculum and its faculty. Dr. Rufus Clements, its president, was a member of the Atlanta City Board of Education.

Paine College in Augusta celebrated its semi-centennial in 1933.

Oglethorpe Established
The Crypt Of Civilization

In 1935, the late Dr. Thornwell Jacobs, then president of Oglethorpe University, had a "crypt of civilization" sealed up under Phoebe Hearst Hall there. In it were placed many artifacts of our time and culture. It is to be opened in another century.

This college, Sidney Lanier's alma mater, was strengthening itself into a vital part of the educational picture. Strong leaders were moving in, distinguished programs were being put into action, and the college, concentrating on doing what it had resources to do exceptionally well, was moving into a good future.

Colleges such as Agnes Scott continued to draw students from many states who were attracted by its high standards and its exceptional program. Here for many years Robert Frost came annually and read his poems and talked with the students. A working arrangement was launched by which this college and Emory, and others, could share facilities and resources. Emory and Agnes Scott, both near Decatur, enriched each other immeasurably, not only in social life, but in the sharing of such visitors as Robert Frost, Arnold Toynbee, Margaret Mead, and others.

740

The Trappist Monks And Their Abbey

Trappist monks of the Benedictine Order came to build a magnificent abbey and monastery near Conyers in Rockdale County. Near land once owned by a film star named Colleen Moore who once built and furnished a $500,000 doll house full of miniature treasures, the abbey has risen there on the Georgia countryside. In the silence, the Trappists, who rarely speak because they have taken vows of silence, have hammered and shaped their wondrous structure to the glory of God and the good of man. The silent, brown-cowled monks look like figures out of the Middle Ages, studying, praying, working, all as silent as the falling snow.

It was on a March day in 1944, when the chill winds blew, that a little band of monks came down from Gethsemane, Kentucky, to start the monastery and abbey of Our Lady of the Holy Ghost in the rural Protestant community in Georgia. Their very appearance was strange to Georgians. They moved into a whitewashed cow barn, the only building on the barren acres, evicting two cows and twenty mules. Within the next few years, they collected a million dollars' worth of materials, worked their fields, and labored with love to erect here among the brown fields the glistening white church to the glory of God. It has vaulted ceilings, Gothic arches, stained glass windows, and a great statue of St. Benedict on the side wall.

Georgians became good neighbors of the gentle monks. Growing gradually accustomed to the strange sight of silent men hammering at their building or toiling in the fields, Georgia began to take a proprietary pride in the project. Many gave materials and money, as did people throughout the nation. The state agricultural experts advised them against row crops, which depleted their soil, and advised more dairy and barnyard produce. The monks began to send their eggs and milk and bread to Atlanta and elsewhere. Once they gave away a cow to some neighbors in the Georgia countryside who had a misfortune.

A Georgian Started It All

The reason that the monastery now stands there in the Georgia countryside was that a Georgian was proud of his state. The Right Reverend Dom Frederick Dunn from Atlanta was the head of the Gethsemane abbey in Kentucky when the plan was started to build another one. He thought of his native Georgia. He was the son of a printer and had grown up in Atlanta. The monks looked at several places, and they finally decided on the site that he had urged, the red, rolling hills of Georgia near Honey Creek.

The monks cut timber from their trees to build the first buildings in which they lived. They also built a rustic chapel. There they assembled nine times a day, beginning at two in the morning, to pray. Their last prayer is at six in the evening. After that, they retire. They do not have newspapers, radio, television, or other diversions of the world. They are men who have retired from the world to pray for its sorrows and contemplate its salvation. They do have contact men, but the monks themselves live in silence and separation. They emerge into the world to vote. After John Fitzgerald Kennedy, who was of the Catholic faith, was elected president, some of their neighboring Protestant pastors came to get information. One said to the monastery official allowed to speak to the outside world, "I want to get more information about the faith of my President."

The monks had to have some lay help in the building of their great structures. But they patiently did most of the work themselves: designing and making the stained glass

windows, laying the terrazzo floor, creating the beautiful gardens, lifting the rafters into place, polishing the marble, laying the blocks — everything except such professional things as drawing the architectural design (they even altered this) and planning the steel structuring.

Silently they go about their work and prayer. They sleep on straw mattresses in bare cells in their clothes. They have no possessions. They eat only vegetables and brown bread. There are men from many places and many lives: a golf pro, an airplane pilot, a Wall Street tycoon, a politician, and a former Marine. They came from many stormy seas into this port of calm.

The bread that the monks bake is from the same recipe as that used by the Cistercian Order since its beginning in the year 1098!

The full name of the order to which these Benedictine-Cistercian monks belong is Cistercians of the Strict Observance, from the original monastery founded at Citeaux in France. The word "Trappist" refers to a reform in the order that was once made at LaTrappe, an abbey in Europe.

How The People Were Making A Living

A change that was to revolutionize Georgia politics and government was coming about gradually before 1950. People were swarming in off the farms to the cities. In 1949, Georgia became a predominantly manufacturing state for the first time instead of a predominantly agricultural state. Much land had been put into the soil bank. The government was paying farmers not to grow certain crops. Besides this, farms were being mechanized. Fewer farmers could produce even more food. There were no longer enough jobs on the farm for everybody who had been working there.

Georgia had lost at least a third of its farms and was to lose more. In 1916, farmers in Georgia had planted 5,000,000 acres in cotton. During the fifth decade, this would diminish to 350,000 acres, with 450,000 more acres of cotton land in the soil bank.

In 1940, there were still 1,500,000 Georgians living on

farms. By 1960, only 400,000 would be left there. Yet Georgia's 1940 farm income of $140,000,000 would rise by 1960 to $800,000,000. With mechanization and better farming methods resulting from research, fewer farmers could grow more food. Cotton was still a big money crop. So was tobacco, but there was also much money coming in to Georgia farmers from peanuts, corn, better hogs and cattle, dairy products, chickens, truck farm vegetables, pecans, peaches and other crops. Some of the best Farmers Markets in the world were helping market crops more efficiently, too. And Georgia was rapidly becoming a leader in pulpwood products.

MORE INDUSTRIES WERE COMING IN

New industries were coming in. Most of them were locating near cities, though some started small plants in the rural areas. Industries already in the state, such as textiles, oldest of them all, were expanding.

In 1915, Henry Ford in Atlanta, opened an assembly plant where 600 people were hired to assemble 100 cars a day for the southeast. In 1945, the Atlanta Ford Plant opened at Hapeville and, by 1957, covered a million square feet and was one of the major automobile assembly plants in the nation. Here, too, was built the Falcon, first compact car to be built in the South. Ford set up the Ford Marketing Institute in Atlanta, where about 2,500 men train for their jobs each year.

General Motors was also assembling cars in Atlanta by 1927. Chrysler set up a $2,000,000 Training Center where its employees from thirteen southeastern states came. Buick-Oldsmobile-Pontiac opened at Doraville in 1947. Others are also in Georgia. Many supporting industries, such as U.S. Rubber, have come in the wake of these industries. The John Smith Company is the oldest car dealer in the metropolitan area. Established in 1869 to make fine carriages, it made its last carriage in 1906, and turned, like many other such firms, to selling the new cars that had appeared on the horizon in America.

The automobile industry has Georgia payrolls that amount to millions, and they spend other millions buying products from Georgia dealers for use in their business.

Georgia was making many products, even in the first

years of the century, and as time went on, more and more of its money came from products manufactured in Georgia. Factory-made products, from cradles to caskets, including automobiles, clothes, and hundreds of other products, added to the state's prosperity.

The Associated Industries of Georgia had a saying, "What Georgia makes, makes Georgia." The State Chamber of Commerce was vigorously presenting to the nation the advantages Georgia offered business and industry. So was the state itself, through its trade and industrial agencies.

From baseball bats to bombers, Georgia was manufacturing things. The huge airplane factories at Lockheed in Marietta made great silver planes that flew around the earth. Hundreds of talented and skillful people came to Georgia to work in these plants

GEORGIA MINERALS — AND THE ROAD PAVED WITH AMETHYSTS

Georgia had begun to develop its natural resources. Among these were minerals. Georgia had about twenty-five kinds of minerals that would eventually bring in some $100,000,000 a year. Such minerals were marble, coal, flagstone, feldspar, manganese, kyanite, copper, chromite, bentonite, corundum, olivine, tripoli, vermiculite, barytes, bauxite, iron, fuller's earth, limestone, mica, sand and gravel, slate, granite, and talc. Georgia's clays had been exported since early days. Later, Georgia clay went into the coating of many fine papers used to produce magazines. Millions of bricks, made in Georgia, began to be shipped all over the world.

Of all the minerals, marble was the most famous and valuable of those that came out of the Georgia earth.

Granite became more and more important and profitable. The biggest quarries were around Elberton in northeast Georgia.

Many semi-precious stones were found in Georgia, and gem-hunting became a popular hobby. In the Georgia museum on the fourth floor of the State Capitol in Atlanta is an exhibit of these Georgia minerals, including exquisitely colored amethysts. Now and then a Georgian tells a tourist, "We even have a road paved with amethyst." This is partly true.

Near Swords, Georgia, there is a road paved with a sparkling stone that has an amethystine content.

The Georgia gold on the capitol dome, brought down by covered wagon from Dahlonega, is always pointed out again. Dahlonega has Gold Rush Day annually, and is preserving as a museum the old courthouse, built during Gold Rush days. Hundreds still stop to pan gold in the little town.

What Was Ahead

Mid-century marked the last years before the decree of the U.S. Supreme Court — which would be handed down on May 17, 1954 — would change a long-time way of life, affecting education, politics and government, social relations, and every other facet of living in the South.

Change was at hand. But much of it was already emerging, even before the court decree, and not all of it was related to the racial question. Much was the result of the new technology, especially that which mechanized farms.

Ahead was what many people felt was the most interesting period of Georgia's entire history: from mid-century to now.

GEORGIA NOW

UNIT 12

CHAPTER 62

GEORGIA IN

THE SPACE AGE

As Georgia moved into the last half of the twentieth century, many changes were coming to the state. Some, such as the changing patterns in racial relations, were convulsive and painful. But most of these people concerned with the changes were doing their best to meet them with courage, intelligence and dignity. Georgians were fighting in Viet Nam, as they had in all wars in which their country had been involved from the beginning.

The tremendous farm-to-city movement was causing changes in government, such as the disappearance of the county unit system and the redistricting of political units. The state now had over four million people. The state was more urban than rural. This in itself was a startling change for a state that had once been one of the world's great crop-producing areas, and almost wholly rural when the century began.

Industry was coming to Georgia in great numbers. Space-age enterprises were beginning to locate in Georgia. Education was moving to meet the new developments. Georgia was establishing vocational-technical schools to sharpen the skills of Georgians who would work in these industries, and was creating more colleges. The state and private enterprise were making organized motions toward northern capital and even to European industries to consider trade with Georgia. Delegations from Georgia visited foreign countries to present the state's advantages and many foreign countries had established consulting agencies in Georgia.

Georgia-made products were being marketed all over the earth. The colleges and universities were joining with business and industry to do research in depth to point the way to new or better products that could be made in Georgia, or natural resources that could be developed to greater advantage. Georgia's per capita income, which was $1,610 in 1960, is expected to be at least $2,353 in 1976, a 46 percent increase. The National Planning Board predicts that by 1996, there will be 1,820,000 Georgians employed. There were 1,309,000 in 1960. Most of the increase will be in manufacturing.

Georgians were coming to a sharper awareness that their greatest natural resource was in the minds and talents of their children. There were more than a million boys and girls enrolled in 1,944 public schools in grades one through twelve, and movements were being planned to set up junior colleges, and to get senior colleges and universities ready for the tremendous influx that the 1970's would bring.

The 1954 decision of the United States Supreme Court had affected Georgia, whose Negro citizens, almost a third of the population, were pressing for more nearly equal rights in education, housing, government, and public facilities. Negroes were elected to the Georgia legislature for the first time since 1907. A number of Negroes had already been serving as members of local school boards in Georgia. Negro children were being admitted to the schools, either by court order or by voluntary action of local school authorities. The Eighty-eighth Congress passed a bill about the constitutional rights of Negroes. The action of Congress came almost exactly ten years after the Supreme Court decision.

Tourists were becoming big business, and the state was developing its attractions and recreation centers, and Georgia citizens themselves were learning more about their state and enjoying their lakes and parks.

It was a time of tremendous change in Georgia. The space age had come and the world was growing smaller by the minute. Georgians determined to be ready for it.

One of the few unchanging things in Georgia was

the state's geographic center: a spot in Twiggs County, eighteen miles southeast of Macon.

The Census Tells An Interesting Story

Of the more than three billion people living on this earth this minute, over four million of them live in Georgia.

Population experts predict that by the year 2000 A.D., there will be six billion persons living on this globe. Georgia's population in 2000 A.D. is estimated at 8,203,-000; that of the United States, which is now less than 200,000,000, is expected to be 380,000,000 by 2000 A.D.

The 1970 population of Georgia will, according to expert estimates, be 4,658,000 by that year. By 1976, it is expected to reach 5,500,000.

The official census is taken every ten years. That practice was started in 1790. This is the way Georgia's population has grown since that year:

1790----------82,548	1880--------1,542,180
1800----------162,686	1890--------1,837,353
1810----------252,433	1900--------2,216,331
1820----------340,985	1910--------2,609,121
1930----------516,823	1920--------2,895,824
1840----------691,392	1930--------2,908,521
1850----------906,185	1940--------3,123,723
1860--------1,057,286	1950--------3,444,578
1870--------1,184,109	1960--------3,943,116

(Although the official census is taken only every ten years, reliable estimates are made for the years in between, for government, business, and others who need statistics for planning. By 1962, Georgia's population was 4,097,500. In 1965, it was 4,224,700.

The important part of the census story for Georgia was that which showed where the people were living. In 1950, the census indicated that thousands had moved off the farms since 1940. The people continued to move into the cities. By 1960, over half of all Georgians lived in fifteen counties, and 53 of the state's 159 counties had fewer than 7,000 people in each.

The 1950 census showed that 3,444,578 people lived in Georgia. By 1960, this had increased 14.5 percent to 3,943,116. Of these, 55.3 percent or 2,190,236 were living in urban centers, and only 1,762,880 were living in rural areas. The urban segment has increased 529.4 percent since 1900, when it was 15.6 percent of the population. In the whole world, only 50 percent were in urban centers, but sociologists were predicting that by 1980 this would rise to 70 percent.

The 1960 census figures showed that the Georgia people were of these races: of the 3,943,116 people living in the state that year, 1,125,893 were non-white. The non-whites were in these categories: Negro 1,122,596; Indians, 749; Japanese, 885; and Chinese, 686. Of Georgia's 1960 population, 25,300 were born in foreign lands.

Georgia is not crowded in many places. There is room to live and enjoy the out-of-doors. Gertrude Stein once said America has more places where nobody is than where somebody is. Georgians have wide expansive space, with only 70 people per square mile, in contrast with New Jersey, for instance, which has 830 people per square mile. The United States, with great open spaces in the West, averages 52 people per square mile. Alaska, the newest state, has less than 1 person per square mile.

Georgians continue to move. Every day over 150 change their places of residence, and half of these move out of Georgia, but many people from outside move in.

HOW OLD ARE GEORGIA'S PEOPLE?

The 1960 census revealed that the largest group among Georgia's four million people are school students between the ages of seven and sixteen. This group constitutes more than a million of Georgia's total population.

The official breakdown of Georgia's age groups is as follows: 12 percent are under five years old; 22 percent are between five and fourteen; 15 percent are between fifteen and twenty-four; 13 percent are between twenty-five and thirty-four; 13 percent are between thirty-five and forty-four; 11 percent are between forty-five and fifty-four; 7 percent are between fifty-five and sixty-four; and 7 percent are sixty-five years or older.

CHAPTER 63

WHAT IS HAPPENING
IN GOVERNMENT
AND POLITICS

When the last half of the century began, Herman Talmadge was still governor of Georgia, and the president in the White House was still Harry S. Truman. Talmadge continued as governor until 1955, when Marvin Griffin succeeded him. Truman's administration ended in 1952, when he was succeeded as president by General Dwight D. Eisenhower.

Griffin was succeeded in office by Ernest Vandiver, a quiet, north Georgia lawyer who had married a niece of Senator Richard B. Russell. After Vandiver came Carl Sanders to be governor from 1962 to January, 1967.

In the presidency, Eisenhower was followed by young John Fitzgerald Kennedy. Georgia remained Democratic in its presidential voting, and supported Adlai Stevenson in his two campaigns. In 1964, however, its electoral college vote went to the Republican candidate, Barry Goldwater.

State Government And The
Governors Of These Years

No governors in the history of Georgia had harder problems to lead their people in solving than the governors who were in office after mid-century. Herman Talmadge, who had served ably in the office for six years, ended his administration in January, 1955. He stayed in private law practice and farming for two years, and was elected to the United States Senate.

EDITOR MARVIN GRIFFIN BECAME GOVERNOR OF GEORGIA

In 1955, a south Georgia editor defeated seven men and a woman in a campaign that made him governor of Georgia. He was Samuel Marvin Griffin, editor of the Bainbridge *Post-Searchlight,* just as his father, Pat Griffin, was earlier. Griffin had been born in Bainbridge on September 4, 1907. In 1929, he was graduated from The Citadel in South Carolina, and four years later he was back in Bainbridge editing his father's paper with his brother, Cheney Griffin, who became mayor of Bainbridge and member of the Georgia General Assembly. Marvin Griffin himself was elected to the legislature in 1935. In 1940, he was executive secretary to the governor, Ed Rivers. Then he served three years in the United States Army, and was in three of the big battles in the South Pacific. He came out as a lieutenant colonel, and went back into politics in Georgia. In the Ellis Arnall administration he became adjutant-general of Georgia. He supported Herman Talmadge in the three-cornered fight for the governor's office. Griffin was elected lieutenant-governor in 1950; four years later, he was elected governor.

He put a great deal of money into education: a science center at the University of Georgia, the nuclear reactor at Georgia Tech, and a $700-a-year raise for the public school teachers.

A dramatic incident of his administration was the arrival of the Gold Wagon Train from Dahlonega, driven by citizens, bringing the 43 ounces of gold that made the dome of the State Capitol a beautiful, shining landmark on the Georgia scene.

Governor and Mrs. Griffin carried with them to the Governor's Mansion the shadow of an old sorrow. In the Winecoff Hotel fire in Atlanta in 1947, they had lost their only daughter. Among the 117 people who died in that catastrophe was a group of high school students who had come to a youth group meeting in Atlanta. She was one of them. They also had a son, Sam, who became a student at Georgia Tech, and later returned to Bainbridge.

Griffin went back to Bainbridge when his term of office was over. He had built up a highly enthusiastic group of followers throughout Georgia. He ran for governor again in 1962, but he was defeated by a young legislator, Carl Sanders of Augusta.

THE 1954 RACIAL DECISION THAT SHOOK THE SOUTH

On May 17, 1954, the United States Supreme Court in Washington handed down a decision that was to end a long-time way of life in Georgia and the rest of the South.

The Supreme Court had in 1896 upheld the "separate, but equal" plan under which southern states had provided separate schools, transportation, and public facilities for white and Negro races. The case was known as Plessy vs. Ferguson. In 1887, Florida had passed the first "Jim Crow" law requiring railroads to transport Negroes either in separate cars or in partitioned sections of white cars. In 1891, in New Orleans, eighteen Negro men had formed a committee to test this law. Homer Plessy, entering the white section of a railroad car on June 7, 1892, was arrested and tried so that this law could be tested. Negroes believed the law to be in conflict with the Constitution of the United States, especially with the thirteenth and fourteenth amendments. The "separate, but equal" law re-

755

mained on the books, however, upheld by the court, from its decision on May 18, 1896, to the decision of the Supreme Court on May 17, 1954. A curious little footnote to the two decisions was this: one justice, named John Marshall Harlan, on the bench in 1896, dissented from the court's verdict. His grandson, Justice John Harlan, was one of the 1954 justices on the Supreme Court bench when the "separate, but equal" rule was ended. The grandfather in his dissent had said, "The arbitrary separation of citizens on the basis of race... is a badge of servitude wholly inconsistent with their civil freedom and equality before the law." But neither the other justices nor the majority of the people in the South saw it that way.

"A GOVERNOR OF GEORGIA WAS BORN YESTERDAY"

On July 4, 1918, Samuel Ernest Vandiver, Sr., a business man and plantation owner in Franklin County, was mingling with the holiday crowd at Lavonia, Georgia. He said, "A future governor of Georgia was born yesterday." He was right. His son, Samuel Ernest Vandiver, Jr., had been born at Canon, a village in the county where the Vandivers lived. In January, 1959, he became the governor of Georgia.

After he went to Darlington, a private school at Rome, he graduated from the University of Georgia in 1940 with a law degree. Then he went to war as an Army Air Corps fighter pilot. When he came back home in 1945, he became mayor of Lavonia, where he had grown up. He was the youngest mayor in the state, only twenty-seven years old. He moved to Winder to practice law, and married Betty Russell, niece of United States Senator Richard B. Russell. He managed the campaign of Herman Talmadge for governor; he was appointed adjutant general, and directed Georgia's Civil Defense program. People all over the state became familiar with his name on the road signs and posters of the Civil Defense plan. He was elected president of the National Civil Defense organization, and was a major general in the National Guard.

He was elected lieutenant governor in 1945. The new Constitution had set up the office. In 1958, he ran for governor and was elected. He came to the job in a time of crisis. The 1954 decision of the United States Supreme

Court, which would integrate schools, was causing a ferment in Georgia thought. At first, Vandiver, who had grown up in Georgia and shared the feelings of many Georgians that this could not be, set his mind and plans against the matter. When Federal Judge W.A. Bootle ruled on January 6, 1961, that two young Negroes, Charlayne Hunter and Hamilton Holmes must be admitted to the University of Georgia, Vandiver, with courage that was acclaimed by many Georgians, reversed his stand rather than see the schools of Georgia closed. The state could not bear a burden of ignorance, he said. He guided the legislature as they enacted legislation to meet the changed conditions.

Vandiver, regarded by Georgians as a man of great personal honesty and integrity, urged the legislature to take back control of Georgia's purse strings. Governors, he said, had had too much financial control. Of every $4 expended in 25 years, $1 had been spent by executive order. He recommended, and they set up, a modern budget bureau to evolve a continuing financial plan for capital and recurring expenditures. Among the achievements of his administration were increased money for the public schools, teachers' salaries, bus drivers' salaries, more money for hospitals and highways, parks, and public buildings. A quiet man whose speeches were never spectacular, Vandiver was respected for the calmness and courage with which he met the worst crisis that his state had faced in many years.

Governor and Mrs. Vandiver took a special interest in the mentally ill patients at the state hospital in Milledgeville. They visited the hospital, and their visit led to a statewide renewal of interest in these patients and many benefits for them. Besides more state money, the patients benefited by public funds raised to build a "chapel of all faiths" there. Governor and Mrs. Vandiver continued to lead an annual motor parade at Christmas to carry thousands of Christmas gifts to patients at the hospital. He planned to run for governor again in 1966, but ill health prevented.

HOW VANDIVER FACED THE INTEGRATION CRISIS

A statewide committee, headed by John Sibley, an Atlanta banker, held hearings throughout Georgia, giving citizens of both races an opportunity to express their thoughts and feelings about the crisis that confronted them. The people wanted to keep their schools open. They were loathe to change a way of life to which generations of living had accustomed them, but they knew that their children must not be allowed to grow up without an education.

How The County Unit System Disappeared

Georgia's county unit system of voting in primary elections was struck down by the federal courts in 1962. A three-judge federal court, on May 28, 1962, declared it unconstitutional. The United States Supreme Court, in an eight-to-one vote, decreed that there can be no legal county unit system.

This system had been in operation most of the time by the political parties since 1877. It was enacted into law by the Neill Primary Act in 1917, but it was still used only in the primaries or "pre-elections." The people voted down a proposal to extend it to the general elections.

This is the way the county unit system worked. Each county had twice as many unit votes as it had representatives in the lower house of the legislature. The eight largest counties, which had three representatives each, had six unit votes each. The next thirty largest counties, with two representatives each, had four unit votes each. The remaining counties, with one representative each, had two unit votes each.

The small rural counties had many leaders who pointed out that the county unit system guaranteed the rural voters a fair voice in their government and kept undue power out of the hands of "city political machines." On the other hand, many who opposed the county unit system pointed out that it was undemocratic, since it made the vote of a citizen in a small county count many times more than that of a citizen who voted in the city. Fulton County, with 566,326 people according to the 1960 census, had six unit votes. It had 14 percent of the population, paid 25 percent of the taxes, but had only 1.46 percent of the voting power. The state's three smallest counties with a total of 6,980 people (Echols, 1,876; Quitman, 2,432, and Glascock, 2,672) also had a combined unit vote of 6. This made the vote of a citizen in one of these three counties worth more in an election than the vote of a citizen of Fulton, the opponents of the county unit system said. A candidate got the entire unit vote of a county if the majority of the voters in that county voted for him. It was much easier to campaign among 6,980 voters than among a half million in metropolitan Atlanta, they argued. They also said that there had been cases in Georgia where the candidate who got the most unit votes was elected, even though he had received fewer popular votes than the loser. They usually gave as an illustration of this the election of the late Eugene Talmadge in his fourth successful bid for the governorship. He received most of the county unit votes, even though his popular vote was 305,777, whereas his opponent, James V. Carmichael received 313,421 popular votes.

Every person's vote now counts alike in Georgia primaries as indeed it has all the time in the general election. "One man, one vote" is the basis of election now.

SANDERS BECAME GOVERNOR IN 1963

Carl Edward Sanders, an Augusta lawyer who had served with distinction in the General Assembly, became the governor of Georgia. He had defeated former Governor Marvin Griffin of Bainbridge.

Sanders, born in Augusta, May 15, 1925, graduated from the University of Georgia law school in 1947, and married Betty Byrd Foy of Statesboro. With their two children, they moved into the old Governor's Mansion in Atlanta in 1963. Plans were underway to build a new home for Georgia's governors. It was being built in 1966.

Sanders had been elected to the legislature in 1954, had served as floor leader in the House, and later as president pro tempore of the Senate. The Augusta Chamber of Commerce had named him Young Man of the Year in 1955 and the Georgia Junior Chamber of Commerce had chosen him as one of the state's five outstanding young men in 1959.

He entered the governorship with a progressive program, in which education was given top priority. "If there is to be a star in the show during my administration, it will be the Georgia child," he said. In 1964, he was given the Golden Key award at Atlantic City for his achievements in education. This is an award presented by a half dozen national education groups each year. The recipient chooses the teacher who did most to help him. Sanders chose his first grade teacher in Augusta.

He was also elected chairman of the Southern Regional Education Board.

Sanders advocated many other progressive things, and moved swiftly to put his ideas into action. Among the things besides better education he proposed for Georgia

Governor Carl Sanders
760

were these: developing the tourist industry in Georgia; changing the organization of the highway department to a ten-member board with a director; creation of a Department of Youth; industrial expansion; consolidation of counties when a majority of the citizens in the counties affected voted for this; the adoption of a Fair Elections Code; better crime prevention and prison rehabilitation systems and other measures. He presented a two-year budget that included the expenditure of $465,000,000 during the fiscal year 1963-1964 and $489,000,000 during the fiscal year 1964-65. Later Georgia revenue increased still more.

Governor Sanders set a precedent by appointing a woman to head a major government agency; he appointed Mrs. W. B. Schaefer, wife of a Toccoa doctor, as director of the welfare department, which became the Department of Children and Family Services. Welfare was receiving 4.21 percent of the state's entire spending. There were 1,745 workers on the program, with 183 at the headquarters in the capital, 1,272 in county departments, and 291 working in state institutions. The federal government provided 77.43 percent of the department budget; the state, 18.88 percent. Mrs. Schaefer, a native of Barnesville, was given one of Georgia's biggest jobs.

Georgians became more aware of what the department did. There were fewer Georgians on welfare rolls than the public thought. Only 4.2 percent of the population received welfare benefits, and more than half of these were getting Old Age Assistance. In 1964, there were 91,929 Georgians over sixty-five receiving Old Age Assistance; 3,085 receiving Aid to the Blind; 47,777 receiving Aid for Dependent Children; and 25,507 receiving Aid to the Disabled. A total of 50,959 Georgians had requested help within the fiscal year but 25,261 of these (or 49.6 percent) had been turned down because they did not qualify for one reason or another. The Department had spent within the year $103,666.41 helping Georgians who did qualify.

A Youth Department was created within this agency. A survey had discovered that more than 5,000 Georgia children were in jail because when they had got in trouble, or had been neglected, there had been nowhere else for them to go.

761

Legislature Controls State Expenditures

In 1963, a constitutional amendment placed authority for all expenditures in the General Assembly. (The state already had a pay-as-you-go plan. It can only spend what it expects to take in that year plus any left-overs from the year before. Buildings, ports, and such are financed through numerous Authority financing bodies.)

Fifty-four senators and 205 representatives are in the General Assembly now. The legislature meets in January each year, for a forty day-session.

Georgia And The Federal Government, And The Presidents

Georgia's close ties with the federal government were especially evident in finances. More and more of the services which Georgians supported and benefited by were aided from federal funds: highway building, health and welfare services and, increasingly, education. The Congressional delegation from Georgia, ten in the House and two Senators, kept the state aware of its status as a part of a federal pattern of government. Every four years a presidential election renewed Georgia's vigorous interest in national politics and government. For many years, Georgia and the rest of the nation could predict that Georgia would go overwhelmingly Democratic, but in this era came a surprising trend toward change.

PRESIDENT KENNEDY APPOINTED A GEORGIAN SECRETARY OF STATE

In 1960, when young John Fitzgerald Kennedy became President of the United States, he chose a Georgian as the highest ranking member of his Cabinet. Dean Rusk, born in Canton and educated in Atlanta, got the job. He was the second Georgian to hold this office. Before him had been John Forsyth, a governor of Georgia, who became Secretary of State in the Cabinet of President Andrew Jackson.

Rusk was the son of a Presbyterian minister in Cherokee County, in Georgia's Indian country. His father had to give up the ministry because of throat trouble, and he supported a wife and five children by farming, and sometimes teaching. When Dean was four, his father got a job as mail carrier and moved his family to Atlanta. Dean Rusk entered the second grade, went on to become president of the senior class and cadet colonel at old Boy's High in Atlanta, and then to Davidson College. He was a Phi Beta Kappa and won a Rhodes Scholarship. These are scholarships to British universities maintained through a fund set up by Cecil Rhodes, an Englishman who became wealthy from diamond mines he founded in Africa.

Secretary Of State Dean Rusk

The country of Rhodesia was named for him.

During World War II, Rusk served in many places, including the India–Burma–China theater. Later he taught at Mills College, married one of his students, and went to law school at the University of California in Berkeley.

He had become president of The Rockefeller Foundation, where he supervised the distribution of $250,000,000 to underdeveloped countries, when President Kennedy met him. The president-elect had known Rusk only a few days when he offered him the position as Secretary of State in his Cabinet. Rusk had once before worked in the State

Department when George C. Marshall was Secretary of State.

GEORGIAN BECAME ASSISTANT SECRETARY OF AGRICULTURE

John P. Duncan, Jr., of Quitman, was chosen by President John F. Kennedy and Secretary of Agriculture Orville Freeman to become Assistant Secretary of Agriculture for Marketing and Stabilization. Mr. Duncan had been president of the Georgia Farm Bureau. He owns an 800-acre farm in Brooks County. Mr. Duncan has traveled much about the world and he believes that food is a key to the solution of the world problems. He said, "The hungry people in Africa, South America, and East Asia where I visited were not much interested in whether we or the Soviets put a man in orbit first or which is ahead in the space race. They are chiefly interested in getting food for themselves and their families. That is where our Food for Peace program is winning friends for us."

THE GEORGIA LEGISLATURE WAS CHANGED

The United States Supreme Court ruled that both houses of the state legislatures should have their representation from districts that were approximately equal in population. The Court later refused to reconsider this, though there was much objection to it by the public and by Congress. Many pointed out that though the senate could have equal districts, as the United States Senate had, the lower house might be chosen from districts that were unequal.

Georgia moved to rearrange its senatorial districts, and redesign them into fifty-four. The state was later given time for replanning.

GEORGIA GOES FOR A REPUBLICAN PRESIDENTIAL CANDIDATE FOR THE FIRST TIME IN 1964

Georgia was the only southern state that remained consistently in the Democratic column despite the strains and stresses of politics. It was known throughout the nation as a one-party state. Some leaders pointed to the disadvantages of this. Georgia did not get its fair share of recognition from either party, they said. The Democrats used their political awards to bargain with the doubtful states because they knew Georgia would always vote Democratic; the Republicans never offered anything because they knew it was useless.

But by mid-century, a strong Republican party group was growing in power in Georgia. The public image of the party was being renewed. People no longer associated the name "Republican" with the hardships and corruption of the postwar Carpetbag government that came in the wake of the Confederacy's fall. Several of the counties in north Georgia had always had strong Republican leaders. Some had elected Republicans to the legislature, and to local offices. But the party had not yet been able to gather enough strength to elect a Congressman, and it was 1962 before they put a candidate for governor in the field. He was a prominent, well-liked lawyer named Edward Smith of Columbus, who knew well enough that his was only a token race; but it was evidence of the growing confidence of the Republicans that they could make Georgia a two-party state. He was killed in an automobile wreck just as the campaign began.

Then in 1964 Georgia elected a Republican Congressman, Howard (Bo) Callaway, descendant of an old, respected Georgia family, and head of the far-famed Callaway Gardens. Georgia also in 1964 increased its Republican state legislators from seven to twenty-two. Moreover, Georgia for the first time in the modern era went Republican in the presidential election. It gave Barry Goldwater, the Republican candidate, 616,600 votes, and Lyndon B. Johnson, the Democratic incumbent, 522,557.

In 1960, Georgia had given Kennedy 458,638 votes to 274,472 for his Republican opponent Richard Nixon. Many Georgians had in past years voted against Al Smith for president because he was a Catholic; but now many of these same voters were enthusiastic supporters of Kennedy, who was also of the Catholic faith. Georgians grieved when the young President was assassinated in Dallas, Texas, on November 22, 1963, as they had grieved when Roosevelt died at Warm Springs on April 12, 1945.

When the 1966 elections loomed, the Republicans, with new strength, confidence and prestige, were offering candidates for many offices, including governor.

765

In the 1964 elections also, eight Negroes were elected to the Georgia legislature's House of Representatives. Some were Democrats and some were Republicans. One was a woman. Two were already in the Senate. Some people were under the impression that this was the first time since the Reconstruction period that followed the Civil War that Negroes had been in the Georgia General Assembly, but there had been representatives from a coastal county early in the present century.

Negroes were serving on boards of education in several Georgia cities and towns. In Atlanta, Dr. Rufus Clements, President of Atlanta University, who had served on the city education board for some years, was joined by Dr. Horace Tate, who had been for some time executive secretary of an organization of Negro teachers.

The 1964 legislative election of ten Negroes gave Georgia more Negro legislators than any state in the United States except Pennsylvania, which also had ten that year, and Michigan, which had eleven. The 1966 General Assembly had ten Negroes, one a woman.

CHAPTER 64

GEORGIA CHANGED ITS
CONGRESSIONAL DISTRICTS

One of the problems Georgians and their leaders had to consider in the mid-sixties was the realignment of congressional districts. The lines of the ten districts had not been changed in thirty years. There were disparities in the size of the districts. The number of people within them ranged from 823,680 in the Fifth Congressional District, which included Atlanta, to 272,154 in the Ninth, which included Gainesville. About 400,000 in each district would divide the representation more equally.

The matter came to a focus when a suit was filed by James P. Westberry, a state senator, and Candler Crim, Jr., two Atlanta citizens, charging that the congressional districting was unconstitutional because the Fifth District of Fulton, DeKalb and Rockdale counties was too populous in comparison with the other nine districts.

The case was filed in the United States Fifth Circuit Court of Appeals. This court agreed that the districts were unequal in population, but ruled out federal intervention to force changes. Those who had brought the case appealed it to the United States Supreme Court, which agreed to hear it. The Justice Department of the United States also entered the case, on the side of the appellants

The reorganization of the congressional districts resulted in the current pattern.

President Johnson And His Georgia Ancestors

Lyndon Baines Johnson, the Texan who served for

Map Of New Congressional Districts

many years in Congress, became Vice-President in the Kennedy Administration and thirty-sixth President of the United States when Kennedy was killed in Dallas, is a descendant of Georgians. He was born on a farm in Texas, August 27, 1908.

Johnson had been riding in a car behind President Kennedy when the fatal shots were fired in Dallas. Rufus Youngblood, of Macon, Georgia, a Secret Service man guarding Johnson, pushed the Vice-President down in his car and protected him with his own body from possible shots fired at him. Youngblood had been a cadet colonel at Tech High and, after leaving college for the armed service during World War II, had returned to get his engineering degree at Tech in 1949. He was given the Treasury Department's highest medal, for "exceptional bravery," in recognition of his efforts to shield Johnson.

Johnson took the oath as President ninety-nine minutes after President Kennedy died, and served out the remainder of Kennedy's term. Then in 1964, he was elected President by a record-breaking landslide vote. He and Vice-President Hubert H. Humphrey received 42,670,000 popular votes, and 486 electoral votes from 44 states. Senator Goldwater and his vice-presidential nominee, Representative Miller of New York, received 52 electoral votes from 6 states.

"LBJ" had been associated in Congress, during the 32 years he had spent there, with many Georgia Congressmen. He had been to Georgia more than once, and had been speaker at exercises at Mercer University. He had known well the late Georgia Senator Walter F. George. Mrs. Johnson had come to Georgia to make the reward to the Outstanding Georgia Homemaker who is chosen each year at the Southeastern Fair.

Two of the first gestures of recognition which the new president made toward Georgia were these: he chose Governor Carl Sanders to be one of the four governors asked to sit with the Johnson family in Congress as the new president made his first speech to the joint houses of Congress, in November 27, 1963, and he picked Emory University's Dr. Willis Hurst as his personal physician. Johnson had once been a patient at Emory and Dr. Hurst was physician there.

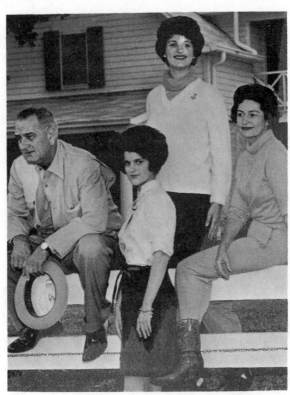

President Johnson And His Family

Georgians Became Ambassadors

W. Tapley Bennett, Jr., of Griffin, became ambassador from the United States to the Dominican Republic. He was in Santo Domingo when a crisis arose in 1965 and, on his counsel, the Johnson Administration sent in aid to protect United States citizens and property there. Ambassador Bennett was honor guest at a press dinner in Atlanta a few weeks thereafter, and President Johnson sent to the dinner a telegram of appreciation and support for him and the position he took in the crisis. Bennett resigned in 1966.

Lucius Battle, also of Georgia, served in the Johnson Administration as ambassador to the United Arab Republic.

CHAPTER 65

MODERN GEORGIANS
AND THEIR DAILY LIVES

A between-census survey of Georgia in 1966 showed that 4,400,000 people were living within the state, with 4,658,000 predicted by 1970. The surprising thing is that most of them — over 55 percent — were living in urban areas, and this is in a state which for more than 200 years had been predominantly rural. The exodus from the farms, caused by mechanization, soil banks, incoming industry, and other factors, had affected Georgia in many ways: reapportionment of the legislature, civil rights actions, housing problems, payrolls, education, and other phases of living.

Work patterns have changed as farms needed fewer workers and industry needed more. Labor officials predict that in the decade between 1960 and 1970 Georgia will add 265,000 jobs, or 508,200 by 1976. Employment is expected to reach 1,817,500 by 1976. It was 1,309,000 in 1960. Estimates vary in job projections for the future as much as in population projections. One survey predicts that by 1975 there will be 5,884,637 people living in Georgia, or a 49.2 percent increase over 1960. Another predicts 5,479,000, a 39 percent increase.

Income in Georgia, though still lower than the national average in many phases, has gone up considerably in recent decades. Between 1940 to 1960, the total personal income of Georgians increased 500 percent. Financial experts say that personal income in Georgia, which was $6.4 million in 1960, will reach $12.9 million by 1976. Per capita income was only $290 in 1939; in 1960, it had reached $1,610; by 1962, it was $1,649; and in 1964, it was $1,864. In the years between

1929 and 1955, it had increased 281 percent, the second largest such gain in the nation. By 1976, per capita income in Georgia is expected to reach $2,343. By 1976, Georgia's output of goods and services is predicted at over 17 billion dollars. In 1947, it was $4,640 million.

"Fortune Magazine" reported in 1965 that of the 500 biggest business organizations in the United States, 400 offices have warehouses here. More than 100 of the nation's largest industrial firms make or assemble products in Georgia.

In Atlanta, the 21-story First National Bank Building, largest office building in the southeast, was built with over a million square feet of floor space.

In 1960, Georgia had 55,019 commercial and industrial firms. This was the fifteenth largest number of any state in the nation. Georgia ranked fifth in the number of new ones acquired within a decade.

With world markets developing for Georgia, and the underdeveloped and emerging nations needing products made and grown here, Georgia's economy and prosperity are likely to continue the trend upward. More earning power of Georgians, as they train in vocational centers and elsewhere for new or better jobs, will enable them to buy more consumer goods, pay more taxes, support better schools, and add to the state's general prosperity.

Tourism has become big business, and has caught the imagination of big and little communities in developing their sites of interest. Recreation centers create jobs, as well as offer opportunities for happier leisure. Better roads and means of travel have brought more tourists in and impelled Georgians to become better acquainted with their own state.

Health services are more widespread. Hospitals and clinics, research and education have all combined to lengthen the lives of Georgians. The average age of a Georgian is now twenty-seven, and life expectancy is longer than it was when the century began. Federal health services and benefits add to the health and well-being of Georgians.

Social tensions remain, but Georgians are striving valiantly to comply with new laws and to change their traditional patterns to conform with them. Difficulties have arisen as old ways clash with new laws, but much progress

772

has been made in education, housing, public services, religion, and other areas where racial conflicts were likely to occur.

There were Georgians whose work had taken them out of the state, sometimes to other countries. Some had achieved world fame. More than one Georgia boy had become an astronaut. Many others were making their living in jobs that did not even exist a decade ago.

The movement of Georgians from farms to cities is part of a national trend that is expected to keep up. In late 1965 the magazine "U.S. News and World Report" listed Georgia as one of twelve states that will grow fastest in the next decade. Most of this increase will be living in the metropolitan area of Atlanta, and earning a living in industry. This population pattern will have a tremendous impact on work, voting, education, and every other area of life. The change was showing up especially in voting strengths. More political power was moving in the cities. Negroes were also registering and voting in greater numbers, especially after the passage of civil rights and voters acts by Congress. In 1960, only 31.3 percent of all citizens of voting age in Georgia actually voted; the United States average was 64.3 percent.

CHAPTER 66

THE CHANGING ECONOMY

New Patterns Develop

Georgians, who once made their living in agriculture, have seen their state's economy gradually achieve a balance between farming and factory, agriculture and industry. In 1910, less than one-eighth of all Georgia workers were in manufacturing. By 1940, one-fourth were. By mid-century, industry outpaced agriculture as an employer and the products of factories brought more money to Georgia than the products of the farm.

Thousands of Georgians have moved to cities or urban areas, but farming is still a basic part of Georgia's life and welfare. In the eighteenth century, 85 percent of the people in the nation worked to produce the food and fiber needed in the country. Now this can be done by only 8.7 percent of them. Moreover, technology has relieved them of most of its drudgery.

The Land And Its Products

The land is always basic to the life of a people. The crops, livestock, and dairy products grown in and on the green fields and pastures of Georgia have helped shape the state's economy, and are indispensable.

The resources of the earth and its forests are worth millions more to Georgia; marble, granite, other stones, iron ores, and naval stores bring much money to the state.

The game and fish in streams and forests have great commercial value, and also draw thousands of hunters and fishermen to the woods, and rivers, creeks, lakes, and ponds throughout the year.

There's Room In Georgia!

Though most Georgians now live in or near the cities, there are wide open space left in Georgia. Georgia has 58,876 square miles and 4,400,000 people.

The revolutionary changes in agriculture, the exodus of so many people from the land, the urbanization of Georgia's population, the industrialization of the economy, and the rising standard of living of the people all were making Georgia a different kind of state. But Georgians have adapted to change since the beginning. Said one Georgia leader, "The one unchanging rule of life is change."

One evidence of change was this: at the University in Athens, first in the old home of former Governor Wilson Lumpkin, a computer was installed that revolutionized the collection and use of data. It worked on many things, from how smart a child is to how fast a pine tree grows. It served business and education. The rate first established, $375 an hour, not counting the programming, sounded high, but in that hour, the "magic monster" could register 6,000 students, type individual class rolls, issue each student a schedule, type master lists for the school administrator and resolve schedule conflicts! There was virtually no limit to what it could do.

Southern states are rapidly climbing in the nation's manufacturing picture. Up to 1960, they still produced only about 20 percent of the nation's manufactured products. But manufacturing was growing faster in the South than in the United States as a whole. Since World War II, it increased nearly five times in value; in Georgia, nine times. Retail sales in Georgia in 1964 totaled $6,733,780,998. In 1939, they had amounted to only $605,002,000.

CHAPTER 67

INDUSTRY BOOMS

IN GEORGIA

Industry, which took precedence over agriculture as a way of earning a living about mid-century, continues to expand in Georgia. New ones are coming in at the rate of one a day, and those already in the state are expanding. In the Atlanta area alone, more than 1,800 plants manufacture or process 3,400 products! Georgia was prospering with industries related to aircraft, automobiles, electronics, chemicals, wood and paper products and scores of others.

Henry Grady, who had long ago pointed out the lack of manufacturing in Georgia, would have been gratified to see how many things were being produced in Georgia in the 1960's. So would Adiel Sherwood, who wrote in his *Georgia Gazetter* in 1827, "Leather, shoes, hats, carriages, saddles, cabinet work, cotton and woolen clothes, etc., are manufactured throughout the state. But little is manufactured in the southern section, even for the blacks: homespun in the upper sections is worn by the most wealthy and respectable inhabitants. Much, however, is still being imported for every part of the state."

The manufacturing that Sherwood was talking about was being done mostly in the plantation shops, or in small plants. There were no large manufacturing enterprises in Georgia then. But they soon began to come in: iron foundries, machine shops, wood factories, flour mills, tanneries, and carriage shops. By 1860, there were 1,800 manufacturing establishments in Georgia, with a $10,000,000 investment, producing $17,000,000 worth of products annually. The War Between the States played havoc with these plants. But after the war, manufacturing started up again, and from 1870 to 1890, the capital invested in them increased four times. Some of this was the result of Henry Grady's promotion of the cotton expositions in Atlanta.

There was a time when Georgia sent its raw resources outside the state. They were manufactured elsewhere, and then Georgians had to buy them back as finished goods.

But then the state began to encourage industry to develop here. "From raw materials to finished product" is more and more the slogan in Georgia now. This development of natural resources has brought unprecedented progress and prosperity. The cotton crop supports a $2,000,000,000 textile industry, plus another $2,000,000,000 in the manufacture of wearing apparel. In 1963, nearly a half billion dollars came from freezing, canning, and preparing such foods as peaches, apples, corn, peanuts, and other crops. The mineral industry brings in more and more millions. Forestry products come very near bringing in a billion. Georgia has the largest area of private woodlands of any of the fifty states. Of the state's 37,500,000 acres, more than 23,000,000 are in woodland. In Augusta, a $70,000,000 plant has been built to manufacture newsprint for the Atlanta newspapers. One steel mill now in Georgia employs over 1,600 Georgians and has a payroll of over $10,000,000! More than 1,600,000 telephones provide many jobs, despite much automation.

Industry has a wide range in Georgia, from the manufacturing of gigantic earth-moving machinery up near Toccoa, to the thread mills in middle Georgia and the shrimp-packing plants along the coast. In between range businesses that would run down the alphabet all the way from A to Z.

Rivers, harbors, ports and other water facilities added greatly to the ease of transporting manufactured goods. From the Savannah port the first cargo, shipped in 1733, was skins, roots, and herbs. Now the Savannah River is navigable for 200 miles, all the way to Augusta, and bears on its surface more than four million tons of cargo a year. The Georgia Ports Authority there adds about 80 million dollars to

Shrimp Boats

Georgia's economy each year. The Savannah harbor is 31 miles long.

In 1744 the first commercial house established, Habersham and Harris in Savannah, shipped lumber, hogs, deerskins, indigo, rice, tobacco and a few bags of cotton to England. In 1768 a "trade at home" campaign developed because Georgia merchants were angered at Britain's trade policies.

Now about 500 foreign ships dock at Savannah each year. They bring in raw sugar, molasses, jute bagging, burlap, petroleum products, gypsum rock, sulphur, finished steel products, manganese and aluminum ores, industrial chemicals, fertilizer materials, and potash, among other things. Many products are exports: paper products, naval stores, roadbuilding equipment, farm machines, cottonseed meal, peanuts, soybeans, lumber, clays, iron and steel scrap, chemicals, and phosphate fertilizer material. Cotton is only 1 percent of what it was in the old plantation days when the cotton kingdom was at the height of its power.

Georgia has unlimited opportunities for manufacturing, say planners and researchers.

"We can scarcely comprehend the vast potentials which remain undeveloped in Georgia," said Dr. Kenneth Wagner, head of Georgia Tech's Industrial Development Branch.

The State of Georgia, local Chambers of Commerce, and university research and planning groups worked together intensively to find what was possible in Georgia. What were the resources here? Where were the people with the money and ability to develop these?

Like Henry Grady in the last century, Georgia leaders made tries all over the nation and the world to show manufacturers and others what Georgia had to offer. It is no longer enough simply to describe to them such generalities as good climate, enough workers, and friendly people. Detailed information is now prepared and presented showing market costs, taxes, labor and labor laws, transportation, building costs, utility rates, plant sites, market date, population, vocational training, educational opportunities and the like.

Industrial development councils have been set up to do research and provide information about the state's possibilities.

Rural areas, which have lost population as farm workers whose jobs disappear flock to cities hunting work, are bidding for industries. In the 1950's 60 percent of the manufacturing was concentrated in 16 counties.

In the 1960's, the State Chamber of Commerce was urging small communities to continue their efforts to lure more industry to Georgia because "just 100 new factory workers mean 296 people, 112 more households, 51 more school children, $590,000 more personal income per year, $270,000 more bank deposits, 107 more passenger cars, 174 more workers employed, 4 more retail establishments and $360,000 more retail sales per year."

In January, 1966, Georgia's unemployment was only 1.4 percent, the lowest in history, and 50 percent below the national average. More than 40,000 industrial jobs had been added within 3 years. In those 3 years, 347 new industries had come in and 424, already here, had expanded.

Early Industry

Georgia's development of its ceramics industry, using

779

native clays here instead of exporting them to be used elsewhere, revived the history of early Georgia clay shipped to England for making exquisite Wedgwood ware. From Stoke-on-Trent, England, came a story of the original journal, now in the Wedgwood library there, kept by a man named Griffiths. He was sent by the original Wedgwood to negotiate with the Indians for the use of white clay. His journey lasted from July 1767 to April 1768. He reported on his visit to the Cherokees. They objected to the white man's digging their clay and leaving holes in their land. But Griffiths was tactful enough to have ransomed a Cherokee Indian maiden who had been captured and taken away. He returned her to her people, and they agreed to negotiate with him for the white clay. "We shook hands and settled the matter," he reported.

Early Georgians prized beautiful tableware, and eight Sevres plates were brought from abroad by the state's first governor, John Adam Treutlen. They are now in the State Archives.

Fine furniture was also made early in this section. Georgia woods were sent to England and made into beautiful furniture there. Silversmiths were early in this land, too. One was the Indian, Sequoyah, inventor of the Cherokee alphabet.

Lockheed In Georgia

By 1966 the Lockheed Corporation had an annual payroll of $156 million, and employed 22,500 persons in Georgia. The Georgia Division was established in 1951 at Marietta, about ten miles north of Atlanta; it covers 76 acres. Lockheed also has a nuclear research laboratory at Dawsonville, Georgia, for the nation's first study of radiation effects on large systems, materials, and component parts. Work done by Lockheed in Georgia reaches out in some way to nearly all parts of the world. The plant has brought engineers, researchers, and other workers from many parts of the nation and the world to Georgia, and has given employment to many Georgians, and new interest to the space age for Georgia.

Lockheed chose Georgia for the building of a $3-million, 46-acre research facility at Marietta in 1964, the largest company-owned one in the South. The area's educational facilities, colleges, universities, technical and vocational training and high schools were cited as reasons why this site was chosen. Other space-age enterprises were locating in Georgia because, for one thing, colleges like Georgia Institute of Technology, the University of Georgia, and others were working with them on problems of research. "Georgia has a future in the aerospace age," said a Lockheed leader. Lockheed is the largest aircraft factory under one roof in America. In 1965, Lockheed was awarded the largest Defense Department contract in history: $2.2 billion to build the C-5A, the world's largest airplane. Marietta became the cargo airlift capital of the world.

Government Workers

A 1963 study showed that 197,311 Georgians were employed in full-or part-time government service. This put Georgia sixteenth among the states in this area of work. Federal government agencies were employing 60,157; there were 31,500 engaged in working for the State government, and another 105,654 in the service of local governments. Of the 1.109,600 non-agricultural workers in the state, 18 percent were in government service.

Textiles, The Oldest
Industry, Was Changing

Georgia's oldest industry, textiles, started about 1811 on Epson Creek in Wilkes County, where the first successfully operated mill was established. It was natural for this industry to grow up in Georgia, for it was here that the great cotton-producing area was located. Now, when research and technology have produced many man-made fibers, Georgia still provides a good place for textile industries. Here the climate, the water power, the sources of electricity, the humidity for spinning and weaving, good transportation and other advantages continue to make Georgia a great textile center. Georgia's textile plants now use more cotton than Georgia fields produce. They import cotton and wool from many other places in the world.

By 1960, 353 textile mills were all over Georgia. They employed over 100,000 Georgians, used more than 3,000,000 spindles and had an annual payroll of nearly a half billion dollars. Pine forests and pulpwood in Georgia were furnishing natural resources for the mills, since this was the chief source of rayon. Cornfields were also important to textiles, since the plants used millions of pounds of starch and other corn products.

The 40 largest companies, which operated 66 plants, employed 35,236 workers, had a 1965 payroll of $151 million, gross sales of $725 million, planned to spend $40 million in expansions and gross 1.36 million in 1966.

Education had also provided strengths for the textile industry, as well as other businesses. Research laboratories and programs to train textile engineers were expanded with the help of industry. In the 1960's textiles were having trouble competing with imported fabrics, from Japan and elsewhere, that could be produced with cheaper labor.

One of the most interesting phases of the textile industry was that of tufted textiles. There were many products from this one part of the textile industry, but the one that the public thought of first was usually the colorful bedspreads often seen flapping along the clotheslines in the northwest area of the state.

The bedspreads had an interesting origin.

TUFTED TEXTILES HAD A STRANGE BEGINNING

Tufted textiles, now so important to Georgia, started with a wedding present. Katherine Evans, a fifteen-year-old Georgian, had seen an old tufted bedspread and decided to make one like it for a friend who was getting married. Other people saw the one she made, liked it, and asked her to make bedspreads for them. She sold the first one in 1901. She bought the sheeting and thread from a cotton mill near her home in Dalton. Katherine drew the design for each spread and then hired neighbors to finish them by hand.

The introduction of machines changed the making of tufted textiles. The machines could tuft the textiles as expertly as the women could, and turn them out faster. The machines were crude at first, but were rapidly improved. With the coming of the machines, the industry grew rapidly.

Making Tufted Textiles

To the bedspreads have been added rugs, carpeting, tapestries, and other creations of beauty and usefulness. Jute from India and latex made from Malayan rubber have kept the tufted textile industry in Georgia in touch with the far places of the world. Research and the setting up of more laboratories and plants to produce products needed to make textiles have brought even greater prosperity to Georgia.

Katherine Evans Whitener, after her retirement, said with wonder in her voice, "That wedding present gave work to a lot of people, didn't it?"

Mrs. Whitener died in Dalton in 1964 at eighty-three. The flag over the American Tufted Textile Manufacturers Association across the street from her home flew at half-mast. She had seen the tufted textile industry grow from her $2.50 bedspread to a multimillion-dollar enterprise that brought more prosperity to her own community and state, and gave work to thousands. The year she died, the United States government reports listed the whole textile industry gross sales as $592,000,000 a year.

Cotton thread, manufactured in Georgia, has an in-

teresting history. Once all sewing thread was silk or linen.
When Napoleon's 1806 embargo cut off silk shipments to
Britain, the Clarks began to make cotton thread. Now they
have plants in Georgia. When Elias Howe invented the
sewing machine in 1846, this increased the demand for
sewing thread. History in Georgia says that an earlier
sewing machine was invented by Dr. Francis Goulding
of Roswell, author of *The Young Marooners*.

Ford Established His Business In Georgia

Henry Ford established a branch of his automobile
business in Atlanta on November 8, 1909.

On December 10, 1947, Ford's grandson, Henry Ford
II, dedicated the new Ford plant built on the 83-acre lot
Ford acquired in Hapeville. On July 22, 1955, the millionth
Georgia-built Ford car rolled off the assembly line. Other
Ford affiliate enterprises, like the parts depot at East Point,
a tractor and implement test center at Vienna, and regional
sales offices, added to Georgia's industrial growth throughout

An Automotive Mechanics Class

784

the twentieth century. By the time Ford observed its Golden Anniversary, more than 2,000 Georgians were working with the organization, and the payroll in metropolitan Atlanta's area exceeded $12,000,000 a year. Officials said the company was buying over $20,000,000 worth of materials from Georgia firms each years.

CHAPTER 68
FEWER FARMS PRODUCE
MORE FOOD AND FIBER

By 1960, 90 percent of the population had shifted to urban centers, putting tremendous strains on the schools and the housing facilities. Many of those who stayed on the farms were working part-time in the small industries that located in many parts of rural Georgia. There remained in Georgia about 100,000 farms, but some of these were part-time farming operations.

The surprising thing, however, was that Georgia's farm income from all its crops and related activities and products had spurted from $140,000,000 in 1940, to about $800,000,000 — almost a billion dollars — in 1961. In January, 1966, the governor told the legislature that it had reached an all-time high of approximately a billion dollars in 1965. Net income per farm increased from $1,228 in 1949 to $3,621 in 1964. The newer research and experiment, the good teaching of vocational agriculture and the help of farm agents and the colleges and high schools, had made the Georgia farmer a very productive part of the economy. Georgia is third in the diversification of crops. Besides diversification, painfully learned because of the boll weevil holocaust of the 1920's, there was hybridization, better fertilization, mechanized farming and other things that were responsible for the agricultural success of Georgia. More and better cash crops were being produced with less labor and less cost: peanuts, corn, hogs, cattle, dairy products, truck crops, pecans, tobacco, soybeans, peaches. They were bringing important money to Georgia.

In 1965, peanuts topped agricultural products for the first time, bringing in over $101 million, to corn's 99, cotton's 90, and tobacco's 79. All rural products — not just crops — totaled over a billion dollars in 1965. Georgia, in 1874, set up the nation's first department of agriculture. It has helped Georgians to grow and market better products, thereby bringing more prosperity to the whole state. Farmers' markets were set up. The one near Atlanta is the biggest of its kind in the world.

Tobacco Growing In Georgia

It is a drama worth watching as trucks roll in bringing fresh produce in a rainbow of colors, dew-fresh and ready for the buyers. Things such as green melons, scarlet tomatoes, beige peanuts, red apples, yellow pumpkins and a multitude of others make the market a colorful place.

In other places besides the colorful farm markets, Georgians began to dramatize the products of their fields and forests and pastures. Cordele had established a watermelon festival; Woodbury set up a pimiento festival; and Blakely and southwest Georgia made the most of their fame as "the world's peanut capital." Honey bees in southeast Georgia add a grace note, not only with their clear crystal jars of honey, but from the bees shipped all over the world. Wilkes County advertised its green pastures. The Hiawassee Mountain Fair gave growers there a chance to display their accomplishments. Where old red, eroded gulleys like scars on the earth had marked the land's devastation from the one-crop system, the land had turned into emerald green pastures, dark woodlands growing money through night and day as trees were turned into pulp products or naval stores, and newly important crops that laced the furrows with things people waited to buy. Scientific farming gave evidence of a new partnership between education, with its training and research laboratories, and the farmer who could put this new knowledge into action.

Georgia farmers have an interest in the world market and in farming operations in other countries. Many of them have visited farms in far places.

Cotton Is Still Important

Though crops are now diversified and cotton is no longer the one big money crop in Georgia, cotton still ranks high in importance.

Georgia's cotton crop of 1963 brought $113,460,000. This was 610,000 bales for ginning, spinning and processing, and 241,500 tons of seed for various products. By the time the crop goes through the manufacturing processes, it will mean almost a billion dollars to the people who are concerned with it, including those in manufacturing, trade and industry of the state.

The Co-operative Extension Service, with headquarters at Athens, said that the 1963 crop was from a record-breaking yield of 455 pounds of lint cotton per acre. The service had launched a program, beginning in 1958, to work toward a 500-pound-per-acre yield and an addition of 400 million dollars to Georgia's income by 1965.

The Bankers Farm Bulletin of the Federal Reserve Bank of Atlanta points out that Georgia is one of four southeastern states in which the farm output has jumped 53 percent in the past two decades, in spite of rapidly shrinking crop acreages. Acreage in production shrank from 22 million acres in 1940 to 13 million in 1961. The Bulletin said it could shrink to 6 million acres by 1970. But production increases, agricultural research and the intelligent use of it by farmers, more knowledge of scientific farming, and better resources account for much of this. "This once again confirms capitalism's dynamic impact," the publication said.

The story of cotton is enmeshed into the story of Georgia, and forms a fascinating part of the Georgia drama. Georgia was the first state to produce cotton commercially. Even today, with all the synthetics and new crops, one can reach out from almost anywhere and touch something made of cotton.

Other Products

Northeast Georgia is no longer primarily apple country, for much industry has come in. But Georgia's picturesque apple country still produces over a half million bushels of apples each year. The delicate pink blossoms on the trees in spring, and the gold or scarlet apples on the green trees in late summer and early autumn make this a picture postcard section. Five counties in north Georgia raise most of the commercial crop of apples. They are Habersham, Cobb, Fannin, Gilmer, and Rabun. Only about 20 percent of the Georgia apple crop is sold within the state. Most of Georgia's apples are sold in Mississippi, Louisiana, Texas, and Florida. Some growers harvest as many as 1,000 bushels per acre from their apple trees. In 1965, Georgia produced its biggest apple crop: 630,000 bushels. Apple trees are now being planted in middle Georgia, in some sections that formerly grew peaches.

In 1908, apples from north Georgia took second prize among 1,500 kinds of apples at the National Apple Growers Festival in Spokane, Washington. They took four first prizes in a similar show at Ithaca, New York, in 1913. In 1925, a huge red apple weighing 5,200 pounds was moulded in the Virginia apple country and shipped by train to Cornelia, Georgia, to mark the center of the apple country. It is still a sight of interest to tourists.

Monument To The Apple, In Cornelia

GEORGIA IS THE CHICKEN CAPITAL OF THE WORLD

A spectacular Georgia sucess story is the story of how the area around Gainesville has become the broiler capital of the world. The packing plants process about 250,000,000 young chickens for broiling each year, in many salable products, from the whole chicken to frozen chicken pie. This chicken and egg industry brings about $250,000,000 into Georgia. This is about a third of the entire sum that comes into the state for exported agricultural products each year.

Georgia hens were laying 2.5 billion eggs yearly by 1962. Surprisingly, part of the increase was due to automation. It enabled Georgia egg producers to handle more hens because push-button management had made it possible to feed, water, light, nest, ventilate and gather eggs by machines. Better breeds of chickens, feed improved by research, and men who kept up with and used the best methods in management also accounted for much of the increase.

THE FORESTS BRING IN MONEY

Money from its swamps and forests was still adding much to Georgia's income. Tree money was nothing new in Georgia. Lumber, from which the first colonists had built houses, was sold to make ships. Turpentine and other naval stores were sold from the trees. The early plantation owners along the coast sent their best lumber to England to be turned into the fine furniture being designed there.

Charles Herty, in this century, showed the world how to make newsprint and other products from Georgia's pines. Pulpwood industries moved in, and started turning the green trees into boxes and paper and other products, and put more money into the pockets of Georgia farmers. More than 1,300 related industries are dependent in some degree on tree products.

By 1960, 1,313 plants were manufacturing some tree products, and the value of the products they turned out totaled $976,675,840, nearly a billion dollars. Farmers who once had toiled through long, weary, back-breaking hours behind the plow, were now having a little more time to sit in their rocking chairs, read the paper, watch TV, or zoom into town in their cars to Rotary or church. Pine trees, planted where cotton used to be, were growing to earn money for the farmers. Tractors and other mechanized vehicles were doing the drudgery, and electricity was better than a hundred servants who had toiled from "can see to can't see" in the fields and the houses back in the days of slavery and of Reconstruction. Nurseries, free or at small cost, provided Georgia farmers nearly a half million pine seedlings a year to plant.

Pines are not the only important trees among the 163 different kinds that grow in Georgia. Gum and oak, as well as pine, are the principal woods used in making furniture. Some woods still go into parts of ships, though not as much as into "Old Ironsides," or the U.S.S. "Constitution." Some wood from St. Simons Island on the coast of Georgia went into this famous old ship.

Georgia leads the nation in the production of pulpwood, and accounts for a fifth of all that produced in the twelve southeastern states. Some Georgia newspapers have set up their own newsprint factories.

Naval stores provide the raw material for more than 300 products now, including paint, varnishes, synthetic rubber, adhesives, soaps and disinfectants, inks, dyes, plastics, paper, and many others.

Gold, Oil, and Iron In Georgia

Geologists, viewing the world's need for gold, say that the nation is going to have to dig gold again, probably with federal subsidies, and that there may be more commercial digging for gold in Georgia before the end of this century. The Department of the Interior had placed gold on the list of metals eligible for exploration assistance.

Iron ore has been found in quantities in south Georgia, but the problem has been finding the proper way to develop it profitably. Quitman, Stewart, and Webster counties are three in which iron has been found in quantity.

The 1958 General Assembly offered $250,000 to the first person who could successfully bring in an oil well producing 100 barrels a day.

Georgia's annual production of minerals, including clays and stones, is over $130,000,000. About 25 minerals are marketed from Georgia each year. Stone alone brings in $50,000,000 annually. Georgia leads the nation in producing marble, granite and kaolin which is often referred to as Georgia's white gold. Kaolin, sometimes called "white mud" is a $50,000,000 industry here. Georgia produces three-fourths of all the nation uses. It is useful for paper-making, ceramics, and medicine, among other things. All slick-paper magazines use it.

Georgia's marble, from white through pale pink to dramatic black and white, has been used in some of the world's most beautiful buildings and statues. The center of the marble industry is around Tate, Georgia, in Pickens County.

Granite, also used in buildings, roads, and monuments,

792

is a valuable Georgia product. A surprising range of by-products come from these stones, such as grit for chickens, powdered marble used in making chewing gum and other things.

Talc and soapstone are used in making cosmetics. Coal, maganese, copper, iron, limestone, and fuller's earth, flagstone, mica, chromite, kyanite, feldspar are other products in Georgia. Barite is a $2,000,000 industry. This is used in the manufacture of barium chemicals for use in products as varied as oil drills, X-rays, films, atomic reactors, television tubes, and ceramics. Bauxite, used in making aluminum, is produced in Georgia.

Experts say that Georgia has many products useful for nuclear reactors. One substance used in creating nuclear energy is a radioactive isotope of theorium, found in monozite, a mineral from the sandy coastal area of Georgia. Titanium, a new-sounding name in Georgia, is used in making paint and is useful to space exploration.

Fairy crosses are probably the most nearly unique stone found in Georgia. They are found in Fannin and Gilmer counties and other parts of the Blue Ridge section. They are crystals of staurolite, which sounds like "starlight," a mineral made up of iron, alunimum, and silicon. Nature shaped these small bits of beauty about 500 million years ago. They are shaped like Maltese crosses, Celtic crosses, St. Andrew's crosses, and Greek crosses. Some people say they are "angels' tears," shed when Christ was crucified.

Georgia Became Part of
the Appalachian Project

Georgia in 1964 became one of the ten states of "Appalachia," an area in which the United States government was concerned with improving the earning power and living conditions for the mountain people living there. Only 35 of Georgia's 159 counties were within this area, however. They were all in north and west Georgia, at the end of the Appalachian chain. This area had 675,000 of the state's 4,000,000 people, or 13 percent of Georgia's population. Their per capita income was $1,169. This was fourth from the bottom in the ten states of the area. More than 36 percent of the 675,000 Georgians living in this area were in families with incomes less than $3,000 a year.

It was in connection with this Appalachia project that President Lyndon Johnson visited Georgia on May 8, 1964. In a speech here that day he referred to his great-great-grandfather, who had been a Georgia tenant farmer in Oglethorpe County.

The world market had become increasingly important to Georgia, and leaders were proposing to make it still more so.

Groups of Georgians, sometimes headed by a governor, go to other countries frequently to talk to business and government leaders about the products Georgia has to offer, and the opportunities here for business locations and investments. Bright and colorful booklets are carried or sent depicting Georgia's advantages.

Many Products Made In Georgia
Are Sold All Over The World

One Georgia product that has become world-famous got its start early in the century. It was Coca-Cola. The formula was concocted in 1886 by John S. Pemberton. By 1900, over $100,000 a year was spent advertising the new drink, and it had been acquired by Asa W. Candler. Bottling plants were being set up throughout the nation and the drink was being sold in every state and Indian territory. The product was to prove such a money-making venture that Candler eventually gave over $8,000,000 to Emory University, where his brother, Bishop Warren Akin Candler, was a guiding force. Today only two people at one time know the closely guarded Coca-Cola formula, and they never travel together. When one dies, another person is let in on the secret.

795

In the first two years of the 1960's, Georgia had sold almost $100,000,000 worth of products — wood, paper, textiles, and machinery — to the European Economic Community (France, Italy, West Germany, Belgium, Luxembourg, and The Netherlands). These sales accounted for 30 percent of all Georgia's exports during those two years. Business reports showed that 44 percent of what Georgia exported was going to European markets, 19 percent to South America, and 14 percent to Asia. Two percent of what went out through Georgia's ports was going to other North American ports. Most went by truck, train, or plane. Of what came into Georgia through its ports, 34 percent came from North Europe, and 10 percent from South America.

About a half-million Georgians work in production or services directly connected with international trade.

Many nations have consular representatives in Georgia. Three countries, Great Britain, West Germany, and Israel, have full-time career consuls in Atlanta. About 20 others are represented by businessmen who are honorary consuls. Most are natives of the country they represent. The consuls attend to such matters as helping people with visas and passports, and providing accurate, dependable information for those who wish to travel to their countries or are considering trade there. They also look after foreign visitors or students here from their countries. The United States Department of Commerce has a field office and a customs house in Atlanta.

Foreign countries co-operate with Georgia in many ways. One was France's sending its great pictures for exhibit in memory of the Georgians who died in the Paris plane crash at Orly Field.

The Magna Carta, first sealed and agreed to by King John in the meadow at Runnymeade in 1215, was brought to Atlanta from England in November, 1965. The document first recognized that all men, even rulers, are subject to law. This was the first time it had been outside England. It was presented at a national convention of the English-speaking Union. Former President Eisenhower was the speaker.

Georgia Built A House For Its Own History

In 1965, the beautiful new 17-story Archives Building near Capitol Hill in Atlanta was dedicated. It cost more than $6,000,000, has over 8,000 books, nearly 20,000 manuscripts, and about 15,000 reels of microfilm relating to Georgia's history. It is reported to be one of the most beautiful archives buildings in the world. To it was brought the famous Confederate window picture story, and the handsome staircase, both from the Rhodes Building on Peachtree Street where the archives were formerly located.

The New State Archives Building

The State Division of Industry and Trade and the Georgia State Chamber of Commerce and its local branches have led the state in promoting tourism. A "Stay and See Georgia" program has put the spotlight on communities which have developed their historic sites or their spots of beauty.

Governor Carl Sanders, in his 1966 State of the State message to the General Assembly, said, "Tourism and recreation in Georgia have now been developed into a billion dollar business."

Four favorite spots with tourists were indicative of the increase. In May, 1965, Callaway Gardens at Pine Mountain recorded its five millionth visitor, even though the gardens are a recent development, opened in 1952. In one month, July, more than 188,000 visited the Gardens. Jekyll Island was reporting record crowds. In north Georgia, Rock City — mistakenly thought by some to be in Tennessee, but actually in Georgia — had a gross income for one month of over $356,000. Stone Mountain Park has already attracted more than a half million visitors.

Historic sights, marked by the Georgia Historical Commission or promoted by local communities, and scenic beauty had done much to lure visitors off the main-traveled roads and into the towns and along the countrysides. The education department's vocational courses were aiding state and local leaders in training service people to become aware of their importance as they rendered courteous, efficient service to the tourists and offered them well-made or-marketed Georgia products.

Georgia's bid for tourists was stepped up in 1963 with the establishment of more Tourist Information Centers by the state. The first one was set up January 20, 1962 on Route 301 just north of Sylvania. It was an immediate success. Over 400 travelers from 15 states registered in one day. Others were soon set up near Ringgold on Interstate Route 75, and on Interstate 85 near the South Carolina line. Still others were blue-printed; some cost $77,500.

Tourists spent $150 million in Georgia during 1962. They stayed an average of 2.12 days. The typical tourist dollar is spent like this: 34¢ for food; 23¢ for automobile expense; 19¢ for lodging; 15¢ for entertainment; and 9¢ for other purposes. The survey showed that the average tourist had three in his party, earned $7,000 to $10,000, and liked the scenery and historic sites.

Tourists suggested that Georgia should improve its roads, eliminate some speed traps, provide more overnight accommodations near sites of interest, and see that food is as good as the well-advertised "Southern home cooking." Georgians themselves, traveling within their own state, were spending over $125 million.

798

Georgia long ago found that it had much to offer people from other states: scenic beauty, the lure of the coast to which people had been coming to relax for two centuries, historic sites, and recreation. More than a thousand honeymooning couples come to the coast each year, especially to the Cloisters on Sea Island. But long years ago, they came to be guests of the hospitable, wealthy coastal aristocrats. Celebrities from Hollywood, Washington, and elsewhere have come to Georgia to hunt, fish, play golf, or relax for many years. The millionaires relaxed at Jekyll when they owned the island, and on the beautiful estates near Thomasville.

President William Howard Taft came to Augusta, to play golf long before President Dwight Eisenhower did. Golf has drawn many to Georgia. The Master's Tournament at Augusta is one of the world's great sporting events. The fame of Bobby Jones, long acclaimed the world's greatest golfer, put Georgia in the spotlight of golf.

Atlanta built a $20 million stadium, attracted professional sports teams and became Dixie's sports capital.

Hunters from Hollywood, New York, Washington and elsewhere have come to south Georgia to shoot game in the

The Atlanta Stadium

luxuriant woodlands there.

Special events, like Thomasville's rose festival, Atlanta's dogwood festival, the Hiawassee Mountain Fair, and the Plum Nelly Clothesline Art show, lure tourists.

Fishing is a tremendous attraction, too. The state has over 700 miles of cold-water trout streams in north Georgia. A restaurant once put up a sign: "The trout you are about to eat is so fresh that last night it slept in the stream outside this window." There are 17 chief rivers running 2,819 miles. There are almost a half million acres of lake surface, and a 126-mile shore line where the sapphire sea washes up on the bronze marshes that Sidney Lanier wrote poems about. There are picturesque waterfalls, and the 2,050-mile Appalachian Trail starting in Georgia and going over the mountain tops to Maine and beyond.

TEN SIGHTS THEY WANT TO SEE

There are many sights they want to see. Some Georgians have listed the ten most interesting sights in the state as (1) Stone Mountain, (2) the gold-domed Capitol, (3) the Cyclorama, (4) the Okefenokee Swamp, (5) Jekyll Island, (6) one of the three Indian Mounds: Ocmulgee, Kolomoki, or Etowah, (7) Amicalola Falls (8) Tallulah Gorge, (9) Providence Canyons, and (10) the Little White House at Warm Springs.

But there are many others just as interesting: Callaway Gardens, the largest inland man-made beach in the world, at Pine Mountain; Frederica on St. Simons; the gold-mining country around Dahlonega; Lake Lanier at Gainesville; the Jefferson Davis Memorial near Irwinville; and Confederate vice-president Alexander Stephens' home, at Crawfordville. Others are Augusta, with its many sites of interest like the McKay Trading Post, where the thirteen soldiers were hanged on the stair; Meadowbrook, the home of George Walton, one of Georgia's three signers of the Declaration of Independence, and the former home of Woodrow Wilson; old Midway Church, where the Puritans settled and where such men as the ancestors of Justice Oliver Wendell Holmes and Samuel F.B. Morse were pastors; the Archives Building in Atlanta; the old State Capitol

Sope Creek Bridge

and Governor's Mansion in Milledgeville; the Old Slave Market in Louisville; and Jerusalem Church in Effingham County. There are many more, especially Savannah.

Georgia's historic homes are pointed out to tourists. The Tourist Division of the Georgia Department of Industry and Trade published a booklet on them, with pictures. Among these are houses at West Point, where Fort Tyler was the last Confederate fort to fall, the Jones plantation house at Birdsville where seven generations of the same family have lived, homes in Wilkes, the plantation house at Stone Mountain, Ben Hill's homes, Barrington Hall at Roswell, the Governor's Mansion in Milledgeville, old homes in Savannah, Augusta, and Macon, and historic homes like the Wren's Nest of Joel Chandler Harris, Jarrett Manor, and Eagle Tavern. Georgia has scores of old homes interesting for both their architecture and their history.

A film to attract tourists to Georgia was narrated by the film actress Susan Hayward, who had married the late Georgian, Eaton Chalkley, and moved to a farm home near Carrollton. It was titled "Susan Hayward Invites You to Georgia." Its premiere showing was at the World's Fair in New York in 1964. In the introduction, the actress said, "Here on the farm in Carroll County, I feel that I'm on one of the biggest sets of all! One that even the late Cecil de Mille, with all his flair for grandeur, might

801

Factors' Walk In Savannah

have envied. This is my home now, and believe me when I say to you that all of Georgia is one vast stage of beauty and relaxed living. It is a real color spectacular. A vibrant, busy member of the family of states, exploding with dynamic growth, strengthening the backbone of America." The scenes in the film included such interesting Georgia sights as Stone Mountain, the gold-domed Capitol, the Georgia Tech-Auburn football game, the Okefenokee Swamp, Jekyll Island, Andersonville, Tallulah Falls, Grant Park, Kennesaw Mountain, Atlanta's skyline, the coast country and many others.

Atlanta's new art center, a new auditorium, and many big new hotels were all contributing to the new interest of people in coming to Georgia to visit or to live.

GEORGIA HAS MANY PARKS

From the Chattahoochee National Forest that spreads

802

all across scenic north Georgia, to Jekyll Island, the world-famous state-owned recreation site on the coast, Georgia has many parks and outing locations.

As people began to have more leisure, Georgia developed more state parks for recreation. People pushed by the pressure of a world full of tensions began to see the value of recreation for both physical and mental health. Georgians, as well as tourists, came by the thousands to enjoy the state's parks. In 1965, more than 5 1/2 million came.

In 1930, there were only nine; by 1966, there were thirty-seven and land had been acquired for more.

Rock City Atop Lookout Mountain

There are national sites in Georgia, not for camping but for interesting sightseeing. Two among many are Fort Frederica on St. Simons Island, one of the nation's few pre-Revolutionary parks and museums, and Ocmulgee National Mounds near Macon, where one of the three tremendous Indian mound sites may be seen.

The United States owns about 5.5 percent of Georgia's land, or 2,034,000 acres, worth almost a $100 million, and containing buildings worth almost a half billion.

The Chattahoochee National Forest was established by proclamation of President Franklin D. Roosevelt on July 9, 1936. It has six ranger districts, with a total of 660,000 acres, spreading over 20 counties. The headquarters is in Gainesville. The forests are valuable for timber, wildlife conservation, and recreation. But the government established it primarily for the purpose of protecting the watershed.

Among the several national cemetery parks are Chickamauga in north Georgia and Andersonville in south Georgia.

Churches Are For the Eye and Spirit

Georgia, 80 percent of whose people are church members, has more than ten thousand churches and synagogues and other places of worship. These, for natives and visitors alike, are interesting to the eye and reposeful for the spirit.

Along the pine-lined roads of south Georgia or gleaming in the sun-splashed valleys among the north Georgia mountains are many jewel-like little white country churches. Near Sharp Top Mountain in Cherokee County is one where the tombstones tell the tale of more than 70 who joined the church in a strange revival and were baptized in a nearby stream where the ice had to be broken. A slave, sent north by his owner to study architecture, designed a church at Perry. The Pink Chapel ruins at St. Simons are left to remind survivors of a murder that forced the killer to build a chapel where his family could worship after neighbors in their regular church were slow to forgive.

Historic churches like Christ Church on St. Simons, near where the Wesleys preached under the trees, attract visitors. Churches in Savannah date back to the beginning.

In Augusta is the church where Woodrow Wilson's father was pastor. At Midway is the church of the Puritans.

Near Conyers is the beautiful Trappist monastery and its Abbey of Our Lady of the Holy Ghost.

On Capitol Hill in Atlanta is a monument to a priest, Father Thomas O'Reilly, who persuaded Sherman's men not to burn the churches there when they were burning Atlanta in the autumn of 1864. The priest's church, The Diocesan Shrine of the Immaculate Conception, then a wooden structure but now a brick church and the oldest one in Atlanta, was used as a hospital. The Ahavith Achim Synagogue at Peachtree Battle Avenue in Atlanta has contemporary art work so beautiful that it is a delight to its own people and to thousands of visitors.

In **Milledgeville** is tiny St. Stephen's Episcopal Church on the grounds of the Old State Capitol. Sherman's men stabled their horses in this church.

Old Jerusalem Church in Effingham County, with its Bible on the altar, and its golden swan of Martin Luther on the steeple, is the church where the old Salzburgers worshipped. The first governor of Georgia, John Adam Treutlen, worshiped there.

Probably the most beautiful little chapel in all Georgia is the little chapel in the green woods by a lake at Callaway Gardens. The stained glass windows depict the four seasons, and organ music from the little chapel often echoes over the hills.

On Jekyll is Faith Chapel, where the millionaires worshiped. At two motels, in Buford and Blakely, are thimble-tiny prayer chapels with crosses, where travelers may meditate or pray. At Bethesda below Savannah is a replica of Reverend George Whitefield's chapel in England. He was the founder of this Bethesda orphanage. At Talbotton is a little Gothic church of beauty. The Strauses, who founded Macy's in New York, have always been interested benefactors of Talbotton institutions because their father, who started the family fortune, once had a store in Talbotton.

Big Bethel Church in Atlanta is nationally known because of its music, and its famed "Heaven Bound" drama, which has drawn thousands.

Transportation:
How The People Come And Go

Transportation has been a big factor in Georgia progress from the beginning. Roads were built over old Indian trails. The rivers were used as highways for travel and getting crops to market. Then railroads began to be built across the state. With the invention of the automobile, paved roads made travel easier. Then came the airplane. Georgia, in the center of the dynamic southeast, became almost at once a crossways for the world.

ROADS RUN ALL OVER THE STATE

Travel in Georgia has come a long way since the time that Oglethorpe made his brave and dangerous 400-mile journey across a state with no roads or bridges to Coweta near Columbus, to keep the Creek Indians friendly to Britain.

Later, there were stagecoaches, and dirt roads for them to go along. Inns grew up for the travelers to rest and spend the night. The coaches could not travel more than forty miles a day, even at their fastest. It took four days in good weather, a week in bad weather, to get from Savannah to Augusta.

Georgia's roads have vastly improved in recent years. The Georgia Highway Department, set up in 1919, gets a big share of the state's tax money, and more federal funds in recent years have made possible better roads through the state. Georgia was allotted 1,103 miles of the national interstate system in the thirteen-year program.

In 1916, Congress first passed the Good Roads bill, providing a federal dollar for every state dollar used to build good roads. Laws have been changed many times since then, making possible more funds, both state and federal, for road building.

The Coastal Highway, from the Savannah River to Florida, opened in 1928. By 1925, Georgia had 3,000 miles of improved highways and 87,000 miles of country roads, but these were not enough. Besides more and better roads within the state, Georgia urgently needed highways connecting with other states that would make it possible for outsiders to travel more easily through Georgia, and for Georgians to travel or send their products afar.

The state launched a mammoth program in improving and expanding its roads that had brought it, by 1962, to the rank of seventh among the fifty states in construction of interstate highways. More highways, the city freeways and connectors, the wide expressways running up and down and across the state, made travel better in Georgia. The dangerous open range laws that once allowed cattle and other livestock to roam at will had been changed to make highways safer.

Some of Georgia's roads along the countrysides and towns have picturesque names: Po Biddy Road, Nowhere Road, and others.

Many of the highways had been named for famous people who were connected with Georgia in some way, like President Franklin Delano Roosevelt, or native Georgians like Senator Richard B. Russell. The Russell scenic highway was a part of a federal road, and led across some of Georgia's most picturesque scenery. It was planned to go through the Tesnatee Gap, along Lordy Mercy Cove, past Duke's Creek where gold was first found in Georgia in 1828, and by Raven's Cliff, with its 500-foot waterfall. The road will be pouring thousands of tourists right into the heart of Georgia's most scenic wonderland for years to come.

In 1965, Georgia had a road system of 87,346 miles, and approximately two million automobiles, buses and trucks were registered in the state.

The Mississippi River is just 400 miles away from Georgia's western boundary. Georgia is the largest state east of it. Georgia, in the heart of the southeast, is within two hours' plane ride of a fourth of the people in the United States.

Railway freight, air freight, trucking cargoes and ships in and out the ports and along the rivers make it possible for Georgia to market its products of farm and factory within and outside the state. In 1965, Georgia truckers were paying nearly $28,000,000 a year in state taxes and nearly $32,000,000 in federal taxes.

During the 4 years, 1963-1966, the state invested $750 million in highways; 677 miles of the interstate highways were also completed or under construction.

The great dams and locks on Georgia rivers have created lakes and centers where power is generated and recreation areas have developed. Millions of dollars invested in them have strengthened Georgia's economy. Among them are the Clark Hill Dam above Augusta, the Hartwell Dam, the Buford Dam creating the Lake Sidney Lanier area around Buford and Gainesville, the Allatoona development in the Rome-Cartersville area, the Oliver Dam at Columbus, the Walter George development at Fort Gaines, the Jim Woodruff Dam at Bainbridge and others. Georgians envision their inland ports along the rivers being connected with the great ocean and gulf. Navigable rivers would make easier the problem of transporting Georgia's products to outside markets, increase travel and recreation, and create more power.

Georgia's waterways became more and more important. There was much interest in a proposed cross-state canal that would shorten the distance between the Gulf of Mexico and the Atlantic Ocean, as the Panama Canal had shortened the distance between the Atlantic and Pacific oceans. This was especially important to the space centers, which had to haul their products from such places as Texas to the Cape Kennedy space center on the east coast of Florida. Georgia leaders pointed out how much a shorter water route through Georgia would save.

GEORGIA'S INTRA-COASTAL WATERWAY

Along the coast, boats skitter along 137 miles of

Georgia's inland waterways. Some are boats in which people travel on business or for pleasure. Others carry cargoes. Almost a million tons of water-borne traffic moves over these bright waters each year. Most of the commodities shipped are pulpwood, lumber, creosote, oil, fuel oil, paper, sand, steel and industrial chemicals. These routes are a part of the Atlantic Intra-Coastal Waterway.

The United States Army Corps of Engineers, which also deepens harbors and rivers, works with flood control, and builds dams at many places further inside the state on inland rivers, works on these waterways.

Georgia is one of the few states with two deep-water ports on the Atlantic: Savannah, where about 1,200 steamships sail out each year, and Brunswick, where about a hundred leave. More than five million tons are shipped from these two ports yearly.

MAKING THE ROADS SAFE

Georgians have taken steps to make their roads and highways safer. The alarming rate at which Americans were getting killed on United States highways (one every 15 minutes, four every hour) prompted Georgia to tighten up its safety laws, require safety checks on cars, and increase its patrol vigilance. The State Department of Education added a state consultant on driver training to help local schools set up courses for the thousands of pupils who each year become old enough to drive cars.

GEORGIA AND AIR TRAVEL

More than three million travelers a year get on and off planes at Atlanta's beautiful new airport. A plane arrives or departs there every two minutes, 365 days a year. The new airport was opened in 1962. An object of interest — and controversy — in its lobby is a $35,000 mobile hanging from the center ceiling. A huge map of Georgia is placed where travelers can see it immediately.

Georgia has twelve major airports: Albany, Athens, Atlanta, Augusta, Brunswick, Columbus, Macon, Moultrie, Rome, Savannah, Valdosta, and Waycross. Airplanes connect Georgia with the nation and the world. Daily non-stop jet service to and from California is provided from Atlanta. Six of the nation's big air trunk lines and two local service

Atlanta Airport

lines operate in Georgia. Atlanta ranks sixth in the nation
in air carrier operation. Its airport is one of the busiest
in the world.

CHAPTER 70

HEALTH SERVICES
ARE EXPANDING

Georgia's State Department of Health is headed by Dr. John Venable, a native Georgian. The Department, which employs about six thousand people, co-ordinates the work of local health departments in Georgia's counties. The present department was created by an Act of March 18, 1933. The State Hospital for the Mentally Ill, at Milledgeville, was transferred from the Welfare Department to the Health Department in 1959. The Gracewood Home for the Mentally Retarded, near Augusta, the Battey Hospital at Rome, and the centers for the rehabilitation of alcoholics are responsibilities of the Health Department. It also supervises the establishment of Hill-Burton hospitals and health centers, the recording of vital statistics of birth and death, programs of sanitation, water pollution control, maternal and child health, communicable disease control and many other health services. The Department has its own building on Capitol Hill.

Health is a chief concern of Georgia. The Department of Health, the United States Communicable Disease Center, medical, dental, and nursing schools, and great hospitals give evidence of this. Environmental health has been one of the chief interests.

Studies in air pollution and the problem of getting enough clean water and ending the pollution of the streams are going on. Industrial hygiene is a service of the health

811

department. Radiation service concerns itself with providing basic safety techniques important to those who live in a world of nuclear energy and want to reduce its hazards. Accident prevention is a concern also.

In 1965, Georgia had 2,839 physicians in private practice and many more in public health services. The state set up in recent years scholarships to finance through college and medical school young doctors who would agree to practice in the rural areas of the state where there are not enough doctors. The Hill-Burton Hospital Act made possible the building of hospitals in many communities that had been without them. Health centers and clinics in the counties and communities have achieved remarkable progress in improving Georgia's health. The federal government has built imposing new hospitals in the state, like the $12,000,000 veterans' hospital built near Decatur, Georgia. Nursing homes throughout the state made more comfortable the convalescence of invalids or the latter days of older people.

Heart disease, the leading cause of death in the nation, is also the leading cause in Georgia, with 12,021 Georgians dying of this in 1962.

How The Health Program Grew

Certain diseases had plagued Georgia from the beginning. Oglethorpe's colonists had malaria and, later, smallpox. Yellow fever was a plague along the coast.

During the nineteenth century, little was actually done in an organized way to protect the health of the state's people, a situation found in most other states during that period. However, as early as 1817, inspection of meat and drugs had been required, and in 1866, the state began to provide for smallpox vaccinations. Registration of birth was also begun in 1823. The first state board of health was set up in 1875, but was voluntary.

It was not until 1903 that the first modern Board of Health urged the state to set up agencies of its own, especially urgent after a serious smallpox scare in 1899.

The Legislature passed a law calling for the State Board of Health with twelve members, one from each Congressional district, usually a doctor. Local boards of health were also required. 812

Regulations pertaining to health became more stringent; water was analyzed, slaughter houses inspected, drugs restricted to prescriptions, nurses registered, mosquito-breeding lands drained, contagious diseases quarantined, and strict sanitary rules about the removal of dead animals enforced.

Yellow fever was not the plague it once had been, but the reservoirs and the swamps were still here in the South where yellow fever germs could lurk. The Public Health Service asked Congress for $5 million to launch a final war against a mosquito known as "aedes aegpti," an insect that had been known to destroy whole armies. Campaigns against the fever in this section early in this century were so thorough that there is no known source where the mosquito could now get the virus in this area. There are still sources, however, in Latin America from which it could be brought in. The Pan American Health Organization has been co-

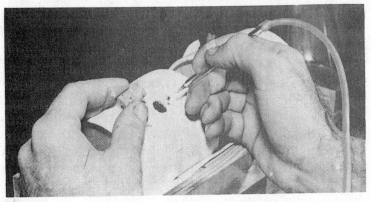

Mosquitoes Are Used In Research

operating with this country in a campaign to wipe out the mosquito that carries yellow fever. The five-year program that was recently planned has an estimated cost of $45,000-000, but experts say it may cost $90,000,000 to wipe out the mosquito from the southeast and eradicate the danger completely.

The phenomenal growth of health services, aided by state and federal money, as well as local support, has been of great benefit to Georgians. Hospitals, health clinics, and more doctors and other trained personnel have resulted in Georgians living longer and living more happily and healthfully.

813

Besides the University Hospital and Medical College in Augusta, other institutions aid Georgia's health. For example, Emory University has a medical school and hospital, and carries on much research for the betterment of human health. Among its facilities is the Yerkes Regional Primate Research Center where the study of animals like orangutans, gorillas, and many monkeys reveal much about similar diseases or health in mankind himself. The animals were given to Emory by Yale University in 1956, when the laboratory was located at Orange Park, Florida.

The Egglestone Hospital for Children is also located on the Emory campus.

Mental Health

There has been growing interest throughout Georgia in recent years in mental health. During the Vandiver administration, a committee headed by Dr. W. Bruce Schaefer, Toccoa physician who had been president of the Medical Association, outlined its recommendations for the improvement of the state's mental health efforts and facilities. That set in motion a program that has benefited Georgia greatly. New buildings have been constructed at the State Hospital, which was opened in 1848 and now has more than 12,000 resident patients and 2,500 out-patients. Vocational services and classes for children in the institution have been set up or expanded. Dr. Irville MacKinnon, a doctor of national prominence, and professor of psychiatry at Columbia University, heads the institution, and leads in improving mental health services in Georgia. A program of preventive activities was increased, and people all over Georgia have become interested in the problem. The Georgia Association for Mental Health in 1963 had thirty-nine chapters in the state. Their purpose was to educate and inform the public about mental health, and to give assistance to those whose mental health was impaired.

Day-by-day work, as well as the more dramatic Christmas parade of gifts for State Hospital patients, has created a new attitude in Georgia toward mental illness.

The Division of Mental Health in the State Department of Health is staffed with able people who are highly skilled in this field. In 1964, as interest increased in combining

814

services across county lines, there was considerable discussion about providing the services of psychologists or psychiatrists for several counties from one health center.

A gratifying recognition of the improvement of Georgia's mental health program came in November, 1964, when the State Hospital at Milledgeville was accredited for a three-year residency training program in psychiatry. In the sixteen Southern states, there are only five other state hospitals accredited to train psychiatrists. The Hospital already had some training affiliations with Emory University's Medical School and the Medical College of Georgia at Augusta.

Besides the state-financed buildings added to the hospital, a Chapel of All Faiths has been built with the aid of money donated by the public.

The Mental Health program was growing in Georgia by 1964. The people of the state had been made aware of the importance of mental health, the Department of Health and the Association for Mental Health had given them plain, sometimes shocking, facts: that approximately 400,000 Georgians (one out of every ten) are now suffering from some form of mental illness, and that at least 100,000 school children are emotionally disturbed. Tackling this problem with new vigor, as they were attacking other problems that confronted them, Georgians could see progress.

There is much interest in decentralizing the huge mental hospital, building smaller ones, and involving Georgians in neighborhood programs to help the mentally ill regain their health.

The Georgia Mental Health Institute was opened in Atlanta in November, 1965. A mental retardation center was located in De Kalb County.

Three Faces of Eve: *Study In Mental Health*
A book which became a best seller in America and a dozen foreign countries, and was made into a film by Hollywood, was *The Three Faces of Eve*.   It was published in 1957. It was at first simply a report, made by two Georgia

psychiatrists from the Medical College of Georgia at Augusta, to the American Psychiatric Association. The two psychiatrists were Dr. Hervey M. Cleckley and Dr. Corbett H. Thigpen of Augusta. The bizarre case was that of one of their patients with whom they had worked. Of course they did not use her real name.

There was so much interest in the case that they wrote a book about her. Hollywood made a movie starring Georgia-born Joanne Woodward. The script was written by a Georgia writer and film producer, Nunnally Johnson of Columbus.

The case was about the strange appearance of three different personalities in the body of one patient. One personality was that of a rather drab, anxious, quite respectable housewife whom they called Eve White. Suddenly, without warning and after repeated headaches which sent her to the doctors, Mrs. White's body was taken over by a flirtatious, shallow personality whom the doctors called Eve Black. Later, a serious, serene young woman named Jane was the third personality who appeared. The odd case is still the subject of comment by doctors and by those who have read the remarkable book.

The United States Communicable Disease Center Is In Georgia

Near Emory in Atlanta is the Communicable Disease Center. It is the only unit of the United States Public Health Service located outside of Washington. It was started in the 1940's as a malaria control center, and has grown into the present structure. It now has about 200 research projects going on.

The Center aids state health units in preventing or handling epidemics. It provides laboratory diagnostic aid, test material, and training staff to help states organize or expand their own communicable disease program.

The Center's staff once helped Georgia's health authorities avert a threatened polio epidemic. During a routine test of the Sabin polio vaccine, tests made with the aid of the center revealed a high incidence of Type III polio contamination in Atlanta. The epidemic was averted.

Among the center's research projects was one on

The First Lady, Mrs. Lyndon B. Johnson, Breaks Ground For Additions To The Atlanta Headquarters Of The U.S. Public Health Service's Communicable Disease Center. (May 11, 1964).

leprosy. Its research may make possible the decrease or control of this deforming disease that afflicts more than fifteen million human beings throughout the world.

The Problem Of A New Constitution

In the early 1960's, Georgians began to hear much of a new constitution being needed.

The state had lived under a document of law since the Third Provincial Congress in the spring of 1776 drew up temporary "rules and regulations of government." There were eight brief sections of this. But even then, it was divided just the way government is divided today, into the three familiar parts: executive, legislative, and judicial.

The Constitution had been revised many times since 1776. In 1943 the legislature, during the administration of Governor Ellis Arnall, set up a commission of twenty-three members to draft another state constitution. When it was completed and reviewed by the General Assembly, it was submitted to the people of Georgia, who approved it by a vote of 60,065 to 34,417.

This constitution was very long, and included much statutory law that many people felt did not really belong in a constitution. There were also many amendments. By the

1960's, plans began to be shaped to draft another constitution. Federal court decisions and decrees came up at the time and had to be dealt with before state law could be clearly shaped. The plans were delayed for a time.

CHAPTER 71

WHAT'S HAPPENING IN
EDUCATION AND THE ARTS

Matters of the mind and spirit have taken on new vigor throughout Georgia. Education has become the chief topic of conversation, the chief recipient of state tax money. The people, willing to tax themselves more to finance education, are at the same time demanding that the education they finance be genuine quality education, from kindergarten through graduate school. Federal funds and new laws passed by Congress and signed by Kennedy and Johnson during their terms as president, made possible in Georgia and throughout the nation more and better ventures in education.

Georgia was already moving forward on its own toward better education. The adoption of a Minimum Foundation Program of Education and its subsequent revision, the strengthening of the state department of education, the growth of the Southern Regional Education Board, the creation of science centers, the addition of nuclear reactors, more citizens' groups working for education, the spreading of junior colleges and vocational-technical schools all were factors in Georgia's forging ahead in education.

The Georgia Education Improvement Council was set up to co-ordinate the educational efforts in the state: elementary, secondary, and higher education.

The Public Schools —
Their Growth And New Ventures

In 1966, Georgia had 195 public school systems, with 1,944 schools, elementary and high school. In them, more than a million boys and girls are taught by about 41,000 teachers, better trained and better paid than ever before.

Georgia had the twelfth largest school system in the nation. The state is putting more money into education, and more federal funds are available. New school buildings are to be seen everywhere in Georgia, but more are needed each year because about 20,000 or 30,000 pupils are added to the rolls each year, more than were there the year before.

Georgia was out in front in the nation in educational television, in consolidating its schools, in building area vocational-technical schools, and in many other modern educational ventures.

WHO'S HERE TO EDUCATE?

In the 1,944 schools in Georgia in the 1965-66 school year were 1,140,967 pupils, from kindergarten to twelfth grade. The enrollment had zoomed past the million mark for the first time in 1959-1960. Besides the pupils actually in school, there were about 600,000 more of pre-school age for whom Georgia had to busy itself getting enough teachers and building enough classrooms and providing enough textbooks.

There were also thousands of college age, and more of them were in college now than in previous years. There were those who did not go to college but wanted excellent vocational training to prepare them for jobs in business and industry. There were also thousands of adults who wanted retraining, either because automation had replaced them in their jobs or because they needed refresher courses to qualify for better jobs or promotions.

The 1966 graduating class, estimated at 52,360, represented an investment of nearly $150 million in tax money, or nearly $3,000 per student.

HALF THE STUDENTS RIDE TO SCHOOL ON THE BUS

Five thousand big, chrome yellow school buses daily carry to and from school a half million pupils, almost exactly half of all those enrolled in Georgia's schools. It was the bus that made consolidation of schools practical, and brought twelve grades of free public school education within reach of children from the remotest rural areas.

Of the school bus drivers, more than three hundred were women, and about a hundred were either teachers or older students. The school buses of Georgia totaled, every day during the 180-day school year, mileage equal to thirteen trips around the world, or more than fifty million miles a year. It cost less than $35 per child per year, or about 30¢ a mile. The average school bus route, from home to school and back, was about thirty miles.

Most school bus accidents are caused by cars running into the back or side of the bus. Chrome yellow was chosen as the color for school buses throughout the nation because research shows it is the easiest color to see.

Bus drivers took a special interest in their charges, and felt themselves a real part of the school and its program. One driver expressed it for them all when he said, "After all, you can't teach them till we get them there!"

A few Georgia children got to school by boat. They were students who live on Sapelo Island, across from Darien.

DR. CLAUDE PURCELL BECAME GEORGIA'S
FOURTEENTH STATE SCHOOL SUPERINTENDENT

On January 13, 1958, Dr. Claude Purcell became superintendent of schools for Georgia. He directed the progress of the nation's twelfth largest school system, and was named one of the country's ablest school executives. He served as chairman of the legislative committee for the powerful American Council of Chief State School Officers, and was often called to Washington to testify before congressional committees on behalf of the increased federal support that brought more federal money to Georgia and other states for education.

Dr. Purcell, a native of Banks County, was a career man in education. He had come up through the ranks from teacher of a one-room school to principal, then to county school superintendent in Habersham County. He was brought into the state department of education in 1942 by Dr. M. D. Collins, then state superintendent of schools. Dr. Purcell ably administered the Minimum Foundation Program, supervised school transportation, and prepared for board approval the first school building plans.

He was appointed by the governor as state school superintendent after the resignation of Dr. Collins, and was later elected and re-elected to the office. In 1962, he was one of twelve American state school superintendents invited as guests of the West German government to review the school programs there.

His administration was commended for the expansion of educational television, better salaries for teachers, more money for schools, more research and experimental programs, grants for teachers for summer study, the sixth year certificate, increase of the teacher scholarship program, and many other facets of progress.

On December 24, 1965, Dr. Purcell resigned. Governor Carl Sanders appointed as his successor Jack P. Nix, who had been director of vocational education.

Jack P. Nix

The Minimum Foundation Program Of Education

In the late 1940's many Georgians undertook a study of the public school system. In 1949, the legislature enacted the Minimum Foundation Program of Education. This guaranteed at least a minimum program of education to every child in Georgia, no matter where he lived. Basically, the program provided that the community would pay part of the cost and the state would pay the balance. Collectively, all the school systems at first paid 15 percent; the state paid 85 percent. The new law was put into effect in 1951, when a 3¢ sales tax provided the state enough money to finance the program.

Programs For Exceptional Children

Georgia set up its first Governor's Honors Program in the summer of 1964, the second state to do this, and the first to provide state funds for it. Under this program, four hundred of the state's brightest juniors and seniors from the high schools were given eight free weeks of creative learning in areas of their talent and interest, under the skillful direction of about forty able teachers. Georgia was one of the first states to have a full-time consultant in the education department to handle programs for exceptional children, which also included the mentally retarded, the emotionally disturbed, those with speech, eye, ear, or limb defects, and others. Many children who need special education attend regular schools, but get help also from specially trained personnel.

Georgia has also set up educational programs through the cooperation of educational agencies with other groups, in prisons, in mental hospitals, and in other places where education is needed.

The Academy for the Blind in Macon, taken over by the state in 1852, and the School for the Deaf at Cave Spring, started in 1848, have attained wide acclaim for the accredited programs they have provided. Both schools have academic and vocational programs, and are free.

The STAR program of the State Chamber of Commerce has done much to add prestige to academic achievement. Annually, the students who rank highest and are recommended are honored with local and state programs. Scholarships, trips abroad, and other awards have done much to spotlight the shining minds in senior classes, and the teachers who helped move them into motion toward their highest achievements.

The STAR program, made up of the first letters of the words Student-Teacher Achievement Recognition, has won national attention, and other states have patterned programs on Georgia's.

The Governor's Conference on Education, sponsored by the Georgia School Boards Association, has annually assembled Georgians to discuss school problems and take pride in school progress.

In 1965, Georgians all over the state were discussing a plan that had been advanced to create bigger school units in Georgia.

In 1964, the state board of education authorized a study of standards for schools, and a study of more efficient and economical ways to organize school districts in Georgia. The reorganization study was done by a group from Peabody College at Nashville, Tennessee, and was directed by Dr. W. D. McClurkin. The Report was sometimes called the Peabody Report, but more often the "McClurkin Report."

Dr. McClurkin pointed out that Georgians had given evidence of their interest in good education and their willingness to support it. He praised Georgians for having consolidated their schools from 6,600 to 1,944 since 1930. By 1966, there were only four one-teacher schools left in Georgia.

Within the same thirty years, he pointed out, the average teacher's salary had gone from $700 a year to more than $5,000. Per-pupil expenditure had gone from $34 per pupil to more than $300, though it was still far below the national average.

He recommended that more schools be consolidated so that Georgia pupils might have a wider curriculum, better libraries, laboratories, lunchrooms, and more staff to teach them.

The statistics revealed that 78 of the 196 school districts had fewer than 2,500 pupils, and only 15 had more than 10,000 pupils.

He recommended that a school system, in order to provide good education, have at least 10,000 pupils, but preferably from 15,000 to 20,000. This would enable each school system to have specially trained personnel which the legislature had already made possible for schools that could qualify: 1 for each 200 pupils. At first these were limited to librarians, counselors, visiting teachers, curriculum directors and principals. But ultimately, they could include speech therapists, psychiatrists, art directors, special education teachers, researchers and many others. Because they were limited to 1 for each 200 pupils, small schools could not qualify for the services that larger schools could get.

Georgians discussed the report and its recommenda-

A Modern Georgia High School

tions, from Rabun to Seminole counties, from the mountains of Dade to the bronze marshes of Flynn. There were some good little schools in Georgia which people were reluctant to give up. Small schools had certain advantages. But the advocates of the McClurkin Report insistently pointed out that there was not enough money to provide all the services for small schools that could be provided in larger systems. Many Georgians, their school leaders, board members, and legislators had already read the books written by former Harvard President James B. Conant, who had been studying United States schools and who had recommended larger school systems also. He advocated that a school system be large enough to have at least 100 in the graduating class.

The Vocational Program Grows

The state has long had one of the best of the country's vocational education programs. Georgians introduced the act in 1917 that launched this program for the nation. They were Congressman Dudley M. Hughes of Danville and Senator Hoke Smith of Atlanta. Senator Walter George and Congressman Braswell Dean put their names to later bills that continued and expanded it. Current Georgians in Congress support it. In 1963, Congress enacted the Perkins Bill which brought more funds for this program.

In high school and adult programs, boys and girls and older Georgians had first been trained to build better farms and create better homes. Later, the trade and industrial distributive education, and business programs were also added.

The state has maintained two vocational-technical boarding schools at Clarkesville and Americus for many years. Recently area vocational-technical schools have also been built; twenty-eight are either finished or planned. Tuition is free to Georgians at all these schools, and training has equipped thousands of Georgians for good jobs in trade and industry. The results have been personal fulfillment, growth of the state's economy, and the influx of more industry ready to locate where well-trained workers are to be found. The vocational division of the education department also began to administer the federal Manpower Training Program.

Besides the work of the vocational agriculture teachers and home economists with the public school program, Georgia's farms and homes have greatly benefited from the work of farm agents and home demonstration agents whose program is based at the University of Georgia in Athens, and is under the United States Department of Agriculture. The University itself trains professional workers in agriculture, forestry and other areas that have benefited both rural and urban Georgia.

More Public School Progress

Educational television has spread over Georgia rapidly. By 1965, Georgia had four stations on the air, and five more scheduled for opening in 1966. Atlanta had set up its own station some years before, and joined in the state network to further the education of Georgians. The stations were connected so that teacher education programs and other such things could make possible greater educational advantages for the state. The first teacher educational program, one on how to teach reading, had as early as 1964 been viewed by 16,000 teachers!

SCHOOL LUNCH BECAME A $40 MILLION ENTERPRISE

Georgia's school lunch program came under the state

Department of Education in 1943. Senator Richard B. Russell was widely regarded over the nation as "the father of the school lunch program." Before this was made a part of the school plan, the only hot lunches had been provided when mothers or concerned teachers warmed soup on the school stove.

By 1966, the school lunch program in Georgia was a $40,000,000 enterprise. The 1950 school lunchrooms, which served more than a million meals each of the 180 school days in the year, got cash reimbursements, and more than $10,000,000 in foods from the United States Government. These funds made it possible for them to serve for 25¢ or 30¢ a hot, nourishing lunch at noon. The health of Georgia's school children improved, and they studied better. One educator said, "It's hard for a hungry child to learn much." Ten thousand school lunchroom workers carried on the program in the schools, under a supervisor or the school principal. Often they arose while it was still dark to get the lunch ready for the children and their teachers. Lifelong habits in good nutrition and in good manners often started or improved in the school lunchrooms of Georgia. Of the $40,000,000, about $30,000,000 or more went to local farmers for fresh foods or to local merchants for school lunchroom supplies.

The Georgia school lunchrooms serve more than 120 million meals during the school year. Both the president and the governor issue proclamations each year that call attention to the importance of the school lunch program.

Basic Adult Education Grows

Adults who did not get a chance to finish school were getting more help as the modern school program and the new federal legislation got into action. In 1960, Georgia had about 355,000 people over twenty-five who did not get to the fourth grade, and the state department of education had some classes in basic education. When the Economic Opportunity Act passed in 1964, more programs were set up, and they were designed to reach all Georgians over eighteen who did not get to the eighth grade. There were classes in how to read and write, but there were also courses in good citizenship, voting, filling out income tax, keeping records, and

Two Buildings In The University of Georgia Science Center

handling many everyday matters that went beyond basic education.

Georgia's "median point" citizen appeared in the census of 1960 as having had nine years of school. Half of all Georgians had had more; half had had less. This was an improvement over 1950, when the median was 7.8 years. With the vigorously expanding educational program of the state during the 1950's and 1960's, the median in Georgia would soon appear as far beyond nine years, and more and more would be listed as not only high school but college graduates.

Those who did not finish high school were finding help, too. The education department was giving General Education Development Tests to those over twenty who did not finish high school, and issuing to them high school equivalency certificates to aid them in jobs or future college plans. These tests were given at twenty centers throughout the state. Between 1947, when the plan was set up, and the fall of 1965, the department had issued 31,836 certificates, and was issuing about 3,000 a year. With each certificate went a letter of encouragement from the state school superintendent. The recipients wrote many notes of appreciation for the help, both the certificate and the letter. One man wrote, "I have framed both of them, and they are on my wall."

Georgia's Teachers

In the public schools of Georgia, there were early in 1966 more than 41,000 teachers. About 95 percent of them had at least four years of college, and more than 10,000 had master's degrees. The state board of education had already approved adding the doctorate to the teacher salary schedule. No beginning teacher could get a teaching certificate in Georgia unless he or she had had at least four years of college. The average teacher's salary had gone past the $5,000 mark but was still below the national average. In 1965-1966, the average in Georgia was $5,350.

The first state salary schedule, which had been adopted in 1937 when the seven months' school law and the free textbook law had also passed, had been based on what kind of certificate the teacher held. The salary ranged from $40 a month in state salary for a teacher who held a county license, to $80 for those who held a "life professional" certificate. Georgia teachers' salaries from the state ranged in 1965-1966 from $3,895 for a beginning teacher with four years of college and a professional certificate, to $6,582 for a teacher with a sixth year (of college) certificate and fourteen years' experience. Teachers' raises over the four years of the Sanders administration had been $1,200 average. Across-the-board raises had been abolished and the biggest raises were going to the best prepared and most experienced teachers.

Visiting teachers, curriculum directors, counselors, and other specialists added to school staffs were making a big difference in the school program, and strengthening education in Georgia. Gradually more and more specialists are being added.

FUTURE TEACHERS GET FREE SCHOLARSHIPS

Georgia needed more and more good teachers. The state set up in 1959 a scholarship program, similar to one for future doctors already existing, to finance college for talented young people who stood high in their classes, wanted to teach, and needed money for their education. They could get up to a thousand dollars a year, and even $1,800 for a fifth year of graduate study in some cases, for college. They did not have to pay a dollar of this back, but they did have to teach in Georgia, and they did have to maintain an excellent grade to stay in the program. By 1966, this program had put about five hundred of the state's brightest young people into Georgia classrooms as teachers, and there were a thousand students in colleges on the scholarships. The state was currently investing $600,000 a year in the program.

A state scholarship commission, set up by the legislature, also had further help for young Georgians in preparing for many professions, either in grants, loans, or in interest-guaranteed plans of borrowing.

What's Happening In The Colleges

Georgia's colleges, both state and private, are going on to new heights of attainment in building programs and academic achievement. Their biggest problem has been finding space for tremendously increased enrollments.

The projected enrollment for 1970 for the colleges in the University system alone is 90,633, or an 80 percent increase over the enrollment in 1960; and by 1976, an enrollment of 109,776, an increase over 1960 of 119 percent. This projection was made by the staff of the Governor's Commission To Improve Education in November, 1963. Private colleges, which enrolled 20,000 in 1963, will have from 25,000 to 30,000 by 1975.

The Southern Regional Education Board was organized in the southeast with the purpose of making more education available for people in this section. If one state did not have a certain type of college, it paid the difference in tuition for one of its students to attend that college in a state which did have it. In 1965, Georgia's Governor Carl Sanders was named chairman of SREB. Its offices have, from the beginning, been located in Atlanta.

The Southern Regional Board created a Commission on Goals for Higher Education. In a booklet, "Within Our Reach," they had had this message for the South: "Within reach of the people of the South lie opportunities that stir the imagination. Economically, this region can be one of the most productive areas on earth. Culturally, its writers, painters, and musicians can bring new glory to American literature, art, and music. Intellectually, its colleges and universities can increasingly become preeminent centers of learning and leadership. These things are possible. These states have the natural resources and the human resources to attain them. The catalyst needed to produce the transformation is higher education of the finest quality."

Georgia colleges have gone on to new achievements in learning, both in liberal arts and in technical and professional fields. They have more deeply demonstrated a sound conviction that the people the world needs most are those who have both an appreciation of old cultures and a grace and skill in the arts of communication and awareness of history, as well as professional ability to handle some job well in an increasingly technical world. The doctor wants to know about Beethoven, and the engineer is likely to discuss Plato's ideas about government.

A new development in Georgia is the spread of junior colleges. Some institutions that have previously been junior colleges have made the transition to senior colleges.

Some colleges have recently observed special anniversaries or events. In 1965, Emory University in Atlanta observed its half-century mark, and Atlanta University had reached its hundredth year. Wesleyan in Macon — the first college in the world chartered to grant degrees to women — had another visit from one of its most illustrious former students, China's Madame Chiang Kai-shek. Young Harris College in the mountains dedicated a room to the memory of the poet Byron Herbert Reece, who had taught there.

Emory in 1965 was observing the fiftieth anniversary of its establishment in Atlanta. Emory-at-Oxford, which remains an important and charming part of Georgia's educational scene, was established in 1834 as a manual school and chartered in 1836 as Emory College, sponsored by the Methodists. It was suspended in 1862 because of the war, and reopened six years later. In 1915 it opened another college, now a university, near Atlanta.

Emory was by 1965 one of the nation's great universities, and in that year launched a $25,000,000 fundraising campaign in its bid to become still greater. Its students are by now mostly graduate students studying at one of its professional schools, such as medicine or law, though

Emory University

it still maintains a top-ranking undergraduate program.

By 1965, Emory's enrollment had passed 6,000 and its faculty, 1,300. It was granting 1,100 degrees yearly, more than half of them graduate and professional. Since 1915, it had graduated about 26,000. Its yearly budget exceeded $35 million. In 1965, its future plans included an eight-story library that was to cost about $5,500,000 and house a million books. Among its priceless possessions is a collection of things connected with John Wesley, including a pulpit from which he had preached to Welsh miners. On the campus of this red-roofed college is a whimsical eye-catcher: a monument to anti-gravity!

Georgia Tech opened its doors October 3, 1888, with 84 students. All but one were from Georgia; one was from Tennessee. Tech is regarded as a great asset in a world to which science is so new that half of all the scientists who ever lived are alive today. The Frank H. Neely Nuclear Research Center and other facilities make it possible for Tech to look at modern concerns and ancient interests, from atoms to stars, to put them in perspective for Georgia and the world. When the 5-megawatt heavy-water reactor was installed in 1963, it was one of two in the United States and more modern than the one at the Massachusetts Institute of Technology.

Tech has accepted the challenge of the space age, while holding on to the basic idea that power rests in the mind of man. Said one commentator, "Modern scientific philosophy holds, with Einstein, that the universe is not completely determinable or measurable. The certainty, measurability, and inevitability of nineteenth century science has been replaced with relativity, probability, and chance. The door is thus opened for creative individual action." Arnold Toynbee wrote that a society begins to decline at its height when it loses its "creative minority of people." So if society survives it will be due to individuals who accept willingly and use wisely the power of man to change the world.

After the Civil War, Lee himself had become a college president, and he had counseled the South to educate its youth. In 1866, he said, "I consider the proper education of the South's youth one of the most important objects now to be attained and one from which the greatest benefits may be expected. Nothing will compensate us for the depression of the standard of our moral and intellectual culture and each state should take the most energetic measures to revive its schools and colleges and, if possible, to increase the facilities of instruction and to elevate the standard of living."

Those who had founded Tech knew that Georgia must move into the industrial revolution. The old liberal arts education, still deeply important to the richness of living, was not enough. The Civil War itself had shown the handicap of being without engineers and other technically trained people. Georgians and their legislators, geared to liberal arts education, were rather vague about what an engineering school provided and Tech had difficulty getting money to survive. In this era, when the state, the South, and the nation itself is indebted in many ways to the technological benefits that have come from this institution, its early difficulties seem suprising. "Tech lights us into the next century," said a Georgian. Up to 1966, its presidents had been these: Dr. Isaac Hopkins, 1888 to 1896; Dr. Lyman Hall, 1896 to 1905; Dr. Kenneth G. Matheson, 1906 to 1921; Dr. M. L. Brittain,

1922-1944; Dr. Blake Van Lee, 1944-1956; Dr. Edwin D. Harrison, since 1957.

In 1965, Atlanta University, the world's largest cluster of colleges started for Negroes, observed its one hundredth anniversary.

The institution started in a boxcar in 1865. It was begun by people who sought to educate the children of slaves who had been freed during the Civil War but who were uneducated and untrained for jobs.

The University attracts visitors and students from many parts of the world. On the hundredth anniversary, Dr. Rufus Clements said, "This week we had visitors from Kenya and from Japan the same day." The University, which now has only graduate students, is the focus of several Negro colleges around its campus: Morehouse, Clark, Spelman, and Morris Brown. Its working arrangement with Gammon Theological Seminary provides education for young ministers.

In the same week that the University observed its anniversary, Governor Nelson Rockefeller, one of the family that has given much money to the colleges and for whose grandmother Spelman College was named, was in Atlanta to speak at Ebenezer Baptist Church, where Rev. Martin Luther King, Sr., and his son, Rev. Martin Luther King, Jr., winner of the 1964 Nobel Peace Prize, are co-pastors.

West Georgia College at Carrollton continued to receive plaudits from the nation for its unique College in the Country, a plan by which the adult education program carried education out to farmers and housewives and others, who enriched it in return by their ideas and their interests.

Tech, with its research center and its nuclear reactor, was sending out graduates who would make a great difference in the future. The University's main campus at Athens had not only a new stadium, but a Science Center and park, and one of the nation's newly established research and dissemination centers designed to study and improve teaching and learning. The Center for Continuing Education on this campus, one of the first two in the nation of its kind, draws adults there for conferences and study and sends them back to business, clubs, communities, and farms with new ideas and widening interests.

834

Besides the network of state colleges, junior, senior, and graduate, that spreads over Georgia, there are some of the nation's best private schools and colleges. Many have long ago attained fame and continue to grow.

Baptists were moving toward the building of a great college center in Atlanta to extend the strength and power of Mercer at Macon. The six Baptist colleges in the state had a greater enrollment than ever, and like other colleges, were having to turn students away.

An example of the growth of the private or denominational colleges was that of Berry, established in 1902 by Miss Martha Berry. In 1956, Berry College had 614 students on its beautiful campus. In 1965, it had 1,113 students.

Two other schools which, like Berry, had been started primarily for the children of the mountains, continued to do an excellent job of educating younger students. Assisted in some phases by the regular public school program, they are also the special proteges of organizations. Tallulah Falls school is the continuing interest of the Georgia Federation of Women's Clubs, and the Rabun Gap — Nacoochee School focuses the attention of the United Daughters of the Confederacy.

There are many other schools in Georgia that have made outstanding contributions to the future education of Georgia children and young people. Space makes it impossible to discuss all of them.

THE UNIVERSITY SYSTEM HAS A BOARD OF REGENTS

The colleges that are supported through state appropriations are linked into a university system, governed by policies set up by a board of regents of fifteen members, appointed by the governor with the assent of the Senate. A chancellor heads the system and each institution has its own president.

How The Junior Colleges
Are Spreading Over The State

The spread of the junior college movement over the nation also involved Georgia. In the wake of pressing demands from students over the nation to get into college (some studies predict there will be 7 million college students

Mercer University

by 1970), some solution had to be found. The existing colleges simply did not have enough room for all who wanted to go, even when entrance requirements were made harder and fewer could qualify.

The junior colleges had advantages: they could be built nearer the students' homes, and would be therefore less expensive for those who could live at home and attend classes; they could provide terminal education for those who wanted only two years of college, as well as the first two years for students who planned to transfer to a four-year college later.

836

Georgia was providing a network of colleges for all Georgia boys and girls who wanted to go to college and could qualify. Georgia's high school graduates had already increased to 52,360 by 1966. More of them than ever planned to enter college. Many planned to enter the junior colleges.

State junior colleges already in operation in 1965 were Middle Georgia College at Cochran, South Georgia College at Douglas, Abraham Baldwin College at Tifton, and Brunswick Junior College. Others were being built or in the planning stage at Albany, Gainesville, Marietta, Dalton, Bibb County, Clayton County, and west Fulton County.

Some junior collegs were in transition to four-year colleges.

De Kalb County had established a junior college. This school, like several others in the state, was located near a vocational-technical school.

Most of the publicly supported junior colleges are under the board of regents that governs the University system. The vocational-technical schools, financed jointly by state and local funds, are under the state board of education. New legislation made it possible for several local school systems to join together to help establish vocational technical schools that would be available to all within their areas.

These Affect The Public Schools and Higher Education, Too

Some things affect both the schools and the colleges of Georgia. The decision on race handed down by the Supreme Court in 1954 was one. Another was the Georgia Educational Improvement Council. Another is the Interstate Compact, in which Georgia has been one of the first states to take an interest.

The Georgia Educational Improvement Council is a permanent body set up to co-ordinate educational forecasts and programs in Georgia. It was recommended by the Governor's Commission To Improve Education, which spent several months studying education in the state. It also co-ordinates the general plans of the Board of Regents, the University system, the State Board of Education, and the public schools to avoid duplication. It projects the future needs of education, and works with the legislature in long-range planning. The Council has an executive secretary, and eleven members. Six are members because of the offices they hold: the state superintendent of schools, the chairman of the state board of education, the chancellor of the University system, the chairman of the board of regents, the chairmen of the education committees of the Senate and the House of the General Assembly, and five members whom the governor appoints from the state at large. The Council is a new experiment in education, not only in Georgia but in the nation.

Georgia And The Interstate Compact

Georgia's governor, legislature, and educators were among the first in the nation to indicate their interest in a new idea in education: the Interstate Compact. Six Georgians were among those from fifty states who attended a conference in Kansas City in the fall of 1965 to discuss this new venture.

The idea of the compact was mentioned in *Shaping Educational Policy* by former Harvard president James B. Conant, who spent some years studying education in the United States. The idea of the compact was for the states to set up a voluntary plan of co-operation to maintain a nationwide (though not national) educational commission to discuss and plan for the best in education. Each state would have seven members, including the governor and two state legislators, and other appointed educators and laymen. The organization, which would become effective when endorsed by ten states, sought to guide, not govern, the states in their future programs for making far-reaching plans for education. Plans called for the states to make pro rata contributions ranging from $7,500 to $22,500 a year, beginning in January, 1968.

The organization is expected to (1) join political, professional and lay groups in a partnership for education, (2) collect, analyze and disseminate information on the needs, resources, and new techniques of education, (3) provide a forum for discussion and recommendation of educational policies, (4) provide information helpful to state governors and legislatures in planning for education, (5) act as a clearing house of information on how such problems are being solved in different states, (6) suggest the best in local administrative policies, and (7) assist in devising the best ways of financing education.

In support of this proposed plan, the Georgia Senate adopted this resolution:

A RESOLUTION

Calling upon the Council of State Governments to study appropriate ways and means to establish a compact among the fifty States of the Union providing for an Interstate Commission to study the goals and standards of education in the United States.

WHEREAS, the State of Georgia is undertaking an unprecedented program to improve the quality of education in our State; and

WHEREAS, the other States of the Union are faced with similar challenges and are also seeking to raise their educational standards; and

WHEREAS, in reality we are faced with a nationwide educational challenge requiring each state to bring new vigor and vitality to public education; and

WHEREAS, each state and the Congress of the United States could benefit greatly from careful research and study of the educational problems in the several States together with the establishment of desirable standards for various educational policies; and

WHEREAS, there now exists no organization capable of developing such information; and

WHEREAS, it is desirable that the States themselves initiate a study of the usefulness of such an interstate research organization.

NOW, THEREFORE, BE IT RESOLVED BY THE SENATE that this body does hereby urge the Council of State Governments to initiate a study of the appropriate ways and means of establishing such an organization and to present to the several States its recommendations and proposals.

BE IT FURTHER RESOLVED that the Secretary of the Senate is hereby authorized and directed to transmit an appropriate copy of this Resolution to the Board of Managers of the Council of State Governments.

Senate Resolution 46. Adopted in Senate February 12, 1965.

A Modern Georgia School

CHAPTER 72

THE U.S. SUPREME
COURT DECISION ON RACE

On May 17, 1954, the Supreme Court of the United States handed down a decision decreeing that the South's "separate, but equal" school systems were henceforth illegal.

The Sibley Commission turned in to the Governor and General Assembly a majority report, recommending that the schools be kept open, and a minority report that dissented from this view. The legislature rescinded the laws of the state that had required separate schools, and adopted a freedom-of-choice plan. One proposal that was tried for a year or two was private tuition grants, but gradually these diminished and virtually disappeared. The Civil Rights Act and an Education Act that provided $40 million in federal funds for Georgia included a provision that the money could not be disbursed to segregated schools.

Before this law passed the Eighty-ninth Congress in 1965, however, Georgia had already moved to abide by the law of the land as decreed by the United States Supreme Court. The first two Negro students were admitted to the University of Georgia in January, 1961. Nine students were also admitted to high schools in Atlanta. Gradually, Negro students entered more and more schools throughout the state. Private schools and colleges often complied voluntarily, even when they did not receive any federal funds.

By the fall of 1965, there were about ten thousand Negro students enrolled in Georgia's previously all-white public schools. For the most part, Georgia came through its school integration crisis with relative dignity and co-operation between the races.

In 1966, most of Georgia's 196 local school systems had plans to desegregate, thereby continuing to receive federal money. Most boards, school leaders, teachers, parents and students wanted their schools to comply with the law and meet the new situation with intelligence and dignity.

CHAPTER 73

PROGRESS IN
THE CULTURAL ARTS

The schools and colleges joined with people in clubs and communities to further the arts in Georgia. The purpose was not only to foster talent but to help people appreciate music, literature, art, architecture, and to find in these areas more grace and strength for living. The new stirrings were not only prompted by the fact that an increasingly mechanized and automated world was bringing more leisure and more time for the arts, but by the realization that these arts were an important part of life and everyday living.

Art And The Memorial Cultural Center

A tragedy gave impetus to Georgia's support of art. When many Georgians died in a plane crash at Orly Field near Paris in June, 1962, after an art tour of Europe, their friends began planning memorials to them. One was a plan for the establishment of an expanded art school in connection with the art museum and galleries of the Atlanta Art Association on Peachtree Street in Atlanta. The Association had sponsored the European tour. The results are living memorials: the Memorial Cultural Center, with 1,800 seats, and the Atlanta School of Art under the auspices of the Atlanta Arts Alliance. Symphony, ballet, theater, opera, and the art school are brought together.

France, honoring the memory of those who died sent to Atlanta for exhibit two great paintings, "Whistler's Mother" and "The Penitent Magdalene." Thousands of Georgians came to view them. A portrait of Lafayette, the great Frenchman who had helped America win its freedom in the Revolution, was also loaned. The Lafayette portrait was painted by Samuel F. B. Morse, inventor of the telegraph, who was also a fine artist.

The Atlanta Art Association has for many years done much to encourage art and art appreciation in Georgia. The beautiful galleries and institute next door, and the Thornton House in the Museum gardens, with its gourmet food, have contributed to the promotion of art. Atlanta University, where such fine arts as painting, music, and drama flourished, has an excellent art collection.

At the University of Georgia in Athens, a beautiful modern art building houses the art collection and classes. Fine artists in Georgia colleges, schools, and communities have served their state well.

One of the most interesting paintings in Georgia is at the back of the stage in the University of Georgia auditorium at Athens. It is a painting of St. Peter's Cathedral in Rome and it has been there almost a hundred years. It was painted by George Cook of Virginia, and presented to the University by Daniel Pratt, an Alabama art collector, in honor of his friend, Dr. Andrew Lipscomb, Chancellor of the University, on August 1, 1867. It was partially burned in 1955 when the auditorium caught fire, but was soon restored.

The Mead Corporation started in Georgia in 1954 the support of awards for fine paintings and the works of outstanding artists. This was one of several moves by business and industry to support the fine arts, as patrons had done in the Renaissance in Europe. The program soon became nationwide, and thousands of artists submitted their paintings.

The First National Bank of Atlanta commissioned artists to paint a series of excellent pictures showing various phases of Georgia's growth and beauty.

Architecture is an art that has taken on new grace in Georgia. The state has always been a mecca for those who were interested in seeing antebellum architecture at its best. Many of the old, white-columned mansions built before the Civil War and handsome homes in places like Savannah, designed by English architects, have appeared in nationally circulated publications. The Governor's Mansion at Milledgeville is a gem. Former homes of Ben Hill, Robert Toombs, and others are still visited by many not only for their historic interest but for their superb architecture.

The Thornton House, which was moved from Union Point in Green County and rebuilt on the grounds of the Atlanta Art Association, is very likely the oldest home in Georgia. It was built in 1780, and is an example of the kind of cottage in which lived settlers who came to Georgia from Virginia and the Carolinas in the eighteenth century. It is a buff color, with a blue-green trim. The yards have been restored as they were orginally, with boxwoods, vegetable and flower gardens, and a white picket fence. Pear and apple trees have been planted around it.

In recent years, skyscrapers have appeared on the skyline of Atlanta, giving drama to the architecture of the city. Public buildings, such as the Atlanta stadium, the library at Tallulah Falls school, the conference center at Jekyll, the library at Tech, and others are in dramatic and interesting contrast to the older forms of architecture in Georgia. Shopping centers such as the one at Lenox Square in Atlanta illustrate the interesting partnership that has developed between art and industry. Many modern building centers have fascinating sculpture as added beauty and interest.

Music, a part of the Georgia story since Charles Wesley wrote hymns here, has grown to be a bigger part in recent years. The State Department of Education has a music consultant who co-ordinates the general program in music and music appreciation. Teachers in the schools and colleges of the state often serve also as choir directors or organists for local churches, thus helping local communities to grow in their awareness of fine music and to develop their ability to make music.

The Music Education Association, the Music Teachers Association, the Organists' Guild and Georgia Federated Music Clubs have worked valiantly in the cause of fine music throughout the state.

Superb Symphony Orchestras Are Numerous

The Atlanta Symphony Orchestra became in two decades one of the top twenty-five orchestras in the nation. Its founder, Henry Sopkin, came to Atlanta "with a thousand pounds of music and the dream of building a major symphony orchestra." Besides the regular concerts, this group has given "Tiny Tots" concerts for children and about fifty concerts for all young people. The public schools co-operated, and his youth concerts became widely known. Nearly fifty thousand students hear the symphony each year. Some of those who play in the Atlanta Symphony Orchestra are also well-known in other fields, such as a traffic engineer who is a clarinetist, and veterans from military service.

Albert Coleman, who came to Atlanta from his native France, leads the well-known 55-piece Pops Orchestra, which he started some twenty years ago.

Augusta's Symphony Orchestra has been under the direction of Harry Jacobs, who was with the NBC and Chicago symphony orchestras and played with the Minneapolis Symphony under Dimitri Mitropoulos. He also heads the fine arts department at Augusta College. Scientists, doctors, and professors are among the players here. This group, too, gives special concerts for children, as do most major musical groups in the state.

Savannah's symphony orchestra was organized in 1953, with Chauncey Kelly as director. He was invited to be guest conductor of the Dominican National Symphony Orchestra.

Governor Sanders, through the State Department of Education, made available in 1965 funds for a pilot project of state youth concerts that took the Savannah Symphony Orchestra to play at a number of Georgia schools. The Education Act passed by Congress in 1965 had provisions under which more music and art and drama could be made available to both public and private schools.

Rome is believed to have the only woman conductor in the state. She is Miss Helen Dean Rhodes. Students from the schools and colleges here join the adult musicians, who include a postman, a woman engineer, and an inventor.

Columbus Symphony Orchestra, which features a Valentine concert, has directors who also direct music in its schools and colleges. The orchestra was developed under the guidance of Robert Barr, who later went to Jekyll and became music director at Glynn Academy in Brunswick, one of the three oldest schools in the state.

Other musical groups throughout Georgia are doing much to help Georgia make and appreciate the finest in music.

The A Cappella Choir of the Woman's College in Milledgeville has sung the "Elijah" annually for over thirty years, and not only makes music in its own college community but has toured many places to sing its songs. Unusual musical groups that have given pleasure to listeners include the Bell Ringers of St. Philip's Cathedral in Atlanta and the madrigal singers in Milledgeville. The Emory Glee Club, which has frequently toured Europe, is known for its excellent concerts. Negro musical groups such as the choirs at the state colleges at Savannah and Albany, the Spelman and Clark College choirs in Atlanta, the Morris Brown Concert Choir, and the Morehouse Men's Glee Club have attracted widespread attention for their fine work. The famed Big Bethel Church Choir is known far outside the state. Other groups, too numerous to list, have done valiant service in helping Georgians make and appreciate music. Georgia has produced outstanding singers of both races: the late James

847

Melton, Beverly Wolfe, Mattiwilda Dobbs, Roland Hayes and many others.

Grand opera — the Metropolitan from New York — first started coming to Atlanta in 1910, and brought singers such as Caruso, Geraldine Farrar, Rosa Ponselle and a glittering galaxy of others. One was murdered.

Georgia music teachers have done outstanding service to the cause of music. Some have written books telling the story of music in Georgia, and others have collected the music especially adapted to Georgia.

Georgia has song writers. One is Johnny Mercer of Savannah.

Ballads from the mountain people of north Georgia and from the plantations of the south country and the coast have vastly enriched the state's music. Country music has made a tuneful addition. Slave songs brought over from Africa or surging up from sorrow or bubbling from their joy as the dark people of Georgia's antebellum days worked in field and forest have been collected and form a rich and beautiful chapter in the music story of the state.

CHAPTER 74

THE COMMUNICATION ARTS

Word artistry in a wide range from newspapers to books and magazines, radio and television is evidenced by the skill and talent of many Georgians.

Byron Herbert Reece, His Plows And His Poetry

On a thirty-acre farm near Wolf Creek in Union County, lived a young Georgia genius who wrote poetry so beautiful that it won him national awards and a Guggenheim Fellowship. He loved the land and he loved words. His poem "The Ballad of the Bones" is a haunted thing, of strange beauty and great depth. A book of poetry, *Bow Down In Jericho,* won him the Georgia Distinguished Writers Award. His novel, *Better A Dinner of Herbs,* was not so beautiful as his poetry, but was very interesting.

He had been born near Choestoe. Since before the Civil War his people had farmed the same land that he now loved and plowed. Two of his great-grandfathers were killed in that war.

There were those who thought he should give up plowing for poetry. "Anybody can plow potatoes," a friend said to him. "Anybody can plow potatoes, but nobody is willing to plow mine but me," he answered. Once he said, "Greenness is as necessary to me as to a blade of grass." He liked nature, the old, eternal hills, the silver rains of spring, and the gold of the autumn harvest. Another poet, Kentucky's Jesse Stuart, encouraged him. National magazines began to notice him. Critics proclaimed his genius.

849

Many people could write jingles, but Byron Herbert Reece was a young poet in the tradition of Keats and Shelley.

With the money he made from his writing, he bought tools for his farm. Sometimes he left the farm for a little while, to go read this beautiful poetry to the people in the cities, or to teach for a little while at a college, or to be a consultant for a writers' group somewhere.

Then illness plagued him. He had contracted tuberculosis. He went to Battey Hospital at Rome, then left the hospital, but he was never well again.

Some critics think that only Sidney Lanier and Byron Herbert Reese in Georgia have written poetry that will endure. The same disease plagued them both. It was the same one that had killed John Keats long ago.

Writers

Nunnally Johnson, formerly of Columbus, Georgia, later of Hollywood, was listed by Gorham Munson in *The Written Word* as "the world's highest paid writer." Munson said, "In 1945, he was paid $150,000 for 8 weeks of work on a screen play. That is, he got $18,645 a week on that job, the highest weekly rate of pay to a writer recorded in history." Later he became a producer. Johnson had sold fifty-two short stories, one right after another to *Saturday Evening Post,* with never a rejection. He was once a reporter on his hometown newspaper.

A Million Georgians Read Georgia's Newspapers

By 1961, Georgia had 242 papers; of those, 31 are dailies. They were being read by more than a million Georgians. Papers had made much progress since that April day in 1763 when James Johnston published the first issue of his *Georgia Gazette* in Savannah. They had reported wars, editorialized about secession, and headlined murders and miracles of industry. There had even been a Cherokee Indian newspaper, printed in the Cherokee language that Sequoyah developed, and also in English.

The first woman editor in Georgia was Mrs. David B. Hillhouse, who edited the *Washington News* in Wilkes

County after her husband died in 1804. She also ran the printing office and did the official printing of Georgia state laws.

The institute of the Georgia Press Association, held each February in Athens, was founded by Miss Emily Woodward of Vienna, who had been president of the press association. The offices of the Georgia Press Association are in Atlanta.

Louis T. Griffith and John E. Talmadge have written the story of Georgia's newspapers in their book *Georgia Journalism 1763-1950*, printed by the University of Georgia Press.

Magazines in Georgia were often well-edited and widely read. One of the nation's best and most famous Sunday magazines in a newspaper is that of the *Atlanta Journal-Constitution*. Started many years ago under the editorship of Angus Perkerson, assisted by his book-writing wife, Medora Field, it was later ably edited by George Hatcher.

Other magazines were the *Georgia Magazine,* the *Georgia Review, Atlanta,* and the *Georgia Quarterly.* Each one of them served well to make people in and outside of Georgia more aware and appreciative of the state.

Georgia ranks sixth in the nation in the number of broadcasting stations. Applications are in for many more radio and television stations. The Georgia Association of Broadcasters vigorously promotes their interests.

WSB, one of the nation's earliest radio stations, later expanded into television, with its center in a building called "White Columns on Peachtree."

Georgia's libraries were growing, and new ones were being established over the state. The first colonists that came in 1733 brought over a thousand books with them. Libraries had been established in many Georgia cities and towns. Andrew Carnegie, the Scot steel magnate who was one of the millionaires that owned Jekyll, began to give money to libraries. Of the $60,000,000 that he gave to libraries in this country, $100,000 came to Atlanta to make possible the library in downtown Atlanta. By 1898, public libraries were beginning to be supported by public funds. A state library commission was set up. Both the public and the high school libraries, however, were being administered through the State Department of Education by mid-century, and bookmobiles were rolling around the mountains and down the long stretches of pine-lined roads in south Georgia, carrying thousands of books to those in remote rural areas. Federal funds had been added to state and local library funds.

By 1966, there were 34 regional libraries serving 125 counties and over 80 bookmobiles. There were also 34 county libraries and 17 independent libraries. Library service for every county in Georgia had been provided. The records showed that Georgians were reading twice as many books as they had a decade ago.

Libraries were also offering music, discussion groups, paintings, story hours, summer reading programs, and information service to the public.

Georgia's Library for the Blind, serving both Georgia and Florida, had 3,500 talking books in 20,000 copies, and 4,600 Braille books.

About 15 million books were also being circulated in school libraries, which owned nearly 7 million volumes.

The Georgia Historical Commission was set up in 1951; by 1963, it had placed about two thousand markers on historic sites throughout Georgia. Of these, 750 marked spots important in the history of the War Between the States. These markers have increased awareness of the history of Georgia.

The markers call attention of tourists and natives to sites where history had happened or interesting figures had lived from the days of the Mound Builders and Indians to past the Confederacy. Some are history; some are legend. Some mark events that shook the world, such as the siege of Savannah and the death of the Polish hero Pulaski. Others remind the passerby that something quaint or colorful happened here, such as Lorenzo Dow's curse on the town that would not listen to his preaching. At some places, dramatic things occurred, such as the Battle of Brier Creek, near Sylvania. Other markers tell of people such as Ol' Dan Tucker, " who combed his hair with a wagon wheel and died with the toothache in his heel." There's another for Daniel Abram Simon, the Wilkes County tavern keeper who is buried standing up, "with his gun in his hand to get a quick shot at the devil on Judgment Day."

Sidney Lanier is honored by a marker at Brunswick, where he wrote poetry under the tree known as Lanier's

Oak, near the Marshes of Glynn that he made famous in his poetry. Another at Auraria near Dahlonega shows where thousands swarmed in to dig for gold in 1829.

The Commission also restored historical buildings,

Monument to Count Pulaski

such as the White House in Augusta, where Thomas Brown hanged the thirteen soldiers; Jarrett Manor at Toccoa, home of Jesse Walton, brother of George Walton of Declaration of Independence fame, and others. It probes Indian mounds, builds museums, and even helps raise historical boats from a river!

The Commission is attached to the office of the Secretary of State.

The beautiful new seventeen-story Archives building near Capitol Hill, dedicated in 1965, houses thousands of books, manuscripts and pictures relating to Georgia history. When it was opened, Carl Sanders, the governor of Georgia, and Ernest Vandiver, former governor during whose administration it was launched, were on the program. South Carolina sent Georgia a copy of the original Georgia charter, which Oglethorpe had left there when he stopped in that state for help and guidance as he was on his way to Savannah to found the state of Georgia.

POSTSCRIPT

"GEORGIA IS TOMORROW COUNTRY"

A wise man was asked, "What is the most important sentence one could put into a book on Georgia history?" He thought for a little while, and then he said, "Put in these four words: 'Georgia is Tomorrow Country.'"

We look back, as in this volume, to a sometimes quieter past, so that we may plan the busy future, and be an intelligent part of it. No one knows what the future is going to be, but that's where we ought to be looking. We can shape it to our liking; so we had better start thinking how we would like it.

Georgia has great blessings, and great problems. Those who were Georgians before you came were aware of blessings, and involved in solving problems. Their courage and concern helped make Georgia what it is today. Your awareness and involvement can help shape the future of Georgia.

What riches do we have?

Georgia has 4,000,000 people; by 2000 A.D. it will have 8,000,000. Its richest resource lies in the minds and talents and attitudes of its people.

Georgia has fertile farms, green pastures, growing crops, better livestock, flowing rivers, great lakes with power dams and recreation centers, woods full of game, forests for lumber and naval stores, rainfall and a climate for growing.

Georgia has vast industry, manufacturing hundreds of things the world needs and will pay for, from baseball bats to prefabricated houses, from automobiles to clocks, from rugs to rocket fuels, from pencils to planes, from ceramics to cereals.

Georgia has big and expanding business, serving its citizens and the world outside, distributing goods and services, here at the hub of the southeast, the doorstep to South America, in touch with lands over all the earth.

Georgia has travel routes, and means of travel: roads lacing the communities together, and interstate highways flashing past to connect it with the nation; millions of cars and trucks and buses coming and going; one of the world's busiest airports, and other airports across the state, with planes large and small zooming through the blue sky.

Georgia has scenery as beautiful as any in the world, and sights to see and things to do that make the state a mecca for tourists from the other forty-nine states, and many a foreign country.

Georgia has thousands of schools and colleges to educate its people, to move minds into motion, to trigger talents, to spark creativity, to train citizens for jobs, to help them enrich their lives with art and music and literature, to care for their health, to use their leisure wisely and happily.

Georgia has thousands of homes: split-level houses, brand-new and shining; old white-columned mansions that awaken nostalgia for a past now gone with the wind; cottages down by a country road or on a lake shore; old, spreading houses in the country that have housed many generations of the same family where the chimney has vines clinging and a rooster crows down by the garden gate; apartment houses, trim and neat, for busy people who like their convenience.

Georgia has ten thousand places of worship where people can go to be near their God. Everywhere they lift spires to the soft Georgia skies.

Georgia has a free government, which the people choose. Power runs like electricity from the voting precincts in the remotest rural village and the most congested city to the gold-domed capitol in Atlanta.

Georgia has instant communication with the world beyond: television stations, radio, newspapers, writers whose voices are heeded in lands afar and at home, word artists who can stir the minds and move the hearts of men and inspire them to think and to act on what they think, and to keep informed about the issues of the day. These articulate people and these miracles of communication keep Georgia's windows open on the world.

Yet There Are Problems Which Georgians Still Must Solve

Georgians must concern themselves with making genuine quality education available to all, providing teachers who can inspire more Georgians to want education and be willing to exert their minds to acquire it. Too few Georgians are high school graduates, and there are not enough college graduates. There are not enough doctorates granted here, and not yet enough research and experiment in education. Georgia needs more well-educated people, with the willingness and ability to solve its remaining problems.

Georgians will have to work hard within the next few years to attain racial harmony. As long as the dark shadow of conflict lies across our path, we cannot get on with the important achievements that would bring more material benefits to all people of all races.

Georgians must vote in larger numbers. Only about 32 percent of all Georgians who could vote take the trouble to vote. Awareness and concern for the issues involved and the candidates offering themselves must be of more importance to Georgia citizens.

In the midst of beauty, there is still ugliness which needs to be eliminated: dilapidated slums, cluttered roadsides, used car piles of rusty junk, unpainted buildings, deteriorating barns and fences, litter along the highways.

Georgians must make Georgia safer. We must stop killing one another on the highways. We need, too, more safety from crime, disease, alcoholism, mental health, and other dark nights of the soul.

Finally, to paraphrase the comment of former president Dwight Eisenhower, who came often to Georgia, in his inaugural address: "This truth must be clear before us: whatever Georgia hopes to come to pass within its boundaries must first come to pass in the hearts and minds of Georgians."

Ours is an open-end society. No tyrant structures it for us. We blueprint it for ourselves, and can build to what we can dream, can achieve whatever we are able to imagine. Faith in ourselves and our future is our built-in bonus, a force more powerful than atom bombs. We look back at what Georgians have done, and then we ourselves resolve to go right out and climb a new mountain or light a fresh star.

Says William Silverman, a modern philosopher, "There is no limit to the potential of the human spirit to conquer and achieve. There is no power to equal the power of the human will to create and to build, to persist and to prevail."

Think on this history of Georgia unrolled before you, these people who were a part of the story of your state in the days before yesterday, what mighty things they accomplished, how nobly they wrought, how big they dreamed so that you might have the great Georgia that is yours today. They evolved a free government, they built great structures, they plowed wide fields, they researched the deep secrets of nature, they fought and conquered mighty foes, they triumphed over disease, darkness, and despair, they created new products and delved into technology to improve old ones, they tried out better ways in human relations, they taxed themselves to educate their children, they wrote their thoughts down into books, they dreamed great dreams and dared great deeds to build this Georgia that is yours.

You and your generation are coming into your heritage. This is your Georgia to build into new greatness. It is the finest tribute you can pay to those who have gone before: to dream big, quiet dreams, and act with courage to make them come true.

As Shakespeare wrote: "What's past is prologue!"

INDEX

Acadians in Georgia, 200, 201

Adams, Abigail, 326

Adams, Henry, 339

Adams, John, 213, 221, 226, 241, 294, 336

Adams, John Quincy, 379, 381, 425, 426

Adams, Samuel, 221, 231

Agnes Scott College, 740

Air travel in Georgia, 809

Allcorn, Frank W., Jr., 724, 725

Alston, Robert, 655

Altamaha River, 20, 21

Alum Cave, 14

Amatis, Nicholas, 129, 130

Amatis, Paul, 129, 130

Amherst, Jeffrey, 412

Amicalola, 11

Amicalola Falls, 43, 44

Amicalola Falls State Park, 44

Anderson, George, 560

Anderson, Robert, 518-521

Andersonville Prison, 539, 559, 566, 588

Andrews, Frances Eliza, 568, 569, 583

Anne, 115-117

Annie Ruby, 12

Anti-Federalists, 368

Appalachian Project, 793, 794

Appalachian Trail, 12

Apple growing in Georgia, 789

Arawaqua, 12

Arnall, Ellis G., 657, 713, 715-719, 817

Ashburn, G.W., 596

Asbury, Francis, 320, 321

Ashe, John, 266

Ashford, W.A., 723

Atkinson, W.Y., 630, 654

Atlanta University, 741, 834

Attakullakulla, 101, 194, 438

Audubon, John James, 31, 57

Augusta, 151, 152

Auraria, 405, 451, 452

Axson, I.K., 191

Aztecs, 68

B

Bacon, A.O., 612

Baker, John, 254

Baldwin, Abraham, 309, 310, 318, 319, 344, 346

Barnett, Nathan, 53

Barnsley Castle, 2

Barnwell, John, 98-100

Barr, Robert, 847

Bartow, Francis, 501

Bartram, John, 208, 209

Bartram, William, 21, 39, 40, 66, 208, 209

Battle, Lucius, 770

Bear River, 25

Beatie, George, 727

Beauregard, Pierre T., 480, 518-521

Beecher, Henry Ward, 487

859

Bell, Vereen, 41
Bellamy, Ralph, 725
Benet, Stephen Vincent, 546, 562
Benjamin, Judah P., 509, 510, 563
Bennett, W. Tapley, Jr., 770
Benning, Henry, 515, 580, 581
Berrien, John, 368, 383–385, 427
Berry, Martha, 661, 662
Berry College, 835
Bethesda, 141, 158–160
Bethune, Thomas Greene, 637, 638
Bevan, Joseph Vallence, 343
Bierce, Ambrose, 535
Bignon, Christopher Poulain du, 30, 37, 78
Bird, Georgia state, 57
Birney, Alice McClellan, 631, 632
Black, Eugene, 604
Blackbeard (see Edward Teach)
Blackbeard's Island, 28
Blood Mountain, 12, 13
Bloody Marsh, 33
Bloody Marsh, Battle of, 173–176
Boll weevil, 657–659
Bolzius, John Martin, 140–143
Booth, John Wilkes, 572, 573
Bootle, W.A., 757
Bosomworth, Thomas, 27, 185, 186

Boudinot, Elias, 449–451, 455, 456, 464, 471, 472
Boudinot, Harriet, 450–451
Bowen, Oliver, 152
Bowie, Jim, 398
Bowlegs, Billy, 42
Bowles, William, 327
Boyd, Thomas, 264, 265
Brady, Matthew, 479
Bragg, Braxton, 529, 533, 534, 538, 543, 548, 552, 557
Bray, Thomas, 109
Brier Creek, Battle of, 266
Brim, Emperor, 64, 103, 121
Brooks, Francis, 172
Brooks, Preston, 487
Brown, John, 488, 491–493
Brown, Joseph Emerson, 498–501, 503–505, 509, 512, 529, 558, 559, 578, 591, 596, 601, 610, 611, 614, 616, 652
Brown, Joseph Mackay, 651
Brown, McEvers Bayard, 36
Brown thrasher, 57
Browne, Thomas, 276, 279–281, 288
Brownson, Nathan, 287, 288, 303, 318, 344
Brumby, Thomas, 641
Bryan, Jonathan, 202, 219, 220, 260
Buchanon, James, 518
Bull, William, 117
Bulloch, Archibald, 222, 225, 235, 238, 240, 245, 246
Bullock, Rufus, 593, 609

Burge, Dolly Sumner Lunt, 568
Burgoyne, John, 253
Burke, Edmund, 182, 183, 216
Burns, Robert, 144, 734
Burnside, Ambrose, 480, 542
Burr, Aaron, 33, 374, 375
Burr, Theodosia, 353
Bushnell, David, 317
Butler, Elizur, 454
Butler, Frances, 377
Butler, Pierce, 228, 374, 375

C

Cabot, John, 93
Calculator, 686
Caldwell, Erskine, 730
Calhoun, John C., 384, 431, 458
Callaway, Howard (Bo), 765
Campbell, Archibald, 257, 259, 262, 265, 266
Campbell, Duncan, 423
Candler, Allen, 639–641, 648, 654
Candler, Asa W., 795
Candler, Warren Akin, 795
Carlyle, Thomas, 29, 175, 396
Carmichael, James V., 713, 717, 759
Carnegie, Andrew, 39, 604, 851
Carr, Mark, 191
Carter, Don, 733
Carteret, Lord, 108
Cartledge, James, 321

Carver, George Washington, 594, 606, 607, 659
Castell, Robert, 105, 120
Catton, Bruce, 477
Causton, Thomas, 127, 148, 164
Chappell, J. Harris, 339
Charles I, 96
Charles II, 97
Charlotte, Queen, 224
Chase, Ilka, 32, 731
Chattahoochee National Forest, 14, 15
Chattahoochee River, 8, 17, 18
Cherokee Indians, 9, 12, 14, 20, 68, 69, 410, 435–473
Cherokee Phoenix, 449–451
Cherokee rose, 55
Chesnut, Mary Boykin, 492, 548, 567
Chesterton, G.K., 2
Chickamauga, Battle of, 533–536
Chivers, Thomas Holley, 636
Churches in Georgia, 804–806
Churchill, Winston, 113, 114, 171, 296, 511, 640
Clark, John, 266, 274, 276, 355, 360, 367, 369, 371, 372, 399
Clark, William, 353
Clarke, Elijah, 17, 264–266, 276–279, 284, 296, 333, 334
Clay, Henry, 379, 380, 483, 484, 486
Clay, Lucius, 723

Davis, Sam, 270, 506

Davis, Varina Howell, 507, 571, 574, 575

Davis, Winnie, 565, 575, 576

Davison, Samuel, 146, 147, 154

Dawes, William, 229

DeAllyon, Vasquez, 72

Dean, Braswell, 825

Decatur, Stephen, 34

Defoe, Daniel, 145

Delamotte, Charles, 145, 148, 314

Dempsey, Charles, 166, 167

Dent, James D., 373

DeSoto, Fernando, 16, 21, 47, 73-84

DeSoto, Isabella, 74, 82

D'Estaing, Charles, 267-271, 274, 275

De Toqueville, Alexis, 411

Dewey, George, 641

Dickens, Charles, 29, 105

Disney, Walt, 526, 636

Dodd, Lamar, 727

Dorsey, Hugh, 683, 686

Douglas, Melvin, 734

Douglas, Stephen A., 502

Dobell, John, 157

Dodge, Anson, 36

Dodge, Ellen, 36

Dolly, Quanimo, 256-258

Domingo, Augustin Baez, 27, 89

Dooly, John, 264, 277, 278

Douglas, William O., 9

Drake, Francis, 94

Dugas, Graham, 656

Duncan, John P., 764

Dunn, Dom Frederick, 741, 742

E

Early, Peter, 360-362

Eaton, Peggy, 384

Education in Georgia, 820-840

Edwards, Harry Stillwell, 594, 636

Egmont, Percival, 102, 109, 110, 116, 132, 165

Eisenhower, Dwight David, 650, 736, 799

Elbert, Samuel, 266, 345

Ellis, Henry, 202-206

Emanuel, David, 137, 355

Emory University, 739, 740, 814, 831, 832

Etowah Mounds, 66

Etowah River, 20

Evans, Augusta J., 515

Everett, Edward, 458

F

Fannin, J. W., 398

Federalists, 300, 368

Felton, Rebecca, 615,616-619

Felton, W. H., 615, 616, 618, 619

Few, Benjamin, 278

Few, William, 278, 303, 309-311

Fitzgerald, P. H., 622

Flag, Confederate, 470, 480, 511

Flag, Georgia, 54

Fleming, Berry, 733

Flint River, 17, 22

Flower, Georgia, 55

Floyd, Charles, 42

Floyd, John, 419, 420

Ford, Henry, 560, 661, 744, 784

Forrest, Nathan Bedford, 514, 531-33, 590, 595
Forrester, William, 154
Forsyth, John, 319, 320, 381-383, 434
Fort Benning, 685, 686
Fort Gaines, 18
Ft. King George, 98-100
Fort McAllister, 21, 560
Fort Mims Massacre, 419
Fort Pulaski, 274, 501, 502
Foster, Stephen, 18-20, 41
Franciscans, 18, 87-89
Frank, Leo, 2, 682, 683, 686
Franklin, Benjamin, 158, 159, 209, 216, 220, 221, 232, 253, 272, 294, 307, 308, 313, 346, 627
Franklin College, 317
Frederica, 33, 152-155
Freeman, Douglas Southall, 522, 587
Fremont, John C., 354, 389, 485, 490
French and Indian War, 193-196
Frost, Robert, 740
Fulton, Robert, 309, 341, 342
Fuser, L. K., 254, 255

G

Gage, Thomas, 220, 228, 229
Galphin, George, 207
Garrick, David, 179
Garrison, William Lloyd, 487
Gates, Horatio, 228, 276, 286

Genet, Edmond Charles, 332, 333
George, Walter, 650, 651, 720, 769, 825
George I, 106, 109, 114
George II, 6, 106-109, 114, 132, 154, 198
George III, 196, 213, 215, 216, 220, 232, 240, 253, 254, 290, 295, 296
"Georgia" (Song), 58
Georgia, University of, 318, 319, 629, 739
Georgia Tech, 832-834
Gershwin, George, 20
Giffen, Newton, 536, 537
Gilmer, George, 336, 352, 454, 459, 461, 462
Glascock, William, 263, 274
Glynn, John, 223, 238
Gold mines, Georgia, 405, 451-453
"Golden Islands," 25
Goldsmith, Oliver, 179
Goldwater, Barry, 753, 765, 768
Graham, John, 188, 207
Graham, Patrick, 188, 189, 199
Gordon, John B., 512, 546, 549, 578, 585, 595, 605, 610-613, 616, 654, 655
Gordonia, 209
Gould, George, 36
Goulding, Francis R., 636, 784
Grady, Henry, 500, 579, 602-605, 612, 627, 687, 777
Grant, Ulysses S., 518, 524-526, 540-542, 546, 554, 570, 571, 578, 579

Hodges, Courtney, 723
Hodgson, Hugh, 272
Holden, Genevieve E., 733
Holmes, Abiel, 34, 190, 329
Holmes, Oliver Wendell, 34, 480
Hood, John Bell, 533, 543, 546, 548, 552-555, 581
Hoover, Herbert, 704
Hopkey, Sophey, 33, 148-150
Hopkins, Harry, 712
Hopkins, Miriam, 734
Horseshoe Bend, Battle of, 420
Horton, William, 178
Houston, Sam, 399, 458, 510
Houston, William, 129
Houstoun, John, 222, 223, 225, 235, 236, 252, 258-260, 318, 345
Howe, Julia Ward, 493
Howe, Robert, 256
Howley, Richard, 260, 344
Hughes, Charles Evans, 677
Hughes, Dudley M., 683, 825
Hull, Hope, 320, 321
Humphries, Thomas, 321
Hurst, Willis, 769

I

Incas, 68
"Indian Mound," 36
Indian Springs, Treaty of, 423-426
Ingham, Benjamin, 138
"Irene" (School), 138
Irwin, Jared, 312, 333, 338, 356

J

Jackson, Absalom, 23
Jackson, Andrew, 360, 365, 379, 419, 420, 423, 428, 431-434, 456-459, 461, 484
Jackson, Graham, 725
Jackson, Henry Rootes, 636
Jackson, James, 53, 221, 231, 254, 258, 260, 287-289, 291, 296-298, 309, 310, 312, 328, 337-340, 344, 346, 368, 369, 372, 416
Jackson, Thomas J., "Stonewall," 493, 530
Jackson, William H., 56
Jacobs, Harry, 846
Jacobs, Thornwell, 182, 740
James I, 95, 113
Jarrett Manor, 412, 413
Jasper, William, 261, 271, 272
Jay, John, 307
Jefferson, Thomas, 62, 307, 312, 346, 351-353, 374, 484, 689
Jekyll Island, 30, 36-38
Jenkins, Charles, 592, 609
Jenkins, Robert, 171
Jenkins Ear, War of, 171-172
Jerusalem Church, 139
Jesuits, 87
Jews in early Georgia, 135-137
Johnson, Andrew, 498, 589-591
Johnson, Herschel V., 501, 591
Johnson, James, 590, 591, 610

867

Polk, Leonidas K., 152, 548, 550, 551
Pope, Alexander, 183
Pope, John, 591, 592
Population figures, 751, 752
Populist Party, 623, 624, 649
Pou, Charles, 733
Poultry industry in Georgia, 791, 792
Poythress, John, 398
Pratt, Rev. Horace, 22
Prescott, Samuel, 229
Prescott, William, 68, 69
Prevost, Augustine, 254, 260, 261, 266-270
Prevost, Mark, 254, 255, 259, 260, 266
Priber, Gottlieb Christian, 155, 156
"The Prophet," 414-416
Providence Canyons, 44, 45
Pulaski, Casimir, 267 272-274
Pulitzer, Joseph, 36, 728
Purcell, Claude, 737, 821, 822
Puritans in Georgia, 189-191
Purry, Jean, 92, 93, 107

R

Rabun, William, 423, 431
Radium Springs, 45
Raikes, Robert, 148
Railroads, early Georgia, 404-405
Rainbow Falls, 14
Raleigh, Sir Walter, 94, 95
Randall, James Ryder, 637

Randolph, John, 359
Rankin, Jeanette, 679
Reck, Baron von, 140
Red Sticks, 69
Reece, Byron Herbert, 732, 849
Removal Treaty, 428
Revere, Paul, 220, 221, 229, 230
Reynolds, John, 21, 130, 198-202
Reynolds, Joshua, 160, 179
Reynolds, Richard J., 29
Rhodes, Helen Dean, 847
Ribaut, 'Jean, 22, 85, 90, 91, 95
Ridge, John, 456, 457, 464, 471, 472
Ridge, Major, 456, 457, 464, 471, 472
Rivers, Eurith, 713-715, 754
Robinson, Jackie, 737
Rock Eagle Mound, 66, 67
Rockefeller, Nelson, 834
Rockefeller, William, 36
Rocky Knob, 12
Rogers, Will, 439
Rome, 20, 79
Roosevelt, Franklin Delano, 14, 40, 43, 648, 650, 692, 706, 707, 712
Roosevelt, Theodore, 232, 640, 641, 643, 648, 677, 678, 701-705, 722, 724, 725, 804
Rosecrans, William S., 534, 538
Ross, John, 453, 455-458, 459, 464, 472
Ruffin, Edmund, 520
Rusk, Dean, 762-764
Ruskin, John, 52

Russell, Richard B., 630
Russell, Richard B. Jr.,
709, 710, 720, 723
Russell, William, 479
Ruth, George Herman
("Babe"), 736
Ryan, Father, 637

S

St. Catherine's Island, 27,
85
St. Johns, J. A., 47
St. Marys (town), 23
St. Marys River, 8, 22-24,
41
St. Simons, 21
St. Simons Island, 33-36
Sallette, Robert, 201, 284
Salzburgers in Georgia,
139-143
Sanders, Carl, 723, 759,
760, 761, 769, 797, 798,
829, 830, 847, 854
Sansom, Emma, 529, 531-
533
Sapelo Island, 29, 30
Savannah, N. S., 401, 402,
403
Savannah, Siege of, 267-
271
Savannah River, 16, 17
Schaefer, Bruce, 814
Schaefer, Mrs. W. B., 761
Schofield, John M., 552
Scotch Highlanders in
Georgia, 143, 144
Scott, Dred, 489
Scott, Winfield, 464, 465,
466-469, 519, 520, 525,
545
Scott, Robert Lee, 723
Screven, James, 254

Sea Island, 30-32
Seal, Georgia, 53, 246, 312
Seal, Trustees', 111
Seminole, Lake, 22
Seminoles, 69, 430-434
Senauki, 131, 132, 134
Sequoyah, 14, 447-449
Seward, William, 391-393,
493, 520, 554, 562, 573
Shakespeare, William, 1
Sheftall, Mordecai, 137
Sheftall, Sheftall, 137
Sherman, William Tecum-
seh, 1, 21, 183, 531,
534, 541-549, 551-558,
561, 570, 571, 582, 583
Sherwood, Adiel, 776
Sibley, Celestine, 733
Sibley, John, 757
Sibley Commission, 757,
758, 841
Sidney, Sir Phillip, 1
Silk-raising, 128-130
Silverman, William, 858
Slaton, Governor John,
652, 681, 682, 684
Slavery in Georgia, 496-
498
Smith, Al, 701, 703
Smith, Edward, 765
Smith, Hoke, 617, 625, 651,
652, 679, 683, 825
Smith, James M., 580,
627
Smith, Kirby, 508
Smith, Lillian, 730
Song, Georgia, 58
Sopkin, Henry, 727, 846
Southern Regional Educa-
tion Board, 830, 831
Spalding, James, 155
Spalding, Thomas, 29, 155,
339, 373, 374

872

875